survey of # Operating Systems

Sixth Edition

Jane Holcombe
Charles Holcombe

Mc
Graw
Hill
Education

SURVEY OF OPERATING SYSTEMS

ISBN 978-1-260-56582-9
MHID 1-260-56582-3

Cover Image: ©*Dave Cutler Studio, LLC*

JANE HOLCOMBE In the early 1980s, Jane Holcombe was the tech support person for a small financial planning company, a role she was assigned at a time when technology was about connecting specialized terminals to expensive industry-specific systems via costly telephone company links. These systems were limited in the reports they generated, and far from user-friendly, and her boss tasked her with researching the emerging technology of the time: IBM Personal Computers. Jane would often discover bookmarked technical magazines on her desk, along with a note from the boss instructing her to check out the articles and research how to move their accounting and contact management systems to PCs. After months of research and after consulting with various experts, she oversaw the move of the accounting and contact management functions to IBM PCs connected via a local area network (LAN) for sharing the data. The network was very slow, and the software for accounting and contact management required memorizing keystrokes for each function. However, the boss was pleased with the ability to make quick changes to the reports these systems generated—something not possible with the old, mainframe-based systems. This project showed Jane the potential of personal computing in business.

One of the many lessons she learned during this time was that one roadblock to bringing PCs into business was the lack of knowledgeable PC support staff. So, her next project was a career move, as she created appropriate courseware and co-founded a company that presented technical PC and network support courses nationwide.

In the early 1990s, she sold her interest in the training company and returned to independent technical consulting and instruction, acquiring experience and certifications for both Novell and Microsoft. Her focus through the 1990s was small business servers and networks. In recent years, she has worked primarily as a technical writer and technical editor.

CHARLES HOLCOMBE has a high-tech background in computing in the nuclear and aerospace fields. In his 15 years at Control Data Corporation, he was successively a programmer, technical sales analyst, salesman, and sales manager in the field marketing force. At corporate headquarters, he ran Control Data's Executive Seminar program, headed sales training for the corporation, was liaison to the worldwide university community, and was market development manager for the Plato computer-based education system. Since then, he has been an instructor and consultant. He has authored and delivered many training courses and is a skilled editor. Currently, he is an independent editor for various clients and collaborates with Jane on writing projects. For a while, he claimed he was semi-retired, but, with his consulting and editing work, he cannot say that any more.

Together the Holcombes have authored textbooks and self-study guides, based on Jane's area of expertise and their collaborative research and testing of new technologies used by consumers, students, and businesses.

About the Contributors

This book was greatly influenced by the comments, suggestions, and feedback from the following group of dedicated instructors. To them we give our heartfelt thanks.

Reviewers

Melissa Williams	*Colorado Technical University*
Susan Guerrant	*Wake Technical Community College*
Robert Doyle	*NMSU/Dona Ana Community College*
Anita Laird	*Schoolcraft College*
David Harris	*Benedictine College*
Iyad A. Ajwa	*Ashland University*
Patrick Dudenhofer	*Cedarville University*
Perry Kivolowitz	*Carthage College*
Chet Cunningham	*Madisonville Community College*
Pam Jensen	*Minnesota West Community and Technical College*

John Blyzka   *Mount San Antonio College*
Jeremy Caudle   *Davidson County Community College*
Audrey Styer   *Morton College*
Ken Araujo   *Francis Marion University*
Navin Madras   *Elizabethtown Community and Technical College*
Bryan Moss   *San Jacinto College*
David Bunde   *Knox College*
Jay Alire   *Emily Griffith Technical College*
Martha McCreery   *Rend Lake College*
Albert Cheng   *University of Houston*
Randy Gambill   *Wilkes Community College*
Mark King   *Aiken Technical College*
Dwayne Towell   *Lipscomb University*
Ali Shaykhian   *Florida Institute of Technology*

Acknowledgments

Once again, just as Jane was beginning a search for another project, and Chuck was busy with editing for his clients, Alan Palmer, Senior Product Developer, notified us that McGraw-Hill Higher Education had approved the sixth edition of our Survey of Operating Systems textbook. Because much has happened with operating systems and with personal computing since we wrote the first five editions, we knew it would require a nearly complete rethinking of the content. Along with director Wyatt Morris and Alan, we wrote a suggested Table of Contents that Alan sent to instructors—some of whom were using the fifth edition. The results of this survey helped us create the outline for the sixth edition.

As with previous editions, knowledgeable peer reviewers scrutinized each chapter, giving us invaluable feedback on the relevancy and accuracy of the content. We can't imagine writing a book like this without these technical reviews.

We thank every member of the talented team of people at McGraw-Hill who ensured the book's integrity. They include Wyatt Morris, Alan Palmer, Jeni McAtee, and Kala Ramachandran from SPi Global. We particularly want to thank Wyatt and Alan for their unstinting support, professionalism, and patience. We love the design of this edition, and we greatly appreciate the expertise of the members of the production group who all worked hard to make the book look wonderful. Creating and laying out the many elements of this complex book design was a huge task, and they handled it skillfully.

We appreciate all who worked so hard to make this book what it is.

Thank you!

About This Book

Important Technology Skills

Information technology (IT) offers many career paths, leading to occupations in such fields as PC repair, network administration, telecommunications, Web development, graphic design, and desktop support. To become competent in any IT field, however, you need certain basic computer skills. This book will help you build a foundation for success in the IT field by introducing you to fundamental information about popular desktop and mobile operating systems, a needed basis for working with all types of computing devices.

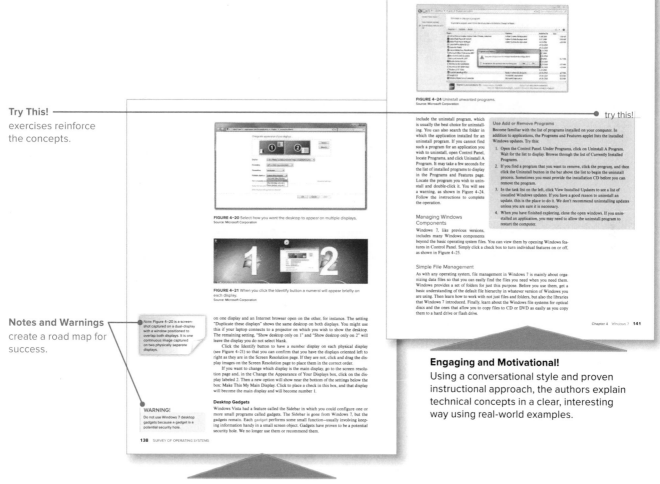

Try This!
exercises reinforce the concepts.

Notes and Warnings
create a road map for success.

Engaging and Motivational!
Using a conversational style and proven instructional approach, the authors explain technical concepts in a clear, interesting way using real-world examples.

Makes Learning Fun!
Rich, colorful text, and enhanced illustrations bring technical subjects to life.

Effective Learning Tools

The design of this colorful, pedagogically rich book will make learning easy and enjoyable and help you develop the skills and critical thinking abilities that will enable you to adapt to different job situations and troubleshoot problems.

Jane and Charles Holcombe's proven ability to explain concepts in a clear, direct, even humorous way makes this book interesting and motivational, and fun.

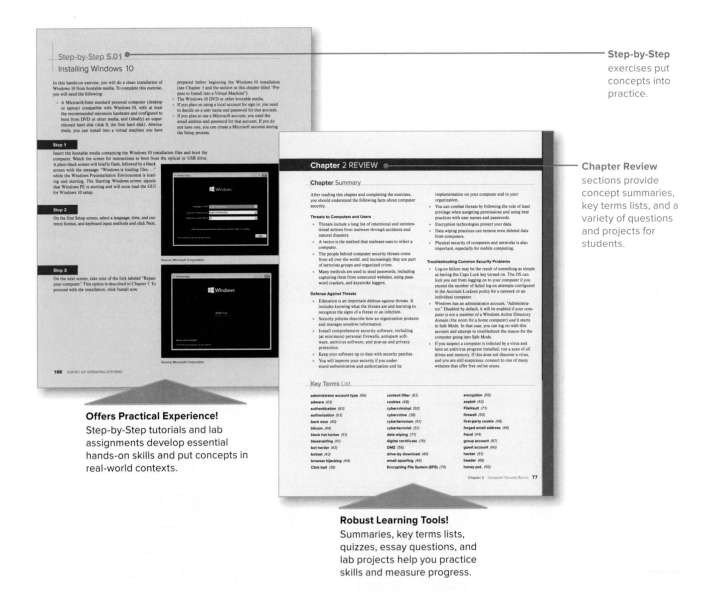

Step-by-Step exercises put concepts into practice.

Chapter Review sections provide concept summaries, key terms lists, and a variety of questions and projects for students.

Offers Practical Experience!
Step-by-Step tutorials and lab assignments develop essential hands-on skills and put concepts in real-world contexts.

Robust Learning Tools!
Summaries, key terms lists, quizzes, essay questions, and lab projects help you practice skills and measure progress.

Each chapter includes:

- **Learning Outcomes** that set measurable goals for chapter-by-chapter progress.
- **Four-Color Illustrations** that give you a clear picture of the technologies.
- **Step-by-Step Tutorials** that teach you to perform essential tasks and procedures hands-on.
- **Try This!** sidebars that encourage you to practice and apply the concepts in real-world settings.

- **Notes** and **Warnings** that guide you through difficult areas.
- **Chapter Summaries** and **Key Terms Lists** that provide you with an easy way to review important concepts and vocabulary.
- **Challenging End-of-Chapter Tests** that include vocabulary-building exercises, multiple-choice questions, essay questions, and on-the-job lab projects.

New to *Survey of Operating Systems*, Sixth Edition

General changes in this Sixth Edition:

- We removed *Windows 8.1,* the Fifth Edition's Chapter 5, and moved appropriate content into *Windows 10,* now Chapter 5.
- We added a new chapter, Chapter 9, *Chrome OS.*
- We added content on the various accounts commonly used on various devices, especially those accounts required for cloud services. Look for this information in Chapter 9, *Chromebooks and Chrome OS,* and in Chapter 11, *Mobile Operating Systems: iOS and Android.*
- In addition to reviewing and updating the content from the Fifth Edition, we worked to tighten the text throughout, improve the flow, and remove topics that are no longer relevant.
- Finally, we updated exercises, figures, and illustrations to support learning.

Chapter 1 Introduction to Operating Systems

- We added introductory information about Chromebooks and Chrome OS.
- We updated text and images throughout the chapter.

Chapter 2 Computer Security Basics

- We updated chapter content and images, as appropriate.

Chapter 3 Desktop Virtualization

- We updated chapter content and images, and increased the number of hands-on Step-by-Step exercises to five (from three in the last edition).

Chapter 4 Windows 7

- We updated the text and appropriate images.

Chapter 5 Windows 10

- Windows 10 is no longer the big news in operating system, so we pared down the content to focus on what we feel is important in this mature OS, including recently added features. We also moved some key terms from the former Windows 8.1 chapter to this chapter.

Chapter 6 Supporting and Troubleshooting Windows

- We updated chapter content and images.

Chapter 7 Apple macOS on the Desktop

- We updated chapter content and images.

Chapter 8 Linux on the Desktop

- We updated chapter content and images.

Chapter 9 Chromebooks and Chrome OS

- This new chapter is a recognition of the importance of Chromebooks and the Chrome OS at school, in the office, and at home. This chapter emphasizes skills for working with both Web apps and Android apps, as well as the tasks of printing and file management in the cloud.

Chapter 10 Connecting Desktops and Laptops to Networks

- We updated content and images, where appropriate.

Chapter 11 Mobile Operating Systems: iOS and Android

- We updated content and images to include tasks for working with multiple accounts on mobile devices and how to secure devices first through primary accounts (Google Android or Apple iOS) associated with the device, and then via settings on the device.

Appendix A: Windows Mouse and Keyboard Shortcuts

- We updated this list.

Appendix B: Chromebook & Chrome Browser Keyboard Shortcuts

- The new Chromebook keyboards are physically different from those found on other laptop computers and have new functions assigned to them, which are listed in this appendix. In addition, because it is an OS derived from the Chrome browser, we list the Chrome Browser shortcut for use within the browser. Finally, we include a list of Chrome editing shortcuts. Most of these will be familiar to both Windows and Apple macOS users.

Contents

5   Windows 10   159

6   Supporting and Troubleshooting Windows   207

7   Apple macOS on the Desktop   249

Introduction

What Will You Learn?

The first five editions of this book were well received by instructors and students. This sixth edition updates the material and presents new information that is relevant to the topic of desktop operating systems, including Windows, Apple macOS, Linux, and Chrome OS. In addition to these operating systems, this edition includes new information on mobile operating systems, as well as chapters on subjects peripheral to operating systems, such as computer security, desktop virtualization, and connecting computers and mobile devices to networks. We carefully revised every chapter as needed, with more illustrations and plenty of hands-on opportunities. We have added content throughout, while working to streamline the book in response to feedback we received from instructors.

How Will You Learn?

We don't want to simply give you an encyclopedia of information because it can feel like you're standing in front of an information fire hose, and we've been there ourselves many times in the past decades. Rather, keeping in mind that "less is more," we present just the key points about operating systems, and guide you in your own exploration of the specifics of the technology. One book simply can't give you everything you need to know about operating systems, but we do hope to empower you and to increase your ability to use widely available tools and resources to figure out the answers to your questions. Such tools as the Internet and the help program in your OS are aids you should turn to when you need to learn more about a topic, and when you want to enhance your skills in working with each of these operating systems—and with computers in general.

Each chapter uses many techniques to help you learn. We start by listing learning outcomes, follow that up with a lucid explanation of each topic, and support it with real-world experience and a liberal use of graphics and tables. To give you hands-on experience and to help you "walk the walk," each chapter contains detailed Step-by-Step tutorials and short Try This! exercises to reinforce the concepts. To build vocabulary to help you "talk the talk," each chapter contains computer term definitions, highlighted in a Key Terms List and compiled into a Glossary at the end of the book. We've also included notes, which provide handy pieces of knowledge to use with your desktop OS. Warnings will help you prevent mishaps.

You can measure what you've learned with end-of-chapter Key Terms, Multiple-Choice, and Essay quizzes. In addition, Lab Projects challenge you to independently complete tasks related to what you've just learned.

Let's Get Down to Work

OK, enough of this introductory stuff. This is the last time in this book that you'll see so many words without illustrations. From now on it's downright exciting. Learn a lot and *have fun!*

Supplements

For teachers using this book in the classroom, a powerful collection of teaching tools written by the authors is available online at **www.mhhe.com/holcombe6**:

- An Instructor's Manual that maps to the organization of the textbook and provides additional instructor tips and activities to use with the book.
- A test bank for each chapter available online in either Word or EZ Test format.
- Engaging PowerPoint slides on the lecture topics, including key points and illustrations from the chapters.
- Solutions to the end-of-chapter quizzes.

Jane Holcombe
Charles Holcombe

chapter

1

Introduction to Operating Systems

©Yuriy Rudyy/Shutterstock

Learning Outcomes

In this chapter, you will learn how to:

LO **1.1** Describe the purpose and functions of operating systems.

LO **1.2** Describe major events in the evolution of operating systems.

LO **1.3** List and compare the common desktop operating systems in use today.

LO **1.4** List the most common mobile OSs, the devices associated with them, and the features found in most of these devices.

Understanding operating systems (OSs) is critical to your future success in life. It is. Just believe us. You don't? You say you drive a car just fine, but you don't understand its engine, transmission, or other systems? So why can't you just use your computer? Why do you have to even know it has an OS? Just as you can use a car without in-depth knowledge of how it works, you can use your computer to write a letter, send email, create a report, surf the Internet, participate in social networking, and much more without understanding operating systems. You only have to know how to turn it on, call up the application program you wish to use, perform tasks, and turn it off.

If you want to get the most out of the computers you use in your work, school, and private life, you need to understand how the most critical software component, the computer's operating system, works.

This chapter provides an overview of microcomputer operating systems—specifically, those commonly found on desktop and laptop computers and the personal mobile devices we use today. We'll begin with a brief look at microcomputers—their components and their general types. Then we'll explore the functions that operating systems perform. Finally, we introduce you to the OSs in all types of microcomputers including those in home and office computers as well as tablets and smartphones. ✺

LO 1.1 | Overview of Microcomputer Operating Systems

This section is an introduction to the common operating systems used in today's computing devices (microcomputers). We begin by answering a few general questions you may have: What is an operating system? What is a microcomputer? What microcomputers are you using today? Then we briefly explore the events that led to the devices we use today as well as the operating systems that make them useable to us.

Operating Systems Defined

An operating system (OS) is a collection of programs that controls all of the interactions among the various system components, freeing application programmers from needing to include such functions in their programs. An application (app) is software that allows a user to perform useful functions, such as writing a report, picking up email, editing graphics, calculating a budget, and much more. Microsoft Word and Adobe Photoshop are applications. Applications send commands to the OS to interact with the hardware.

Microcomputers Defined

Consumers encountered their first microcomputers in 1977 with the introduction of the Apple II, Radio Shack TRS-80, and the Commodore PET. The Apple II best combined the critical elements that defined a microcomputer at the time: these included a keyboard, monitor display, available peripherals, an operating system, useful applications, and a reasonable price tag. Today, microcomputers are everywhere, and many of us have them in various forms.

Our friend Brianna uses a PC at work and an Apple iMac at home, and she always has her smartphone handy. She will soon take night classes in which she will use either a tablet or a laptop that she will carry to and from school. She is considering a Chromebook, running the Chrome OS, because the school requires that students use the Internet-based Google Cloud and its associated apps. She wants to learn more about the computers she uses each day, beginning with the hardware.

A typical PC with components.
©Denis Rozhnovsky/Alamy

Hardware Components

- A computer is a device that performs calculations. A typical modern computer is an electronic device that can perform a huge number of useful tasks for its owner.
- Any computer, small or large, has a central processing unit (CPU) that performs the calculations, or processing for the computer.
- A microcomputer is a computer small enough and cheap enough for the use of one person. The CPU in a microcomputer is a microprocessor, although many still refer to it simply as a CPU or processor.
- An important invention that led to the miniaturization of computers was the integrated circuit (IC), a small electronic component made up of transistors (tiny switches) and other miniaturized parts.
- Interaction with a computer is input/output (I/O). When we send something into the computer, we call it input. You are inputting through input devices when you type on the keyboard, tap on a touch screen, or talk to a computer through a microphone. Output is processed information of many types: sounds sent

through the speakers, visual output to the display screen or printer and data files saved or sent over a network.

- In a microcomputer, the internal components include at least one microprocessor, random-access memory (RAM) that acts as the main memory for holding active programs and associated data, firmware, and various other supporting circuitry, all installed onto a motherboard.
- The typical microcomputer also has some form of storage, such as a hard drive, and it has at least one means each for input and output.

Note: Random-access memory (RAM) is volatile: when you turn off the computer the contents in RAM disappear.

Firmware

Each computer device you use has special software resident in integrated circuits called firmware containing small programs for providing basic communications between the operating system and the hardware.

- System firmware contains program code that informs the processor of the devices present and how to communicate with them.
- Most components and peripheral devices that connect to a computer (such as the video and network adapters, USB ports, and digital cameras) have their own firmware, which is often limited to small programs for providing basic communication between the operating system and the component.

Although you may never be aware of the firmware on a mobile device, on an older PC or laptop you may see evidence of the system and other firmware as they perform tests of the hardware. Carefully, watch the screen as you power up the computer, as shown in Figure 1-1. If status and error messages display in plain text on a black background during startup, they are the result of tests run by the system firmware or the tests by additional firmware on the computer's components. More recent computers may show a message only if there is a serious problem with the computer.

Today's Microcomputers

The miniaturization of computers led to computers being built into all types of machinery, including vehicles, aircraft, and appliances. Computers touch our lives 24/7, and each has some form of operating system.

Servers. A server is a computer that provides one or more services to other computers over a network. What services do servers provide? A file server stores data files for network-connected users. If a server has one or more printers connected to it that it shares with users on the network, it is a print server. We call a server doing both tasks a file and print server; even though it sounds like two services, they combine into one service.

```
Phoenix — Award BIOS v6.00PC
Copyright (C) 1984-2003, Phoenix Technologies, LTD


Main Processor : AMD Athlon (tm) 64 X2 Dual Core Processor 3000+
Memory Testing : 1720000K OK
```

FIGURE 1–1 An example of a firmware start-up message on an old PC.
Source: Phoenix Technologies Ltd.

A PC laptop.
©Rashevskyi Viacheslav/Shutterstock

A MacBook laptop.
©Norman Kin Hang Chan/123RF

©Zeynep Demir/Shutterstock

Other services include messaging services (email and fax), Web services, and many others. It takes specialized software to provide each type of server service, and complementary client software to request each type of service over a network. A computer on the user end of these services is a client. Today's client computers include the PCs, laptops, tablets, and smartphones discussed in this book. A server can offer multiple services at the same time while also being a client to other servers.

A desktop or laptop computer can act as a server for a few network clients. However, a server to which hundreds or thousands of clients must connect requires much more capable hardware to provide more storage, faster processing, and faster network access. It also requires specialized software, beginning with the operating systems. There are versions of Windows, Apple macOS, Linux, and UNIX especially designed as servers. The hardware for a high-quality server can run into the tens of thousands of dollars and upward, versus the much lower cost of a consumer-grade PC at a few hundred dollars.

Desktops and Laptops. A desktop computer, often called a personal computer (PC), is a computer designed to spend its useful life in one location—on a desk. A typical desktop computer consists of a box containing the main components, a display screen, a keyboard, and a pointing device (mouse). The box and the display screen may be combined into one case—referred to as an all-in-one.

A laptop computer has a flat screen and a keyboard, each integrated into a panel with a hinge holding the two together and allowing you to close the laptop and slip it into a case for easy portability. There are many sizes and types of laptop computers. Laptops are often used as portable replacements for desktop PCs. The common operating systems for desktops and laptops are Apple's macOS (previously named OS X) for Apple brand desktop and laptops, Microsoft Windows, and Linux for other brands of PCs and laptops, the Chrome OS for Chromebox system units that are essentially PCs that come configured with the Chrome OS, and the Chrome OS for the Chromebook laptops. There are several manufacturers who sell Chromebooks, but Google does not provide Chrome OS as a separate consumer product.

In this book, we use the term personal computer (PC) for a desktop computer running Windows or Linux and Mac for the Apple iMac desktop computers as well as the MacBook laptop computers. Both types of Apple computers run macOS.

Mobile Devices. Microcomputers today include a long list of devices that don't have *computer* in their name, including mobile devices. A mobile device has all or most of its electronic circuitry, such as the microprocessor, controllers, and memory, on a single microchip. This is known as system-on-a-chip (SoC). Mobile devices use wireless technologies and include a wide variety of products ranging from single-purpose computers to multifunction mobile devices. Some mobile devices run proprietary OSs, while others run scaled-down versions of desktop OSs. A mobile device commonly stores its OS in firmware, as an embedded OS.

The most popular mobile devices are smartphones. A smartphone works as a cell phone, but also lets you connect to the Internet, view your email, and install and run a variety of apps for entertainment, education, and work. Modern smartphones have high-quality touch screens. Examples of smartphones are Apple's iPhones and various models by Motorola, Nokia, HTC, Samsung, LG, and others. Examples of operating systems designed specifically for use on smartphones include Google's Android and Apple iOS Windows Phone (versions 7, 8, and 8.1), and Windows 10 Mobile.

Another very popular type of mobile device is a tablet. A tablet has a touch screen, has no integrated keyboard (usually), is larger than a smartphone, and is much more portable than a laptop. There are many lines of tablet products, such as the Apple iPad, Microsoft Surface, Samsung Galaxy, Google Nexus, Sony Xperia, and Kindle Fire.

Based on your preferences and needs, you can purchase a tablet with one of these OSs preinstalled: Apple iOS, Microsoft Windows, Android, or Chrome OS.

Internet of Things. And lastly, microcomputers exist in devices belonging to the Internet of things (IoT). These are devices we don't normally think of as computing devices. They include kitchen appliances, thermostats, utility meters, components in automobiles, light bulbs, and industrial control devices. They are not necessarily mobile, but they communicate on networks, often the Internet. IoT devices are increasingly used in industrial automation, connecting wirelessly, or via Ethernet, to automation networks.

try this!

Functions of Microcomputer Operating Systems

When using her PC at work or her Mac at home our friend Brianna spends much of her time in a specific application, such as a word processor, a graphical drawing program, or a Web browser. However, she must also perform tasks outside of these applications, beginning with the simple task of logging onto the computer, launching an application, and managing files. Since each type of computer requires different skills to complete tasks, she wants to gain a better understanding of the OSs to perform better on the job and be more comfortable working with the different computers. She wants to learn what an OS is and what functions it performs, which we describe in the following sections.

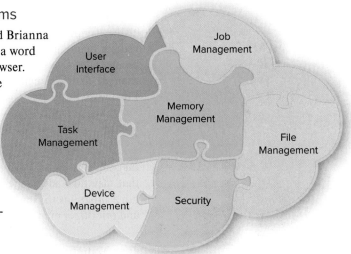

The functions of an operating system.

The Big Picture

When a computer is turned on an operating system starts up (or "boots up," a derivation of the expression "lifting yourself by your own bootstraps"). Its main component, the kernel, remains in memory while the computer is running, managing low-level (close-to-the-hardware) OS tasks.

When a programmer, also known as a "developer," writes an application, he or she designs the application to interact with the operating system and to make requests for hardware services through the operating system. To do this, a programmer must write the program to use the correct commands to request operating system services. The operating system, in turn, interacts with the hardware on behalf of the application and fulfills the requests the application made. An operating system performs several functions. We'll study them next.

User Interface

The user interface (UI) is the software layer, sometimes called the shell, through which the user interacts with the OS. The UI includes the command processor, which loads programs into memory, as well as the many visual components of the operating system (what you see when you look at the display).

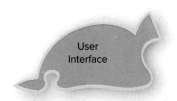

Command-line Interface. On a computer running Linux (without a graphical shell), this visual component consists of a character-based command line that requires text input. This is the command-line interface (CLI). Windows and macOS both have an

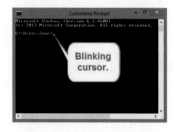

FIGURE 1–2 The Windows Command Prompt.
Source: Microsoft Corporation

Note: Although Linux traditionally had a CLI, most current versions of Linux for the desktop come with both CLIs and GUIs.

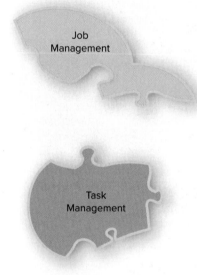

optional CLI that runs in a window. Figure 1-2 shows the Windows 10 Command Prompt for the user Jane: white characters against a black screen, with a blinking **cursor** waiting for you to type a command at the keyboard. A cursor in a CLI is merely a marker for the current position where what you type on the keyboard will appear. Only a limited set of characters can display on the screen. To become proficient at working in a CLI, you must memorize the commands and their modifiers and subcommands.

Graphical User Interface. Apple's macOS, Microsoft's Windows, and even mobile operating systems each provides an information-rich **graphical user interface (GUI)**, fully integrated into the operating system. It is through this GUI that you communicate with the OS and the computer. The GUI offers menus and small graphical icons that allow you to use a pointing device to select programs to run and to perform many other tasks, such as opening a word processor file.

Although you do not have to memorize commands, working within a GUI does require learning the meaning of the various graphical pieces that make up the GUI and how to navigate among them to access your programs and data. In addition, you must learn how to activate a program (start it running) so that you can get your work or play done. Figure 1-3 shows the Apple's macOS GUI. Notice the icons and other graphical components, such as the bar at the bottom containing icons for starting apps. Three windows are open on the desktop. In a GUI, you move a graphical pointer around using a pointing device—usually a mouse, trackball, touch pad, or touch screen. The pointer allows you to select or manipulate objects in the GUI to accomplish tasks. For example, to delete an item in macOS drag it into the Trash, shown on the bottom right of Figure 1-3. By contrast, in a CLI, you would type a command such as "delete report.txt."

Job Management

Job management, also known as process scheduler, is an operating system function that controls the order and time in which programs run. Two examples of programs that may take advantage of this function are a scheduling program that schedules other programs to run on a certain day and time, and a print program that manages and prioritizes multiple print jobs.

Task Management

Task management is an operating system function found in multitasking operating systems. **Multitasking** implies that a computer is running two or more programs (tasks)

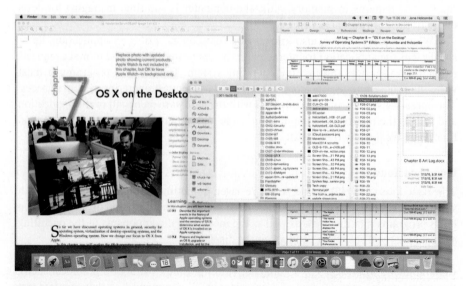

FIGURE 1–3 The macOS GUI.
Source: Apple Inc.

at the same time. In reality, a computer cannot simultaneously run more tasks than the number of processors that exist within the computer. Until recently, most microcomputers had only a single processor, so they accomplish multitasking through a scheme that makes order out of chaos by determining which program responds to the keystrokes and mouse movements. New processors can have multiple CPUs within a single chip, so they have true multitasking coexisting with task switching.

try this!

View Active Tasks in Windows or macOS

You can see what tasks are running on your Windows or macOS computer. Try this:

1. On a Windows computer with a keyboard, press CTRL-SHIFT-ESC to open Task Manager, a utility that lets you view tasks as running applications and their processes. Select the Processes tab and notice the large number of active processes.

2. On an macOS computer press COMMAND+SPACEBAR to open the Spotlight search box, and then type "activity" and select Activity Monitor from the results list. Notice the list of processes in the column labeled Process Name.

Task management controls the focus (where the system's attention is at any given moment). It allows the user to switch between tasks by giving the focus to the application the user brings to the foreground. In graphical operating systems, the foreground application runs in the current window, the window that is on top of other windows on the screen. This window receives input from the keyboard, mouse, and/or touch screen when the user types. While active in memory, a program runs as one or more small components called processes. The OS's task management function manages these processes.

File Management

File management, also referred to as data management, is an operating system function that allows the operating system to read, write, and modify data, while managing the logical storage of the data. Each operating system has at least one scheme of logical organization, called a file system. A file system is the logical structure used on a storage device (hard disk, optical disc, thumb drive, etc.) for managing and storing files. The file system also includes the program code that performs these tasks. An operating system uses a technique called formatting to write the logical structure to a storage device. The operating system maps the logical organization of the file system to physical locations on the storage device, most often a conventional hard disk drive or solid-state drive (SSD), so that it can store and retrieve the data.

File Management

Normally, a single storage device will have only a single file system, residing in an area defined as a partition, but some operating systems allow a storage device to have more than one partition. A partition may be an entire drive volume or just a portion of a drive, and an operating system automatically assigns some identifier, such as C for the first hard drive recognized by Windows. Windows follows the drive letter with a colon, so that a complete drive name is C:. We call this a logical drive.

Note: As a rule, the term *folder* is used in a GUI, while the term *directory* is used in a non-GUI operating system.

Within the logical structure of a file system, data is organized into entities called files that are saved to storage devices. File management also allows users to organize their files, using other special files that act as containers. One of these special files, called a folder or directory, can contain lists of files as well as other folders, along with the physical location of the files and folders. Figure 1-4 shows the Windows 10 File Explorer with folder icons identifying various folders. The Navigation pane on the left includes two drive icons for the local disks C: and D:.

Device Management

The device management function controls hardware devices by using special software called device drivers that are installed in the operating system. A device driver supplements or replaces firmware—even parts of the system firmware. It contains code for controlling a component; usually allowing much more control of a device than the device's firmware alone. A device driver is unique to a device; the manufacturer of the device creates it to work with a specific operating system. For instance, a printer

Device Management

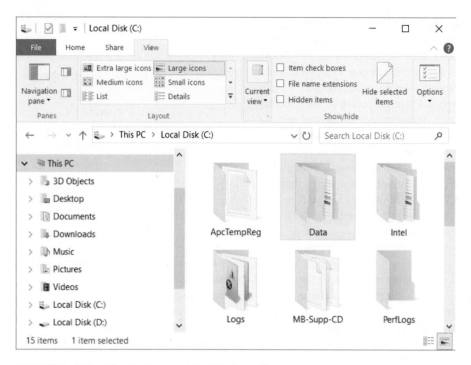

FIGURE 1–4 The File Explorer app in Windows 10.
Source: Microsoft Corporation

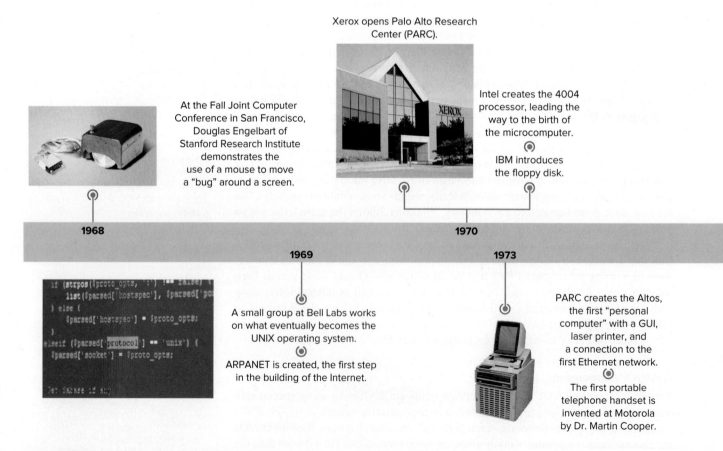

Xerox opens Palo Alto Research Center (PARC).

At the Fall Joint Computer Conference in San Francisco, Douglas Engelbart of Stanford Research Institute demonstrates the use of a mouse to move a "bug" around a screen.

Intel creates the 4004 processor, leading the way to the birth of the microcomputer.

IBM introduces the floppy disk.

A small group at Bell Labs works on what eventually becomes the UNIX operating system.

ARPANET is created, the first step in the building of the Internet.

PARC creates the Altos, the first "personal computer" with a GUI, laser printer, and a connection to the first Ethernet network.

The first portable telephone handset is invented at Motorola by Dr. Martin Cooper.

1968

1969

1970

1973

or video adapter may come with separate device drivers for Windows, macOS, and Linux. OSs today are plug- and- play (PNP), which makes them intelligent enough to detect an installed or connected device and automatically search for and install the needed device driver.

Note: The timeline running along the bottom of the next several pages shows highlights of computing history. Some are described in this chapter. Many are not.

Memory Management

Memory management is an operating system function that manages the placement of programs and data in memory, while keeping track of where it put them. Modern operating systems use a scheme for making optimal use of memory, even allowing more code and data to be in memory than what the physical RAM used as system memory can hold. However, if you have insufficient memory for the type and number of apps you use, you may notice your computer slowing down. Adding more memory to a computer will usually allow you to run applications faster. However, there is a limit to how much RAM memory you can physically install in a computer, and there is also a limit to how much memory each operating system can use. We will address the limits for each operating system in upcoming chapters.

Memory Management

Security

The built-in security features of an operating system provide password-protected authentication of the user before allowing access to the local computer and may restrict what someone can do on a computer. This protects the computer and the data it contains from unauthorized access. For example, Rachel is the accounting clerk in a small company. She has confidential information on her computer, and she doesn't want just anyone to be able to walk up to her computer and access the information stored there. Rachel can set up her computer so that others cannot access the data on

Security

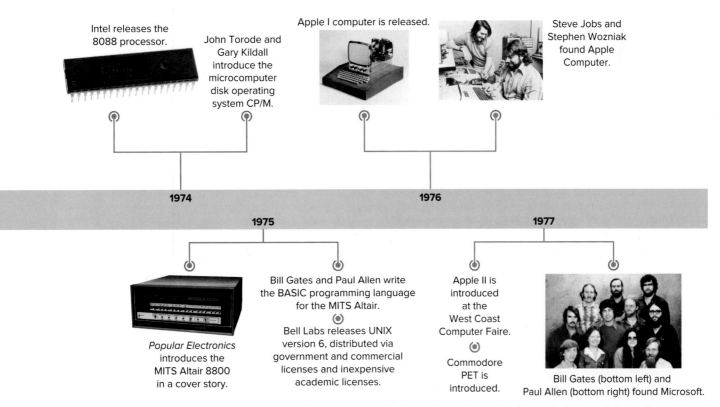

Intel releases the 8088 processor.

John Torode and Gary Kildall introduce the microcomputer disk operating system CP/M.

Apple I computer is released.

Steve Jobs and Stephen Wozniak found Apple Computer.

1974

1976

1975

1977

Popular Electronics introduces the MITS Altair 8800 in a cover story.

Bill Gates and Paul Allen write the BASIC programming language for the MITS Altair.

Bell Labs releases UNIX version 6, distributed via government and commercial licenses and inexpensive academic licenses.

Apple II is introduced at the West Coast Computer Faire.

Commodore PET is introduced.

Bill Gates (bottom left) and Paul Allen (bottom right) found Microsoft.

her computer. Security is a large topic—one that would take many books and weeks of your time to really master—but to go much farther in this book without addressing computer security would be foolish, so Chapter 2 is devoted to computer security basics. There you will learn about threats to computers, what security is built in to the operating systems discussed in this book, and the steps you can take to protect yourself from threats.

LO 1.2 | Yesterday's Operating Systems

The complex operating systems you see on your desktop, laptop, and mobile devices didn't just magically appear one day. They evolved through many small steps over several decades. An operating system as a separate entity didn't exist in the early years of digital computing (defined roughly as from World War II into the 1950s). At that time, each computer was dedicated to a single purpose, such as performing trajectory calculations for weapons or mathematical analysis for a science lab. Each program included system functions as well as the main function of the computer.

In those early days, the "user" was a government agency, research institute, or large business. Each organization ordered computers to meet their needs, as narrow as they may seem today. It was common for programmers to write the system I/O routines (the stuff of today's OSs) right into their programs. By the mid-1960s, as data storage on disk systems became more common, we needed operating systems to manage these disks and to perform other common system-level routines. As new technologies emerged, computers became more capable, leading to the need for an underlying operating system.

In this section, we explore the history of present-day computing devices and their operating systems. We start with UNIX, arguably the oldest OS still in use today. Its beginnings predate microcomputers.

Note: The MITS Altair 8800 was an important predecessor to the Apple II, TRS-80, and PET computers. Although featured in a cover article of the January 1975 issue of *Popular Mechanics,* it was not for everyday use. Whether you bought the $395 kit or the fully assembled $495 version, the input method was switches that you flipped to program it, and the result of these efforts (the output) was a pattern of blinking lights. As a portent of the future, the Altair 8800 gave Bill Gates and Paul Allen their very first sale of a ROM-based interpreter for the BASIC programming language.

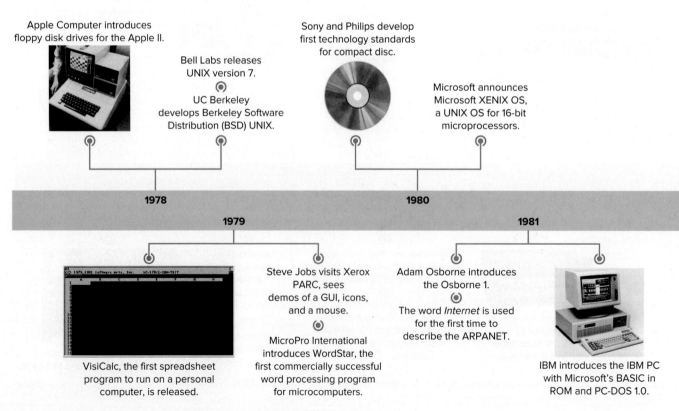

Apple Computer introduces floppy disk drives for the Apple II.

Bell Labs releases UNIX version 7.

UC Berkeley develops Berkeley Software Distribution (BSD) UNIX.

Sony and Philips develop first technology standards for compact disc.

Microsoft announces Microsoft XENIX OS, a UNIX OS for 16-bit microprocessors.

1978

1980

1979

1981

VisiCalc, the first spreadsheet program to run on a personal computer, is released.

Steve Jobs visits Xerox PARC, sees demos of a GUI, icons, and a mouse.

MicroPro International introduces WordStar, the first commercially successful word processing program for microcomputers.

Adam Osborne introduces the Osborne 1.

The word *Internet* is used for the first time to describe the ARPANET.

IBM introduces the IBM PC with Microsoft's BASIC in ROM and PC-DOS 1.0.

©Ralph Morse/Getty Images, ©ANATOL/Shutterstock, Source: Visicorp, ©Bettmann/Getty Images

UNIX—The Operating System for All Platforms

UNIX has a longer history than the other operating systems described in this book, and it is still in use today. In fact, Apple's Mac macOS is a certified UNIX operating system. UNIX grew out of an operating system developed for an early Digital Equipment Corporation (DEC) computer and went through several generations of changes before it emerged from the Bell Labs Computing Science Research Center (Bell Labs) as UNIX version 6 in 1975, a portable operating system for minicomputers and mainframe computers. A portable operating system is one that you can use on a variety of computer system platforms, with only minor alterations required to be compatible with the underlying architecture. Minicomputers and mainframe computers allowed multiple remote users to connect and use the computer's resources, and UNIX supported the time-sharing and multitasking features that made this possible.

The University of California at Berkeley licensed UNIX, modified it, and distributed it to other schools as Berkeley Software Distribution (BSD) version 4.2. Later versions followed. The schools paid licensing fees to Bell Labs. Students and others improved on and added to UNIX, freely sharing their code with each other. This tradition still prevails today with such versions of UNIX as FreeBSD, NetBSD, OpenBSD, and OpenSolaris. Commercial versions of UNIX today include AIX, OpenServer (derived from SCO UNIX), and HP/UX.

Today UNIX is still used on very large computer systems (referred to as mainframes) and less commonly on Intel desktop systems, as well as on a variety of midsize computers. Versions of UNIX run on many of the world's

try this!

Research the History of UNIX

Learn more about the UNIX operating system.
Try this:

1. Point your browser to **opengroup.org/unix**.
2. Look for a link to The UNIX Evolution: An Innovative History. There is also a link to the UNIX Infographic that summarizes the history up to just a few years ago.
3. Browse through the list of topics to learn more about what is currently happening with UNIX.

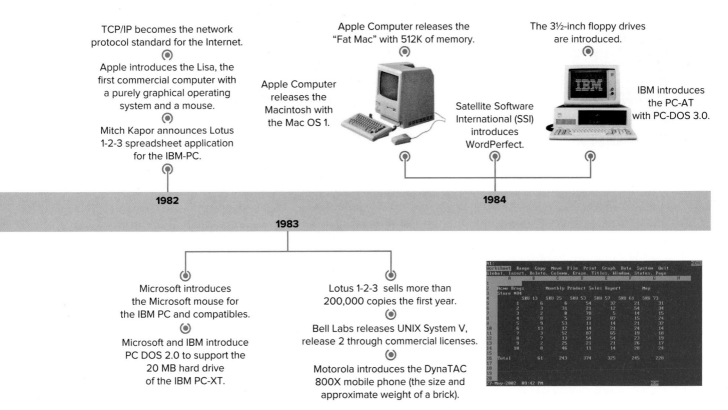

TCP/IP becomes the network protocol standard for the Internet.

Apple introduces the Lisa, the first commercial computer with a purely graphical operating system and a mouse.

Mitch Kapor announces Lotus 1-2-3 spreadsheet application for the IBM-PC.

Apple Computer releases the "Fat Mac" with 512K of memory.

Apple Computer releases the Macintosh with the Mac OS 1.

Satellite Software International (SSI) introduces WordPerfect.

The 3½-inch floppy drives are introduced.

IBM introduces the PC-AT with PC-DOS 3.0.

1982

1984

1983

Microsoft introduces the Microsoft mouse for the IBM PC and compatibles.

Microsoft and IBM introduce PC DOS 2.0 to support the 20 MB hard drive of the IBM PC-XT.

Lotus 1-2-3 sells more than 200,000 copies the first year.

Bell Labs releases UNIX System V, release 2 through commercial licenses.

Motorola introduces the DynaTAC 800X mobile phone (the size and approximate weight of a brick).

©Interfoto/Alamy, ©Twin Design/Shutterstock, Source: Convergent Technologies, Unix system

Internet servers. Most versions of UNIX also offer several different user interfaces. Some use character mode, like the traditional shells, such as the Bourne shell and the C shell. Others use a graphical interface such as GNOME or KDE. As mentioned earlier, Apple's macOS operating system is based on a version of UNIX, and it has a graphical user interface.

Even fierce UNIX advocates do not see UNIX taking over the desktop any time soon. However, it is very secure and stable. Versions of UNIX run on many of the world's Internet servers.

The Evolution of Desktop Operating Systems

The miniaturization of computer components inevitably led to the evolution of desktop operating systems available to consumers.

Small Steps

Operating systems evolved through many small steps over several decades, some in the form of technical advances and others in evolutionary changes in how people used computers, especially as they saw the need to use computers as multipurpose devices. The "user," at first a government agency, research institute, or large business, would define the computer's purpose at any given time by the program chosen to run. In the 1950s, some early "operating systems" managed data storage on tape for mainframe computers, but it was much more common for application programmers to write system I/O routines (the stuff of today's OSs) right into their programs. By the mid-1960s, as disk systems became more common on large computers, we needed operating systems to manage these disks and to perform other common system-level routines.

The computer enthusiasts who bought the earliest microcomputers of the 1970s, such as the MITS Altair 8800, were infatuated with the technology. What we now consider slow CPU speeds, very limited memory, clumsy I/O devices, and lack of software was exciting and new technology at the time. They would network with like-minded

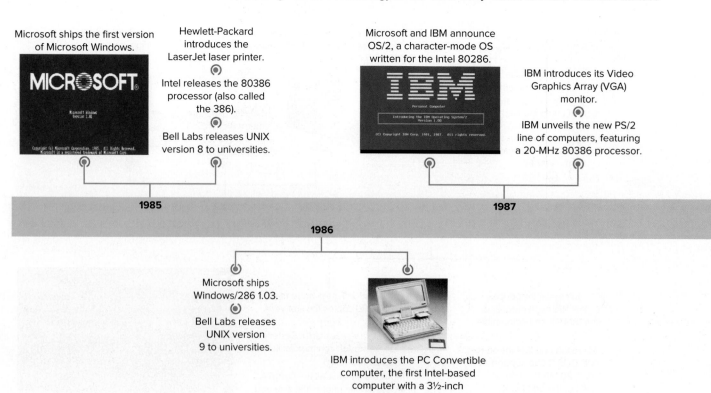

Microsoft ships the first version of Microsoft Windows.

Hewlett-Packard introduces the LaserJet laser printer.

Intel releases the 80386 processor (also called the 386).

Bell Labs releases UNIX version 8 to universities.

Microsoft and IBM announce OS/2, a character-mode OS written for the Intel 80286.

IBM introduces its Video Graphics Array (VGA) monitor.

IBM unveils the new PS/2 line of computers, featuring a 20-MHz 80386 processor.

1985

1987

1986

Microsoft ships Windows/286 1.03.

Bell Labs releases UNIX version 9 to universities.

IBM introduces the PC Convertible computer, the first Intel-based computer with a 3½-inch floppy disk drive.

Sources: Microsoft Corporation, IBM Corporation, ©Science & Society Picture Library/Getty Images

people, have informal meetings and discussions, and then gather in self-help groups and form clubs such as the Home Brew Computer Club in California's Silicon Valley. They shared their techniques for creating hardware and programming language software for these computers. Almost every one of these early microcomputers exceeded the expectations of their makers and users, but before long, and for a variety of reasons, most of the early entrepreneurial companies and their products disappeared.

Early Apple Computers and Their OSs

In 1976, Steve Jobs and Stephen Wozniak—two friends working out of a garage—founded Apple Computer, based on their first computer, the Apple I. Their real notoriety began in 1977 when they introduced the Apple II at the West Coast Computer Faire in San Francisco. This created interest in the brand, and the addition of disk drives in 1978 made it a sought-after product for the technically adventurous consumer. The OS for the Apple II did not have a GUI interface—which first appeared in later Apple computers.

The Killer App for the Apple II For a microcomputer to truly become a successful, widely accepted product—used in businesses as well as by hobbyists—it had to be a tool that performed an important task; it had to have an application that many people needed enough to purchase a computer. We call that application a killer app.

One such killer app was VisiCalc, an electronic spreadsheet program introduced in 1979 for the Apple II computer (running the Apple OS). Before microcomputers and programs like VisiCalc, people created spreadsheets manually, on large grid-printed sheets of paper. Consider one scenario: the manager of a small retail store would enter a column of numbers—say, sales for one product in the store—day-by-day for a month. Then he would add up the daily columns to get the total sales for that product for that month. The next column was for the next product, and so on. The process was tedious and error prone, but very valuable to the manager of the store. VisiCalc automated this

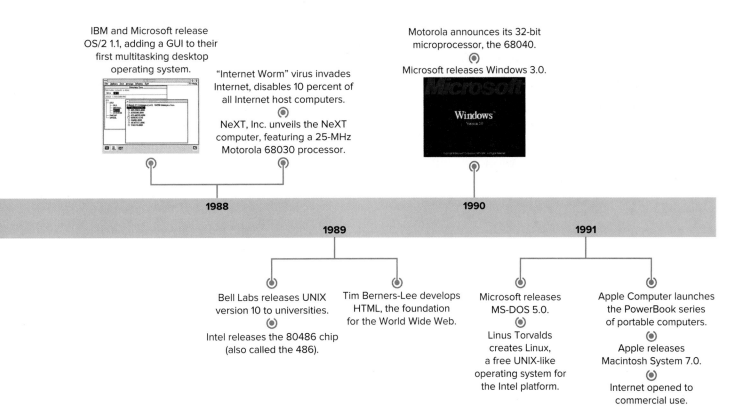

IBM and Microsoft release OS/2 1.1, adding a GUI to their first multitasking desktop operating system.

"Internet Worm" virus invades Internet, disables 10 percent of all Internet host computers.

NeXT, Inc. unveils the NeXT computer, featuring a 25-MHz Motorola 68030 processor.

Motorola announces its 32-bit microprocessor, the 68040.

Microsoft releases Windows 3.0.

1988

1989

1990

1991

Bell Labs releases UNIX version 10 to universities.

Intel releases the 80486 chip (also called the 486).

Tim Berners-Lee develops HTML, the foundation for the World Wide Web.

Microsoft releases MS-DOS 5.0.

Linus Torvalds creates Linux, a free UNIX-like operating system for the Intel platform.

Apple Computer launches the PowerBook series of portable computers.

Apple releases Macintosh System 7.0.

Internet opened to commercial use.

Sources: IBM Corporation and Microsoft Corporation

thankless job, remembered the formulas for the calculations, and allowed people to recalculate a whole column of numbers after changes were made.

VisiCalc gave people a reason to buy a personal computer, contributing to the success of the Apple II. However, as the 1980s arrived, Apple failed to come out with a successor to the Apple II in a timely fashion.

The Lisa Computer—a pretty face with no apps. In 1982, Apple introduced the Lisa, the first commercially available computer with a purely graphical operating system—and a mouse. However, this computer was not the needed successor to the Apple II because it lacked something very important for consumers—applications. It was not successful.

try this!

Watch Old TV Commercials for the IBM PC and Lotus 1-2-3

It has been over 30 years since the introduction of the IBM PC in 1981 and the killer app Lotus 1-2-3 in 1983. See how these products were introduced to the public in TV advertisements. Try this:

1. Point your browser to http://mentalfloss.com/article/48627/lotus-1-2-3-three-decades

2. Read the article and watch the first two videos. Some of us can verify the accuracy of the portrayal of office workers at the time (except for the singing and dancing part).

3. The third video is no longer available.

4. The fourth video reviews the history of Lotus 1-2-3 with great clips of the news coverage and events and people behind the product.

Apple Macintosh and the Mac OS. Apple's Macintosh computer, released in 1984, overshadowed the Lisa and marked the beginning of consumer excitement and the near-cult following of the Apple computer products. The Macintosh came with Mac OS System 1, a GUI operating system that used a mouse. Apple improved the Mac OS over the years to include many easy-to-use features. Most importantly, there were soon plenty of apps for this computer.

Apple revised and improved the operating system to support multiple users, but it was weak in memory management and lacked full multitasking.

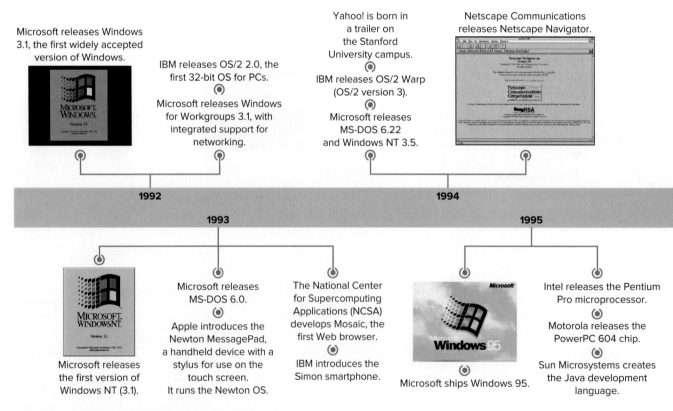

Microsoft releases Windows 3.1, the first widely accepted version of Windows.

IBM releases OS/2 2.0, the first 32-bit OS for PCs.

Microsoft releases Windows for Workgroups 3.1, with integrated support for networking.

Yahoo! is born in a trailer on the Stanford University campus.

IBM releases OS/2 Warp (OS/2 version 3).

Microsoft releases MS-DOS 6.22 and Windows NT 3.5.

Netscape Communications releases Netscape Navigator.

1992

1994

1993

1995

Microsoft releases the first version of Windows NT (3.1).

Microsoft releases MS-DOS 6.0.

Apple introduces the Newton MessagePad, a handheld device with a stylus for use on the touch screen. It runs the Newton OS.

The National Center for Supercomputing Applications (NCSA) develops Mosaic, the first Web browser.

IBM introduces the Simon smartphone.

Microsoft ships Windows 95.

Intel releases the Pentium Pro microprocessor.

Motorola releases the PowerPC 604 chip.

Sun Microsystems creates the Java development language.

Sources: Microsoft Corporation and Netscape Communications Corporation

The final release of the classic Mac OS family was Mac OS 9, introduced in 1999. In 2001, it was replaced by a completely new operating system—Mac OS X, based on UNIX. This is the OS on the Apple desktop and laptop computers currently in use, although Apple officially changed the name to macOS in 2016. We will use this latest name throughout the book to refer to the OS for the Apple Mac.

The IBM PC

IBM introduced the IBM PC in 1981, taking advantage of the void left by Apple, who had not introduced a true successor to their Apple II. The IBM PC far exceeded IBM's sales forecast of a quarter of a million units during its predicted 5-year product lifetime. According to one account, IBM took orders for half a million computers in the first few days after introducing the IBM PC. The early enthusiasts bought it despite the roughly $5,000 price tag for a typical configuration. The IBM logo on the product implied that it was a serious business computer, inspiring business users to buy it.

IBM PC DOS. The selection of an OS for the IBM PC came from a fateful series of events. IBM representatives visited Microsoft, then a fledgling software company, with two objectives. Acquire a BASIC interpreter to install in firmware on their PCs and find an OS that would start up from disk (diskette at first) on these new systems because Microsoft's BASIC interpreter was available on other microcomputers including the MITS Altair 8800, and it was popular with early users. IBM subsequently licensed Microsoft's BASIC interpreter and installed it in the firmware of the IBM PC.

When the IBM folks talked to Bill Gates about providing an OS, he sent them to another company, Digital Research, the creators of the then-popular CP/M OS. Digital Research refused to sign a contract with IBM, so the IBM guys went back to Bill Gates. Consequently, Microsoft bought an OS from another company, and this was the basis of the first version of the IBM PC Disk Operating System (DOS).

Note: In the years after its introduction, thousands of applications were written for PC DOS (and MS-DOS), but Lotus 1-2-3 (spreadsheet), dBase (database management), and WordPerfect (word processing) were the de facto business standards at the end of that decade. All contributed to the mass adoption of PCs at work, at school, and at home.

Note: Many of us still open a command line interface (CLI) in Windows to use certain advanced troubleshooting tools. There are two CLIs that come with Windows: the Command Prompt and the Windows Power Shell.

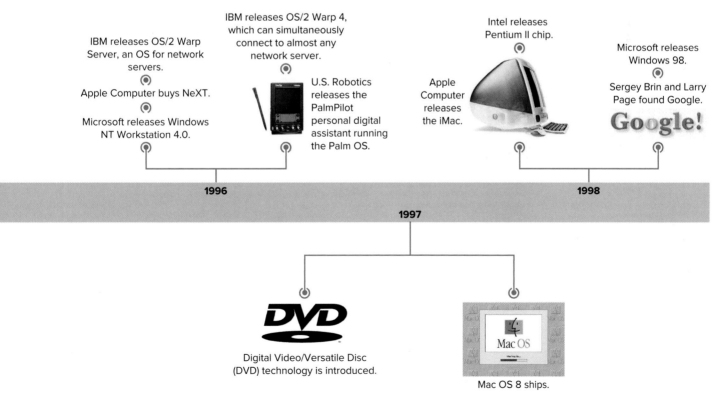

IBM releases OS/2 Warp Server, an OS for network servers.

Apple Computer buys NeXT.

Microsoft releases Windows NT Workstation 4.0.

IBM releases OS/2 Warp 4, which can simultaneously connect to almost any network server.

U.S. Robotics releases the PalmPilot personal digital assistant running the Palm OS.

Apple Computer releases the iMac.

Intel releases Pentium II chip.

Microsoft releases Windows 98.

Sergey Brin and Larry Page found Google.

Google!

1996

1998

1997

Digital Video/Versatile Disc (DVD) technology is introduced.

Mac OS 8 ships.

©Science & Society Picture Library/Getty Images, ©Bloomberg/Getty Images, Sources: Google LLC, Philips, and Apple Inc.

The Killer App for the IBM PC. While VisiCalc, the killer app for the Apple II, was still an important app, it did not take full advantage of the increased memory in the IBM PC. The IBM PC still needed a killer app. That app was a spreadsheet app that ran on the DOS operating system and used all the 640 KB of memory available to software (OS plus application) on the IBM PC. This new app was Lotus 1–2–3, which was noticeably faster than VisiCalc and had additional features, including database functions and a program for creating graphs from the spreadsheet data.

PC DOS versus MS-DOS. PC DOS was the version for IBM computers. MS-DOS refers to the several versions of DOS developed by Microsoft and made available to non-IBM PC manufacturers. "DOS" in both names stands for "disk operating system." DOS did not have the more advanced capabilities of today's OSs. It was single-tasking, with no support for virtual memory, no native GUI, and no built-in security function. While it could use much more memory than the OSs that preceded it, DOS had very limited memory support compared to the OSs developed over the last three decades to support our much more advanced computer hardware.

DOS had a text-mode command-line interface that required users to remember cryptic commands and their subcommands to perform file management functions and to launch DOS applications. Figure 1–5 shows a good example of how cryptic DOS was.

PC DOS 1.0 supported single-sided 5.25-inch floppies. After that, each major version of DOS was released to support new disk capacities. MS-DOS 6.22 was the last widely used version of that OS. Some forms of DOS are now available from third-party sources, but the need for this type of OS is dwindling.

OS/2

In 1987, Microsoft and IBM introduced their jointly developed Operating System/2 (OS/2), intended to replace DOS. However, it required a much more advanced and expensive computer than DOS required, had very limited support for DOS apps, and lacked a killer app.

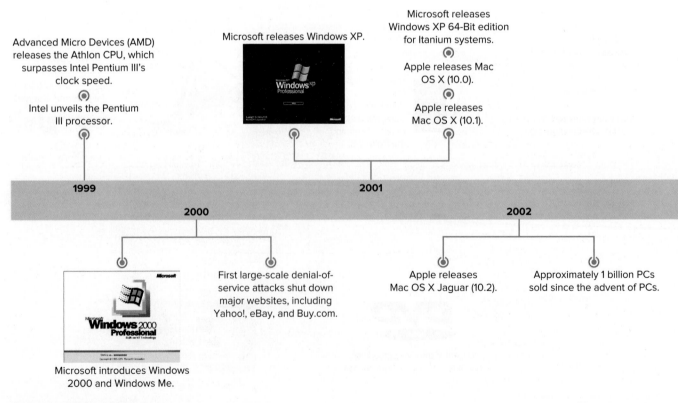

Advanced Micro Devices (AMD) releases the Athlon CPU, which surpasses Intel Pentium III's clock speed.

Intel unveils the Pentium III processor.

Microsoft releases Windows XP.

Microsoft releases Windows XP 64-Bit edition for Itanium systems.

Apple releases Mac OS X (10.0).

Apple releases Mac OS X (10.1).

1999

2000

2001

2002

Microsoft introduces Windows 2000 and Windows Me.

First large-scale denial-of-service attacks shut down major websites, including Yahoo!, eBay, and Buy.com.

Apple releases Mac OS X Jaguar (10.2).

Approximately 1 billion PCs sold since the advent of PCs.

Source: Microsoft Corporation

```
A:\>format c: /s /u

WARNING: ALL DATA ON NON-REMOVABLE DISK
DRIVE C: WILL BE LOST!
Proceed with Format (Y/N)?y


Formatting   502M
Format complete.
System transferred

Volume label (11 characters, ENTER for none)?

  526,106,624 bytes total disk space
      212,992 bytes used by system
  525,893,632 bytes available on disk

        8,192 bytes in each allocation unit.
       64,196 allocation units available on disk.

Volume Serial Number is 3A4E-17DA


A:\>_
```

FIGURE 1–5 The MS-DOS prompt showing the Format command and the resulting output to the screen.
Source: Microsoft Corporation

In 1994, IBM introduced OS/2 Warp, an improved version of OS/2 with a GUI. After about 18 months, IBM retreated from the battle for the desktop and targeted sales of OS/2 Warp to the high-end server market. It never rivaled Windows or UNIX in terms of sales. In 2003, IBM announced it would not develop future versions of OS/2, and in December 2004 IBM sold its PC division to China-based Lenovo Group. OS/2 support was discontinued in 2005.

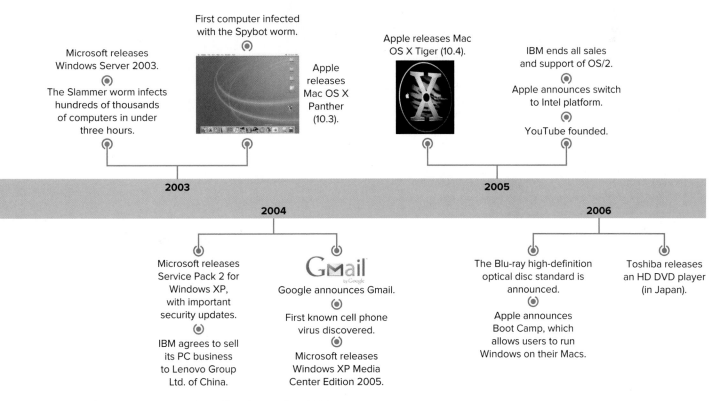

Sources: Apple Inc., ©Kim Kulish/Corbis/Getty Images, Google LLC.

Microsoft Windows

Microsoft Windows is an OS with a GUI. It began life in 1985 as a simple GUI shell on top of MS-DOS. Since then, it has slowly evolved into a much more advanced OS, dominating the desktop for much of its life. Windows' fate is tied to the PC. Therefore, as more people use mobile devices for many of the functions previously assigned to PCs, PC sales have declined. Windows computers have also faced tough competition in the K-12 education market, where Apple iPads and Chromebooks are important tools for students. Following is a brief look at the various Windows versions.

Windows 1 through 3. In 1985, when the first version of Windows appeared, it consisted of a not-very-good GUI by today's standards, balanced precariously on top of MS-DOS. The GUI code was separate from the OS code. It was slow and had a flat look—you couldn't lay one graphic on top of another. The ability to overlap graphical elements, such as windows and icons, did not show up until a later version.

In 1990, Microsoft introduced Windows 3.0, which supported capabilities contained in the Intel processors in the latest PCs. The most important feature of Windows 3.0 was that it would run DOS apps better than previous versions, so that you could keep your old DOS apps, while gradually moving to the expanding number of Windows apps. Windows 3.0 still had its quirks, but for the first time, IT managers saw a potential GUI replacement for DOS as the desktop OS of choice.

In the spring of 1992, Microsoft brought out a minor upgrade, Windows 3.1, which many organizations adopted as the standard desktop OS. The fact that Microsoft's entire suite of productivity applications was also available in versions for Windows 3.*x* helped encourage adoption.

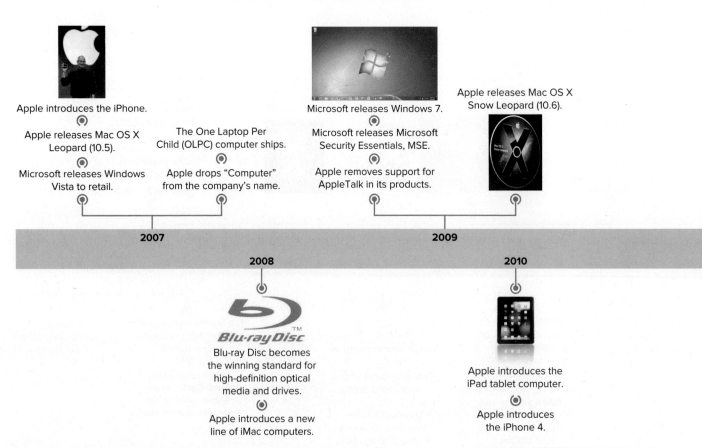

Apple introduces the iPhone.

Apple releases Mac OS X Leopard (10.5).

Microsoft releases Windows Vista to retail.

The One Laptop Per Child (OLPC) computer ships.

Apple drops "Computer" from the company's name.

Microsoft releases Windows 7.

Microsoft releases Microsoft Security Essentials, MSE.

Apple removes support for AppleTalk in its products.

Apple releases Mac OS X Snow Leopard (10.6).

2007

2009

2008

2010

Blu-ray Disc becomes the winning standard for high-definition optical media and drives.

Apple introduces a new line of iMac computers.

Apple introduces the iPad tablet computer.

Apple introduces the iPhone 4.

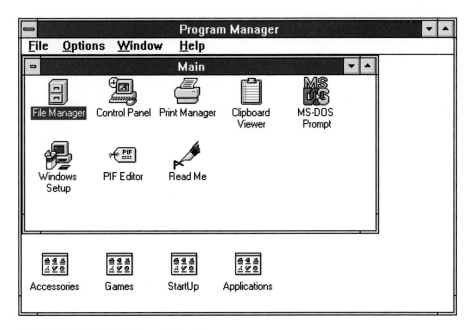

FIGURE 1–6 The Windows 3.1 desktop.
Source: Microsoft Corporation

Figure 1-6 shows the Windows 3.1 desktop. Notice that there is no task bar at the bottom of the screen, just the Program Manager window (the main window) with other windows nested in it.

Windows for Workgroups. DOS and Windows OSs through Windows 3.*x* included only the operating system functions. If you wanted to connect to a network, you added a network operating system (NOS) on top of your installed OS.

Google Glass Explorer "smart glasses" prototype available for $1,500 to a limited number of "Glass Explorers."

Microsoft releases Windows 8.1.

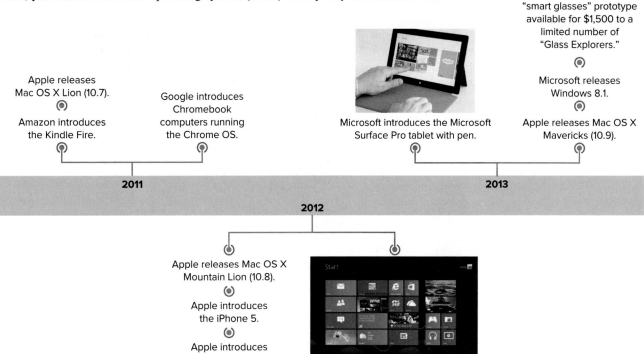

Apple releases Mac OS X Lion (10.7).

Amazon introduces the Kindle Fire.

Google introduces Chromebook computers running the Chrome OS.

Microsoft introduces the Microsoft Surface Pro tablet with pen.

Apple releases Mac OS X Mavericks (10.9).

2011

2013

2012

Apple releases Mac OS X Mountain Lion (10.8).

Apple introduces the iPhone 5.

Apple introduces the iPad mini.

Microsoft Windows 8 and the Microsoft Surface tablet are released.

This separate network operating system might be from 3COM or Novell, or it might be Microsoft's LAN Manager NOS, developed in the late 1980s. You had to install the correct client software for the type of network and servers to which you connected.

Beginning in October 1992 with Windows for Workgroups 3.1, Microsoft included both the client and server software in all of its Windows OS products. This enabled peer-to-peer networking, meaning desktop computers could act as servers to their peers. This worked well in a small work group environment of 10 or fewer computers. Windows for Workgroups 3.1 was followed a year later by Windows for Workgroups 3.11, with some improvements. It was still a GUI running on top of MS-DOS.

Windows NT. Because it had the same user interface as Windows 3.1, Windows NT was introduced in 1993 as Windows NT 3.1. That was where the similarity ended. It was a server operating system, which included server protocols in its integrated network support. Furthermore, unlike Windows 3.*x* and Windows for Workgroups, the GUI did not sit on top of DOS, but was an entirely new operating system.

Note: The acronym *NTFS* is the preferred usage when talking about the file system first introduced in Windows NT. The longer name for it, the "New Technology File System," is rarely used.

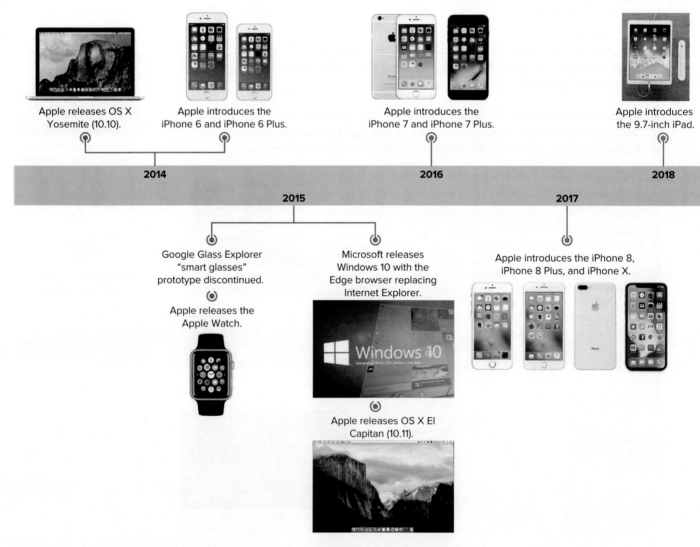

Apple releases OS X Yosemite (10.10).

Apple introduces the iPhone 6 and iPhone 6 Plus.

Apple introduces the iPhone 7 and iPhone 7 Plus.

Apple introduces the 9.7-inch iPad.

2014

2015

2016

2017

2018

Google Glass Explorer "smart glasses" prototype discontinued.

Apple releases the Apple Watch.

Microsoft releases Windows 10 with the Edge browser replacing Internet Explorer.

Apple introduces the iPhone 8, iPhone 8 Plus, and iPhone X.

Apple releases OS X El Capitan (10.11).

With Windows NT, Microsoft introduced the New Technology File System (NTFS) with an entirely new logical structure for storing files. This file system is expandable and uses a transaction processing system to track changes to files, so that it can roll back incomplete transactions. It also includes several other features, including file compression, file encryption, file and folder security, and indexing. NTFS is the default file system in the current versions of Windows.

The next version, Windows NT 3.5, released in 1994, was the first Windows OS to have separate editions: Windows NT Workstation and Windows NT Server. Both of these used the same kernel and interface, but the Server version had enhancements and components that were needed only on a network server. The Workstation version was a robust desktop operating system targeted to corporate and advanced users. It had a higher price tag than Windows 95 (introduced in 1995), which was intended for consumers.

In 1996, Microsoft introduced Server and Workstation editions of Windows NT 4.0, which had a GUI similar to that of Windows 95 as well as other improvements and enhancements to the OS.

Windows 95. Windows 95, released in 1995, was a continuation of the Windows 3.*x* model with the graphical environment simply "sitting" on top of the DOS operating system. It did have some improvements in the operating system, including the GUI, which made it the most popular microcomputer operating system up to that time.

Windows 98. Windows 98 was an evolutionary development in the Windows desktop operating system, including improvements in both visible and under-the-hood components. It offered more stability than its immediate predecessor, Windows 95, meaning that it was less likely to stop in its tracks just when you were about to complete that book order on Amazon. Figure 1–7 shows the Windows 98 desktop. Its biggest drawback was lack of security. It did not have a local security accounts database for local authentication, and it did not support the NTFS file system; therefore, it did not have file and folder security.

FIGURE 1–7 The Windows 98 desktop with open windows.
Source: Microsoft Corporation

The Windows XP Start Menu.
Source: Microsoft Corporation

Windows Me (Millennium Edition). Windows Me (Millennium edition), introduced in 2000, targeted the home market, especially the home game user. It was essentially Windows 98 with improved music, video, and home networking support. Windows Me was installed on many computers that were sold to individuals, but it was not an OS that organizations adopted.

Windows 2000. In 2000, Microsoft introduced the Windows 2000 family of OS products, which brought together the best of Windows 98 (the GUI) and Windows NT. Windows 2000 was available in several editions that covered OS needs from the desktop (Windows 2000 Professional) to the enterprise server. Figure 1–8 shows the Windows 2000 desktop.

Windows XP. In 2001, Microsoft introduced Windows XP, intended only for the consumer desktop, not for the server environment.

There were several Windows XP editions, but the three most common were Windows XP Home edition, Windows XP Professional, and Windows XP Media Center. All were 32-bit OSs, had the same improved GUI, and shared many of the same features, but only Windows XP Professional included several important network- and security-related features. Additionally, Microsoft offered Windows XP 64-bit edition, which supported only 64-bit software and was limited to computers with the Intel Itanium processors.

The Windows XP desktop was very different from that of its main predecessor, Windows 98. Figure 1–9 shows the Windows XP desktop with several open windows. Microsoft redesigned and reorganized the Start menu, shown here.

The last service pack for the 32-bit version of Windows XP was SP3. Support for Windows XP Service Pack 3 (SP3) and for the 64-bit version with Service Pack 2 ended in April 2014, per Microsoft's published policy, the Microsoft Support Lifecycle.

Windows Vista. Microsoft released the first retail edition of Windows Vista early in 2007. Seen more as an upgrade of Windows XP, it included improvements in how Windows handles graphics, files, and communications. The GUI had a new

FIGURE 1–8 The Windows 2000 desktop showing the Start menu and open windows.
Source: Microsoft Corporation

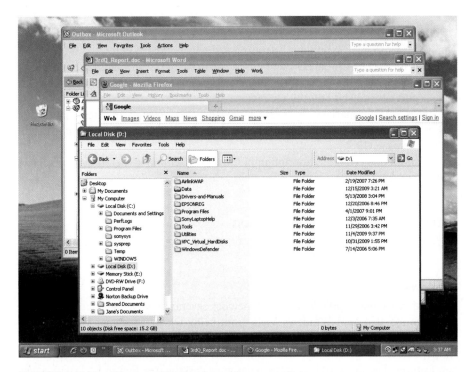

FIGURE 1–9 The Windows XP desktop with open windows.
Source: Microsoft Corporation

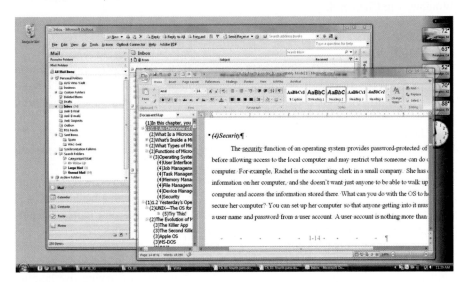

FIGURE 1–10 The Windows Vista desktop showing the transparent windows of the Aero feature.
Source: Microsoft Corporation; text ©Jane Holcombe

look compared to previous versions of Windows (see Figure 1-10). It also had a feature called Aero, which included translucent windows, live thumbnails, live icons, and other enhancements to the GUI. Windows Vista was not widely adopted due to problems with speed on older hardware as well as high hardware requirements. Mainstream support for Windows Vista ended in April 2012.

try this!

Are You Running 32-bit or 64-bit Windows?

If you have a Windows computer handy, see if it is running a 32-bit or 64-bit version. Try this:

1. In the Windows 7 or Windows 10 Start menu Search box (or in the Windows 8.x Start screen), type "system."
2. In the search results list, select "System." Do *not* select "System Information."
3. This opens Control Panel to the System page.
4. The System Type field will say "32-bit Operating System" or "64-bit Operating System."

LO 1.3 | Today's Desktop Operating Systems

Today's desktop microcomputer operating systems include Windows 7, Windows 8, Windows 10, macOS, Chrome OS, and Linux. All of these OSs are multiuser/multitasking operating systems, with support for virtual memory and security. Each comes in versions that support either 32-bit or 64-bit processors.

Table 1-1 summarizes the current desktop OSs covered in later chapters of this book, listing the publisher, platform, and types of applications that you can run natively on each OS.

What follows is a brief description of these OSs, with more detail in the chapters devoted to each OS.

Today's Windows for the Desktop

Today's Windows for the desktop include Windows 7, Windows 8, and Windows 10.

Windows 7

Released in October 2009, Windows 7 includes several improvements correcting the shortcomings that kept Windows Vista from being widely accepted. Windows 7 is faster than Windows Vista in several ways, from starting up, to going into and out of sleep mode, to recognizing new devices when you connect them. Windows 7 has many new features. The short list includes a redesigned desktop (see Figure 1-11) with a new taskbar that has many new features of its own, such as jump lists. Learn more about Windows 7 in Chapter 4.

Windows 8 and 8.1

Windows 8, released in October 2012, came with better security and improved wireless connectivity as well as support for some newer hardware, such as USB 3.0 ports and improved touch screen support for simultaneous multiple touches and gestures.

The most controversial changes to Windows 8 were to the GUI, or rather GUIs. The default GUI, centered around the Start screen shown in Figure 1-12, is a departure from the Windows 7 desktop with its three-dimensional look. Objects in this new GUI appear flat, without shading and borders so that they do not take up extra screen space. This is necessary because Windows 8 runs on a wide range of computing devices: PCs, laptops, and tablets. The Windows 8 Start screen contains tiles that represent apps. Each tile can show active content, such as newsfeeds, stock quotes, slideshows, and more, depending on the tile's app.

The second Windows 8 GUI, a modified version of the Windows 7 desktop (without the Start menu) has a very flat look to it in spite of having overlapping

TABLE 1–1 Summary of Current Desktop/Laptop Operating Systems

Desktop/Laptop OS	Company	Platform	Applications Supported
Windows 7	Microsoft	Intel/Microsoft	DOS, 16-bit Windows, 32-bit Windows, 64-bit Windows applications
Windows 8 and Windows 10	Microsoft	Intel/Microsoft	DOS, 16-bit Windows, 32-bit and 64-bit Windows applications for the Desktop and for the Windows 8 Modern GUI
macOS	Apple	Intel/Apple Mac	Mac applications
Linux	Various	Intel/Microsoft	UNIX/Linux applications
Chrome OS	Google (Alphabet)	Intel/Microsoft	Chrome Web Store apps and Android apps via Google Play

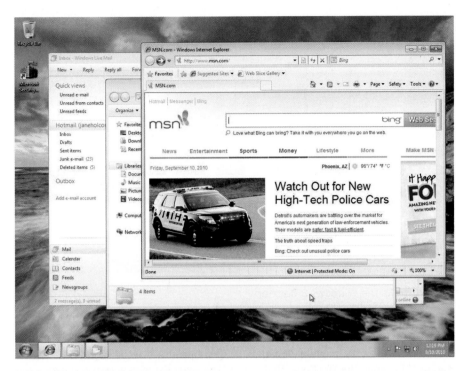

FIGURE 1–11 The Windows 7 desktop.
Source: Microsoft Corporation

FIGURE 1–12 The Windows 8 Start screen.
Source: Microsoft Corporation

windows. Figure 1-13 shows the Windows 8 desktop. In 2013, Microsoft released an update to Windows 8—Windows 8.1—with changes to the Start screen and the desktop that they hoped would satisfy critics of the Windows 8 GUIs.

Although Windows 8 came after Windows 7, it never sold sufficiently to match the market share achieved by Windows 7 (or Windows XP). This was despite the changes made in Windows 8.1. Therefore, this book does not include a separate chapter on Windows 8.*x*.

Note: In 2013, Windows 8 was followed by the important Windows 8.1 Update. Therefore, going forward in this book, we use the term Windows 8.*x* to refer to both releases.

Windows 10

In 2015, Microsoft introduced Windows 10, skipping the logical naming progression to Windows 9. Windows 10 includes a modified, but recognizable, Start menu on the

FIGURE 1–13 The Windows 8 desktop.
Sources: Microsoft Corporation; photos ©Jane Holcombe

desktop (returned by popular demand). It also includes new or improved features. Figure 1-14 shows the Windows 10 desktop. The short list of new features are:

- A new Start menu.
- Windows Hello biometric authentication using facial features or fingerprint.
- The Cortana personal assistant.
- The Microsoft Edge browser (replacing Internet Explorer).
- Universal apps that run on all Windows 10 systems.
- The Xbox app that brings game features to Windows 10.
- Support for multiple desktops within the GUI.

Further, for a period of one year after its introduction, Windows 10 was available as a free upgrade to consumers running Windows 7 Service Pack 1 (SP1) or Windows 8.1 Update on PCs, laptops, and tablets. Learn more about Windows 10 in Chapter 5.

FIGURE 1–14 The Windows 10 desktop.
Source: Microsoft Corporation

Apple macOS

Whereas the Linux and Microsoft OSs are available to install on hardware from many manufacturers, the Apple Inc. strategy has been to produce proprietary hardware and software for better integration of the OS and the hardware. They do not license macOS to run on other manufacturers' computers. This has historically resulted in a higher price for a Mac than for a comparable PC. For several years, beginning in the mid-1990s, Macintosh computers used the Motorola PowerPC chip with an architecture enhanced for graphics and multimedia. Since 2005 the Apple Mac line of computers have been Intel-based.

The Mac OSs in common use today are versions of macOS (X is the Roman numeral for 10). When first introduced in 2001, it was named macOS and it was a revolutionary change from the previous Mac OS 9 because Apple based macOS on NextStep, an OS with a UNIX kernel. Until macOS, the Macintosh OSs were strictly GUI environments, with no command-line option. macOS, with its UNIX origins, gives you the option of a character-based interface, but most users will happily work solely in the GUI (see Figure 1–15). Apple has released several versions of macOS renaming it macOS in 2016. Learn more about macOS and its features in Chapter 7.

Linux

Linux is an operating system modeled on UNIX and named in honor of its original developer, Linus Benedict Torvalds. He began it as a project in 1991 while a student at the University of Helsinki in his native Finland. He invited other programmers to work together to create an open-source operating system for modern computers. They created Linux using a powerful programming language called C, along with a free C compiler developed through the GNU project called GNU C Compiler (GCC). Linux has continued to evolve over the years, with programmers all over the globe testing and upgrading its code. Linus Torvalds could not have predicted in 1991 how well accepted the new operating system would be over 20 years later.

Linux is available in a variety of distributions, and it can be modified to run on nearly any computer. A distribution is a bundling of the Linux kernel and software—both enhancements to the OS and applications, such as word processors, spreadsheets, media players, and more. The person or organization providing the distribution may charge a fee for the enhancements and applications, but cannot charge a fee for the Linux code itself. Many distributions are free or very inexpensive.

Note: A distribution is also called a "distro" or "flavor."

Linux natively uses a command-line interface, and Figure 1–16 shows an example of a Linux directory list at the command line. Windows-like GUI environments,

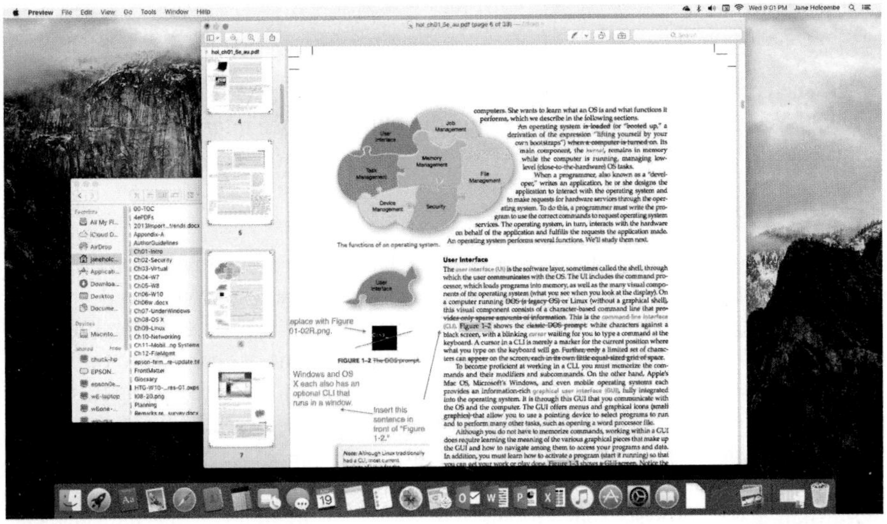

FIGURE 1–15 The macOS GUI.
Source: Apple Inc.; text ©Jane Holcombe

```
[cottrell@localhost ppp]$ ls -l
total 56
-rw-------    1 root     root          78 Feb 27 17:09 chap-secrets
-rw-r--r--    1 root     root         927 Apr 14 12:38 firewall-masq
-rw-r--r--    1 root     root         825 Apr 14 12:38 firewall-standalone
-rw-r--r--    1 root     root           0 Apr  8 09:08 ioptions
-rwxr-xr-x    1 root     root         310 Dec 26  2000 ip-down
-rwxr-xr-x    1 root     root        3564 Mar 20 22:17 ip-down.ipv6to4
-rwxr-xr-x    1 root     root         362 Dec 26  2000 ip-up
-rwxr-xr-x    1 root     root        5745 Mar 11 17:42 ip-up.ipv6to4
-rwxr-xr-x    1 root     root         918 Mar 11 17:43 ipv6-down
-rwxr-xr-x    1 root     root         918 Mar 11 17:43 ipv6-up
-rw-r--r--    1 root     root           5 Feb 27 17:09 options
-rw-------    1 root     root          77 Feb 27 17:09 pap-secrets
drwxr-xr-x    3 root     root        4096 Jul  5 15:02 peers
-rw-r--r--    1 root     root          93 Apr 14 12:38 pppoe-server-options
[cottrell@localhost ppp]$
```

FIGURE 1–16 A Red Hat Linux directory listing (the ls command).
Source: Red Hat Inc.

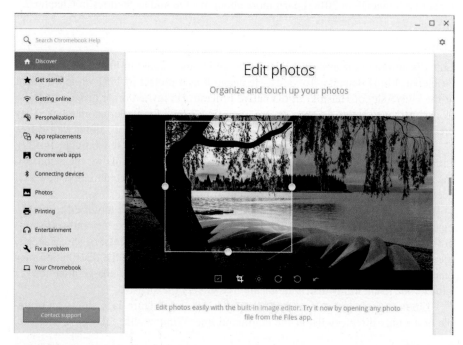

FIGURE 1–17 The Chrome OS GUI.
Source: Google LLC

called shells, are available that make it as accessible to most users as Windows or macOS. We will discuss selecting a Linux distribution in Chapter 8 along with other Linux-specific details.

Chrome OS

In the last three decades, computer-based work has gradually migrated away from our desktop computers and local networks to the cloud. We access cloud-based apps for online learning, completing projects and labs, submitting papers, collaborating with coworkers and fellow students, and for taking exams. At home, we connect to online services for entertainment, managing our finances, and much more. Recognizing this movement, Google created Chrome OS, an operating system based on a Linux kernel with a GUI based on the Chrome web browser. Of course, Chrome is also its default browser.

At first, it wasn't taken seriously by many professionals because it was not much more than a web browser, but Google has continued to improve the Chrome OS. Today, several manufacturers offer laptops, desktops, and tablets dedicated to the Chrome OS (see Figure 1-17).

LO 1.4 | Today's Mobile Operating Systems

Mobile computing today has followed the trajectory of all computing, thanks to the miniaturization of components and new technologies. And like PCs, mobile devices became more desirable thanks to apps. However, don't look for a single "killer app" for mobile devices. Rather, the most popular mobile devices are those with a large number of compelling apps. Also, unlike the early PCs, which were seen more as office productivity tools, today's mobile devices are very personal devices used for communicating and entertainment as well as for work- and school-related tasks.

Of the two mobile OSs featured in this book, Apple licenses iOS only for use on Apple mobile. Google does not charge manufacturers licensing fees for using Android, but may require that certain Google apps and features be included. They license it for free under the Android Open Source Project. This helps hold down the cost of Android smartphones.

Mobile Devices

There are many manufacturers of mobile devices, but the ones we will focus on are those that use the Apple iOS or Android, operating systems. Two things they have in common are support for a variety of wireless technologies and the ability to customize them with a variety of apps. Table 1–2 gives a summary of these OSs and the devices that use them. Following is a brief description of the hardware features of these devices:

- Network adapters for various types of wireless networks.
- Great high-quality color touch-screens that allow the OS to respond to several types of touch gestures.
- One or two (front and back) digital cameras.
- Built-in speakers and/or speaker ports for external speakers.
- Rechargeable batteries with battery life to get you through a normal day of use.
- An accelerometer that detects the physical tilt and acceleration of the device.
- Solid-state drives (SSDs).

Note: The iPod Touch runs iOS, but we are not covering this device. With its small screen and NO cell phone support, it is simply a digital music player with tablet features.

Note: This book does not include coverage of the Watch OS, the operating system in the Apple Watch smartwatch.

Connectivity

The "smart" in smartphone comes from the computing ability that makes it a tool for work, home, and school. The "phone" in smartphone recognizes the ability to connect to a cellular network for voice communication. Typically, you purchase a smartphone from a cellular provider, and connect the phone to the provider's network as your first ownership task.

Many tablets also have cellular network support for which you pay a premium—both for the cellular hardware in the tablet and for the cellular service.

To help control the cost of cellular data plans, we are fortunate to also have Wi-Fi connectivity in virtually all smartphones and tablets. If you enable Wi-Fi on your

TABLE 1–2 Summary of Current Mobile OSs and Related Devices Featured in This Book			
Mobile OS	**Source of OS**	**Smartphones/Tablets**	**Sources for Apps**
Apple iOS	Apple	Apple iPhone and iPad	Apple Apps Store
Android	Google	Smartphones and tablets from various manufacturers	Apps from Google Play and many other sources

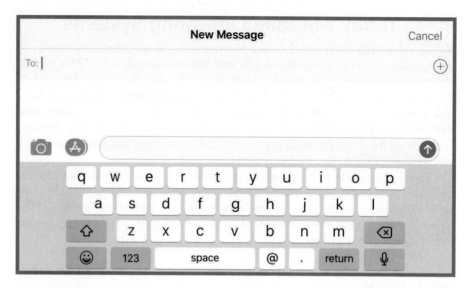

FIGURE 1–18 The virtual keyboard on an iPhone.
Source: Apple Inc.

smartphone, you can save on your cellular data usage by connecting to an Internet-connected Wi-Fi network.

Another common wireless option is Bluetooth, a wireless networking technology for connecting over very short distances (a few yards or meters). Bluetooth is used to connect a mobile device to other computers and to wireless devices, such as keyboards, headphones, speakers, and printers.

We will discuss how to enable and configure different types of network connections for mobile devices in Chapter 11.

Mobile Operating System Features

When discussing mobile operating systems, it is difficult to separate the OS from the hardware, so the OS features we describe are closely tied to the previously listed hardware features of the mobile device.

Touch Screen and Virtual Keyboard Support

A mobile OS supports the touch screen by interpreting the various screen gestures we make. It also supports a feature called **virtual keyboard**. When you touch an area of screen that requires input from a keyboard, the OS will display the virtual keyboard, an on-screen image of a keyboard with labeled keys that you can tap. Figure 1-18 shows the virtual keyboard on an iPhone. Many mobile devices will optionally connect to an external keyboard—usually via a Bluetooth wireless connection. Learn more about these features in Chapters 10 and 11.

Screen Rotation

Mobile operating systems take advantage of the hardware accelerometer by rotating the image on the screen to accommodate the position and allow you to read the screen. This feature is called **screen rotation**. Figure 1-19 shows the screen of an iPhone in "portrait" orientation, and Figure 1-20 shows the screen of the same iPhone in "landscape" orientation.

FIGURE 1–19 An iPhone screen in portrait orientation.
Sources: Apple Inc.; photos ©Jane Holcombe

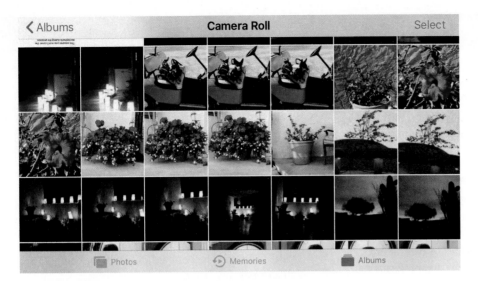

FIGURE 1–20 An iPhone screen in landscape orientation.
Sources: Apple Inc.; photos ©Jane Holcombe

Updateable

As with desktop operating systems, the ability to update a mobile OS is important to the usability and security of the mobile device. In general, you can update an OS depending on the constraints of the hardware limits imposed by the cellular provider.

Availability of Apps

Today's mobile devices are desirable because of the number of useful apps, making the availability of a large selection of compelling apps more important than a single killer app that millions desire. Both Apple iOS and Google Android have a large number of quality apps available to them, as well as many trivial and nonessential apps. Each mobile OS has one or more online sources, such as the Apple Store, shown in Figure 1-21.

Security

Mobile devices are targeted by the same security threats that target other computers. Being able to update the OS is only part of what you need to do to protect yourself and your data. Third-party solutions are available for some mobile OSs, and all of them come with some built-in security features. We will explore the security options for the iOS and Android mobile operating systems in Chapters 10 and 11.

Data Synchronization

Data synchronization is an important feature supported by mobile OSs, especially for people who use multiple devices and wish to access the same data across all devices. For instance, you can access your contacts list and other data from anywhere with whatever device you are using. We will examine the synchronization options for mobile devices in Chapter 11.

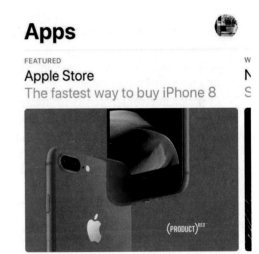

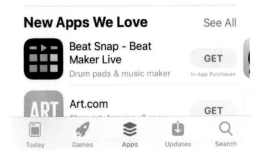

FIGURE 1–21 The Apple Store for iOS apps and other Apple products.
Source: Apple Inc.

Chapter 1 REVIEW

Chapter Summary

After reading this chapter and completing the exercises, you should know the following facts about operating systems.

An Overview of Microcomputer Operating Systems

- An operating system is a collection of programs that control all of the interactions among the various system components.
- A computer is a device that calculates. A central processing unit (CPU) is the component that performs the calculation for a computer.
- A microcomputer is a computer small enough and cheap enough for the use of one person. The integrated circuit (IC) is one of the inventions that made microcomputers possible.
- Interaction with a computer is called input/output (I/O).
- The CPU in a microcomputer is a microprocessor, which, along with several other important components (memory, firmware, and more), is installed onto a motherboard.
- System firmware contains the program code that informs the CPU of the devices present and how to communicate with them.
- A device driver is a special program containing code for controlling a component.
- Common microcomputers in use today include desktops, laptops, tablets, and smartphones.
- Windows, Chrome OS, and Linux will run on a desktop PC or compatible laptop computer. Mac OS runs on the iMac desktop and MacBook laptop models.
- A server is a computer that provides one or more services to other computers.
- Smartphones and tablets are the two most popular mobile devices.
- Operating systems provide these functions:
  - User interface
  - Job management
  - Task management
  - File management
  - Device management
  - Memory management
  - Security

Yesterday's Operating Systems

- UNIX is the oldest operating system still in use. It comes in versions for large computers, as well as microcomputers.

- The complex and powerful OSs we now use evolved over many decades.
- Early microcomputers were introduced in the 1970s. The Apple computers came with the Apple OS.
- Certain "killer apps," notably VisiCalc and Lotus 1-2-3, made microcomputers appeal to organizations and ordinary people.
- IBM introduced the IBM PC in 1981 with Microsoft BASIC in ROM. They offered PC DOS for computers with a floppy disk drive.
- In the 1980s, Microsoft made MS-DOS available to third-party PC manufacturers.
- OS/2 was first developed in a joint effort between Microsoft and IBM. IBM soon continued development of it without Microsoft, bringing out OS/2 Warp, a GUI version. IBM discontinued support for OS/2 in 2005.
- Microsoft Windows evolved from the first version in 1985 to Windows 10, introduced in 2015.
- The Apple Mac computer, introduced in 1984, came with the Mac OS System. This OS line continued through Mac OS 9, introduced in 1999, and phased out after OS X was introduced in 2001.

Today's Desktop Operating Systems

- Today's desktop operating systems include Windows 7, Windows 8, Windows 10, macOS, Chrome OS, and Linux.
- Windows 7, released in 2009, included many improvements over Windows Vista; many businesses adopted this for their desktop PCs.
- Windows 8 was introduced in October 2012 with two GUIs. In 2013, Microsoft released the Windows 8.1 Update with changes to the Start screen and desktop.
- Windows 10 was introduced in 2015 with changes to the GUI and several new features.
- Apple's macOS based on NextStep, an OS with a UNIX kernel, runs only on Apple Mac desktop and laptop computers.
- Linux can run on nearly any computer. It natively uses a command-line interface, but GUI shells are available.
- Google's Chrome OS comes on Chromebooks and the Chromebox.

Today's Mobile OSs

- People use mobile devices for communicating and personal entertainment as well as for work- and school-related tasks.

- Apple's iOS runs on Apple's iPhone and iPad products (as well as on the iPod touch). Apps are only available from the Apple Apps Store.
- Google's Android OS runs on smartphones and tablets from many manufacturers. Apps are available from Google and from many other sources.
- Features in mobile devices include:
  - Multiple types of wireless network adapters.
  - High-quality color touch screens.
  - One or two (front and back) digital cameras.
  - Built-in speakers and/or speaker ports.
  - Rechargeable batteries with battery life sufficient for a normal day of use.
  - An accelerometer that detects the physical tilt and acceleration.
  - Solid-state drives (SSDs).
- Smartphones and some tablets support cellular connections and are usually bought through cellular providers.
- Smartphones and tablets offer Wi-Fi connections, a cheaper alternative to cellular for accessing the Internet with the device.
- Bluetooth is a wireless networking technology for connecting over very short distances.
- A mobile OS displays a virtual keyboard when you touch an area of screen that requires text input.
- A mobile OS takes advantage of the hardware accelerometer in a device by rotating the image on the screen to accommodate the position of the screen so that it is readable to the user.
- Most mobile operating systems can be updated.
- Popular mobile OSs have a large number of available apps.
- All mobile OSs have security features, and third-party solutions are available.
- It is important to have good options for synchronizing data across all devices used by an individual.

Key Terms List

accelerometer *(29)*	graphical user interface (GUI) *(6)*	partition *(7)*
application (app) *(2)*	input/output (I/O) *(2)*	personal computer (PC) *(4)*
central processing unit (CPU) *(2)*	integrated circuit (IC) *(2)*	plug-and-play (PNP) *(9)*
client *(4)*	Internet of Things (IoT) *(5)*	portable operating system *(11)*
command-line interface (CLI) *(5)*	job management *(6)*	processes *(7)*
computer *(2)*	kernel *(5)*	random-access memory (RAM) *(3)*
Chrome OS *(28)*	killer app *(13)*	screen rotation *(30)*
cursor *(6)*	Mac *(4)*	security *(9)*
device driver *(7)*	memory *(3)*	server *(3)*
device management *(7)*	memory management *(9)*	smartphone *(4)*
directory *(7)*	microcomputer *(2)*	solid-state drive (SSD) *(7)*
distribution *(27)*	microprocessor *(2)*	system firmware *(3)*
embedded OS *(4)*	mobile device *(4)*	system-on-a-chip (SoC) *(4)*
file management *(7)*	motherboard *(3)*	tablet *(4)*
file system *(7)*	multitasking *(6)*	task management *(6)*
firmware *(3)*	New Technology File System (NTFS) *(21)*	user interface (UI) *(5)*
folder *(7)*	operating system (OS) *(2)*	virtual keyboard *(30)*
formatting *(7)*		

Key Terms Quiz

Use the Key Terms List to complete the sentences that follow. Not all terms will be used.

1. A/an _____ controls the interaction between a program and a computer's hardware, freeing application programmers from the task of including such functions in their programs.

2. The _____ is the main component of an OS that always remains in memory while the computer is running, managing low-level OS tasks.

3. The desktop operating systems described in his chapter all have an optional character mode _____

4. The Google _____ is based on their popular web browser. The physical memory of the computer will hold.

5. When you run several applications at once and switch between them, you are experiencing the _____ feature of an operating system.

6. Interaction with a computer involving getting data and commands into it and results out of it is called _____.

7. The role of a/an _____ is to provide services to other computers on a network.

8. Software that allows the operating system to control a hardware component is a/an _____.

9. A/an _____ is a hardware component in a mobile device that an OS uses when it rotates the image on the screen so that it is readable in its current position.

10. The _____ function of an OS includes the visual components as well as the command processor that loads programs into memory.

Multiple-Choice Quiz

1. Which of the following operating systems cannot be licensed to run on a PC?
   a. macOS
   b. Windows 10
   c. Windows 7
   d. Linux
   e. Windows 8

2. Which of the following is a small electronic component made up of transistors (tiny switches) and other miniaturized parts?
   a. Peripheral
   b. Integrated circuit (IC)
   c. Tablet
   d. Mouse
   e. Vacuum tube

3. Introduced in 1983, this application program became the "killer app" that made the IBM PC a must-have business tool.
   a. Microsoft Word
   b. VisiCalc
   c. BASIC
   d. PC DOS
   e. Lotus 1-2-3

4. Which of the following is not available as a desktop operating system?
   a. Chrome OS
   b. macOS
   c. Windows 10
   d. Linux
   e. iOS

5. Which of the following is a computer input device? Select all correct answers.
   a. Mouse
   b. Printer
   c. Keyboard
   d. RAM
   e. ROM

6. On a network, the purpose of this type of computer is to allow users to connect over the network to save and access files stored on this computer, as well as to print to printers connected to this computer.
   a. Desktop computer
   b. File and print server
   c. Tablet
   d. Laptop
   e. Smartphone

7. Which acronym describes technology in which all or most of a device's electronic circuitry is on a single microchip?
   a. IoT
   b. UI
   c. RAM
   d. SSD
   e. SoC

8. macOS is built on NextStep, an OS based on what kernel?
   a. Linux
   b. UNIX
   c. DOS
   d. Windows
   e. Chrome OS

9. In the 1950s, a typical computer end user would have been a _____.
   a. computer gamer
   b. medical doctor
   c. politician
   d. government agency
   e. secretary

10. What acronym describes networked devices that contain microcomputers but are not thought of as computing devices, such as refrigerators, automobile components, light bulbs, and industrial control devices?
    a. IoT
    b. RAM

c. NTFS

d. SSD

e. SoC

11. Which of the following accurately describes the overall trend in computing during the past 70-plus years?

a. Toward physically larger, more-powerful computers.

b. Toward physically larger, less-powerful computers.

c. Toward physically smaller, less-powerful computers.

d. Toward physically smaller, more-powerful computers.

e. Toward physically smaller, single-use computers.

12. When working with a mobile device, if you touch an area of screen that requires text input, the OS will display this for your use.

a. Help screen

b. Virtual keyboard

c. A Bluetooth button so that you can connect a keyboard

d. CLI

e. Screen gestures

13. Using this type of wireless network connection when browsing the Internet with a smartphone or tablet can save you data fees.

a. Bluetooth

b. Wi-Fi

c. USB

d. Cellular

e. Ethernet

14. What file system is the default for current Windows OSs?

a. iOS

b. IC

c. RAM

d. NTFS

e. SSD

15. Which of the following is a technology you would use to connect your smartphone to a wireless headset?

a. Bluetooth

b. Wi-Fi

c. USB

d. Cellular

e. Ethernet

Essay Quiz

1. Describe the benefit to programmers of having an operating system when that programmer is creating a new application.

2. Based on your own observations, do you believe there are more differences or more commonalities among the different operating systems across devices: PCs, laptops, tablets, and smartphones?

3. Review the timeline provided in this chapter and select an event that you believe is the most significant event and give a reason for your choice.

4. Linux comes in distributions from many sources. Define the term *distribution* in this context.

5. In general terms, describe a mobile OS's use of a device's accelerometer.

Lab Projects

LAB PROJECT 1.1

Pick a typical day for you, and create a journal of all the interactions you have with computers from the time you wake up in the morning until you go to bed at night. *Hint:* Even a gas pump contains a computer.

LAB PROJECT 1.2

If you use both a desktop (or laptop) computer and a mobile device, describe the similarities and differences you notice in working with the GUI on each device. If you do not use both types of devices, find someone who does (classmate or other) and interview that person for this project. Create a report of these results to submit to your instructor or to use in a discussion of results with your classmates.

LAB PROJECT 1.3

Poll classmates or coworkers to determine how they use their mobile devices. Are they primarily entertainment devices? If so, describe why this is the case. How many people polled used a mobile device as a primary computer?

In that case, what tasks did they perform on the mobile devices? Were there tasks they preferred to do on a desktop or laptop? Create a report describing the results and be prepared to discuss with other students who completed this project separately.

chapter

2 Computer Security Basics

©Chad Baker/Ryan McVay/Getty Images

Learning Outcomes

In this chapter, you will learn how to:

LO **2.1** Describe security threats and vulnerabilities to computers and users.

LO **2.2** Identify methods for protecting against security threats.

LO **2.3** Troubleshoot common security problems.

Why do operating systems include security features? Why do we need to apply security patches to operating systems? Why has computer security become a multibillion-dollar business worldwide? Why? Because it's dangerous out there! And, as you will learn in this chapter, "out there" seems to be everywhere, because no place or technology is safe from threats. That includes the Internet, corporate extranets, desktop and laptop computers, cell phone, tablet, other mobile devices, and all your Internet-connected entertainment and environmental controls in your house. Here you'll learn about the threats, and the methods, practices, and technologies for protecting your computer systems.

In this chapter, we first attempt to instill a healthy dose of paranoia in your mind so that you avoid inviting malware and becoming victims of scams, and we identify methods for securing your computing devices. Then, in later chapters, you will learn how to implement OS-specific security. 🜨

LO 2.1 | Threats to Computers and Users

What are you risking if your computer or mobile device is not secure? The short answer is that you risk your identity, the work you have created, your company's integrity, and your own job if you are responsible for loss of the company's equipment or data. Today, government regulations, such as the Sarbanes–Oxley Act or the Health Insurance Portability and Accountability Act (HIPAA) require that organizations protect certain personal information, such as health and personal financial data. The consequences to an organization that does not comply with these regulations, or that experiences a breach of security involving such data, can be very severe.

We'll begin the long answer with an overview of common threats and how they gain access to computers. Many of the threats described are severe enough to be considered cybercrimes. A cybercrime is illegal activity performed using computer technology.

Malicious Tools and Methods

We call software threats malware, a shortened form of "malicious software." This term covers a large and growing list of threats, including many that you no doubt know about, such as viruses, worms, Trojan horses, or spam. But have you heard of pop-up downloads, drive-by downloads, war driving, bluesnarfing, adware, spyware, back doors, spim, phishing, or hoaxes? Read on and learn about the various types of malware and their methods of infecting computers and networks.

Malware development has become a huge industry that targets all computing devices, with the greatest growth in malware targeting mobile devices.

Vectors

A vector is a method that malware uses to infect a computer. While some malware may use just a single vector, multivector malware uses an array of methods to infect computers and networks. Let's look at a few well-known vectors.

Click Bait. Click bait is content in an email, Web page, social networking page, or within any online app, that is designed to lure you to click on it and its associated link in order to open a Web page or run a video. Click bait may simply be the link itself in an email or a headline or photo containing just enough information to make you curious so that you will click on the link.

Social Networking. Social networking is the use of social media, which is any service (Internet-based or other) that provides a place where people can interact in online communities, sharing information in various forms. Community members generate social-media content. A social networking site is a website that provides space where members can communicate with one another and share details of their business or personal lives. Facebook is a very popular social networking site. LinkedIn is a social media site targeted to professionals who use it for business contacts. Twitter (Figure 2–1) allows users to send and receive short text messages (tweets) of up to 140 characters.

We see social media as a vector for malware and social engineering (defined later in this chapter) as well as a rich source of personal information on individuals. We are horrified to see the personal details that people reveal on their Facebook and Twitter sites, and recent developments have shown that our personal data is being harvested through our social media activities, as well as that of our contacts. Thousands of companies profit from the use of our data collected during a variety of online activities without our knowledge, and without our receiving any real compensation. This activity, called "surveillance capitalism" by Harvard Business School professor Shoshana Zuboff.

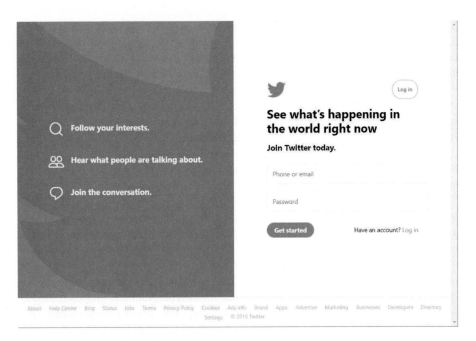

FIGURE 2–1 The Twitter Log in page.
Source: Twitter Inc.

Email. Some malware infects computers via email. The simple act of opening an email containing the Nimda virus can infect a computer, depending on the software you are using to read the message.

Regardless of the email client you use, clicking on a link in an email message can launch malware from a website.

try this!

More About Social Media

Check out the latest in social media. Try this:

1. Open your favorite search engine, such as **Google.com** or **Bing.com**.
2. Enter the key words "social media."
3. Browse through the results and create a list of at least 10 social-media sites.
4. Return to the search engine and enter "social media security."
5. Browse through the results and look for recent articles on social media security concerns. Read some of the articles and discuss them with your classmates.

Malicious Code on Websites. Some malware infects computers by lurking in hidden code on websites. An unsuspecting user browses to a site and clicks on a link that launches and installs malware on her computer.

Trojan Horses. A Trojan horse, often simply called a Trojan, is both a type of malware and a vector. The modern-day Trojan horse program gains access to computers much like the ancient Greek warriors who, in Virgil's famous tale (the epic poem *The Aeneid*), gained access to the city of Troy by hiding in a large wooden horse presented as a gift to the city (a Trojan horse). A Trojan horse program installs and activates on a computer by appearing to be something harmless, which the user innocently installs. It may appear as just a useful free program that a user downloads and installs or a video, but it is a common way for malware to infect your system.

Although it is hard to fit all threats into tidy categories, we consider threats similar to the "Complete a Quick Survey" exploit to be a Trojan because it appears to be something harmless, tempting you to comply. If you complete the survey it may take some action, such as pretending to scan your computer for problems, but the results will be bogus, offering to fix the problems it claims to find and asking for payment. A threat that causes you to take action out of fear is scareware.

Searching for Unprotected Computers. Still other malware searches throughout a network for computers that do not have the latest security updates and/or do not have real-time antimalware installed. The malware can then install itself.

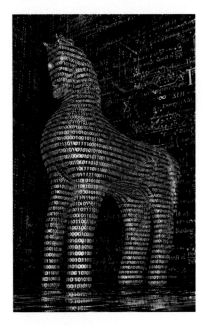

Trojan horse
©posteriori/Shutterstock

Sneakernet—The Oldest Vector. Yet another vector is as old as PCs. In the days when it was uncommon for computers to connect to any network, users shared data between computers by carrying a floppy disk containing data or programs from one computer to another. The slang for this practice is sneakernet. Sometimes, the floppy disk contained malware, making sneakernet the oldest vector for PCs. Sneakernet still exists, but the storage device used today is the flash drive, and the computers are usually also connected to a network, which extends the risk when malware infects a single computer. In August 2010, the U.S. Deputy Defense Secretary declassified the information that a flash drive, inserted into a U.S. military laptop in 2008 on a military post in the Middle East, was the vector for malicious code that caused a significant breach of military computers.

Back Doors. In computing, a back door is a way in which someone can gain access to a computer, bypassing authentication security. Sometimes a program's author installs a back door into a single program so she can easily access it later for administering and/ or for troubleshooting the program code. Or an attacker may create a back door by taking advantage of a discovered weakness in a program. Then any program using the back door can run in the security context of the invaded program and infect a computer with malware. In one well-known situation, the Code Red worm took advantage of a specific vulnerability in Microsoft's Internet Information Server (IIS) Web server software to install a back door. The result was that the worm displayed a message on every Web page on the IIS server. The message included the phrase, "Hacked by Chinese." Then the Nimda worm took advantage of the back door left by the Code Red worm to infect computers.

Rootkits. A rootkit is malware that hides itself from detection by anti-malware programs by concealing itself within the OS code or any other program running on the computer. Someone who has administrator (root) access to the computer installs a rootkit, giving an attacker administrator privileges to the computer. He can then run any type of malware to quietly carry out its mission.

Pop-Up Downloads. A pop-up is a separate window that displays (pops up) uninvited from a Web page. The purpose of a pop-up may be as simple as an advertisement, but a pop-up can be a vector for malware. A pop-up download is a program downloaded to a user's computer through a pop-up page. It requires an action on the part of a user, such as clicking on a button that implies acceptance of something such as free. The program that downloads may be a virus or a worm.

Drive-By Downloads. A drive-by download is a program downloaded to a user's computer without consent. Often the simple act of browsing to a website, or opening an HTML email message, may result in such a surreptitious download. A drive-by download may also occur when installing another application. This is particularly true of certain file-sharing programs that users install to allow sharing of music, data, or photo files over the Internet. Some drive-by downloads may alter your Web browser home page and/or redirect all your browser searches to one site. A drive-by download may also install a virus, a worm, or even more likely, adware or spyware (which we describe later in this chapter).

War Driving. Secure all Wi-Fi networks with the latest standard of Wi-Fi security and require passwords to access the network. A Wi-Fi network that connects to the Internet through a router is a hotspot and should be protected from unauthorized access. Someone who detects an unprotected hotspot can access the Internet for free. Further, the reason we see this as a vector is that they also can capture keystrokes, email, passwords, and user names from the wireless traffic, giving them ways to send malware to connected users or use the information they gather to steal users' identities.

Some people actively seek out unsecured Wi-Fi networks, a practice called war driving. A war driver moves through a neighborhood in a vehicle or on foot, using a mobile device equipped with Wi-Fi wireless network capability and software that identifies Wi-Fi networks. The software detects the level of security (or lack of) on each detected Wi-Fi network.

Note: A less-dramatic term for "war driving" is "access point mapping."

Using an unsecured hotspot can expose you to threats. If you need to be inspired to secure your Wi-Fi network, check out the Internet, where numerous websites describe how to war drive, as well as how to protect your data from theft. There are even many war driving videos on YouTube, as shown in Figure 2-2.

Bluesnarfing. Similar to war driving, bluesnarfing is the act of covertly obtaining information broadcast from wireless devices using the Bluetooth standard, a short-range wireless standard used for data exchange between desktop computers and mobile devices. Bluetooth devices have a range of from 10 centimeters to 100 meters, depending on the power class of the device. Using a smartphone, a bluesnarfer can eavesdrop to acquire information, or even use the synchronizing feature of the device to pick up the user's information—all without the victim detecting it.

Password Theft

A password is a string of characters that you enter, along with an identifier, such as a user name or email address, to authenticate yourself. If someone steals your passwords they can gain access to whatever you thought you were protecting with the password. Stealing passwords is theft with intent to break into computers and networks.

Stealing Passwords through Websites. There are numerous programs and techniques for stealing passwords. One commonly used technique is to invade an unsecured website to access information unwitting users provide to the site, such as user names and passwords, and such personal information as account numbers, Social Security numbers, birth dates, and much more.

Stealing Passwords with Password Crackers. Another technique used for stealing a password is a program called a password cracker. Some password crackers fall into

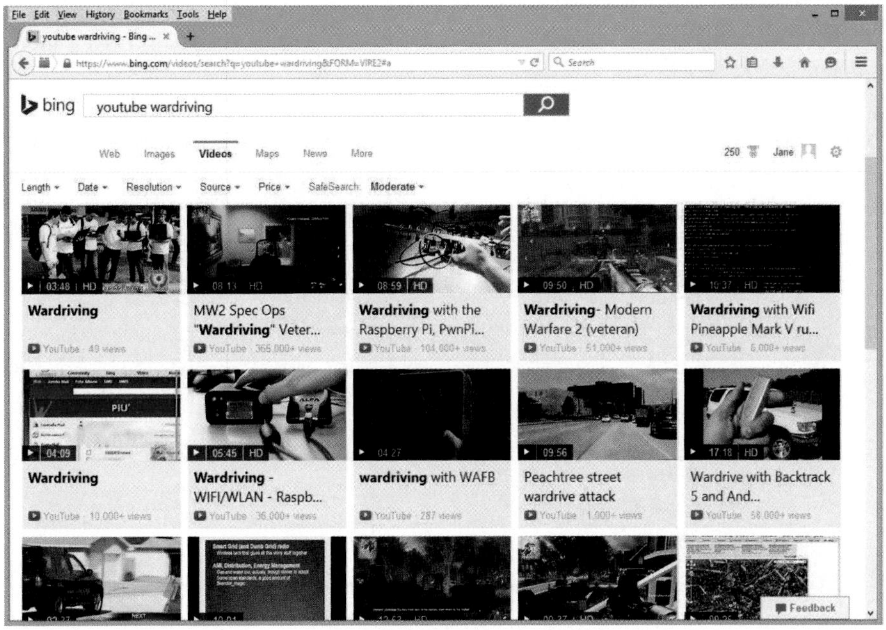

WARNING!

There are password crackers for every operating system, every type of computing device, and all the social networking services in use today. Learn more when you search on the key words "password cracker" using your favorite search engine.

FIGURE 2-2 Online videos show examples of war driving.
Source: Microsoft Corporation

the category of "brute-force" password crackers, which simply means the program tries a huge number of permutations of possible passwords. Often, because people tend to use simple passwords such as their initials, birth dates, addresses, etc., the brute-force method works. Other password crackers use more sophisticated statistical or mathematical methods to steal passwords.

Stealing Passwords with Keystroke Loggers. A method for stealing passwords, as well as lots of other information, is the use of a keystroke logger, also called a keylogger. This is either a hardware device or a program that monitors and records every keystroke, usually without the user's knowledge. In the case of a hardware logger, the person desiring the keystroke log must physically install it before recording. Some models are Wi-Fi enabled. When properly configured, a Wi-Fi keystroke logger can send reports on captured data via email, and the owner can also remotely access the keystroke logger. Without a network connection, a hardware keystroke logger must be physically retrieved to access the collected data.

A software keystroke logger program does not require physical access to the target computer but simply a method for downloading and installing it on the computer. This could occur through one of the vectors described earlier in this chapter. Once installed, such a program can send the logged information over the Internet via email, or using other methods, to the person desiring the log.

Some parents install keystroke loggers to monitor their children's Internet activity, but such programs have the potential for abuse by people with less-benign motivations, such as stalkers and identity thieves. A simple Internet search of "keystroke logger" will yield many sources of both hardware and software keystroke loggers. See Figure 2–3. The latter are now the more common.

Zero-Day Exploits

We call a malware attack an exploit when it takes advantage of some vulnerability in our computers or networks. Experts are constantly discovering these vulnerabilities and attempting to stay ahead of the bad guys with appropriate defense techniques. However, sometimes someone finds a software vulnerability in an operating system or application such as those we study in this book that is unknown to the publisher of the targeted software, and someone devises a way to exploit that vulnerability. We call this unknown exploit (often a virus) a zero-day exploit, and it is very difficult to protect against such a threat.

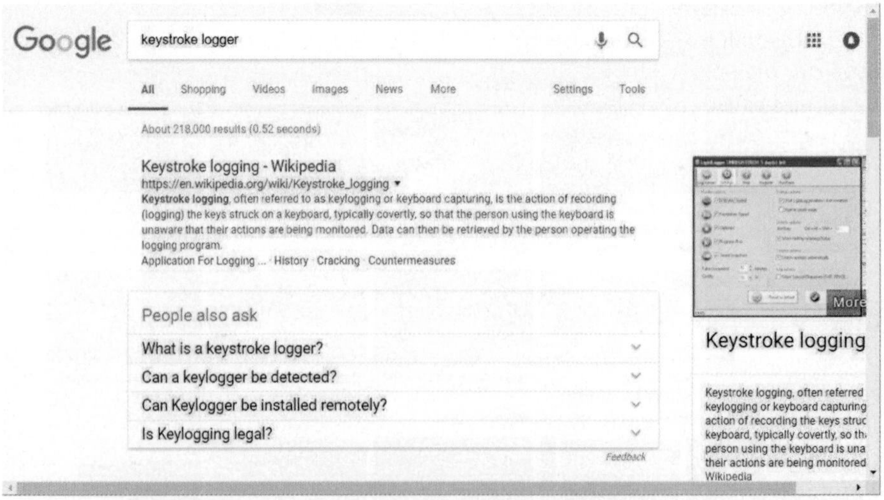

> *Note:* Advanced keystroke loggers may also capture screenshots of all activity on a computer.

> *Note:* Two major flaws (or bugs) were revealed in Intel and AMD microprocessors, named Meltdown and Spectre. Exploits that take advantage of these flaws take over computers at the lowest, most vulnerable level.

FIGURE 2–3 Search on "keystroke logger" to learn more about the devices and software available.
Source: Google LLC

Viruses

While, in the broadest sense, "virus" is a term used for all malware, technically, a virus is one class of malware: a program installed and activated on a computer or mobile device without the knowledge or permission of the user. Viruses usually attach themselves to a file, such as a Microsoft Word document, and replicate and spread as you copy or share the infected file. Like a living virus that infects humans and animals, a computer virus can result in a wide range of symptoms and outcomes. Loss of data, damage to or complete failure of an operating system, or theft of personal and financial information are just a few of the potential results of computer virus infections.

Note: "In the wild" is a term frequently used to describe the overall computing environment, including private networks, and Internet and all other public networks. "In the zoo" refers to a controlled and isolated environment where viruses can be analyzed during the development of patches. This type of environment is also called a "sandbox."

Worms

Like a virus, a worm is a program installed and activated on a computer without the knowledge or permission of the user. But a worm replicates itself on the computer, or throughout a network. In other words, a worm is a network-aware virus that does not require action from the unwitting user to replicate, and it can have a similar range of outcomes. The Netsky and MyDoom worms caused chaos and loss of productivity just by the huge amount of network traffic they generated. The typical worm resides in a single file that it replicates onto multiple machines. However, the Nimda worm changed all that by inserting its code into other executable files on the local drive of each machine to which it replicated itself, making it difficult to locate and remove the worm.

WARNING!

A worm can replicate itself via Bluetooth, infecting mobile devices when people are in crowded public places, such as sports bars. Turn Bluetooth off when not in use and when in close proximity to strangers.

Botnets and Zombies

A botnet is a group of networked computers that, usually unbeknown to their owners, are infected with programs that forward information to other computers over a network. A bot, short for robot, is a program that acts as an agent for a user or master program, performing a variety of functions—for both good and evil. An individual computer in a botnet is a zombie because it mindlessly serves the person who originated the botnet code. A bot herder is someone who initiates and controls a botnet. Botnets have grown to be one of the biggest threats on the Internet.

Spyware

Spyware is a category of software that runs surreptitiously on a user's computer, gathers information without the user's permission, and then sends that information to the people or organizations that requested it. A virus may install Internet-based spyware, sometimes called tracking software or a spybot, on a computer. Spyware can be used by companies to trace users' surfing patterns to improve the company's marketing efforts; it can be used for industrial espionage; it is used by law enforcement to find sexual predators or criminals (with appropriate legal permissions); and it is used by governments to investigate terrorism.

Note: Keystroke loggers are a form of spyware.

Adware

Adware is a form of spyware that collects information about the user in order to display targeted advertisements to the user, either in the form of inline banners or in the form of pop-ups. Inline banners are advertisements that run within the context of the current page, just taking up screen real estate. Pop-ups are a greater annoyance, because they are ads that run in separate browser windows that you must close before you can continue with your present task. Clicking to accept an offer presented in an inline banner or a pop-up may trigger a pop-up download that can install a virus or worm.

Browser Hijacking

We received a call the other day from Dave, a finance officer at a large farm implement company. Every time he opened his browser, the home page pointed to a site advertising adware removal software. This is an example of browser hijacking, a practice that has been growing. Some unscrupulous people do this so that their website will register more visitors and then they can raise their rates to advertisers.

Dave was able to reverse this by changing the default page in settings, but it was very annoying. He was lucky; hijackers can make it very difficult to defeat the hijack by modifying the registry (a database that stores configuration settings in the Windows OS) so that every time you restart Windows or your Web browser the hijack reinstates.

Spam and Spim

Spam is unsolicited email, often called junk email. This includes email from a legitimate source selling a real service or product, but if you did not give the source permission to send such information to you, it is spam. Too often spam involves some form of scam—a bogus offer to sell a service or product that does not exist or tries to include you in a complicated moneymaking deal. We call spam perpetrators spammers, and spam is illegal. Spam accounts for a huge amount of traffic on the Internet and private. Some corporate network administrators report that as much as 60 percent of the incoming email traffic is spam.

Spim is an acronym for spam over instant messaging, and the perpetrators are spimmers. A spimmer sends bots out over the Internet to collect instant-messaging screen names, and then a spimbot sends spim to the screen names. A typical spim message may contain a link to a website, where, like spam, the recipient will find products or services for sale, legitimate or otherwise.

Social Engineering

Social engineering is the use of persuasion techniques to gain the confidence of individuals—for both good and bad purposes. People with malicious intent use social engineering to persuade targeted people to reveal confidential information or to obtain something else of value. Social engineering is as old as human interaction, so there are countless techniques. Following are just a few categories of computer security threats that employ social engineering.

Fraud. Fraud is the use of deceit and trickery to persuade someone to hand over money or other valuables. Fraud is often associated with identify theft (discussed later), because the perpetrator will falsely claim to be the victim when using the victim's credit cards and other personal and financial information.

One form of fraud is ransomware, a type of scareware that threatens to do damage or lock a user out of a computer unless the user pays a "ransom." There is no guarantee that your data will be unencrypted once the payment is made. A more frightening variation of ransomware claims that the victim has been observed in an illegal act, such as distributing child pornography, and threatens to report this to the authorities unless the victim pays a ransom. Ransomware may require payment through an online payment system, such as bitcoin.

Phishing. Phishing is a fraudulent method of obtaining personal and financial information through Web page pop-ups, email, and even paper letters mailed via the postal service. Think of the metaphor of a fisherman preparing and casting his bait in an ocean full of fish. Even if only one in a hundred fish take the bait, he is statistically likely to have many successes. A phishing message ("bait") purports to be from a legitimate organization, such as a bank, credit card company, retailer, and so on. In a typical phishing scenario, the email or pop-up may contain authentic-looking logos, and even links to the actual site, but the link specified for supplying personal financial information will take recipients (the "phish") to a "spoofed" Web page that asks them to enter their personal data. The Web page may look exactly like the company's legitimate Web page, but it's not.

While the typical phishing attack casts a wide net by sending out millions of messages, some phishing attacks are more targeted. We call these spear phishing, and the target of a spear-phishing attack is usually one that has a high probability of delivering a very valuable return. Such an attack may come in the form of a message with a greeting that includes your name and content that includes some of your personal information. If you work in a large organization, the attack may have language that seems to come from a coworker, detailing department information or referring to a recent (perhaps unnamed) meeting. The source of the message may actually be your coworker's valid address if the attacker managed to hijack the email account. Or it may be a forged email address. Someone forges an email address by modifying the sender's address in the email message's header—the information that accompanies a message but does not appear in the message. We also call this type of forgery email spoofing.

Be very suspicious of email requesting personal or financial information. Legitimate businesses will never contact you by email and ask you for your access code, Social Security number, or password.

WARNING!
Phishing (and spear phishing) are just old-fashioned scams in high-tech dress.

Hoaxes. A hoax is a deception intended either for amusement or for some gain with malicious intent. Hoaxes take many forms. One example is an email message appearing to be from someone you know claiming she took an unplanned trip to London where she was mugged in the subway. The email address looks legitimate, but when you respond, you receive a message from someone else stating that your friend is now in jail and needs bail money. Sounds outlandish? We received such a message, but we were suspicious and called our friend who reported that she was safe at home and that several other of her friends had responded to the message and received the plea for money.

Note: This type of hoax is also known as an imposter scam.

Enticements to Open Attachments. Social engineering is also involved in the enticements to open attachments to emails. Called "gimmes," you find these enticements either in the subject line or in the body of the email message. Opening the attachment then executes and infects the local computer with some form of malware. A huge number of methods are used. Sadly, enticements often appeal to the less-noble human characteristics such as greed (via an offer too good to be true), vanity (physical enhancement products), or simple curiosity (with a subject line that appears to be a response to an email from you). More tragic, these enticements may appeal to people's sympathy and compassion by way of a nonexistent charity or by fraudulently representing a legitimate charity.

Identity Theft

Identify theft occurs when someone collects personal information belonging to another person and uses that information to fraudulently make purchases, open new credit accounts, and even obtain new driver's licenses and other forms of identification in the victim's name. There are many ways not directly involved with computers for thieves to steal your identity. However, the use of computers and mobile devices for social networking and purchasing has greatly expanded the scope of this type of crime, turning it into a huge business involved in the theft of large numbers of persons' data from large databases. These criminals sell such identity information for pennies per

Step-by-Step 2.01

Take a Phishing IQ Test!

It is often difficult to discern which emails are legitimate and which are "phishing." Test your ability to detect a phishing scam. To complete this test, you will need a computer or mobile device with an Internet connection.

Step 1

Use your Web browser to connect to the phishing test at **www.sonicwall. com/phishing/**. If this URL no longer works, use a search engine to find a phishing test.

Step 2

After reading the instructions and helpful hints, start the test. Click on the button labeled, Take the Phishing IQ Test.

Step 3

You will be presented with several messages and you must decide whether each is legitimate or phishing.

Source: SonicWall

Step 4

When you finish, the program will grade you on your choices and you will see the correct answers. Each message also has a detailed explanation as to why it is either legitimate or phishing. Read these explanations carefully.

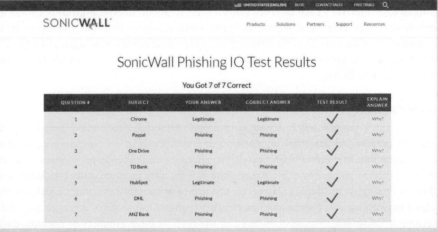

SonicWall Phishing IQ Test Results

You Got 7 of 7 Correct

QUESTION #	SUBJECT	YOUR ANSWER	CORRECT ANSWER	TEST RESULT	EXPLAIN ANSWER
1	Chrome	Legitimate	Legitimate	✓	Why?
2	Paypal	Phishing	Phishing	✓	Why?
3	One Drive	Phishing	Phishing	✓	Why?
4	TD Bank	Phishing	Phishing	✓	Why?
5	HubSpot	Legitimate	Legitimate	✓	Why?
6	DHL	Phishing	Phishing	✓	Why?
7	ANZ Bank	Phishing	Phishing	✓	Why?

Source: SonicWall

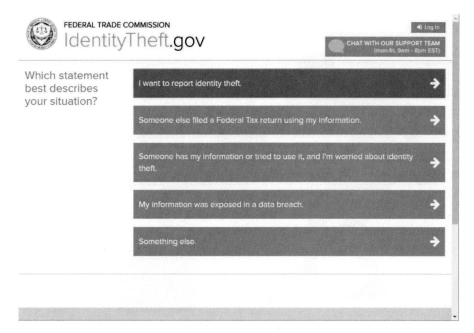

FIGURE 2-4 The FTC Identity Theft Web page.
Source: Federal Trade Commission

record. Several websites maintained by the U.S. government offer valuable information for consumers who wish to protect themselves from identify theft. A starting place is the website **www.idtheft.gov**, by the President's Task Force on Identity Theft (see Figure 2-4); it includes steps to take if you have been a victim of identity theft. Connect to this website in the Try This.

try this!

Learn More About Identity Theft

Learn more about identity theft and what to do if you are a victim of identity theft. Try this:

1. Open your browser; enter **www.idtheft.gov** into the address box. The actual URL is **www.identitytheft.gov**, but the shorter version works and is easier to type.
2. This site, shown in Figure 2-4, gives clear step-by-step instructions for what to do if you are a victim of identity theft.
3. Notice that you can print out each checklist.
4. For prevention tips, direct your browser to **ftc.gov/idtheft**. This is also a link found on the bottom of the **IdentityTheft.gov** page accessed in the previous steps.

Exposure to Inappropriate or Distasteful Content

The Internet, and especially the World Wide Web, is a treasure trove of information. It is hard to imagine a subject that cannot be found somewhere on the Internet. However, some of this content may be inappropriate or distasteful. To some extent, only an individual can judge what is inappropriate and distasteful; however, there are circumstances in which certain content harmful to some individuals—such as young children—is considered a threat.

Invasion of Privacy

One can also view many of the threats discussed so far as invasions of privacy. Protecting against privacy invasion includes protecting your personal information at your bank, credit union, at online and brick-and-mortar retail stores, athletic clubs, and at any organization in which you are a customer, member, or employee. All steps you take to make your computer more secure also contribute to the protection of your privacy. Don't forget physical security and the ability of people to gather information by **shoulder surfing**, which entails reading information off your screen while you work on your computer in a busy office or public location.

Invasion of privacy by shoulder surfing.
©Troy Aossey/Getty Images

Misuse of Cookies

One form of privacy invasion involves the misuse of something called cookies. Cookies are very small files a Web browser saves on the local hard drive at the request of a website. The next time you connect to that same website, it will request the cookies saved on previous visits—often giving you the convenience of automated log-ins to each site. Cookies are text files, so they cannot contain viruses, which are executable code, but they may contain the following:

- User preferences when visiting a specific site.
- Information you may have entered into a form at the website, including personal information.
- Browsing activity.
- Shopping selections on a website.

WARNING!

From now on, when you browse the Web, look for links to the privacy statement or site policy at each website you visit.

Users are not overtly aware of the saving and retrieving of cookies from their local hard disk, although most good websites clearly detail whether or not they use cookies and what they use them for. You can find this information in the privacy statement or policy of the site. Cookies are accessible by the website that created them, or through some subterfuge of the website creator. A cookie contains the name of the domain that originated that cookie. A first-party cookie is one that originates with the domain name of the URL to which you directly connect. A third-party cookie refers to a cookie that originates with a domain name beyond the one shown in the current URL. An ad embedded in a Web page—often called banner ads—can use cookies to track your Web surfing habits, and third-party cookies play a part in this type of tracking, making third-party cookies less desirable than first-party cookies.

Computer Hardware Theft

Good security includes something as simple as locking doors, keeping hardware locked away from prying eyes and sticky fingers. That's obvious. What may not be obvious to you, especially if you use a laptop as your principal computer, is what happens if someone steals your computer. You would be astonished at how many computers,

Guard against computer theft.
©Image Source, all rights reserved.

especially laptops and mobile devices, are stolen each year, and unless your computer has been properly secured, and all the data backed up, there goes your business information, your data files, your financial information, your address book, everything! Although a large percentage of computer thefts occur just so the thief can sell the hardware quickly and get some quick cash, an increasing number of thieves are technically sophisticated and will go through your hard drive looking for bank account, credit card, and other financial data so they can steal your identity.

Accidents, Mistakes, and Disasters

Accidents and mistakes happen. We don't know of anyone who hasn't accidentally erased an important file, pressed the wrong button at the wrong instant, or created a file name he can't remember. Disasters also happen in many forms. Just a few are fires, earthquakes, and weather-induced disasters such as tornadoes, lightning strikes, and floods. Predicting such events is imperfect at best. The principal way to protect against accidents, mistakes, and disasters is to make frequent, comprehensive backups. You can make backups of an entire hard drive using programs that make an image of the drive, or you can use programs that back up your critical data files on a periodic basis. Organizations that have a lot of valuable data even make multiple backups and keep copies off-site. Then, in case of fire, flood, earthquake, or other natural disaster that destroys not only the on-site backups but also the computer, they can still recover.

Keeping Track of New Threats

We cannot begin to cover all the methods currently used to victimize computer users. However, various organizations work to keep track of these threats, counter them, and inform the public. The Federal Trade Commission (FTC) Bureau of Consumer Protection is one such organization. It maintains a website (**www.ftc.gov/bcp/**), shown in Figure 2-5, containing a list of documents about various consumer issues and threats. These documents are worth reviewing from time to time to learn about new threats. This site also posts the latest related news and hosts a blog.

Computer accidents are common.
©Mikael Damkier/Shutterstock

FIGURE 2–5 The FTC Bureau of Consumer Protection website.
Source: Federal Trade Commission

The People Behind the Threats

The people behind computer security threats are as varied as are their motivations. They come from all walks of life and are scattered all over the globe. The umbrella term for a person who breaks laws using computer technology is cybercriminal. Other terms further define the people behind these threats.

Organized Crime

Organized crime is a growing source of these threats. Organized crime cartels exist in every major country in the world, with certain areas notorious for their homegrown crime organizations. Organized crime specialists work at stealing bank account login information and also are the source of many fraud attempts and money laundering via online shopping.

Cyberterrorists

Terrorists cause destruction without regard to its effect on humanity. Terrorists of all types have embraced cybercrime as a method by which individuals can wreak havoc on victims worldwide without putting themselves in physical danger. Such an attack is cyberterrorism, and a person who carries it out is a cyberterrorist.

Hackers

As any group of people engaged in similar endeavors grows and matures, it develops a set of terms and participant competency rankings. For years, the term "hacker" has been used, particularly by the press, to mean someone who uses sophisticated computer programming skills to invade private computers and networks to cause havoc, steal passwords, and steal identities and money. But the people who work to invade computer systems actually fall into several classifications describing their actions. For instance, in some circles, a hacker is someone with a great deal of computing expertise, a white hat hacker. Like the classic good cowboy who wore a white hat in old westerns, a white hat hacker is not a cybercriminal and only explores computer system weaknesses for the purpose of making systems more secure, an activity considered to be ethical.

Hacker.
©Den Rise/Shutterstock

Crackers

A cracker is a member of a group of people who proudly call themselves hackers, but are regarded as black hat hackers. This again harks back to the old cowboy westerns in which the bad guys wore black hats. They may be after financial gain or simply get a kick out of causing damage after breaking into computers and making phone systems do things they aren't supposed to do (the latter is called phone phreaking). White hat hackers call these people "crackers" and want nothing to do with them because being able to break security doesn't make you a hacker any more than being able to hot-wire a car makes you an automotive engineer. The basic difference is this: Hackers build things and look for vulnerabilities in order to improve security; crackers break into systems illegally and do harm.

Script Kiddies

A script kiddie is someone who lacks the knowledge to personally develop a security threat, but uses scripted tools or programs created by others to break into computer systems to cause damage or mischief. The name implies enough knowledge to run computer scripts or programs.

Click Kiddies

A click kiddie is similar to a script kiddie, but with even less knowledge than a script kiddie, requiring a GUI to select and run a hacking tool. A click kiddie browses the Web, searching for sites that make it even easier by providing forms the click kiddie can fill out, enter a target IP address, and click to initiate an attack. Such sites provide the additional benefit of anonymity to the perpetrator.

Packet Monkeys

Packet monkeys are similar to script kiddies and click kiddies in that they need to use programs created by others to perform their attacks. They typically have little understanding of the harm they may cause, and their exploits are often random and without a purpose other than the thrill of trying to get away with something. Hackers call packet monkeys "bottom feeders."

Packet monkeys create denial-of-service attacks by inundating a site or a network with so much traffic (data packets) that the network is overwhelmed and denies service to additional traffic.

LO 2.2 | Defense Against Threats

No simple solutions exist to the damaging and mischievous threats that lurk on the Internet and on private networks, but doing nothing is not an option. We need to make our best efforts to thwart these threats, even if we cannot deter a determined and skilled invader. Most people do not have the necessary skills, motivation, or access to sophisticated tools, so implementing basic security will keep the majority out. Here are some basic defensive practices that you can apply in operating systems to avoid being a victim.

Education

This chapter may be just the beginning of your education about how threats, such as viruses, get access to computers and networks and how your own behavior can make you vulnerable to such threats as identity theft. Beyond understanding how these things can happen, also be actively alert to signs of a virus or that someone is using your credit cards or using your identity to obtain credit for themselves. Then you can take steps to defend against threats and recover from damage from threats.

Be suspicious of anything out of the ordinary on your computer. Any unusual computer event may indicate that a virus, some sort of browser hijack, or other form of spyware, adware, and so on has infected your computer. Signs to look for include:

- Strange screen messages.
- Sudden computer slowdown.
- Missing data.
- Inability to access the hard drive.

Similarly, unusual activity in any of your credit or savings accounts can indicate that you are a victim of identity theft, including:

- Charges on credit accounts that you are sure you or your family did not make.
- Calls from creditors about overdue payments on accounts you never opened.
- Being rejected when applying for new credit for reasons you know are not true.
- A credit bureau reports existing credit accounts you never opened.

Keep yourself informed by checking out reliable sources. ZDNet publishes articles on many technology topics. Just one of their regular security columns is the Zero Day blog, which gives an overview of the latest security-related news. Another good site for keeping up with security news is **www.schneier.com**.

Along with education about threats comes paranoia. However, if you use a computer at home, work, or school, and are on a network and/or the Internet, a touch of paranoia is healthy. Just don't let it distract you from your day-to-day tasks. Take proactive, responsible steps, as we outline here.

Paranoia 101: Don't Be a Victim

One important tool is a healthy skepticism (with a touch of paranoia) whenever you are online. Tech companies like Facebook, Google, Apple, Microsoft, and Amazon earn billions of dollars from your data without your permission and without compensation to you. Our goal here is to make you more aware of what you are giving away so that you can look for ways to avoid revealing too much about yourself.

Note: The use of your personal data hurts the economy because these tech companies, especially Facebook and Google, have relatively few employees, and therefore put very little back into the economy in the form of wages.

Nothing Is Free

Nothing is free, especially when it comes to online services, such as email and social media. Do you have a free email account with Google, Yahoo, Apple, or Microsoft? It isn't free. You are paying for it with your personal data. Some providers claim to use only the metadata. This is the data attached to the email identifying the source of the message and its destination. That data alone tells providers a lot about you and those with whom you communicate. Others don't stop at the metadata, but also scan the content of your email. Both types of data are used to target you with advertisements and other messages.

try this!

Title

Learn about the latest news involving personal data gathered through social media. Try this:

1. Open a Web browser and enter the search string, "social media data breach:"
2. Skip the results that are clearly advertisements. In most browsers, ads are at the top of the list of results and the link is preceded by "Ad."
3. Look for links to recent articles and read several articles.
4. Discuss your findings, including any recent breaches and developments in laws to protect against data breaches or misuse of personal data.

What can you do to protect yourself?

Look for security and privacy controls for your accounts. This includes email, social media, and any online service. Also, be more aware of free services, and consider if you truly need those services. If you decide you do, investigate purchasing an equivalent service. For instance, if you "rent" your own domain name, you can then pay for a hosting service to host your email. This has the added benefit of allowing you to have several email accounts linked to that domain name. These could include multiple accounts for you to use in different circumstances as well as accounts for friends, family, and employees. These services are relatively inexpensive, but you will need to decide who among you will be the administrator of this service, adding and removing accounts and doing other maintenance.

At one time, using a custom domain name, we hosted our own email server in our home office, but this involved more responsibility and cost than we wanted, so after a few years, we moved our email services to a hosting service with Jane as the administrator.

What Are You Revealing about Yourself?

Consider behavior modification. Your own behavior can make you vulnerable to data mining as well as to scams. Anytime you play a computer game online, enable apps within social media, or respond to online surveys (within social media or otherwise), you are providing data for someone, regardless of the security and privacy settings you may have for your various accounts. This is because you are voluntarily offering clues to your likes, dislikes, hobbies, friends, family connections, and more. It may be hard to resist responding to a simple question like, "What was your first car?" or "Do you remember this _____?" This second is usually accompanied by a photo of some obsolete tool or kitchen utensil. Responding to these questions adds more data points to the great database(s) in the cloud. Consider what you are revealing about yourself before you decide to participate in these services, survey, or games.

Note: If you belong to social media in order to keep up with friends and family, consider adopting a "look, but don't click" approach.

Resist Click Bait

Among all the distractions competing for our attention, click bait may be the most difficult to ignore, but you must try if you do not want to reveal more about yourself to persons unknown to you or risk inviting a malware infection.

Government Regulations

Slowly, governments are gaining some understanding of the threats to individuals and governments from the vast amounts of personal data collected without our permission or compensation. The European Commission's General Data Protection Regulation (GDPR) is one attempt to protect user data within the European Union (EU), as well as personal data exported from the EU. The United States Congress lags behind these efforts, but some legislation is in process at this time.

Security Policies

> *Note:* Password complexity requirements may state that a password must include a combination of both lowercase and uppercase alphabetical characters, numerals, punctuation, and math symbols.

Every organization should have a set of established security policies describing how they protect and manage sensitive information. Security policies define data sensitivity and data security practices, including security classifications of data, and who (usually based on job function) may have access to the various classes of data. For instance, a security policy may state, "Only server administrators and advanced technicians may access the server room, and must not give access to any other individuals." Security policies should also describe the consequences of breaking policy rules.

Security policies should exist in both document form and software form. For instance, at work or school, if you are logging into a network with a central login, such as a Microsoft domain, administrators may configure the servers to enforce a password policy that accepts only strong passwords. How they define a strong password depends on the settings selected, such as minimum password length or complexity. In addition, they may require that you create a new password every month, and that you cannot repeat any of the previous 10 passwords.

Windows has security policies implemented from the domain level on the computers as well as on the users that log on to the domain. Windows also has a local security policy that affects the local computer and users, but can be overridden by domain policy when the computer and user are logged on to a Windows domain. The Local Security Policy console shown in Figure 2-6 allows an administrator to set local security policy. This is a very advanced task.

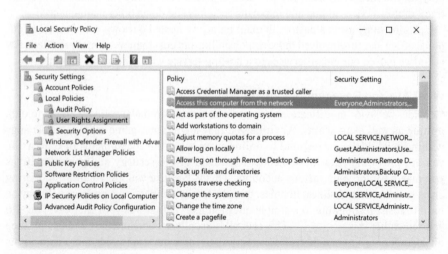

FIGURE 2–6 The Windows Local Security Policy console.
Source: Microsoft Corporation

Firewalls

A **firewall** is either software or a physical device that examines network traffic. Based on predefined rules, a firewall rejects certain traffic coming into a computer or network. The two general types of firewalls are network-based hardware firewalls and personal firewalls that reside on individual computers. We recommend that you always have a reliable personal firewall installed, even if your computer is behind a hardware firewall. An attack can be from another computer behind the firewall, and that is when your personal firewall becomes your last line of defense between your computer and the world. Let's look at these two general types of firewalls.

Network-Based Firewalls

A network-based firewall is a hardware device designed to protect you against the dangers of having an unprotected connection to the Internet. It sits between a private network and the Internet (or other network) and examines all traffic in and out of the network it is protecting. It will block any traffic it recognizes as a potential threat, using a variety of techniques. Table 2-1 lists some of the most common technologies normally included in a firewall, although some of these are not strictly firewall technologies. Your ISP and most corporations employ hardware firewalls, expensive and specialized computers manufactured by companies such as Cisco, Palo Alto Networks, Fortinet, and others, and these sophisticated firewalls require highly trained people to manage them. Such a firewall probably protects the network at work or at school.

At home or in a small office, most people have a consumer-grade hardware firewall that comes in a small device that performs many of the same functions performed by a more professional-grade firewall. The most common name for these devices is broadband router or cable/DSL router. They combine the function of a firewall, a router (a device that "routes" traffic from one network to another), an Ethernet switch, and even a wireless access point all in one tiny box. These inexpensive devices can handle the traffic of just a few computers, while the more serious devices employed by ISPs and large organizations can handle thousands of simultaneous high-speed transmissions. These consumer-grade devices now come with the "one button" configuration that automatically configures a simple connection to the Internet, with the latest security turned on. You can also access the built-in Web page to make manual changes to the settings. Figure 2-7 shows the security page of a Cisco Wireless Router, which

FIGURE 2–7 The Security page from a Cisco Wireless Router's configuration utility.
Source: Cisco Systems

TABLE 2-1 Firewall Technologies

Technology	Description
IP packet filter	An IP packet filter inspects (or filters) each packet that enters or leaves the network, applying a set of security rules defined by a network administrator. Packets that fail inspection may not pass between the connected networks.
Proxy service	Sometimes referred to as an application-layer gateway, a proxy service watches for application-specific traffic. For example, a Web proxy only examines Web browser traffic. Acting as a stand-in (a proxy) for internal computers, it intercepts outbound connection requests to external servers and directs incoming traffic to the correct internal computer. You can configure a proxy service to block traffic from specific domains or addresses.
Encrypted authentication	Some firewalls require external users to provide a user name and password before they can open a connection through a firewall. Since the authentication information (user name and password) must pass over the Internet, it is important to encrypt it. This authentication involves the use of one of several encryption protocols. Encrypted authentication is a security service that is not limited to firewalls and is not always implemented on a firewall.
Virtual private network (VPN)	Not a true firewall technology, a virtual private network (VPN) is a virtual tunnel created between two endpoints over one or more physical networks, done by encapsulating the packets. Other security methods usually applied include encryption of the data and encrypted authentication. When set up in combination with properly configured firewalls, a VPN is the safest way to connect two private networks over the Internet.

includes support for all the technologies listed in Table 2-1 and many more features, including support for the 802.11N standard for Wi-Fi communications and security. The setting labeled "Firewall" is just one option for securing your home network. Even with this device, you would need to research the impact of the various settings before changing from the default settings.

The firewall administrator configures a firewall to allow traffic into the private network or prohibit traffic from entering the private network based on the types of computers residing within the private network, and how they will interact with the Internet. If all the computers on a private network are desktop computers that connect to the Internet to browse Web pages and access FTP sites, the firewall protecting the network has a simple job. It simply blocks all in-bound traffic that is not the result of a request from a computer on the internal network; it matches incoming traffic with previous outgoing traffic that made requests that would result in incoming traffic. Then, when you connect to a website, outgoing traffic from your computer to the website requests to see a page. That page comes to you as incoming traffic and a firewall will allow it through based on your initial request.

But if the private network includes servers that offer services on the Internet, then the firewall must allow initiating traffic to come through, but it does not allow all incoming traffic through. In this case, an administrator configures a firewall to allow incoming traffic of the type that can only communicate with the internally based servers. The various types of traffic include email, Web, FTP, and others. Each type of traffic has a certain characteristic the firewall can recognize. Figure 2-8 shows a firewall protecting a network containing both servers and desktop computers (shown as clients).

A network professional would look at the simplified example of a firewall shown in Figure 2-8 and immediately talk about setting up a DMZ, named for a wartime demilitarized zone. In networking, a DMZ is a network between a private (inside) network and public (outside) network. An organization puts any servers that it wishes to have offer services to the Internet in the DMZ.

Personal Firewalls

Because many attacks come from within a private network, personal firewalls have become standard. The Windows Defender Firewall is included in Windows. macOS comes with a firewall, and there are many third-party firewalls for Windows, macOS, and Linux. There are two places where you can configure the Windows Firewall. One is the Windows Defender Firewall Control Panel, shown in Figure 2-9. Using the links in the pane on the left, you can make changes to the Firewall. A more advanced

Note: A server created as a decoy to draw malware attacks and gather information about attackers is called a honey pot. A honey pot may be located outside a corporate firewall, within a DMZ, or inside the corporate network.

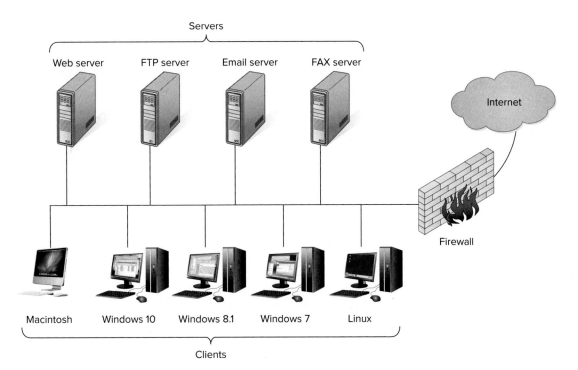

FIGURE 2–8 A private network protected by a firewall.

FIGURE 2–9 The Windows Defender Firewall Control Panel.
Source: Microsoft Corporation

configuration tool is Windows Defender Firewall with Advanced Security, a Microsoft Management console shown in Figure 2–10.

If you have installed a third-party firewall—either separately or as part of a security suite—the Windows Defender Firewall will be turned off. Opening the Windows Defender Firewall applet in Control Panel will show you a message stating that your computer is unprotected and you need to turn on Windows Defender Firewall. This message may simply mean that Windows Defender Firewall is disabled because you are using a third-party firewall.

Note: Zone Labs (**www.zonelabs .com**) offers many excellent security products, including Zone Alarm, a personal firewall.

Security Software

A logical progression through the appropriate defense against computer security threats would have us look at authentication and authorization at this point. However, because we include activities that require that you access the Internet, we will first

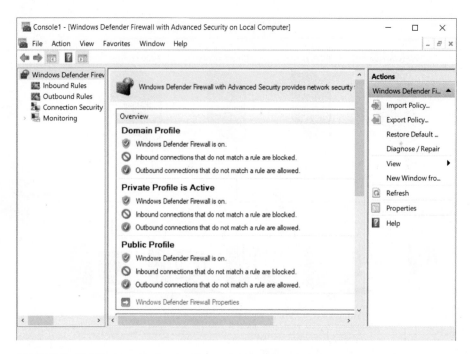

FIGURE 2–10 Windows Defender Firewall with Advanced Security.
Source: Microsoft Corporation

talk about the comprehensive security software that should be in place before you connect to the Internet. This does not mean that security software is more important than authentication and authorization. They are all important pieces of every security defense strategy.

Comprehensive security software may come in one bundle of software from one source, or it can be separate software from many sources. The pieces should include (at minimum) a personal firewall, antivirus software, anti-spam software, and an email scanner. Figure 2-11 shows the console for Bitdefender with security components and various tools for managing the security package, such as the Update that

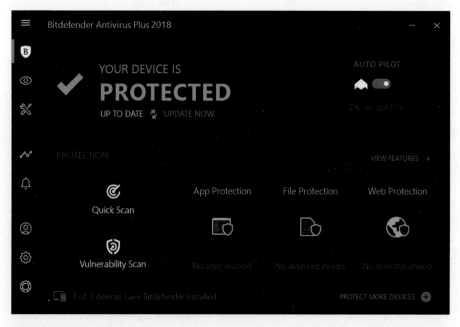

FIGURE 2–11 Security software with many bundled components.
Source: Bitdefender Antivirus Plus 2018

automatically checks the Bitdefender site for updates and then downloads and installs them. The following sections will describe security components included with common security software.

Antispam Software

A spam filter is software designed to combat spam by examining incoming email messages and filtering out those that have characteristics of spam, including certain identified keywords. In an organization with centralized network and computer management, spam filter software installed on central mail servers can remove spam before it gets to a user's desktop. Network administrators may use Internet-based spam filtering services that block spam before it reaches the corporate network.

Individuals connected to the Internet from home or in small businesses are often on their own when it comes to eliminating spam. Luckily, many email clients, such as Microsoft Outlook, offer spam filtering. Without a spam filter you must sort through your own email to find and delete the spam. Spam filters are not perfect—they can filter out legitimate messages, while allowing some spam messages through. For this reason, most spam filters require some configuration on the part of the user using rules or filters that will automate the process of removing spam from known sources. And the user will still often need to review a list of suspected spam messages. Figure 2–12 shows the Microsoft Outlook Junk Email Options dialog box with several tabbed pages of settings that allow you to configure the spam filter.

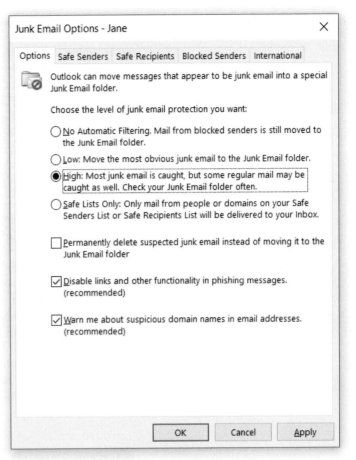

FIGURE 2–12 The Outlook Junk Email Options page.
Source: Microsoft Corporation

Antivirus Software

An antivirus program can examine the contents of a storage device or RAM looking for hidden viruses and files that may act as hosts for virus code. Effective antivirus products not only detect and remove viruses, but they also help you recover data that has been lost because of a virus. To remain current, they require frequent updating as to the virus threats to watch for. An antivirus program includes an antivirus engine (the main program) and a set of patterns of recognized viruses, usually contained in files called definition files. Retailers of antivirus software commonly charge an annual fee for updates to the antivirus engine and the definition files. There are excellent free services for home users. One example is AVG antivirus from GRIsoft. Software companies that offer free security software usually also offer a feature-rich commercial version to which you can upgrade for a fee. The free version gives you a chance to see if you like using it before you put out any money. Once installed, most antivirus programs will automatically connect to the manufacturer's website and check for these updates.

Note: Microsoft offers free security software for Windows: Microsoft Security Essentials for Windows 7, and Windows Defender for Windows 8, 8.1, and 10.

Pop-Up Blockers

Many free and commercial programs are available that effectively block various forms of adware, especially pop-ups, which are the easiest to block and the most annoying because a pop-up advertisement appears in its own window and must be closed or moved before you can see the content you were seeking. A program that works against pop-ups is a pop-up blocker, and all major Web browsers now have built-in pop-up blockers.

Note: The most important browser setting is often a few layers down in the Settings dialog for that browser. Be sure to explore these settings.

We have found a few websites where blocking all pop-ups has blocked much of the content we were seeking. In that case, we may configure the pop-up blocker to make an exception for that site. You can enable the pop-up blocker feature on the Privacy page of the Internet Options dialog box for Internet Explorer. Once enabled, click the Settings button to open the Pop-up Blocker Settings page. Turn on the pop-up blocker for the Google Chrome browser by opening Advanced Settings, Content Settings. The Popups setting is one of many listed there, as shown in Figure 2–13.

To configure the pop-up blocker in Firefox, open Options and select the Content tab, where you will find the setting to turn the pop-up blocker off or on. You can also open the Exceptions dialog for Firefox, and add any website where you wish to enable pop-ups.

Privacy Protection and Cookies

Web browsers and security programs offer privacy protection options. In Microsoft Internet Explorer, you can configure privacy settings, through the Internet Options dialog box, accessible from either the Control Panel or the Tools menu in Internet Explorer. This is also where you determine how Internet Explorer handles cookies. The settings range from "Block all cookies" to "Allow all cookies," with a variety of settings in between. Experiment with the settings by choosing one and then spending some time browsing the Internet. The balance here is between the convenience of cookies for automated login to frequently accessed sites and the risk of an invasion of privacy. We recommend that you allow first-party cookies for the convenience (explained earlier) and block third-party cookies because the tracking methods often associated with third-party cookies are an invasion of privacy.

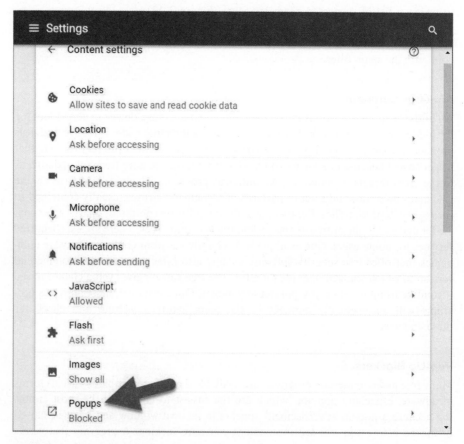

FIGURE 2–13 The Chrome Pop-Up Blocker setting.
Source: Microsoft Corporation

Parental Controls and Microsoft Family

The feature for protecting children from inappropriate content is known as Parental Controls in macOS. Look for Parental Controls in the System Preferences window or turn it on or off for a user in the Users and Groups dialog box. With a Microsoft account you can take advantage of a new free service called Microsoft family. This allows you to either create new accounts for family members or invite a relative with a Microsoft account to join your family. You can protect children in your Microsoft family by creating activity reporting, screen time limits, and content restrictions. Learn more about the benefits of Microsoft family at **account.microsoft.com/family**. See Figure 2-14.

Content Filtering

You can use software that blocks content, called a content filter, to enable protection from inappropriate or distasteful content. A common type of content filter used on the Internet is a Web content filter, a software program designed to work with a Web browser either to block certain sites or to allow only certain sites. As with most types of software, you can find both free and commercial versions of Web content filters on the Internet. In fact, you may already have a Web content filter in your Web browser that you only need to enable and configure.

> *Note:* To learn more about content filters, use your favorite search engine to search on the key words "Web content filter."

Many services are available on the Internet to evaluate website content and give each site ratings based on such parameters as language, nudity, sex, and violence. A content filter may use one or more of these rating services, and allow the administrator to choose the rating level to permit or exclude. Not all websites are rated, so if you enable a Web content filter, you will also have to decide what it should do in the event the user connects to an unrated site.

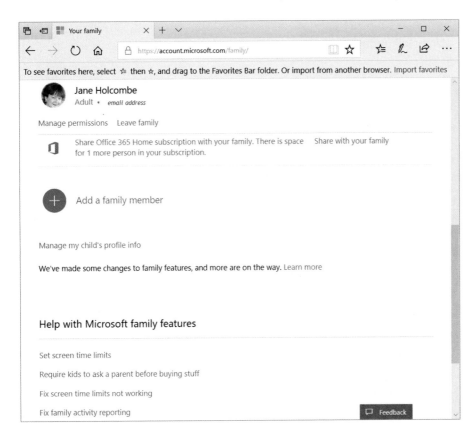

FIGURE 2–14 Add a family member using the Microsoft family feature.
Source: Microsoft Corporation

You can see the update history on your Windows computer. Try this:

1. Open Control Panel. In Windows 7, open it from the Start menu. In Windows 8.*x* and 10, right-click on the start button and select *Control Panel.*
2. Tap or click on the Windows Update link in Control Panel to open it.
3. In the task pane (on the left) in Windows Update, click or tap View Update History.
4. This opens the View Update History control panel, where you can scroll through the list of installed updates.

Software Updates

You should be sure to keep your operating system and applications up to date with security patches, especially if you are running Windows. Microsoft continues to update each version of Windows for several years (see the Microsoft Support Lifecycle at www.microsoft.com), and the versions discussed in this book automatically check for the updates that plug security holes that malware perpetrators exploit. Windows keeps a list of all the updates installed on your computer, as shown in Figure 2–15.

Authentication and Authorization

One of the first defenses against threats is authentication and authorization by a security system built into the operating systems on your local computer and on network servers. The OSs surveyed in this book support authentication and authorization. In fact, Linux, Windows, and macOS require it.

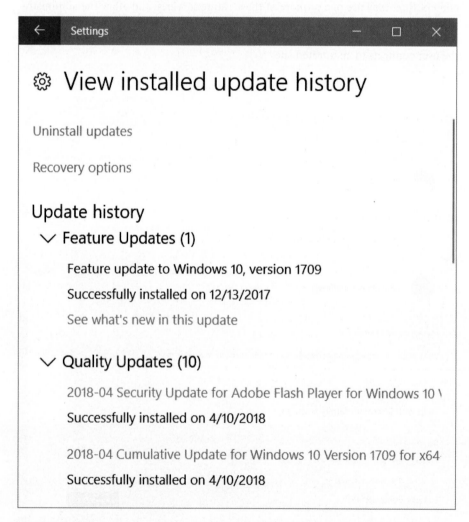

FIGURE 2–15 Windows Update maintains a history of updates.
Source: Microsoft Corporation

After you, as the administrator, have set up an account for Rachel in accounting she must enter her username and password when she logs on to her computer. Before giving her access to the computer, security components of her operating system will verify that she used a valid user name and password. This validation of the user account and password is authentication.

A recently hired part-time clerk, Kirsten, works at night entering accounts payable information into Rachel's computer. To allow Kirsten to also log on to Rachel's computer, you can create a new user account for Kirsten. Although only Rachel and Kirsten can log on to this computer, Rachel does not want Kirsten to be able to access the payroll information, also stored there, because this is private information. What might you do to help Rachel with this problem? One thing you could do (if her operating system supports it) is to set up Rachel's computer so that she can assign special permissions to the files and folders on her hard disk, giving each user account the level of permission it needs. For instance, one of Kirsten's tasks is to add accounting information to the accounts payable files, so you could give Kirsten's account the authorization that will allow her to write to the files in the accounts payable folder. You will not give Kirsten's account access to any of the other folders, and you will only give Rachel's account full control of the folders that she needs to use.

Authentication

Authentication is the verification of who you are. Authentication may be one-factor, two-factor, or even three-factor. One-factor authentication is your use of a user name and password as you log on to your computer. In this case, you are authenticated based on something you know—your user name and password. One type of two-factor authentication involves the use of something you know plus something you have, referred to as a token. If you use a cash card at an ATM, you are familiar with two-factor authentication, because the something you know is your PIN (personal identification number) code, while the token is your cash card. Another type of two-factor authentication, common with many online services today, requires your authentication with a username and password followed by the service sending a one-time authentication code via a method you previously agreed to, such as a text message to your smartphone or the use of an authenticator app. For even more security, consider three-factor authentication, adding biometric data, such as a retinal scan, voice print, or fingerprint scan to the token and password.

Note: There are several authenticator apps by Google, Microsoft, Blizzard Entertainment, and others.

Automatic Login

Right about now you're thinking that we're wrong about Windows and macOS requiring authentication. Your computer is running the latest version of Windows or macOS but you don't have to enter a username or password to access your desktop and all your personal settings and data. So, obviously, you are not authenticated. Right? Wrong! Windows, macOS, and Linux always require authentication, but each has a feature called automatic login that the OS installation program system turns on under certain circumstances, such as when you bring home a PC or Mac that you just bought in a retail store. Automatic login authenticates anyone who powers up your computer using the same credentials, and they have access to everything that you normally do. You should never enable automatic login on a computer at school or at work.

Authorization

Authorization determines the level of access to a computer or a resource (files, folders, printers, and so on) to an authenticated user. Authorization includes authentication plus verification of your level of access to a computer or resource, including permissions and/or user rights. When you connect to a shared folder on your LAN, the security system of the computer hosting the folder will perform authorization, authenticating you and verifying that your account has some level of access to the folder. This level of access is called a permission. Permission describes an action that you may perform on an object. An example of a permission found on a file system is the read permission that allows reading of the contents of a file or folder, but by itself it does not allow any other action on that file, such as deleting or changing it. Another component that affects level of access is a user right. A **user right** defines a system-wide action that a user or group may perform such as logging on to a computer or installing device drivers.

Passwords

The most common method of authentication is the use of a password and an identifier, such as a user name. A password is an important piece of the security puzzle. Don't take your password for granted. In fact, password should be plural, because you should use unique password for every account, and you should put a great deal of thought into creating passwords that truly help you protect yourself. This is important because, secure authentication is your basic defense against an invasion of your privacy, and your password is central to having secure authentication. Most experts recommend using passwords that are at least eight characters long and that contain a mixture of numbers, letters (both uppercase and lowercase), and nonalphanumeric characters. It's easy to guess passwords that use common words—such as the name of a pet—and therefore they offer little in the way of real security.

Establish a method for creating strong passwords—whether it is some scheme that you think up or software that helps you create these passwords. Begin by thinking of a phrase that is easy to remember such as: "I love the Boston Red Sox." Then take the first letter of each word in that phrase and string the letters together. In our example, the result is: iltbrs. Now turn it into a more complex password by capitalizing some of the alpha characters and inserting numbers and other symbols between the letters: i-l,T.b+r-s. If this meets the minimum password requirements, you have a password. Now, the trick is to remember this password without the use of sticky notes!

A great alternative to "do-it-yourself" password creating is to use password management software. A **password manager** will create strong passwords, remember them for you, and even insert the correct password when you need it. Secure the password manager itself with a single strong password. Use a single password manager, such as Dashlane or LastPass, to manage the passwords across all your devices. Figure 2–16 shows the Sites page of the LastPass password manager.

Best Practices with Passwords and Accounts

You may actually have habits that make you vulnerable to identity theft or another type of attack on your computer, data, or personal information. Consider the following questions:

- Do you have too many passwords to remember?
- When you have an opportunity to create a new password, do you use your favorite password—the one that you use everywhere?
- At school or work, do you have your password written on sticky notes or your desk calendar?
- Have you used the same password for more than a few months?

If you can answer yes to any of these questions, you are at risk! And the risk is not only with your password. Because many websites allow you to provide a user name to use when you log in, you may also be reusing the same user name and password combination. Now a hacker doesn't even have to guess your account name.

Create Strong Passwords. A strong password is one that meets certain criteria, and these criteria change over time as hackers create more techniques and tools for discovering passwords. An administrator should have a password that is a minimum of

Use unique and complex passwords.
©Zmeel Photography/iStockphoto

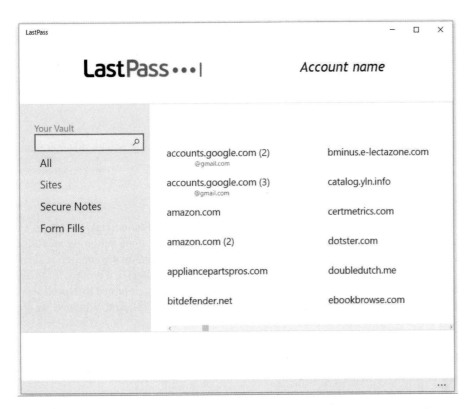

FIGURE 2-16 The Sites page of the LastPass password manager.
Source: LogMeIn, Inc.

15 characters long. Additionally, a strong password includes a combination of letters, numbers, and other symbols, as allowed by the security system accepting the password. Common sense requires that your personal password should be easy for you to remember, but difficult for others to guess.

Always use strong passwords for the following types of accounts:

- Banks, investments, credit cards, and online payment providers.
- Email.
- Work-related accounts.
- Online auction sites and retailers.
- Sites where you have provided personal information.

Avoid Creating Unnecessary Online Accounts. Many websites ask that you create an account and join, but what are the benefits of joining? Why do they need information about you?

Don't Provide More Information Than Necessary. Avoid creating accounts with websites that request your Social Security number and other personal and financial information. Avoid having your credit card numbers and bank account information stored on a website. Although it's not easy to do online, you can do this with a merchant in person: If asked for your Social Security number, ask these four questions:

1. Why do you need it?
2. How will you protect it?
3. How will you use it?
4. What happens if I don't give it to you?

You may have to make a decision as to whether to do business with that merchant if you don't receive satisfactory answers.

Security Account Basics

A security account is an account that can be assigned permission to take action on an object (such as a file, folder, or printer) or the right to take some action on an entire system, such as install device drivers into an operating system on a computer. A security account may identify a single entity (individual or computer) or a group of entities. Security accounts exist in security databases, such as those maintained by Novell servers, UNIX or Linux systems, macOS desktop and server OSs, and Windows server and desktop operating systems.

User Accounts

All operating systems discussed in this book have robust security that begins with using user and group accounts and the requirement to log in to the computer with a user account. The most common type of security account is an individual account, called a user account, assigned to a single person. In the security database on each device, a user account contains, at minimum, a user name and password used to authenticate a user. Depending on the structure of the security accounts database, a user account may contain additional identifying information. Typically, a user account will include the user's full name, a description, and a variety of other fields including email address, department, phone numbers, and so on.

Built-In User Accounts

Each OS has a very special, very privileged built-in account—a super user—that can perform virtually all tasks on a computer, from installing a device driver to creating other security accounts. In Windows this privileged built-in user is Administrator, and it is disabled by default. In those operating systems with their ancestry in UNIX—macOS and Linux—root is the most powerful user account, as it is in UNIX. We'll discuss these accounts in the appropriate chapters.

At the other end of the privilege spectrum, we have a guest account, found in Windows, macOS, and Linux. This account is the least privileged and is disabled by default in Windows. If this account is enabled, a stranger can log in with the account (usually with no password), but cannot see anyone else's files and cannot make changes to the system.

Standard Versus Administrator Accounts

Linux and the versions of Windows and the OS featured in this book all have the notion of types of user accounts. In Windows, a standard user account is for an "ordinary" user without administrator status. A Windows child account is basically a standard account with the additional restrictions applied through Microsoft family. A user logged on with a standard account can change her password and other personal settings, but cannot change computer settings, install or remove software and hardware, or perform other system-wide tasks. In contrast, a user logged on with an account that is an administrator account type can perform system-wide tasks that affect the overall operating system and other users. For example, an administrator can create new users, change user settings, install applications and operating system components, install hardware (and the drivers for that hardware), and access all files on a computer. Ignoring the built-in, but disabled, Administrator account, the first account created in any of these systems must be an administrator account type, and then you may use this account to create additional accounts. When an administrator creates a new account, the default type is Standard.

In macOS, there is a check box in the Accounts dialog for a user: the "Allow user to administer this computer" check box, shown in Figure 2–17. If this is checked, the user account is an administrator account; if it is unchecked, the account is a standard account. As with the Windows administrator accounts, an macOS administrator account can install programs and do a range of system-wide tasks. An macOS standard user is limited much as a Windows standard user is.

The administrator type of account in Linux includes the all-powerful root, and some other accounts, but the standard account type is not as clear. For instance, "standard user" is the term used to describe the long list of accounts some distributions will create automatically if you choose a special installation. Since this includes the root account and others with a wide range of permissions, it is not the same as the standard type of account used in Windows and macOS.

Group Accounts

A **group account** is a security account that contains one or more individual accounts, and, in some security accounts databases, may contain other groups. Group accounts allow us to manage resources for multiple users and make administration of accounts much easier. Group accounts exist in the security accounts databases of all the OSs discussed here—some are built in and privileged users can create others. We will concern ourselves only with those groups that exist in the security accounts database on a desktop computer and not with the security accounts that exist on a network server, such as a Windows Domain Controller. We call the accounts on a desktop computer local user and group accounts. The built-in local groups in Windows include Administrators, Users, and Guests, but other groups are created for various services

FIGURE 2–17 Select this check box to change a standard user to an administrator in macOS.

Source: Microsoft Corporation

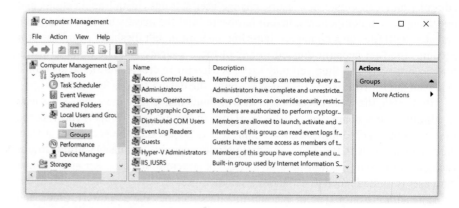

FIGURE 2–18 The Local Users and Groups node in Computer Management showing all groups on the local computer.
Source: Microsoft Corporation

and applications as they install into Windows. Figure 2–18 shows the Local Users and Groups node of the Computer Management console, an advanced tool for managing users and groups in Windows.

Computer Accounts

Computers (and sometimes devices) may also have security accounts within a security accounts database maintained by a network server, such as in a Microsoft Windows Active Directory domain. This means your computer actually joins a domain before you, as a user, can log on to the network. When this occurs, new group accounts appear in the accounts database on your desktop Windows computer as it integrates into the domain. The details of this relationship are beyond the scope of this book, but be aware that this is the case if your computer is part of a Windows Active Directory Domain. How could this affect you? If you bring your personal laptop to the office, you will not be able to log on to the corporate network in the same way that you do from your desktop until an administrator makes your computer a member of the domain. If it's not desirable to join your personal laptop to the network, there are other methods to give you access to the corporate network.

User Account Control

Before Windows Vista, if you wanted to make changes to your system such as installing a new device or program, you had to log on as an administrator. This meant, if you were already logged on with an account that did not have administrative access, you would have to log off and log on again with an administrator account before you could perform a major system task. To avoid this annoyance, many people stayed logged on all day every day using an account with administrator access. This meant that if malware infected your computer, it would have full control over your computer because it would have the same level of access as the logged-on user. To prevent this, Microsoft introduced **User Account Control (UAC)** in Windows Vista to prevent unauthorized changes to Windows.

Microsoft has continued to update the UAC feature. In Windows 10, you can configure it in User Account Control Settings, shown in Figure 2–19. There are four settings. The most restrictive will notify you whenever an app tries to install software or make changes and whenever you try to make changes to Windows settings. The next level (the default) will notify you only when apps try to make changes to your computer, but not when you make changes to Windows settings. The third level will notify you only when apps try to make changes to your computer, but will not dim the desktop. The final, and least secure will never notify you when an app tries

Note: the Local Users and Groups manager is not available in the Home editions of Windows 7 or Windows 10, nor is it in the basic Windows 8.*x* edition. It is in the Pro and Enterprise editions of Windows.

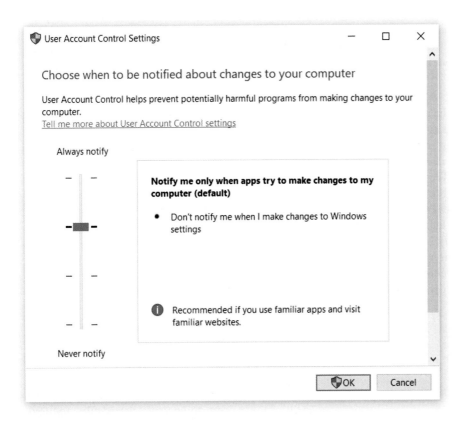

FIGURE 2–19 The Windows 10 User Account Control Settings.
Source: Microsoft Corporation

to install software or make changes to your computer or when you make changes to Windows settings.

OS X also has a function similar to Windows UAC, but it is more subtle. Certain dialog boxes have a lock symbol on the lower left. It will appear locked in some instances and unlocked in others. If you are in a dialog box, such as Users & Groups, you will find that when the lock symbol shows it is locked you can still make certain changes, such as changing your own picture, without a problem, but unlocking the lock reveals more settings that only an administrator may change. If you wish to access the advanced settings, you simply double-click on the lock and enter the user name (it will default to the currently logged-on user) and password of an administrator account, as shown in Figure 2-20. So, even if you have logged on with an account with administrator privileges, it acts like Windows UAC by requiring you to take an extra step before making system-wide changes.

Best Practices When Assigning Permissions

The most important practice in assigning permissions to accounts in any operating system is to use the rule of least privilege. Give permissions to each user or group that allows each user the amount of access required to complete assigned tasks, but do not give users more access than required. Thus, the user has the least privileges necessary to function.

Encryption

Encryption is the transformation of data into an unreadable format (cipher text) that you can decrypt (decipher) only by using a secret key or password. A **secret key** is a special code used to decrypt encrypted data. You can encrypt data you are sending over a network. In addition, you can encrypt data files that are stored on a local computer or network server. Encryption protects sensitive or valuable data and only

FIGURE 2–20 Click the Lock to make advanced changes in a macOS Settings box.
Source: Microsoft Corporation

someone who knows the password or holds the secret key can decrypt the data back to its original state. The secret key may be held in a digital certificate (also called a security certificate, or simply a certificate), which is a file stored on a computer.

Encrypting Network Traffic

Without being aware, you participate in encrypting network traffic when you do online banking or shopping. Look at the address line and you will see the protocol prefix "http" replaced by "https." This means that you are now using Secure HTTP (HTTPS), which encrypts the communications between you and the bank or e-commerce server. HTTPS uses the Secure Sockets Layer (SSL) security protocol. For this encryption method, the user certificates contain identifying information used for verifying the holder of the certificate (your bank or the online retailer), including the holder's public key for use in encrypting a message for the user. Only the user holds the private key to decrypt the message. Your Web browser and its security protocols manage it all for you. If the browser detects a problem with a certificate as a page is loading, you will receive a warning that a website's security certificate is invalid. You should not continue loading the page and should block this website via your browser's security settings.

Windows Encrypting File System

Encryption is very useful for data stored on a laptop or in professional settings, where data theft is a concern. The Microsoft NTFS file system allows you to encrypt selected files and folders (not an entire drive) through a feature called Encrypting File System (EFS). Turn on encryption through the Advanced button of the Properties dialog box of a folder residing on an NTFS volume, and then all files created in that folder become encrypted. Figure 2–21 shows the Advanced Attributes dialog that opens from the Advanced button on the Properties of a folder named Data. Clicking the check box labeled Encrypt Contents To Secure Data will turn on encryption for this folder. Anyone who is logged on with your credentials has access to EFS encrypted data. If you copy or move an encrypted file to another NTFS-formatted volume, the encryption is maintained. If you copy or move an encrypted file to a volume that is not formatted with NTFS, the file is saved without encryption.

Whereas EFS is a useful tool, it is not without problems, including the risk that you will lock yourself out of your own files if you change your password. Only enable EFS if you have a knowledgeable administrator (such as at school or work) who will take certain precautions to ensure that someone can aid you in recovering your encrypted files should you be unable to access them yourself.

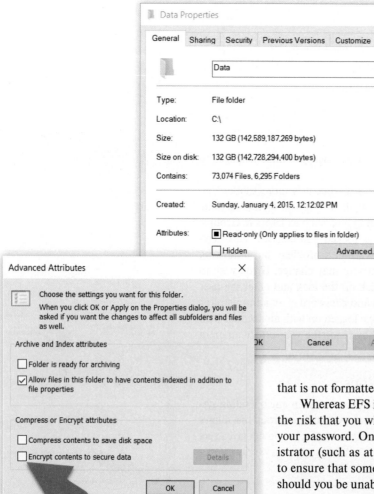

FIGURE 2–21 Turn NTFS encryption on or off using the Properties of a folder in Windows 10.
Source: Microsoft Corporation

Encrypting with Windows BitLocker

BitLocker Drive Encryption is a feature of the Ultimate and Enterprise editions of Windows Vista, Windows 7, Windows 8, and Windows 10 Pro and Ultimate. It allows you to encrypt an entire drive. You or anyone else who is logged on with your credentials has access to the encrypted drive. When using BitLocker in Windows 7, Windows 8, or Windows 10, you can use a feature called BitLocker to Go to encrypt external hard drives and flash drives. When you create a BitLocker to Go volume, you select the method for unlocking. Because this is a portable drive, you can assign a password or a smart card to unlock the drive. See the BitLocker Control Panel in Figure 2-22.

Windows Vista cannot create a BitLocker to Go volume, but can read one provided the user has the means to unlock the volume, owing to the program BITLOCKERTOGO.EXE, a BitLocker to Go Reader, that is installed on each BitLocker to Go volume. You will still need to unlock the drive, using a password or smart card.

Encrypting with macOS FileVault

MacOS has a feature called FileVault that began life as an encryption tool for all the files in your Home folder, and it has been improved in recent versions. Enable macOS FileVault in the Security and Privacy Settings dialog box. Someone logged on with your credentials can access the encrypted files.

Data Wiping

When you move computers from user to user or remove a computer from service within an organization and sell it or give it away, you should remove the data on the computer. This goes beyond a simple delete operation, because there are many methods for "undeleting" such files. To be sure that a determined person will not access your old files, you must remove them completely. The permanent removal of data from a storage device is data wiping.

A reformat of the hard drive is one method, but it's not truly very secure, and it's a problem if you wanted to keep the operating system and programs on the disk. Another method is to use data wiping software that uses an algorithm for writing over an entire drive volume, or just those portions of a drive that contain data—whether it has been deleted or not. You can perform data wiping on any storage media that is rewritable, including hard drives, optical drives, and solid-state storage. Both free and commercial data wiping programs will do the trick for most purposes. Such programs are available for all storage types. Those written for hard drives can take advantage of

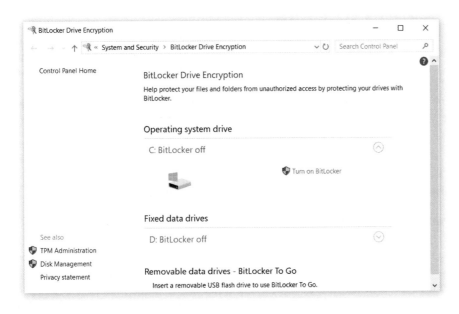

FIGURE 2–22 The Windows 10 BitLocker Control Panel.
Source: Microsoft Corporation

a government-approved ability built in to newer hard drives—Secure Erase. You cannot recover data once you have used such a data-wiping program.

Physical Security

Physical security of computers and networks is yet another huge topic that we can only touch on here. Physical security for desktop computers and networks includes limiting who has access to the building or room in which the desktop computers or network servers reside. Physical security is part of a school or other organization's security policy, and that policy must define its implementation. Small organizations often simply rely on the trustworthiness of their employees—with mixed results—while larger organizations implement formal physical security protection. This can include a mode of identifying someone trying to get entry to a building or room. This mode can be a guarded entrance with confirmation of a person's credentials, key card access, or a variety of other methods depending on the security needs of the organization. Securing laptops and other mobile devices has its own challenges, addressed next.

Security for Mobile Computing

In addition to the practices outlined above as defenses against threats, special considerations are required when traveling with laptops or other mobile computing devices. We will discuss specific security options for mobile devices in Chapter 11. Following are a few general tips.

Be Extra Wary of the Danger of Theft

The very portability of laptops and other mobile computing devices obviously makes them more susceptible to physical theft, so you should be alert to that threat and never leave them unattended while traveling.

Encrypt Sensitive and Confidential Data

In addition to applying permissions, you should further protect any sensitive data on a mobile device with encryption, if available for that device.

LO 2.3 | Troubleshooting Common Security Problems

Most problems have a simple cause, and that is as true with security problems as it is with most computer-related problems. Therefore, when troubleshooting any problem, you should first ask yourself, "What is the simplest (dumbest?) thing that could cause this problem?" The second question should be, "What has changed?" These two questions will keep you from going off in a panic looking for a high-tech solution before at least considering one or more simple solutions. In this section, we discuss some common security problems we have encountered and our recommended solutions.

Troubleshooting Log-On Problems

There are certain nearly universal log-on problems. They include the following.

Caps Lock Key Turned On

Everyone does it! You're in a hurry, and when you type in your user name and password, you don't notice the placement of your hands and one or both of them are incorrect. You receive an error message indicating that the user name or password is incorrect, as in Figure 2-23. No problem; you type it in again, but don't notice that you have the caps lock on. Some operating systems, including Windows, will warn you of this, but other operating systems will not. Therefore, be careful about the placement of your hands and ensure that Caps Lock is off before entering your user name and password.

FIGURE 2–23 Log-on error message.
Source: Microsoft Corporation

Too Many Log-On Attempts

On a bad day, like your first day back at work after a vacation, you may try several times before you enter the password correctly. If you're logging on to a corporate network, it is counting all these tries and you may exceed a limit on the number of log-on attempts. This limit is part of account policies, which you learned about earlier in this chapter. Exceeding the number of log-on attempts (account lockout threshold) may result in your user account being locked out of the computer and the network for a period of time (account lockout duration), and you will see a message similar to that in Figure 2-24. There is usually a third parameter used for account policy: the period of time after which the counter for the number of log-on attempts resets to zero.

If a message like this appears when you are trying to log on to a network at school or work, you will have to call an administrator for help. An administrator may be able to override the lockout so that you can try again. Type carefully this time!

If no administrator is available, you will have to wait for the account lockout time to expire. An administrator configures these settings, usually to comply with a company's security standard (see Figure 2-25). So, it could be a matter of minutes, or it could even be days! Although at the time it can be a huge inconvenience, this is your protection against password crackers, who may need to make many tries before they guess the correct password.

FIGURE 2–24 Log-on lockout message.
Source: Microsoft Corporation

FIGURE 2–25 The Windows Account Lockout policy, where an administrator can set values for lockout duration, threshold, and a period of time after which the counter resets.
Source: Microsoft Corporation

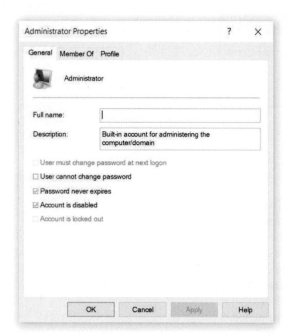

FIGURE 2-26 The Properties dialog box for the Administrator account shows it is disabled by default. Source: Microsoft Corporation

Using the Administrator Account in Troubleshooting

Windows has an administrator account, named Administrator. It is disabled by default, as shown in Figure 2-26. The Administrator account is enabled if your computer starts in Safe Mode and if the computer is not a member of a Windows Active Directory domain. In this case, you can log on with this account and attempt to troubleshoot the reason for the computer going into Safe Mode.

Troubleshooting a Suspected Malware Attack

If you suspect a computer is infected by a virus and you have an antivirus program installed, first use it to run a scan of all drives and memory to see if you can discover and remove the virus. If this does not discover a virus but you are still suspicious, or if you do not have an up-to-date antivirus program installed, you can connect to one of many websites that offer free online scans. An online virus scanner does not fully install, so it should not conflict with your installed security software. Just one example of such a scanner is Housecall, found at **housecall.trendmicro.com**. This scanner is by Trend Micro, which also offers a commercial security suite at **www.trendmicro.com**.

Step-by-Step 2.02

Perform an Online Virus Scan on a PC or Mac

Try one of the online virus scanners. All you need is a Windows computer or a Mac running maxOS 10.7 and up, with a Web browser and a connection to the Internet. Use the online scanner at Trend Micro, or one recommended by your instructor.

Step 1

Open your browser and connect to **http://housecall .trendmicro.com**. Ensure that you are at this website, and were not redirected to one of the many download sites that entice you to download and install questionable software.

Source: Trend Micro Incorporated

Step 2

On the Trend Micro HouseCall page, select 32-bit or 64-bit for one of the Windows downloads, or select Mac for an apple Mac desktop or laptop. The Home Network button opens the download page for HouseCall's Home Network scanner.

Step 3

Click the Save File button. The HouseCall launcher will download into your Downloads folder.

What do you want to do with HousecallLauncher64.exe (2.4 MB)?
From: go.trendmicro.com

Run | Save | ∧ | Cancel | ×

Source: Trend Micro Incorporated

Step 4

Open your Downloads folder, locate the HouseCall Launcher, and double-click or tap it to install and run the program.

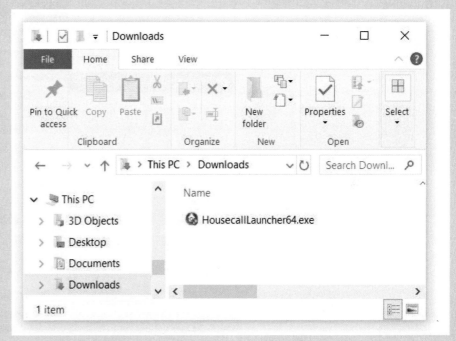

Source: Microsoft Corporation

Step 5

Respond to any User Account Control prompt to enable the program to run. Then it will take a few minutes to load the program, checking for updates and doing other housekeeping. When prompted, accept the Trend Micro End User License Agreement and select Next.

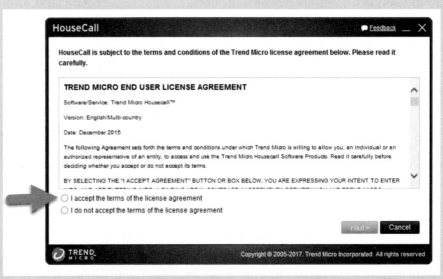

Source: Trend Micro Incorporated

Follow the on screen instructions to run the scan. In the lab, open Settings and select Quick scan because a full system scan can take several hours, depending on the amount of programs and data on your computer. At home, you may want to perform a full system scan.

Source: Trend Micro Incorporated

When finished, the results dialog box displays.

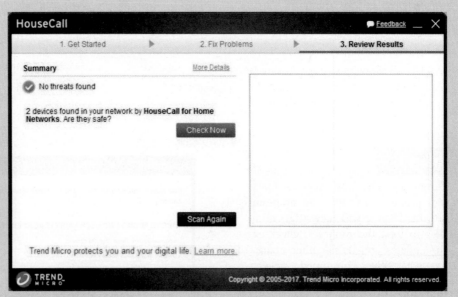

Source: Trend Micro Incorporated

Chapter 2 REVIEW

Chapter Summary

After reading this chapter and completing the exercises, you should understand the following facts about computer security.

Threats to Computers and Users

- Threats include a long list of intentional and unintentional actions from malware through accidents and natural disasters.
- A vector is the method that malware uses to infect a computer.
- The people behind computer security threats come from all over the world, and increasingly they are part of terrorists groups and organized crime.
- Many methods are used to steal passwords, including capturing them from unsecured websites, using password crackers, and keystroke loggers.

Defense Against Threats

- Education is an important defense against threats. Know what the threats are and learn the signs of a threat or an infection.
- Don't be a victim. Nothing is free. Don't reveal personal information online. Resist click bait.
- Security policies describe how an organization protects and manages sensitive information.
- Install security software, including personal firewalls, antispam software, antivirus software, and pop-up and privacy protection.

- Keep your software up to date with security patches.
- Improve your security with authentication and authorization.
- Combat threats with the rule of least privilege when assigning permissions and using best practices with passwords.
- Encryption technologies protect your data.
- Data wiping practices can remove even deleted data from computers.
- Physical security of computers and networks is important, especially for mobile computing.

Troubleshooting Common Security Problems

- Log-on failure may be the result of something as simple as having the Caps Lock key turned on. You will be locked out if you exceed the number of failed log-on attempts configured in the Account Lockout policy.
- Windows has an administrator account, "Administrator." Disabled by default. Enabled if your computer is not a member of a Windows Active Directory domain it starts in Safe Mode. In that case, log on with this account and attempt to troubleshoot the reason for the computer going into Safe Mode.
- If you suspect a computer is infected by a virus, run a scan of all drives and memory.

Key Terms List

administrator account type *(66)*

adware *(43)*

authentication *(63)*

authorization *(63)*

back door *(40)*

bitcoin *(44)*

black hat hacker *(51)*

bluesnarfing *(41)*

bot herder *(43)*

botnet *(43)*

browser hijacking *(44)*

click bait *(38)*

content filter *(61)*

cookies *(48)*

cybercriminal *(50)*

cybercrime *(38)*

cyberterrorism *(50)*

cyberterrorist *(50)*

data wiping *(71)*

digital certificate *(70)*

DMZ *(56)*

drive-by download *(40)*

email spoofing *(45)*

Encrypting File System (EFS) *(70)*

encryption *(69)*

exploit *(42)*

FileVault *(71)*

firewall *(55)*

first-party cookie *(48)*

forged email address *(45)*

fraud *(44)*

group account *(67)*

guest account *(66)*

hacker *(51)*

header *(45)*

honey pot *(56)*

hotspot *(40)*	ransomware *(44)*	spyware *(43)*
identify theft *(45)*	rootkit *(40)*	standard user account *(66)*
keylogger *(42)*	scareware *(39)*	third-party cookie *(48)*
keystroke logger *(42)*	secret key *(69)*	token *(63)*
malware *(38)*	Secure HTTP (HTTPS) *(70)*	Trojan horse *(39)*
Microsoft family *(61)*	Secure Sockets Layer (SSL) *(70)*	user account *(66)*
Parental Controls *(61)*	security account *(66)*	User Account Control (UAC) *(68)*
password *(41)*	shoulder surfing *(47)*	user right *(64)*
password cracker *(41)*	social engineering *(44)*	vector *(38)*
password manager *(64)*	social media *(38)*	virus *(43)*
permission *(63)*	social networking *(38)*	war driving *(41)*
phishing *(45)*	spam *(44)*	white hat hacker *(51)*
pop-up *(40)*	spam filter *(59)*	worm *(43)*
pop-up blocker *(59)*	spear phishing *(45)*	zero-day exploit *(42)*
pop-up download *(40)*	spim *(44)*	zombie *(43)*

Key Terms Quiz

Use the Key Terms List to complete the sentences that follow. Not all terms will be used.

1. A/an _____ defines what a user or group can do to an object such as a file or folder.

2. Programs on a website may send very small text files called _____ to a Web browser, along with a request that the Web browser save the file on the user's computer.

3. Unsolicited email, usually sent to market a service or product (legitimate or otherwise), is called _____.

4. _____ occurs when someone collects personal information belonging to another person and uses that information fraudulently.

5. In Windows, a/an _____ defines a system-wide action a user or group may perform, such as logging on to a computer or installing device drivers.

6. _____ includes authentication, plus determination of a person's level of access to a computer or a resource.

7. The EFS feature in Windows NTFS and macOS FileVault feature are both examples of _____ at the file system level.

8. _____ is verification of who you are.

9. A parent wanting to protect a child from inappropriate Web content may use a/an _____.

10. A person or program with administrative access can install malicious code as a/an _____, which hides itself from detection within the operating system.

Multiple-Choice Quiz

1. What is the name for the defining rules and practices for protecting and managing an organization's sensitive information?
   a. Firewalls
   b. Security policies
   c. Security software
   d. Content filtering
   e. Antivirus

2. This type of annoyance appears uninvited in a separate window when you are browsing the Web and can provide a vector for malware infections.
   a. Inline banner
   b. Pop-up

   c. Spam
   d. Adware
   e. Back door

3. With this Windows feature turned on (as it is by default) a logged-on user only has the privileges of a standard account, even if that user is an administrator, and must provide credentials to perform most administrative tasks.
   a. Account lockout threshold
   b. EFS
   c. Lockout policy
   d. UAC
   e. Account lockout duration

4. This term describes unsolicited messages received via instant messaging.
   a. Spam
   b. Spyware
   c. Zombie
   d. Spim
   e. Bot

5. You open your browser and, rather than pointing to your home page, it opens to a Web page advertising adware removal or antivirus software. You reconfigure the browser to point to your home page, but when you restart the browser, it again points to the wrong Web page. This behavior is a symptom of what type of malware?
   a. Spyware
   b. Worm
   c. Browser hijacking
   d. Keystroke logger
   e. Trojan horse

6. What type of malware installs on a computer without the knowledge or permission of the user, and replicates itself on the computer or throughout a network?
   a. Virus
   b. Utility
   c. Worm
   d. Scam
   e. Spim

7. What term is used for a seemingly harmless program that has malicious code hidden inside?
   a. Worm
   b. Trojan horse
   c. Antivirus
   d. Optimizer
   e. Cookie

8. What utility or feature of a browser is used to inhibit the annoying windows that open when you are browsing the Web?
   a. Content filter
   b. Firewall
   c. Antivirus
   d. Spam filter
   e. Pop-up blocker

9. Strange screen messages, sudden computer slowdown, missing data, and inability to access the hard drive may be symptoms of what?
   a. War driving
   b. Spam
   c. Encryption
   d. Virus infection
   e. Fraud

10. This device sits between a private network and the Internet (or other network) and examines all traffic in and out of the network it is protecting, blocking any traffic it recognizes as a potential threat.
    a. Router
    b. Firewall
    c. Bridge
    d. Worm
    e. Keystroke logger

11. After several failed log-on attempts, a message appears stating that your account was locked out. This is the result of exceeding this setting in Account Lockout policy on a Windows computer.
    a. Password length
    b. Account lockout threshold
    c. Account lockout duration
    d. Maximum password age
    e. Password complexity requirements

12. This type of malware conceals itself within the OS code and gives someone administrative access to a computer.
    a. Rootkit
    b. Pop-up download
    c. Drive-by download
    d. Worm
    e. Hoax

13. What is the term used to describe the use of persuasion to gain the confidence of individuals?
    a. Hoax
    b. Fraud
    c. Phishing
    d. Social engineering
    e. Enticement

14. What term describes the action of a password cracker that simply tries a huge number of permutations of possible passwords?
    a. Keystroke logging
    b. Brute force
    c. Statistical analysis
    d. Mathematical analysis
    e. Phishing

15. This firewall technology inspects each packet that enters or leaves the protected network, applying a set of security rules defined by a network administrator; packets that fail are not allowed to cross into the destination network.
    a. Proxy service
    b. VPN
    c. IP packet filter
    d. Encrypted authentication
    e. DMZ

Essay Quiz

1. Explain automatic log-in and why you should not allow it in a situation in which you require security.

2. Consider the following statement: User Account Control limits the damage that someone can do who accesses your computer when automatic log-in is enabled. Elaborate on this statement, describing why it is true, and why there is still a great risk.

3. Why should you disable the Guest account?

4. In your own words, describe why the use of Internet cookies can be an invasion of privacy.

5. Differentiate between permission and user right.

Lab Projects

These Lab Projects ask you to research various topics. In your answers, please provide links to websites you discovered that support your essay or project responses.

LAB PROJECT 2.1

Research identity theft/fraud to answer the following questions.

1. What is the estimated cost of identity theft/fraud in the United States in a recent year? What is the trend compared to previous years?

2. Identity theft can involve computers, but in many cases, computers play only a small part in identity theft. Find a recent article on an identity theft ring and describe how the thieves operated.

3. Share your findings with others in your class and compare the information you found.

LAB PROJECT 2.2

Research the latest malware threats. Many organizations, including antivirus vendors and security services, post information on the Internet about the latest malware threats. Use an Internet search engine to research the latest threats, which you may find at one of the top security software manufacturers, such as McAfee or Symantec. Using the information from one of these sites, make a list of five current threats and research each to learn more about it. Briefly describe each threat and how you will use security software or behavior to defend your computer from each one.

LAB PROJECT 2.3

Organizations require trained specialists to keep their computers and networks secure. One way prospective employers can determine how much someone knows about security is by requiring job applicants to hold certain appropriate security certifications that require study, experience, and passing exams. Find and research a security certification and give a brief description of this certification, including the organization that is behind this certification, who should seek it, what domains (topics) are included in the exam, and the job titles this certification would apply to.

chapter

3 Desktop Virtualization

Source: Microsoft Corporation

Learning Outcomes

In this chapter, you will learn how to:

LO **3.1**   Describe the various types of virtualization used in everyday computing and ways you might use desktop virtualization.

LO **3.2**   Select and install a desktop virtualization option for a Windows desktop host computer.

LO **3.3**   Select and install a desktop virtualization option for a macOS host computer.

When a software company such as Microsoft is developing new software, before it is released to the public, they make it available in beta form to people outside of the company to test. One way to get to know a new OS is to take advantage of the opportunity to try it out, but not all of us have an extra computer to use for such testing. That is when desktop virtualization comes in handy, letting you run Windows or Linux in a special environment on your computer, while keeping your existing operating system intact. All you need in addition to specialized virtualization software is a computer with the processing power and enough RAM and hard drive space to support the number and types of OSs you wish to run. You also need appropriate licenses for all the software, including the OSs running in the virtual machines.

In this chapter, we explore the exploding phenomenon of desktop virtualization and prepare you to install the desktop OSs described in this book into virtual machines. This will save you the cost and physical desktop space for multiple computers. ✦

LO 3.1 | Virtualization Overview

In this section, we define virtualization and many of the terms associated with it, describe its background, and discuss how it has led to the virtualization of desktop operating systems.

Virtualization Is Everywhere

Virtualization is the creation of an environment that seems real, but isn't, and today it seems like virtualization is everywhere. There are many types. You can spend time in a **virtual world**, such as Second Life (Figure 3-1). A virtual world often lets a user select an animated computer-generated human, an **avatar**, to represent him or her within it. People use virtual worlds in online training, marketing of products, and in games of many types. When a virtual world includes three-dimensional images and involves other senses, giving the participant a feeling of actually being present in that time and space, we call it **virtual reality (VR)**.

Augmented reality (AR) is different from virtual reality, although the lines are sometimes blurred. Augmented reality involves viewing something in real time through a camera or other device while the image (or other input) is digitally modified. AR can involve any of the senses. AR technology is finding its way into gaming, retailing, job training, and education.

Many organizations use **storage virtualization** in which client computers can utilize many networked hard drives as though they are one. Network engineers work with **network virtualization** involving a network addressing space that exists within one or more physical networks, but which is logically independent of the physical network structure. Then there is **server virtualization**, in which a single machine hosts multiple servers, each of which performs tasks as independently from the others as separate physical machines would. Companies that provide low-cost web hosting services can create a separate virtual web server for each customer.

With only a small leap from these we come to **desktop virtualization**, the virtualization of a desktop computer into which you can install an operating system,

> *Note:* Pokemon GO is a very popular augmented reality (AR) game that brought out both the excitement and dangers presented by the distraction of using augmented reality games in public places.

FIGURE 3–1 Select an avatar to represent you in Second Life, then explore this virtual world where you can interact with others in a variety of destinations.
©Casimiro PT/Shutterstock

its unique configuration, and all the applications and data normally used by a single person. This virtual desktop may reside on a server, allowing a user to access it over a network from a computer with specialized client software, or it may exist on the local computer.

Each individual virtual environment in both server virtualization and desktop virtualization is a **virtual machine (VM)**—the software emulation of all hardware with which an operating system must interact. But wait, there's more! There is **application virtualization**, in which a user connects to a server and accesses one or more applications rather than an entire desktop environment. This chapter is devoted to today's desktop virtualization, but first we will look at the past.

Your (Great?) Grandparent's Virtual Machines

Today's virtual machines have a long pedigree: They can trace their roots back to the 1960s when mainframe computer manufacturers, such as IBM, added the ability to create multiple separate environments on a single computer. A user connected using a **dumb terminal** that was little more than a keyboard and display with a connection to a host computer (mainframe or minicomputer) with little or no native processing power (hence the term *dumb*).

A dumb terminal connected to the host computer, sending keystrokes and displaying the keystrokes and responses on the display. During a single terminal session, a user connected to a discrete area on the host called a partition. The partition to which each user connected was not like today's virtual machines, but was an area where the user had access to programs and data. After the advent of the IBM PC in the 1980s, a PC configured to emulate a dumb terminal often replaced the dumb terminal.

For years, this model prevailed for those organizations that wished to have a central system where all the programs and data resided, with the individual users connecting from whatever served as a terminal. The 1990s implementation of this model included servers or minicomputers running **terminal services** to which users connected nearly seamlessly to partitions from their desktop PCs using **terminal client** software. These were not, however, virtual machines because the entire hardware and operating system environment was not part of the partition to which users connected. They did not have a fully configurable desktop operating system, such as Windows, to work with beyond their application and data.

A 1970s-era computer terminal.
©Bill Johnson/Getty Images

Today's Virtual Desktops

Today connect to a virtual desktop from your local computer to a server on which the virtual environment resides or by using locally hosted virtual machine. We will briefly discuss the server-based model and then look more closely at options for virtual machines on your desktop computer.

Server-Based Virtual Desktops

In the past few decades, many large organizations have adopted the thin client for their desktop users. A **thin client** is a dedicated terminal or a PC with terminal client software. In either case, a thin client usually lacks such common peripherals as

Note: Thin clients are the modern day dumb terminals.

expansion slots and optical drives. The purpose of a thin client is to connect to a server, allowing the user to work in a server-hosted environment. When that environment provides the entire OS experience and the working applications, it is a virtual machine. This virtual machine may reside on a server and be accessed by a client computer (thin or not), or it may reside on a desktop computer. One term for hosting and managing multiple virtual desktops on network servers is **virtual desktop infrastructure (VDI)**. Today, VDI applies to any server product that provides virtual desktop support.

Local Virtual Desktops

When desktop virtualization resides on a desktop computer, the interactive user (the one sitting in front of that computer) can switch between the **host OS** (the operating system installed directly on the computer) and a **guest OS** (the operating system installed within a VM). Figure 3-2 shows Windows 7 running in a virtual machine on a macOS desktop. If the computer has enough processing power, RAM, and disk space, it may simultaneously run multiple virtual desktops.

Type I and Type II Hypervisors

A **hypervisor**, also called a **virtual machine monitor (VMM)**, is the software layer that manages underlying hardware allocated to one or more virtual machines. Hardware virtualization allows multiple operating systems to run simultaneously on a single computer. A hypervisor normally emulates a computer separate from the underlying computer, using a virtual processor compatible with that of the underlying machine—mainly either an Intel processor or an AMD processor.

There are two types of hypervisors, Type I and Type II. A **Type I hypervisor**—sometimes called a bare-metal hypervisor—can run directly on a computer without an underlying host operating system. A **Type II hypervisor** requires a host operating system.

Type I hypervisors first appeared on high-powered servers. At the time, desktop computers lacked the hardware support in the processors and firmware required for virtualization of some hardware. Of course, that desktop computers became more powerful, and Type I hypervisors are available from the major hypervisor manufacturers—notably Citrix, Microsoft, Oracle, and VMware. These companies offer a

FIGURE 3-2 A Windows 7 client OS running in a virtual machine in macOS.
Source: Microsoft Corporation

selection of products that centrally manage desktop virtual machines, delivered to the desktop (laptop or PC) over a network.

Most of the hypervisors we use in our examples in this chapter are Type II hypervisors requiring an underlying operating system. Whatever hypervisor you use, you will find more and more organizations deploying server-based virtual machines that are the users' everyday work environment. The reason for this is easier central management of the operating systems and user environment.

You have several choices for Type II hypervisors for desktops, but today some of these run only on computers with hardware-assisted virtualization features, which means they require a computer with either the Intel Virtualization Technology for x86 (Intel VT-x) or AMD Virtualization (AMD-V) architecture extensions, which improve the performance of virtual machines on the host. Some hypervisors, such as the one that comes with Windows 8 and Windows 10, require even newer features.

There are several choices of desktop hypervisors, depending on both the hosting OS and the desired guest OSs. Once you select a hypervisor, work through the following tasks.

Note: If your computer's documentation indicates that the processor supports virtualization but a hypervisor requiring this fails to install due to lack of support, look in the documentation for the computer for instructions on enabling this feature.

1. Prepare the host computer:
   - Select a computer that is not important for your everyday work.
   - Confirm that the computer's hardware and operating system meet the minimum requirements for hosting the hypervisor you intend to install.
   - Back up your hard drive.
   - Remove any conflicting software.

Note: If you decide to install two or more different hypervisors on a single host system, do not try to run different hypervisors at the same time.

2. Install the hypervisor, such as Oracle's VirtualBox hypervisor.

3. Create a virtual machine, selecting from a list of guest OSs that the hypervisor supports.

4. Install the guest OS. This normally requires the full retail version of the OS. You may also use a compatible precreated virtual machine. You must have a legal license or a trial version for each guest OS. The guest OS can be installed directly from a physical disc (CD or DVD) or from a bootable ISO file, which is an image of the contents of a CD or DVD.

5. Install appropriate utilities for the guest OS. The hypervisor publisher provides these utilities, and they include special software for making a virtual machine work better for the guest OS.

6. Finally, once you have an OS installed into a virtual machine, you need to realize that the guest OS and host OS are sharing the same physical hardware, and the mouse and keyboard aren't easily shared. Normally, you give a VM control of a mouse by moving the pointer into the VM and clicking inside the guest window. The virtual machine captures the mouse and keyboard, giving the VM the focus. To release the mouse and keyboard, simply move the cursor outside the VM window and click or tap. Another way to release the mouse and keyboard from VM control is with a host key, a key or combination of keys. If a hypervisor will not release the mouse and keyboard from a VM, look for an icon for the host key in the border of the window surrounding the virtual machine. Figure 3–3 shows the bottom right border of a VirtualBox window in macOS. The arrow points to icons indicating that the host key is the left down arrow combined with the Mac Command key.

Major Hypervisor Sources

The major hypervisor manufacturers are Citrix, VMware, Parallels, Microsoft, and Oracle. There are other players in the field, described in articles and reviews in technical publications and websites.

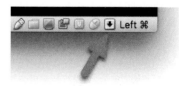

FIGURE 3–3 Look at the bottom of the VirtualBox VM window to learn what combination of keys is the host key.
Source: Oracle Corporation

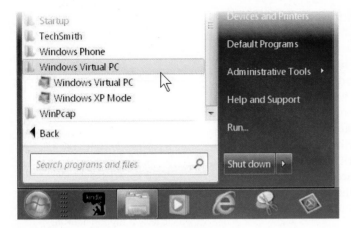

FIGURE 3-4 The Windows 7 Start menu showing Windows Virtual PC and Windows XP Mode.
Source: Microsoft Corporation

LO 3.2 | Virtual Machines on Windows Desktops

You have several options—either fee-based or free—for running Linux, DOS, or Windows on a Windows desktop computer. At this writing you cannot run any version of macOS in a VM on a Windows PC, due to licensing issues. The hypervisors we describe here for Windows hosts are free. Two are from Microsoft (Windows Virtual PC, and Client Hyper-V) and one is from Oracle (VirtualBox).

Microsoft does not require that you register to acquire a free Microsoft Windows desktop hypervisor. However, the installation program will verify that your host OS is a legitimate version of Windows before the Microsoft virtualization product will install.

Windows XP Mode and Windows Virtual PC on Windows 7

Microsoft provides both **Windows XP Mode** and Windows Virtual PC as free, optional components of Windows 7. The main purpose of Windows XP Mode for Windows 7 is to run legacy Windows XP applications that will not run well in Windows 7. It uses a runtime version of Windows Virtual PC. You can install Windows XP Mode and/or Windows Virtual PC. Once installed, these features appear on the Start menu, as shown in Figure 3-4.

Microsoft recommends Windows XP Mode and Windows Virtual PC for small and midsize businesses with Windows 7 desktops. For larger organizations, Microsoft recommends their server-based Azure Virtual Machines.

With Windows Virtual PC, you can also create VMs to run other guest systems, including older versions of Windows, and most versions of Linux. Once installed, it is so well-integrated into Windows 7 that you can start programs installed in the Windows Virtual PC VM from Start menu shortcuts of the host OS. Beyond that, if you have a certain data-file type that you prefer to run in a program that is in the VM, you can assign that file type to the program in the host. Then, double-clicking on such a data file will launch the VM and the program within it.

Only three editions of Windows 7 support Windows Virtual PC and Windows XP Mode. They are Windows 7 Professional, Enterprise, and Ultimate. You may only need to enable them in the Windows Features Control Panel, shown in Figure 3-5. The Try This! will show you how to locate

FIGURE 3-5 The Windows Features Control Panel showing Windows Virtual PC available, but not enabled.
Source: Microsoft Corporation

try this!

Enable Windows Virtual PC or Windows XP Mode on a Windows 7 computer with the Professional, Enterprise, or Ultimate edition. Try this:

1. In the Start menu's Search box enter "windows features."
2. In the search results list, select Turn Windows Features on or off. This opens the Windows Features dialog box.
3. In the Windows Features dialog box, the features list alphabetically. Scroll down to see if Windows Virtual PC is listed. If it is not, you will need to connect to the Microsoft site and install it. If it is listed but not checked, you will need to check it to enable it. Then follow the instructions.

this dialog box and determine if Windows Virtual PC is listed and how to enable it if it is listed but not active.

Downloading and Installing Windows XP Mode in Windows 7

If you cannot start the installation of Windows XP Mode from the Windows Features dialog, you will need to connect to the Windows XP Mode Download page at **Microsoft.com**. Step-by-Step 3.01 describes how to do this.

Step-by-Step 3.01

Downloading and Installing Windows XP Mode

Complete this exercise using a computer running one of the supported editions of Windows 7: Professional, Enterprise, or Ultimate. Only do this exercise if you cannot start the Windows XP download and install from your Start menu or from the Windows Features Control Panel. Be prepared to install security software into the Windows XP Mode virtual machine when it starts up for the first time. Your instructor may provide this software for you.

Step 1

Open your browser and use a search engine, such as Google or Bing, to search on "windows xp mode download." Select the link to the correct download page at the Microsoft Download Center. Do not use any other download service. Double-check that the link is at **microsoft.com** before clicking on it.

Source: Microsoft Corporation

Step 2

On the Windows XP Mode page of the Microsoft Download Center click the Download button.

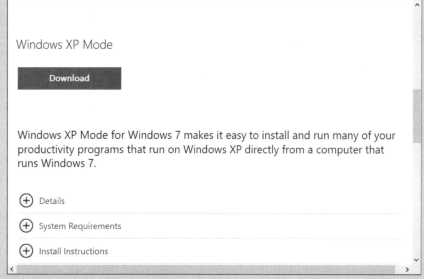

Source: Microsoft Corporation

Step 3

Two installation files for XP Mode are listed. The N version came without Media Center, so it is smaller. Select one and click Next.

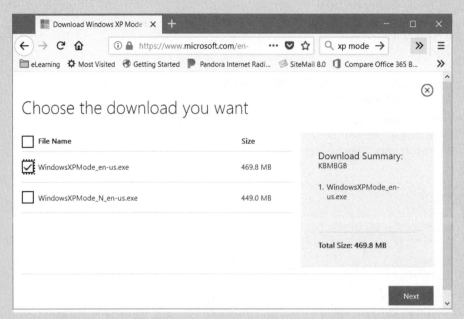

Source: Microsoft Corporation

Step 4

After the download completes, open your Downloads folder and locate the Windows XP Mode executable file, shown here. Double-click to start the setup program.

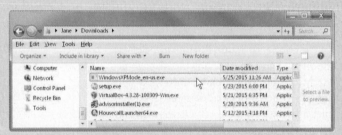

Source: Microsoft Corporation

Step 5

Follow the instructions on the screen, accepting defaults, as in the case of the location, and proceeding through the pages of the setup.

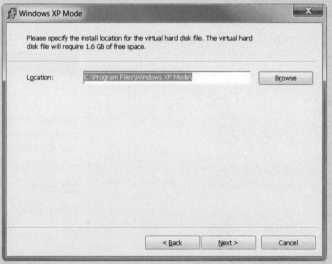

Source: Microsoft Corporation

Setup installs a virtual hard disk.

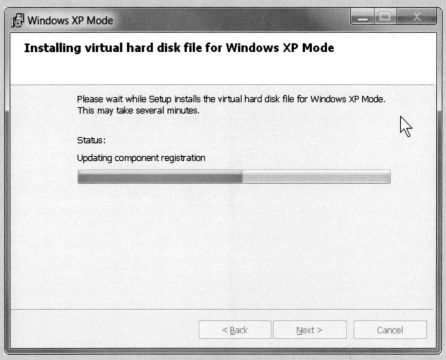

Source: Microsoft Corporation

Accept the license agreement and click the Next button.

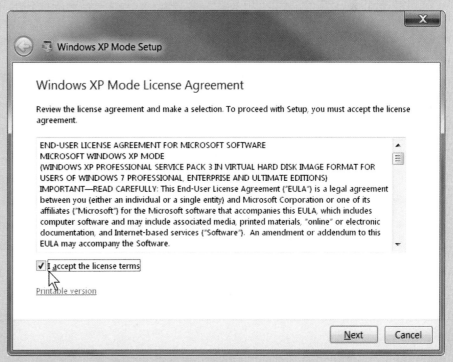

Source: Microsoft Corporation

When this screen appears, select the first option and click Next.

Source: Microsoft Corporation

Setup will share the files on your computer with Windows XP Mode. This is normally what you would want to do. Click Start Setup unless instructed otherwise.

Source: Microsoft Corporation

The first time Windows XP Mode starts, install the antivirus software provided by your instructor.

Step 11

Windows XP Mode comes with Internet Explorer version 8, which is no longer supported. We strongly recommend that you not use a browser within Windows XP Mode, but only old apps that will no longer run in Windows 7.

Step 12

To exit from Windows XP Mode first select Log Off from the Windows XP Start menu. A Log Off Windows dialog box opens. Click Log Off in this box.

Source: Microsoft Corporation

Source: Microsoft Corporation

Step 13

You are not done yet! The Log On to Windows dialog box displays in the virtual machine. Select the Action menu and then select Sleep or Close. When you select Close, the virtual machine will hibernate, and the XP Mode window will close.

Source: Microsoft Corporation

Removing Windows XP Mode

To remove Windows XP Mode open the Programs and Features Control Panel, locate Windows XP Mode in the list of programs and double-click on it. The uninstall program will delete the XP Mode virtual hard disk and all data saved to the disk. It will not delete data you saved on the host drive.

If you also installed the full Windows Virtual PC, removing Windows XP Mode will not remove the hypervisor.

WARNING!

Whenever you download software, be sure to download only from the publisher's website. For instance, only download Microsoft software from **microsoft.com**. Many download sites offering a legitimate program may also be seeded with links to other software—often with download buttons that are more prominent than the one for the software you want.

Installing Windows Virtual PC in Windows 7

If you have a version of Windows 7 that supports Virtual PC, you may be able to enable it or initiate a download from the Windows Features dialog, shown back in Figure 3–5. If you cannot enable Windows Virtual PC through the Windows Features dialog, connect to the Windows Virtual PC page in the Microsoft Download Center (shown in Figure 3–6). Click the Download button and follow the instructions to download your Windows Virtual PC software.

Once the download is complete, locate the correct file. If you are running 64-bit Windows 7, select the file with "x64" in its name. If you are running 32-bit Windows 7, select the file with "x86" in its name. Click to place a check in the box by the correct file name, and then click Next.

A dialog box will give you the choice of opening or saving the file. Select Save and click OK. After the download completes, open your Downloads folder and locate the file. Double-click it to start the setup program. Follow the prompts after that, including allowing the system to restart. After it restarts, go to the Start menu, and confirm that Windows Virtual PC is listed in All Programs. This is your starting point for Step-by-Step 3.02 in which you will create a virtual machine in Windows Virtual PC.

Removing Windows Virtual PC

Windows Virtual PC is installed as an update to Windows 7, so to remove it, you must go into the Programs and Features Control Panel, select View Installed Updates, and

FIGURE 3–6 The Windows Virtual PC Download page.
Source: Microsoft Corporation

Creating a Virtual Machine in Windows Virtual PC

This exercise assumes you have a Windows 7 computer with the Professional, Enterprise, or Ultimate edition and that you have enabled Windows Virtual PC, as described in the previous text.

Step 1

Open the Start menu and locate and launch Windows Virtual PC.

Step 2

Click the Create Virtual Machine button to open the Create Virtual Machine Wizard.

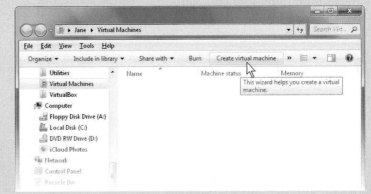

Source: Microsoft Corporation

Step 3

On the first page of the Wizard, enter the name for the new virtual machine. Leave the location as is and click the Next button.

Source: Microsoft Corporation

Step 4

On the next page either accept the default Memory setting or enter the amount recommended by your instructor. Leave the check in the box by Networking unless told to remove it by your instructor. Click Next to continue.

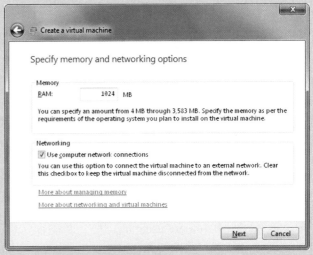

Source: Microsoft Corporation

Step 5

On the Add a Virtual Hard Disk page keep the default setting (the first option) unless instructed otherwise. Click Create to create the new virtual machine.

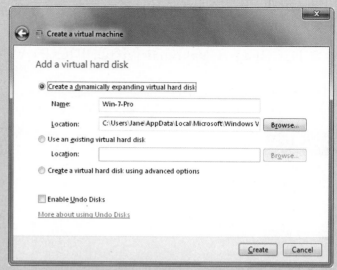

Source: Microsoft Corporation

Step 6

Open Windows Virtual PC from the Start menu to see the new virtual machine listed.

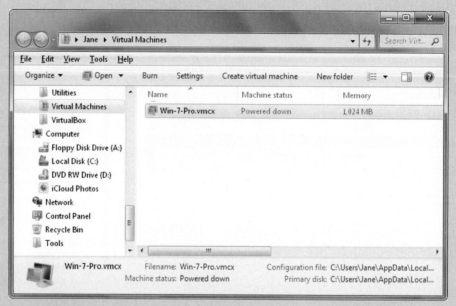

Source: Microsoft Corporation

Step 7

Now prepare the virtual machine to use the installation program of the OS you plan to install. Windows Virtual PC can install the new OS from a DVD drive or an ISO image file. With the new virtual machine selected in the Virtual Machines folder, click the Settings button. If you are using an ISO image make sure it is on a local hard drive.

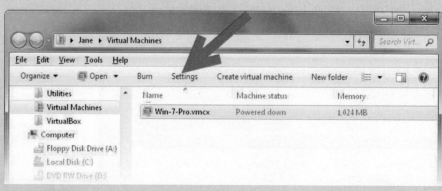

Source: Microsoft Corporation

Step 8

In this step, you enable the VM to boot from either a DVD or an ISO image. In the Settings dialog box for the virtual machine, select the source: DVD drive or ISO image. If you select ISO image, you will need to browse to the location of the ISO image. Then click OK.

Source: Microsoft Corporation

Step 9

When you are ready to install the OS into the VM, open the Virtual Machine folder and either double-click the virtual machine or select it and click the Open button in the toolbar. This will start the installation, which should proceed like a normal OS installation, but it will all happen within the VM window.

then in the Installed Updates page scroll down to the Microsoft Windows category, as shown in Figure 3-7. Double-click Windows Virtual PC. When the Uninstall an Update prompt appears, click the Yes button. When prompted to restart the computer, close all open windows and then click the Restart Now button.

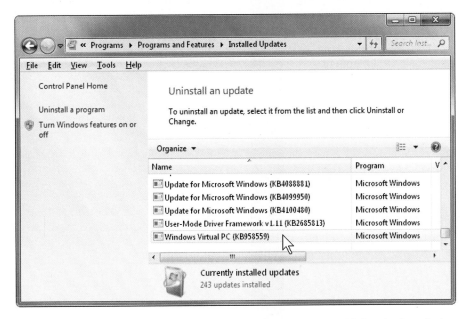

FIGURE 3–7 To remove Virtual PC double-click Windows Virtual PC in the Installed Updates page of Programs and Features.
Source: Microsoft Corporation

Client Hyper-V on Windows 8.x and Windows 10

The hypervisor introduced in Windows 8, Client Hyper-V, is a Type I (bare metal) hypervisor. This characteristic of Client Hyper-V is not apparent because you enable it from within Windows, but the host, or parent OS itself, runs in a virtual machine separate from the client VMs that you create. It is based on the Hyper-V hypervisor found on Windows Servers. Client Hyper-V includes the Windows To Go Virtual Hard Disk (VHD) feature that allows you to create a virtual hard disk (VHD) on a USB drive, take it to another computer, and boot from it. This is an example of a Type 1 hypervisor at work.

Client Hyper-V is only available in the Pro and Enterprise editions of Windows 8.x and Windows 10. It requires at least 4 GB of RAM (more is better) and a CPU with the Second-Level Address Translation (SLAT) feature found in many Intel and AMD CPUs. To check if your Windows 10 computer supports Hyper-V, open System Information, scroll to the bottom of the System Summary, and look for four items that begin with "Hyper-V." If the Value column contains a Yes, that feature is available.

Note: The Microsoft Windows Server versions of Hyper-V have more advanced capabilities for hosting server operating system clients.

Enabling Hyper-V and Creating a Virtual Machine

If you have an edition of Windows that supports Hyper-V, enable Client Hyper-V using the Windows 10 Control Panel titled Windows Features, as described in Step-by-Step 3.03, an exercise that steps through enabling Client Hyper-V and creating a virtual machine.

Step-by-Step 3.03

Working with Client Hyper-V in Windows

In this hands-on exercise, you will enable Client Hyper-V in Windows. Then you will create a new virtual machine. To complete this exercise, you will need the following:

- A desktop or laptop with the Pro or Enterprise edition of Windows 8 or Windows 10 installed, with all current updates. The steps were written specifically for Windows 10 but are very similar in Windows 8.
- To be logged in with a user account with administrator privileges.
- Sufficient installed RAM to support the existing programs and the addition of Client Hyper-V. We recommend a minimum of 8 GB of memory.
- A reliable and fast Internet connect.

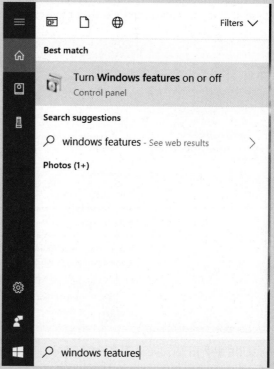

Step 1

From the Windows 10 desktop, enter the following in the Taskbar Search Box: **windows features**. From the results, select **Turn Windows features on or off**.

Source: Microsoft Corporation

Step 2

Step 1 opened the Control Panel dialog box, Windows Features, with the list of available features. Some features have multiple selectable components, indicated by a plus sign to the left of the check box by the feature. An empty box indicates that it is not enabled. A check in a box means the feature is enabled. If Hyper-V is not enable, click the checkbox to enable it. Then click OK.

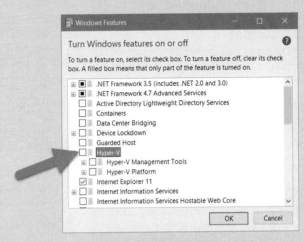

Source: Microsoft Corporation

Step 3

Follow the progress as Windows locates the required files and makes changes to the system. Watch for this message and click **Restart now**.

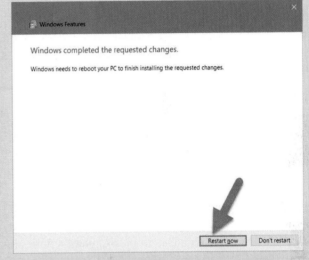

Source: Microsoft Corporation

Step 4

After the restart, sign in and click the Start button. The Hyper-V Manager will appear in the list of programs under **Recently added**. Click it to start the Hyper-V Manager.

Source: Microsoft Corporation

Take a moment to familiarize yourself with the Hyper-V Manager. On the left, below the Hyper-V Manager node, is the name of the host computer. The middle pane contains Virtual Machines (once created), as well as Checkpoints and Details of those VMs. A Checkpoint is a saved "snapshot" of a virtual machine at a single point in time. The pane to the right contains actions you can take. If your Hyper-V Manager shows different options, you may have a different version than the one in the example.

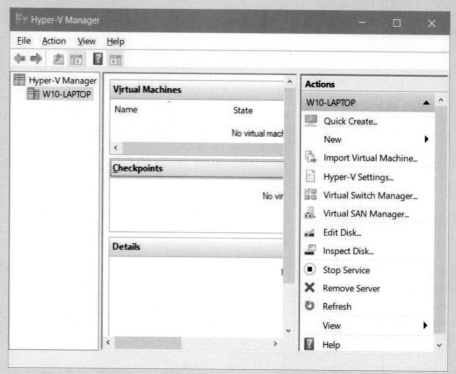

Source: Microsoft Corporation

A Hyper-V shortcut is added to the Windows Administrative Tools folder in the Control Panel, but this is not as convenient as launching it from a pinned shortcut on the Taskbar. With the Hyper-V Manager window open, locate the shortcut for the running app on the taskbar and right-click it. Then select the option Pin to taskbar.

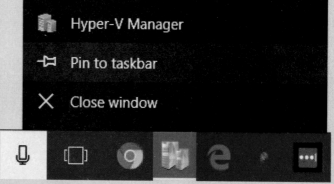

Source: Microsoft Corporation

Return to the Hyper-V Manager window. Under Actions select New. From the pop-up menu, select Virtual Machine to start the New Virtual Machine Wizard.

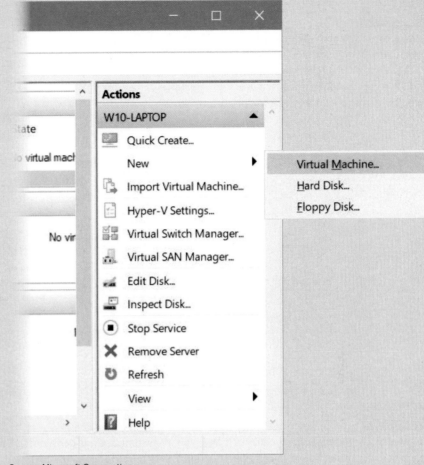

Source: Microsoft Corporation

In the New Virtual Machine Wizard, take time to scroll through the items on the left, reading the explanation for each item in the right pane. Do not select any options while viewing these items. Then select Finish to quickly create a virtual machine with the default settings for the items listed in the left pane.

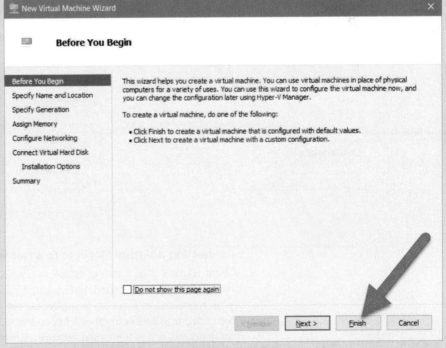

Source: Microsoft Corporation

Return to the Hyper-V Manager window. The VM you created is shown in the Virtual Machines list in the middle pane. Because you used the defaults, it is simply named New Virtual Machine.

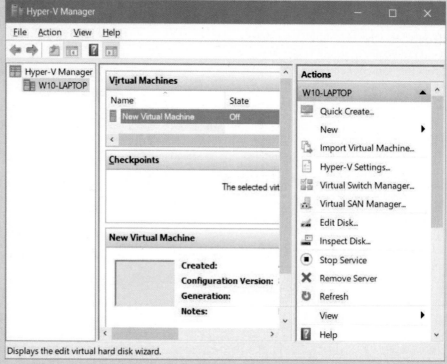

Source: Microsoft Corporation

To rename a virtual machine, click on it and type a new name. Consider naming this virtual machine with your initials plus a number. Later, when you install a client operating system into the virtual machine, simply rename it so that it is easily identified, such as using the OS and version of that OS. You now have a virtual machine into which you can install an operating system. You will need Hyper-V Manager to complete the next exercise, Step-by-Step 3.04. Now you are ready to install an operating system into the new virtual machine.

Source: Microsoft Corporation

Source: Microsoft Corporation

Connecting a Virtual Machine to a Network

Client Hyper-V uses a virtual switch to connect VMs to a network. The three types of virtual switches are external, internal, and private. An external virtual switch gives the VMs connected to it access to a physical network. An internal switch allows the VMs connected to it access to other VMs connected to that switch as well as to the physical computer, but not to a physical network. A private switch allows communication among the VMs connected to that switch, but not to the physical computer or physical network.

Client Hyper-V includes an internal switch named Default Switch. New virtual machines can connect to this switch, but in order to give a virtual machine access to the external network (and to the Internet), you need to create a new switch of the external type, and then connect the VM to that switch. Step-by-Step 3.04 walks through the tasks required to create a virtual switch and to connect a VM to that switch.

Step-by-Step 3.04

Creating a Virtual Switch for Client Hyper-V VMs

In this hands-on exercise, you will create a new virtual switch using Hyper-V Manager.

To complete this exercise, you will need the following:

- A desktop or laptop with Windows 8 or Windows 10 Pro or Enterprise edition installed and with Client Hyper-V enabled, as a result of completing Step-by-Step 3.03.

- To be logged in with a user account with administrator privileges.
- Sufficient installed RAM to support the existing programs and the addition of Client Hyper.

Step 1

From the Windows 10 desktop, open Hyper-V Manager. In the Actions list, click on Virtual Switch Manager.

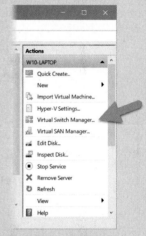

Source: Microsoft Corporation

Step 2

In the Virtual Switch Manager, choose the type of switch and then click Create Virtual Switch.

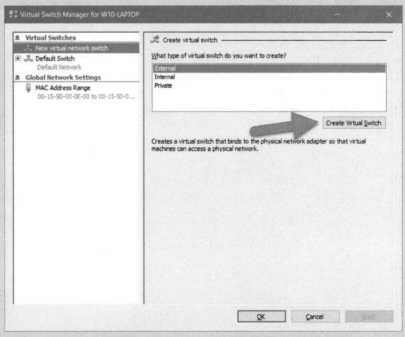

Source: Microsoft Corporation

In the Virtual Switch Manager, locate the Name field in the right pane, select the entire name, and overwrite it with a new descriptive name.

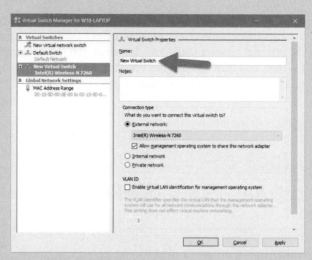

Source: Microsoft Corporation

In our example, we used the name "Access to External Network."

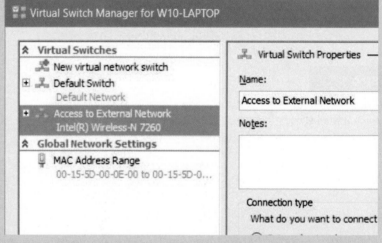

Source: Microsoft Corporation

Now open the Hyper-V Manager. In the Virtual Machines pane, click on the virtual machine you created in Step-by-Step 3.03. Under Actions, note that the actions for the host computer are at the top, and the actions for the selected virtual machine are next. In the Actions for the virtual machine click Settings.

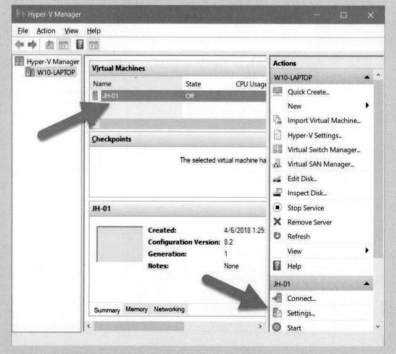

Source: Microsoft Corporation

In the Settings dialog for the virtual machine, click on Network Adapter under the list of Hardware on the left. Then, in the right-hand pane, click on the drop-down box under Virtual switch and then click on the switch you previously created and click the OK button.

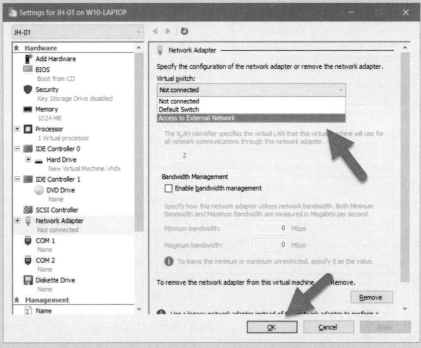

Source: Microsoft Corporation

The Virtual Machine Connection window will open. Our virtual machine is turned off, and we have not yet installed an operating system into this virtual machine. You are now ready to install an operating system into a virtual machine. In the coming chapters, you may use this virtual machine to install one of the operating systems you will study. For now, close this window.

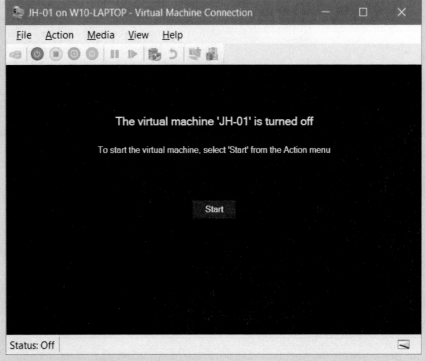

Source: Microsoft Corporation

Removing Hyper-V

Because Hyper-V is enabled through the Windows Features Control Panel, you need to remove it the same way. Locate the Hyper-V node shown in Step 2 of Step-by-Step 3.03 and click to clear the check box, and then click OK. The Windows Features dialog box will display progress information while it initiates the change, and then it will display a message stating that it needs to restart to complete the changes. Click

Note: Possibly the biggest name in desktop virtualization is VMware with several products. We did not use these excellent products in our examples because they are not available for free except as free trials that expire.

the Restart Now button, and it will make changes as it shuts down and again when it restarts Windows.

Oracle VirtualBox

Oracle VirtualBox is a versatile free hypervisor that comes in versions for a variety of host operating systems, among them Windows, Linux, and macOS. It will run guest versions of Windows, Linux, and DOS. It is available for download at **www.virtualbox .org**. Because it also runs on a macOS host, we will use it in the next section when we discuss Virtual Machines on macOS.

LO 3.3 | Virtual Machines on macOS

You may want to use virtualization software on a Mac to test a distribution of Linux or a version of Windows or to run certain Windows apps that aren't available for macOS. There are several options for doing this, including Apple Boot Camp (not really a virtualization tool), VirtualBox, and Parallels. Apple Boot Camp is a multiboot solution, but VirtualBox and Parallels offer virtualization on the Apple desktop. Parallels Desktop by Parallels is a commercial product, and you can learn about it at **www.parallels .com/products/desktop/**.

Apple Boot Camp—A Dual-Boot Option

Apple Boot Camp is available with macOS. It is a dual-boot option, meaning it allows you to install Windows onto a separate disk partition, and then you can choose to boot into either OS. This is an either-or situation; you need to restart to change from one OS to the other. The advantage of a dual-boot solution is performance—each OS is running directly on the Mac with no performance loss from being in a virtual machine. However, today's hypervisors, when used on a recent Apple computer running macOS, perform well enough to discourage us from dedicating the disk space to a multiboot solution such as Apple Boot Camp.

Oracle VirtualBox

The free version of Oracle VirtualBox will run on a variety of host operating systems including Windows, Linux, and macOS. It supports as guest OSs versions of Windows, Linux, and DOS. Figure 3–8 shows Windows 10 running in Virtual-Box in macOS. Step-by-Step 3.05 describes how to download and install Oracle VirtualBox.

FIGURE 3–8 Windows 10 running in VirtualBox on an macOS host.
Source: Microsoft Corporation

Step-by-Step 3.05

Installing Oracle VirtualBox

Using a file you will download or a file provided to you by your instructor, install Oracle VirtualBox. The instructions provided are for installing it into macOS using a disk image file (.dmg). To complete this exercise, you will need the following:

- A computer running a version of macOS supported by the latest version of VirtualBox. You can find older versions on the VirtualBox website, if necessary.

- A computer that meets the hardware requirements for the version of VirtualBox you will install.
- The user name and password of an administrator account for this computer (even if you have logged on as an administrator, you will need these credentials to install new software).
- A broadband Internet connection.

Step 1

On a computer running macOS, open the browser (Safari) and type "virtualbox.org" in the address box. Click on the Download link button and follow the prompts to download the disk image file.

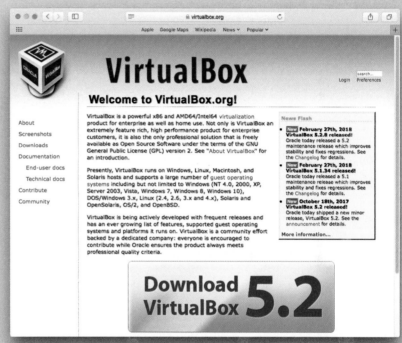

Source: Oracle Corporation

Step 2

Locate and double-click the VirtualBox disk image. It will be on the desktop or in the Downloads folder in Finder. This will open the VirtualBox drive. If you wish to read the documentation, open the UserManual.pdf file. Also, note that the VirtualBox Uninstall tool is located here, for when you decide you do not need this program.

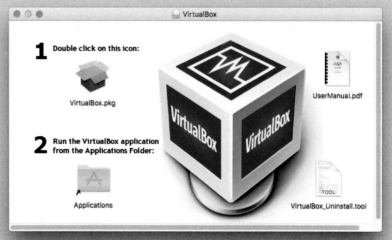

Source: Oracle Corporation

To start the VirtualBox installation, double-click on the VirtualBox.pkg icon. The VirtualBox installation wizard runs. At first it runs a test to verify that the computer can support VirtualBox. Follow the instructions and proceed through the pages, including providing the user name and password for an administrator account for the computer. Then you can either accept the defaults for a standard install or select a differ- ent destination and installation type.

Source: Oracle Corporation

In a very short time, the installation is complete, and you will find VirtualBox listed in Applications. Launch VirtualBox and then open the Machine menu at the top of the screen. Select New.

Source: Oracle Corporation

The New Virtual Machine app will guide you through the creation of a virtual machine. This process does not require the guest OS, but you do need to know which OS you will install into the virtual machine you are creating. You are simply configuring the machine to accept the guest OS. When prompted to name the virtual machine, use a meaningful name, such as the name and version of the OS you plan to install. Then select the OS you will install and continue.

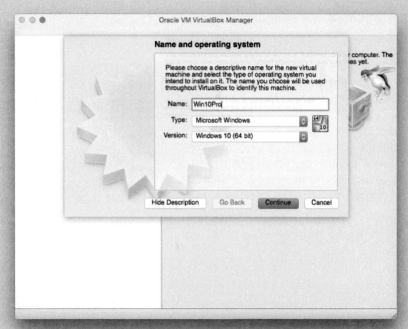

Source: Oracle Corporation

On the Memory size page accept the default and click Continue.

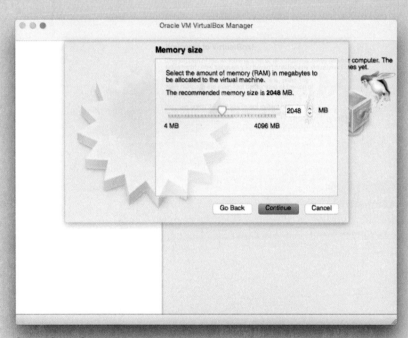

Source: Oracle Corporation

On the Hard Drive page, select Create a Virtual Hard Drive Now and click Create. On the Hard Drive File Type page, select the first type, which is VDI, the default for VirtualBox, and the one you should choose if you only plan to use this VM in VirtualBox. If you plan to use this VM in another hypervisor, select a type used by that hypervisor. Then click Continue.

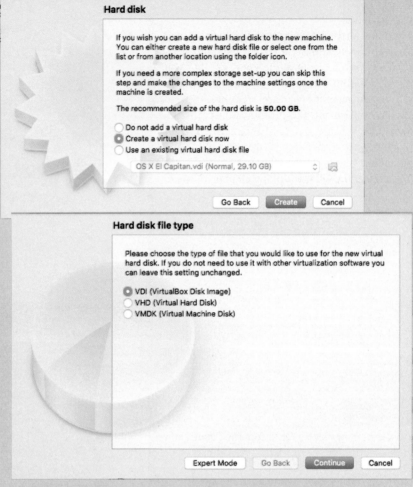

Source: Oracle Corporation

On the Storage on Physical Hard Disk page, select Dynamically Allocated and click Continue.

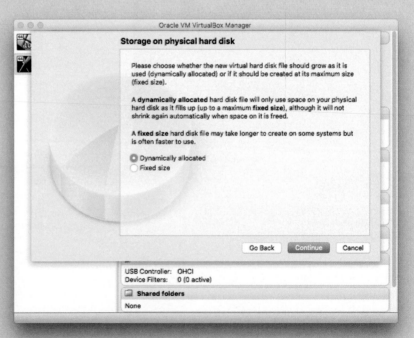

Source: Oracle Corporation

Step 9

On the File Location and Size page, the name will match the name you gave to the virtual machine. Accept the defaults for name, location, and size on this page and click Create. On the next page, you will see a summary of the virtual disk settings. Confirm that these are correct and click the Done button to complete the creation of the virtual disk. Then you will see another summary page for all the settings for this virtual machine. Confirm the settings and click Done.

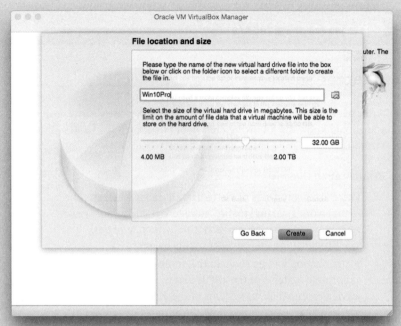

Source: Oracle Corporation

Step 10

When the console window opens, check that your new virtual machine is listed. It is now ready for the installation of the OS.

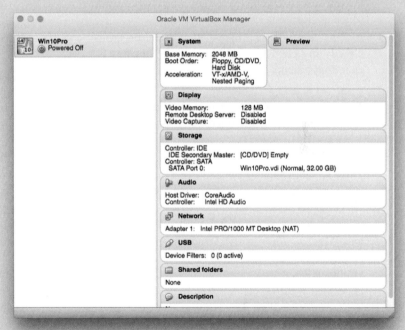

Source: Oracle Corporation

Step 11

When you are ready to install an operating system, double-click on a virtual machine. This will launch the First Run Wizard, which will guide you through the process of beginning the installation of your OS.

Step 12

Secure the virtual machine. Assign a strong password to any user account you create within the guest OS, then update the OS with all security updates, and install antivirus and other security software.

Chapter 3 REVIEW

Chapter Summary

After reading this chapter and completing the exercises, you should know the following facts about desktop virtualization.

Virtualization Overview

- There are many types of virtualization today, such as virtual worlds, virtual reality, storage virtualization, network virtualization, server virtualization, and desktop virtualization—the subject of this chapter.
- Virtualization had its roots in the dumb-terminal/mainframe systems of the 1960s and the terminal service/terminal client systems of the 1990s.
- You can host today's virtual desktops on network servers or on PCs.
- A hypervisor, or virtual machine monitor (VMM), is the software that emulates the necessary hardware on which an operating system runs.
- A Type I hypervisor (a "bare-metal hypervisor") runs directly on a computer without an underlying host operating system.
- A Type II hypervisor requires a host operating system.
- The major sources of hypervisors are Citrix, VMware, Parallels, Microsoft, and Oracle.

Virtual Machines on Windows Desktops

- There are both commercial and free hypervisors for running Linux, DOS, or Windows on a Windows desktop computer.
- Windows XP Mode is a free hypervisor that installs on a Windows 7 host with a Windows XP guest OS preinstalled. It does not require hardware-assisted virtualization.
- Download Windows XP Mode from the Microsoft website and install it.

- Remove Windows XP Mode through Windows from the Programs and Features Control Panel.
- The free Windows Virtual PC requires both Windows 7 and hardware-assisted virtualization.
- Download and install Virtual PC from the Microsoft website. It installs as an update, so to remove it you will need to uninstall it from the Installed Updates Control Panel.
- Client Hyper-V is the Type I hypervisor that is included with Windows 8 Pro and Windows Enterprise editions.
- Client Hyper-V has more rigorous hardware requirements than other desktop hypervisors, requiring at least 4 GB of RAM and a CPU with the Second-Level Address Translation (SLAT) feature.
- Enable Client Hyper-V through the Windows Features Control Panel.
- Remove Hyper-V by deselecting it in the Windows Features Control Panel.
- Oracle VirtualBox is free and runs on several hosts including versions of Windows, Linux, and Max macOS, and it will run on hardware that does not support virtualization.

Virtual Machines on macOS

- You have several choices for hypervisors for macOS that will run versions of Windows and Linux.
- Apple Boot Camp is not actually a hypervisor but a dual-boot option that allows you to dual boot between macOS and Windows. This gives each OS full use of the hardware, but only one can be loaded at a time.
- Oracle VirtualBox is a free hypervisor and will run versions of Windows, Linux, and DOS.

Key Terms List

application virtualization *(83)*
augmented reality (AR) *(82)*
avatar *(82)*
desktop virtualization *(82)*
dumb terminal *(83)*
guest OS *(84)*
host key *(85)*
host OS *(84)*
hypervisor *(84)*

ISO file *(85)*
network virtualization *(82)*
Second-Level Address Translation (SLAT) *(96)*
server virtualization *(82)*
storage virtualization *(82)*
terminal client *(83)*
terminal services *(83)*
thin client *(83)*

Type I hypervisor *(84)*
Type II hypervisor *(84)*
virtual desktop infrastructure (VDI) *(84)*
virtual machine (VM) *(83)*
virtual machine monitor (VMM) *(84)*
virtual reality (VR) *(82)*
virtual world *(82)*
virtualization *(82)*
Windows XP Mode *(86)*

Key Terms Quiz

Use the Key Terms List to complete the sentences that follow. Not all terms will be used.

1. The software layer that emulates the necessary hardware on which an operating system runs in a virtual machine is a/an _____.

2. Viewing something in real time through a camera or other device while the image is digitally modified is an example of _____.

3. Many organization use _____ in which many networked hard drives are seen as one by the client computers.

4. _____ is the creation of an environment that seems to surround the participant and feels real.

5. When you run a desktop OS within a hypervisor, it is called _____.

6. In the 1960s, a/an _____ was the very simple interface device to a mainframe computer.

7. In the 1990s, people often used _____ software on a PC to connect to applications on a specialized server or minicomputer.

8. A/an _____ is a low-cost PC, usually without such common peripherals as expansion slots, and optical drives, and is used to allow a user to connect and work in a server-hosted environment.

9. In desktop or server virtualization, the software emulation of all hardware with which an operating system must interface is a/an _____.

10. Second Life is an example of a/an _____.

Multiple-Choice Quiz

1. In which type of virtualization does a user connect to a server and work within a program, without an entire virtualized desktop environment?
   a. Storage virtualization
   b. Application virtualization
   c. Terminal services
   d. Thin client
   e. Virtual world

2. What term describes the hosting and management of multiple virtual desktops on network servers?
   a. Thin client
   b. Terminal services
   c. Minicomputers
   d. Virtual desktop infrastructure (VDI)
   e. Partitioning

3. Which of the following does not require a host OS?
   a. Type II hypervisor
   b. Type I hypervisor
   c. Oracle VirtualBox
   d. Windows Virtual PC
   e. Windows XP Mode

4. What hypervisor, described in this chapter, is a "bare metal" hypervisor?
   a. Windows 10
   b. Windows Virtual PC
   c. Windows XP Mode
   d. Oracle VirtualBox
   e. Client Hyper-V

5. What type of hypervisor requires a host OS?
   a. Type II
   b. Type I
   c. Boot Camp
   d. A bare-metal hypervisor
   e. A dual-boot hypervisor

6. If you wanted to run Windows 7 on a Mac running macOS which option would give you the best performance, but would not run Windows in a virtual machine?
   a. Windows XP Mode
   b. Hyper-V Client
   c. Oracle VirtualBox
   d. Parallels
   e. Apple Boot Camp

7. Which of these is a free hypervisor that runs on Windows, macOS and Linux OSs?
   a. Client Hyper-V
   b. Windows Virtual PC
   c. Oracle VirtualBox
   d. Apple Boot Camp
   e. Windows XP Mode

8. Which acronym stands for a feature of many Intel and AMD CPUs required by Microsoft's Client Hyper-V?
   a. AR
   b. SLAT
   c. VMM
   d. VDI
   e. VR

9. Which of the following solutions should you select if you wish to run a Windows guest on macOS, but you need frequent access to both the host and guest OSs?
   a. Windows XP Mode
   b. Windows Virtual PC
   c. Oracle VirtualBox
   d. Boot Camp
   e. Client Hyper-V

10. Which of the following will release the mouse from the control of a virtual machine?
    a. Guest key
    b. Host key
    c. Host OS
    d. VDI
    e. Terminal service

11. Which of the following is synonymous with hypervisor?
    a. Terminal service
    b. Bare metal
    c. Virtual hard drive
    d. Virtual machine
    e. Virtual machine monitor (VMM)

12. Your Windows PC has an AMD processor installed that includes AMD-V technology and the motherboard fully supports this processor. Which is the most capable version of a Microsoft hypervisor you can install on this machine, provided the computer meets all the other requirements?
    a. VirtualBox
    b. Client Hyper-V
    c. Windows XP Mode
    d. Boot Camp
    e. Parallels Desktop

13. What legal issue must you consider when installing a guest OS into a hypervisor?
    a. Copyright of guest OS
    b. Antivirus
    c. Licensing of guest OS
    d. Guest key
    e. Supplying security credentials

14. After downloading VirtualBox to an iMac with macOS which of the following is the name of the object you should double-click to install VirtualBox on your computer?
    a. VirtualBox.pkg
    b. VirtualBox.iso
    c. VirtualBox.exe
    d. VirtualBox.pdf
    e. VM.bat

15. Which of the following is a multiboot option for running Windows as a second OS on an macOS computer?
    a. VirtualBox
    b. Windows Virtual PC
    c. Windows XP Mode
    d. Boot Camp
    e. Parallels

Essay Quiz

1. What is the purpose of each of the two most important files created by a Type II hypervisor when preparing a new virtual machine?
2. Describe a feature of Client Hyper-V that allows you to take a virtual machine to another computer on a common small handheld device.
3. Explain why an IT person would want to use a hypervisor on a desktop computer.
4. Provide a reason why you would not run macOS in a virtual machine on a Windows computer.
5. You have Windows XP Mode installed on your Windows 7 computer, and you would like to do a side-by-side comparison of Windows XP Mode and Windows XP in a VirtualBox VM. What precautions should you take and how many computers are required for this comparison?

Lab Projects

LAB PROJECT 3.1

Find out how virtualization is being used in an organization in your area. Arrange an interview with an IT manager, network engineer, or other knowledgeable IT staff person from an organization in your area. Consider approaching someone at a regional hospital or medical clinic because privacy laws require that they meet certain minimum standards in IT, and they often have the best IT staff in a community. Ask if they are using virtualization, and if so, what type. What are their future plans for virtualization? Report your findings to your classmates.

LAB PROJECT 3.2

If you installed a hypervisor on your computer, find another one that will run on your OS. Install the second hypervisor and attempt to open the virtual machines created for the first hypervisor. Compare the similarities and differences. Will the new hypervisor work with the virtual machines you created with the first one? Decide which one you prefer working with. If it is the second, then keep it; if you preferred the first one, uninstall the second.

LAB PROJECT 3.3

Find out the latest about Type I and Type II hypervisors. Browse the Internet using the keyword *virtualization* and watching for recent articles and news releases. Consider turning on Google alerts with the key term *virtualization*. Watch the number of alerts you receive over just a period of a few days.

chapter

4 Windows 7

©Eloy Alonso/Reuters/Landov

Learning Outcomes

In this chapter, you will learn how to:

LO **4.1** Install and configure Windows 7.

LO **4.2** Use the features of Windows 7.

LO **4.3** Manage Windows 7.

LO **4.4** Configure local security in Windows 7.

Windows Vista was released in 2007. The resistance to Windows Vista was so strong that Microsoft prolonged the life of Windows XP, allowing sales of new PCs with OEM (original equipment manufacturer) Windows XP installed until October 2010. This was one year after the release of Windows Vista's successor, Windows 7, and nine years since the introduction of Windows XP. History repeats itself. Although Windows 8 was introduced in 2012, many individuals and organizations decided not to upgrade, but to continue using Windows 7. In this chapter, we consider the issues of installing and configuring Windows 7, followed by an overview of Windows 7 features and the basics of managing an installed OS. Finally, we'll explore issues for configuring local security in Windows 7. ●

LO 4.1 | Installing Windows 7

In this section, we will explore the options you have for installing Windows 7. We begin by identifying the upgrade paths available should you decide to install Windows 7 on an existing Windows desktop or laptop, answering such questions as, "Can I upgrade from Windows XP to Windows 7?" and "Can I upgrade from Windows Vista to Windows 7?" Then we will describe your options for moving your data and settings to a new installation of Windows 7 and detail the actual steps for doing a clean installation of Windows 7, following by important postinstallation tasks.

The Windows 7 Lifecycle

Before installing Windows 7, consider the lifecycle of this operating system. It was introduced in 2009, and Microsoft's mainstream support for this version ended January 13, 2015. Windows 7 is presently in the extended support phase of its product lifecycle, which ends January 14, 2020. The features of mainstream support important to most of us are the security updates, nonsecurity updates, and some free support. The only one of these free services clearly available during the extended support phase is security updating, but paid support is still available. Learn more about the Microsoft Product Lifecycle at **https://support.microsoft.com/en-us/lifecycle**.

Recommended System Requirements

Microsoft designed Windows 7 to provide better performance and to be more reliable on the same hardware required by its predecessor, Windows Vista. Table 4–1 shows the Windows 7 minimum requirements.

Windows 7 Editions

Microsoft no longer offers Windows 7 as a retail product in their Microsoft Stores, but other retailers make it available. As with earlier versions of Windows, Microsoft offered Windows 7 as several separate products, called editions. The differences between editions are mainly in the included components, targeted to specific types of users. The more features the more expensive the edition. The three retail editions of Windows 7 were Home Premium, Professional, and Ultimate. Other Windows 7 editions were bundled with hardware as OEM Windows. The Enterprise edition of any version of Windows is not available at retail, but sold only to customers of the Microsoft Software Assurance plan, a distribution channel for bulk licensing to organizations. The Enterprise editions have added features required by a large enterprise. These features include support for mass distribution, linking with enterprise security, compliance, collaborative productivity, and more.

Windows 7 also came in two scaled-down editions called Starter and Home Basic. The Starter edition was an OEM edition with many features removed or disabled, including the ability to change the desktop wallpaper or join a Windows domain. The Home Basic edition was available in emerging markets and was not available in the United States, most of Europe, the Middle East, Australia, New Zealand, and Japan.

> **WARNING!**
>
> If you plan to run Windows XP Mode, Microsoft recommends a PC with Intel-VT or AMD-V enabled in the CPU, plus you will need a minimum of 2 GB of memory and an additional 15 GB of free disk space.

TABLE 4–1 Windows 7 Minimum Requirements

	Windows 7 32-Bit Editions	Windows 7 64-Bit Editions
Processor	1 GHz 32-bit x86	1 GHz 64-bit x64 processor
System memory	1 GB	2 GB
Available hard drive space	16 GB	20 GB
Support for DirectX 9 graphics with WDDM 1.0 or higher driver (DirectX 10 required for certain games)	✓	✓
Graphics memory (to support Aero)	128 MB	128 MB
Audio output (if desired)	✓	✓
Internet access (for keeping the OS updated)	✓	✓

Upgrade Paths

An upgrade of an operating system, also called an in-place installation, is an installation of a newer operating system directly over an existing one.

The only in-place installation possible from an earlier version of Windows to Windows 7 is from Windows Vista.

From Windows Vista to Windows 7

Table 4-2 lists the direct upgrade paths from Windows Vista to Windows 7. Blank fields indicate that you must do a clean install. You cannot directly upgrade from Windows XP or older versions to Windows 7.

An upgrade has its risks, since you end up with a new OS on an old computer with many of the problems of the old installation as far as unnecessary installed programs, old hardware, and possible data loss or permission problems. With the Windows 7 Upgrade product, you can still do a clean installation, by starting the Windows 7 Setup from within the previous Windows version. At the screen that asks you to select the type of installation, Upgrade or Custom, simply select Custom, and follow the prompts from there.

Note: The Windows 7 Upgrade product is different in two ways from the full Windows 7 retail product. The first is in how you install it, and the second is a licensing issue. The upgrade product is cheaper than the full product because it is intended to replace the previously installed licensed Windows.

Preparing to Install Windows 7

The preparation steps for installing Windows 7 vary based on whether you are doing an upgrade from Windows Vista, a side-by-side multiboot installation, or a clean installation. Here is a brief overview of each of the installation types:

- An upgrade, also called an in-place installation, installs directly into the folders in which the previous version of Windows installed. Windows 7 setup manages to preserve the old settings, while removing the old OS before installing the new OS. You can only upgrade from a Windows Vista edition that is upgradeable to the edition of Windows 7 you plan to install (see Table 4-2). However, if you simply aren't quite ready to break all ties with your old installation of Windows, then consider the next option.

- A multiboot installation leaves an old OS in place, installing a new OS in a separate partition or hard disk. This allows you to select the OS you wish to boot into every time you start the computer, and this is what we did on Jane's computer when Windows 7 was first available, because she still wanted an installation of Windows Vista for screenshots and comparison while writing about both Windows Vista and Windows 7. To install Windows 7 to multiboot, do a clean installation on a separate partition or hard disk, which means you will select the Custom installation choice. Windows 7 setup will preserve the earlier version of Windows and create a Windows Boot Manager menu, as Figure 4-1 shows, which will display for a short period at every restart. We often refer to a multiboot configuration with just two choices of operating system as a dual-boot configuration.

Note: Use the Custom option when you want to do either a multiboot or a clean installation.

TABLE 4-2 Upgrade Paths to Windows 7					
Windows Vista Edition (with SP1 or SP2)	Windows 7 Home Basic	Windows 7 Home Premium	Windows 7 Professional	Windows 7 Enterprise	Windows 7 Ultimate
Business			✓	✓	✓
Enterprise					✓
Home Basic	✓	✓			✓
Home Premium		✓			✓
Ultimate					✓

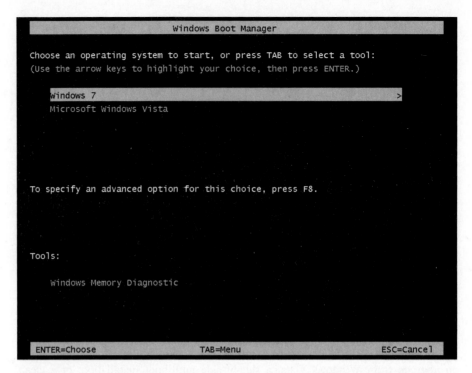

```
                          Windows Boot Manager

Choose an operating system to start, or press TAB to select a tool:
(Use the arrow keys to highlight your choice, then press ENTER.)

   Windows 7                                                            >
   Microsoft Windows Vista




To specify an advanced option for this choice, press F8.




Tools:

   Windows Memory Diagnostic






ENTER=Choose                          TAB=Menu                   ESC=Cancel
```

FIGURE 4–1 The Windows Boot Manager menu showing two choices: Windows 7 and Windows Vista.
Source: Microsoft Corporation

- A **clean installation** is an installation of an OS onto a completely empty hard disk or one from which all data is removed during the installation. A clean installation takes the least amount of disk space and is a new beginning for the new OS. You most often install on a totally clean hard drive, although, in the case of a multiboot installation, you can direct Windows 7 setup to install as a clean installation on a different partition or drive from that of the existing OS. To start a clean installation, select the Custom installation choice. To automate a clean installation onto many desktops, organizations use other, more advanced methods, such as hands-free, scripted install, or they use an **image**, which is an exact duplicate of the entire hard drive contents, including the OS and all installed software. The use of images is very popular in medium-to-large organizations that have dozens, hundreds, or thousands of desktop computers.

Regardless of the type of installation you plan to do, you must ensure the hardware minimums are met, determine how to boot into the Windows setup program, and decide if you will activate immediately or later and if you wish to register the product with Microsoft. You can verify that your computer meets the recommended minimums by comparing the system configuration with Table 4-1.

Registration versus Activation

At some point, Windows setup will prompt you to register your product and to activate it. Many people confuse activation with registration. These are two separate operations for Microsoft software, although other popular software products combine these two functions, requiring that you give an email address and other personal information before the program is considered "legal" and activated.

Registration is when you inform Microsoft who the official owner or user of the product is and provide contact information, such as name, address, company, phone number, email address, and so on. Registration is generally optional with Microsoft products. **Activation** of Microsoft products is called **Microsoft Product Activation (MPA)** and

Note: IT professionals use scripted installations or some type of imaged installations. These methods often take a great deal of preparation and knowledge and are best used when you must install an OS on many computers, using identical configurations as in a department, classroom, or computer lab.

is an antipiracy tool, meaning that Microsoft wishes to ensure that you are using your software per the software license, which normally limits its use to a single computer.

Microsoft Product Activation does not scan the contents of the hard disk, search for personal information, or gather information on the make, model, or manufacturer of the computer, and it sends no personal information about you as part of the activation process.

Activation is mandatory for retail versions of Windows 7 and you must do it within 30 days of installing the software. When prompted to activate during the installation, if you choose to activate at that time you enter a product key code from the Windows 7 packaging. The activation program communicates with Microsoft (you must have an Internet connection to do this online) and generates a product ID from the product key code and then combines it with a value that represents your hardware components to create an installation ID code. The activation program sends this code to Microsoft, which returns a 42-digit product activation code. Activating automatically online is the best way to do this.

If you do not have an Internet connection when you try to activate, or if the activation program detects a problem, you will see a message telling you to call Microsoft. While sitting by the computer, call the number provided. You will need to read the installation ID to a representative and enter the resulting 42-digit activation code in the Activate Windows by phone dialog box.

Note: If you know that you will make major changes to the hardware in the first 30 days of using the new Windows 7 installation, then do not activate during installation, but wait until you have made the changes. This is because major hardware changes trigger the activation process again. Major hardware changes include: upgrading of the motherboard, CPU, hard drive, network interface card (NIC), graphics card, or RAM.

Consider Windows Update Settings

Before you begin the Windows installation program, you need to give some thought to how you want Windows to acquire the necessary updates that may improve its performance and make it more secure. Then, during Windows installation, you will configure Windows Update, a Windows utility that can automatically connect to the Microsoft site and download and install updates. If you own the computer in question, then we recommend that you choose to have the updates downloaded and installed automatically. If the computer is part of a corporate or school network, then you need to ask your instructor or the IT staff how they want to handle updates.

Prepare to Transfer Settings and Data

Unless you are doing an in-place installation of Windows 7, you will want a way to transfer your data, email, and settings for Windows and your applications. Microsoft provides a utility that will do this for you, whether you plan to dual-boot between an older version of Windows and Windows 7 or do a clean installation. This utility, Windows Easy Transfer (WET), is available on the Windows 7 DVD. Before you run it, make sure you have an appropriate location where you want to transfer the files. This can be directly to a new computer, providing you have a special cable to use or a network connection between the two computers. However, you are most likely to do this using an external hard drive or USB flash drive. Just make sure that the location has plenty of free space for the files you will transfer. Make this location or drive available to the old computer, then insert the Windows 7 DVD into that computer and browse to the Support folder. Locate and double-click on the file MIG.WIZ to launch the Windows Easy Transfer wizard, shown in Figure 4–2. Carefully follow the instructions in the wizard for selecting the files and settings from the old computer to the location or drive.

Then, after Windows 7 is installed on the new computer, run the Windows Easy Transfer utility by entering "easy transfer" in Start | Search Programs and Files. You will need to enter the location of the files into Windows Easy Transfer, and then identify your computer by selecting "This is my new computer." Then follow the instructions to transfer the files.

Prepare to Install into a Virtual Machine

If you have a hypervisor installed on a lab computer and plan to install Windows 7 into a virtual machine, you will need to first create a VM for the installation (as described in Chapter 3), and then ensure that the virtual machine will boot from the drive or

FIGURE 4–2 Windows Easy Transfer for Windows 7.
Source: Microsoft Corporation

ISO file containing the Windows 7 Setup files. By default, virtual machines in all the hypervisors discussed in Chapter 3 will connect and boot from an optical drive (CD or DVD) at startup, but you first need to configure the VM to use the drive. Figure 4–3 shows the Client Hyper-V Settings for a virtual machine named W7. In the left pane, the BIOS settings are selected, and the right pane shows the order in which the VM will search for boot devices. If the Windows 7 setup files are in an ISO image file, change the DVD settings for that virtual machine to point to the location of the ISO file before starting the VM, and then restart the VM and follow the prompts.

The Installation

When you start the Windows 7 setup program, the **Windows Preinstallation Environment (Windows PE)** starts. This is a scaled-down Windows operating system. Much like the old Windows setup program, it has limited drivers for basic hardware support for 32-bit and 64-bit programs. Windows PE supports the Windows setup GUI, collecting configuration information. The Windows 7 installation program requires very little user input. Step-by-Step 4.01 will walk you through the steps for performing a clean installation.

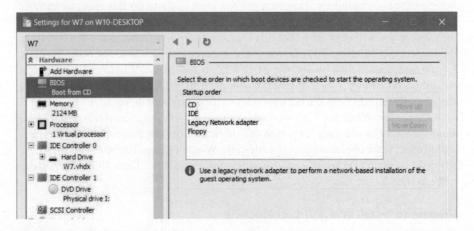

FIGURE 4–3 These settings allow a virtual machine to boot from the drive containing the installation program.
Source: Microsoft Corporation

Step-by-Step 4.01

Installing Windows 7

In this step-by-step exercise, you will do a clean installation of Windows 7. To complete this exercise, you will need the following:

- A Microsoft/Intel standard personal computer (desktop or laptop) compatible with Windows 7, with at least the recommended minimum hardware and configured to boot from DVD, and an unpartitioned hard disk (disk 0, the first hard disk). Alternatively, use a virtual machine you have prepared before beginning the Windows 7 installation (see Chapter 3).

- The Windows 7 DVD or ISO file.

- The Product ID code. If you are using a retail version, look for this on the envelope or jewel case of your Windows 7 DVD. If you are not using a retail version, your instructor will provide a Product ID code or other instructions.

- A 15-character (or less) name, unique on your network, for your computer.

- A strong password for the user account created during setup.

Step 1

Using an ISO file or DVD, boot the computer or virtual machine. When using a DVD, watch the screen for instructions to boot from the optical drive. As the computer or VM boots, a plain black screen will briefly flash, followed by a black screen with the message: "Windows is loading files . . ." while Windows Preinstallation Environment is loaded and started. The Starting Windows screen signals that Windows PE is starting and will soon load the GUI for Windows 7 setup.

Step 2

On the first Install Windows page, select a language, time, currency format, and keyboard input methods. Then select Next.

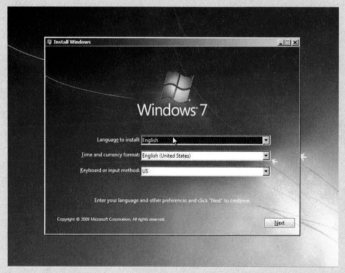

Source: Microsoft Corporation

Step 3

At the center of the next screen is the Install Now button, but you should notice two important links on the bottom left. One is labeled "What to know before installing Windows." Click on it to see if you have overlooked a preparation step. The second link, labeled "Repair your computer," is an important one to remember. If, after you install Windows 7 your system will not start, pull out your Windows 7 DVD, boot from it, and select this option.

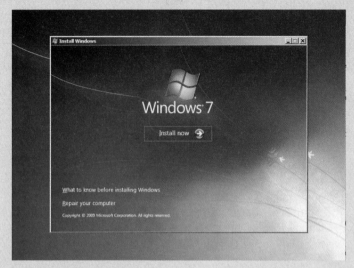

Source: Microsoft Corporation

Step 4

On the license page read the Microsoft Software License Terms, then click to place a check in the box labeled "I accept the license terms" and click the Next button.

Step 5

On the next page you are asked, "Which type of installation do you want?" Select Custom to perform a clean installation.

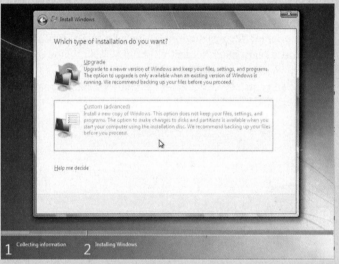

Source: Microsoft Corporation

Step 6

On the next page, select the target drive for the installation and click Next. On most systems, this page will show a single disk with much more free space than shown here.

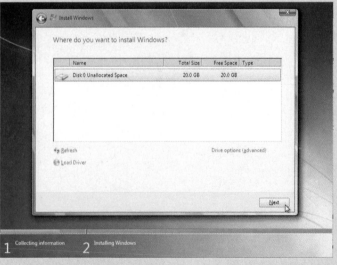

Source: Microsoft Corporation

Step 7

Next, Windows 7 setup goes through the installation phases, restarting several times and returning to this page that displays progress with a green check by each completed phase.

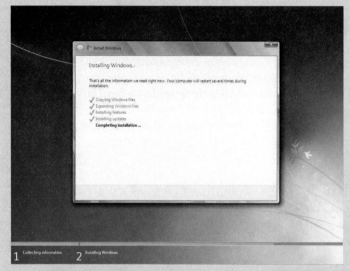

Source: Microsoft Corporation

Step 8

When it reaches the Completing Installation phase, the message "Setup will continue after restarting your computer" displays. After this, as Windows 7 restarts, the message "Setup is checking video performance" displays. Next enter a user name for the first user account (this will automatically be a Computer Administrator type, although that detail is not mentioned) and a name for the computer.

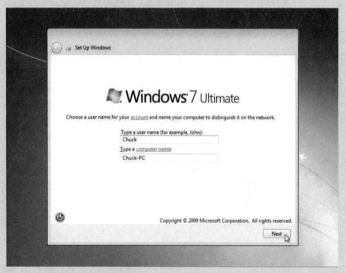

Source: Microsoft Corporation

Step 9

Next create the password for the user account, entering it twice, and type a password hint that will help you to recall the password but not reveal it to others. The password hint will display anytime you enter an incorrect password when logging on.

Source: Microsoft Corporation

Step 10

On the next page enter the 20-character Product Key. Notice the check box labeled "Automatically activate Windows when I'm online." Already checked by default, this means it will activate automatically if your computer connects to the Internet. If not activated within 30 days, Windows will stop functioning. Click Next to continue the final configuration steps.

Source: Microsoft Corporation

Step 11

On the next page configure the Automatic Update Settings. Unless your instructor tells you otherwise, click the first option: "Use recommended settings." Windows setup will then continue. On the next page, select your time and date settings, and click Next.

Step 12

Now select your computer's current location. If you are at home, select Home Network; if you are at school or work, select Work Network; if your computer has mobile broadband or you are using a public Wi-Fi network, select Public Network. There will be a short delay while Windows connects to the network and applies settings.

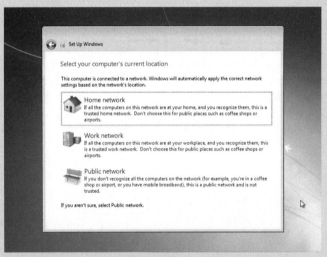

Source: Microsoft Corporation

Step 13

The Welcome page displays, followed by a message: "Preparing your desktop ..." Soon the desktop displays and, depending on the setting you selected for updating and whether you have an Internet connection, you will see a message that Windows is downloading and installing updates. Some updates require restarting Windows to complete installing the update.

Source: Microsoft Corporation

Postinstallation Tasks

After you install Windows 7, perform the necessary postinstallation tasks. They include verifying network access (assuming you connected to a network), installing security software, and installing at least the critical updates, including Service Packs. You should complete these tasks before moving on to customizing the desktop for yourself or another user and performing other desktop management tasks.

Verifying Network Access

Once you have completed the installation, look for the network status icon on the task-bar. If it does not show a red *x*, then you have a network connection. If it shows a yellow exclamation mark, you have a local network connection, but do not have a connection to the Internet, although a router is present. Hover the mouse cursor over the icon. In the example shown here, the icon indicates a connection to a network named "ShortMoose" as well as to the Internet. If the network has no name, the top line would simply say "Network." In reality "ShortMoose" is the name of a wireless broadband router to which this computer connects via Ethernet. In Chapter 10, you will learn more about connecting to a private network as well as to the Internet.

The network status icon.
Source: Microsoft Corporation

Installing Security Software

It's difficult to say which is more important: downloading and installing the all-important updates or installing a security package. We opt to install the security program before completing all the updates. If you do not have another program available to use, consider the free Microsoft Security Essentials, shown in Figure 4-4, available at www.microsoft.com/security_essentials. It includes general malware protection and free, automated updates. If you do not have another preferred security program, download and install this easy-to-use package as soon as possible.

Installing Updates

Now that you have verified that the computer has network access and installed security software, your next task is to install updates. Although some updates do install at the end of the Windows 7 installation, you will need to ensure that additional updates install.

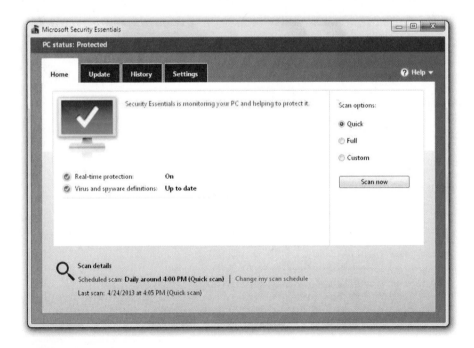

FIGURE 4-4 Microsoft Security Essentials.
Source: Microsoft Corporation

try this!

Configure Windows Update

If you are logged on as an administrator, you can make changes to Windows Update. To configure Windows Update, try this:

1. Open the Start menu, in the Search Programs and Files box type "Windows Update," and select Windows Update from the results list.
2. In the task pane of Windows Update, click Change Settings.
3. Using the drop-down lists and the check boxes, select the desired settings.
4. Click OK to close the Windows Update Change Settings box. Close Windows Update.

How you actually obtain updates will depend on the organization (school or business) where you install Windows. In some organizations, the IT department may distribute updates for new installations on CD even before connecting a computer to a network. Other organizations may make them available on a shared folder on the private network. In most cases, if you have an Internet connection, you will configure Windows Update to automatically download and install updates. Figure 4–5 shows the options for configuring Windows Update.

If, during setup, you configured updates to download and install automatically, you can let nature take its course. In addition, we like to be more proactive, because it can take Windows Update a few days before it downloads and installs all the updates for a new installation. Therefore, even with automatic update configured, we recommend you use the Windows Update program to manually access the updates immediately after upgrading or installing Windows. This will still take several iterations, but you will bring it up-to-date sooner this way.

Virtual Machine Additions

If you installed Windows 7 into a virtual machine, be sure to install the virtual machine additions for Windows. Whatever hypervisor you are using will remind you to do this, usually when you start the newly installed OS in the virtual machine. Each hypervisor product has a different name for these additions, and you may simply need to respond to a pop-up window or you may need to look in one of the menus on the window surrounding your virtual machine to initiate the installation of the additions.

FIGURE 4–5 Windows Update Settings.
Source: Microsoft Corporation

TABLE 4–3 Features in the Windows 7 Retail Editions

	Home Premium	Professional	Ultimate
Desktop navigation features such as Shake, Peek, and Snap	✓	✓	✓
Instant Search searches external hard drives, networked PCs, and libraries	✓	✓	✓
Internet Explorer 8 (Upgrade this to the latest Internet Explorer.)	✓	✓	✓
Windows Media Center (It requires a TV tuner and other hardware required for some functions.)	✓	✓	✓
HomeGroup for easy file-and-print sharing on a home network (HomeGroup requires a network and PCs running Windows 7.)	✓	✓	✓
Windows XP Mode for running Windows XP programs not compatible with Windows 7		✓	✓
Windows Touch	✓	✓	✓
Domain Join wizard for joining a Windows domain		✓	✓
Backup to a home or business network		✓	✓
BitLocker			✓
Switch among 35 languages			✓

LO 4.2 | Windows 7 Features

This section offers an overview of Windows 7, including the separate Windows 7 products and some key features offered in Windows 7. Table 4–3 lists Windows 7 features and the editions in which each feature is included. We will examine just a few of these features in the following sections.

The Windows 7 Desktop

The Windows 7 Desktop was only an evolutionary, not revolutionary change from that of its predecessors. For instance, the Windows 7 GUI can contain shortcuts in various locations, such as the desktop or the Start menu. A shortcut is an icon that represents a link to one of many types of objects. Double-clicking on a shortcut has the same results as taking the same action directly on the linked object. An object can be a folder, a data file, a program, or any other type of object an icon can represent in Windows. Shortcuts on the desktop are often, but not always, distinguished by a small bent arrow, as seen here on the shortcut for Mozilla Firefox. Shortcuts on the Start menu, such as those shown in Figure 4–6, typically do not have the bent arrow. The shortcuts highlighted in yellow in Figure 4–6 are pinned to the Start menu and will remain there until they are unpinned by the user. More on pinning later in this chapter. The shortcuts highlighted in mauve are shortcuts of recent programs that Windows dynamically adds to the Start menu. A horizontal line (barely visible) divides these two areas of the Start menu.

A desktop shortcut.
Source: Microsoft Corporation

Aero

Windows Aero is Microsoft's name for a group of GUI desktop features and visual themes introduced in Windows Vista and improved somewhat in Windows 7. Windows 7 Aero

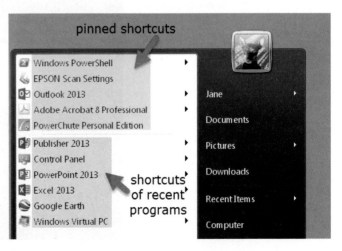

FIGURE 4–6 Shortcuts (at left) on the Start menu.
Source: Microsoft Corporation

includes transparent windows (referred to as "Glass"), Windows animations, Flip 3D, Aero Shake, Aero Snap, and Aero Peek.

Figure 4-7 is an example of the Windows 7 desktop with Aero enabled. **Flip 3D** lets you switch through your open windows as if they were a stack of cards or photos. Use the WINDOWS KEY+TAB combination to use Flip 3D, shown in Figure 4-8. It requires a video card that supports (at minimum) DirectX 9.0 and Shader Model 2.0. Figures 4-7 and 4-8 also show one of the desktop themes available with Windows 7.

Aero Snap lets you manipulate windows quickly. For instance, to maximize a window, drag it until its title bar touches the top edge of your display. Restore a maximized window by dragging it away from the top of the display. **Aero Shake** lets you quickly minimize all but one window by giving that window a quick shake. **Aero Peek** allows you to peek at the underlying desktop by hovering your mouse over the Show Desktop

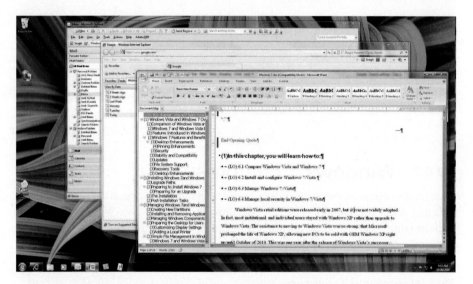

FIGURE 4–7 Windows 7 with Aero enhancements, including transparent Glass.
Source: Microsoft Corporation

FIGURE 4–8 Using Flip 3D in Windows 7.
Source: Microsoft Corporation

button, the small vertical bar at the far right edge of the taskbar. Aero Peek makes all open windows temporarily transparent.

Jump Lists and Pinning

Windows 7 improves the Start menu and taskbar with the Jump Lists and pinning features. The old pinned area of the Start menu is still available, and programs are often pinned there, but you can also pin items on the taskbar. When you right-click on a program shortcut on the Start menu or taskbar, a Jump List displays, as in Figure 4-9. This is a list of recently opened items such as files, folders, and websites. It automatically lists only the recently opened items, but you can select an item and "permanently" pin it to a Jump List. Practice pinning items in Step-by-Step 4.02.

Pinning allows you to place icons for applications and destinations on the taskbar and Start menu. Once pinned, an item's icon remains on the toolbar regardless of whether the program is open or closed. Simply click it to open the application or destination. When a program is running, its icon appears as a square button on the toolbar, as demonstrated by the Microsoft Outlook button on the toolbar in Figure 4-10, which shows a portion of a Windows 7 taskbar with the various icons labeled.

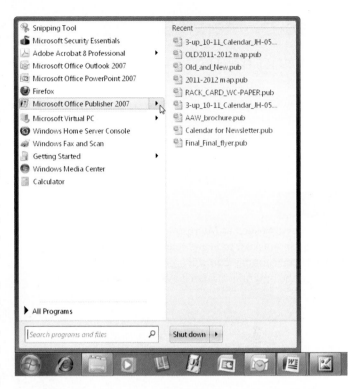

FIGURE 4–9 A Jump List (in the right column) for Microsoft Office Publisher.
Source: Microsoft Corporation

Figure 4-11 shows the Jump List for Microsoft Word that includes both Word documents and other types of files, such as recently embedded TIF files in Word documents.

Pin a program and then use that program's Jump List to pin several data files to the one program. When you pin a program to the taskbar, you use that one icon to open the program and switch to the program, and then you can select an item from the program's Jump List, which, like most pinned items, carries an automatically generated list of recently opened files for that item, but you can also add items to this list. There are several ways to pin programs. Learn more about pinning and Jump Lists in Step-by-Step 4.02.

Note: We pin the apps we use the most to the taskbar, and now find we rarely launch apps from the Windows 7 Start menu.

Notification Area

The notification area, also called the system tray, is not new in Windows 7, but it is greatly improved over that of previous versions of Windows. The notification area holds status indicators and pop-up menus for a variety of devices and programs installed on your computer. It is so handy that many installation programs—both by Microsoft and by other software publishers—insert their own handy icons here. Before Windows 7, this practice resulted in clutter that detracted from the value of this feature. Windows 7

FIGURE 4–10 Pinned items on a taskbar, along with the button for a running program.
Source: Microsoft Corporation

FIGURE 4–11 Right-click a pinned item to view its Jump List.
Source: Microsoft Corporation

Step-by-Step **4.02**

Pinning Items

Practice pinning programs to the taskbar, and then pin files within a program's Jump List. In this step-by-step exercise, you will need the following:

- A computer with Windows 7 installed—either a conventional installation or an installation in a VM.

Step 1

Start a program, such as Microsoft Word. Then right-click the program's taskbar icon and select Pin This Program to Taskbar. The running icon will appear the same, but when you close the program, a pinned icon will remain.

Source: Microsoft Corporation

Step 2

You can also pin a program to the taskbar by dragging it. Open the Start menu and browse through the pinned items list or the All Programs menu until you locate the icon for a program you wish to pin. Then drag and drop the program icon onto the taskbar.

Source: Microsoft Corporation

Step 3

Windows 7 automatically generates Jump Lists, but you can ensure that an item stays on a Jump List by pinning it. To pin an item, right-click an icon on the Start menu to display the Jump List. Then hover the mouse cursor over an item in the list until the pushpin icon displays. Click the pushpin icon to pin the item.

Source: Microsoft Corporation

Step 4

Now you can see the distinction between the recent items Windows 7 automatically pins to the Jump List and those you choose to pin.

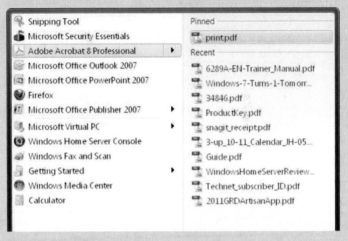

Source: Microsoft Corporation

Step 5

To unpin a program from the taskbar simply right-click on it and select Unpin This Program from Taskbar. To unpin an item from a Jump List, right-click on it and select Unpin from This List.

changed all that. To begin with, it does not display as many icons here itself, and best of all, it changed how icons appear and behave. Further, all those additional status icons are tucked away, but readily available with a click on the Show Hidden Icons button, as shown in Figure 4-12.

Figure 4-13 identifies the objects in the notification area. The Network icon shown indicates an Ethernet (wired) network, whereas an icon with five vertical bars in graduated sizes indicates a wireless network. If the network adapter is disconnected,

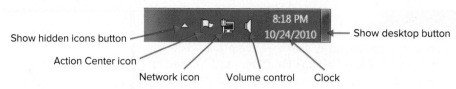

FIGURE 4–13 The Windows 7 notification area.
Source: Microsoft Corporation

Show hidden icons button

Action Center icon

Network icon   Volume control   Clock

Show desktop button

FIGURE 4–12 The hidden status icons revealed by clicking the Show hidden icons button shown here on the left side of the notification area.
Source: Microsoft Corporation

a red X will appear on the icon. If there is another problem with the network, it will have a yellow triangle with a black exclamation mark. Hover the mouse cursor over an icon to see a brief description; right-click to display a context menu, and click on the icon to open the related program.

Action Center

The Windows Action Center, represented in the taskbar notification area by the small flag icon, will briefly display a message balloon when there is a problem with your security programs or backup. Then it will quietly sit there with a white X against a red circle until you resolve the problem. A single click opens a message box, as shown in Figure 4-14. To open Action Center (see Figure 4-15) either click on the Open Action Center link in the message box or double-click the Action Center icon on the taskbar.

Libraries

Windows 7 introduced libraries. A library looks like a file system folder, but it is not, even though the four default libraries in Windows 7 carry the names of special folders: Documents, Music, Pictures, and Videos. While a folder is a container for files and other folders (called subfolders), a library only contains links to the locations of files and folders.

A library stores information about the locations of folders and files, displaying them as if they were all in one location, thus making it easier for you to find related information or types of files. For instance, in our example, the Documents library shows two default locations: My Documents (in this case D:\Yoda\Documents) and Public Documents (D:\Users\Public\Documents), as shown in Figure 4-16. Locations can be on the local computer or on shared locations on a network.

FIGURE 4–14 The Action Center message box appears after a single click of the Action Center icon.
Source: Microsoft Corporation

FIGURE 4–15 Open the Windows 7 Action Center by clicking on the Action Center link in the message box shown in Figure 4–14.
Source: Microsoft Corporation

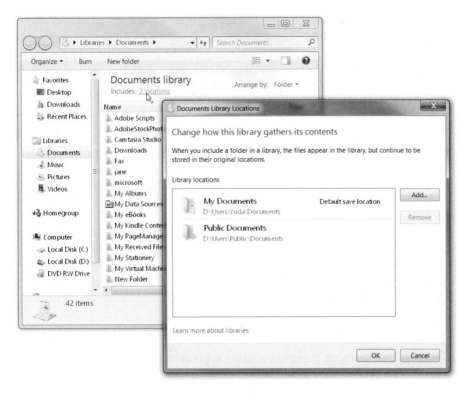

FIGURE 4–16 The two default locations for the Documents library.
Source: Microsoft Corporation

File System Support

Regardless of the file system used on a disk or disc, what you see in Windows Explorer remains the same: folders and files. Windows 7 supports the file systems described below.

FAT File Systems

The **FAT file systems** include FAT12, FAT16, FAT32, and exFAT. Each has a logical structure that includes a file allocation table (FAT)—hence the name of the file system— and a directory structure. The file allocation table enables the OS to allocate space for files, while a directory gives the OS a place for identifying information about each file. The FAT file system used many years ago on the diskettes and hard drives of the early PCs running IBM's PC-DOS and Microsoft's MS DOS is now called the FAT16 file system. The versions that are important to know about today are FAT32 and exFAT.

Recent versions of Apple macOS support FAT32, as well as exFAT (discussed next), so consider using one of these on a flash drive that you intend to use in both Windows and Apple macOS computer.

The Extended File Allocation Table (exFAT) file system is intended for use with solid-state storage devices, such as flash drives. While exFAT theoretically supports volume sizes up to 64 zettabytes (ZBs), the recommended maximum is 512 terabytes (TBs).

Windows NTFS File System

The NTFS file system is available in all versions of Windows beginning with Windows NT, but excluding the Windows 95, Windows 98, and Windows Me versions. The main NTFS logical structure is a **master file table (MFT)** that is expandable, and therefore can be modified in future versions. Windows uses a transaction processing system to track changes to files, adding a measure of transaction-level recoverability to the file system, similar to what your bank uses to track transactions, and it will roll back incomplete transactions.

Over the years Microsoft improved NTFS. From the beginning, the NTFS file system provided file and folder security not available on FAT volumes. Today, in addition to file and folder security and transaction processing capability, NTFS supports many features. The short list includes file compression, file encryption, and an indexing service. NTFS is the preferred file system for hard drives in Windows and the default created when you install Windows.

File Systems for Optical Discs

Optical discs require special Windows file system drivers. The CD-ROM File System (CDFS) allows Windows OSs to read CD-ROMs and to read and write to writable CDs (CD-R) and rewritable CDs (CD-RW). The Universal Disk Format (UDF) is a file system driver required for Windows to read DVD ROMs and to read and write DVD-R and DVD-RW.

In addition to the traditional method for writing to optical drives (basically, a write once method), Microsoft introduced a new file system for optical drives in Windows Vista, which allows you to write to an optical disc, notably the DVD-RW and CD-R optical discs, adding files at any time, as long as the disc has room. Learn how to select between these two methods in the section titled "Managing Windows."

Security

In Windows 7, Microsoft improved existing security features such as User Account Control, BitLocker, and Windows Defender.

Improved User Account Control

As described in Chapter 2, User Account Control was introduced in Windows Vista. This security feature is designed to prevent malware from installing without the user's knowledge. It is less annoying in Windows 7, with fewer tasks requiring user intervention and use of an elevation prompt. Additionally, if you log on with an account with administrative privileges, you can adjust the User Account Control elevation prompt behavior.

> *Note:* BitLocker and BitLocker To Go will encrypt an entire volume, regardless of the file system (NTFS, FAT, or exFAT).

BitLocker and BitLocker To Go

BitLocker, introduced in Windows Vista Enterprise and Ultimate editions, is also limited to the Enterprise and Ultimate editions in Windows 7. In Windows 7, as in Vista, you can encrypt the boot volume, but you can also encrypt any internal hard drive. Further, a feature called BitLocker To Go lets you encrypt external drives, such as flash drives. Later in this chapter you will learn how to use BitLocker in Windows 7.

AppLocker

AppLocker, a new feature in Windows 7, allows an administrator of a Windows Active Directory domain to control which applications each user can run, reducing the chance of malware running on the user's computer. This feature applies only to computers at work or school that are part of a Windows Active Directory domain.

Windows Defender

Introduced in Windows Vista, Windows Defender is a free built-in antispyware utility integrated into the Windows 7 Action Center where you can configure spyware scanning and updates.

Program Compatibility

If you need to run an old application that does not work well in Windows 7, open Help and Support from the Start menu, search on "compatibility," and check out the recommendations there. One recommendation is to run the Program Compatibility Troubleshooter. This will walk you through creating settings that may help your program to run better. Or you can do this manually by tweaking the compatibility settings for that application in the Properties for the application or its shortcut.

If the application still will not run, download and install Windows XP Mode, as described in Chapter 3. Install the application into the Windows XP VM. Windows 7 will even allow you to create a shortcut on the Start menu to an application installed in Windows XP Mode.

Recovery Tools

With each version of Windows, Microsoft has enhanced the recovery tools for repairing damage to the operating system. One of the most venerable of these tools is Task Manager, which has been in Windows through several versions and was extensively improved along the way. Task Manager allows you to see the state of individual processes and programs running on the computer, to view resource usage (CPU, memory, and disk), and to stop errant programs, when necessary.

You can access many of these tools while Windows is up and running, but in case a serious problem prevents Windows from starting, you can access an entire menu of tools by booting your system from the Windows 7 disc. Choose the language settings, click Next, and click the option Repair Your Computer. Select the OS you want to repair (if you installed more than one), click Next, and the System Recovery Options menu will display (see Figure 4-17). The following tools are available from this menu:

Note: Task Manager has abilities beyond managing tasks. If your Windows computer seems unusually slow, open Task Manager and select the Performance tab to determine if CPU or memory usage is high. Select the Networking tab to see state and speed of your network connections.

- Startup Repair scans for problems with missing or damaged system files and attempts to replace the problem files.
- System Restore allows you to create a restore point, which is a snapshot of Windows, its configuration, and all installed programs. Many restore points are created automatically when you make changes to your system. If your computer has problems after a change, use System Restore to roll it back to a selected restore point.
- System Image Recovery will let you restore a complete PC Image backup, providing you created one ahead of time.

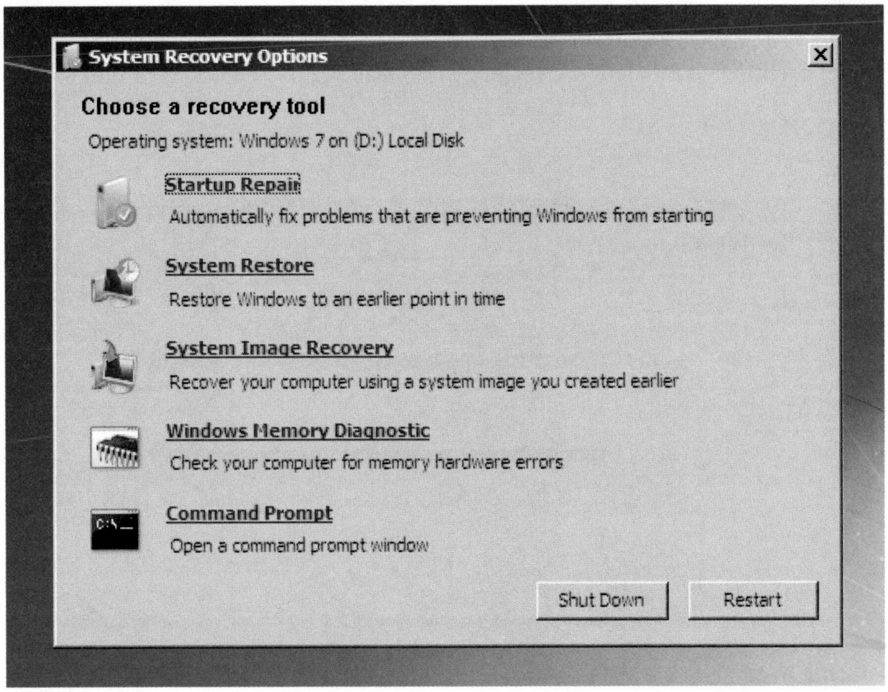

FIGURE 4–17 The Windows 7 System Recovery Options.
Source: Microsoft Corporation

- **Windows Memory Diagnostic Tool** tests the system's RAM because RAM problems can prevent Windows from starting normally. If this tool detects a problem, replace the RAM before using any other recovery tool.
- **Command Prompt** provides a command-line interface in which you can use command-line tools to resolve a problem.

LO 4.3 | Customizing and Managing Windows 7

Once you have installed Windows 7, and completed the postinstallation tasks, it's time to customize Windows for the user. In this section, you will practice some of the common procedures for customizing and managing Windows 7, use Computer Management tools for a variety of tasks, install and remove applications, manage Windows components, and prepare the desktop for users, including modifications to display settings and adding a printer.

Computer Management

After you install Windows 7, if you add a new hard drive to your computer and need to partition it or do any other maintenance, open the Computer Management console and expand the Disk Management node. Figure 4–18 shows the disks on our Windows Vista/Windows 7 dual-boot computer. Windows Vista is installed on Disk 0 (drive C:) and Windows 7 is installed on Disk 1 (drive D:).

If you add a hard drive—internal or external—to a Windows computer, use Disk Management to partition and format the drive, if necessary. New external drives often come pre-formatted with FAT32, which does not provide security and cannot automatically repair damage to the disk. Therefore, if you wish to use the NTFS file system, open Computer Management and reformat your new drives. This will destroy all data on the target partition. There is also a method for converting a FAT partition to NTFS from the Command Prompt, which it will do without losing data. Although the danger of data loss is small, we recommend backing up your data before converting a FAT partition. To do this conversion, open a Command Prompt and enter **convert** *d:* **/fs:ntfs,** where *d:* is the letter of the target partition you wish to convert to NTFS. See Figure 4–19. You cannot use the

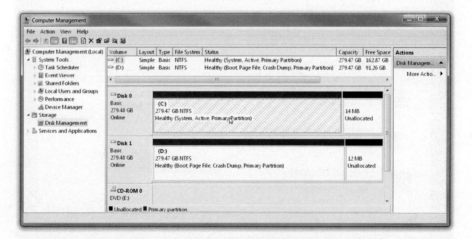

FIGURE 4–18 The Disk Management node in the Computer Management console.
Source: Microsoft Corporation

```
Command Prompt                                    [ - ] [ □ ] [ X ]

Microsoft Windows [Version 6.1.7601]
Copyright (c) 2009 Microsoft Corporation.  All rights reserved.

C:\Users\Jane>convert d: /fs:ntfs
```

FIGURE 4–19 Convert a FAT partition to NTFS from the Windows Command Prompt.
Source: Microsoft Corporation

convert command to go to any other format. If you want to convert from NTFS to another format, you must back up the drive, format it, and restore the data.

Preparing the Desktop for Users

In the many years, we have worked with PCs running Windows OSs, we have noticed one phenomenon: A user who previously had to be shown the location of the on/off button will quickly figure out how to personalize the desktop. It seems like one day we help unpack the PC and a week later we come back to see dozens of shortcuts arrayed over desktop wallpaper of a child's crayon drawing. Whenever possible, we encourage such personalization because it means the person is making the computer his or her own and learning how to move around in Windows at the same time. Whether you are preparing a PC for yourself or another user, there are steps to take after you complete the immediate postinstallation tasks and before you install the necessary everyday applications. These include customizing the display settings—mainly the resolution—and adding a local printer.

Customizing Display Settings

After installing Windows 7, you may need to customize the display settings for resolution and (if you are lucky) for multiple displays.

Display Resolution. The Windows 7 installation program is very good at quickly installing Windows, but we still find that we need to tweak the display resolution settings because Windows setup may install a generic display driver that does not support the native resolution of the display. This is especially true when you install it into a virtual machine. In that case, you will install the virtual machine additions appropriate for the hypervisor and installed version of Windows, which will include better video adapter support. Then you will be able to select a higher resolution for the virtual display.

When you have installed Windows 7 on a desktop computer with a flat-panel display, if it installed the appropriate driver for the video adapter and the display, then Windows will normally select the correct resolution. A flat-panel display has one native resolution, which will show as the recommended resolution.

A related issue is that because today's display systems (the video adapter and display combined) are capable of very high resolution, you may need to enlarge icons and other objects to make them more visible on the desktop. In fact, when you increase the resolution, it will prompt you to "Make it easier to read what's on your screen." This is where you change the size of items on your screen. Practice adjusting screen resolution in Step-by-Step 4.03.

Note: A higher display resolution results in a smaller less readable screen font. To make it easier to read labels on icons and menus, change the size of text and objects on the screen, as shown in Step-by-Step 4.03.

Step-by-Step 4.03

Adjusting the Display Resolution

In this step-by-step exercise, you will familiarize yourself with the Windows 7 Appearance and Personalization settings and make a few changes to the desktop. You may see different settings than those shown in these steps, depending on the capabilities of your display. To complete this task, you will need the following:

- A PC or VM with Windows 7 installed.
- Administrative access.

Step 1

First change the screen resolution. A quick way to open the Screen Resolution page of the Appearance and Personalization applet is to right-click on an empty area of the desktop and select Screen Resolution from the context menu.

Source: Microsoft Corporation

Source: Microsoft Corporation

Step 2

Click on the down arrow in the drop-down list labeled Resolution, look for a recommended resolution, and select it. Click OK.

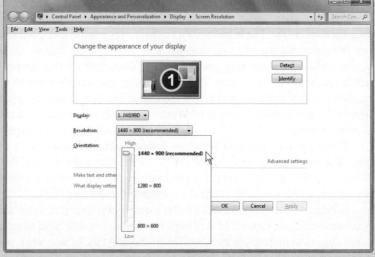

Source: Microsoft Corporation

Step 3

If you have increased your resolution, you will see this page, on which you can select the size of the text and other screen objects. This page is also available from the Screen Resolution page by clicking the link labeled "Make text and other items larger or smaller." Watch the Preview as you select a different size.

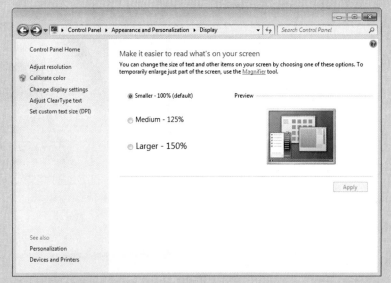

Source: Microsoft Corporation

Step 4

If you changed the text and object size, you will need to log off and then log on again for the change to take effect.

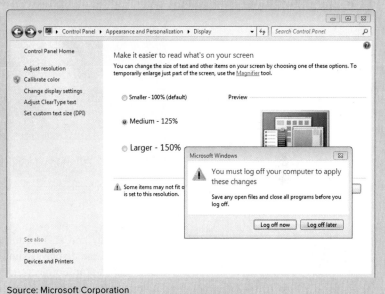

Source: Microsoft Corporation

Multiple Displays. Although most PCs today only have a single display, more and more jobs require the increased screen real estate of multiple displays. Windows has supported multiple displays for several versions. All you need to add more display space to a typical desktop PC is a dual-headed video adapter and a second display. For most laptops the only cost is for a second display, because laptops usually come with a display connector for an external display that you can use simultaneously with the built-in display. We have worked with dual displays for over a decade on our computers, and we have found that it can be a bit weird to work with displays of different sizes. Therefore, the ideal situation is to use identical displays.

When you have multiple displays, you can configure how Windows uses these displays on the Screen Resolution page. Our preferred mode is "Extend these displays," which leaves the taskbar on the main display (labeled 1 in Figure 4-20) and extends the desktop to the secondary display. It is great to have a document open

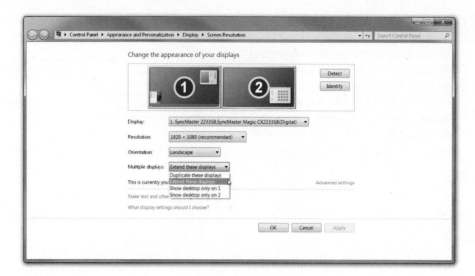

FIGURE 4–20 Select how you want the desktop to appear on multiple displays.
Source: Microsoft Corporation

FIGURE 4–21 When you click the Identify button a numeral will appear briefly on each display.
Source: Microsoft Corporation

on one display and an Internet browser open on the other, for instance. The setting "Duplicate these displays" shows the same desktop on both displays. You might use this if your laptop connects to a projector on which you wish to show the desktop. The remaining setting, "Show desktop only on 1" and "Show desktop only on 2" will leave the display you do not select blank.

Click the Identify button to have a number display on each physical display (see Figure 4–21) so that you can confirm that you have the displays oriented left to right as they are in the Screen Resolution page. If they are not, click and drag the display images on the Screen Resolution page to place them in the correct order.

If you want to change which display is the main display, go to the screen resolution page and, in the Change the Appearance of Your Displays box, click on the display labeled 2. Then a new option will show near the bottom of the settings below the box: Make This My Main Display. Click to place a check in this box, and that display will become the main display and will become number 1.

Desktop Gadgets

Windows Vista had a feature called the Sidebar in which you could configure one or more small programs called gadgets. The Sidebar is gone from Windows 7, but the gadgets remain. Each **gadget** performs some small function—usually involving keeping information handy in a small screen object. Gadgets have proven to be a potential security hole. We no longer use them or recommend them.

Adding a Local Printer

Installing a new printer in Windows should be a nonevent because Windows is a plug-and-play OS, and new printers are plug-and-play. Therefore, you simply follow the setup guide for the new printer. In many cases, Windows will already have the printer driver and will install it without requiring a DVD from the manufacturer, but there can be another reason to run a setup program from the printer manufacturer. A new printer, especially one that includes other functions—primarily document scanning, copying, and faxing—will also include special software beyond the standard printer driver. Most common is software for scanning and organizing your documents.

Before connecting a printer, be sure to read the printer's setup guide—usually a hard-to-miss oversized sheet of paper with the basic instructions for setting up the printer. Often, a printer setup guide will instruct you to install the printer's software before connecting it, especially if it connects via USB. It will also guide you through making both the power connection and the connection to the computer. How will your printer connect to the computer? The most common wired printer interface is USB, but some printers also use IEEE 1394 (FireWire).

If a printer uses a cable (USB or IEEE 1394) you will first connect the printer, and then turn it on. If it connects via a wireless method, you will turn on the printer and establish the wireless connection. Once Windows detects a printer, it installs the driver and configures the printer for you. It will be added to the Devices and Printers applet, shown in Figure 4–22, and be available to all applications that can use a printer. The printer with the white check mark on a green circle is the default printer that Windows will use unless you select a different printer. Double-click on a printer icon to open the printer page with status information and links to the printer properties, print queue, and other pages for managing and controlling the printer and its features.

> *Note:* In the example in Figure 4–22, not all devices in the Printers and Faxes categories are physical printers or faxes. Some are software "printers" such as Adobe PDF that take a file from one format (a Word document or a graphic file) and "prints" it to a file in a new format, such as Adobe PDF, a file format commonly used for electronic document exchange that does not require users to have the same software that was used to create these documents, just software that can read them.

Connecting to a Network Printer

If you are installing a Bluetooth or Wi-Fi printer, or if a printer is available on your school or corporate network, and an administrator has configured it with appropriate permissions so that you can connect and print to it, you can do just that. To do so,

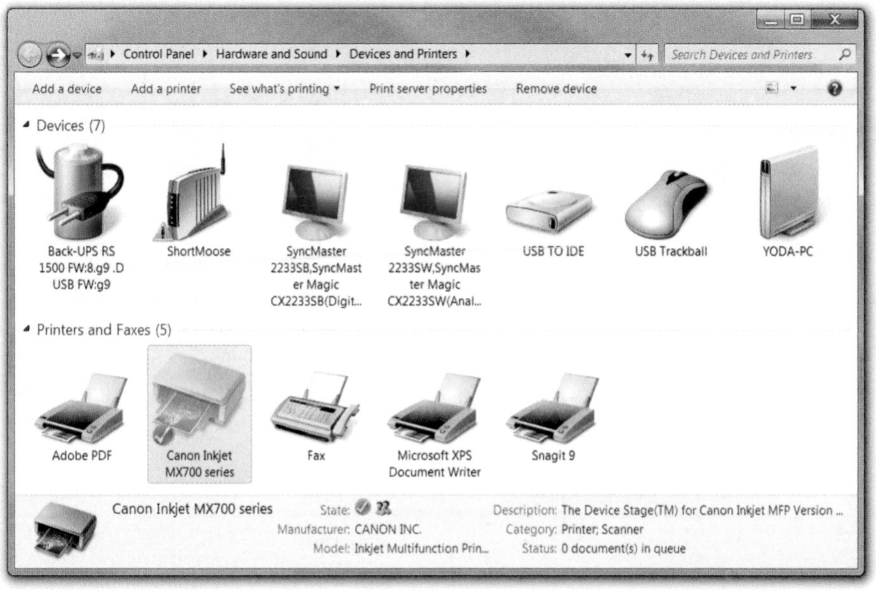

FIGURE 4–22 The Devices and Printers Control Panel.
Source: Microsoft Corporation

open Devices and Printers and click Add a printer. In the **Add Printer wizard**, select "Add a network, wireless or Bluetooth printer." It will take time to search for all available network printers and then display them in the box. Select the Printer Name of the printer you wish to connect to, click Next, and follow the instructions. This will install the appropriate printer driver on your computer so that Windows can format each print job for that printer before sending it to the network printer.

Installing and Removing Applications

By now, you are ready to install applications into Windows to make your computer the tool you need for work, home, or school. If you purchased a computer with Windows preinstalled, you may also need to remove some of those preinstalled applications you have no desire or need to use.

Installing Applications

Today, each mainstream application comes with its own installation program that will walk you through the installation process. Some offer just a few options, installing with very little user input, while others will give you the option to do a custom install, in which you select the components to install and the location for the installed files. These programs copy the application files and make necessary changes to Windows, such as associating one or more file types with the application so that when you double-click on, say, a file with a DOCX extension, it knows to open Microsoft Word.

After completing an application installation, you should make sure to update the application. If you have an Internet connection, most applications will check for updates. This is very important today when malware targets our business productivity software. If your applications are from Microsoft, you can update them through Windows Update, which will list updates under Optional Updates, as shown in Figure 4–23.

Removing Applications

When it comes time to remove an application, you should first look for an uninstall program for the application. If the application has a submenu off the Start menu, it may

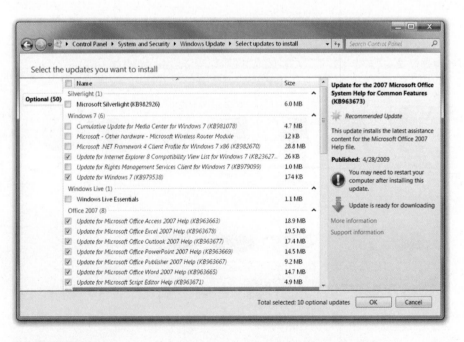

FIGURE 4–23 Update Microsoft Applications through Windows Update.
Source: Microsoft Corporation

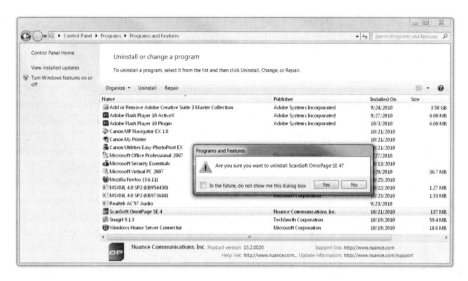

FIGURE 4–24 Uninstall unwanted programs.
Source: Microsoft Corporation

include the uninstall program, which is usually the best choice for uninstalling. You can also search the folder in which the application installed for an uninstall program. If you cannot find such a program for an application you wish to uninstall, open Control Panel, locate Programs, and click Uninstall A Program. It may take a few seconds for the list of installed programs to display in the Programs and Features page. Locate the program you wish to uninstall and double-click it. You will see a warning, as shown in Figure 4-24. Follow the instructions to complete the operation.

Managing Windows Components

Windows 7, like previous versions, includes many Windows components beyond the basic operating system files. You can view them by opening Windows features in Control Panel. Simply click a check box to turn individual features on or off, as shown in Figure 4-25.

try this!

Use Add or Remove Programs

Become familiar with the list of programs installed on your computer. In addition to applications, the Programs and Features applet lists the installed Windows updates. Try this:

1. Open the Control Panel. Under Programs, click on Uninstall A Program. Wait for the list to display. Browse through the list of Currently Installed Programs.

2. If you find a program that you want to remove, click the program, and then click the Uninstall button in the bar above the list to begin the uninstall process. Sometimes you must provide the installation CD before you can remove the program.

3. In the task list on the left, click View Installed Updates to see a list of installed Windows updates. If you have a good reason to uninstall an update, this is the place to do it. We don't recommend uninstalling updates unless you are sure it is necessary.

4. When you have finished exploring, close the open windows. If you uninstalled an application, you may need to allow the uninstall program to restart the computer.

Simple File Management

As with any operating system, file management in Windows 7 is mainly about organizing data files so that you can easily find the files you need when you need them. Windows provides a set of folders for just this purpose. Before you use them, get a basic understanding of the default file hierarchy in whatever version of Windows you are using. Then learn how to work with not just files and folders, but also the libraries that Windows 7 introduced. Finally, learn about the Windows file systems for optical discs and the ones that allow you to copy files to CD or DVD as easily as you copy them to a hard drive or flash drive.

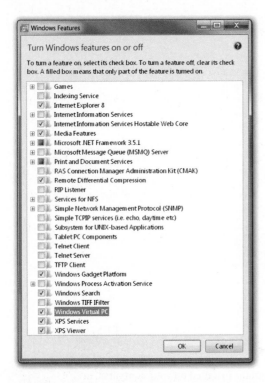

FIGURE 4–25 Use the check boxes to turn Windows features on or off.
Source: Microsoft Corporation

Windows 7 Default File Hierarchy

All versions of Windows create one set of folders for the operating system, another set for application program files, and an additional set, **personal folders**, for each user account to hold user data files. The 32-bit and 64-bit distributions of Windows differ only in the location in which they store programs. The 32-bit distributions of Windows 7 stores all programs in the Program Files folder, while the 64-bit distributions store only 64-bit programs in this folder and store 32-bit programs in the folder named Program Files (x86). Figure 4–26 shows the folder hierarchy for a 64-bit installation of Windows 7. The default location for the majority of the Windows operating system files is in C:\Windows.

The default location for user data is C:\Users\<username> where <username> is the log-on user name. In Figure 4–27, note the folder for the user Jade. Within this folder are the personal folders created by Windows to hold various types of data or, as in the case of the Desktop folder, to hold files from a certain location. The Downloads folder holds files you download with your Internet browser.

Navigating Windows Explorer

There are several ways to manage your files in Windows. The primary tool for saving files is the individual application you use to create and modify files of a certain type: for instance, a word processing program, spreadsheet program, photo editing program, or other application. When you issue the

FIGURE 4–26 The Windows 7 64-bit default folder hierarchy.
Source: Microsoft Corporation

FIGURE 4–27 Windows 7 personal folders for the user Jade.
Source: Microsoft Corporation

command within an application to save a file, you can navigate to the location of your choice and either save the file in an existing folder or create a new folder before saving. Similarly, when you decide to open an existing file from within an application, you can navigate to a location and open the desired file.

Although you can also do many file management tasks within an application, the primary tool for copying, moving, renaming, and deleting files is **Windows Explorer**. Microsoft introduced some features to the Windows Explorer folder windows, which we highlight here. Figure 4–28 shows the anatomy of a Windows Explorer folder window. By default, the Menu bar appears only when you press the ALT key, and you can use the Organize button and other buttons on the toolbar to modify the appearance and functionality of the Windows Explorer folder windows.

try this!

Explore Windows Folders

If you are sitting at a computer with Windows 7, explore the folder hierarchy. Try this:

1. Click Start | Computer or use the shortcut keys: Windows Key+E to open Windows Explorer.

2. In Windows Explorer, double-click the icon for the Local Disk (C:). Note the folders in the root of drive C:.

3. Double-click the icon for Program Files and note the folders under Program Files. If you have a 64-bit installation of Windows, double-click the icon for Program Files (x86) and note the folders in this folder.

4. Now browse to the Users folder and open the folder for the account with which you logged on and explore the contents of this folder.

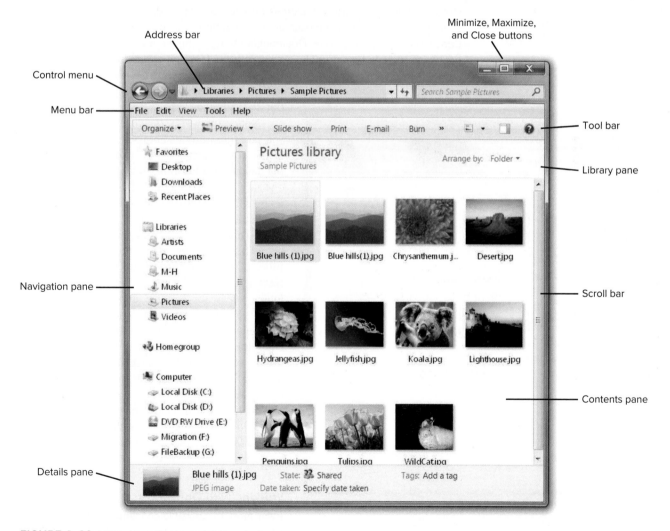

FIGURE 4–28 A Windows Explorer folder window.
Source: Microsoft Corporation

Navigate through Windows Explorer with mouse operations. When you hover the mouse over the navigation pane, small clear triangles appear next to each folder object that can be expanded. Click the triangle and it turns solid black and points down to the right in the navigation pane at the now-visible objects contained in the original folder. Click an object's icon in the navigation pane to open it in the contents pane. If you wish to open objects (folders, files, etc.) in the contents pane, you double-click on the object. You can move files and folders from one location to another by dragging and dropping the object you wish to move. Right-click on an object to access other possible operations.

Working with Libraries

Recall what you learned earlier in this chapter about libraries. A library points to one or more locations. Familiarize yourself with libraries by clicking the Windows Explorer pinned icon on the taskbar (it looks like a bunch of folders in a stand) and clicking on any library in the navigation pane. For instance, when you do this to the Documents pane, its contents appear in the contents pane and above that pane is the Library pane. The word *Includes* appears in the Library pane, and after that appears the number of locations. But this is also a link—click it to open the Documents Library Locations window.

You can add locations to a library and create libraries of your own. This is very handy if you want to organize all the files related to a project but those files are stored in folders in various locations on your local hard drive, external hard drives, or network servers. You can back up data in a library as if it were stored in one location. To add a location to the Documents library, simply click the Add button, which opens the Include Folder in Document window. Use this to browse to the folders you wish to add, select the folder, and click the Include Folder button. Windows then adds the new location to the library.

Notice the words *Default save location*. When you save files into this library, you are putting them in the default location for saving files. To change the default save location, first you need more than one save location in a library. Then all you need to do is right-click the desired location and select "Set as default save location."

To create a new library, first click on Libraries in the navigation pane, then notice the New Library tool that appears on the toolbar. Click New Library, which will create a new library folder, ready for a name and locations. If you missed entering the name when you created it, right-click on the New Library, select rename, enter the name, and press Enter. With the new library selected in the navigation pane, the contents pane will indicate that the library is empty. Click the "Include a folder" button to begin adding locations to this new library. You can continue to add locations. Figure 4–29 shows a new library named M-H with two locations—one on a network server named HTC-SERVER.

FIGURE 4–29 A new library, M-H, with two locations: Manuscripts and Screenshots.
Source: Microsoft Corporation

Working with Optical Discs

Even most inexpensive consumer-grade PCs come with optical drives capable of burning (writing data, music, or videos to disc), and optical discs are

Note: Open Windows Explorer quickly by pressing the Windows key and "e" key together.

Note: By default, Windows Explorer hides extensions for known file types, an inconvenience for power users. To make file extensions visible, open Windows Explorer and press Alt-T to open the Tools menu, select Folder Options, then click the View tab. In Advanced Settings clear the check box labeled Hide extensions for known file types. Click OK to close Folder Options.

great for those files you wish to remove to make more room on the computer's hard drive. Whatever your need for burning CDs or DVDs, you should first understand the two formats Windows 7 uses when it burns discs: the ISO Mastered format and the Universal Disk Format (UDF) Live File System.

Use the Mastered format when you want to be able to use a CD or DVD in a conventional CD or DVD player or in any computer (older Apple Macs or PCs). The trouble with using this format is that each item you select to copy to the PC is stored temporarily in available hard disk space (in addition to the space used by the original file) until you finish selecting all you wish to copy, and then they are copied in one operation. This makes it difficult to copy files from a hard drive when you have very little free hard drive space on any hard drive in your computer.

Use the Live File System to burn a disc when you will only use the disc on newer Apple Macs and PCs running Windows XP or new OSs. Using Live File System you can directly copy items to the drive without requiring extra hard drive space. You can copy items individually, over time—either by leaving the disc in the drive or by reinserting the disc multiple times. If all the systems in which you plan to use a disc are newer PCs or Macs, then keep the default setting, which uses the Live File System. Step-by-Step 4.04 will walk you through copying files to an optical disc using the Live File System format.

Step-by-Step 4.04

Burning a CD or DVD

In this step-by-step exercise, you will burn a DVD using the Live File System, which allows you to copy files much as you would to any hard drive or flash drive. To complete this exercise, you will need the following:

- A computer with a DVD/CD drive and with Windows 7 installed—either a conventional installation or an installation in a VM.
- A blank CD or DVD.

Step 1

Insert a blank disc into the optical drive. When the Autoplay dialog opens, select Burn Files to Disc.

Source: Microsoft Corporation

Step 2

In the Burn a Disc dialog, provide a title for the disc (the default is the current date), enter a name, and then click Next.

Live File System format

Mastered format

Source: Microsoft Corporation

Step 3

Windows formats the disc.

Source: Microsoft Corporation

Step 4

After the disc is prepared, this message displays. You can now copy files to the disc from Windows Explorer—either click the button labeled "Open folder to view files" (just one way to open Windows Explorer) or close the box and continue working, copying files to the disc as you would normally copy files to a hard disk or USB drive.

Source: Microsoft Corporation

Step 5

For instance, you can drag and drop folders and files to the disc, as we have done here with the folder titled "06-A+SG_7E." When you use the Live File System, you can continue to add files to the disc as long as it has available space. You can do that now, or add files to it later.

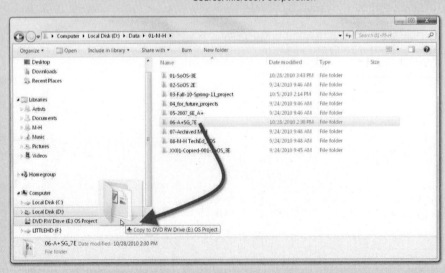

Source: Microsoft Corporation

LO 4.4 | Managing Local Security in Windows 7

If your Windows computer is on a corporate network, the company will centrally manage it, including the security issues. A computer that is not part of a corporate network depends on the knowledge of the user for its security. Security implemented solely on a desktop or laptop computer is local security. Here we will look at administering local user accounts, local security for files and folders, Windows BitLocker drive encryption, Windows Defender anti-spam protection, and Windows Firewall.

Administering Local User Accounts

Local user accounts reside in the local accounts database on a Windows computer. You use a local account to give someone access to the Windows computer and local data. More than one person can log on to a Windows desktop computer as an interactive user (the one sitting at the keyboard), through a feature called Switch Users, but only one person at a time can physically use that Windows desktop computer's mouse, keyboard, and display. Typically, only one interactive user uses a desktop computer. Therefore, most users have little or no experience managing local accounts other than their own, and those same users rarely need to make any changes to their own account. This section gives you a chance to create and manage a local user account.

User Accounts Applet

The primary tool for administering local user accounts is User Accounts, a Control Panel applet shown in Figure 4-30. Either browse to it from Start | Control Panel or enter "user accounts" in the Start menu Search box and select User Accounts from the list of results. In the example shown here, the user Yoda is an Administrator and the account is password protected.

Working with User Accounts in Windows

You must log on with an account that is a member of the Administrators group to see all the local user accounts on your computer. Then open User Accounts and click Manage Another Account. The Manage Accounts window, shown in Figure 4-31, will show the existing accounts. In the example shown there are only two accounts: Yoda and Guest; the Guest account is disabled, which is the default for this account.

FIGURE 4–30 The User Accounts Control Panel.
Source: Microsoft Corporation

Windows 7 also has a local account built in named Administrator, disabled by default during a clean installation or an upgrade. The exception to this is when you upgrade a Windows Vista installation that only has the Administrator and has no other active local account that is a member of the local Administrators group, which would be a rare occurrence. In that case, the local Administrator account is enabled, so it would be visible in Local Users when an administrator selects Manage Another Account.

When you are performing an upgrade to Windows 7 on a Vista PC in a Microsoft Active Directory Domain, it will disable the local Administrator account regardless of the contents of the local accounts database. You can enable this account after installation, but we strongly recommend that you not do it because *this* account is all-powerful and immune to the User Account Control (UAC) security feature, whereas other accounts that are simply members of the local Administrators group are not immune to UAC.

Therefore, while the built-in Administrator account is logged on, the computer is more vulnerable to a malware attack. So, it's good practice to not enable the Administrator account for everyday use, as you may never need this account.

User Account Control

Recall from Chapter 2 that User Account Control (UAC), introduced in Windows Vista and improved in Windows 7, is designed to protect the computer from having malware installed. In Vista or Windows 7, even if you log on as an Administrator, UAC will inform you that a program is trying to perform something for which it needs elevated permissions (administrator).

Windows 7 has eliminated many of the events that would have triggered a UAC prompt in Windows Vista. For instance, if you are logged on with an Administrator type account, you will not see the Consent Prompt appear for certain advanced administrative tasks, such as opening the User Account Control Settings window. A Standard user will need to provide credentials.

FIGURE 4–31 The Manage Accounts window shows existing accounts.
Source: Microsoft Corporation

Step-by-Step 4.05

Creating a New Account in Windows 7

In this step-by-step exercise, you will create a new Standard user account. To complete this exercise, you will need the following:

- A computer or virtual machine with Windows 7 installed.
- Be prepared to log on using an Administrator account (not necessarily *the* Administrator account).

Step 1

Click Start | Control Panel | User Accounts and Family Safety | User Accounts. In the User Accounts window, click Manage Another Account. | Create a New Account. Enter a name for the account, read the descriptions of the Standard user and Administrator user account types, but leave Standard user selected and click Create Account.

Source: Microsoft Corporation

Step 2

The Manage Accounts window opens with the new user added.

Step 3

The new account does not have a password. To password protect the account, you can either allow the user to log on and create a password, or you (as an Administrator) can create a password that the user will need to use when logging on. To create a password for this account, double-click on the account icon and click Create a Password.

Step 4

In the Create Password window, enter the new password twice in the New password and Confirm new password boxes. It is optional to enter a password hint, and we recommend you do that. Then click the Create Password button.

Step 5

The new user account appears in User Accounts as a Standard user account and is password protected. Close all open windows. Notice the other changes you can make to this account. When you are finished, close User Accounts.

Local Security for Files and Folders

Windows 7 supports the use of permissions to protect files and folders on local NTFS volumes. Additionally, it offers encryption on NTFS volumes, allowing you to turn on encryption for a folder, as described in Chapter 2. In this section, we will look at applying permissions on local NTFS volumes.

File and Folder Permissions

The NTFS file system allows you to control who has access to specified files and folders by assigning permissions. These permissions restrict access to local users and groups as well as to those who connect to these resources over the network. However, in the case of those connecting over a network, the share permissions (not related to NTFS permissions) take effect first and may block access to the underlying files and folders. Only NTFS volumes allow you to assign permissions to files and folders directly. In this section, we will focus on the security features of NTFS, including file and folder permissions.

On a volume formatted with the NTFS file system, each folder and file has a set of security permissions associated with it using the following mechanism. Each file and folder on an NTFS volume has an associated Access Control List (ACL), which is a table of users and/or groups and their permissions to access the file or folder. Each ACL has at least one Access Control Entry (ACE), which is like a record in this tiny ACL database that contains just one user or group account name and the permissions assigned to this account for that file or folder. An administrator, or someone with Full Control permission for the file or folder, creates the ACEs.

To view the ACEs in an ACL for a file or folder, open the Properties dialog box and select the Security tab. Figure 4–32 shows the Security page for a folder named

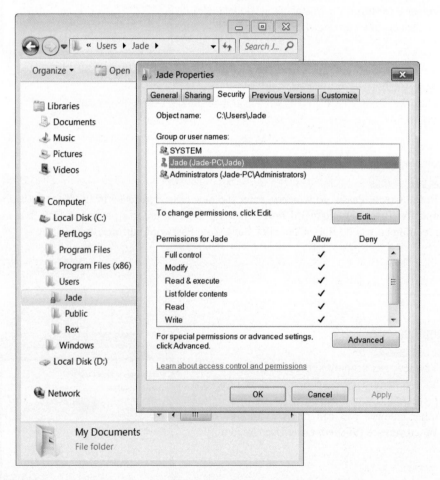

FIGURE 4–32 The list of permissions Windows creates on a user's personal folder.
Source: Microsoft Corporation

Jade, which is the top-level personal folder automatically created by Windows the first time the user Jade logged on. Notice the list of permissions for the user Jade. This is an ACE. These are the default permissions set by Windows on the user's personal folders.

Change the permissions on a folder or file by opening its Security page and clicking the Edit button to reveal the page shown in Figure 4-33, where you can add a user or group, remove a user or group, and specify the permissions assigned to the file or folder for each user or group. Table 4-4 compares the standard permissions on folders versus those on files.

These permissions apply to files and folders on an NTFS volume and protect those resources from both locally logged-on users and those who may connect over a network. Windows only assigns network shares to folders, so you must assign the permissions to the shared folder. This entirely different set of permissions is applied before a network user accesses the NTFS folder and file permissions. We will explore sharing files on a network and setting share permissions in Chapter 10.

NTFS Permission Inheritance

The folders and files on a volume are in a hierarchy, with the drive itself at the top, followed by the root folder and subfolders. Every subfolder and its contents inherits these permissions. If you wish one of the subfolders to have different permissions, you must first navigate to it and open its Properties dialog to explicitly set those permissions on the Security page. When you view permissions on a file or folder, the permissions inherited from the parent are visible but unavailable, as shown in Figure 4-34 by the gray checks and lack of boxes, and you will not be able to modify those permissions at that level. New permissions can be assigned, but inherited permissions cannot be altered. You can modify them in the folder in which they originated or you can choose to block inheritance on a folder or file to which you wish to assign different (usually more restrictive) permissions. To do this, you must access the Advanced Security Settings, then click the Change Permissions button, and deselect the check box labeled Include inheritable permissions from this object's parent.

BitLocker Drive Encryption

If you have very high security needs and have either the Ultimate or Enterprise version of Windows Vista or Windows 7, consider enabling BitLocker Drive Encryption. Microsoft introduced it in Windows Vista as an optional feature for encrypting only the drive on which the Windows OS resides. It was enhanced in Windows 7 to include drives beyond the system drive, including internal hard drives and externally attached drives. This last feature is called BitLocker To Go.

FIGURE 4–33 Modify the permissions for the folder named Jade.
Source: Microsoft Corporation

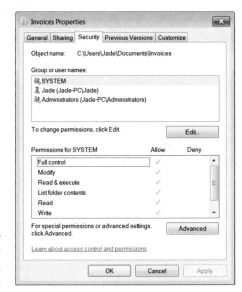

FIGURE 4–34 Inherited permissions are grayed out.
Source: Microsoft Corporation

TABLE 4–4 Comparison of Folder and File Standard Permissions	
Standard Folder Permissions	**Standard File Permissions**
Full control	Full control
Modify	Modify
Read and execute	Read and execute
Read	Read
Write	Write
List folder contents	

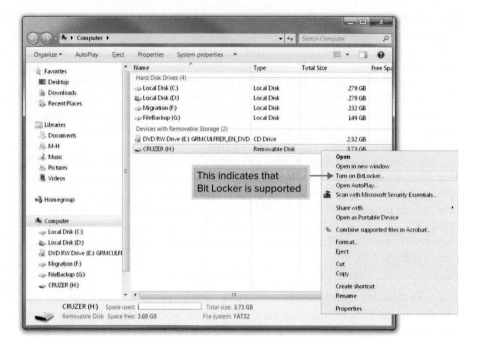

FIGURE 4–35 Right-click a drive and look for the option Turn on BitLocker.
Source: Microsoft Corporation

BitLocker is off by default. When you enable it, BitLocker encrypts the entire contents of a drive, storing an encryption and decryption key in a hardware device that is separate from the encrypted hard disk. To do this, the computer must have either a chip with Trusted Platform Module (TPM) version 1.2 or higher or a removable USB memory device (a USB flash drive will do). When you use TPM, the drive and computer are married because the chip resides in the computer.

To encrypt the drive on which Windows is installed, BitLocker requires a hard drive with at least two partitions: one that contains Windows (the "system" partition), and a second partition (the "boot" partition) created by BitLocker and not directly usable by the user. When you perform a clean installation of Windows 7, it creates the hidden boot partition. This partition is critical to booting up your computer, and without it Windows cannot be started from the encrypted partition.

In Windows 7, when you wish to encrypt a drive—either internal or external—you simply open Windows Explorer, right-click a drive, and select BitLocker from the context menu, as shown in Figure 4-35. The existence of this choice on the menu indicates that the selected drive supports BitLocker.

BitLocker To Go may be the BitLocker feature most ordinary folks will use because many people carry flash drives, and when they have confidential information, such as medical records, it is important to protect that data. However, you will only be able to access the data on the drive on the computer on which you encrypted it or on a computer where you can make the keys available, which is limited to computers running Windows 7 or newer.

The tool for managing BitLocker for all your drives is the BitLocker Drive Encryption Control Panel shown in Figure 4-36. Notice the lock and key on the encrypted drive, named Cruzer.

try this!

View the BitLocker Status of All Drives at Once

Quickly view and manage the BitLocker status of your drives on a Windows 7 computer. Try this:

1. Enter "bitlocker" in the Start | Search box, and select BitLocker Drive Encryption from the results.
2. Click the link labeled TPM Administration to see if your computer supports TPM.
3. If you have a flash drive and have permission to do so, insert it into your computer and turn on BitLocker for that drive.

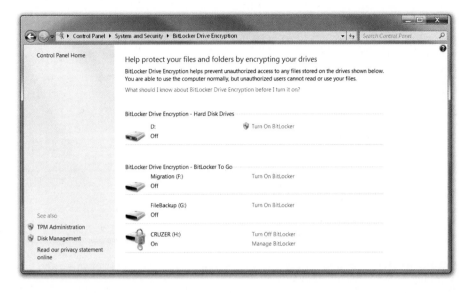

FIGURE 4–36 BitLocker is turned on for Drive H:.
Source: Microsoft Corporation

Once you encrypt a drive with BitLocker, Manage BitLocker becomes a choice on the context menu for that drive in Windows Explorer, so you can access the management options for the drive from either location. Open the BitLocker Drive Encryption Control Panel by entering "manage bitlocker" in the Start menu's Search box or from within the main Control Panel window.

Windows Defender

The version of Windows Defender included with Windows 7 only protects against spyware. To see if Windows Defender is running on your computer click Start, type "defender," and select Windows Defender from the results list. If you see the message shown in Figure 4-37, Windows Defender is off, and if no other security software enabled, click the link "Click here to turn it on." However, if you have Microsoft Security Essentials, or almost any full-featured third-party security software installed, it will include antispyware software, and you will not need Windows Defender.

Microsoft Security Essentials

Microsoft Security Essentials (MSE) offers much broader real-time protection against malware as well as scheduled scans. MSE is available for Windows 7 and earlier versions as a free download from Microsoft. When you install MSE, Windows Defender is disabled because it is not necessary. Recently, when we connected to the Microsoft site for the free download, we were directed to a page that guided us through the installation of free antivirus from Microsoft and the selection of recommended settings.

Windows Firewall

Most security software suites come with a personal firewall. Windows Firewall has been a feature of Windows since Windows XP Service Pack 2. Each newer version of Windows has added its own enhancements to this personal firewall. So there is really no excuse for not using a personal firewall on your PC.

To open the Windows Firewall type "windows firewall" into the Start Search box and select it from the results. The example shown in Figure 4-38 is on a computer connected to a private network. Notice that it shows we are not connected

FIGURE 4–37 Windows Defender is turned off.
Source: Microsoft Corporation

FIGURE 4-38 On this page "Public networks" refers to public Wi-Fi networks and other untrusted public networks.
Source: Microsoft Corporation

to a public network, which refers to an open Wi-Fi network like you would encounter if you used your laptop in an airport terminal or at your favorite coffee shop. The computer in question actually is connected to the biggest public network in the world—the Internet—but a firewall on a router guards our connection to the Internet.

Chapter 4 REVIEW

Chapter Summary

After reading this chapter and completing the Step-by-Step tutorials and Try This! exercises, you should understand the following facts about Windows 7.

Installing Windows 7

- The Windows 7 system requirements are nearly identical to the requirements for Windows Vista.
- As with earlier versions, Windows 7 is bundled as several products called editions—each with a set of features. Windows 7 has three retail editions: Home Premium, Professional, and Ultimate.
- You cannot directly upgrade Windows XP to Windows 7, and the ability to upgrade from Windows Vista to Windows 7 depends on the editions involved in the upgrade—both for Windows Vista and for Windows 7.
- You must decide on the type of installation: upgrade, multiboot, or clean installation. You achieve the latter two by using the Custom option in the Windows setup program.
- Retail editions of Windows must be activated, a process that confirms you are using a legal product, not a pirated copy.

- Decide how you want the Windows Update program to download and install updates because Windows 7 setup will query you about this.
- Unless you are doing an in-place installation to Windows 7, run a program, such as Windows Easy Transfer (WET) in the old installation to gather the settings and data you want to transfer to your new Windows installation. Then, after installing Windows 7, run the WET utility from the new installation to complete the transfer.
- The Windows 7 setup program runs a special scaled-down Windows OS, Windows PE.
- Immediately after installing Windows, verify network access, install security software, and finish updating Windows. If you installed Windows into a VM, do the same tasks, but also run the virtual machine additions for the hypervisor.

Windows 7 Features

- The Windows 7 desktop is enhanced with such features as Jump Lists and pinning.

- Windows 7 supports several file systems: FAT, exFAT, NTFS, and file systems for optical discs.
- Security features such as User Account Control, BitLocker, and Windows Defender are improved in Windows 7, and BitLocker To Go and AppLocker have been added.
- If an old app does not run in Windows 7, first use the Program Compatibility Troubleshooter. If it does not solve the problem, download and install Windows XP Mode and test the old app in that VM.
- Windows 7 has enhanced or added new recovery tools, including Startup Repair, System Restore, System Image Recovery, and Windows Memory Diagnostic Tool.

Customizing and Managing Windows 7

- Familiarize yourself with the tools in the Computer Management console, especially the Disk Management node, which will allow you to perform a variety of tasks on disks.
- If necessary, adjust the display resolution, and change the text and object size.
- If a computer has multiple displays, use the Display Resolution control panel to configure the displays for the way the user will use them.
- Install and uninstall a program using the program's own installation program. Some programs do not come with an uninstall option. In that case, use the Programs applet in the Control Panel to uninstall the program.
- Turn Windows features on and off in the Control Panel Programs applet.
- During installation, Windows creates a default folder hierarchy into which it installs operating system files and program files.
- The first time a user logs on, Windows creates the user's personal folders under the Users folder at the root of the drive on which Windows installed. If this is an NTFS volume, Windows will set permissions for the user's personal folders.

- Libraries appear to be folders when viewed in Windows Explorer, but a library is not a folder—it is an object that keeps track of one or more locations where certain folders and files are stored.
- If you burn an optical disc with the Mastered format you will be able to use it in a conventional CD or DVD player, or in older Apple Macs or PCs, but the burn process for this format requires hard drive space to temporarily store the files before burning to disc.
- If you burn an optical disc with the Live File System you will be able to directly copy items to the drive without requiring extra hard drive space. You can also add files to a disc formatted with the Live File System.

Managing Local Security in Windows 7

- Local user accounts reside in the local accounts database on a Windows computer, and the User Account Control Panel applet is the primary tool for managing these accounts.
- You must log on as an Administrator to see all the local user accounts on your computer.
- User Account Control (UAC) has been improved in Windows 7 with fewer events that trigger UAC prompts.
- As with previous versions, Windows 7 supports the use of permissions on local NTFS volumes, as well as folder encryption.
- Each folder and file on an NTFS volume has a set of security permissions, Access Control Entries (ACEs), stored in an Access Control List (ACL). These permissions are inherited through the folder hierarchy.
- BitLocker Drive Encryption in Windows Vista can only encrypt the boot volume (the volume on which Windows resides). In Windows 7, it can encrypt other disk volumes, as well as external disks. This last feature is called BitLocker To Go.
- Windows Defender is a built-in antispam utility. Microsoft Security Essentials (MSE) is a broader antimalware program that is free from Microsoft. Windows Firewall is a personal firewall that comes with Windows.

Key Terms List

Access Control Entry (ACE) *(150)*

Access Control List (ACL) *(150)*

Action Center *(130)*

activation *(116)*

Add Printer wizard *(140)*

Aero Peek *(126)*

Aero Shake *(126)*

Aero Snap *(126)*

AppLocker *(132)*

BitLocker *(132)*

BitLocker To Go *(132)*

clean installation *(116)*

dual-boot *(115)*

FAT file systems *(131)*

Flip 3D *(126)*

gadget *(138)*

image *(116)*

Jump List *(127)*

library *(130)*

Live File System *(145)*

local security *(147)*

Mastered *(145)*

master file table (MFT) *(131)*

Microsoft Product Activation (MPA) *(116)*

Microsoft Security Essentials (MSE) (123)

multiboot (115)

personal folders (142)

pinning (127)

Program Compatibility
   Troubleshooter (132)

restore point (133)

shortcut (125)

Startup Repair (133)

System Image Recovery (133)

System Restore (133)

Task Manager (133)

upgrade (115)

Windows Aero (125)

Windows Defender (132)

Windows Easy Transfer (WET) (117)

Windows Explorer (143)

Windows Memory Diagnostic Tool (134)

Windows Preinstallation Environment
   (Windows PE) (118)

Windows Update (117)

Key Terms Quiz

Use the Key Terms List to complete the sentences that follow:

1. To preserve your installed programs and settings in place, install a new version of Windows as a/an _____.

2. Each file or folder on an NTFS volume has a/an _____ associated with it, containing security permissions.

3. _____ is a feature that lets you switch through your open windows as if they were a stack of cards or photos.

4. A/an _____ folder contains pointers to multiple locations on your computer and network, displaying the contents as if they were all stored in a single location.

5. _____ is a scaled-down Windows operating system that supports the Windows setup GUI.

6. The _____ feature allows you to temporarily make all open windows transparent when you hover your mouse over the Show Desktop button.

7. A/an _____ is a snapshot of Windows, its configuration, and all installed programs.

8. _____ is a Windows tool that has been greatly improved from version to version; it allows you to see the state of individual processes and programs running on a computer, and to stop programs, if needed.

9. _____ is a new feature in Windows 7 that allows you to encrypt a removable drive.

10. When you right-click on a program shortcut on the Windows 7 Start menu or taskbar, a _____ displays containing recently opened items and items you may have pinned there.

Multiple-Choice Quiz

1. What *retail* edition of Windows 7 includes BitLocker?
   a. Enterprise
   b. Home Basic
   c. Home Premium
   d. Professional
   e. Ultimate

2. What is the name for the desktop feature in Windows 7 that allows you to quickly minimize all but the current window with a simple mouse movement?
   a. Aero Snap
   b. Flip 3D
   c. Aero Shake
   d. AppLocker
   e. UAC

3. This Windows 7 feature requires a video card that supports (at minimum) DirectX 9.0 and Shader Model 2.0.
   a. BitLocker
   b. Windows Aero
   c. Instant Search
   d. Windows Defender
   e. Windows XP Mode

4. What alternative term correctly describes an upgrade of an operating system?
   a. Clean installation
   b. In-place installation
   c. Multiboot
   d. Optional installation
   e. Managed installation

5. After you complete a multiboot installation, you will see this special menu at every restart.
   a. Select OS
   b. F8
   c. System
   d. Windows Boot Manager
   e. Computer Management

6. You have Windows Vista Ultimate edition and want to upgrade to Windows 7. Which of the following editions would you select for an in-place installation of Windows 7?
   a. Ultimate
   b. Home Premium
   c. Home Basic
   d. Enterprise
   e. Business

7. What installation type should you choose in Windows setup if you want to do either a multiboot or a clean installation?
   a. Upgrade
   b. Custom
   c. Dual-boot
   d. In-place
   e. Advanced

8. The Disk Management node exists in this console utility.
   a. Administrative Tools
   b. Control Panel
   c. Windows Explorer
   d. Computer Management
   e. System and Security

9. If you are setting up a multimonitor system, which Display option will let you put different windows and other objects on each multiple display, giving you more work space?
   a. Landscape
   b. Extend these displays
   c. Show desktop only on 1
   d. Duplicate these displays
   e. The recommended resolution

10. What feature of Windows is represented in the taskbar notification area by a small flag icon?
    a. AppLocker
    b. System Restore
    c. Action Center
    d. Task Manager
    e. BitLocker

11. What new feature of Windows 7 appears to be something it isn't, but allows you to organize and work with data from various locations as if they were together in one place?
    a. Windows Aero
    b. BitLocker To Go

c. Library
d. Notification Area
e. Instant Search

12. What all-powerful user account built into Windows is disabled by default?
    a. Administrator
    b. Standard
    c. Local
    d. Guest
    e. Parental

13. During Windows setup one account is created for the user of that computer, and you provide a name and password for it. What type of account is this?
    a. Standard
    b. Administrator
    c. Parental
    d. Local
    e. Guest

14. What is the term used in the Windows Firewall Control Panel in Windows 7 to refer to Wi-Fi networks at coffee shops and other retail locations?
    a. Private networks
    b. Work networks
    c. Home networks
    d. Public networks
    e. Internetworks

15. What antispyware program comes bundled with Windows 7?
    a. Microsoft Security Essentials
    b. UAC
    c. BitLocker
    d. BitLocker To Go
    e. Windows Defender

Essay Quiz

1. Describe Flip 3D, including what it does and how to use it.

2. Your Windows XP computer is more than adequate for Windows 7. You would like to do a clean installation of Windows 7, discarding your old Windows XP installation, but you researched the hardware and software and you found that while all the hardware is compatible, one critical old application is incompatible and will not run in Windows 7. What is your best option for continuing to use this old application on a Windows 7 computer until you find a compatible replacement? Describe both the best solution and one other option, including the type of installation of Windows 7 required for each, and any other requirements beyond the minimums.

3. Windows setup now includes updating Windows. Does the inclusion of this step mean that you will not have to update immediately after installing Windows? Your answer must be more than a yes or no. Include why your answer is true.

4. A technician added a second display to your Windows 7 PC. After you log in the first time using the dual displays, you notice that the taskbar is on the right display. You prefer it on the left. Describe the steps you would take to place the taskbar on the left display.

5. Describe how UAC works to protect your computer from malware.

Lab Projects

LAB PROJECT 4.1

Using a computer with Windows 7 installed, open an app, pin the app to the taskbar, and repeat this for the three or four apps you use the most. Close all the apps, and then open each again from the pinned shortcut on the taskbar. Open two or more files in each app so that the file names appear on the Jump List for each app. Write a few sentences about how this did or didn't work for you compared to launching these apps from the Start menu.

LAB PROJECT 4.2

How successful is Windows 7? What is the latest information on the global operating system market share for Windows 7? Is Windows 7 more successful or less successful than Windows XP? How has Windows 10 affected the use of Windows 7? Research the answers to these questions and write about your findings.

LAB PROJECT 4.3

Use the Internet to research the conditions under which you read a flash drive on a Windows XP PC after the flash drive has been encrypted with BitLocker To Go on a Windows 7 computer, then test it: Prepare the flash drive as necessary. Copy data onto the flash drive. Then use BitLocker To Go to encrypt the drive, using the option to create a password (be sure to remember the password). Then take the flash drive to a Windows XP computer and insert the drive. Are you prompted to supply a password? Are you able to access the data on the drive? Describe how you prepared the flash drive and the results.

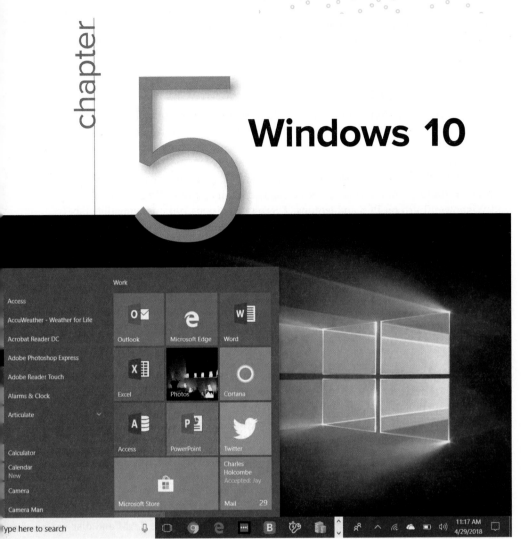

chapter

5 Windows 10

Learning Outcomes

In this chapter, you will learn how to:

LO **5.1** Select a Windows 10 edition and the method of installation, and then install and configure Windows 10 on a laptop or PC.

LO **5.2** Perform appropriate postinstallation tasks to prepare Windows 10 for everyday use.

LO **5.3** Practice working with the new features of the Windows 10 GUI.

LO **5.4** Configure local security in Windows 10.

Source: Microsoft Corporation

Windows 10 was released in July 2015 as a cross-platform OS, designed to give the user the same UI across all their devices—PCs, laptops, tablets, and smartphones. Windows 10 may be the last official Windows version, as Microsoft has stated that they will continually upgrade and add features to this OS rather than release separate versions at intervals as they have done over the past 30 years. Keep in mind as you progress through this chapter that what is true today may not be true by the time you read this book. We hope to get you started with the basics of the operating system so you can continue to learn and use new features as they appear in Windows on your devices. ✻

LO 5.1 | Installing Windows 10

Perhaps you plan to purchase a new computer with Windows 10 preinstalled, or like many of us, you might decide to upgrade the operating system on your existing Windows PC or laptop.

In any event, you need to decide which edition of Windows 10 you will use and how to migrate data from your old computer or installation of Windows to Windows 10. Additionally, you may want all your old settings to apply in the new installation. Therefore, we begin by describing the Windows 10 editions, move on to reviewing the system requirements for this new OS, and then consider how you might upgrade from

Windows 7 or Windows 8. Before installing Windows 10, decide how to sign in to the OS and take some necessary steps before installing it onto an older computer. After all this preparation, install Windows 10.

Windows 10 Editions

Note: Another edition, Windows 10 IoT Core, comes preinstalled on small, inexpensive mobile devices that fall into the Internet of Things (IoT) category.

Windows 10 comes in several editions. The Education Edition—for school staff, administrators, teachers, and students—is only available through academic Volume Licensing. And Microsoft has multiple levels of Enterprise Editions, also only available through Volume Licensing.

Retail Editions are available to any individual. The remainder of this chapter describes installing, configuring, and securing two retail editions: Windows 10 Home and Windows 10 Pro on PCs and laptops. These two editions run on compatible tablets. Table 5–1 compares selected features of these two editions.

Windows 10 Home

Windows 10 Home Edition runs on PCs, laptops, and tablets and is aimed at consumers who do not need some of the premium features of Windows 10 Pro. Owners of PCs or tablets with Windows 7 Home Basic, Windows 7 Home Premium, or the "basic" edition of Windows 8.*x* were able to upgrade to this edition for free for a year after the July 29, 2015, launch of Windows 10.

Windows 10 Pro

Note: In 2017, Microsoft introduced another edition, Windows 10 S. We have chosen not to discuss this edition because by 2018, we could not find any manufacturer who sold computers with this preinstalled, and it was not adopted by a significant number of people.

Windows 10 Pro runs on PCs, laptops, and tablets. It is equivalent to the Windows 8.*x* Pro, Windows 7 Professional, and Windows 7 Ultimate that offer features required for businesses, such as those described in Table 5–1. Users running any of these systems, with appropriate updates, could upgrade for free for a year after the July 29, 2015, Windows 10 launch.

System Requirements

The minimum hardware requirements to install Windows 10 on an Intel- or AMD-architecture computer are very modest, and you will want much more RAM and disk space than the minimum described if you plan to install several programs and store

TABLE 5–1 Comparison of Selected Features in the Windows 10 Retail Editions for PCs and Laptops

Features	Windows 10 Home	Windows 10 Pro
Maximum physical RAM memory	4 GB in 32-bit OS 128 GB in 64-bit OS	4 GB in 32-bit OS 512 GB in 64-bit OS
BitLocker & BitLocker To Go		✓
Continuum	✓	✓
Cortana personal digital assistant	✓	✓
Domain Join support for joining a Windows domain		✓
Encrypting File System (EFS) on NTFS volumes		✓
Group Policy Management for Windows domain		✓
Hyper-V client	✓	✓
Hyper-V host (64-bit OS only)		✓
Microsoft Edge Web Browser	✓	✓
Windows Apps	✓	✓
Virtual Desktops	✓	✓
Windows Hello biometric login	✓	✓
Works on PCs, tablets, and laptops	✓	✓

data locally. Fortunately, even today's budget-level computers come with hardware that far exceeds the requirements for Windows 10, so we do not expect you to have a problem with the minimum requirements. Having said all that, here are the minimum system requirements:

- 1-GHz or faster processor or a 1-GHz system on a chip (SoC) (such as in a mobile device)
- Minimum 1-GB RAM for 32-bit Windows 10 or 2-GB RAM for 64-bit Windows 10
- 16 GB available hard disk space for 32-bit Windows 10; 20 GB for 64-bit Windows 10
- DirectX 9 graphics device with Windows Display Driver Model (WDDM) 1.0
- 1,024 × 600 minimum screen resolution (1,366 × 768 recommended)
- Internet access

Further, a multitouch-capable touchscreen, touchpad, or touch mouse is required if you wish to take advantage of Windows 10's multitouch support that senses several simultaneous touch gestures.

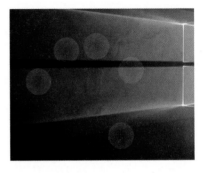

A touch screen on a Windows 10 PC showing the author's five simultaneous touches.
Source: Microsoft Corporation

Upgrading to Windows 10

Upgrading to Windows 10 is an easy decision for many—both because it is (or was) free (see below) and because the system requirements are modest. The actual upgrade installation is also smoother and faster than for previous versions. In this section, we discuss the free upgrade and what versions of Windows and which editions (free or not) you could upgrade to Windows 10.

Free Upgrade to Windows 10

Windows 10 was released July 29, 2015, and for a period of one year after that date it was a free upgrade for many existing installations of legally licensed and updated Windows 7 and Windows 8.1. A Windows 7 computer required Service Pack 1 (SP1) installed to qualify for the free upgrade to Windows 10. A Windows 8 computer had to have Windows 8.1 Update 1 installed. A qualifying computer also had to have Windows Update configured to download and install updates automatically.

Beginning in late spring of 2015, users with qualifying Windows 7 and Windows 8.1 systems noticed a new Windows logo icon near the right side of their taskbars. Hovering the mouse over this icon showed that it was titled Get Windows 10. Clicking on this icon opened a wizard, shown in Figure 5-1, which checked the system for compatibility and allowed you to reserve your free upgrade.

This reservation had to be made before July 29, 2015. Once you reserved an upgrade, Windows Update would then quietly download the upgrade to your system. Then, beginning on July 29, 2015, people who had made a reservation were notified that their free Windows 10 was available to install. This was done via a pop-up message over the Get Windows 10 icon. When you clicked on that message icon, the installation would begin from the files previously downloaded.

Those who upgraded during this one-year period had the added benefit of free continued security updates as well as other feature and functionality updates to Windows 10 *for the supported lifetime of the device.*

Some computers that would otherwise qualify, but were Domain Joined (members of a Windows domain), could not be upgraded while online. They had to upgrade using an ISO image file. The Get Windows 10 wizard and the setup program both check that a Windows installation is legally licensed, but you can also check for yourself. To do that in either Windows 7 or Windows 8.1, open the Control Panel System applet and look on the bottom of the page for the words "Windows is activated." It's as easy as that! Figure 5-2 shows the System applet in Windows 8.1 Pro.

The Get Windows icon displayed on the Windows 8.1 taskbar.
Source: Microsoft Corporation

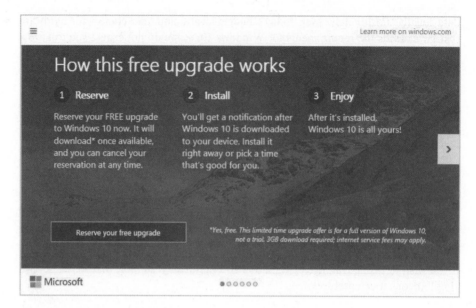

FIGURE 5–1 The Get Windows 10 wizard as it appeared before the user reserved an upgrade.
Source: Microsoft Corporation

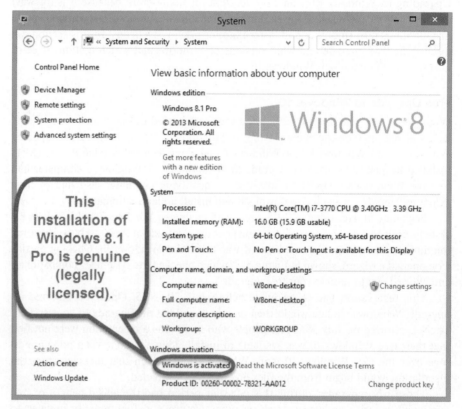

FIGURE 5–2 Use the Control Panel System applet to confirm that an installation of Windows is genuine.
Source: Microsoft Corporation

Upgrading Editions

To upgrade an existing installation of Windows to Windows 10, the old version must be Windows 7 Service Pack 1 (SP1) or Windows 8.1 Update 1. However, it is important to understand which editions of each are directly upgradable, and to which Windows 10 editions. Table 5-2 shows the upgrade paths for Windows 7 SP1 to Windows 10, and Table 5-3 describes the upgrade paths from Windows 8.1 Update 1 to Windows 10.

TABLE 5–2	Upgrade Paths from Windows 7 (with Service Pack 1) to Windows 10 Retail Editions	
From	**To**	
Windows 7 Starter	Windows 10 Home	
Windows 7 Home Basic		
Windows 7 Home Premium		
Windows 7 Professional	Windows 10 Pro	
Windows 7 Ultimate		

TABLE 5–3	Upgrade Paths from Windows 8.1 Update 1 to Windows 10 Retail Versions	
From	**To**	
Windows 8.1	Windows 10 Home	
Windows 8.1 with Bing		
Windows 8.1 Pro	Windows 10 Pro	
Windows 8.1 Pro for Students		

The Downside to Upgrading

When upgrading an existing system to Windows 10, some features are removed. You should understand this ahead of time and consider if these are features you will miss. For instance, Windows Media Center is removed by Windows 10 Setup. While Media Center was included in certain editions of Windows 7, it was a feature you would have paid for if you added it to Windows 8 or 8.1. Here is as a list of those features that we know are removed, along with a few remarks:

- Windows Virtual PC with Windows XP Mode
- Windows Media Center
- Windows 7 Desktop gadgets
- The ability to disable automatic Windows Update for Windows 10 Home
- Solitaire, Minesweeper, and Hearts games (Setup installs a new version of Solitaire. Minesweeper is a free app at the Windows Store. Several non-Microsoft versions of Hearts are also free.)
- Support for USB floppy drive driver (if present) will be removed.
- The Windows Live Essentials OneDrive app (Rather than being a separate app, in Windows 10 OneDrive is integrated into File Explorer.)

Preparing to Install Windows 10

Before installing any operating system, there are preparation tasks—some requiring simple decisions, others requiring action beforehand.

Update Windows 7, Windows 8, or Windows 8.1

Before you upgraded a computer to Windows 7, you could connect to the Microsoft site and run the Windows 7 Upgrade Advisor to determine if your existing hardware, drivers, and software were compatible with the new OS. Similarly, when preparing to upgrade to Windows 8 or 8.1, you could connect and run the Windows 8 Upgrade Assistant for the same type of evaluation of your system. For Windows 10, Microsoft does a similar test, currently available through the Get Windows 10 app installed by Windows Update.

WARNING!

Beware of scams involving phone calls or emails claiming to be from Microsoft. Microsoft does not phone or email customers to inform them of the Windows 10 upgrade or to ask for personal information. After Windows 10 was introduced, people received phone calls and emails claiming to be from Microsoft. These were bogus. The phone calls involved a variety of phishing scams, and the email messages contained links or downloads that could install malware.

First ensure that you have one of the upgradable Windows versions and editions described in Table 5–2 or Table 5–3. Then open Windows Update and ensure that your Windows 7 or Windows 8.1 installation is up to date. Only then will you be able to run the Get Windows 10 app to determine if your hardware, installed drivers, and software are compatible with Windows 10.

Back Up Your Data

If you are doing an in-place upgrade, your data and settings will be preserved, but you should still back up any important data stored on that computer before upgrading. If, like many people, you save your data to the cloud using a file-storage service, such as Dropbox or Microsoft's OneDrive, then you may consider that file storage to be your backup. Or you may use a cloud-based backup service that is separate from the cloud-based file-storage service you use for saving your working files.

As an example, Jane had Windows 8.1 Pro on her primary work PC. She did and still does store data from recent and current projects—both personal and business—on Microsoft's OneDrive, and has archives of past projects stored offline. Therefore, with a copy of the archive elsewhere, she could skip doing a local backup and restore the archive from the backup.

Update Firmware

If you are planning to use an existing computer with a functioning operating system installed, we suggest a rather advanced task for those who don't mind challenges: Update the system firmware while the previous OS is intact. This is especially important on a computer that is several years old because a firmware update may make the difference between using all the computer's features with the new version of Windows versus experiencing instability problems, such as the system hanging up when you try to shut down. Some manufacturers install update-manager software that checks for and downloads drivers and firmware, in which case, your system may be up to date. Otherwise, you may need to do a little searching for the computer model on the computer manufacturer's site to see if there are any firmware updates for that model. Then, follow the manufacturer's instructions for updating the firmware.

Acquire Updated Drivers

As with firmware updates, your existing computer may have a utility installed by the manufacturer that checks for updates to the system drivers for that model computer. Over time, these utilities have morphed into full-blown marketing apps for the manufacturer, but the updating function is useful because it may ensure that you have the latest drivers for the installed OS, and they may be acceptable to Windows 10. Windows 10 Setup will check your system to ensure that it has current device drivers. If Windows 10 does not have new drivers and the previously installed drivers are incompatible, Setup may install a generic driver, providing there is a reasonably compatible driver. If Setup issues an error message, you may need to acquire an updated Windows 10 driver. Alternatively, if Setup installed a generic driver, you may still need to install an updated driver from the manufacturer to take advantage of all of a device's features.

Microsoft Product Activation

Microsoft Product Activation (MPA) is an antipiracy tool that ensures you are using your software per the software license. One important change in the Windows 10 activation process is that you do not have to manually enter an alphanumeric string of characters called a product key during activation because Windows 10 comes "pre-keyed" and will automatically provide the key to Microsoft during the activation process. The product key only works with one instance of the Windows 10 product.

If there is no Internet connection, it will try to activate the product key once the computer is connected. If it fails to activate after several tries, a message will display with instructions on how to manually activate the product—usually via telephone.

Choose How to Sign In to Windows 10

Decide ahead of time how you will sign in to Windows 10. Your choices are to sign in to Windows 10 with (1) a local account that exists only on the Windows 10 computer, (2) a Microsoft account, or (3) a Windows Active Directory account if your computer is a member of a Windows Active Directory domain (at work or school).

Signing In with a Local Account. When you install Windows it creates a local account, but in Windows 8 or 8.1 and Windows 10 you can sign in using either a local account or a Microsoft account. If you use a local account, it only gives you access to local resources; you will need to sign in separately to any Microsoft services you use. Figure 5–3 shows a Sign-In screen for a local account. This account has not been customized with a picture, which you can do at any time after you install Windows 10.

Signing In with a Microsoft Account. A **Microsoft account (MSA)** is a free account with Microsoft that gives the subscriber access to Microsoft services, such as **Outlook.com**, Messenger, OneDrive, and Xbox LIVE. If you use an MSA, the Sign-In screen will display the name and the email address associated with your MSA. We prefer to use the MSA because this one sign-in gives you access to the local computer as well as to your Microsoft services. Then you can access all your data across other devices and services, and you can synchronize your settings on other Windows 8.1 and Windows 10 devices that use the same sign-in. Learn more about syncing your devices in the section titled *Postinstallation Tasks.*

You can use your existing MSA, create one ahead of time by going to the Microsoft site, or wait and create a new MSA during Windows 10 installation. Figure 5–4 shows the MSA sign-in page for Windows 10.

Signing In with a Domain Account. If your computer is running Windows 10 Pro, Windows 10 Enterprise, or Windows 10 Education, it can join a Microsoft Active Directory Domain (based on Windows Server), and you will be required to sign in

Note: If you do not enter a password when you create a local account, sign in will not require a password, and the Sign-In screen will not show the password box. We strongly recommend that you create a password for your local account unless you are the only person with physical access to your computer.

Note: In Windows 8 and 8.1, Microsoft required a Microsoft account to use certain Modern apps, such as Mail and Calendar. In Windows 10, they pulled back from this stand. For instance, if you wish, you can now use the Mail app without using Microsoft account—perhaps using a Google account.

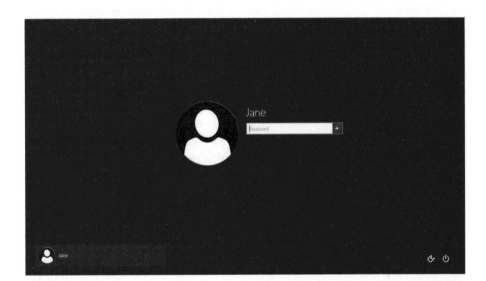

FIGURE 5–3 The initial Sign-In screen for a local account. Personalize it with an image.
Source: Microsoft Corporation

User Name Appears Here
email address appears here

Password

FIGURE 5–4 The Sign-In screen for a Microsoft account, personalized with an image of the authors' pet.
Source: Microsoft Corporation

using a domain user account. In this case, you may not be involved in the installation of Windows or selection of the account at all but have a fully configured computer delivered to your desk. You will then enter your domain credentials, as instructed by a domain administrator.

Prepare to Install into a Virtual Machine

If you have a hypervisor installed on a lab computer and plan to install Windows 10 into a virtual machine, you will need to first create a VM for the installation (as described in Chapter 3), and then ensure that the virtual machine will boot from the drive containing the Windows 10 Setup files. By default, virtual machines in all the hypervisors discussed in Chapter 3 will connect to a computer's physical DVD drive as a virtual DVD drive and can boot from that drive at startup. Therefore, if you have a Windows 10 DVD, insert it into the host computer's DVD drive before starting the VM. At startup, the VM will boot into the Setup program. If the Windows 10 files are in an ISO image file, change the DVD settings for that virtual machine to point to the location of the ISO file before starting the VM, and then restart the VM and follow the prompts.

The Installation

If you purchase Windows 10 online as a full retail product or as an upgrade from Windows 7 or Windows 8.1, you can do either a Web-based install or a more conventional Windows Setup install which you can do from a download from the Microsoft Store or from a USB drive purchased at the Microsoft Store, on-line or at one of the physical store locations. Packaging is shown in Figure 5–5.

Web-Based Setup

Microsoft's online **Web-based setup** is quick and combines the more traditional Windows Setup program with the features of the Windows Upgrade Advisor and the settings and data migration tools described in Chapter 4. Web-based setup requires very little interaction and is very fast. If you select this option, follow the on-screen instructions to install it.

FIGURE 5–5 The Windows 10 retail packaging.
Source: Microsoft Corporation

WARNING!

A clean install will delete anything currently stored on the drive you select for the installation.

Traditional Windows Setup

The traditional Windows Setup is available for Windows 10. To install Windows 10 using this program, you must have the Windows 10 Setup files on bootable media.

Bootable Media. The retail editions of Windows 10 are no longer available directly from Microsoft on DVD.

Purchase Windows 10 online and choose the option "Install later by creating Media," and you will have the option to download to a USB drive or to an ISO file. If you install it to a USB drive, you will have a bootable USB Setup drive.

Choose ISO, and Microsoft will download an ISO image file containing a copy of the entire contents of a disc. After downloading it to a Windows computer, simply double-click the file and the Windows Disc Image Burner dialog will display. Insert a blank disc in your disc drive, click Burn, and it will create the disc.

Beginning Windows Setup. Once you have the media, you can either boot your computer from it (a clean install) or, if upgrading, first sign in to your Windows 7 or Windows 8.1 Update 1 computer and insert the disc. If it does not automatically run setup, open Windows Explorer or File Explorer (⊞+E), browse to the disc, and double-click the Setup file.

Step-by-Step 5.01 will walk you through the steps for a clean install of Windows 10 from bootable media. An upgrade can also be done from bootable media. When you start the installation, the Windows Preinstallation Environment (Windows PE) starts as it did in Windows 7, Windows 8, and Windows 8.1.

Note: Exercise 5.01 requires a computer that can boot from either a USB or a DVD drive. If your computer fails to do this, change the boot order setting in the computer's system settings. The actual steps for doing this vary by manufacturer. For instructions, do an online search using your computer model name and the key words "boot order."

Note: Windows PE was introduced in Chapter 4. It is a scaled-down Windows operating system with basic hardware support for 32-bit and 64-bit programs that is used during Setup and also during certain recovery scenarios.

Installing Windows 10

In this hands-on exercise, you will do a clean installation of Windows 10 from bootable media. To complete this exercise, you will need the following:

- A Microsoft/Intel standard personal computer (desktop or laptop) compatible with Windows 10, with at least the recommended minimum hardware and configured to boot from DVD or other media, and (ideally) an unpartitioned hard disk (disk 0, the first hard disk). Alternatively, you can install into a virtual machine you have prepared before beginning the Windows 10 installation (see Chapter 3 and the section in this chapter titled "Prepare to Install into a Virtual Machine").
- The Windows 10 DVD or other bootable media.
- If you plan on using a local account for sign in, you need to decide on a user name and password for that account.
- If you plan to use a Microsoft account, you need the email address and password for that account. If you do not have one, you can create a Microsoft account during the Setup process.

Step 1

Insert the bootable media containing the Windows 10 installation files and boot the computer. Watch the screen for instructions to boot from the optical or USB drive. A plain black screen will briefly flash, followed by a black screen with the message: "Windows is loading files . . . " while the Windows Preinstallation Environment is loading and starting. The Starting Windows screen signals that Windows PE is starting and will soon load the GUI for Windows 10 setup.

Step 2

On the first Setup screen, select a language, time and currency format, and keyboard or input methods and click Next.

Source: Microsoft Corporation

Step 3

On the next screen, click Install now.

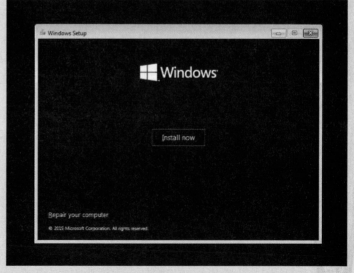

Source: Microsoft Corporation

Step 4

When the license screen appears, read the Microsoft Software License Terms, then click to place a check in the box labeled "I accept the license terms" and click the Next button.

Step 5

On the screen after the license screen you are asked, "Which type of installation do you want?" Select Custom to perform a clean installation.

Source: Microsoft Corporation

Step 6

On the next screen, you select the target drive for the installation. Anything currently stored on the drive you select will be deleted. If Windows 7 or Windows 8 was previously installed on the system on which you are doing a clean installation, this screen will show two partitions on the drive, as shown here. The smaller one is reserved by the operating system. In this case, select the larger of the two partitions and click Next.

If you are installing into a virtual machine or onto a clean hard drive without a previous installation of Windows, there will be only a single partition. Select it and click Next.

Source: Microsoft Corporation

Step 7

Windows 10 Setup will now go through the installation phases. It may restart several times and return to this page that displays progress with a green check by each completed phase.

Source: Microsoft Corporation

Step 8

A screen with the Windows logo in the center and a progress animation over the words "Getting ready" displays. Eventually, a screen displays with an explanation of what will occur if you click the button at the bottom labeled "Use Express settings." Select this button unless your instructor or administrator gives you different instructions. Also note that this is the first time the Ease of Access icon displays (on the lower left). Select this to have audio and visual aids to make Setup more accessible. Ease of Access settings are also available after Windows is installed. Look for it on every Sign-In screen, in Windows Setup, and in the Control Panel.

Source: Microsoft Corporation

Step 9

After a short delay while Setup configures your system, this screen will display asking, "Who owns this PC?" Your response to this screen depends on your situation. In a classroom lab, you will probably select "My organization." At home, you will select "I do." Select one of the choices; then click Next.

Source: Microsoft Corporation

After another short wait, a Sign-In screen opens. The actual screen depends on your choice in Step 9. If you selected "My Organization," then you will follow the screen prompts and enter your credentials for signing in to the organization's network.

If this is your own computer and you do not need to sign in to a Windows domain, sign in with a Microsoft account or create a local account (see Step 11).

For this exercise, we will sign in with a Microsoft account. If you wish to do that, enter the email address and password associated with your Microsoft account in this screen. Then click Sign in and skip to Step 12.

Alternatively, if you want to create a new Microsoft account, click on Create one!

If you wish to create and sign in with a local account, click on "Skip this step" and proceed to step 11.

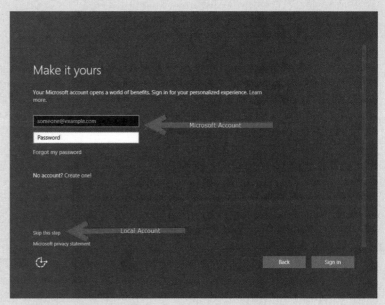

Source: Microsoft Corporation

If you wish to sign in with a local account, create a user by entering a user name and password at this screen. Then, click Next and skip to Step 14.

Source: Microsoft Corporation

Step 12

After signing in with your Microsoft account credentials, this screen will display if you have configured your Microsoft account with two-step verification for extra security and provided a telephone number where you can receive text messages. Just the last two digits of the phone number are shown in the first box. If this is correct, enter the last *four* digits in the second box, click Next, and a numeric code will be texted to your phone.

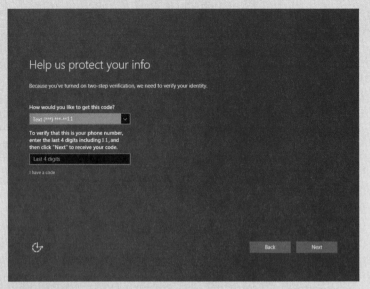

Source: Microsoft Corporation

Step 13

On the following page, enter the verification code that was sent to your phone and click Next.

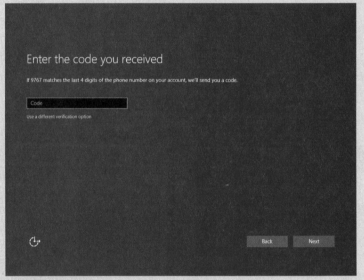

Source: Microsoft Corporation

Step 14

After a short wait, you will see a screen suggesting that you create a PIN to use for signing in. You may choose "Skip this step" or "PIN me." If you choose to skip the step, proceed to Step 15. If you choose "PIN me" you will see the "Set up a PIN" message. If you want to do this, we suggest that you clear the four-digit PIN checkbox and enter a PIN of at least six digits. Be sure to memorize it.

Step 15

The next page urges you to set up Cortana. For now select "Not now," and Setup will finish and sign you into the Desktop.

Source: Microsoft Corporation

LO 5.2 | Postinstallation Tasks

You will need to do some tasks soon after installing Windows 10. In earlier versions of Windows, we would normally instruct you to install security software at this point, but, like Windows 8 and 8.1, Windows 10 comes with the Windows Defender security enabled during setup. We will look at Windows Defender later in this chapter. Your postinstallation tasks should include installing drivers, if necessary running Windows Update, and backing up Windows and your data files. But first, take a few minutes to familiarize yourself with the new GUI so that you can do these postinstallation tasks.

Get Acquainted with the New GUI

The Windows 10 GUI (and there is only one) is the Desktop; it opens up with the Recycle bin shortcut on the upper left and a taskbar with Start button along the bottom. This section is a brief introduction to some of the new features that you may need to work with when you do the postinstallation tasks. They include the new Start menu, the File Explorer file management tool, and the new Edge Web browser. Later, after taking care of any postinstallation tasks, we will look more closely at Windows 10 features.

Keyboard Shortcuts

A keyboard shortcut is a key combination or a key-mouse combination that initiates an assigned action, saving you several mouse, keyboard, or touch actions. Windows 10 supports most of the keyboard shortcuts included in previous versions, as well as a few new ones. Throughout this textbook we provide special notes, pointing out some of our favorite keyboard shortcuts. Many of them take advantage of the Windows key ⊞ located near the bottom left of most keyboards or as a special physical button on some tablets or on the Microsoft Touch Mouse.

The Windows 10 Start Menu

Click or tap the Start button (on the far left of the task bar) to open the Start menu, as shown in Figure 5-6, which shows the Start menu in Desktop mode, covering a portion of the Desktop. This is how the Start menu appears on a computer with a keyboard attached. Click or tap the menu icon on the upper left of the Start menu to toggle the Quick link titles on or off. In Windows 10, scroll vertically to see more tiles on the Start menu.

> *Note:* A menu icon consisting of three horizontal lines is commonly called a hamburger icon. You will find this icon in Microsoft Windows and various Google settings and apps.

FIGURE 5–6 The Windows 10 Desktop with the Start menu open on the left.
Source: Microsoft Corporation

Note: Later in this chapter, learn about the special user interface mode for tablets: Tablet mode.

The Power menu options.
Source: Microsoft Corporation

Note: Later in this chapter, we will use the features of the Start menu's search box (now occupied by Cortana) to get help, find apps and settings, and access the other features of Windows 10.

Click or tap Start again to close the Start menu. Microsoft calls the Start menu simply "Start," but in this book, we will continue to use the term "Start menu." After its absence in Windows 8 and 8.1, the Start menu returned by popular demand, combining a selection of features from the Windows 7 Start menu and the Windows 8 Start screen along with new or improved features, that change as Microsoft continues to update Windows 10.

User Tile and Quick Links. In the left column of the Start menu is the User tile for the currently signed-in user, with an optional picture. What we called a shortcut on the Start menu in Windows 7 is now called a Quick link. This is not exactly like the Windows 7 Start menu, but it does have a Quick link that opens the Power menu containing options to shut down, restart, or put Windows into Sleep mode. To make room for touch, the Quick links and tiles become larger on a tablet, and menu choices are spaced farther apart. You can launch programs from Quick links, from tiles on the Start menu, from links pinned to the Taskbar, and from the All Apps list, which we look at next.

All Apps. In recent updates to Windows 10, the All Apps list appears by default on the Start Menu, providing a sorted list of installed apps, as shown in Figure 5-6. Hover the mouse near the border between the All Apps list and the tiles to see the vertical scroll bar on the right side of the Apps list. Drag the scroll bar up or down to browse through the list. Folder items have a drop-down button to the right that opens a list of the contents of that folder. Earlier installation of Windows 10 did not display the All Apps list by default, but had an All apps quick link above the Windows icon that would open the list on the Start menu.

Start Menu Settings. To explore options for personalizing the Start menu, open the Start page in Settings, as shown in Figure 5-7. Experiment with turning settings off and on to suit the way you work.

File Explorer

Another feature to check out before beginning your postinstallation tasks is File Explorer, the Windows 10 file management utility. This renamed and updated replacement for Windows Explorer first appeared in Windows 8. Microsoft has made more changes in the File Explorer UI in Windows 10, but nothing that should keep you from finding your way around if you are experienced with either Windows Explorer or Windows 8 or 8.1 File Explorer. Even the File Explorer icon on the taskbar (Figure 5-8), while updated somewhat, is recognizable from previous versions. In Figure 5-9 notice the ribbon containing menu buttons near the top of the window and the list of Quick links under Quick access on the left. When browsing your folders, select one you open frequently and click the Pin to Quick Access button on the left side of the ribbon. Briefly acquaint yourself with File Explorer by selecting it from the taskbar and browsing the folders.

Lock Screen

The Lock screen is a screen that prevents you from accidentally triggering some action that you did not intend to occur on a device with a touch screen. The classic example is "pocket dialing" someone on a smartphone while the phone is in your pocket. By default, the Lock screen displays under certain conditions including: when you first start up your computer, after a period of inactivity, when you choose Lock from the User tile, or when you use the Windows Key+L shortcut.

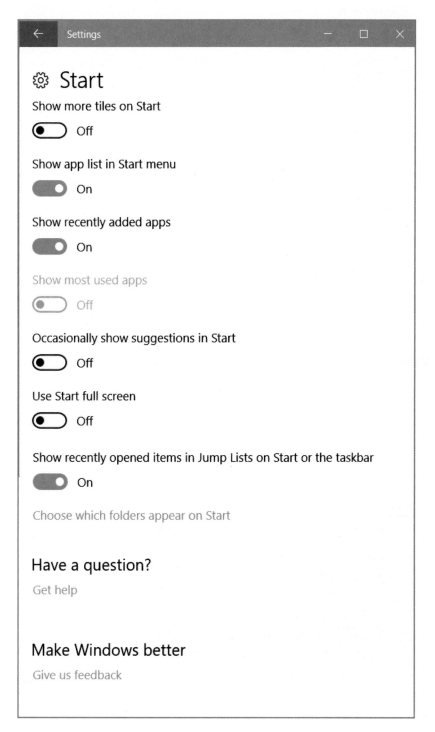

FIGURE 5–7 The Windows 10 Start Settings.
Source: Microsoft Corporation

Microsoft Edge

The last feature we will preview before discussing the postinstallation tasks is the Windows 10 Web browser, **Microsoft Edge**. This is an alternative to the decades-old Internet Explorer (IE), which is also included in Windows 10 for backward compatibility with some websites.

When browsing with Edge, if a website is incompatible with the new browser, Windows will automatically switch to IE. You can also choose to open IE manually.

Note: Windows 10 also supports Mozilla Firefox, Google Chrome, and Opera browsers.

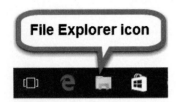

FIGURE 5-8 The File Explorer icon on the taskbar.
Source: Microsoft Corporation

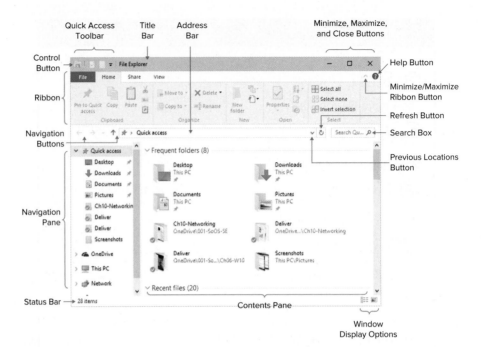

FIGURE 5-9 The Windows 10 File Explorer file management tool.
Source: Microsoft Corporation

FIGURE 5-10 The Microsoft Edge icon is pinned to the taskbar by default.
Source: Microsoft Corporation

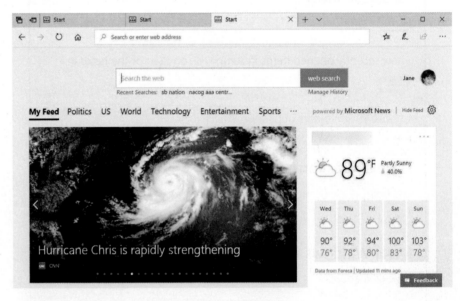

FIGURE 5-11 The Microsoft Edge browser window.
Source: Microsoft Corporation

Note: Microsoft Edge is a Windows app, which means that it runs in Windows 10 on all devices, adjusting itself for the various screen sizes. Take a closer look at Windows apps later in this chapter.

One way to launch IE is to type "Internet Explorer" in the Search box at the bottom of the Start menu. The top item in the results list should be Internet Explorer, with the description "Desktop app." Click it to open IE.

Launch Microsoft Edge from its taskbar icon, shown in Figure 5-10. Notice the clean look of the Microsoft Edge window in Figure 5-11. This image shows My Feed, my customizable news feed containing snapshots of news articles from a variety of sources. The large image in My Feed is a weather map from CNN. Clicking the arrows on the right or left of the picture will scroll through other news articles. To personalize My Feed in Edge, simply click the gear-shaped button labeled Hide Feed, shown below the user tile. This opens the Customize page for My Feed.

Install and Troubleshoot Drivers

Windows Setup detects your hardware devices and installs appropriate drivers. If Setup detects a noncritical device that does not work with one of the available drivers, you may be prompted to provide the driver files, or setup may quietly install a generic driver that works with a device, but doesn't take advantage of all its features. Or you may have a noncritical device that simply does not work after Windows 10 is installed. Therefore, one postinstallation task is to watch for error messages and devices that do not seem to function properly and install updated drivers. You have some choices for this that we will explore next.

Install Updated Drivers from Manufacturers

If you were prepared to install new drivers during setup, but did not have an opportunity to install them, then immediately after setup check for problems with the installed drivers in the form of error messages or a component not functioning properly. If you see such symptoms, install those drivers that you prepared ahead of time. In most cases, when manufacturers supply a compatible driver, it comes as an executable. If you downloaded the driver file, it will normally be in your Downloads folder, or you may have the driver file on an external device. In either case, open File Explorer, locate the file, and double-click it to run the driver setup. If the driver file is not an executable file, the manufacturer will provide other instructions for installing the file.

Troubleshoot Drivers with Device Manager

We recommend that you troubleshoot driver problems with Device Manager, a Control Panel applet that displays the list of hardware and the status of each device. Familiarize yourself with this utility before you have problems. In Step-by-Step 5.02, use Device Manager to look for problem drivers in the new Windows 10 installation and to correct problems, if necessary.

Step-by-Step 5.02

Using Device Manager in Windows 10

In this exercise, you will open Device Manager to detect and resolve driver problems in Windows 10. To complete this exercise, you will need the following:

- A computer running Windows 10, preferably with a mouse and keyboard.
- You should be signed in with an administrator account, which you are if you are signed in as the user created during Windows 10 Setup.
- An Internet Connection will allow Device Manager to search online in Steps 6 and 7.

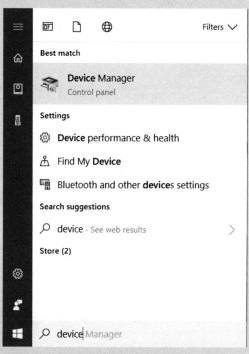

Source: Microsoft Corporation

Step 1

In the Start menu's Search box, type "device manager." In the search results list, notice that the results are shown in categories. Click on Device Manager, shown here at the top of the list.

Another way to open Device Manager is to use the ⊞+x shortcut to open the Power User Menu, and then select Device Manager.

Notice that the name of your computer displays at the top of the contents pane in Device Manager. Below that the devices are arranged in nodes. If Device Manager detects a problem with a device, the node will expand to show the device, along with a yellow error icon. In this example, no errors were detected, but we clicked on the Mice and other pointing devices node to expand it and to learn more about the detected pointing devices. Notice that the mouse was detected, as well as the built-in touchpad (Lenova Pointing Device).

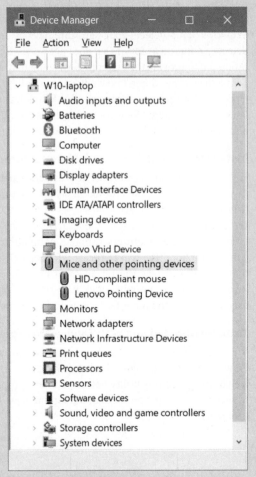

Source: Microsoft Corporation

If Device Manager shows an error for a device, double-click that device. If there is no error, select a device, as we did, and double-click it to open the Properties. The box below Device Status shows that this device is working properly. If there is a problem, an error message appears here. How you would troubleshoot a problem depends on the error. Device errors are often caused by the driver. Click the Driver tab to see your options for managing the driver.

Source: Microsoft Corporation

The Driver page has several buttons for managing drivers. Click on the Driver Details button.

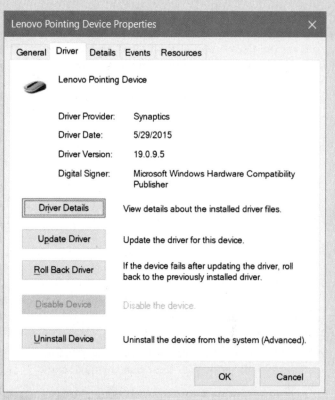

Source: Microsoft Corporation

The Driver File Details page shows the location and name of the driver file. There may be more than one file, as shown here. Click OK to close Driver File Details and return to the Properties dialog box.

Source: Microsoft Corporation

Step 6

Back on the Driver page of the Properties dialog box, click the Update Driver button. On the Update Driver Software Page, click the top option titled *Search automatically for updated driver software* and follow the instructions.

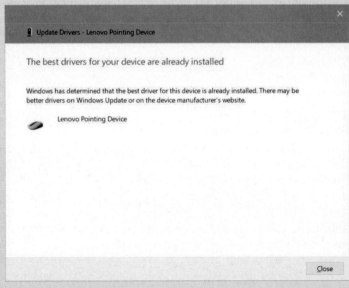

Update Drivers - Lenovo Pointing Device

How do you want to search for drivers?

→ **Search automatically for updated driver software**
Windows will search your computer and the Internet for the latest driver software for your device, unless you've disabled this feature in your device installation settings.

→ **Browse my computer for driver software**
Locate and install driver software manually.

Cancel

Source: Microsoft Corporation

Step 7

A message and progress bar displays while Windows searches for a driver on your local computer and on the Internet.

Update Drivers - Lenovo Pointing Device

Searching online for drivers...

Cancel

Source: Microsoft Corporation

Step 8

In our example, Windows determined that the best driver was already installed, displaying this message. If this is the case on your computer, click the Close button to return to the Properties dialog box where you can click the OK button to end the exercise. If a message displays that a driver is being downloaded or installed, follow the instructions and when it completes, click the OK button to close the last dialog box.

Update Drivers - Lenovo Pointing Device

The best drivers for your device are already installed

Windows has determined that the best driver for this device is already installed. There may be better drivers on Windows Update or on the device manufacturer's website.

Lenovo Pointing Device

Close

Source: Microsoft Corporation

If you update a device driver, then the Properties for that device shows that the Roll Back button is live. Click the Close button to end the exercise.

Source: Microsoft Corporation

If you upgrade a driver and then have problems with the device, or if Windows becomes unstable immediately after a driver upgrade, open the Properties dialog box for the device and use the Roll Back Driver button to remove the new driver and restore the old driver. The last two buttons on the Driver tab of the Properties dialog box for a device, Disable and Uninstall, trigger drastic measures that you would not normally take without advice from a very knowledgeable person.

Personalize Windows 10

After just a few minutes of using a new installation of Windows, you will feel the need to make it your own with your own preferences. Perhaps you want to change the size of icons on the desktop and taskbar or change pictures on the Lock screen, Desktop, or Sign-In screen. And we all have our own color preferences, which you can configure for the taskbar and windows. Begin by tweaking display settings, and then move on to the other ways to personalize Windows 10.

Tweak Display Settings

The Desktop context menu is one way to access Display settings. Open the context menu (Figure 5-12) by right-clicking an empty area of the Desktop. From the context menu select Display settings. In Windows 10, this opens the Display page of the Settings app where you change settings to suit how you work. Figure 5-13 shows the Display settings. Since Windows 10 was first released, Microsoft has made several changes to Settings, so you may see different options. Scroll through the settings and select those options you would like to change.

Note: To display the Desktop context menu on a touch screen, press on an empty area of the Desktop and hold until a small square appears, then immediately release.

Note: If you are using Windows 10 in a virtual machine, you will be able to view the Display settings but not change them.

Identify, Detect, and Connect to Displays. Scroll down in Display Settings and click on Identify. A number will appear on each display connected to your computer.

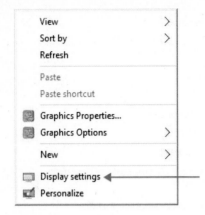

FIGURE 5–12 The Desktop context menu.
Source: Microsoft Corporation

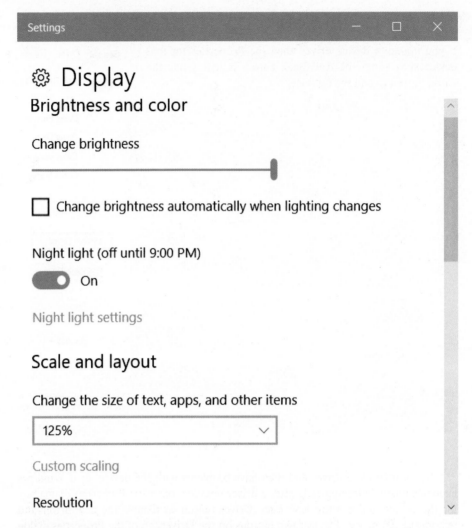

FIGURE 5–13 The Windows 10 Display settings.
Source: Microsoft Corporation

This is very helpful when you have multiple displays, so that you can select which display is the main display, the one that will show the Sign-In screen and will be the primary screen for the Desktop. Click Detect to detect all connected displays, and click Connect to a Wireless Display to initiate a connection with a wireless display.

Change the Size of Items on the Desktop. The Scale and Layout setting gives you some control over the size of displayed items; on the desktop computer, with 23 inch displays, the choices were 100%, 125%, 150%, or 175%, but on the laptop this was limited to either 100% or 125%. The default is 100%, and if you change it, you will need to sign out and sign in again for it to take effect.

Orientation and Lock Rotation. The Orientation setting allows you to change the orientation from landscape (normal on desktops and laptops) to Portrait, as well as both of these orientations reversed, or "flipped." You normally will not change this setting. On a tablet, the Orientation setting will be grayed out, as shown in Figure 5-14, because sensors in a tablet will detect when you physically rotate the device and change the orientation without modifying these settings. Sometimes when using a tablet you want the tablet to stay in one orientation, even as you physically rotate it. For that reason tablets have the setting Lock rotation of this display, also shown in Figure 5-14.

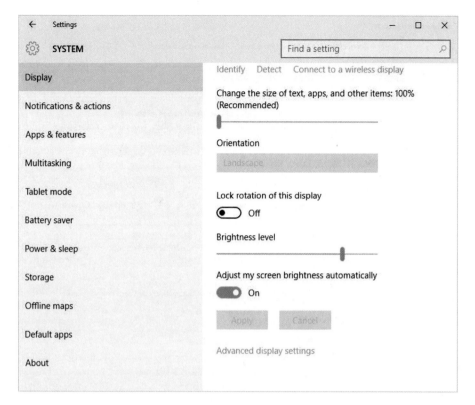

FIGURE 5–14 The Display settings on a tablet.
Source: Microsoft Corporation

Brightness Level. A Windows 10 laptop or tablet will automatically dim the screen when running on battery or, if the device has ambient light sensors, it will brighten the screen when it detects bright light. One laptop would dim the screen to an unacceptable level, even when it was plugged into an outlet. To avoid this, we turned this setting off, and manually set the brightness level to the highest setting. Experiment with this setting before following our example. The setting that allows Windows to automatically adjust brightness works very well on most tablets. Look for the Night light settings, which allow you to change the color temperature at night from blue to a warmer color.

Note: The actual settings will depend on the type of computer and the Windows 10 feature updates installed.

Resolution Settings. Scroll down to the resolution settings, which should be at the recommended setting on any modern flat screen display, as this is the native resolution determined by the display's design.

Ease of Access

Windows includes Ease of Access settings to make Windows more accessible for all types of needs. The Ease of Access and Power buttons, shown here, are on the bottom right of the Sign-In screen so that you can change some Ease of Access settings at sign-in. At this writing, the best place to find a complete list of Ease of Access settings or links to related settings is in Control Panel. In the Start menu, Search box type "Ease of Access," and click or tap the result titled Ease of Access Center to open the Control Panel, as shown in Figure 5–15. There is a long list; some settings are out of view, and you can scroll down to see them.

The Ease of Access button (left) and the Power button.
Source: Microsoft Corporation

Configure Windows Update

Windows 10 is configured for automatic updates by default. In fact, in both retail editions, Windows 10 Home and Windows 10 Pro, updates are mandatory. In Windows 10

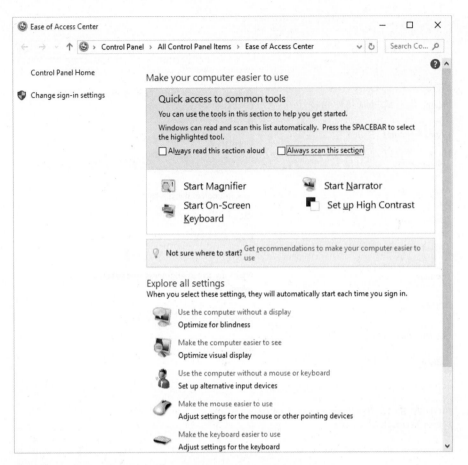

FIGURE 5-15 The Ease of Access Center in Control Panel.
Source: Microsoft Corporation

Pro, you can defer upgrades that would add new features. Deferred upgrades will keep new Windows features from downloading and installing for several months.

However, you should manually trigger updates soon after the installation to ensure that your installation is completely up to date, and to help resolve any remaining driver issues. Additionally, we recommend configuring Windows Update to update all your installed Microsoft software, not just Windows components. Step-by-Step 5.03 walks through the steps for using Windows Update, available through the Settings GUI.

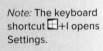

Note: The keyboard shortcut ⊞+I opens Settings.

Step-by-Step 5.03

Configuring and Using Windows Update

Open Windows Update from the Windows Settings GUI, configure Update to update other Microsoft software, and check for more updates. To complete this exercise, you will need the following:

- A computer running Windows 10 Pro.
- You should be signed in with an administrator account or have the user name and password of an administrator account for the computer.

Open Start and select the Settings gear icon to open the Windows 10 Settings GUI. Alternatively, open Settings with the keyboard shortcut ⊞+I. Notice the grouping of settings into categories. Locate and select the Update & Security category. Then click on Windows Update.

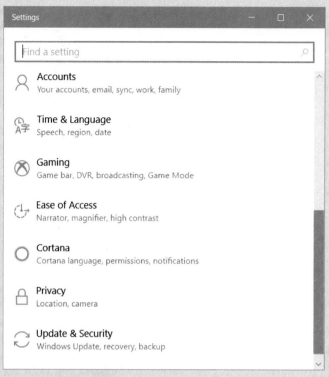

Source: Microsoft Corporation

To see what choices you have for configuring Windows Update, scroll through the options. Shown here are the first two pages of options. To see what updates have been installed click on View Installed Updates. Scroll down and select Advanced Options to see other important updates.

Source: Microsoft Corporation

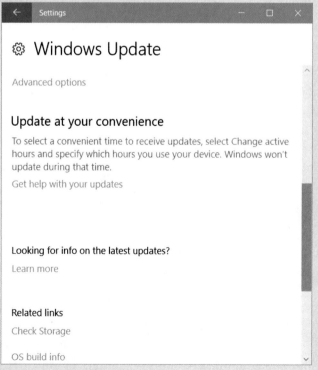

Source: Microsoft Corporation

On the Advanced Options page, ensure that installed Microsoft apps are kept up to date by clicking or tapping to place a check in the box labeled "Give me updates for other Microsoft products when I update Windows."

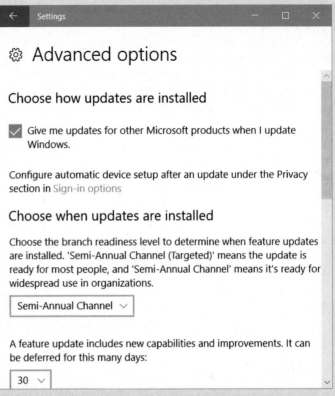

Source: Microsoft Corporation

When you are done with Update settings return to the main Settings page using the back arrow at the top left of the title bar, or simply click the close (x) button on the top right to exit from Settings.

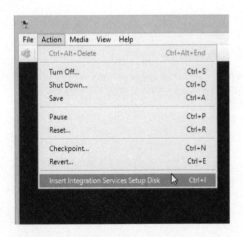

FIGURE 5–16 If you are using Hyper-V, open the Action menu on the Virtual Machine Connection window and select the last option (Integration Services).
Source: Microsoft Corporation

Make Windows 10 Run Better in a Virtual Machine

If you installed Windows 10 into a virtual machine, an important postinstallation task is to install the software into the virtual machine that will make the OS run better. The name for this software and how it installs varies by hypervisor. In Microsoft's Hyper-V, the software is labeled Integration Services, while Oracle VirtualBox uses the name Guest Additions. You may have already seen a message pop-up in Windows 10 in your virtual machine. If so, follow the instructions given. Otherwise, look for an option in the hypervisor window surrounding the virtual machine, as we did when we installed Windows 10 into a Hyper-V virtual machine on a PC running Windows 8.1 Pro. In that case, we opened the Action menu from the Virtual Machine Connection window and selected Insert Integration Services Setup Disk, as shown in Figure 5–16.

If you installed Windows 10 into Oracle VirtualBox, open the Devices menu and select Install Guest Additions.

Remove Unwanted Software

If you purchase a computer with Windows 10 preinstalled, the first time you turn on your new computer you will go through the personalization tasks to configure your sign-in and to customize the Desktop. This Microsoft feature is the **Out of Box Experience (OOBE)**, the last phase of the Windows installation.

Then, when you arrive at the Desktop, you may find software installed by the manufacturer that you do not wish to use. Manufacturers received a lot of bad press a few years ago for some of the "junk" software, referred to as bloatware, that was preinstalled. Since then, new computers we have worked with have not had as much junk software, although we still find software that we simply do not use.

This preinstalled software falls roughly into two categories: trial software from various software publishers and free utilities provided by the manufacturer and labeled with the manufacturer's name.

Trial software is free to use for a period of time, usually 30 days. At the end of that time, the trial software will cease to function unless you pay a fee to activate it. The two most common types of trial software are security, such as McAfee Antivirus, and productivity, such as Microsoft Office. When you launch one of these, it clearly states that it is trial software and the length of the trial period. They also remind you before the trail period expires. What you choose to do about these trial apps depends on your own preferences and needs.

Apps installed by the computer manufacturer can usually be identified by the manufacturer's name in All Apps. Figure 5-17 shows the software installed by the manufacturer Lenovo. You may want to wait until you are more familiar with these apps before removing any.

When you decide to remove an app, open All Apps and scroll through the list to locate the app. You may need to open a folder, as in the case of Lenovo Reach, shown in Figure 5-18. Once you locate the app, right-click on it to bring up the context menu, also shown in Figure 5-18. Then select Uninstall.

FIGURE 5–17 The All Apps list showing software installed by the computer manufacturer Lenovo.
Source: Microsoft Corporation

Migrate or Restore Data

Your next task is to migrate or restore local data from a previous installation. If you did an in-place upgrade, your data should be intact, but if you did a clean installation, you may have a data backup to restore.

If you are migrating data from a Windows 7 computer and used the Windows 7 Backup and Restore utility before installing or upgrading, you are in luck because Windows 10 can do a restore from a Windows 7 backup. The Backup and Restore utility from Windows 7 is included in the Windows 10 Control Panel. Follow the steps in the Try This! to open this Backup and Restore utility.

Back Up Data and the System

Windows 10 includes both the Windows 7 Backup and Restore utility, and a File History tool for automatically backing up your local data. It also includes an image backup utility. You should configure these, or a third-party backup utility, soon after installing Windows 10.

Use Backup and Restore (Windows 7) to Back Up Files

Microsoft returned the Windows 7 Backup and Restore utility to Windows 10, and you can choose to use this to back up your data from any location on your local computer to the backup media of your choice.

Turn on File History

If you store your data files on the local hard drive, you will want to turn on File History. File History will automatically back up files in your Libraries, Desktop, Contacts, and Favorites. Therefore, you will need to save your files in those locations. It also backs up any OneDrive files that are available offline. File History is not turned on by

try this!

Use Backup and Restore (Windows 7)

Backup Windows 10 with the Windows 7 Backup and Restore utility. Try this:

1. In the Start Search box type "backup."
2. From the search results list select Backup Settings, as shown in Figure 5-19.
3. In the Backup Settings page click Go to Backup and Restore (Windows 7).
4. In the Backup and Restore Control Panel select Set up Backup, following the prompts to create a backup.
5. When you are finished, close the Backup and Restore window.

FIGURE 5–18 To remove an app, right-click on it, and select Uninstall.
Source: Microsoft Corporation

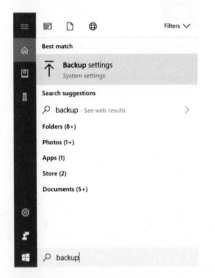

FIGURE 5–19 Select Backup settings from the search results.
Source: Microsoft Corporation

default; if you have a spare external drive connected to your computer or if you can back up to a network location, turn on and configure File History by opening Settings, selecting Update & Security. In Update & Security select Backup. On the Backup page, shown in Figure 5–20. When you first turn it on, you will be prompted to select a location. Once File History is turned on it works automatically, not only saving files as they change, but saving versions of each file, so that you can restore a file to a certain day and time.

Create a System Image Backup

If you installed Windows 10 from bootable media, you already have the means to reinstall or repair the OS, if necessary. In the case of a new computer with Windows 10 preinstalled, look for some program from the manufacturer for creating an image of the factory-installed software in case you need to return the computer to its original state. Or you can create a System image using the Windows 10 utility. To do this open Control Panel. From the All Control Panel Items page select Backup and Restore (Windows 7). On that page, select Create a system image. This opens the page shown in Figure 5–21. Here you can create a System Image backup that you can use to restore Windows if it becomes irreparably damaged.

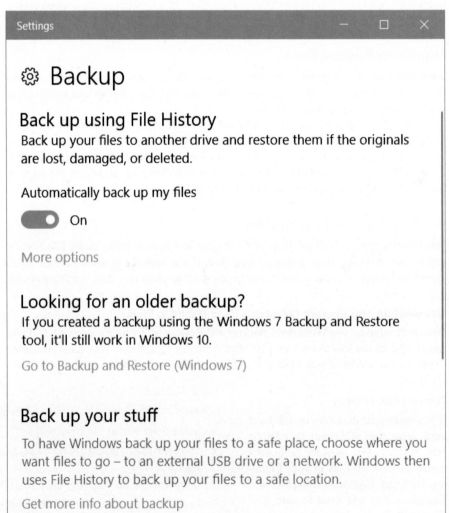

FIGURE 5–20 Open File History in the Backup Settings page.
Source: Microsoft Corporation

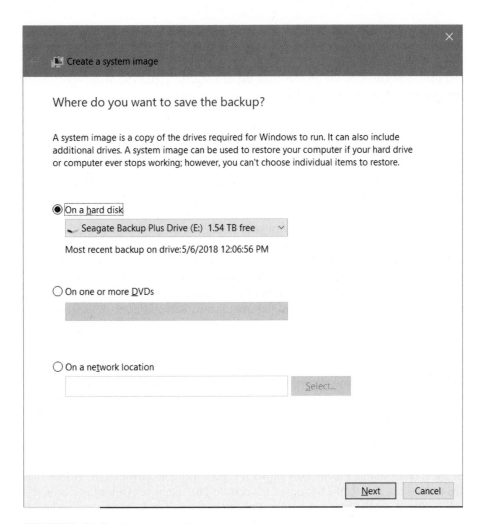

FIGURE 5–21 Create a system image.
Source: Microsoft Corporation

LO 5.3 | Working with Windows 10 Features

Microsoft has announced plans to release frequent updates to Windows 10, adding features along with bug fixes and security patches. Even though they used the update system to add features to Windows operating systems in the past, they continued to bring out new versions every three years or so, which meant that they held most features back until they could present them bundled in a new version. Now they are moving away from that practice, relying on incremental changes made through Windows Update, and adding features when they have them ready to release.

The Windows 10 GUI Modes

Earlier we introduced the Start menu, and now we will look at it more closely. When you start up Windows 10 on a PC or laptop, the Desktop strongly resembles the Windows 7 Desktop, clear of clutter, just showing the taskbar with the Start button and other features, and the Recycle bin shortcut near the top left. As you use your computer, you may add other objects to the Desktop or taskbar in addition to those placed there by default. Microsoft has changed the look of many of these objects, but not so much that you wouldn't recognize them. When you click on Start, the Start menu opens with features borrowed from the Start menu in Windows 7 and the Start screen in Windows 8 and 8.1.

As in Windows 7, the Start menu contains links and is customizable, letting you add or remove links to various folder locations such as Documents, Downloads, Pictures, Music, and Videos. The Start menu also highlights new apps right after they are installed, and contains the alphabetical list of installed apps. The Windows 10 GUI has two modes: Desktop and Tablet.

Desktop Mode

When you open the Start menu in Windows 10 in Desktop mode, the Start menu covers only a portion of the Desktop, as shown back in Figure 5-6. Desktop mode also displays apps windowed so they are easier to move around with a keyboard and mouse (or touchpad). You can use touch gestures in Desktop mode, but the GUI is not as convenient for touch use as it is in Tablet mode. In Desktop mode, the Start menu contains a column along the left with your most used items at the top. Near the bottom are Quick links for File Explorer, Settings, and Power, topped off with the User tile. In addition, out to the right on the Start menu are groups of Windows 8-style live tiles. A live tile is a rectangle on the Windows 8 Start screen or Windows 10 Start menu that works like a shortcut or quick link to launch a program. The "live" part of the name refers to a tile's ability to display active content related to the app, without launching the app.

Tablet Mode

When Windows 10 wakes up on a tablet without an attached keyboard, the Start menu automatically opens in Tablet mode (full screen) to work better with a touch screen. In this mode, all your apps run full screen. To switch between Desktop mode and Tablet mode on a Windows 10 desktop or laptop, simply click or tap the Action Center icon in the keyboard shortcut Notification area on the right of the taskbar (Figure 5-22), or use the keyboard shortcut ⊞+A. When the Action Center opens (Figure 5-23) tap or click Tablet mode. Figure 5-24 shows the Start menu in Tablet mode. Notice that the taskbar remains on the bottom of the screen. The column of Quick links is on the left and the Apps list does not display. The 3rd Quick link from the top opens the All Apps list, full screen. In Tablet mode, a Back icon, in the form of a left-facing arrow, appears on the taskbar. Click or tap this to go back to the last open app.

Selecting Tablet mode from the Action Center may only turn it on temporarily. Depending on the computer and other variables, the next time you restart a computer

FIGURE 5–22 The Action Center icon is on the taskbar.
Source: Microsoft Corporation

Note: The keyboard shortcut ⊞+A opens Action Center.

Note: The Action Center replaces the Windows 8 and 8.1 Charms bar. Action Center opens on touch devices with an edge gesture: a swipe from the right-side of the screen.

FIGURE 5–23 Open Action Center and select Tablet mode.
Source: Microsoft Corporation

FIGURE 5–24 The Windows 10 Start menu in Tablet mode.
Source: Microsoft Corporation

with keyboard attached it will go back to the default Desktop mode. Learn more about personalizing Windows 10 in Step-by-Step 5.04.

Continuum

Continuum is a feature that is ideal for anyone working on a two-in-one device—a tablet with a detachable keyboard. With the keyboard attached, Windows 10 will display the PC-style Desktop mode. Detach the keyboard and the Continuum feature automatically changes to Tablet mode on the fly, converting the Start menu and open apps to full screen. Touch gestures let you move through the open apps. In addition, the Continuum feature enables a Windows 10 Mobile device to connect to monitors and keyboards.

try this!

Turn On Tablet Mode at Startup

Even if you have an attached keyboard, you can have Tablet mode enabled every time Windows 10 restarts. Try this:

1. Open Settings by either of two methods: select Settings from the Start menu or use the keyboard shortcut, ⊞+I.
2. In Settings select Personalization, and then select Start.
3. Enable the option "Use Start full screen."
4. Close out of settings, and the Start menu will open full screen.
5. To return to Desktop mode, return to the Start page in Settings and disable the option "Use Start full screen."

Step-by-Step 5.04

Personalize the Windows 10 Desktop

The Windows 10 Desktop is more than just the Start menu, although that is an important feature. In this exercise, you will customize the Start menu and locate the Power User menu that gives you access to some of the utilities you used in previous versions of Windows. To complete this exercise, you will need:

- A PC or laptop running Windows 10.

Step 1

Open Settings | Personalization | Start.

Step 2

On the Start page scroll down and click or tap "Choose which folders appear on Start."

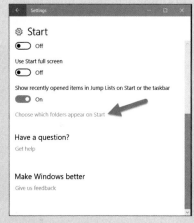

Source: Microsoft Corporation

Step 3

Scroll through the list and select a folder to appear on Start. We selected the Downloads folder.

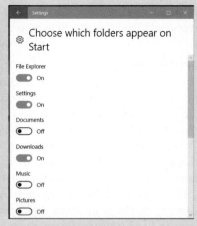

Source: Microsoft Corporation

Step 4

Close Settings and open Start to confirm that the folder you selected was added.

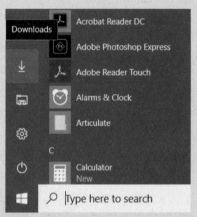

Source: Microsoft Corporation

Step 5

Customize the Desktop. Open Settings again and return to the Personalization page. Select Background. The background can be a picture, solid color, or a slideshow. As you choose different options, the Preview (at the top) changes.

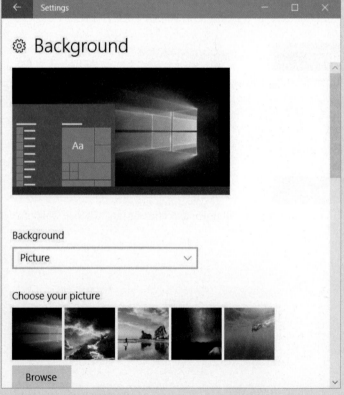

Source: Microsoft Corporation

Step 6

Click on the box labeled Picture in the Step 5 example, and it will open to three choices: Picture, Solid color, and Slideshow. If it was not already selected, select Picture. You can select a different picture from the choices shown or browse to select a personal picture. The Preview reflects your changes, as shown here.

Source: Microsoft Corporation

Step 7

Change the fit of the picture on the Desktop by scrolling down and clicking or tapping the box under Choose a fit. This opens a list of fit treatments that temporarily cover up other settings. The choices include Fill, Fit, Stretch, Tile, Center, and Span. Experiment with different fits and see how they change the picture on the Desktop. Select one that you like.

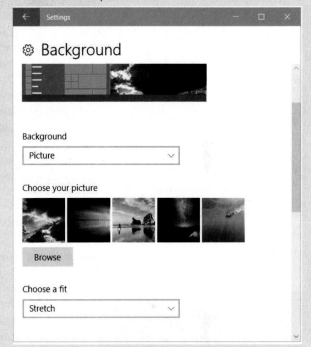

Source: Microsoft Corporation

Step 8

Now select Colors on the Personalization page. This opens the Colors pane. With the first option deselected, you can select an accent color. If it is selected, Windows picks a color to go with your previously chosen background color.

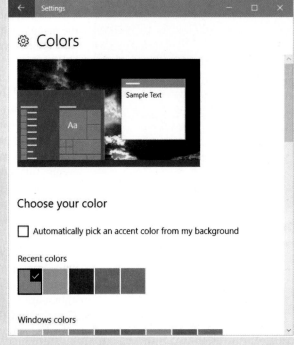

Source: Microsoft Corporation

Step 9

Choose an accent color and add color to the Start menu, taskbar, and Action Center. You can also turn on or turn off the transparency of Start, taskbar, and Action Center. We prefer to have transparency turned off.

Step 10

Experiment with other Personalization options, such as choosing a picture for the Lock screen and selecting apps to appear on the Lock screen. When you have completed the changes you want, exit from Settings and return to the Desktop.

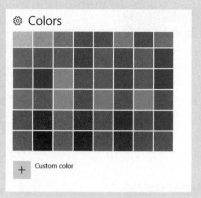

⚙ Colors

+ Custom color

Source: Microsoft Corporation

Getting Started with Cortana

Cortana is an intelligent search system that searches the Web, your computer or device, and any cloud storage you use from that computer. It also learns about you, not by spying but by paying attention to things you give her permission to watch, using the Notebook feature. Let's start with the basics.

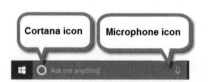

FIGURE 5–25 The Cortana and Microphone icons.
Source: Microsoft Corporation

Communicating with Cortana

Interact with Cortana in several ways. You can simply enter a search string in the search box, as you did in previous versions of Windows, but Cortana can do much more for you. Click or tap the Cortana icon (Figure 5-25) when you want to open her Home page where she keeps pertinent information for you. If you have a working microphone on your computer, click or tap the microphone icon on the right side of the search box, and start talking to Cortana. With either action, the area above the search box will open as she replies, as shown in Figure 5-26. This is the Home page where Cortana displays a configurable set of information for you as she learns more about you.

Control what Cortana displays in the Home page by changing settings. Click the menu icon at the top of the Cortana menu bar to expand it and see the label for each Quick link icon, as shown in Figure 5-27.

FIGURE 5–26 Cortana's Home pane.
Source: Microsoft Corporation

Note: The autocorrect in apps for both PCs and mobile devices is another example of a predictive technology.

Select What Cortana Learns about You

Notebook, shown in Figure 5-28 is where you tell Cortana the things you want her to know about you and what she can use to learn more. This is where you change your name or its pronunciation, add favorite places, connect your online services (such as Office 365), and generally tell her your interests in the areas of dining, events, finance, transportation, movies, TV, music, news, sports, and travel. Move the mouse pointer to the right edge to activate the scroll bar, indicating that there are more items listed below.

Cortana can help you with many everyday tasks involving your installed apps, such as creating a play list, or creating an email. Cortana can go online to track a package based on information in an email. As Cortana learns, it will make appropriate suggestions and give reminders via posts on its Home page that opens up along the left of the screen. Providing a notice or other information in anticipation of a need is called a **predictive notification**, a feature long available in Google Now. This requires some history, but you can configure just how much of your life is revealed to Cortana. Need a little cheering up? Ask Cortana to tell you a joke.

Hey Cortana

The voice activation option, called Hey Cortana, was introduced in Windows Phone 8.1 and made available in Windows 10 for those devices that support voice input. This takes some training of the app by the user to ensure that Cortana responds to the voice query. You can either type your query or talk, and in both cases, you do not need to remember a syntax, but ask questions as you would if talking to or texting with a person.

Using Apps in Windows 10

When working on the Desktop in Windows 10, you will find your apps behaving much like traditional Windows apps did in Windows 7. Launch an app from the Apps list and then pin it to the taskbar or create a shortcut on the Desktop. Windows 10 introduced Universal apps, later renamed to Windows apps, which are an evolutionary change from the Modern apps of Windows 8. Your old Windows apps will still run, but managing multiple running apps in Windows 10 is easier with the new Task view and Virtual Desktop features.

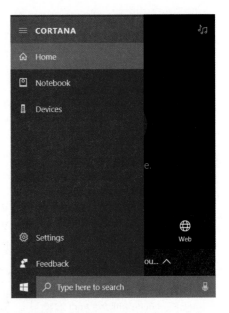

FIGURE 5–27 The Cortana Quick links.
Source: Microsoft Corporation

Windows Store Apps versus Windows Desktop Apps

For Windows 10, Microsoft invested a large amount of effort into the notion that an application should be written once and run on many platforms—universally, so to speak. Therefore, while Windows 8 and 8.1 had Modern apps that covered the entire screen and added a title bar to them in Windows 8.1, Windows 10 introduced the Universal app that runs in Windows 10 on PCs and across all the devices this operating system supports, from the conventional PC to tablets and smartphones.

Microsoft replaced the term Universal App with Windows Store App. With any name, this is an app that conforms to the different screen sizes and other features, such as input type (e.g., keyboard and mouse versus touch screen), making the switch automatically. Figure 5-29 shows Photos, a Universal app, running in a window. On a tablet or smartphone, it will run full screen.

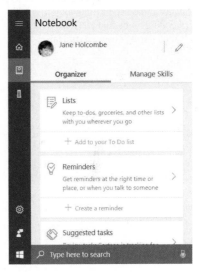

FIGURE 5–28 The Cortana Notebook.
Source: Microsoft Corporation

FIGURE 5–29 A Universal app, Photos, in a window in Desktop mode on a Windows 10 PC.
Sources: Microsoft Corporation; photos ©Jane Holcombe

Windows 10 also supports legacy Windows Desktop apps. They run as they did in Windows 7 and on the Desktop in Windows 8 and 8.1. Windows Desktop apps only run in Windows on PCs and laptops, but Microsoft does have versions of these apps (e.g., Microsoft Office) that run on iOS and Android mobile operating systems.

Task View

Windows 10 **Task view** lets you quickly view all your open apps, improving on the Windows 7 Aero Flip 3D feature. Access Task view by clicking or tapping the Task view icon located to the right of the Search box on the taskbar. It opens with large tiles for each open app, as shown in Figure 5–30.

Virtual Desktops

Windows 10 includes a feature that has long been available in OS X and Linux: support for multiple Desktops—Microsoft calls it **Virtual Desktop**. This is a great way to

Note: On a PC with multiple displays, Task view shows the open windows on each display. This is one of the authors' favorite Windows 10 features.

Note: Beginning with the April 2018 Update, Microsoft moved the New desktop shortcut from the bottom right side to the upper left of Task view and added a Timeline of your activities that you can scroll through using a vertical bar on the right side of the screen.

FIGURE 5–30 Look for the Task view icon to the right of the Search box on the taskbar.
Sources: Microsoft Corporation; photos ©Jane Holcombe

FIGURE 5–31 Task view lets you quickly see your open apps.
Sources: Microsoft Corporation; photos ©Jane Holcombe

group your projects. For instance, on your home PC you could create a new Desktop while working on personal finances with Windows for Quicken, Excel, a calculator app, and your personal banking website open in one Desktop. Then you could also open a second Desktop where you work on a genealogy project. Task view, as shown in Figure 5-31 includes tiles at the bottom of the screen for two separate Desktops. From Task view simply click or tap to select a Desktop. When working in a Virtual Desktop, switch to other active Virtual Desktops by using the shortcut keys **Ctrl+⊞+left arrow** and **Ctrl+⊞+right arrow**.

Note: Two new keyboard shortcuts let you quickly move between Virtual Desktops: Ctrl+⊞+ left arrow and Ctrl+⊞+right arrow.

Microsoft Store

The updated Microsoft Store, Figure 5-32, is available from the Windows 10 Start menu. It requires an Internet connection and a Microsoft account. This one store provides Microsoft apps and services. It offers games, music, movies, and TV.

Be aware that many apps, especially games, have in-app purchases that can be quite expensive. Even if you already have a payment method configured for Microsoft services (such as Office 365) purchased outside the Microsoft Store, you will need to configure a payment method for within the Store, and it will ask for an account password with each purchase—even with in-app purchases. You do not need a payment option to download and install free apps.

The Store Settings page, shown in Figure 5-33, has an option for automatically updating apps. This is turned on by default, and we recommend keeping this setting. This is also where you can control whether or not the Live Tile shows products. Scroll down to Account on this page where a link, Manage your devices, will take you to the page in your Microsoft account settings where you can manage your devices on which you install apps.

The Try This! walks you through installing a free app from the Windows Store.

Xbox Integration

If you have an Xbox One, use the Xbox app on your Windows 10 computer to access all your Xbox data, such as friends, activity, and game history. Additionally, you can record video game clips. With the Xbox app open, use keyboard shortcuts. ⊞+G opens the **Xbox Game bar** containing buttons for working with Xbox recording games, taking screenshots of games, and configuring Xbox. In the Game bar, either click or tap the record button or press ⊞+Alt+G to record the last 30 seconds of a game. Or use the ⊞+Alt+R shortcut to start a recording and repeat

WARNING!

In-app purchases can quickly mount up. The Windows 10 Store app requires a password for each purchase. This is another reason to have a strong password.

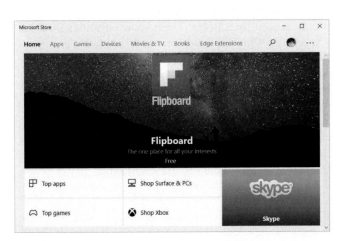

FIGURE 5–32 The Microsoft Store Home page.
Source: Microsoft Corporation

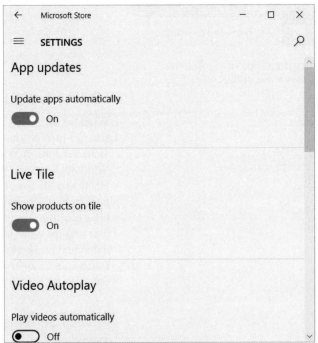

FIGURE 5–33 The Store Settings page.
Source: Microsoft Corporation

Note: Use ⊞+G to open the Xbox Game bar. Then use ⊞+Alt+G to record the last 30 seconds and ⊞+Alt+R to start recording a game. Repeat ⊞+Alt+R to end the recording of a game.

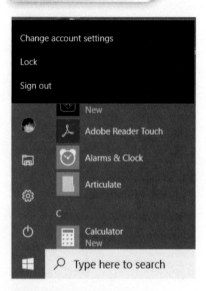

FIGURE 5–34 The User menu.
Source: Microsoft Corporation

that shortcut to stop the recording. Take screenshots of a game with ⊞+Alt+Print Key.

If your Xbox One device can access live TV, you can stream it from your Xbox One to your Windows 10 PC using the Xbox app. The Xbox app also supports **picture-in-picture (PIP)** in which one show displays on the screen while another displays in a small box. This has been a feature in TVs for decades.

Changing the User Picture

In the left column of the Start menu is the User tile displaying an image associated with your account. You can choose a custom picture. Click or tap the User tile to open the menu shown in Figure 5-34. From this menu, you can change your account settings, lock the screen, or sign out. The Try This! describes how to change your account picture in Windows 10.

LO 5.4 | Securing Windows 10

Windows 10 is the most secure version of Windows out-of-the-box because the default settings turn on the most critical security features. These include features from previous versions of Windows, such as Windows SmartScreen, Windows Defender, and Windows Firewall. Windows 10 security is also enhanced by new features: Windows Hello and Microsoft Passport. Although we include a description of Microsoft Passport here, it is one of several security features of Windows 10 designed for an Enterprise environment in which Windows 10 can be centrally managed to protect both the user and the enterprise. The other features we explore in this section are available to individual users who do not have the benefits of using Windows 10 in an enterprise. Further, in Chapter 10, Connecting Desktops and Laptops to Networks, you will learn security settings for popular Web browsers, including Microsoft Edge.

Privacy Settings

The Windows 10 Settings app's Privacy page, shown in Figure 5-35, contains many settings you should explore; carefully consider the trade-off between privacy and the convenience of allowing certain apps have access to your location and other personal

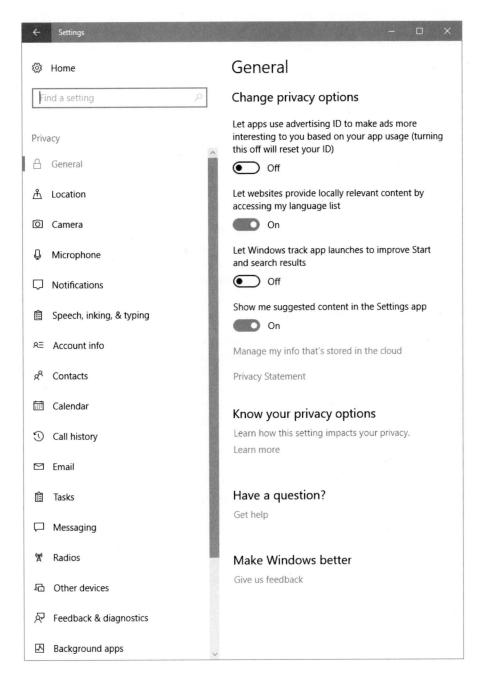

FIGURE 5–35 Windows 10 Privacy settings.
Source: Microsoft Corporation

information. On the General pane, the link titled "Manage my info that's stored in the cloud" will take you to the online Privacy dashboard for your Microsoft Account. This is where you can see the data saved by Microsoft, make some changes to what type of data is collected, and download an archive of that data.

Windows Hello

Windows Hello, a biometric sign-in feature, lets you sign in to your Windows 10 device with a biometric sign-in: fingerprint, facial recognition, or iris scan. It requires the existence of special hardware in the Windows 10 computer. To sign in with a fingerprint, your computer must have a compatible fingerprint scanner. The facial and iris scanning requires a special depth camera that uses infrared light to see features under the less-than-ideal settings in the real world, such as poor light conditions and users wearing makeup or having facial hair.

Microsoft Passport

While Windows Hello allows you to log in to your Windows 10 device using biometrics, Microsoft Passport lets you securely sign in to network resources without sending a password or PIN over the network; the authentication is tied to the hardware. For greater security, combine the secure local authentication of Windows Hello with Microsoft Passport authentication to network resources. Presently, Microsoft Passport gives you access to resources, such as Microsoft's Azure Active Directory services, and Web servers, but there is limited support beyond Microsoft's products. That may change, as Microsoft is among many companies representing such industries as banking, software, hardware, and more who joined the industry consortium FIDO Alliance (Fast Identity Online) to contribute their technology and work together to develop solutions that will allow users to securely access online services and conduct financial transactions without using password authentication and to reduce the risk of fraud.

Note: Learn more about the FIDO Alliance at **https://fidoalliance.org**.

Windows Defender Security Center

Windows Defender automatically provides antispyware and antimalware protection if needed. Installing a third-party security app replaces some features of Windows Defender. Launch the Windows Defender Security Center app by entering "windows defender security" into the Search box. Figure 5–36 shows the Home page of the Windows Defender Security Center. From here you can quickly see the overall security status of your device, even if some of this protection is provided by third-party software.

Windows Defender Firewall

Note: Updates to Windows 10 include additional security features. Open Windows Defender Security Center and compare it with Figure 5–36. You may see new tools, such as Account Protection and Device Security, depending on the update status of your installation of Windows 10.

Access the Windows Defender Firewall status and settings (Figure 5-37) from the Windows Defender Security page. This page contains links to firewall and network-related settings and tools.

Select Advanced settings to open the Windows Firewall with Advanced Security management console, shown in Figure 5-38. This is a very advanced tool for a knowledgeable administrator. Using this console, you can set inbound and outbound rules for the traffic identified by its source or app name, allowing or blocking certain types of traffic.

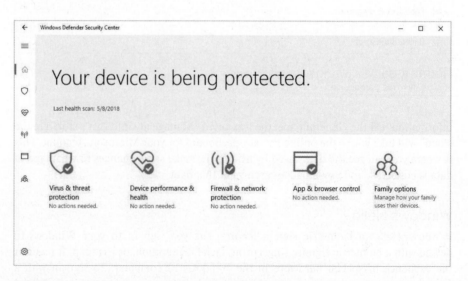

FIGURE 5–36 The Windows Defender Security Center.
Source: Microsoft Corporation

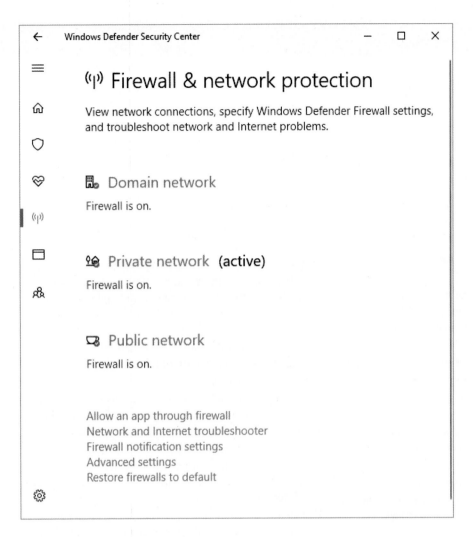

FIGURE 5–37 Windows Defender Firewall and network protection status page.
Source: Microsoft Corporation

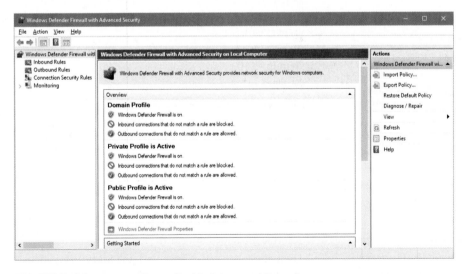

FIGURE 5–38 Windows Firewall with Advanced Security.
Source: Microsoft Corporation

Chapter 5 REVIEW

Chapter Summary

After reading this chapter and completing the exercises, you should understand the following facts about Windows 10.

Installing Windows 10

- The two retail editions of Windows 10 are Windows 10 Home and Windows 10 Pro. Both editions run on PCs and compatible tablets.
- Windows 10 has operating modes that work on PCs, tablets, and two-in-ones.
- The minimum hardware requirements to install Windows 10 on a computer with Intel or AMD architecture are modest, so even budget-level computers today come with hardware that far exceeds Windows 10's requirements.
- Upgrades from certain retail editions of Windows 7 and Windows 8.1 were free for the first year after Windows 10's introduction date.
- Windows 10 includes Cortana, a personal virtual assistant integrated with the new Microsoft Edge Web browser.
- Cortana's voice activation option, Hey Cortana, is available in Windows 10 for those devices that support voice input. Type a query or talk using natural language.
- To upgrade an installation of Windows to Windows 10, the old version must be either Windows 7 Service Pack 1 (SP1) or Windows 8.1 Update 1.
- Prior to upgrading, there are several things you should do:
  - Update Windows 7, Windows 8, or 8.1 if they are not already updated.
  - Back up your data.
  - Update the firmware, if an update is available.
  - Acquire updated drivers if the manufacturer has not automatically updated them.
  - Choose whether you will sign in to Windows 10 with a local account, a Microsoft account, or a Windows Active Directory account.
- Windows 10 comes "prekeyed" and will automatically provide the product key to Microsoft during the product activation process.
- If you purchase Windows 10 online, you can do a Web-based setup that requires very little interaction and is very fast.
- To do a traditional Windows setup, you must have the Windows 10 Setup files on bootable media. If you purchase a physical retail package, you will have bootable media in either DVDs or a USB flash drive. If you purchase Windows 10 online and choose the option "Install later by creating Media," you will have the option to download to a USB drive or to an ISO file.

Postinstallation Tasks

- The Windows 10 Start menu: Apps are on the left and tiles on the right.
- Quick links replace the previous shortcuts.
- File Explorer is the Windows 10 file management utility. It is essentially the renamed and updated replacement for Windows Explorer.
- Microsoft Edge, a new Web browser, is an alternative to Internet Explorer (IE), which Microsoft also included in Windows 10 for backward compatibility with some websites.
- Install drivers. Windows Setup detects your hardware devices and installs appropriate drivers if it has them. If it doesn't, you will have to find them, either online or from the manufacturer.
- Tweak the display settings from the Settings app, and make Windows more accessible with a long list of Ease of Access settings.
- Updates are mandatory in Windows 10 Home and Windows 10 Pro, and you can add updates for other Microsoft software.
- Make Windows 10 run better in a virtual machine. If you installed Windows 10 in a virtual machine, an important postinstallation task is to install the software in the virtual machine that will make it run better. The name of this software varies by hypervisor.
- Remove bloatware software from a computer that has Windows 10 preinstalled.
- Migrate or restore data.
- Back up both data and the system using either third-party utilities or the utilities available in Windows 10: Windows 7 Backup and Restore utility, File History, and image backup.

Working with Windows 10 Features

- Windows 10 default Desktop shows just the taskbar with the Start button, some other features, and the Recycle bin shortcut near the top left.
- On a computer with a keyboard, the Start menu opens in Desktop mode covering a small portion of the

Desktop. Apps are windowed to make them easy to move around by keyboard, mouse, or touchpad.

- When Windows 10 wakes up on a tablet without an attached keyboard, the Start menu automatically opens in full-screen Tablet mode. You can manually switch between Screen mode and Tablet mode.

- The Continuum feature detects when the keyboard is attached so that Windows 10 will display the PC-style Desktop mode.

- Personalize the Start menu by adding Quick links to folders. Personalize the Desktop background and colors.

- Get started with Cortana, Windows 10's virtual assistant. Cortana learns as you use it and it will make appropriate suggestions and reminders. It includes a voice-activation option, Hey Cortana.

- When working in Desktop mode, all apps behave much as traditional Windows apps did in Windows 7. You can launch an app from the Apps list and then pin it to the taskbar or create a shortcut on the Desktop.

- New Universal apps run on all the devices this operating system supports, from the conventional PC to tablets and smartphones.

- Windows 10 Task view lets you quickly view your open apps, improving on the Windows 7 Aero Flip 3D feature. Access Task view by clicking or tapping the Task view icon.

- Windows 10 supports multiple Virtual Desktops. This is a great way to group your projects.

- The Windows Store requires a Microsoft account and offers services, software, games, music, movies, and

TV. To make purchases through the Store, add a payment method through the Store. The Store requires a password for each purchase.

- The Xbox app in Windows 10 accesses a user's Xbox One device.

- Open the User menu from the User tile on the Start menu to change the user picture, lock the computer, or sign out.

Securing Windows 10

- When Windows 10 installs, it enables the most critical security features. Explore the Privacy Settings to balance your privacy needs with convenience.

- Windows Hello, a new feature, lets you sign in to your Windows 10 device with a biometric sign-in type: fingerprint, facial recognition, or iris scan. It requires the existence of special hardware in the Windows 10 computer.

- Microsoft Passport lets you securely sign in to network resources without sending a password or PIN over the network. Once Passport authenticates you locally, it gives you access to resources, such as Microsoft's Azure Active Directory services, and some Web servers.

- Windows Defender automatically provides anti-spyware and antimalware protection. Launch the Windows Defender app by entering "defender" into the Search box.

- Windows 10 Firewall has a simple interface for basic settings. If you select the option labeled "Allow an app or feature through Windows Firewall," a page opens with a list of allowed apps and features.

Key Terms List

bloatware *(187)*	**Microsoft account (MSA)** *(165)*	**User tile** *(174)*
Continuum *(191)*	**Microsoft Edge** *(175)*	**Virtual Desktop** *(196)*
Cortana *(194)*	**Microsoft Passport** *(200)*	**Web-based setup** *(166)*
Desktop mode *(173)*	**multitouch** *(161)*	**Web Note** *(176)*
Device Manager *(177)*	**Out of Box Experience (OOBE)** *(186)*	**Windows 10 Home Edition** *(160)*
Domain Joined *(161)*	**picture-in-picture (PIP)** *(198)*	**Windows 10 Pro** *(160)*
Ease of Access *(183)*	**predictive notification** *(194)*	**Windows Hello** *(199)*
FIDO Alliance *(200)*	**Quick link** *(174)*	**Windows Key** *(173)*
File Explorer *(174)*	**Start button** *(173)*	**Windows Setup** *(167)*
Hey Cortana *(195)*	**Tablet mode** *(190)*	**Windows Store App** *(195)*
keyboard shortcut *(173)*	**Task view** *(196)*	**Xbox Game bar** *(197)*
Lock screen *(174)*	**two-step verification** *(172)*	
live tile *(190)*	**Universal app** *(195)*	

Key Terms Quiz

Use the Key Terms List to complete the sentences that follow. Not all terms will be used.

1. Although this sounds like you are greeting a female friend, _____ is a feature of Windows that lets you activate your personal assistant with your voice.

2. In _____ the Start menu covers the entire screen, and universal apps are full screen.

3. The _____ feature of Windows 10 lets you quickly view all open apps.

4. The _____ feature is similar to ones long available in OS X and Linux, in which you can organize your open apps into individual groupings, with one grouping on your screen at a time.

5. A Start menu _____ works like a shortcut with the added ability to display active content related to the app.

6. Sign in to Windows 10 with a/an _____ to have access to Microsoft services, as well as to programs and files on your local computer.

7. Windows 10 on a two-in-one device uses a new feature called _____, by which it detects when the keyboard is disconnected and automatically changes to Tablet mode.

8. An example of _____ is when Cortana provides a notice in anticipation of a need it discovered by learning about you and your interests.

9. A/an _____ automatically runs full screen on a Windows 10 tablet, and windowed on a computer with a keyboard.

10. _____ is the biometric sign-in feature in Windows 10, requiring special hardware.

Multiple-Choice Quiz

1. This Windows 10 feature is very useful on a computer or device with a touch screen, preventing some unintended actions.
   a. Windows Defender
   b. Lock screen
   c. Continuum
   d. User tile
   e. Multitouch

2. Windows 10 introduced this new Web browser.
   a. Microsoft Edge
   b. Cortana
   c. Microsoft Passport
   d. Continuum
   e. Windows Defender

3. What are the words to look for in the Windows 7 and Windows 8 System app to determine if an installation is legally licensed?
   a. Hello Windows!
   b. Hey Cortana!
   c. License is legal.
   d. Windows is activated.
   e. Genuine Windows!

4. What is the name of the Windows 10 personal assistant that first appeared in Windows Phone 8.1?
   a. Microsoft Edge
   b. Cortana
   c. Microsoft Passport
   d. Continuum
   e. Windows Defender

5. This method for authenticating to network resources does not send passwords or PINs across the network.
   a. Microsoft Edge
   b. Cortana
   c. Microsoft Passport
   d. Continuum
   e. Windows Defender

6. When working in Virtual Desktops in Windows 10, what feature will allow you to see a tile representing each Virtual Desktop, as well as all open apps?
   a. Quick link
   b. Predictive notification
   c. Task view
   d. Windows Hello
   e. Picture-in-picture (PIP)

7. This security antimalware and antispyware app comes with Windows 10 and is enabled during installation.
   a. Microsoft Edge
   b. Cortana
   c. Microsoft Passport
   d. Continuum
   e. Windows Defender

8. Windows 10 includes this renamed and updated file management utility.
   a. Continuum
   b. Windows Passport
   c. Task view
   d. Universal app
   e. File Explorer

9. Which of these will be removed when upgrading a computer from Windows 7 to Windows 10? Select all correct answers.
   a. Windows Hello
   b. Windows Media Center
   c. Desktop gadgets
   d. Windows XP Mode
   e. Minesweeper

10. Click or tap this to open the Windows 10 Start menu. Select all correct answers.
    a. ⊞ Key
    b. Start button
    c. Product key
    d. ⊞+I
    e. ⊞+C

11. Which of the following is the acronym for Microsoft's antipiracy tool?
    a. PIP
    b. OS
    c. MSA
    d. ISO
    e. MPA

12. What optional authentication feature for your Microsoft Account requires that you provide a method for Microsoft to contact you with a special code?
    a. Hey Cortana
    b. Windows Hello
    c. Two-step verification
    d. Windows Defender
    e. Microsoft Passport

13. This feature of Windows Edge allows you to make annotations on a Web page, save the annotated page, and share it with others.
    a. Cortana
    b. Web Note
    c. Microsoft Password
    d. Windows Hello
    e. Quick link

14. Which retail edition of Windows 10 will you buy for your home PC if you need to use BitLocker To Go?
    a. Windows 10 Starter
    b. Windows 10 Education
    c. Windows 10 Enterprise
    d. Windows 10 Home
    e. Windows 10 Pro

15. Windows 8 introduced Modern apps and Windows 10 introduced this type.
    a. Continuum
    b. Windows Passport
    c. Windows Defender Firewall
    d. Universal app
    e. File Explorer

Essay Quiz

1. During the one-year period in which Windows 10 was a free upgrade for compatible systems running either Windows 7 Service Pack 1 or Windows 8.1 Update 1, describe the steps you would have had to go through to do a clean install on a qualifying computer.

2. You plan to do a clean install of Windows 10 Pro onto a computer that is currently running Windows 7, and you plan to reinstall the Windows apps that are currently on that computer. Describe what steps you will take to see if your existing hardware and applications are compatible with Windows 10 and to prepare for any incompatibilities.

3. I have Windows Live Essentials OneDrive app installed on my Windows 7 computer that I plan to upgrade to Windows 10. Describe what will happen during the upgrade and what I should do afterward.

4. Describe the differences between signing in with a local account and signing in with a Microsoft account.

5. Describe Windows Hello and Microsoft Passport and explain the relationship between these two features in making secure connections to network resources.

Lab Projects

LAB PROJECT 5.1

When Microsoft released Windows 10 as a free upgrade to many existing Windows computers, their hope was to replace old versions of Windows with one that would be continually upgraded as time went on. They also hoped to gain market share of desktop and laptop computers. Research how successful this program was in terms of the percentage of qualifying computers that were upgraded and in terms of the resulting market share of Windows 10 on all PCs worldwide.

LAB PROJECT 5.2

Experiment with the Web Note feature. Find a website with content that interests you and use Windows 10 Web Note feature to add notes, highlight important facts, and circle items. Then share with a classmate by emailing a copy of the page. Is this a feature you will use? Discuss this with your classmates.

LAB PROJECT 5.3

Because this chapter is a simple introduction and overview of the Windows 10 operating system, the authors omitted or only briefly mentioned many interesting topics, such as those related to features added to Windows 10 in feature updates. For instance, the Timeline feature was added to Task View in the April 2018 Update, but was only given a margin note in this chapter. Research this feature to learn how to scroll through your Timeline of tasks performed on your Windows 10 computer and resume one or more of those tasks. Then, research how to enable or disable Timeline's tracking of activities associated with your Microsoft account across your devices. Write up your findings and share them with your classmates.

chapter

6 Supporting and Troubleshooting Windows

Learning Outcomes

In this chapter, you will learn how to:

LO **6.1** Define the role of the registry in Windows, and back up and modify the registry when needed.

LO **6.2** Describe the Windows user options and power options, and, given a scenario, select appropriate startup options.

LO **6.3** Install and manage device drivers.

LO **6.4** Troubleshoot common Windows problems.

©Synergee/Getty Images

The world of personal computing has changed considerably during the decades since Windows was first introduced as a GUI operating system for PCs and laptops. The Windows PC or laptop, once required for students and people in innumerable jobs, has been losing ground to tablets and smartphones, as these devices offer more and more functionality. However, Windows still has a significant presence for millions worldwide, especially in the business world. If you are one of them, you may occasionally find yourself needing to troubleshoot Windows. This chapter will guide you through a tour of some of the under-the-hood components and the tools for working with them. Begin with the registry, a critical component of Windows. Then consider user options, power options, and various ways to start up Windows for resolving problems. Then move on to the topic of installing and managing device drivers, and lastly look at methods for troubleshooting common Windows problems. ☀

LO 6.1 | Understanding the Registry

The registry is one of several features that make Windows so adaptable that we can add the hardware and applications to turn a Windows computer into the computing tool we need. Ironically, it is also one of the most complicated and least understood features of Windows. The structure of the registry has remained virtually the same through the last several versions of Windows. In this section, you'll learn about the registry—its role in Windows and how to modify it when needed.

The Registry Defined

The Windows **registry** is a database of all configuration settings in one installation of Windows. It includes settings for:

- Device drivers
- Services
- Installed application programs
- Operating system components
- User preferences

Windows creates the registry during its installation, and it continues to make modifications to it as you configure Windows and add applications and components. During startup, Windows depends on the registry to tell it what services, drivers, and components to load into memory, and how to configure each of them. The registry remains in memory while Windows is active.

Automatic Registry Changes

The Windows registry will automatically change when:

- Windows starts up or shuts down.
- Windows Setup runs (which occurs more often than you may think; for example, each time Windows gets updated).
- Changes are made through a Control Panel applet or the newer Settings tool.
- A new device is installed.
- Any changes are made to the Windows configuration.
- Any changes are made to a user's desktop preferences.
- An application is installed or modified.
- Changes are made to user preferences in any application.

Registry Files

Although considered only a single entity when Windows is running, the registry is stored in a number of binary files on disk. A **binary file** contains program code. The Windows registry files include the following:

- BCD
- default
- ntuser.dat
- sam
- security
- software
- system

> *Note:* Remember that the registry contains only settings, not the actual device drivers, services, or applications to which the settings apply. Windows will not work as you expect it to if these other components are damaged or not available.

TABLE 6-1 Locations of the Hives within the Registry

Hive File	Registry Location
BCD	HKEY_LOCAL_MACHINE\BCD00000000
default	HKEY_USERS\.DEFAULT
ntuser.dat (of the currently logged-on user)	HKEY_CURRENT_USER and HKEY_USERS
sam	HKEY_LOCAL_MACHINE\SAM
security	HKEY_LOCAL_MACHINE\SECURITY
software	HKEY_LOCAL_MACHINE\SOFTWARE
system	HKEY_LOCAL_MACHINE\SYSTEM

The Windows developers named the portion of the registry represented in each of these registry files a *hive*. Table 6–1 shows where the data from each registry hive is located in the registry. Hive files are the permanent portions of the registry, with all the changes saved from use to use. With the exception of ntuser.dat and BCD, these registry files are in a disk folder named config, located below C:\Windows\System32. Figure 6–1 shows the contents of the config folder in Windows 10. Look for the files that match the list above (except ntuser.dat and BCD). Notice that the registry files listed in the config folder have file names without file extensions. If you have Windows Explorer (Windows 7) or File Manager (Windows 8, 8.1, and Windows 10) configured to show hidden files, you will see other files in this location, including files with log extensions that have file names that match the registry files. The operating system uses LOG files for logging transactions to the registry files. Other hidden files with matching file names and SAV extensions are backup copies of registry files created at the end of the text mode stage of setup.

try this!

View Hidden Files and Extensions in Windows Explorer/File Explorer

By default, Windows hides hidden files and extensions in the GUI. Make them visible in Windows Explorer/File Explorer. These steps work in Windows versions 7 and Windows 10. Try this:

1. In Windows 7, open the Start menu and select Control Panel. In Windows 10, enter "control panel" in the Search box and select the result titled "Control Panel Desktop app."
2. In **Control Panel** search on "folder options" and open **Folder Options** (Windows 7) or **File Explorer Options** (Windows 10) from the results.
3. In Folder Options/File Explorer Options select the **View** tab.
4. On the View tab enable the radio button labeled **Show hidden files, folders, and drives.**
5. Ensure that there is *no* check in the boxes labeled **Hide extensions for known file types** and **Hide protected operating system files.**
6. Click or tap the OK button.
7. Open Windows Explorer/File Explorer and browse to the **config** folder, usually found at C:\Windows\System32. Extensions and hidden files are now visible.

BCD

The BCD file resides in the Boot folder in the hidden system partition. As with other registry files, it is a binary file. It contains the Boot Configuration Database (BCD) store used by Windows during the bootloader phase of startup, providing the bootloader with information it needs to locate and load the operating system files.

WARNING!

In the Try This, you disable a setting that hides protected operating system files. Only do this temporarily on a lab computer. Do not do this on a work or school computer unless you have technical support available.

DEFAULT

The default hive contains user desktop settings, called a user profile, used when there is no logged-on user. You do need desktop settings for the GUI even before you log on. You'll see evidence of this profile in the desktop settings used for the Logon screen shown in Figure 6–2.

Note: The Boot Configuration Database in the BCD file is used during the bootloader phase of startup.

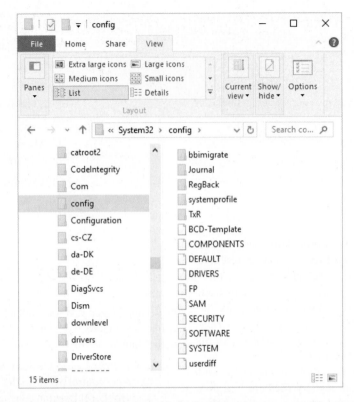

FIGURE 6–1 This view of the Windows 10 config folder shows most of the registry files.
Source: Microsoft Corporation

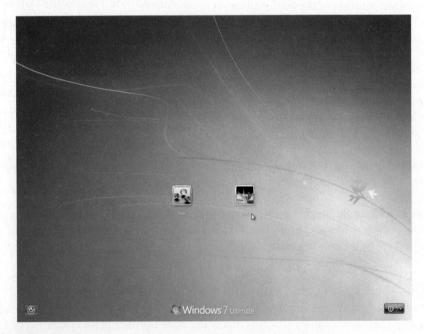

FIGURE 6–2 The default user profile is used until a user logs on.
Source: Microsoft Corporation

NTUSER.DAT

The ntuser.dat hive file contains the user profile for a single user. These settings include application preferences, screen colors, network connections, and other personal choices. Each user who logs on to the computer has a separate ntuser.dat file. During startup, Window uses the other registry hives to load and configure the operating system. One of the last tasks of the operating system at startup is to request a user logon. When a user logs on, the settings from that user's ntuser.dat file apply and become part of the current registry. The first time a user logs on to a computer, Windows uses the ntuser.dat file from the C:\Users\Default folder to create the initial profile for the user. It saves the ntuser.dat file in the top-level personal folder for that user, and it is a hidden file so it is only visible if your Folder Options are set to Show hidden files, folders, and drives.

Note: We described personal folders in Chapter 4.

SAM

The SAM hive contains the local security accounts database; SAM is an acronym for Security Accounts Manager.

Note: The SAM hive also stores user passwords, and it is used to authenticate users.

SECURITY

The SECURITY hive contains the local security policy settings for the computer, including rules for password complexity and for how the system will handle numerous failed attempts at entering a password.

SOFTWARE

The SOFTWARE hive contains configuration settings for software installed on the local computer, along with various items of miscellaneous configuration data.

SYSTEM

The SYSTEM hive contains information used at startup, including device drivers to load as well as the order of their loading, and configuration settings, instructions for the starting and configuring of services, and various operating system settings.

The Temporary Portion of the Registry

The information stored in HKEY_LOCAL_MACHINE\HARDWARE is temporary information, gathered during the hardware detection process of the detect-and-configure-hardware phase of Windows startup. Windows does not save it to disk in a file, as it does other portions of the registry.

Viewing and Editing the Registry

View and edit the hierarchical structure of the active registry using the Registry Editor utility, Regedit. Its executable file, regedit.exe, is located in the folder in which the operating system is installed (by default that is C:\Windows), but it does not have a shortcut on the Start menu or other handy locations in the Windows GUI. This is for a very good reason: It should not be too handy. The Try This! will walk you through opening Regedit and viewing the registry locations shown in Table 6-1.

The first time Regedit runs on a computer, it looks like Figure 6-3. Each folder represents a key, an object that may contain one or more settings as well as other keys. Each of the top five folders is a root key (also called a subtree in Microsoft documentation). Each root key is at the top of a hierarchical structure containing more keys. Each key may contain one or more settings as well as other keys. A key that exists within another key is a subkey. Each setting within a key is a value entry. When you click on the folder for a key, it becomes the active key in Regedit, its folder icon "opens," and the contents of the key show in the right pane, as you see in Figure 6-4. Table 6-2 gives an overview of the information stored within each root key of the registry.

In Regedit, each value entry appears in three columns labeled: Name, Type, and Data. The Type column shows a label that describes the format of the data in that registry value, also called data type. There are many data types in the registry; take a few minutes to study Table 6-3, which shows just a few registry data types, to give you an idea of how diverse the data in the registry can be.

WARNING!

Do not directly edit the registry with a tool such as Regedit unless it is absolutely necessary; there are many safer ways to make a change to the registry. For example, when you change settings in a Control Panel applet, that applet in turn modifies the registry.

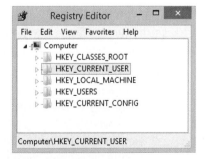

FIGURE 6-3 The registry root keys.
Source: Microsoft Corporation

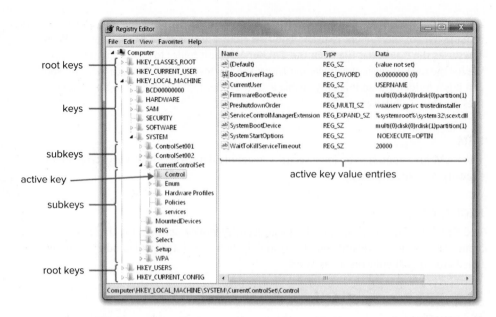

root keys

keys

subkeys

active key

subkeys

root keys

active key value entries

FIGURE 6–4 Registry components.
Source: Microsoft Corporation

TABLE 6–2	Contents of Registry Root Keys
Root Key	**Description**
HKEY_CLASSES_ROOT	Shows relationships (called associations) between applications and data file types defined by file extension. Thanks to the information in this key, you can double-click on a data file and the correct application will open and load the file. This root key contains all the information located in HKEY_LOCAL_MACHINE\SOFTWARE\Classes.
HKEY_CURRENT_USER	Contains the user profile for the currently logged-on user, storing all the user settings that affect the desktop appearance and the default behavior of installed applications.
HKEY_LOCAL_MACHINE	Contains the system information, including detected hardware, application associations, and information for hardware configuration and device drivers.
HKEY_USERS	User profiles for all local user accounts, including the profile of the currently logged-on user (also shown under HKEY_CURRENT_USER), the default profile, and profiles for special user accounts used to run various services. Except for the default profile, each is labeled with a security ID (SID), a unique string of numbers preceded by S-1-5 that identifies a security principal (an entity that can be authenticated) in a Windows security accounts database, including users and groups.
HKEY_CURRENT_CONFIG	Contains configuration information for the current hardware profile, which is a set of changes (*only* changes) to the standard configuration in the Software and System subkeys under HKEY_LOCAL_MACHINE.

try this!

Start Registry Editor

Open Registry Editor and explore the contents of the registry. Try this:

1. Press ⊞+R. This opens the Run box. Type "regedit" and click OK.
2. Respond to any User Account Control dialog to continue.
3. Once Regedit is open, be careful not to make any changes. Browse through the registry structure, much as you would navigate in Windows Explorer/ File Explorer.
4. Notice the folders in the navigation pane and the various folders and settings in the contents pane on the right. Keep Registry Editor open as you read this chapter section.

Backing Up the Registry

It is very important to remember that the last thing you should consider doing, even if your best friend or brother-in-law insists you do it, is to directly edit the registry using Regedit or a third-party registry editing tool. We strongly recommend that you not use the registry cleaning tools promoted all over the Internet. While you should rarely if ever edit the registry, you should know how to back up the registry in case you decide that you have no choice but to use Regedit. Here are two methods for backing up

TABLE 6–3   Windows Registry Data Types (The Short List)

Data Type	Description
REG_BINARY	Raw binary data. It shows some hardware data in binary. Ironically, it shows binary data in hexadecimal and might look like this: ff 00 ff ff 02 05.
REG_DWORD	A 4-byte-long number (32 bits), stored in binary, hexadecimal, or decimal format. It may look something like this in hexadecimal: 0x00000002.
REG_EXPAND_SZ	A single string of text including a variable, which is a value that an application will replace when called. An example of a common variable is %*systemroot*%, which, when Windows uses it, is replaced by the path of the folder containing the Windows system files. Example: A registry entry containing %*systemroot*%\regedit.exe becomes c:\windows\regedit.exe.
REG_MULTI_SZ	Multiple strings of human-readable text separated by a special NULL character that it does not display. Example: wuauserv gpsvc trustedinstaller
REG_SZ	A sequence of characters representing human-readable text. It may use this data type when the data is quite simple, such as a string of alphanumeric characters—for example, ClosePerformanceData—or to represent an entire list: comm.drv commdlg.dll ctl3dv2.dll ddeml.dll.

the registry. The first, using System Restore, is a very broad approach that backs up the entire registry and more. The second method, backing up a portion of the registry with Regedit, is a more targeted approach.

Creating a Restore Point

Our favorite method is to simply create a restore point using System Restore. While Windows creates restore points on a regular basis, you can create one any time you want, knowing that you will have a snapshot of Windows at that point in time. Step-by-Step 6.01 will walk you through this process.

> *Note:* Describing a registry location is similar to the way we describe file and folder locations on disk; we use a notation that shows the path from a root key down through the subkeys: HKEY_LOCAL_MACHINE\SYSTEM\CURRENT CONTROLSET\CONTROL.

Step-by-Step 6.01

Creating a Restore Point

In this step-by-step exercise, you will create a restore point. For this exercise you will need a computer running Windows. The illustrations are from Windows 10. You will need to respond to a User Account Control (UAC) prompt. In which case, if you logged on as a standard account, you will need to enter an administrator password.

Step 1

Open the Run box in Windows using the keyboard shortcut ⊞+R. In the Run box type "sysdm.cpl." Do not type the quotation marks! Click OK.

Step 2

This brings up the System Properties dialog. Select the System Protection tab. Then click the Create button located at the bottom, as shown here.

Source: Microsoft Corporation

Step 3

Type a descriptive name for the restore point. Then press the Create button.

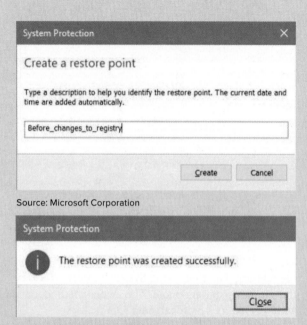

Source: Microsoft Corporation

Step 4

It will take a minute or two, during which a progress message will display in the System Protection box. When Windows has created the restore point, this message will display. Click the Close button.

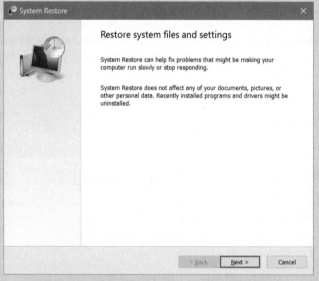

Source: Microsoft Corporation

Step 5

The System Properties dialog box from Step 2 will remain open. To see the restore points, click the System Restore button. If a page displays with a recommended restore point, click Choose a different restore point. Then click the Next button. If a simpler page without the recommended restore point displays, as shown here, simply click Next.

Source: Microsoft Corporation

Step 6

Caution: you want to only view the existing restore points—you do not want to actually roll back to a previous restore point. Simply view the list of restore points, noticing the descriptions. Press Cancel to exit from System Restore. Press Cancel again in the System Properties dialog.

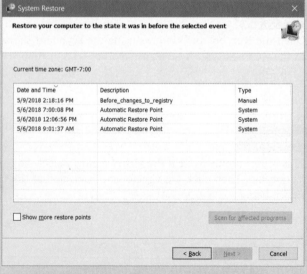

Source: Microsoft Corporation

Use Regedit to Back Up the Registry

Despite knowing the danger of directly editing the registry, you might find yourself in a position in which editing the registry is the only way to solve a problem. This may be the case when an administrator or help desk person has given you specific instructions for virus removal or some other necessary change. Do this only after attempting all other avenues, including using system restore to restore your computer to a previous state or doing a total restore of your computer from a complete backup set. But if all else fails, and you know the exact change that you must make to the registry, then before you attempt to edit the registry, use Regedit to back up the portion of the registry you plan to edit. To back up a registry key, right-click on the folder for the key in Registry Editor and select Export, as shown in Figure 6–5. Provide a location and name for the file, and Regedit will create a .reg file. If you need to restore the file, simply double-click on it.

LO 6.2 | Windows User and Power Options

Windows 7 combined both the user options and power options on one menu. Beginning in Windows 8, these options are separated. We will examine both types of options so that you understand how to use them. As part of the discussion on power options, we will also describe the Windows shutdown and startup procedures. Understanding these can help you to troubleshoot problems that may occur as Windows starts up. It may seem a little backwards, but we will talk about power options, including Sleep, Hibernate, Shutdown, and Restart before describing how the different versions of Windows start up. This is because beginning with Windows 8, Fast Boot is the default startup mode, and it depends on a Hybrid Shutdown. It helps to understand Hybrid Shutdown before learning about Fast Boot.

Windows 7 Shutdown Button

The Windows 7 Shutdown button, if clicked, will shut down Windows and turn off the computer. The Shutdown button has a smaller button alongside it, and when you click it, the Shutdown options menu opens, shown in Figure 6–6. It includes *Switch user, Log off, Lock, Restart,* and *Sleep.* We call the first three options user options and the last two, *Restart* and *Sleep,* power options.

User Options

Beginning with Windows 8, Microsoft moved the user options to the User menu. Open this menu in Windows 8 or 8.1 by clicking or tapping the User tile on the Start screen. In Windows 10, open the Start menu and click or tap on the User tile in the left column. Figure 6–7 shows the Windows 10 User menu. In Windows 7, selecting *Switch user*

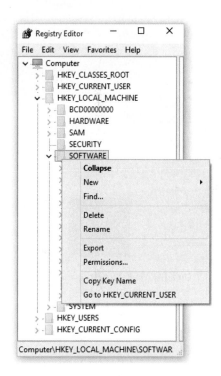

FIGURE 6–5 Back up a registry key and all its subkeys and values.
Source: Microsoft Corporation

Note: Back up the entire registry by opening Regedit's File menu, and selecting Export.

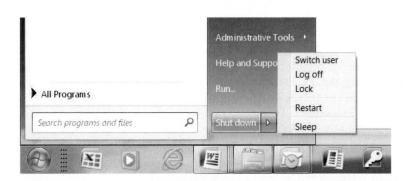

FIGURE 6–6 The Windows 7 Shutdown options menu includes Switch user, Log off, Lock, Restart, and Sleep.
Source: Microsoft Corporation

FIGURE 6–7 The Windows 10 User options menu.
Source: Microsoft Corporation

Sleep
Shut down
Restart

FIGURE 6–8 The Power menu.
Source: Microsoft Corporation

Note: A small difference between the user options menu in these different versions of Windows is the naming of the option called *Change account picture,* in Windows 8.1, versus *Change account settings* in Windows 10. Either one will take you to the Your Account pane on the Accounts page of the Settings app.

Note: A computer recovers more quickly from Sleep than from Hibernate, but Sleep requires power, while Hibernate does not. As a user experience, Hibernate and Sleep are essentially the same: They return you to your open apps and data so that you continue working where you left off.

keeps the current user's session in memory without closing any programs, and presents the logon screen. Another user can then log on and run in a separate user session with her own user profile, seeing her files, but not accessing the first user's open session.

Figure 6–7 shows the Windows 10 User options menu. In Windows 8, 8.1, and Windows 10, although the User options menu does not include *Switch user* there is a method for switching users. If there is another user account on that computer, that user name and profile picture will display at the bottom of the User menu. Selecting another user saves the current user's session in memory and shows the Sign-in screen for the selected user.

Where Windows 7 provides the user options *Log off* and *Lock* on the Shutdown options menu, Windows 10 displays *Change Account settings, Lock,* and *Sign out* on the User menu.

Power Options

While Windows 7 offers Restart, Sleep, and (in some cases) Hibernate from the Shutdown options menu, Windows 8, 8.1, and Windows 10 offer these choices from the Power menu, shown in Figure 6–8. Access the Power menu In Windows 8 and 8.1 from the Settings bar or Sign-in screen. Windows 8.1 also added the Power button to the Start screen. In Windows 10, the Power button is located on the Start menu. In all versions of Windows since Windows 7, Hibernate is not a default option but you can enable it in Control Panel's Power Options. We will describe the difference between Sleep and Hibernate next.

Sleep

If you select the Sleep option, the computer stays on in a very-low-power mode; the system state and user session (applications and data) are saved in RAM, and the screen turns off. Wake up your computer (resume) by clicking a mouse button, tapping a touch screen, or pressing keys. On some computers, you may press the power button to bring Windows out of Sleep mode, but try these other actions first. When the computer resumes from Sleep, you may need to enter your password before you are back in Windows with all your apps open and data intact.

When should you use Sleep? A common scenario is when you must interrupt your work on a laptop or tablet, as when you board a plane. Select Sleep mode before boarding, and when you have settled in your seat, resume and continue working.

Do not use Sleep for a long period of time because when the battery runs down, Sleep mode ends. Microsoft has safeguards built in, but we have never been comfortable using Sleep for an extended period of time because we have seen problems with network connections after bringing a computer back from Sleep mode.

Hibernate

If you select the Hibernate option, Windows saves to disk an image of the contents of RAM, including the OS, open apps, and all the associated data, in a file named hiberfil.sys, and then the OS sends the command to power down the computer. Hibernate does not require power.

When should you use Hibernate? If it is available, you may want to use it on a laptop or tablet when you would use Sleep. To resume, press the power button, and the Lock screen or the Sign-in screen will greet you. The apps that were open before you hibernated Windows will be open with the data intact.

The Windows 7 Shutdown

When you select *Shutdown* from the Windows 7 Start menu, several events occur. Windows does the following:

1. Sends messages to all running apps to save data and settings.
2. Closes the session for each logged-on user.
3. Sends a shutdown message to all running services and then shuts them down.
4. Sends a shutdown message to all devices.
5. Closes the operating system's session.
6. Writes pending data to the system drive.
7. Sends a signal to power down the computer.

Windows 8, 8.1, and Windows 10 Hybrid Shutdown

When you select *Shutdown* from the Windows 8, 8.1, or Windows 10 Power menu it does a Hybrid Shutdown, during which Windows does the following:

1. Sends messages to all running apps to save data and settings, and then shuts down the apps.
2. Closes the session for each logged-on user.
3. Hibernates the Windows session and saves it in a file. It does not hibernate the User session.

Because the hibernate process saves an image of the system session to disk, the operating system does not have to reassemble all its parts every time it starts up.

> *Note:* Restart is also a troubleshooting tool because a problem, such as system instability, that goes away after a restart may have been caused by a temporary problem. The problem is resolved by shutting down and restarting to let Windows reload all its components. You can then note if the problem reoccurs after you open an app or take some other action.

Restart

The method of using the power switch to shut down and start up a device and its operating system is called a cold boot. In contrast, a warm boot restarts the firmware and operating system without a power down and power up cycle. When you select the *Restart* option, all versions of Windows do a full shutdown and a full system startup. This is important to know because a Restart will seem slower on a Windows 8, 8.1, or Windows 10 computer than a cold boot because it will not do the Hybrid shutdown described above, nor the Windows Fast Boot, described later. A Restart is often required when updating Windows or installing an app to complete the installation.

Windows 7 Startup Phases

The Windows 7 startup has several phases on a typical desktop PC. These include:

1. Power-on self-test
2. Initial startup
3. Bootloader
4. Hardware detection and configuration
5. Kernel loading
6. Logon

In the first two phases, the hardware "wakes up" and system firmware searches for an operating system. Through the remaining phases, the operating system builds itself, much like a building, from the ground up, with more levels and complexity added at each phase.

Power-On Self-Test

When you power on your computer, the CPU loads firmware programs into memory. Firmware is software installed in nonvolatile memory chips. This memory may be read-only memory (ROM), erasable programmable read-only memory (EPROM), or a similar technology. All computing devices contain firmware. The common traditional name for the firmware in computers is ROM-BIOS, as defined in Chapter 1, but newer computers come with much more sophisticated firmware that complies with a specification called Unified Extensible Firmware Interface (UEFI).

Among the first firmware programs that run are those that perform the power-on self-test (POST)—a series of tests of the system hardware that determines the amount of memory present and verifies that devices required for OS startup are working. The POST most often only displays a brief black screen before Windows loads.

Initial Startup

During the initial startup, the firmware bootstrap loader program uses hardware configuration settings stored in nonvolatile memory, commonly called CMOS, to determine what devices can start an OS and the order in which the system will search these devices while attempting to begin the OS startup process. The order may be optical drive or USB drive, then hard drive. On a computer with UEFI with Secure Boot turned on, this will normally be drive C only, unless you modify firmware settings, which is an advanced task. The bootstrap loader then looks in the location specified for Windows OS startup code, called the bootloader, and loads it into memory.

Bootloader

Bootmgr is the bootloader file that begins the loading of OS components for all current versions of Windows. Once bootmgr loads, the OS starts the file system, reads the Boot Configuration Database (BCD) file to learn the location and names of the remaining Windows OS files to load into memory at startup. Then it starts the winload.exe program, which is the OS loader boot program. Together, bootmgr and winload.exe manage the startup phases that follow.

Detect and Configure Hardware

The Detect and Configure hardware phase includes a scan of the computer's hardware and creation of a hardware list for later inclusion in the registry.

Kernel Loading

During the kernel loading phase, the Windows kernel (ntoskrnl.exe) loads into memory from the location indicated in the BCD. Hardware information passes on to the kernel, and the hardware abstraction layer (HAL) file for the system loads into memory. The system hive of the registry loads, and components and drivers listed in the registry as required at startup are then loaded. All of this code is loaded into memory, but is not immediately initialized (made active).

Once all startup components are in memory, the kernel (ntoskrnl.exe) takes over the startup process and initializes the components (services and drivers) required for startup. Then the kernel scans the registry for other components that were not required during startup but are part of the configuration. It then loads and initializes them.

The kernel starts the session manager, which creates the system environment variables and loads the kernel-mode Windows subsystem code that switches Windows from text mode to graphics mode.

The Session manager then starts the user mode Windows subsystem code (csrss. exe). Just two of the session manager's other tasks include creating the virtual memory paging file (pagefile.sys) and starting the Windows logon service (winlogon.exe), which leads us to the next phase.

> Note: Windows versions after Windows 7 have the same startup procedures and the files have the same names and roles as those used in Windows 7. But in the newer versions startup is made more secure by Trusted Boot and starts much faster when it uses Windows Fast Boot. We describe both later.

Logon

More things happen during the logon phase than simply authenticating the user, and they happen simultaneously. They include the following:

User Logon. The key player in this phase is the Windows Logon service, which supports logging on and logging off, and starts the service control manager (services.exe) and the local security authority (lsass.exe). At this point, depending on how your computer was configured, you may not be required to actually enter a user name and password. Figure 6-9 shows just one possible logon screen that you may see in Windows 7, in which you simply enter a password for the user name shown.

Program Startup. During program startup, logon scripts (if they exist) run, startup programs for various applications run, and noncritical services start. Windows finds instructions to run these programs and services in many locations in the registry.

Plug-and-Play Detection. Plug-and-play detection uses several methods to detect new plug-and-play devices, and when it detects a new device, it allocates system resources (memory and other OS resources) to the devices and installs appropriate device drivers.

Windows Secure Boot and Fast Boot

On a computer running Windows 8 or newer, all you see during startup may be the manufacturer's logo and, after a brief pause, the Lock screen. The system code in these newer versions of Windows is not much different from that of Windows 7, so it must go through a process similar to that of Windows 7 startup to assemble all the pieces of the OS along with settings, drivers, services, and apps. In view of what you learned earlier in this chapter about how Windows 7 starts up, you may wonder how these newer versions can get all of this done so quickly. We explain that mystery now.

Note: The actual screen or dialog box that appears before you log on varies with your computer's configuration.

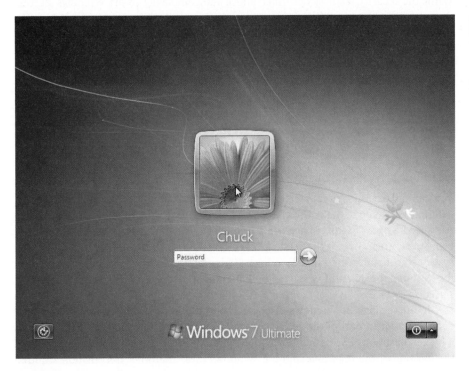

FIGURE 6-9 Log on to Windows 7.
Source: Microsoft Corporation

Firmware Startup

When you turn on your computer, the CPU loads firmware into memory and the power-on self-test occurs regardless of the OS installed, because it occurs before the OS is in control. If you have installed Windows 8, 8.1, or Windows 10 on an older computer with ROM-BIOS, the startup may be a bit longer than that same version of Windows on a UEFI-compliant computer, but it should be faster than Windows 7 on that same computer. Computers that come with Windows 8, 8.1, or Windows 10 preinstalled by the manufacturer must have UEFI firmware and must have security features of UEFI enabled by default to protect Windows during the startup process. Secure Boot is the UEFI firmware feature that loads only trusted operating system bootloaders. From there, as with the Windows 7 startup process described previously, the Windows components take over, with the addition of Windows Trusted Boot, described later.

While Windows proceeds with the phases of startup, up to the point when anti-malware software loads, a UEFI firmware feature called Measured Boot logs the process, and antimalware software can analyze this log to determine if malware is on the computer or if the boot components were tampered with. In an enterprise environment with Windows Active Directory servers, Windows 8, 8.1, or Windows 10 can send this log to a trusted server that can assess the PC's startup and track the security and health of the PC.

Trusted Boot and Early Launch Anti-Malware

Trusted Boot is a feature, introduced in Windows 8, that examines each system file required for the boot process before it loads into memory. Another security component, called Early Launch Anti-Malware (ELAM) does the same for all device drivers before they load into memory, thus preventing drivers containing malware from loading.

Fast Boot

While the security features described above add complexity to the Windows startup, these newer versions of Windows start up very rapidly. The reason for this is the Fast Boot feature, which takes advantage of the hibernated kernel of the Hybrid Shutdown, described earlier in this chapter. Fast Boot simply brings the hibernated system session out of hibernation, saving all the work of the Kernel Loading phase. Additionally, on a computer with multiple CPU cores, the cores work in parallel when processing the hibernation file. Hybrid Shutdown is the default when you select the Shutdown option, and Fast Boot is the default when you power up your computer.

Modifying System Startup

You can modify the system startup on your Windows computer in many ways. First, determine if you can make the change you want through the GUI, such as using the Advanced System Settings page. As a last resort, you can directly edit these settings using the correct tool for the version of Windows in question. We'll look at modifying system startup for Windows 7, Windows 8/8.1, and Windows 10 including the settings for choosing the default OS started on a multiboot system and the length of time the selection menu displays.

In all versions of Windows discussed here, the Boot Configuration Database is actually a hidden part of the registry, stored in a registry file named BCD, located in a hidden partition. The basic information stored in BCD provides locale information, the location of the boot disk and the Windows files, and other information required for the startup process. View the contents of BCD using the BCDedit program, a utility that needs to run from a Command Prompt or Windows PowerShell with

Note: During startup, as part of Trusted Boot, each operating system file is examined before it is loaded into memory. If one appears to have been altered, an unmodified version of the file is used.

Note: Learn about special startup modes for troubleshooting later in this chapter.

elevated privileges, meaning that it runs with the privileges of a local administrator, as described in Step-by-Step 6.02.

The Command Prompt is a command-line interface (CLI) that you can launch from within Windows, from Safe Mode, or as a Recovery option. There are many commands that administrators use that run either in a Command Prompt or in another more advanced command-line interface, Windows PowerShell. Both of these CLIs accept certain commands and can be used to run scripts that advanced technical people use to automate tasks, but Command Prompt is a much simpler and limited interface. Command Prompt, in all its forms, only accepts text input. PowerShell accepts text input, but it also accepts objects, as defined by object-oriented programming. A software object has fields that define its state, and each object has a set of behaviors. Modern operating systems use object-oriented programming.

To change Windows startup settings, one method is to use the Startup and Recovery page of System Properties. Step-by-Step 6.02 will walk you through making a change to BCD using the Startup and Recovery page, and then you will use BCDedit to view the changes made to the BCD file. Another method for configuring Windows System Startup is to use the MSCONFIG utility, described later in this chapter under *Using Windows Troubleshooting and Recovery Tools*.

Step-by-Step 6.02

Modifying Windows System Startup

In this step-by-step exercise, you will modify the system startup for Windows using the Startup and Recovery page of System Properties. The steps work in Windows 7, Windows 8, 8.1, and Windows 10. The images are from Windows 10, but these are nearly identical to what you will see in the other versions.

Step 1

Use the keyboard shortcut ⊞+R to open the Run box. In the Run box, type "sysdm.cpl" (do not type the quotation marks). Click OK. In System Properties, click the Advanced tab.

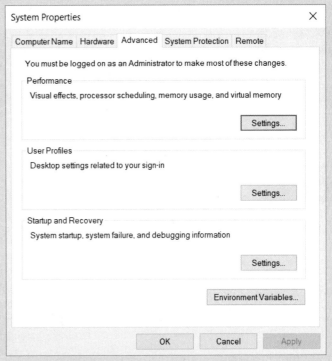

Source: Microsoft Corporation

Step 2

On the Advanced tab of System Properties, locate the Startup and Recovery section near the bottom and click the Settings button to open the Startup and Recovery page. If your computer is a multiboot computer, you can choose the default operating system that it will select if you do not respond to the menu during the time that it displays the list of operating systems. Notice the time selected is 30 seconds.

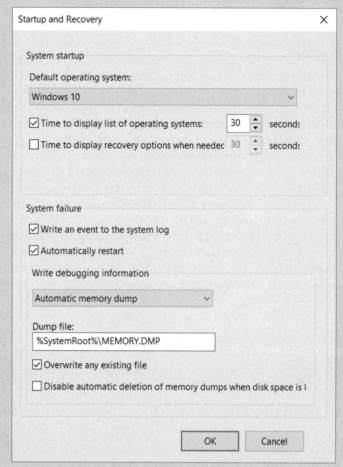

Source: Microsoft Corporation

Step 3

Change the selected time to 35 seconds and click OK to close the Startup and Recovery page. Click OK again to close System Properties. Windows will save the changes in a file named BCD, and they will take effect the next time Windows starts.

Step 4

To see the changes you made, you will need to run BCDedit, an editor that will let you see the contents of BCD. If you are using Windows 7, go to Step 5. If you are using a later version, skip to Step 6.

Step 5

In Windows 7, open Start Search and type **cmd.** Then right-click **cmd,** and select *Run as administrator* from the context menu, as shown here. Respond to the User Account Control (UAC) prompt (if required). The Command Prompt will then open. The Title bar of the window should say Administrator: Command Prompt. If it doesn't, carefully repeat this step. With the Command Prompt window open, skip to Step 7.

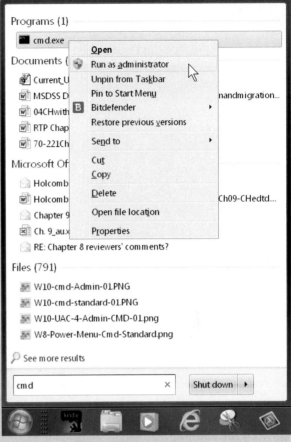

Source: Microsoft Corporation

Step 6

In Windows 8, 8.1, or Windows 10, right-click on the Start button and select either Command Prompt (Admin) or Windows Power-Shell (Admin) from the Power User menu. This will first open the User Account Control (UAC) box. After you respond to the UAC message, the Command Prompt or Windows PowerShell window will open.

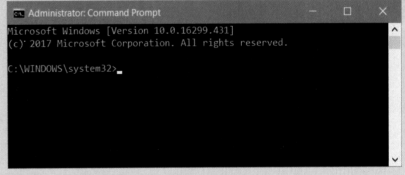

Source: Microsoft Corporation

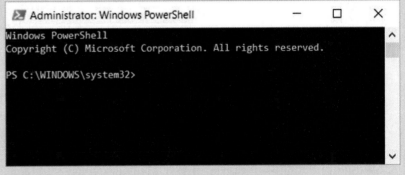

Source: Microsoft Corporation

At the prompt in either window, type "bcdedit" and press Enter. The result should look something like the example here. Notice the Timeout setting, which you changed in the earlier steps.

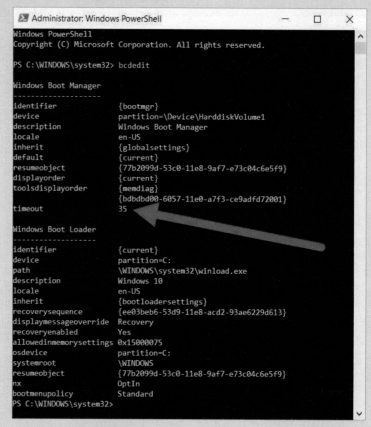

Source: Microsoft Corporation

To close the Command Prompt or PowerShell windows, type Exit and press Enter.

LO 6.3 | Installing and Managing Device Drivers

A huge number of devices work in Windows. There are the ones we take for granted, such as hard drives, flash drives, video adapters, network interface cards, displays, sound cards, and printers, as well as keyboards, mice, and other pointing devices. Then there are others, such as cameras, scanners, video capture cards, and game controllers. In this section, we learn about installing device drivers and managing installed device drivers.

Installing Device Drivers

All devices need device drivers, and the latest versions of Windows come with huge caches of device drivers. Windows and virtually all devices for PCs are plug-and-play (PnP), which is the ability of a computer and OS to automatically detect and configure a hardware device. To work, the computer, the device, and the OS must all comply with the same plug-and-play standard. Therefore, when you connect a device, Windows recognizes it, and then finds and installs the appropriate driver.

But there are exceptions. For example, in some cases, even though the device is plug and play, you need to install the driver (and with it the companion software) before connecting the device. There is also the issue of when you should power on an external device. Some require that you power up the device before connecting it to the PC, while others require that you connect the device and then power it up. The supreme authority for each device is the manufacturer, so you really need to read the manufacturer's quick-start guide or user manual before connecting a new device.

Permissions

Regardless of how easily a device driver installs, you need administrator privileges to install or uninstall a device. In all current versions of Windows, you can install a device driver while logged on as either a computer administrator or a standard user. When logged on as an administrator, you will simply need to click Yes in the UAC Consent Prompt, whereas a standard user will need to provide computer administrator credentials in the Credentials Prompt.

Fortunately, unplugging a device does not uninstall the driver from your computer—it just gives the device a status of "not present." Therefore, once a device is installed, any local users may disconnect and reconnect the device without restriction and it will operate.

Working with Signed versus Unsigned Device Drivers

Because a device driver becomes a part of an operating system, a poorly written device driver can be a vector for malware and cause problems, including system crashes. For this reason, bad device drivers have long been the top cause of operating system instability. Windows has features that help users avoid badly written program code.

One of the latest additions to protections against bad device drivers is Early Launch Anti-Malware (ELAM) during Windows 8, 8.1, or Windows 10 startup, described previously in this chapter. But one of the long-standing central features that protects against all types of bad program code is code signing, the use of a digital signature provided by Microsoft as its seal of approval on program code. A digital signature is encrypted data placed in the signed file. Windows decrypts the digital signature by a process called file signature verification. The digital signature includes information about the file so that the operating system can detect any alterations to the file. Driver signing is simply code signing of device drivers that indicates the integrity of the file or files and that the device driver has passed Microsoft's test for compatibility. This does not mean all nondigitally signed device drivers are bad. What it does mean is that Microsoft has provided a process that manufacturers can choose to use to have their device drivers tested and signed by Microsoft. This is part of the process of having a device added to Microsoft's compatibility list.

If you attempt to install a program that contains unsigned code, you may get a warning. It is then up to you if you want to continue using the unsigned code. If you trust the source, continue. By default, you cannot install unsigned drivers in 64-bit Windows; the installation will simply fail.

Managing Installed Devices

The Devices and Printers Control Panel applet, as well as the PC Settings Devices page in Windows 8, 8.1, and Windows 10 are simple tools for managing devices. The Device Manager Control Panel, available in all versions of Windows, is a more advanced tool. Learn about each of these.

Devices and Printers

You can manage many devices in all three versions of Windows through the user-friendly Devices and Printers Control Panel applet (see Figure 6-10). Open Devices and Printers in Windows 7

try this!

Install a Plug-and-Play Device

Locate a plug-and-play USB device never before installed on your computer, such as a printer or wireless NIC. Try this:

1. Read the documentation for the device. If required, install the device driver before connecting the device.
2. Follow the instructions for the order in which you must power on and connect the USB device to a USB port. You may see a balloon by the notification area as Windows automatically recognizes it.

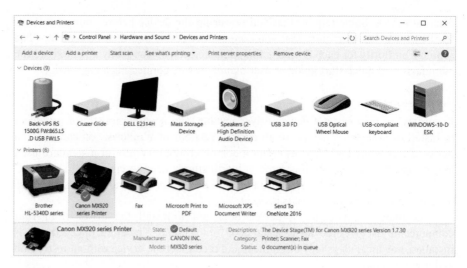

FIGURE 6–10 The Devices and Printers page.
Source: Microsoft Corporation

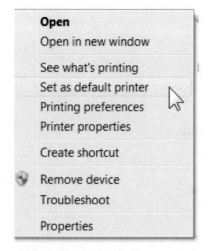

FIGURE 6–11 Set the default printer.
Source: Microsoft Corporation

Note: Some "printers" are actually software to which you can send files for special formatting. Figure 6–10 shows three (Microsoft Print to PDF, Microsoft XPS document Writer, and Send to OneNote 2016) or four, if you count Fax. If you need to convert files to PDF format more often than you need to print them to a physical printer, make *Microsoft Print to PDF* your default printer.

from the Start menu; open it in Windows 8, 8.1, and Windows 10 by searching on "devices and printers." This gives you an overview of the most obvious devices attached to your computer. From here you can access the Properties dialog and other appropriate applications and actions by double-clicking on the device (for the default action) or right-clicking and selecting an action from the context menu. For instance, double-clicking on the Fax object will open Windows Fax and Scan. If you have installed special faxing and scanning software from the manufacturer, that software will open in place of Windows Fax and Scan.

In Figure 6–10, the Canon printer has a round green icon with a white check mark indicating it is the default printer that will be used unless you select a different printer when you select the Print command in an app. To change the default printer, right-click on a printer's icon and then select *Set as Default Printer* from the context menu, shown in Figure 6–11.

Expect newer devices to have a special "home page" that is part of the Device Stage feature. For instance, in Windows 7, double-clicking a printer's icon brought up the printer's print queue. That still happens if your installed printer does not have the Device Stage feature. If it has Device Stage, double-clicking on it will bring up a new page from which you can make many choices for managing the device, including a link to open your printer's print queue. Figure 6–12 shows the Device Stage page for a printer.

Windows 8 and Windows 8.1 PC Settings

In Windows 8 or 8.1, the Devices page of PC settings lists printers and other devices. From this page you can add a plug-and-play device that Windows did not automatically detect and install by clicking the *Add a device* button.

Add or remove devices in PC Settings in the Windows 8 or 8.1 Modern GUI, but for more management tools, go to the Windows Desktop and use the same tools you used in Windows 7: Devices and Printers and Device Manager.

Windows 10 Settings

Microsoft has improved the Settings tool in Windows 10, moving more of the functionality of Control Panel into Settings during feature updates. In Windows 10, launch Settings from the Start menu. In Settings, click or tap Devices to open the Devices pane, shown in Figure 6–13, and then select the type of device you want to add or remove. However, Control Panel still exists, and is often the tool to open when you

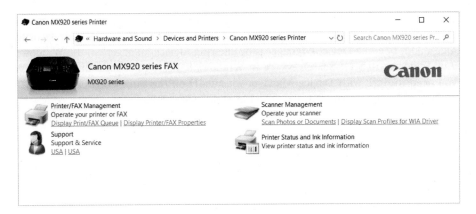

FIGURE 6–12 The Device Stage page for a printer.
Source: Microsoft Corporation

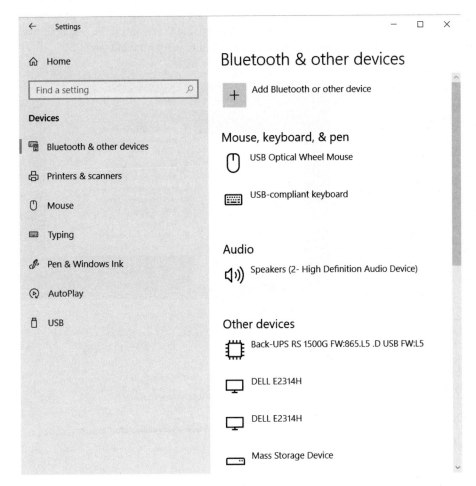

FIGURE 6–13 Add a new device in the Devices page of Windows 10 Settings.
Source: Microsoft Corporation

need to adjust settings or troubleshoot. In fact, some links within the various Windows 10 Settings panes will take you to appropriate pages in Control Panel.

Using Device Manager to Manage Device Drivers

Device Manager is a tool that allows an administrator to view and change device properties, update device drivers, configure device settings, uninstall devices, and roll back a driver update. Rollback is quite handy for those times when you find the new device driver causes problems. Device Manager has been in the last several versions of Windows and is still available in the current versions of Windows. Our favorite method for opening Device Manager is by entering "device manager" in the Windows 7 or Windows 10 Start Search box or in Windows 8, Search Settings. But if you find you need to work with Device Manager repeatedly on the same computer, consider making a desktop shortcut, as described in Step-by-Step 6.03.

Step-by-Step 6.03

Getting to Know Device Manager

In this step-by-step exercise, you will create a shortcut to Device Manager on the desktop to make it more convenient to open. You'll then examine the information shown in Device Manager. This exercise can be completed on a computer running any of the versions of Windows discussed in this chapter. The screenshots are from Windows 10. You will need to either be logged on with an administrator account or be prepared with the credentials of an administrator on that computer.

Step 1

Right-click on an empty area of the Desktop; select New | Shortcut.

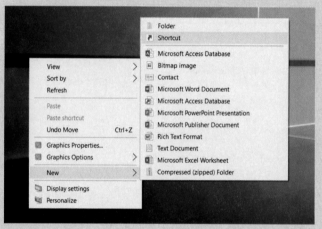

Source: Microsoft Corporation

Step 2

In the Create Shortcut wizard, a text box prompts you to enter the location of the item. Simply enter the file name and extension for the Device Manager console: devmgmt.msc. Double-check your typing. Click the Next button.

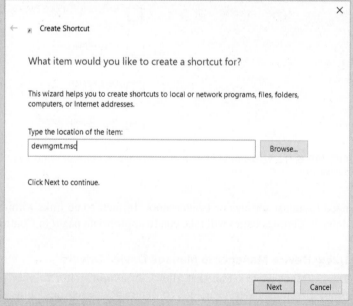

Source: Microsoft Corporation

On the following page of the Create Shortcut wizard, in the text box labeled "Type a name for this shortcut," type "Device Mgr," and click the Finish button.

Locate the new shortcut on the desktop.

Test your new shortcut by double-clicking on it to open Device Manager. Use the View menu to experiment with various ways of changing how it can display information—you have three options for viewing devices and two options for viewing resources that you can choose from the View menu. You will normally view devices by type because this approach is simpler and more understandable. Another option allows you to view hidden devices, which is handy when you want to remove a device driver for a device that is no longer connected or installed in the computer. We do not normally recommend doing this.

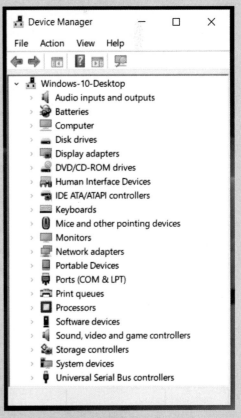

Step 6

When viewing devices by type, there is a node for each device type, such as Audio inputs and outputs, Batteries, Computer, Disk drives, and so on. Familiarize yourself with Device Manager by opening the nodes. Notice that the buttons on the button bar change as you click on the top node (the computer itself), then click on a type node (such as Display adapters), and click on a device under a type node.

Step 7

Double-clicking a device opens its Properties dialog box, where the Driver tab lets you manage a device. Do not make any changes, and when you are finished, close all open windows. You will use other features of Device Manager in the troubleshooting section of this chapter.

Source: Microsoft Corporation

LO 6.4 | Using Windows Troubleshooting and Recovery Tools

A short list of the handiest and most effective tools for troubleshooting Windows problems and recovering from virus infections includes the various Startup options, the System Configuration utility, and Device Manager. Explore these tools in this section.

For Startup Failures: The Windows Recovery Environment

In Chapter 4, we described the Windows Preinstallation Environment (Windows PE), the scaled-down Windows operating system that supports the Windows Setup GUI. This environment is available for Windows 7 and newer versions of Windows. It has limited drivers for basic hardware and support for the NTFS file system, networks, and programs. However, this is still a very robust and specialized operating system, and when needed, it supports a powerful group of diagnostics and repair tools called the **Windows Recovery Environment (Windows RE)**. Computer manufacturers who preinstall Windows have the option of adding their own repair tools to Windows RE.

Note: When configuring a new installation or troubleshooting a problem, keep a journal of any changes you make. A record of the changes will help you return stability to your computer. This can be in the form of a note in a paper notebook or a word processing document. The advantage of the first method is that it will be available to you if Windows becomes unstable. The advantage of using a word processor, such as Microsoft Word, is that you can take screenshots and copy them into the document.

If your Windows computer fails at startup, and if the damage is not too extensive, Windows RE will start and load the Windows Error Recovery page with the options: Launch Startup and Repair (Windows RE's built-in diagnostics and recovery tool) and Start Windows Normally. It is always worth trying the second option to see if the cause of the problem was something transient. Then, if it still doesn't start up normally, select the Launch Startup Repair and follow the instructions on the screen.

In situations where Windows starts, but you notice problems, you may want to use modified startups to troubleshoot and recover from the problem. We will look at them next.

Troubleshooting with Modified Startups

As you work with Windows computers, you may run into computers that fail to start normally or that behave oddly after startup. Windows offers several methods for starting with certain components disabled. Some of these are available through a special menu of startup options; others (including some of the same methods) are available through the System Configuration utility.

The Advanced Boot Options Menu in Windows 7

To access a list of startup options in Windows 7, restart the computer and press F8 before the graphical Windows start screen appears. This will bring up a special menu of startup options entitled "Advanced Boot Options Menu," shown in Figure 6-14. Following are brief descriptions of these options.

Repair Your Computer. If you select this option, Windows PE (the environment used by Windows setup) loads and first requires that you supply a keyboard input method, then requires that you log on, and finally displays the Windows RE System Recovery

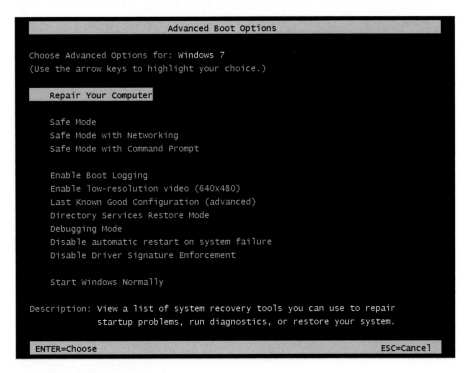

FIGURE 6–14 The Windows 7 Advanced Boot Options menu.
Source: Microsoft Corporation

Options menu shown in Figure 4–17 in Chapter 4. From here you can select one of the following recovery tools, also described in Chapter 4:

- Startup Repair
- System Restore
- System Image Recovery
- Windows Memory Diagnostic
- Command Prompt

The System Recovery Command Prompt, is a command-line interface where you can enter commands to repair Windows. This is a very advanced task, but one command we have used in the past with some success is "chkdsk /r," a command that can repair certain logical damage to a disk.

Safe Mode. Safe Mode is a mode for starting Windows with certain drivers and components disabled. Access Safe Mode from the Advanced Options Menu in Windows 7, as shown in Step-by-Step 6.04. In Windows 8, 8.1, and Windows 10, access it from the Advanced Startup option on the General page of PC Settings, which we describe later. Safe Mode does not disable Windows security. You are required to log on in all variants of Safe Mode, and you can access only those resources for which you have permissions. If Windows will not start normally but starts just fine in Safe Mode, use Device Manager within Safe Mode to determine if the source of the problem is a faulty device. Run System Restore while in Safe Mode and roll back the entire system to a restore point from before the problem occurred.

Three Safe Mode variants are available:

- **Safe Mode** starts without using several drivers and components that it would normally start. It loads only very basic, non-vendor-specific drivers for mouse, video (loading Windows' very basic vga.sys driver), keyboard, mass storage, and system services. Because network components are not started, plain Safe Mode does not support networking.

- **Safe Mode with Networking** is identical to plain Safe Mode, except that it starts the networking components. Use the following debug sequence with Safe Mode with Networking:
  - If Windows will not start normally but starts OK in plain Safe Mode, restart and select Safe Mode with Networking.
  - If it fails to start in Safe Mode with Networking, the problem area is network drivers or components. Use Device Manager to disable the network adapter driver (the likely culprit), then boot up normally. If Windows now works, replace your network adapter driver.
  - If this problem appears immediately after upgrading a network driver, use Device Manager while in Safe Mode to roll back the updated driver. When an updated driver is available, install it.

- **Safe Mode with Command Prompt** is Safe Mode with only a command prompt as a user interface. In a normal startup, Windows loads your GUI desktop, but this depends on the program explorer.exe, the GUI shell to Windows. In place of this GUI shell, Safe Mode with Command Prompt loads a command prompt (cmd.exe) window. This is a handy option to remember if the desktop does not display at all. Once you have eliminated video drivers as the cause, corruption of the explorer.exe program may be the problem. From within the command prompt, you can delete the corrupted version of explorer.exe and copy an undamaged version. This requires knowledge of the command line commands for navigating the directory structure, as well as knowledge of the location of the file that you are replacing. You can launch programs, such as the Event Viewer (eventvwr.msc), the Computer Management console (compmgmt.msc), or Device Manager (devmgmt.msc) from the command prompt.

Enable Boot Logging. While boot logging occurs automatically with each of the three Safe Modes, selecting Enable Boot Logging turns on boot logging and starts Windows normally. Boot logging causes Windows to write a log of the Windows startup in a file named ntbtlog.txt and save it in the systemroot folder. This log file contains an entry for each component in the order in which it loaded into memory. It also lists drivers that were not loaded, which alerts an administrator to a possible source of a problem.

Enable Low-Resolution Video (640×480). This option starts Windows normally, except the video mode is changed to the lowest resolution (640×480), using the currently installed video driver. It does not switch to the basic Windows video driver. Select this option after making a video configuration change that the video adapter does not support and that prevents Windows from displaying properly.

Last Known Good Configuration. Last Known Good (LKG) Configuration is a startup option that will start Windows normally and select the configuration that existed at the last successful user logon (the "last known good configuration"), ignoring changes made after the last logon. This works if you made changes that caused obvious problems. On the very next restart, selecting this option will discard the changes. But if you have logged on since the changes occurred, those changes will be part of the last known good configuration, and this recovery option won't work. Windows 7 is the last version to offer this option.

Directory Services Restore Mode. This option only works on Windows Servers acting as domain controllers.

Debugging Mode. This is a very advanced, (dare we say) obsolete, option in which Windows starts normally, and information about the Windows startup is sent over a serial cable to another computer that is running a special program called a debugger.

Disable Automatic Restart on System Failure. The default setting for Windows is for it to restart after a system crash. However, depending on the problem, restarting may simply lead to another restart—in fact, you could find yourself faced with a continuous loop of restarts. If so, press F8 at the next restart and select the Disable automatic restart on system failure option. Windows will attempt to start normally (just once for each time you select this option) and may stay open long enough for you to troubleshoot. Do not attempt to work with any data file after restarting with this option because the system may be too unstable. If you are not able to solve the problem, then you will need to restart in Safe Mode to troubleshoot.

Disable Driver Signature Enforcement. If you are unable to install a driver due to Driver Signing, and you trust the manufacturer, select this option, which will start Windows normally, disabling driver signature enforcement just for that startup.

Start Windows Normally. Use this option to start Windows normally with no change in behavior. You would use this after using F8 to view the Advanced Options menu and deciding to continue with a normal startup. It does not restart the computer.

Return to OS Choices Menu (Multiboot Only). Selecting this option on a multiboot computer will return to the OS Choices Menu (OS Loader menu).

Step-by-Step 6.04

Using Windows 7 in Safe Mode

In this step-by-step exercise, you will start Windows in Safe Mode. The screen will not be identical, but you can experience Safe Mode in any of these OSs. Be prepared to provide credentials to access Safe Mode because security is still in place when you access Safe Mode. Once in Safe Mode, you can run most Windows troubleshooting tools just as you would after a normal start.

Step 1

Restart the computer, pressing F8 as soon as the power down completes and before the splash screen appears. On the Advanced Boot Options menu, (Figure 6-14) use the up and down arrows to move the cursor around. Position the cursor on Safe Mode and press Enter.

Step 2

When prompted, provide credentials. Safe Mode loads with a black desktop background and the words *Safe Mode* in the corners of the screen. It also opens Windows Help and Support to the page on Safe Mode. Browse through the help information and click on the link labeled "Diagnostic tools to use in safe mode."

Source: Microsoft Corporation

Step 3

On the resulting page, locate links to start several very handy tools in Safe Mode. In the following steps, practice opening some of these utilities.

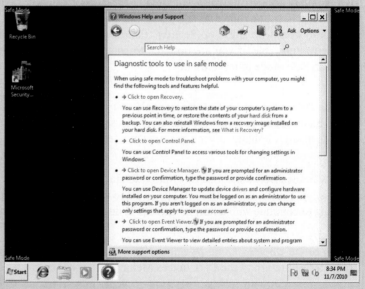

Source: Microsoft Corporation

Step 4

Click the link labeled *Click to open Recovery.* On the Recovery page notice the links to other tools. Click the button labeled *Open System Restore.* On the page labeled *Restore files and settings,* click Next to see a list of the restore points on your computer. Click Cancel to leave System Restore and close the Recovery windows to return to Help and Support.

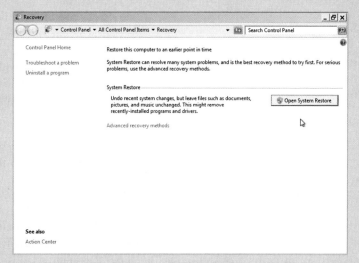

Source: Microsoft Corporation

Step 5

Next, use the link that will open Control Panel. You can open most tools you would need from this page.

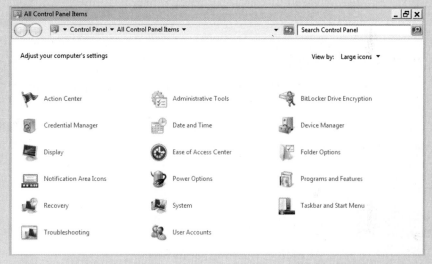

Source: Microsoft Corporation

Step 6

When you are finished exploring Safe Mode, close all open windows, and either shut down or restart Windows, allowing it to start normally.

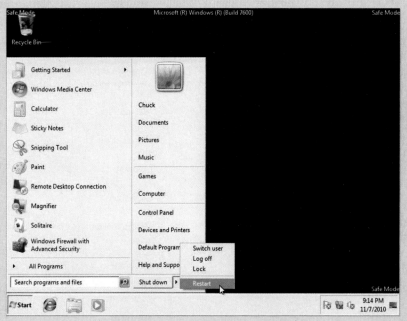

Source: Microsoft Corporation

The Advanced Startup Options in Windows 8, 8.1, and Windows 10

Previously, in this chapter, you learned that if your Windows computer fails at startup and the damage is not too extensive, Windows RE will start and load the Windows Error Recovery page. Another option is to boot from the Windows installation DVD disc or USB drive, but if Windows was preinstalled on your computer and UEFI boot is in effect, you may not be able to boot from disc unless you modify the UEFI settings, disabling Safe Boot security. How you do that differs from manufacturer to manufacturer.

The options you access from the Windows Error Recovery page are those that you can also access from the Update and Security page in Settings in Windows 10. The quickest way to get to this page is to search on "advanced startup" and select the result that says "Change advanced startup options." It is good to practice the Windows Advanced Startup options before you really need them for troubleshooting or recovery of the operating system. Step-by-Step 6.05 will walk you through a tour of the Windows 8 and 8.1 Advanced Startup options.

Step-by-Step 6.05

Exploring Windows 10 Advanced Options

If you have access to a computer running Windows 10 and can sign in with an administrator account for that computer, you can do this exercise.

Step 1

Open the Start menu and select Settings. In the Settings Home page, select *Update and Security.* On that page, select Recovery. Scroll down to see the options shown here in two images. Then, locate *Advanced startup* and click the *Restart now* button below it.

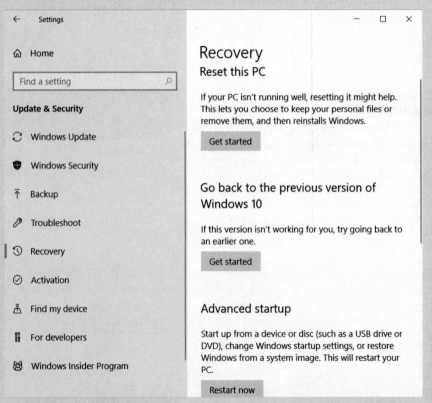

Source: Microsoft Corporation

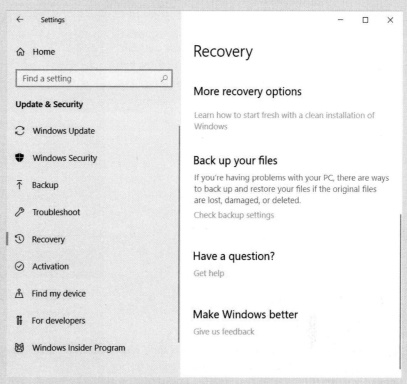

Source: Microsoft Corporation

Windows Recovery Environment (Windows RE) launches. The resulting screen will resemble this, but it may have more options showing depending on the system and the Windows 10 version. To restart in a troubleshooting mode, select Troubleshoot.

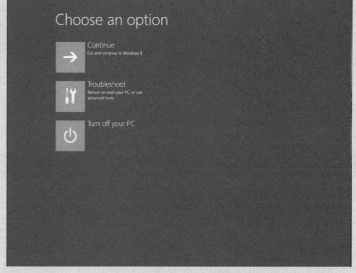

Source: Microsoft Corporation

Step 3

On the Troubleshoot screen, you will see these options, plus you may see one or more options added by the manufacturer of your computer. From this screen select *Advanced options*.

Source: Microsoft Corporation

Step 4

Again, the Advanced Options screen shown here may look different on your computer. For instance, on a computer with UEFI you will see a UEFI Firmware Settings option. Or you may see *Go back to the previous version*. From this screen select *Startup Settings*.

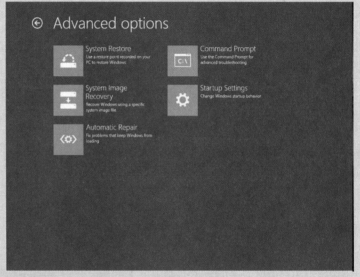

Source: Microsoft Corporation

Step 5

The Startup Settings screen shows the options coming up on the next screen, which will display after you click Restart. Select Restart now.

Source: Microsoft Corporation

Step 6

After a brief pause, the second Startup Settings screen displays with real choices. This is the replacement for the Windows 7 Advanced Boot Options menu. Press the 5 key to start Windows in Safe Mode with Networking.

Source: Microsoft Corporation

Step 7

At this point, you will see a normal sign-in screen. Enter your credentials to sign in and Windows will start in Safe Mode. If you successfully started Safe Mode with Networking, the browser will open to the Windows 10 Help page at the Microsoft site where you can browse through categories of solutions and/or use the Virtual Agent to open a chat session and look for help. If you stump the Virtual Agent, you have the option to connect to a live agent via chat or phone.

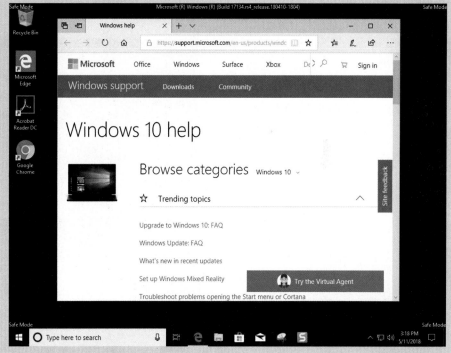

Source: Microsoft Corporation

Step 8

Spend a few minutes exploring more options available to you in Safe Mode. Just one way to do that is to right-click on the Start button to open the Power User menu to quickly access tools, such as Apps and Features, Power Options, Event Viewer, System, Device Manager, Network Connections, Disk Management, Computer Management, and PowerShell.

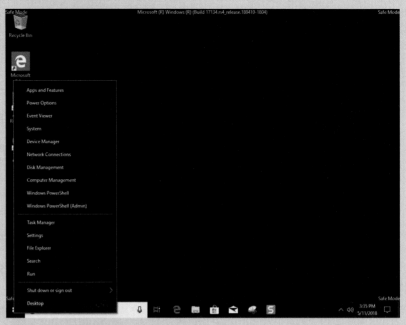

Source: Microsoft Corporation

Step 9

When you are finished exploring the options in Windows Safe Mode, shut down or restart from the Power link on the Start menu or from the Power User menu, shown here.

Source: Microsoft Corporation

Refresh. *Refresh* was an option on the Windows 8.*x* Troubleshoot page in Recovery. In Windows 10, the old Refresh option is still available (but not by that name) as part of the *Reset this PC* option, shown in the illustration by Step 3 in Step-by-Step 6.05. In Windows 10, when you select Reset this PC you will have the options to keep personal files. This option refreshes the operating system without affecting your files. This is a very quick solution to a scenario that previously required advanced tasks and much time.

In addition to saving your user accounts and other personal data and settings, this option saves all your installed apps that came with Windows, as well as any apps purchased through the Windows Store. Then it reinstalls Windows and reinstalls all the saved apps. However, it changes PC settings back to the defaults, removes apps installed from disc or sources other than the Windows Store, and saves a list of all removed apps on the desktop.

To begin Refresh from the Troubleshoot screen of Windows RE, click or tap the *Reset your PC* option. Follow the prompts and select the option labeled *Keep my files*. If asked, provide your Windows installation or recovery media on disc or flash drive. It will then take several minutes, showing progress messages. After one or more reboots, the Lock screen displays, and you can click to open the sign-in screen. After signing in you will need to reinstall the apps that were removed by the refresh.

Reset your PC. In Windows 8.*x*, *Reset your PC* only had one mode: it removed everything and reinstalled Windows, taking it back to the defaults. In Windows 10, when you select *Reset this PC*, and then select *Remove everything*, it will remove your personal files before removing and reinstalling Windows, returning your computer to like-new Windows 10, ready for a new user to sign in and install apps. This complete resetting of Windows is appropriate if you plan to donate a computer or hand it over to someone else for their use.

Troubleshooting with MSCONFIG and Task Manager

System Configuration, more commonly known by its executable name MSCONFIG, is a GUI tool for temporarily modifying system startup. The easiest method for starting MSCONFIG is to open the Run box (⊞+R), type "msconfig," and press enter. MSCONFIG allows you to modify and test startup configuration settings without altering the settings directly. Use the options on the MSCONFIG General and Boot tabs to restart Windows in various troubleshooting modes, including Safe Mode, offered on the Boot menu.

MSCONFIG gives you access to settings buried within the registry through a moderately friendly user interface and it allows you to make temporary changes to try to pinpoint the source of a startup problem. For instance, open the Services tab page and stop a service from launching at startup, restart Windows, and see if that solves the problem. If it does not, then go back into MSCONFIG, enable that service, and disable another. Repeat until you locate the problem. If disabling services does not solve the problem, then move on to the programs.

MSCONFIG comes in all the versions of Windows discussed in this chapter. It works the same in all of these versions with one big exception. The Startup page in Windows 7, shown in Figure 6-15, contains a list of programs that Windows starts

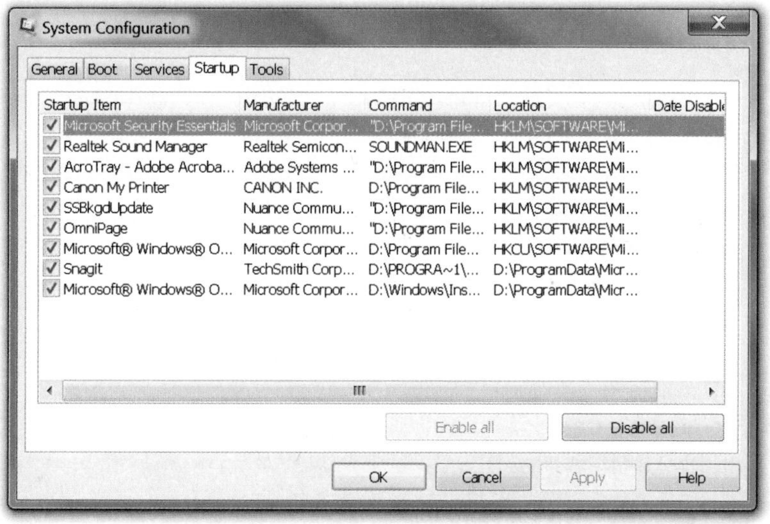

WARNING!

The recovery options *Keep my files* and *Remove everything* both require a lot of power while writing to storage and restarting the computer. Therefore, do not do either of these on a computer that is not plugged into a power source.

WARNING!

If you select the Safe option on the Boot page, it will also change settings on the General page. Therefore, any time you make changes, note the changes and be aware that before the system will restart normally, you will need to return to the General page and select Normal startup.

FIGURE 6–15 System Configuration (MSCONFIG) lets you test startup scenarios.
Source: Microsoft Corporation

try this!

Explore MSCONFIG

Open MSCONFIG and explore the option pages. These steps will work in Windows 7, Windows 8, 8.1, and Windows 10. Try this:

1. Open the Run box and type "msconfig" and press the Enter key or click or tap OK.

2. Explore the five tabs (General, Boot, Services, Startup, and Tools) of the System Configuration dialog box.

3. If you make any changes, make sure you remember them. Click Apply, then OK, and click the Restart button in the final message box.

4. After testing a modified restart, open MSCONFIG again and be sure to select Normal startup before restarting.

automatically, allowing you to disable programs one (or more) at a time at startup so that you can determine if a program is causing startup problems. In Windows 8, 8.1, and Windows 10, this tab contains a link only to the Task Manager utility where a new Startup page contains the list of programs, as shown in Figure 6–16.

Troubleshooting Device Problems

You will quickly learn if Windows detects a problem with a device when you open Device Manager. You will see an expanded device type, and the problem device will have an exclamation mark in a yellow triangle on the icon, as Figure 6–17 shows. The problem may be with the device itself, its device driver, or the ability of the operating system to automatically configure it. In Figure 6–17, Windows has placed the problem device under Other devices because it does not have enough information about it. This usually means that there is no installed device driver.

If you see the exclamation symbol on a device, double-click the device icon to open its Properties dialog box. You will see more information, as shown in the example in Figure 6–18. Follow the instructions in the Device Status box. In the example, it recommends running Update and provides the Update button (not normally shown on this page). Clicking update opened the Update Driver Software page with two choices: Search automatically for updated driver software and Browse my computer for driver software. Select the second one if you have the driver disc or have the driver on your local computer or on a network share. Select the first choice to have Windows search on the Internet. In the scenario shown, we selected the first choice and it found the driver, downloaded it, and installed it with no more interaction from us. In

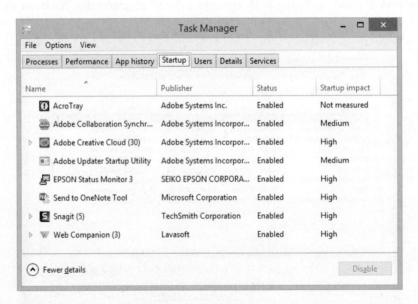

FIGURE 6–16 In Windows 8.1 and Windows 10 use the Startup tab in Task Manager to disable/enable individual programs.
Source: Microsoft Corporation

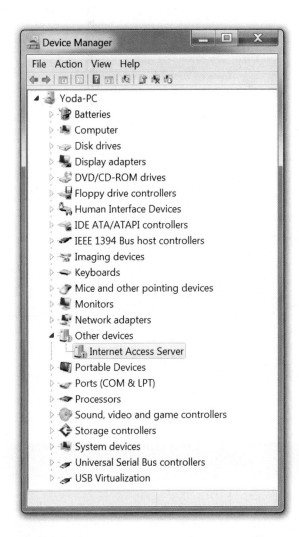

FIGURE 6–17 Device Manager indicates a problem with a device.
Source: Microsoft Corporation

FIGURE 6–18 On the General page of a device's Properties dialog, the *Device status* box describes the problem and recommends action to solve it.
Source: Microsoft Corporation

our example, the device was recognized and placed under the Network Infrastructure Devices category, as shown in Figure 6-19.

For other Device problems, open Device Manager and check out the Driver page of the Properties for the device. For instance, if you update a device driver and then find that the device fails or is not working as well as before the update, use the Roll Back Driver button on the Driver page to remove the updated driver and return to the previously installed driver. This button is active only after you have updated a driver, as shown in Figure 6-20. You can also use this page to update a driver, disable it, or uninstall it. You might disable a driver to see if it relates to another problem. Uninstall it if you do not need a device or if you believe there was a problem with the installation and plan to reinstall the driver.

WARNING!

If you are logged in as a standard user you will not be able to make changes to any settings in Device Manager, but it is still a good tool to use to see the status of devices. You can then report problems to a help desk if you are at school or work.

FIGURE 6–19 After installing the device driver, Windows places the device under the Network Infrastructure Devices category.
Source: Microsoft Corporation

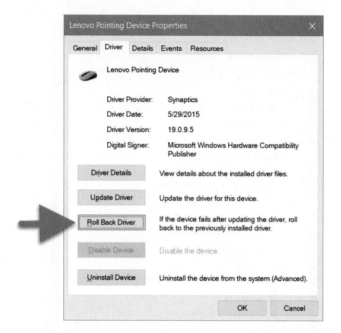

FIGURE 6–20 The *Roll Back Driver* button is active only after a driver update.
Source: Microsoft Corporation

CHAPTER 6 REVIEW

Chapter Summary

After reading this chapter, and completing the Step-by-Step tutorials and Try This! exercises, you should understand the following facts about what is under the Windows desktop:

Understanding the Registry

- The registry is a database of all configuration settings in Windows. The Control Panel applets provide a safe way to edit the registry.
- Windows creates the registry during setup and modifies it any time a setup or installation program runs after that and during startup and shutdown as well as when device drivers and apps are installed.
- The permanent portion of the registry is in several files, called hives. They include system, software, security, sam, default, and ntuser.dat.
- View the registry in a hierarchical folder structure in Registry Editor.
- A registry key is a folder object that can contain one or more sets of settings as well as other keys.
- There are five top-level keys, or root keys.
- A key that exists within another key is a subkey.

- Settings within a key are value entries. Each value entry has a name, type, and data.

Windows User and Power Options

- Windows 7 combines user and power options on the Shutdown menu.
- Windows 7 user options are Switch user, Log off, and Lock. Power options are Restart, Sleep, and (sometimes) Hibernate.
- Windows 8 and later versions have power options on the Power menu and User options on the User tile.
- There are several phases of the Windows startup process.
- If necessary, modify system startup using the Startup and Recovery page in System Properties. You can also modify the BCD file directly to modify startup, but only very advanced techs should do this.

Installing and Managing Device Drivers

- A device driver is program code, created by the device manufacturer, that allows an OS to control the use of a physical device.

- You need Administrator privileges to install any device driver in Windows.
- Once a device is installed, a standard user may disconnect and reconnect the device without restriction—the driver will not be uninstalled.
- Code signing exists to avoid problems caused by badly written code.
- When an administrator installs or connects a plug-and-play device to a Windows computer, the computer will automatically detect the device and install and configure the driver.
- Plug-and-play devices connected to USB or IEEE 1394 (Firewire) can be disconnected without restarting.
- Device Manager is the Windows tool for managing and troubleshooting device problems.

Using Windows Troubleshooting and Recovery Tools

- Windows offers a variety of startup options, and some are well suited for troubleshooting.
- A yellow exclamation mark on a device in Device Manager indicates a problem. Open the properties dialog box to see an explanation.
- Use Device Manager to uninstall, update, and remove device drivers. You can also use it to disable a device without removing the driver.

Key Terms List

binary file *(208)*

bootloader *(218)*

bootstrap loader *(218)*

code signing *(225)*

cold boot *(217)*

Command Prompt *(221)*

Consent Prompt *(225)*

Credentials Prompt *(225)*

data type *(211)*

Device Stage *(226)*

digital signature *(225)*

driver signing *(225)*

Early Launch Anti-Malware (ELAM) *(220)*

Fast Boot *(220)*

file signature verification *(225)*

Hibernate *(216)*

hive *(209)*

Hybrid Shutdown *(217)*

key *(211)*

Last Known Good (LKG) Configuration *(233)*

logon phase *(219)*

Measured Boot *(220)*

MSCONFIG *(241)*

power-on self-test (POST) *(218)*

registry *(208)*

root key *(211)*

Safe Mode *(232)*

Safe Mode with Command Prompt *(232)*

Secure Boot *(220)*

security ID (SID) *(212)*

Sleep *(216)*

subkey *(211)*

System Recovery Command Prompt *(232)*

Trusted Boot *(220)*

Unified Extensible Firmware Interface (UEFI) *(218)*

value entry *(211)*

warm boot *(217)*

Windows PowerShell *(221)*

Windows Recovery Environment (Windows RE) *(230)*

Key Terms Quiz

Use the Key Terms List to complete the sentences that follow.

1. A/an _____ is a portion of the Windows registry that is saved in a file.

2. _____ is a feature in Windows 7 that provides a special home page for a device containing options for managing the device.

3. When viewed with a registry editor, a/an _____ is a registry key located at the top level.

4. Many things occur during some of the startup phases. For instance, during the _____ programs start and plug-and-play devices are detected.

5. _____ is the use of a digital signature provided by Microsoft as its seal of approval on program code.

6. _____ is the more advanced of the two command-line interfaces included with Windows 10.

7. A/an _____ contains program code.

8. The _____ utility is very handy for troubleshooting startup problems, allowing you to temporarily disable programs you suspect are causing problems.

9. _____ is a startup mode for starting Windows with certain drivers and components disabled.

10. A/an _____ is a unique string of numbers preceded by S-1-5 that identifies a security principal (as in Table 6–2) in a Windows security accounts database.

Multiple-Choice Quiz

1. Which of the following is not in the registry?
   a. Device driver settings
   b. Services settings
   c. User data files
   d. User preferences
   e. Application program settings

2. Any change to Windows or an installed application results in a change to this special database.
   a. Microsoft SQL Server
   b. Microsoft Excel
   c. ntuser.dat
   d. Registry
   e. Default

3. Most of the Windows registry files are stored in this location.
   a. *systemroot*\System32\config
   b. D:\Windows
   c. *systemroot*\System32\Registry
   d. *systemroot*\Windows
   e. *systemroot*\WINNT

4. If you select this option from the Power menu in Windows 8, 8.1, or Windows 10, both the system state and the user session are saved in memory, requiring a small amount of power.
   a. Fast Boot
   b. Hibernate
   c. Hybrid Shutdown
   d. Sleep
   e. Measured Boot

5. Beginning in Windows 8, the contents of the Startup tab page in MSCONFIG have been moved to this utility.
   a. System Configuration
   b. Task Manager
   c. BCDedit
   d. Windows RE
   e. PowerShell

6. Which statement is true?
   a. Only the Administrator may disconnect or reconnect an installed device.
   b. Only members of the Administrators group may disconnect or reconnect an installed device.
   c. Only members of the Guests group may disconnect or reconnect an installed device.
   d. Any member of the local Users group may disconnect or reconnect an installed device.
   e. No one may disconnect or reconnect an installed device.

7. What UEFI security feature loads only trusted operating system bootloaders?
   a. Fast Boot
   b. Secure Boot
   c. Measured Boot
   d. Trusted Boot
   e. Early Launch Anti-Malware (ELAM)

8. Which of the following is a Device Manager feature only available after an installed driver updates?
   a. Uninstall Device
   b. Roll back Driver
   c. Disable Device
   d. Update Driver
   e. Remove Driver

9. What registry hive does the bootloader use during startup to locate the operating system files it must load?
   a. BCD
   b. winload.exe
   c. bootmgr
   d. ntoskrnl.exe
   e. winlogon.exe

10. What page in System Properties would you open to modify the length of time the OS selection menu displays during Windows startup?
    a. Startup and Recovery
    b. Device Manager
    c. BCDedit
    d. Local Security Policy
    e. Computer Management

11. What choice on the Windows 7 Advanced Boot Options menu gives you a selection of tools that includes Startup Repair, System Restore, System Image Recovery, Windows Memory Diagnostic, and Command Prompt?
    a. Safe Mode with Command Prompt
    b. Debugging Mode
    c. Directory Services Restore Mode
    d. Last Known Good Configuration
    e. Repair Your Computer

12. Which of the following Windows 7 startup options will not do you any good if you have restarted and logged on after making a change that caused problems in Windows?
    a. System Restore
    b. Repair Your Computer
    c. Enable Boot Logging
    d. Safe Mode with Command Prompt
    e. Last Known Good Configuration

13. When Windows 8, 8.1, or Windows 10 does this, it hibernates the Windows session and saves it in a file but does not save the user session.
    a. Sleep
    b. Hybrid Shutdown
    c. Switch user
    d. Restart
    e. Hibernate

14. You upgraded a device driver, and Windows immediately failed and restarted. The problem is that it seems to be in a continuous restarting loop. What boot startup option will restart normally and give you an opportunity to try to troubleshoot the problem after a normal reboot?
    a. Debugging mode
    b. Enable boot logging

    c. Safe Mode with command prompt
    d. Disable automatic restart on system failure
    e. Safe Mode with networking

15. Which of the following is the executable name for the GUI utility that allows you to temporarily modify system startup?
    a. SYSCON
    b. MSCONFIG
    c. SYSEDIT
    d. regedit
    e. BCDedit

Essay Quiz

1. Describe at least five actions that will automatically change the Windows registry.

2. Your Windows 7 computer is having display problems when starting. You suspect that the cause is a video driver update that you installed. You managed to log on at the first restart after the update, despite being barely able to see the distorted logon dialog box. Then you found that, even though you had logged on, it was hopeless to try to work with the GUI. Describe how you would confirm that the problem is the video adapter and how you will correct the problem.

3. Describe a limit present in both Windows 8/8.1 and Windows 10 when it comes to using the PC Settings options for Devices.

4. A fellow student asked for your help in diagnosing a problem with a Windows computer. He believes there is a problem with the network adapter. He works in a small office and does not know the credentials for the Administrator account on that computer. The person who does know is out of town and is unwilling to give him the password until he can convince her that there truly is a problem. He wants to use Device Manager to see the status of the network adapter. What advice can you give him?

5. Describe what boot logging does and how you would use it as a troubleshooting tool.

Lab Projects

LAB PROJECT 6.1

Your Windows 7 computer will not start, and you believe the cause is a network card you recently installed.

1️⃣ Describe the steps you will take to isolate the problem.

2️⃣ Demonstrate the steps to your instructor.

LAB PROJECT 6.2

A fellow student asked for your help because his Windows 10 computer is unstable. He is considering using Reset your PC. Describe the two options under Reset your PC and if

possible do a reset of a Windows 10 computer. Be sure you have permission to do this, and do not use a production computer. After the refresh, go into Windows and describe any changes you found.

LAB PROJECT 6.3

You are having a problem with your Windows computer that is isolated to a single graphics editing program that you use every day in your work. When you described the problem to the customer service support person for this product, she told you that the only fix for it is to edit a key under HKEY-LOCAL_MACHINE\SOFTWARE.

She has assured you that this fix will work without causing any problems, but you are wary of doing this.

1. Describe the steps you will take before making the suggested registry changes.

2. Demonstrate only the steps you would take before modifying the registry. Do not actually modify the registry.

chapter

7 Apple macOS on the Desktop

©Roman Tiraspolsky/Shutterstock

Learning Outcomes

In this chapter, you will learn how to:

LO **7.1** Describe the important events in the history of Apple operating systems and the versions of macOS determine what version of macOS is installed on an Apple computer.

LO **7.2** Prepare and implement a macOS upgrade or installation, and list the postinstallation tasks.

LO **7.3** Navigate and manage macOS on the desktop, including describing the Home folder, using Finder, performing file management tasks, and working with features and settings.

LO **7.4** Manage local security in macOS.

LO **7.5** Troubleshoot common macOS problems.

So far we have discussed operating systems in general, security for operating systems, virtualization of desktop operating systems, and the Windows operating systems. Now we change our focus to Apple macOS.

In this chapter, you will explore the macOS operating system beginning with an overview of the history and versions; then you'll learn how to install it, manage the desktop, and troubleshoot common macOS problems. Finally, you'll learn the basics of local security in macOS on the desktop.

LO 7.1 | macOS History and Versions

In this overview, we explore the history of Apple's operating systems and the versions of the current line, which has had several name changes over the years from Mac OS X to OS X, then yet another change in 2016 to macOS. In this book, unless needed for clarification, we will call the recent versions "macOS." And yes, there are several versions/releases of the OS, and each version has its own name and number.

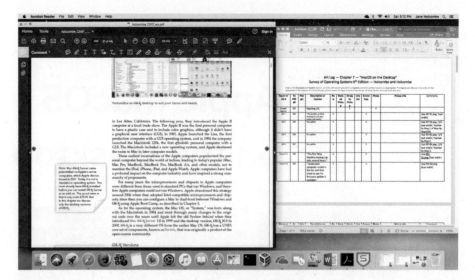

Personalize the macOS desktop to suit your tastes and needs.
Source: Apple Inc.

A Brief History of the Apple Operating Systems

Apple Computer (now officially Apple Inc.) was founded on April 1, 1976, by Stephen Wozniak, Steven Jobs, and Ronald Wayne. They developed and manufactured their first product, the Apple I computer, in a garage in Los Altos, California. The following year, they introduced the Apple II computer at a local trade show. The Apple II was the first personal computer to have a plastic case and to include color graphics, although it didn't have a graphical user interface (GUI). In 1983, Apple launched the Lisa, the first production computer with a GUI operating system, and in 1984 the company launched the Macintosh 128k, the first *affordable* personal computer with a GUI. The Macintosh included a new operating system, and Apple shortened the name to Mac in later computer models.

These earliest incarnations of the Apple computers popularized the personal computer beyond the world of techies, leading to today's popular iMac, Mac Pro, MacBook, MacBook Pro, MacBook Air, and other models, not to mention the iPod, iPhone, iPad, and Apple Watch. Apple computers have had a profound impact on the computer industry and have inspired a strong community of proponents.

For many years the microprocessors and chipsets in Apple computers were different from those used in standard PCs that ran Windows, and therefore Apple computers could not run Windows. Apple abandoned this strategy around 2006 when they adopted Intel-compatible microprocessors and chipsets; since then you can configure a Mac to dual-boot between Windows and macOS using Apple Boot Camp, as described in Chapter 3.

As for the operating system, the Mac OS, or "System," was born along with the Macintosh in 1984 and went through many changes to the original code over the years until Apple left the old System behind when they introduced Mac OS X Server 1.0 in 1999 and the desktop version, OS X 10.0 in 2000. This was a very different OS from the earlier Mac OS/System. This OS has a core set of UNIX components, known as Darwin, that was originally a product of the open-source community.

macOS Versions

Apple has issued several major releases of macOS beginning with the initial release for the desktop, 10.0, code-named Cheetah during its development.

Note: Mac OS X Server came preinstalled on Apple's server computers, which Apple discontinued in 2011. Today it is renamed macOS Server and it is not a stand-alone operating system. You must already have macOS installed before you can install macOS Server as an add-on. The good news is that it only costs $19.99. But in this chapter we discuss only the desktop versions of macOS.

Although Apple did not publicly use the code names for releases 10.0 and 10.1, for each subsequent version they tied the code name to the product and used it heavily in marketing and packaging. Apple continued to name macOS versions for species of big cats until 10.9, Mavericks, named after a popular California surfing location.

Between the major releases Apple has made minor releases (10.13.5, 10.13.6, etc.). Each major release adds many improvements and new features—both minor and major. Recent versions include features first introduced by Apple in their iOS operating system for their popular portable devices, the iPod, iPhone, and iPad.

As you may notice while comparing the illustrations in this book to macOS on your lab computer, you always have the ability to customize the look so that no two installations need to be identical. The screenshots you see in this chapter all use either one of the backgrounds that comes with macOS or a white background for ease of viewing the captured windows and message boxes. Table 7–1 lists the major releases, their names, and release dates.

Apple's OS for their laptops and desktops has had many versions and minor releases since 2001. It is important to know both the version of macOS and the vintage of your computer before you decide to upgrade to a new version of macOS because the latest versions do not run on the older Macs, nor can you upgrade directly from some older versions of macOS to the latest version.

Whenever a new version is available, connect to the Apple website at **www.apple .com** and search on the product name of the new upgrade. Go to the Web page and select Tech Specs. This will list the requirements, including the macOS version, amount of memory and free disk space, the supported Apple computer models, and the requirements for special features of the new version.

To help you prepare for the next macOS upgrade, Step-by-Step 7.01 walks you through the process of checking out the macOS version and Mac computer vintage information.

TABLE 7–1 Release Dates of Versions of Apple's Desktop OS	
Major Release	**Release Date**
Mac OS 10.0 Cheetah	March 2001
Mac OS 10.1 Puma	September 2001
Mac OS 10.2 Jaguar	August 2002
Mac OS 10.3 Panther	October 2003
Mac OS 10.4 Tiger	April 2005
Mac OS 10.5 Leopard	October 2007
Mac OS 10.6 Snow Leopard	August 2009
Mac OS 10.7 Lion	July 2011
OS X 10.8 Mountain Lion	July 2012
OS X 10.9 Mavericks	October 2013
OS X 10.10 Yosemite	October 2014
OS X 10.11 El Capitan	October 2015
macOS 10.12 Sierra	September 2016
macOS 10.13 High Sierra	September 2017
macOS 10.14 Mojave	September 2018

Step-by-Step 7.01

Checking Version and Hardware Information in macOS

It is simple to check the installed version of macOS as well as the model information for a Mac. This exercise will walk you through the steps for checking out this information and more. You need:

- An Apple desktop or laptop computer running macOS.
- The user name and password of an account for this computer.

Step 1

Log on to an Apple Mac computer running macOS. Click the Apple menu in the top-left corner of the screen and select *About this Mac*.

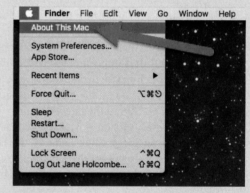

Source: Apple Inc.

Step 2

The window that pops up displays the version of the installed macOS. It also lists the computer model and date of manufacture and other basic information about the computer: processor, memory, startup disk name, graphics adapter, and serial number. You may want to return to this window as you read the next section.

Source: Apple Inc.

Click the *System Report* button to see detailed technical information about the hardware, network, and software. Explore the three categories. When finished, close the open window.

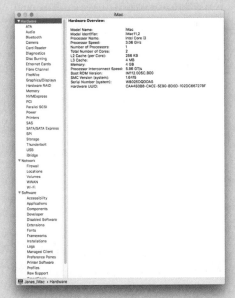

Source: Apple Inc.

LO 7.2 | Installing and Upgrading macOS

This section details the process of installing and configuring macOS including the minimum hardware and software requirements, the installation process, and the postinstallation task of updating software. If you purchase a new Apple computer with macOS preinstalled, the OS will need to be personalized for you.

Setting Up a New Mac

The first time you turn on a brand-new Mac computer or a Mac with a fresh installation of macOS the macOS Setup Assistant runs. Follow the instructions on the screen to sign in with your Apple ID or to create a local computer account that you will use to log in and to select user preferences, such as country, time zone, language, and keyboard layout. As with the Windows OSs, this first account has administrator privileges. The Setup Assistant will then lead you through setting up and configuring many features of macOS. You will have the option to run the Migration Assistant to help you transfer data from other computers or from a backup. When you complete these tasks you will have a customized system ready for the way you work.

Preparing to Install macOS

A new Apple Mac computer has macOS preinstalled, but people with existing Macs will often upgrade to a new version of macOS so we begin by discussing the minimum hardware requirements for upgrading to macOS.

Access a Fast Internet Connection

The latest macOS upgrade requires downloading a large file and may take hours to download. If your Internet connection is metered, meaning you pay for a certain amount of data usage per month, then you may want to take your computer to an Apple store and take advantage of their free fast Internet access to download the upgrade.

Note: When you exceed the data usage limit in a metered Internet connection, you are billed at a higher rate for the additional data.

Back Up Your Computer

Before installing or upgrading macOS, be sure to do a full backup. The best way to do this is to use an external hard drive and Time Machine, the backup software included with macOS since Snow Leopard (10.6). Time Machine requires a dedicated drive that is always available whenever the computer is on. This can be an external USB, FireWire, or Thunderbolt hard drive, a networked hard drive, an internal hard drive (in addition to the startup drive), or a separate partition on a drive. If you have one of these drives available and connected to your computer, open the Apple menu, a drop-down menu that appears when you click the Apple icon on the far left of the menu bar; select System Preferences. In System Preferences, select Time Machine. Turn on Time Machine and follow the instructions. The first backup will take hours. Figure 7–1 shows the Time Machine app ready to setup and configuration. After selecting a backup disk, configure a complete backup.

Check the Computer Model and macOS Version before Upgrading

Before upgrading to the latest version of macOS verify the version of the Mac OS already installed as well as the model (and vintage) of the computer, using the instructions in Step-by-Step 7.01. If your Mac computer is too old, you may not be able to upgrade its OS. Mojave (10.14), released in September 2018, was compatible with the following (or newer) models: MacBook (Early 2015), MacBook Air (Mid 2012), MacBook Pro (Mid 2012), Mac Mini (Late 2012), iMac (Late 2012), iMac Pro (2017), and Mac Pro (Late 2013, Mid 2010, and Mid 2012).

If the OS is too old you will not be able to directly upgrade. Upgrading to macOS Mojave required OS X 10.8 or later. You may need to first upgrade to an interim version before upgrading to the latest version. Even if you have an upgradable version, run Software Update from the Apple menu, a drop-down menu that appears when you click the Apple icon on the far left of the menu bar. Running Software Update will bring your OS up to the latest incremental update before you upgrade.

Other Hardware Requirements

Check out the requirements before you upgrade. Ensure that you have adequate memory and disk space. Presently, you need 14.3 GB of free space and 2 GB of RAM to install the latest version. However, you will want much more of both for running programs and storing data.

FIGURE 7–1 Select a disk for your Time Machine backups.
Source: Apple Inc.

Disable Disk Encryption

FileVault disk encryption has been included with macOS since Snow Leopard (10.6). If you have encrypted your files with either FileVault or a third-party program, temporarily disable it or turn it off. This is just a precaution to avoid any possible incompatibilities during the upgrade process or delays caused by the process of unencrypting. After a successful upgrade, enable encryption, unless you are using a third-party program that the new macOS version no longer supports.

Decide Where to Install macOS

Normally, you install macOS as an upgrade over a previous version. You can also install macOS onto a separate drive or separate partition on the same drive as your present version. This allows you to dual-boot between the two versions. The drive or partition must be empty when you begin the installation. The last OS installed will be the one that boots up by default, but you can change this on the fly by pressing the Option key as you turn on your computer. That is a good way to temporarily boot to the alternate OS. If you wish to change the default, then open the Startup Disk option in System Preferences and the drive you select will be the default startup drive.

Prepare to Purchase the Upgrade Online

Buy the latest version of macOS at the online App Store. Step-by-Step 7.02 includes instructions for accessing the App Store and purchasing the upgrade. You can no longer order it on DVD; you must do an online upgrade or, if you want to do a clean installation, download the installation image and burn it to a DVD or USB flash drive.

Note: Before creating passwords, review the information on creating strong passwords in Chapter 2.

Note: In Step-by-Step 7.02 and other exercises, we mention a macOS feature called the Dock. The **Dock** is a screen object resembling a floating tray usually located at the bottom of the desktop window. Like the Windows Taskbar, the Dock holds icons for commonly used programs, as well as for open applications. Click an icon to open a program. Learn how to configure the Dock later in this chapter.

The Installation

There are rarely surprises with a macOS installation—mainly because the installation is usually an upgrade; one can legally license this OS only on Apple Mac computers. If you do an upgrade, then at the end of the upgrade, you should only need to log in with the account you used before the upgrade.

Even when you buy a new Apple computer, which always has the OS preinstalled, you get to experience the final stages of the installation the first time you start the computer. That is when the Setup Assistant appears, and you will need to answer a few questions, including providing a user name and password.

Step-by-Step 7.02

Upgrading macOS

This exercise describes the steps for upgrading macOS. If you have an Apple computer that meets the hardware requirements but is not using the latest version, you can perform an upgrade during this exercise.

- An Apple computer that meets or exceeds the hardware requirements.

- An Apple ID.
- A broadband Internet connection.

Step 1

Begin an upgrade by first updating your current installation of macOS. Do this from the Apple Menu's Software Update option or by connecting directly to the App Store. To connect to the App Store, double-click on the App Store icon on the Dock.

Source: Apple Inc.

In the App Store, select Updates. When prompted, sign in to the Store and download the updates.

Source: Apple Inc.

While the update is downloading, an icon will display on the Dock with a progress bar.

After downloading and installing all updates to the last version, select the new version from the Store. After it downloads the *Install macOS* window displays. Click *Continue*.

Source: Apple Inc.

Read the license agreement and click the *Agree* button to accept the terms of the license agreement.

Source: Apple Inc.

Step 6

On the next screen, you will normally see only one location for installing the upgrade. If you decide to select another disk, click *Show all disks*. Otherwise, click *Install* to continue.

Source: Apple Inc.

Step 7

A progress bar displays for a short time, and then the computer reboots and you see an Install macOS message box (against a plain background) with progress bar. After this, the message changes to *Install Succeeded* and it reboots again. What happens next depends on whether you did an upgrade over an older version of macOS or installed onto a clean hard drive.

Step 8

If you did an upgrade over an older version of macOS, your apps will be intact, as will your settings, including your local user account. After the restart the logon screen displays, where you log in and meet the new version of macOS.

Source: Apple Inc.

Step 9

If you did a clean install onto an empty hard drive, you have more work to do. The Setup Assistant runs and you will need to answer screens of questions to complete the configuration of your computer, including a new user name and password.

Postinstallation Tasks

A benefit of Apple's requirement that you purchase macOS through the online App Store is that the installation image you download includes the latest updates to macOS. This requirement began with Mountain Lion, and eliminates the need to update macOS immediately after an upgrade or install. If you install macOS from an image you created days or weeks ago, you will need to check updates, as described earlier. Other postinstallation tasks include installing apps into a clean installation, updating apps, and enabling disabled components.

Installing Apps

If you did a clean install, you will need to install all your apps and personalize your computer to your own preferences.

Updating Apps

Apple does not include updates for your apps in the image, so you should check out available updates. An easy way to do this is by simply checking to see if a number appears on the top right of the App Store icon. When that happens, double-click the icon, the App Store window will open, as shown in Figure 7–2, and you can initiate the download and install the update from there.

Alternatively, when you do not see a message or indication of an update but want to see if any are available, open the Apple menu and select *Software Update,* which will also open the App Store window and check for updates.

In yet another scenario, you open an app and a message displays stating that an update is available. Unless you know of a reason to not update the software, simply respond to messages to start the download, including one allowing incoming network connections from the update

try this!

Install Software Updates

It is simple to install updates. Try this:

1. Click the Apple menu in the top-left corner of your desktop, select About this Mac, and click Software Update in the window that displays.
2. In the Updates page of the App Store, see if any updates are available and respond to any messages to begin the Install.
3. Click Agree on any License Agreement page that displays (if you agree, of course). There may be several.
4. Click Restart, if requested.
5. It can take several minutes for the updates to install.

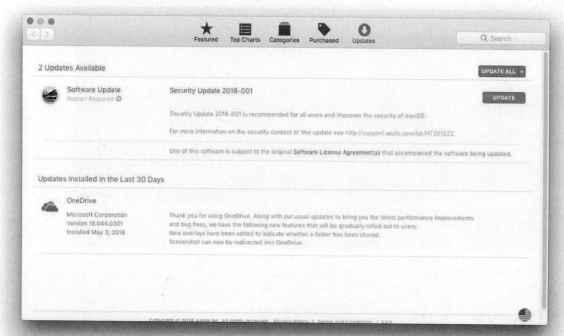

FIGURE 7–2 The Updates page of the Apps Store.

program. Then you may see a message box giving choices to accept or reject individual updates and to start the install. A progress message will display while the update downloads. After the download completes, respond to more messages to continue, to accept the license terms, to select a destination drive, and finally to install the update.

Enable Disabled Components or Apps

If you disabled any components, such as FileVault, before upgrading macOS enable them after completing the upgrade. We describe FileVault later in this chapter.

LO 7.3 | Navigating and Managing the macOS Desktop

Navigating in macOS is much like it is in the Windows desktop. You move around by clicking graphical objects. Tasks include customizing the desktop, installing and removing applications, and adding a printer. You will learn how to set up system preferences, manage files, print, and create and manage user accounts. We also describe the features you use for your everyday work on a Mac, including launching programs and working with the newer macOS features.

The Desktop Menu Bar

One of the biggest differences between the macOS GUI and the Windows desktop is that Windows has a Taskbar at the bottom of the screen with general functions and notifications, and each app has its own menu bar at the top of its window. But macOS has a menu bar across the top of the screen with general functions and which also contains drop-down menus for the current app, and a notification area on the far right that serves some of the same functions as the right end of the Windows Taskbar. Depending on how macOS is configured, the notification area displays the day and time and contains icons for features such as the Spotlight search feature that searches local files and folders. Spotlight is also at the top of every Finder window. Figure 7–3 shows the macOS desktop

Note: The window for an app in macOS does not contain the menu bar, but it does contain buttons for accessing many of the same features available through the menu bar and the round window control buttons in the upper left corner for closing (red), minimizing (orange), and maximizing (green) the window.

FIGURE 7–3 Key features of the macOS desktop.
Source: Apple Inc.

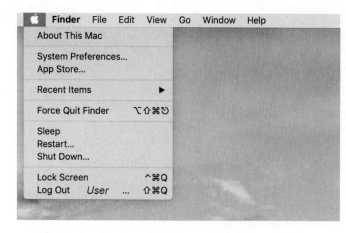

FIGURE 7–4 The Apple menu.
Source: Apple Inc.

with key features labeled. COMMAND+SPACE BAR opens the Spotlight search box. Spotlight presents results as soon as you start typing because Spotlight does a live search. Beginning in macOS 10.11 El Capitan, Spotlight searches everywhere, including the Web, and it is integrated into Safari. Another improvement in Spotlight is that you can ask natural language questions, as we have grown to expect to do with Apple's Siri and Microsoft's Cortana.

Click on the Apple icon on the left of the menu bar to open the Apple menu shown in Figure 7–4. This is where you find the version information (and details of the hardware and software), initiate a Software Update, connect to the App Store, open System Preferences to configure settings, put the computer into Sleep mode, restart the computer, shut down, and log out.

File Management in Finder

Like Windows, the macOS desktop has a file manager, Finder, as its foundation. When you launch macOS, Finder owns the desktop, as evidenced by the Finder menus at the top of the screen, but a Finder window is not open by default. Open the Finder windows from the smiling Finder shortcut on the Dock or with the shortcut keys: COMMAND+SHIFT+H. Apple is gradually replacing this focus on files in macOS by a focus on apps, which we discuss more in the sections on the Dock and Launchpad. However, Finder is your file management tool in macOS and in the following sections we look at the Finder views, then practice creating folders, and learn other file management tasks.

Note: Do you lose sight of your cursor when there is a lot of clutter on your desktop? Simply shake the mouse (or quickly swipe back and forth on a touchpad) and the mouse moves and temporarily enlarges on the screen.

Note: COMMAND+SHIFT+H opens the Home folder. COMMAND+SHIFT+D opens the Desktop folder that contains files and folders that appear on your macOS Desktop.

Home Folder

Each person who logs on to an macOS computer has his or her own Home folder. When you open a Finder window, the Home folder for the currently logged-on user is identified in the Sidebar, the panel on the left of the Finder window, by an icon representing (what else?) a house. When you select your Home folder the house icon displays at the top of the window, as shown in Figure 7–5. Any time you want to open the Home folder, click on it in an open Finder window or simply press COMMAND+SHIFT+H. Several folders are created in the Home folder by macOS. They include Desktop, Documents, Downloads, Movies, Music, Pictures, and Public. You can also create custom folders to help you organize your files. The Documents folder is the default location that many apps use when saving your data files.

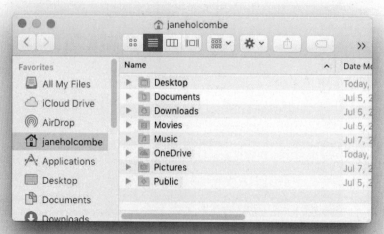

FIGURE 7–5 The Home folder has a house icon and displays the user's name.
Source: Apple Inc.

The Finder menus—Finder, File, Edit, View, Go, Window, and Help—offer a variety of file management and configuration tools. The Finder menu, shown in Figure 7-6, lets you manage Finder itself, as does the menu in this position for any open app. The About Finder option gives its version number. Since Finder is part of the OS, it has the same version number as the OS, but when you open the About menu for an app that is not part of the OS you will see a different version number, and often, much more information about the app. The Window menu arranges window views, and the Go menu offers shortcuts to folders used for storage both on the computer and out on a network.

Select Preferences from the Finder menu and personalize Finder's default behavior. For instance, use the Sidebar options (see Figure 7-7) to add or remove items from Finder's Sidebar.

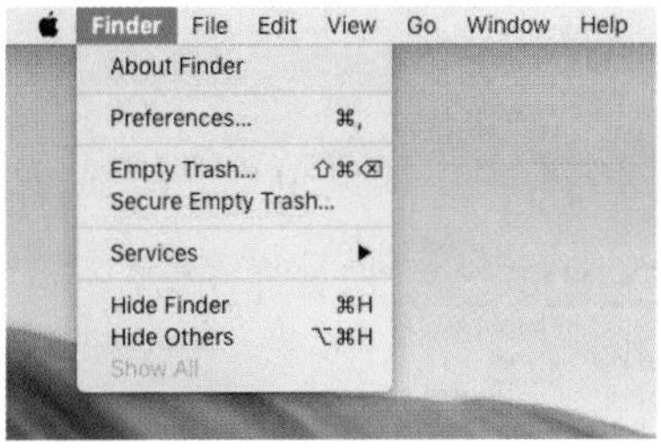

FIGURE 7-6 The Finder menu.
Source: Apple Inc.

Finder Views

Finder has four views or ways of displaying objects: Icon, List, Column, and Cover Flow/Gallery. Finder saves the preferred view of the first folder or disk opened in a new Finder window. The unifying factor in all four viewing modes in macOS is the ability to navigate the file and folder structure of your disks and to open files and folders by double-clicking them. If you are sitting at a Mac, follow the instructions in the Try This exercise, and then, while reading the following paragraphs describing the four views, experiment with the different views. You can set view options from the View menu, or from the View buttons, which we labeled in Figure 7-8.

> *Note:* Beginning in macOS 10.9 (Mavericks), Finder includes Finder Tabs, which act much like the tabs in Safari and other browsers. This reduces clutter by allowing you to have multiple tab pages in one window.

Icon View. In Icon view, shown in Figure 7-9, you simply see the icon for each object in the selected location. This example shows the Applications folder open in Icon view. macOS stores application executables in this folder; double-click an icon to launch its app. We describe other methods for launching apps later in this chapter.

List View. List view, shown in Figure 7-10, displays content in an indented outline format that allows you to see the contents of enclosed folders. This is a powerful means of viewing and organizing your folders and files without having to open new windows for each subfolder, a process that can make your virtual desktop as messy as a real one!

To expand a folder, click the triangular icon to the left of the folder icon. To close the folder, simply click the icon again to hide the contents of that folder. The List view offers a wealth of information about folders and files such as date last opened, date added, size, and kind (e.g., application or file). If you double-click a folder, that folder opens either in the same folder window or in a new window, as in the other two view options.

Column View. In Column view, shown in Figure 7-11, when you select a file by clicking it once, the file's icon or a preview of its contents, either text or graphics, displays in a column to the right. If you click on a folder, the contents display in the column to the right, and if you click on a subfolder, yet another column opens with that folder's contents.

try this!

Explore Finder Views

Open Finder and browse through it while reading about the different types of views. Try this:

1. Open a Finder folder by clicking the Finder icon on the Dock.
2. Click each object in the left pane and then settle on one object that displays many files and folders in the right pane.
3. Locate the View buttons on the Finder window toolbar.
4. As you read through the description of Finder views here in the chapter, select the appropriate View button to select a view.

try this!

Sorting Files in List View

In List view, four columns offer information about your files: Name, Date Modified, Size, and Kind. The default view is an alphabetical sort by name. You can change that order. Try this:

1. Open a Finder folder by clicking the Finder icon on the Dock.
2. Double-click a folder or hard disk.
3. Click the title of any of these columns, and you will see your files sorted by that attribute. Sorting based on the size and data columns is useful when you want to recover hard disk space. Look for big, obsolete files this way.
4. Click the same title again to see the files sorted by that attribute in reverse order. Used most often with the Date column, this technique is effective when you want to search for recently changed or out-of-date files.

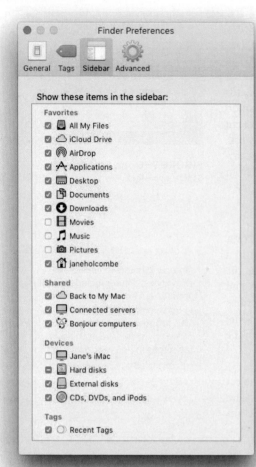

FIGURE 7–7 Use Finder Preferences to add or remove items from the Sidebar.
Source: Apple Inc.

When a window is in Column view, you can change the size of columns by dragging the bottom of the column divider.

Cover Flow View. Cover Flow view, shown in Figure 7–12, opens a pane containing small images of each object in the currently selected folder. Below this pane is a list pane. Select a file or folder in this list and it will appear in the center of the Cover Flow.

Creating Folders in the Finder

Organize your documents and applications in the contents pane. Create a new folder to contain copied or moved files or folders by choosing New Folder from the File menu in the Finder or by right-clicking an area of the contents pane and selecting New Folder. Practice creating a new folder in Step-by-Step 7.03.

Copying, Pasting, and Deleting Files and Folders

Copy and paste files and folders into local or network locations.

- To copy, select the item and choose Copy from the Edit menu (or press COMMAND+C).

- To cut, select the item and choose Cut from the Edit menu (or press COMMAND+X).

- To paste, first either copy or cut a file or folder. Then open the destination location and select Paste from the Edit menu (or press COMMAND+V).

- To delete, choose Delete from the Edit menu (or press COMMAND+DELETE). This moves the file or folder into the Trash. To empty the Trash, select Empty Trash from the Finder menu (or press COMMAND+SHIFT+DELETE).

- If you drag a file or folder and drop it onto a different drive, that operation is a copy, meaning that you have copied the file or folder to the new location and the original remains in the old location. To copy a file or folder onto the same drive with a drag operation, hold down the OPTION key as you let go of the file or folder. Otherwise, it will be a move (discussed next).

FIGURE 7–8 Change the view from the Finder View menu or by clicking one of the View buttons on the toolbar.
Source: Apple Inc.

Note: COMMAND+SHIFT+A opens the Applications folder.

FIGURE 7–9 The Finder window with the Applications folder open in Icon view.
Source: Apple Inc.

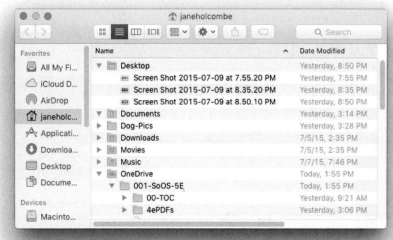

FIGURE 7–10 The Finder window in List view.
Source: Apple Inc.

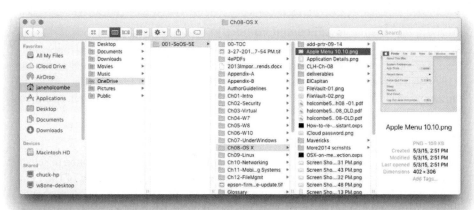

FIGURE 7–11 The Finder window in Column view.
Source: Apple Inc.

Note: In Mojave, Coverflow was replaced by Gallery view.

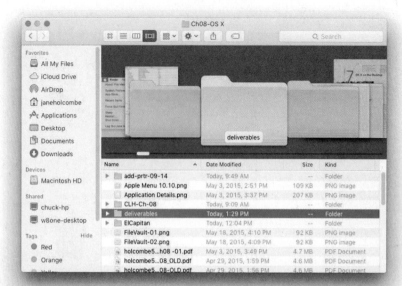

FIGURE 7–12 The Finder window in Cover Flow view.
Source: Apple Inc.

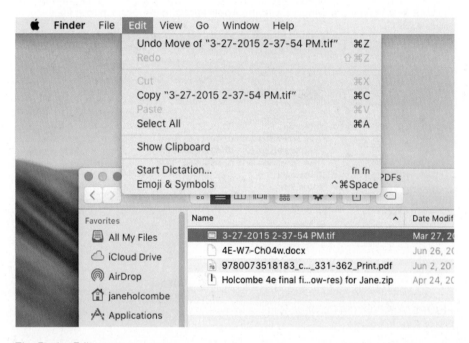

The Finder Edit menu.
Source: Apple Inc.

Moving and Renaming Files and Folders in Finder

If you drag a file or folder and drop it in a different folder on the same drive, that operation is a move, meaning that it is first copied to the new location and then automatically deleted from the old location. When you cut and paste a file or folder, it results in a move regardless of the locations. In Step-by-Step 7.03 you create a folder, and then drag files into the new folder.

Renaming Files and Folders in Finder

Open Finder and locate the file or folder you want to rename; click on it once to select it, and then after a short pause click again. This will highlight the name of the item and you will be able to edit the file name without changing the extension. (You should almost never change a file's extension.) When you are ready to save the item with the new name, either click away from the item or press RETURN.

Step-by-Step 7.03

Creating a New Folder and Organizing Files

In this exercise, you will create a folder within an existing folder, rename it, and move files into it. To complete this exercise, you will need the following:

- A Mac computer with macOS installed.

- A user name and password that will allow you to log on to your computer.
- Files in at least one of the folders of your home directory.

Step 1

Open Finder by clicking its icon (the rectangular, blue and white icon with a face image) on the Dock. If the Home folder is not visible in the Sidebar, first check Finder Preferences, as described earlier, and make sure there is a check by your Home folder. If it is still not visible, it may be hidden. Hover your mouse over the word "Favorites" at the top of the Sidebar. If the word on the right is "Show," click it to make the Home folder visible. Click on your Home folder in the left pane to see its contents on the right. Switch to Column view.

Step 2

Create a new folder. Press COMMAND+SHIFT+N or select New Folder from the Finder's File menu. A new folder, called "untitled folder," will appear in the list of files and folders.

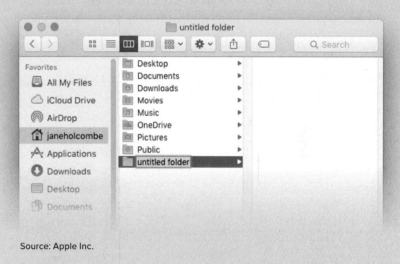

Source: Apple Inc.

Step 3

Type a new name for the folder and press ENTER to save it. Or click the folder once, pause, and then click it a second time to highlight its name, and then type a new name and press ENTER to save the file with the new name.

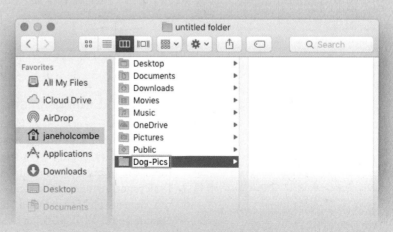

Source: Apple Inc.

Step 4

If a column is not already open to the right of the new folder, double-click on the folder.

Step 5

On the menu bar, select File, New Finder Window. Position the new window next to the window for the new folder. In the newly opened window, navigate to a folder containing files or folders you wish to move to the new folder. In this example, the window on the left shows the new folder "Dog-Pics." The window on the right shows that we selected a file named "Jazzy_3-08-08.jpg."

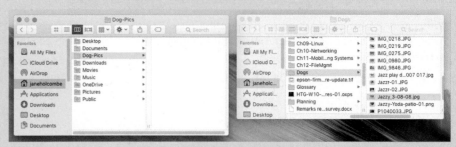

Source: Apple Inc.

Step 6

Select a file or folder that you want to place into this folder by clicking it once and then dragging it to the window containing the new folder. If you want to select multiple files or folders, hold down the COMMAND key while clicking each file until you have selected all the files.

Step 7

When you are finished selecting items, press COMMAND+C to copy them. Then click in the empty folder area in the other Finder window. Press COMMAND+V to paste into the new folder. When you have completed the task, close all open windows.

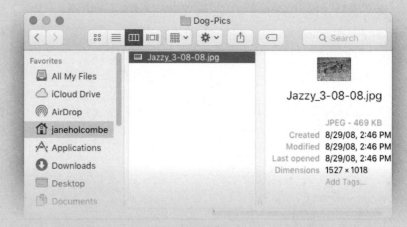

Source: Apple Inc.

The System Preferences icon on the Dock.
Source: Apple Inc.

Changing Settings in macOS

Open **System Preferences** from the Apple menu or from the Dock where its icon is a gray box containing a gear. This is the macOS equivalent of the Windows Control Panel. Figure 7–13 shows the main System Preferences window. Notice the *Show All* button in the title bar; this will always return you to the main System Preferences window. The icons are in rows by category. The actual icons in each row depend on the installed features and devices. While any logged-on user can change some settings, others can only be changed by an administrator, and some can be configured to be changed by either type of user. We describe the System

Show All button

Note: Click the Show All button to return to the main Preferences window from any individual Preferences window.

FIGURE 7–13 System Preferences organized by category.
Source: Apple Inc.

Preferences categories by row below, using category names that are no longer visible in System Preferences.

- **Personal**—Desktop, security, and privacy settings for the currently logged-on user.

- **Hardware**—Settings for hardware devices. Some of these are obviously associated with a single device, but Energy Saver controls the conditions under which different components are put into a low-power sleep mode and/or awakened.

- **Internet and Wireless**—Settings that apply to any form of network available to the computer and to certain services that rely on networking.

- **System**—Software settings that apply to all users of the computer.

- **Other**—Settings that apply to miscellaneous services and devices that do not quite fit into the other categories. This row does not exist in Figure 7-13.

If you have trouble with the default organization of the System Preferences icons, you can sort them in alphabetical order by clicking the View menu (in the Menu bar at the top of the screen) and selecting *Organize Alphabetically.* When you do that, the settings in the System Preferences window are sorted, and the shading that previously separated the categories disappears. However, you don't really need to change the View; simply select the setting name from the View menu, as shown in Figure 7-14. This is helpful when you know the name of a Preference pane but do not recall its category.

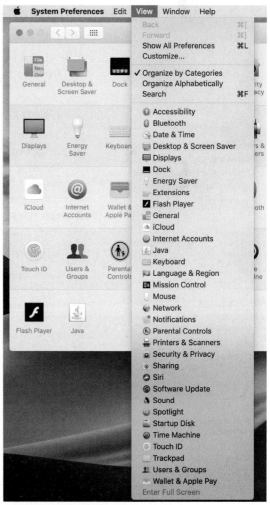

FIGURE 7–14 The View menu lets you change the appearance of the System Preferences folder.
Source: Apple Inc.

Launching and Switching between Apps with the Dock

While early versions of Mac OS used the Finder as a task switcher, macOS delegates the task of launching frequently used apps and switching between open apps to the Dock, shown in Figure 7-2. A subtle line "engraved" in the Dock separates program icons from icons representing disks, folders, and documents. A single click on an icon on the Dock launches the program.

When you launch a program, a small dot appears under the app's icon on the Dock; simply click on one of these icons to quickly switch between tasks. The Trash icon sits on the Dock, waiting for you to drag unwanted files, folders, and apps into it. Add a file, folder, application, or Internet bookmark to the Dock by simply dragging it there. If you want to remove something from the Dock, just drag it off and onto the desktop until the word "Remove" appears over it, as shown in Figure 7-15; release the mouse button. The icon disappears. An icon on the Dock behaves like a Windows shortcut, pointing to a file, program, or location. Therefore, removing it from the Dock only removes the icon.

try this!

Add an Icon to the Dock

Add a shortcut icon to the Dock. Try this:

1. Open the Application folder in Finder and select something you would like to call up quickly from the Dock.
2. Click the item's icon and drag it onto the Dock. Before letting go of the mouse button, move the icon over the Dock to position it between existing Dock icons. Depending on the type of icon, you will be able to position it to the right or left of the divider.
3. Release the mouse button when you are satisfied with the position of the icon.
4. To reposition the Dock on the screen, click the Apple menu and select Dock. From the Dock menu click to select one of the position options. Notice the change in the appearance of the Dock as well as the orientation of the icons.
5. To remove the icon, drag it to the Trash icon.

Using the Heads-Up Program Switcher

There are several ways to switch among open apps, but we find using the Dock, as described above, and using the Heads-Up Program Switcher to be the methods we use the most. Simply press and hold the COMMAND key and tap the TAB key. The heads-up display of open app icons appears in the middle of the screen. Keep the COMMAND key down while you repeatedly tap the TAB key to cycle through the app icons. When the app you want is selected, release the COMMAND key.

View and Manage All Programs in Launchpad

Launchpad, a feature introduced in macOS Mountain Lion, resembles the home screen on Apple iOS devices (shown in Chapter 11). Click the Launchpad "rocket" icon on the Dock to open Launchpad. With Launchpad open, the menu bar at the top of the screen and objects on the desktop disappear, but the Dock remains visible. Now you can view all the existing apps installed on your computer and launch one with a single click. If you have more program icons than will fit on a page, scroll to see additional pages, just as in iOS.

Figure 7-16 shows Launchpad open with one page of app icons. When there are more apps than will fit on one page, Launchpad creates additional pages. The number of pages is indicated by dots positioned just above the Dock. Click a dot or swipe to move to another page. Customize Launchpad by clicking on an icon and holding the mouse button until all the icons in Launchpad start jiggling. Then drag the selected icon to different positions on the page or pages. If you drag an icon on top of another program icon (without releasing it), a horizontal band opens in the middle of the screen. Drop the icon into this band to group it into a folder with the other icon. When we dragged the Mail icon on top of the messages icon, the band opened with the suggested folder

The Heads-Up Program Switcher.
Source: Apple Inc.

FIGURE 7–16 The Launchpad contains app icons.
Source: Apple Inc.

FIGURE 7–15 To remove an icon simply drag it off the Dock until the word "Remove" appears, then release the mouse button.
Source: Apple Inc.

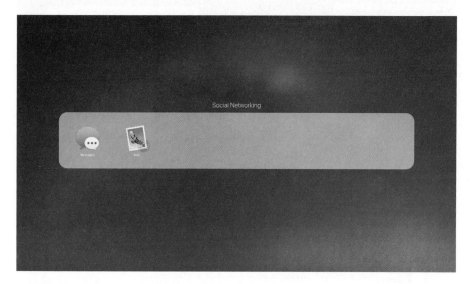

FIGURE 7–17 Group apps that you use together in a folder in Launchpad.
Source: Apple Inc.

FIGURE 7–18 Add other apps to a Launchpad folder.
Source: Apple Inc.

name of "Social Networking." When we dropped the Mail icon, Launchpad created the folder and showed the name above the band, as shown in Figure 7-17. After you create a grouping of apps in Launchpad, you can easily drag and drop more apps into the group, as shown in Figure 7-18.

Declutter the Desktop with Mission Control

Mission Control is a window-management program that combines the functions of the Exposé, Dashboard, and Spaces features. "Exposé" was the term Apple previously used to refer to the feature that let you view all open windows on the screen at once. Dashboard is a screen containing small applets that act somewhat like Windows widgets. A Space is a virtual screen; macOS supports up to 16 Spaces. Use Spaces for separating work, play, and school projects into virtual desktops. Or open an app full screen and place it in its own Space. In recent versions, full-screen apps hide the desktop menu bar and give you the maximum space in which to work.

Note: A more generic term for Apple's Spaces feature is desktop, easily confused with the virtual desktops discussed in Chapter 2, but altogether different. Linux and Windows 10 each have features similar to Spaces.

Open the **Mission Control** screen (see Figure 7-19) to manage these features. Open Mission Control from the Launchpad or check out the keystroke or key combination to open Mission Control in the Mission Control preferences pane, shown in Figure 7-20. The Mission Control shortcut is usually CTRL+UP ARROW. Use it once to open Mission Control. Use it again to close Mission Control.

When you open Mission Control, each window displays as a tile, and a thin bar is across the top with the current space or spaces identified as "Desktop 1," "Desktop 2," and so on. Move your cursor to the top of the screen and the bar will broaden, showing thumbnails for the current spaces, as shown in Figure 7-19. To add a space, simply click

FIGURE 7–19 Mission Control.
Source: Apple Inc.

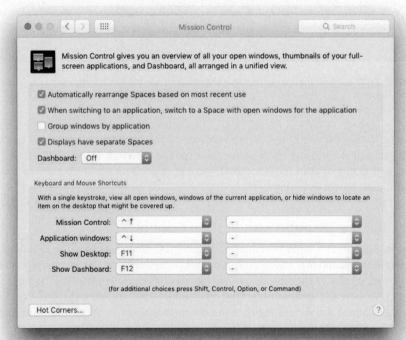

Note: To see a list of all keyboard shortcuts for macOS open the Shortcuts tab of the Keyboard pane in System Preferences.

FIGURE 7–20 Change Mission Control settings in this preferences pane.
Source: Apple Inc.

on the plus (+) at the top right and a desktop will be added showing a thumbnail. Drag an open window from below to another desktop on the bar. Switch between spaces by selecting a space within Mission Control or with the CTRL+RIGHT ARROW key or CTRL+LEFT ARROW key.

Note: Press CTRL+RIGHT ARROW key or CTRL+LEFT ARROW key to switch between Spaces.

Split View

The last few versions of macOS include the ability to make two full-screen apps share the screen, a feature called **Split View**. To begin, open the two apps you wish to have share the screen. In one of the apps click-hold the green button on the top left of the app window. When you release the button, the screen will split behind the app, and the second app will open in the other half of the screen when you click its green button. This is great when you need information from one app while working in another app. Figure 7–21 shows an example of Split View. An app window in Split View is automatically assigned its own desktop space. Click the green button to exit Split View.

Note: Split View hides both the desktop menu bar as well as the window title bar on each app window. Move the cursor to the top of the screen to access these bars.

Notification Center

The **Notification Center** displays important status messages, notifying you of events, such as a new email or text message or the availability of a new update. These messages pop down on the top right of the Desktop. To open the Notification Center itself, click on its icon containing three vertical bars at the far right of the desktop menu bar. In Notification Center, shown in Figure 7-22, you will see all your messages at once. Click the tiny icon in the bottom-right corner of the open Notification Center to open the Notifications preferences window (the open windows in Figure 7-22), where you can configure settings for notifications. Alternatively, open Notifications preferences from System Preferences.

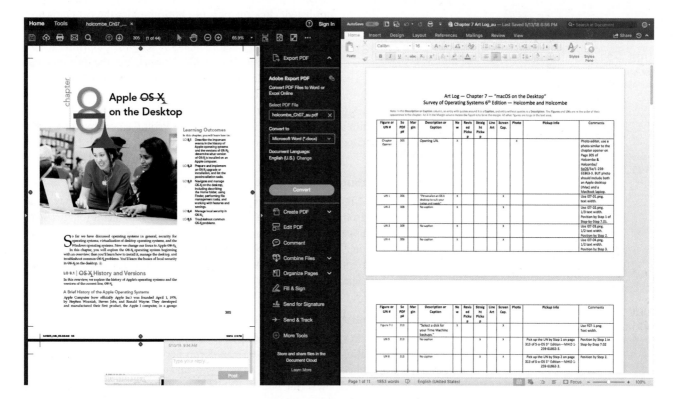

FIGURE 7–21 Full screen apps can be viewed side-by-side in Split View allows to full screen apps to share the screen.
Source: Apple Inc.

FIGURE 7–22 Open Notification Center to see all current notifications.
Source: Apple Inc.

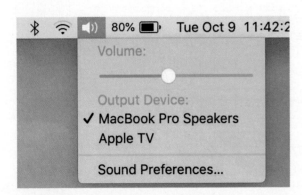

FIGURE 7–23 Some Menu Extras have menus; others have controls. This one has both.
Source: Apple Inc.

Menu Extras

The macOS Menu bar has a variety of icons on the right side—some open up menus, while others, like the speaker icon, open controls as shown in Figure 7-23. These icons that give you quick access to some System Preferences settings are called **Menu Extras**. Add Menu Extras to the Menu bar through the individual preferences panes in System Preferences. For instance, the day and time are visible on the Menu bar because of a setting enabled on the Clock page of the Date & Time preferences pane. This setting is *Show date and time in menu bar*. Similarly, the Volume Control is on the menu bar because of a setting titled *Show volume in menu bar*.

Printing in macOS

No matter what type of printer you have, almost every macOS application manages the printing process in the same way, including giving you the ability to create an Adobe PDF document from any Print menu.

Installing a Printer

Installing a printer in macOS is a nonevent. You simply connect the printer, power up, and it installs without any fuss or obvious activity. The OS quietly searches for the driver, downloading it from the Internet if the computer has an Internet connection.

To verify that the printer did install, open Printers and Scanners in System Preferences. With the Print tab selected, installed printers are listed on the left. If your new printer is not listed, click the plus (+) button under the list (shown in Figure 7-24) to initiate the printer detection process. This is often necessary before macOS recognizes a printer over a Wi-Fi connection. If this doesn't work, use the disc that was packed with the printer or, if you do not have a disc, contact the manufacturer for help finding a driver.

Most of your printer interaction takes place in the Print dialog box within applications. During printing, the Print Center icon appears in the Dock, allowing you to view, hold, or delete jobs.

Setting Printing Options

A printer has a variety of configurable options, which you may modify from the Print menu in any application's File menu (or the Print and Scan preferences pane). These options are specific to the printer model. You should explore these options for your own printer so that you are aware of its capabilities and can plan to take advantage of them.

Where to Find the Print Queue

When you are ready to send a job to the printer, simply open the Print menu in the application, select the printer, and if you need to change paper size, orientation, or scale, click the Page Setup button and make those changes. When you are ready to print, click the Print button. While a job is printing, an icon displays on the Dock, and if you're fast, you can open it in time to see the print queue, which closes when the print job is finished. Otherwise, you can find the print queue for an individual printer by calling up the Print and Scan preferences pane. Select a printer from the list on the left and double-click on any printer or click the *Open Print Queue* button to view its print queue, check the ink or toner level, print a test page, or open a printer utility that will let you do certain printer maintenance and testing.

Siri

Siri, Apple's voice-activated personal assistant, first appeared in iPhones. In the years since its introduction Siri has gained functionality and become a popular feature of Apple iPhones. Now it is available on Apple's desktops and laptops, thanks to support for Siri in macOS. When you install the latest version of macOS the Setup Assistant prompts you to enable and configure Siri. If you decline, you can take time to do it later. When (or if) you are ready to do that, simply click the Siri icon in System Preferences. Then in the Siri preferences pane click to put a check in the box by *Enable Ask Siri.* That will trigger a drop-down box, shown Figure 7–25. It is warning you that Siri sends information to Apple to process your requests. They are giving you the opportunity to learn a bit about how your personal data is used by Apple when you use Siri. If after reading this you want to proceed, click the Enable button in the drop-down box.

Next, click on the button labeled *Siri Suggestions & Privacy* and yet another drop-down box displays, as shown in Figure 7–25. Here you can enable or disable what apps Siri will monitor in order to learn more about you. All options are selected by default. Click the check box to deselect any app you wish excluded from this information gather process. Then Click the Done button.

AirPlay

Apple added **AirPlay**, a feature that was first introduced in iOS, to macOS in Mountain Lion. Use AirPlay to connect to an Apple TV, which acts as an intermediary device for sending your iTunes songs, video, pictures, and other data from your computer to a high-definition (HD) TV via Wi-Fi.

LO 7.4 | Managing Local Security in macOS

Although most malware attacking desktop computers target Microsoft Windows, macOS is not impregnable, and anyone who connects to a network, plugs in a flash drive, or inserts an optical disc in their computer is vulnerable—not to mention the threats you can encounter browsing the Web and even in the messages you receive.

Apple is aware of the threats and has built in many security features that are on by default. Make sure you have updated your software, as described earlier in this chapter. It also doesn't hurt to add an antivirus program to your Mac. However, the greatest threats may be from scams and frauds, and your best defense against them is self-education and skepticism (even paranoia) when faced with messages that ask

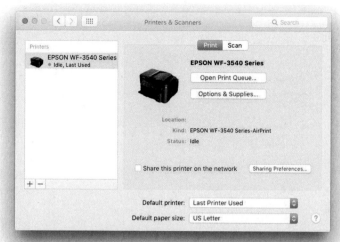

FIGURE 7–24 Click the plus (+) at the bottom of the list to add a new printer.
Source: Apple Inc.

FIGURE 7–25 Enable and configure Siri in its Preferences pane.
Source: Apple Inc.

FIGURE 7–26 Decide what apps Siri will use to learn more about you.
Source: Apple Inc.

Source: Apple Inc.

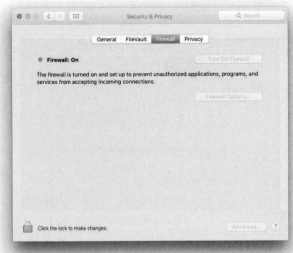

FIGURE 7–27 Firewall is on.
Source: Apple Inc.

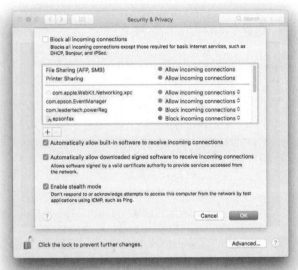

FIGURE 7–28 Incoming connections are allowed for sharing and for certain apps.
Source: Apple Inc.

WARNING!

Anytime you unlock a settings pane, be sure to lock it again when you finish.

for information or require that you click on a link. In this section, we examine the macOS security features that do a pretty good job of protecting you from everything but social engineering.

So where do you begin? Start your relationship with your Mac by exploring the security features of macOS and ensuring that you are using every security option available to you.

Check Out the macOS Firewall

How does your Mac connect to the Internet? Is it through a broadband router at home, or through a Wi-Fi hotspot at the school cafeteria or the local coffee shop? However, your computer connects—whether it is a network you trust (at home or school) or an untrusted network, such as many of the public Wi-Fi hotspots, you need to ensure that you have the macOS Firewall turned on. While the most recent versions of macOS turn it on by default, you should check it out and familiarize yourself with it.

To view and modify Firewall settings, open the Security and Privacy pane in System Preferences and click on Firewall. Ensure that the firewall is on. If it is not, turn it on. You may need to click on the lock icon on the lower left of the window to unlock the settings, in which case you will need to provide a password. Then click the button labeled **Turn on Firewall.** Figure 7-27 shows the Firewall turned on.

After ensuring that the firewall is on, you may need to click the lock icon (if not already unlocked) and provide a password. Now, click the Firewall Options button to view the settings. Figure 7-28 shows this page. This requires some explanation. You could block all incoming connections if all you are doing is simple Web browsing and sending and receiving email. During these operations you initiate the connection to a Web server or mail server. The traffic that comes to your computer because of these actions is not seeking to initiate a connection to your computer; it is simply responding to your request for Web pages or email messages. Therefore, you could block all incoming connections, but still browse the Internet and send and receive email.

Our example in Figure 7-28 is more complicated because we have enabled sharing services on the Mac. If you install or enable services on your Mac that require incoming traffic (not initiated from within), it will configure the Firewall to allow this type of traffic. However, if you do not plan to do any type of sharing and have not enabled any service requiring incoming traffic, Firewall will block all incoming connections and it will turn on stealth mode, which it will gray out so that you cannot disable it. If you later wish to use a sharing service, the installation will change the setting to allow incoming connections for that service.

Gatekeeper

Gatekeeper, a feature introduced in macOS Mountain Lion, limits the online sources from which you can download programs. You will not find an icon labeled Gatekeeper, but you can configure Gatekeeper settings by selecting one of the options labeled *Allow applications downloaded from* on the General page of the Security & Privacy preferences pane. Here is a description of each of those settings (shown in Figure 7-29):

1. **Mac App Store**: Only install apps from the App Store. The most restrictive setting.

2. **Mac App Store and identified developers**: Download and install apps that include a Developer ID signature as well as apps from the Apps Store. Less restrictive.

3. **Anywhere**: Download and install apps from any location, as long as other security features of macOS allow this action. The only restrictions will be from other security components. This turns Gatekeeper off.

Kernel ASLR

Using a security feature called **address space layout randomization (ASLR)**, macOS Mountain Lion and newer OSs load the core operating system code, the kernel, into random locations in memory, rather than loading into the same memory addresses every time. This prevents malware from accessing operating system functions based on their known location in memory.

Digitally Signed and Sandboxed Apps

All apps available through the App Store are digitally signed. A digitally signed app will issue a warning if its code is modified. In addition, each app available through the App Store is **sandboxed**, meaning that it cannot access any code or device it is not authorized to access. It is in a virtual sandbox where it can only play with those "toys" it is permitted to access.

FIGURE 7–29 View and change the Gatekeeper settings by selecting one of the options under *Allow applications downloaded from.*
Source: Apple Inc.

FileVault

FileVault is the macOS file and disk encryption feature. Earlier versions only encrypted the Home folder, but in recent versions of macOS FileVault encrypts everything on your startup drive every time you log out. With FileVault disk encryption turned on, your files are accessible only while you are logged on. Unless someone has access to your password, or you walk away from your computer without logging out, no one can open the encrypted files. An administrator must turn on FileVault using the FileVault page of the Security pane, as shown in Figure 7-30. On the next screen (Figure 7-31), choose how you wish to unlock your disk: with your iCloud account or with a **recovery key**. If you choose to use a recovery key, it will be created and displayed on the screen. Be sure to copy down the recovery key and store it in a safe place. You only need one recovery key on each computer. The encryption of your disk will begin after a restart, and it may take hours to complete. During this time you cannot turn off FileVault.

> **WARNING!**
> Do not turn on FileVault if you cannot allow the computer to run until encryption is completed. It can take several hours for FileVault to encrypt your disk, which it does after a restart.

> **WARNING!**
> If you forget your password or recovery key, you will not be able to access your startup drive and any data stored on it.

FIGURE 7–30 Click the *Turn On FileVault* button in the FileVault page of the Security preferences pane.
Source: Apple Inc.

FIGURE 7–31 Choose how you want to unlock the disk.
Source: Apple Inc.

Secure Virtual Memory

macOS uses a swap file, much as Windows does. The swap file is disk space the OS uses as if it is memory, so they call it virtual memory. All multitasking operating systems use virtual memory to allow you to have several applications open. While you are actively using your word processor, most other open applications are just waiting for you to switch back to them. Therefore, the operating system temporarily saves at least part of the code and data for these other apps to the swap file. Clever hackers can access the data in a swap file, so Apple includes a feature in macOS called Secure Virtual Memory, which encrypts the swap file. In earlier versions, Secure Virtual Memory was only turned on when you turned on FileVault but beginning with Mountain Lion, Secure Virtual Memory is on by default, without a way to turn it off in System Preferences.

Keychain

The keychain is part of a credentials management system using the name "keychain" as a metaphor for a physical keychain. The password to the keychain gives the user access to all the passwords or "keys" on that keychain. Each keychain is a secure database of a user's passwords, collected the first time it asks you to supply a user name and password to something, such as shared folders on your school or work network, at websites, FTP sites, and more.

Two default keychains, System and System Roots, belong to the OS. The first time you log in, macOS creates your first keychain, called login, using your account password as a master password for the keychain. Then as you go about your business, logging in to various servers to access email and other resources, as well as various websites, the credentials you supply are saved in your keychain, provided you respond to a prompt asking if you want to save the password. Although some websites have login programs that will not allow this, many do, and if you save the password for a website in your key chain, it will complete the login boxes (a process called AutoFill in Safari) each time you reconnect to one of these sites.

Safari turns AutoFill on by default, and you can turn it off if you do not want keychain to remember your credentials. Look for a setting similar to AutoFill, or one that mentions remembering passwords in any Internet browser to enable keychain with that browser.

For most of us, the login keychain is sufficient for all our needs, but you can create multiple keychains, each with a separate purpose, such as for your online shopping or as a place to save your personal credit information. Create additional keychains if you need varying security levels. For instance, you can configure one keychain so that the keychain locks if there is idle time over a certain threshold. This is where you keep your keys for accessing online banking accounts. Then create another keychain that will not have such a restriction because it is for low-security activity, such as a website you access purely for entertainment, such as Pandora. To create multiple keychains for various purposes, use Keychain Access, a utility found in Finder | Applications | Utilities, shown in Figure 7–32.

There's more to this topic. Now that most of us work on multiple devices, we need a keychain that will work across those devices as we access the same networks and websites. The last few versions of Apple's OSs include support for iCloud Keychain. This is a keychain stored in iCloud and is accessible to all your devices that support it and that you have enabled. Turn on iCloud Keychain in iOS 7.0.3 or later in Settings | iCloud. Do the same in macOS 10.9 Mavericks or later in the iCloud page of System Preferences.

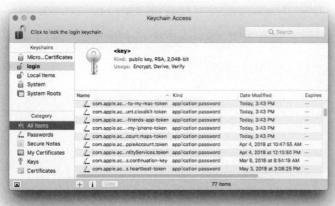

FIGURE 7–32 The Keychain Access utility.
Source: Apple Inc.

Managing Local User Accounts

macOS supports multiple local user accounts. At home, school, or work, you can set up a single computer with multiple accounts so that each person is restricted to his or her own home folder, preserving preferences from one session to another. As in Microsoft Windows, two users can log in to the same computer at the same time, but only one can have control of the "console," the keyboard, screen, and mouse, at any given time. macOS preserves each account's session in memory and users can switch back and forth using fast user switching. Alternatively, users can log in and log out when they finish working or step away.

Parental Controls

Access Parental Controls in System Preferences through the Parental Controls pane or through the settings for individual users in the Users & Groups pane. Parental Controls have four categories of restrictions you can apply to a Standard or Guest account. They are:

- **Apps**—The desktop (Finder) for ease of use and/or to restrict which apps the user can open. Allow or deny the ability to modify the Dock.
- **Web**—Restrict access to adult websites or allow access only to certain websites.
- **People**—Control access to multiplayer games through Game Center, or limit mail and/or messages to a list of allowed contacts.
- **Time Limits**—Assign time limits during weekday and/or weekend and prevent access during defined times.

When you turn on Parental Controls for an account, it becomes a managed account.

Note: You cannot apply Parental Controls to an administrator-type account.

Parental Controls.
Source: Apple Inc.

Types of Users and Privileges

There are several types of user accounts; two of them, Administrator and Standard, are like the Windows account types of the same name. The others are Sharing Only, Guest account, and Root account. We describe the main functionality of the account types here.

Administrator Account. The Administrator account type, also simply called "admin," is for advanced users or for the person who will administer this computer. The first account created during installation is an Administrator. Open the Accounts preferences pane from System Preferences and view the local accounts on a Mac. Notice the description "Admin" on the left under the first account name in Figure 7–33.
An Administrator account can do the following:

- Change all system preference settings and install software in the main application and library folders.
- Create, modify, and delete user accounts.

Standard Account. This account type is for ordinary users in an organization with tech support to take care of configuring and supporting computers. A Standard account type gets into far less trouble because of these restrictions:

- File access is limited to only the user's Home folder and the Shared folder (/Users/Shared/) that is accessible to other users without restriction.
- Access is denied to higher-level system preferences, such as network settings, sharing, software update settings, user setup, and date and time settings.

FIGURE 7–33 The Users & Groups preferences pane.
Source: Apple Inc.

Sharing Only Account. You can create a Sharing Only account for someone who only needs to access shared folders on your Mac over a network. With a Sharing Only account type someone can connect remotely and log in with the local account but will not have her own set of Home folders on the local computer. A person with a Sharing Only account cannot log on locally at the computer where the Sharing Only account resides.

Guest User. Guest is an account type with very limited access, but macOS no longer allows you to assign this account type to a new user. Instead, it creates a single Guest account, called Guest User. This account does not require a password, has access only to the Guest Home folder, and when a guest logs out, all files and folders created during that session in the Guest's Home folder are deleted. Enable the Guest Account in the Users & Groups preferences pane. To further restrict the Guest account, turn on Parental Controls, described previously.

Root Account. The Root account, often called a super-user account, exists mainly for the use of the OS. It is not enabled for interactive users in the standard installation of macOS. Root is only for people familiar with the inner workings of UNIX, and changing things on your computer using this account can result in serious system dysfunction and lost data. We will not describe how to enable it. Root gives you complete control over all folders and files on the Mac.

You rarely will require the amount of control over macOS system files that the Root account allows. Apple specifically organized macOS to limit the need to change the system files and folders.

Automatic Login

Automatic Login bypasses the login page and logs into the selected user account when the computer powers on. With Automatic Login turned off (the recommended setting), macOS prompts a user to enter passwords to log in. In recent versions of macOS, an administrator configures automatic login by selecting the Login Options at the bottom of the Users & Groups preferences pane. This opens a page where you can enable or disable Automatic Login for individual local users, as well as modify the appearance of the login window (if Automatic Login is disabled).

Creating and Deleting User Accounts

The first user account is created when you install macOS, and it is automatically an administrator-type account. After the installation process is complete, you can create additional user accounts, as described in Step-by-Step 7.04. We recommend that you take an additional step and enable an option on the user account page for the first user labeled *Allow user to reset password using Apple ID.* This setting will make life easier for you if you should forget your password for this account, which we discuss later.

> **WARNING!**
>
> Only use Automatic Login in a very safe environment, such as your home, where the convenience outweighs any threat to your data.

Step-by-Step 7.04

Creating a New User/Deleting a User Account

In this exercise, you will add a new user to your computer and delete a user. To complete this exercise, you will need the following:

- A Mac computer with macOS installed.

- You must be logged on to the computer as an administrator.
- If Automatic Login is turned on, turn it off before beginning this exercise.

Open the Users & Groups preferences pane. Click the lock on the bottom left. In the box that opens enter your password and click *Unlock*.

Source: Apple Inc.

Back in Users & Groups click the button with the plus sign at the bottom left. Enter a Full Name and press the Tab key. This will generate an account name based on the full name, by removing the space. At this point, you can change the account name, but once you create the user in the next step, the account name is permanent. Notice that we shortened the account name.

Source: Apple Inc.

If you see a drop-down box concerning Automatic login, click the button labeled Turn Off Automatic Login. Then create a password, and enter it in both the Password and Verify boxes. Enter a password hint, and then click Create User.

Source: Apple Inc.

The new user appears in the sidebar of Users & Groups, and the settings for that user display on the right. The new user in this example is a Standard User. If you want to change this account to an administrator-type account, click to place a check in the box labeled *Allow user to administer this computer* on this page. If the new user is a child, you may want to enable Parental Controls.

Source: Apple Inc.

To delete a user account you will need to ensure that Users & Groups is unlocked for changes. If the lock on the bottom left is locked, click it and enter your password. Then select the user account in the sidebar of Users & Groups and click the minus button (–) at the bottom of the sidebar. When prompted, select an option for saving or deleting the user's Home folder, and then click *Delete User*.

Source: Apple Inc.

LO 7.5 | Troubleshooting Common macOS Problems

In this section, you learn where to find basic help and a guide to the system utilities and keyboard shortcuts that can help you get out of trouble. You'll also learn how to handle the larger files that you'll encounter in today's computing environment.

Where to Find Help

When problems arise in macOS or within an application, where do you go to find help? Explore the options for solving problems and you may find that some of them direct you to the same sources.

Note: COMMAND+SPACEBAR opens the Spotlight bar on the desktop.

Help with the OS

There are several ways to get help with macOS from within the OS itself, such as clicking on the help menu (Figure 7-34) and entering a search string or browsing through the other options. This is a good place to start if you are new to macOS.

FIGURE 7–34 Begin a search for a problem solution by exploring the options on the Help menu.
Source: Apple Inc.

With the improvements in Spotlight search and Siri, we rely more and more on simply asking a question in natural language and selecting a likely source for help among the results it produces. Quickly open the Spotlight bar on the desktop with the COMMAND+SPACEBAR shortcut. Or go directly to Apple's Support Center at **www. apple.com/support**, select the product being used, and search there.

Alternatively, members of the network of Apple user groups around the world can get support from other users and learn more about their computers. Apple user groups are a useful and affordable way to increase your knowledge of your system and the software you choose and use. For more information, see **www.apple.com /usergroups/**.

If self-help fails and your computer is still under warranty, contact Apple directly, using the information that came with your computer. Technical support is expensive if your computer is outside its warranty period. Novice users who use their computers enough to increase the likelihood of multiple requests for support should consider signing up for an AppleCare service and support package to keep technical support costs down. Find more information at the AppleCare site (Figure 7-35) at **www. apple.com/support/products/**.

Help within Applications

If a problem with an open application persists, click the Help menu from the menu bar. In many cases, there will be a local help utility and an option to find online help for the application. Search through the help utility to find an answer to your problem or search the software publisher's website or the Web at large using a brief description of the problem or a part of the error message in the search string.

When to Quit

When you finish working with an app, you can quickly quit the app by pressing COMMAND+Q or by opening the app's menu (shown in Figure 7-36), and selecting Quit. If an open application is behaving strangely—maybe it freezes, displaying

> *Note:* COMMAND+Q quits the current app. COMMAND+OPTION+ESC opens the Force Quit Applications box for the current app.

FIGURE 7-35 The AppleCare site.
Source: Apple Inc.

FIGURE 7-36 An application's Quit option.
Source: Apple Inc.

FIGURE 7–37 Select the application from the Force Quit Applications box.
Source: Apple Inc.

FIGURE 7–38 An application failed.
Source: Apple Inc.

Note: If you change a password, macOS lets you keep your login keychain and assigns the new password to the keychain. When you reset a password, macOS creates a new login keychain for that user, and you will need to manually enter passwords and allow them to be saved in the new keychain.

the "busy" icon for no apparent reason—quit the application and restart it. This will resolve many transient problems.

Sometimes an application will not politely quit; that's when you must use Force Quit—either from the Apple menu or with the key combination of COMMAND+OPTION+ESC. This will bring up the Force Quit Applications box, shown in Figure 7–37. It shows you all the running applications, so you can select the correct one. A force quit allows you to safely remove an application from memory without requiring a restart of your computer and without adversely affecting the rest of the programs running in memory.

macOS Failure to Quit

Sometimes, when you attempt to shut down, log off, or restart, you see a message similar to Figure 7–38, stating that you haven't been logged out because an application has failed to quit, like the one shown here. Return to the app and close it out properly. If that does not work, use the Force Quit tool. If the application still refuses to quit, do a hard power-down by pressing and holding the power button for several seconds.

Forgotten Password

Most calls to help desks are for forgotten passwords. Here we describe your options for recovering from this minor disaster.

Resetting a Password in macOS Snow Leopard or Older

The first-created user account on your computer is automatically designated an administrator. If you happen to forget or lose the administrator password, and if you have macOS Snow Leopard (10.6) or older, reset the password with the help of the installation disc. To do this insert the DVD and from the Install screen choose Utilities | Reset Password. Select the hard drive that contains the System folder, and use the first pop-up menu to select the name of your account. Enter your new password twice. You should keep the DVD in a safe place, because anyone with the macOS DVD can gain complete access to your system.

Resetting a Password

With macOS Lion (10.7) or newer how you reset a password depends on the scenario. We will look at each scenario next.

You are logged in with an administrator account. If macOS is running and you are logged in with an administrator account and wish to reset the password for another account, open System Preferences | Users & Groups. If the lock is in the locked position, click it and enter your password. Select the user in the Users and Groups sidebar, and then select *Reset Password*. Enter a password, verify it by entering it a second time, provide a password hint, and then click *Reset Password*.

You have forgotten your password and cannot log in and FileVault is off. If you cannot get into macOS because you have forgotten your password, and if you don't have FileVault turned on, then at the login screen when you enter a wrong password, the Password Hint box will pop up. If the hint doesn't help, or if there is no hint, click Reset password with Apple ID. The Reset Password box will display, and you can enter your Apple ID and password, and then click Reset Password. Follow the instructions from there.

You have forgotten your password and cannot log in and FileVault is turned on. If FileVault is enabled on your computer, you may be able to use the FileVault recovery key to reset your login password. For detailed instructions, you will need to go to another computer and search **support.apple.com** for the article titled "If you forget your login password and FileVault is on."

The article cited walks you through the necessary steps to attempt to login again with your Apple ID. If that fails, and you cannot reset the password using your Apple ID, select the option to "reset it using your Recovery Key." Then enter your recovery key and reset the password. Be sure to save the new password in a safe location. Or memorize it.

Note: There is a difference between the Change Password and Reset Password options in Users & Groups. The *Change Password* button appears on the account page for the currently logged-on user, and that user must provide his or her current password before entering a new password. When you choose *Reset Password,* which an administrator can do for another user, you need to provide only the new password.

Disappearing Sidebar Items

Our mantra is "Disaster is only a mouse-click away." We could write an entire book on the foibles of blithely moving objects around in any GUI. One minor but annoying problem we have had in macOS is the disappearance of Applications in the Finder Sidebar. Here is a simple solution to standard items disappearing from the Sidebar: Simply open the Finder menu, select *Preferences,* and then click *Sidebar* in the button bar. In the list of items, ensure that all the items you wish displayed have a check mark, and then if items are still missing from the Sidebar, hover your mouse over the word "Favorites." If the word "Show" appears on the right, select it to unhide items.

Useful System Utilities

The utilities described here for macOS are useful for basic troubleshooting. As with any situation, if you find yourself in deep water, seek expert advice. Here is a quick guide to macOS hard disk and network software utilities.

Note: If your system is crashing a lot, it may have damage to the hard disk. Running a diagnostic test with Disk Utility will reveal if there is damage.

Disk Utility

Found in the macOS Utilities folder (Applications | Utilities), Disk Utility, shown in Figure 7–39, offers summary and usage statistics for all volumes attached to the computer. The utility also includes Disk First Aid, accessed from the button on the

FIGURE 7–39 The Disk Utility.
Source: Apple Inc.

FIGURE 7–40 Advanced page of the Network preferences pane.
Source: Apple Inc.

button bar, which enables you to verify or repair OS Standard, OS Extended, and UFS formatted disks, including hard disks and CD-ROMs. The software also works as a one-stop shop for erasing and partitioning volumes.

Network Preferences

Have you ever had a problem with your home Internet connection and found yourself talking to a help desk person from your Internet service provider (ISP)? The help desk often wants you to provide information about your network connection, such as the IP address and other configuration settings. To do that in macOS open the Network pane in System Preferences, select the network connection in the sidebar, and click the Advanced button, and then click the appropriate tab. For instance, the TCP/IP tab shows the IP configuration, while the Wi-Fi tab shows the network or networks to which your computer connects as preferred networks and the type of security used. Figure 7–40 shows the TCP/IP settings.

Using Terminal in macOS

macOS includes another source of utilities for troubleshooting the many programs an advanced user can run from its Command-line interface (CLI) Terminal, a window where you can get in touch with macOS UNIX roots. macOS security applies to your activities while working in Terminal. In this section, we give an overview of Terminal features and opportunities for you to practice using the commands in Terminal. Terminal includes many of the same CLI commands as Linux, the topic of Chapter 9.

Launch Terminal

Launch Terminal from the Utilities folder located in the Applications folder. The first thing you will see is the character mode user interface, or shell. Terminal uses the BASH shell, which we will discuss further in Chapter 8. Launch Terminal and add it to the Dock so that it is easy to quickly launch. See how in the Try This!

The default Terminal $ prompt, as shown in Figure 7–41, begins with the computer name followed by a colon (:) with a tilde (~) representing your home directory. These are followed by the user name of the currently logged-on user and the $ sign. After opening Terminal, notice that just like all other windows in macOS it has its own menu at the top of the screen, as shown in Figure 7–41. Use the Shell menu to launch a new Terminal window so that you can have multiple windows open at once. The Terminal window also supports multiple tabs. Select New Tab to open a new tab in the current Terminal window.

Shell Commands in Terminal

A shell command is a command entered through a CLI shell. There are well over a thousand commands available in Terminal, and one way to quickly see a list is to use the command completion feature. Simply type the first letter and Terminal will try to guess what you are typing, completing the command for you. If you press the TAB key twice at an empty Terminal Command Prompt, it will first pause and prompt you by

Add the Terminal to the Dock.
Source: Apple Inc.

Note: For a short list of frequently used commands see the *UNIX Command Summary* at **www.bsd.org/unixcmds.html.**

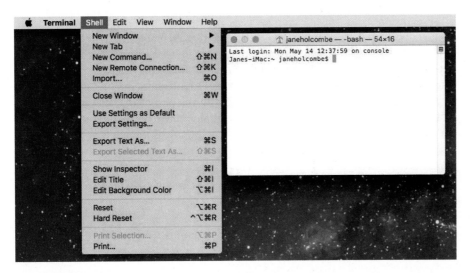

FIGURE 7–41 The Terminal Shell menu.
Source: Apple Inc.

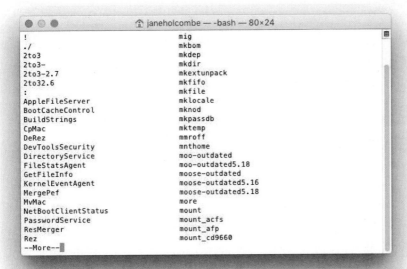

FIGURE 7–42 Press the TAB key twice; then type y to see the complete command list.
Source: Apple Inc.

asking if you want it to display all the possibilities. Press **y** to proceed or **n** to cancel. If you let it proceed, it will display all commands, as shown in Figure 7-42. Notice the word "More" at the bottom of the window. When you see this, press the spacebar to see another window full of the results. Move the scroll bar up to see the commands that scrolled out of the window area. This is not a very satisfying way to see the commands, but it gives you a sense of the quantity of commands.

Before you start typing commands at the $ prompt, you should understand that macOS Terminal is case sensitive and case aware, as are both Linux and UNIX. Commands are (mostly) in lower case, but options may vary, and whenever you type a directory or file name in Terminal, pay attention to case.

Working with Manual Pages

Once you know the name of a command that you want to use, tap into the power of the **man** command to learn how to use that command. This command lets you view the manual page for a Terminal command, called a manpage, usually many "pages." Simply type the **man** command followed by the name of the command.

Note: UNIX-based macOS Terminal provides for the temporary use of the Root account security context when you precede a command with the sudo command and provide your password. This works only if you have logged in as an Administrator. Because of this feature, Terminal does not need the option to "Run as administrator" that the Windows Command Prompt uses.

For instance, to see the manual page for the **ls** command type **man ls.** The documentation for the command will display one screen at a time. A colon (:) and a blinking cursor display on the last line of the window, indicating that there is more of the manpage to display. When you are ready to move to the next screenful of the manpage press the spacebar (or press RETURN to advance one line at a time). To go back up, press the up arrow. When it gets to the end of the manpage "(END)" replaces the colon. You can quit a manpage at any time by pressing the **q** key. Practice in Step-by-Step 7.05.

Note: Whenever the screen gets too cluttered, simply use the clear command.

Step-by-Step 7.05

Using the Man Command

Open two Terminal windows in macOS and practice using the **man** command in one window as a guide for working in a command in the second window.

Step 1

At the $ prompt type **man ls** and press ENTER.

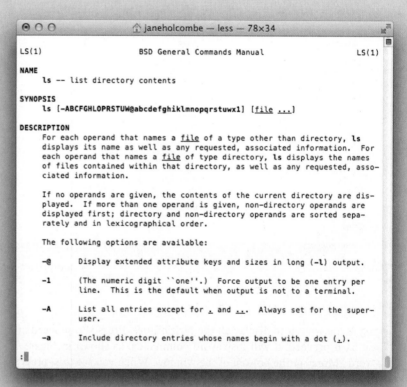

Source: Apple Inc.

Step 2

Notice what the manpage says will occur if no operands (options) are entered at the command line. Test this by opening a second Terminal window while leaving the one with the manpage open. To do this, click the **Shell** menu and then select **New Window.**

Step 3

Use the **ls** command without any options. In the new window, type **ls** and press ENTER. This displays a list of the nonhidden files and directories in the current directory.

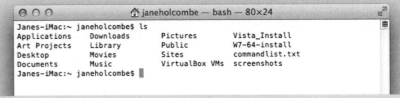

Source: Apple Inc.

Step 4

Back in the first Terminal window, the first page of the **ls** manpage describes the -a option. In the second Terminal window, add the -a option to the **ls** command to see a list that includes both hidden and nonhidden files and directories. Type **ls -a** and press ENTER. All the normally hidden entries appear. They are the files and directories that begin with a period (.).

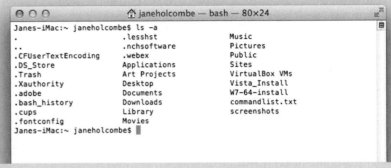

Source: Apple Inc.

Step 5

You know which entries are hidden and which are not, but so far, it is not clear which is a file and which is a directory. The second page of the **ls** manpage describes the -F option. To see all entries (as in step 4), and to also see directories identified with an ending slash (/), type **ls -aF** and press ENTER. Be sure to type the correct case.

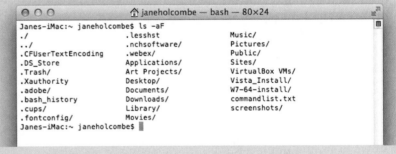

Source: Apple Inc.

Step 6

The output of the **ls** command with the -**aF** identifies all the directories with the forward slash (/). Notice the . and .. entries. The single period (.) represents the current directory and the double period (..) represents the parent directory—the directory above the current directory.

Step 7

In the window where you have been experimenting with the **ls** command, use the **cd** (change directory) command to move up to the parent directory. Type **cd ..** and press ENTER. This changes the current directory to the parent directory.

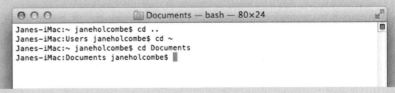

Source: Apple Inc.

    Return to the Home directory: Type **cd ~** and press ENTER.

    Change to the Documents directory: Type **cd Documents** and press ENTER.

Step 8

When you are finished with the **ls** manpage in the first window press **q** to quit.

Chapter Summary

After reading this chapter and completing the Step-by-Step tutorials and Try This! exercises you should understand the following facts about macOS:

macOS History and Versions

- Stephen Wozniak, Steven Jobs, and Ronald Wayne started Apple Computer, now Apple Inc., in April 1976.
- Apple introduced the Macintosh in 1984, the first affordable personal computer with a GUI.
- Apple introduced Mac OS X Server 1.0 in 1999 and the desktop version OS X 10.0 in 2000. It has a UNIX core, known as Darwin.
- Over the years, Apple has released both major and minor revisions of their desktop/laptop OS and renamed it a few times. The current name is macOS.
- Find the version information on the Apple menu's *About This Mac* option.

Installing and Upgrading macOS

- macOS installs only on proprietary Apple hardware, which normally comes with the OS preinstalled.
- Before upgrading, check the version of the installed OS; you may need to upgrade to another version before upgrading to the latest version.
- You cannot upgrade some older Mac computers to the latest version. If the model is upgradable, check the firmware and make sure it has enough RAM and disk space.
- Disable disk encryption before upgrading.
- macOS is no longer available on DVD; you must do an online upgrade or download the installation image and burn it to DVD or USB flash drive.
- If you buy a new Mac, you complete the personalization of the installation with the macOS Setup Assistant.
- After the installation, enable OS components or apps that you previously disabled. If you did a clean installation, you will need to install and update apps and personalize the computer to your own preferences.
- The online installation of macOS includes all the latest updates, so you no longer need to immediately update the OS.

Navigating and Managing the macOS Desktop

- The macOS desktop has a menu bar across the top containing general functions as well as the drop-down menus for the current app.

- The Apple menu opens when you click the Apple icon in the upper left of the macOS window. Use this menu to shut down, restart, log out, and a few other tasks.
- The Finder in macOS is the GUI face of macOS with a variety of file management tools.
- Each person who logs on to a macOS computer has a Home folder identified in the Finder window with a house icon and the user's name. The Documents folder in Home is the default location used by many apps for each user's data files.
- System Preferences is the macOS equivalent to the Windows Control Panel.
- Switch between apps using the Dock or the Heads-Up Program Switcher.
- Drag icons on and off the Dock and configure the Dock to be on the left side, right side, or bottom of the screen.
- See icons for all your installed programs using Launchpad. Group program icons together in folders.
- Declutter the desktop with Mission Control, which lets you create and manage desktop Spaces.
- Notification Center displays messages at the top right of the screen. Open Notification Center to see all messages.
- Menu Extras are icons you can install at the top right of the menu bar; they open menus or controls.
- Most printers install automatically, appearing in the application's Print menu.
- If a printer does not automatically install, use the Print box, click Add Printer to detect the printer.
- Use AirPlay to send local media files through an Apple TV device to a high-definition (HD) TV via Wi-Fi.

Managing Local Security in macOS

- The macOS Firewall is enabled by default. If you install or enable services on your Mac that require incoming traffic, it will configure the Firewall to allow this type of traffic.
- Gatekeeper limits sources from which you can download apps. The most restrictive setting limits program downloads to the App Store. The Anywhere setting turns off Gatekeeper altogether.
- Using ASLR, macOS loads the kernel into random locations in memory.
- macOS apps are digitally signed and sandboxed, meaning that an app cannot access any code or devices it is not authorized to access.

- If you have important and sensitive information on your Mac, ensure that you securely encrypt your startup drive with FileVault.
- The keychain is a secure database of a user's passwords. By default, macOS creates a keychain for you the first time you log in, using your account password as a master password for the keychain.
- Create an iCloud Keychain to save your passwords across all your devices.
- macOS supports multiple local user accounts.
- The first user account in macOS is automatically designated an administrator.
- The types of user accounts in macOS are Administrator, Standard account, Sharing Only account, Guest account, and Root account.
- The Administrator account type can create new accounts, change all system preference settings, and install software in the main application and library folders.
- The Standard user account type can only access files in the user's home folder and the Shared folder (/Users/Shared/).
- The Sharing Only account type gives a remote user access to shared folders on the local computer, but this account cannot log on locally and does not have a local home folder.
- You cannot assign the Guest account type to any user other than the Guest User account created by macOS by default. It does not require a password, only has access to the Guest Home folder, and when the Guest logs off, the folder's contents are deleted.
- The Root account has complete control over all folders and files on the Mac. Only the OS uses this account and it is disabled for interactive users by default.
- Automatic Login bypasses the login page and logs into the designated user account when the computer powers on.

Troubleshooting Common macOS Problems

- When you need help with macOS, do a natural language search in Spotlight. If you have narrowed the problem to one application, use that application's Help utility.
- If an application freezes, press COMMAND+OPTION+ESC to force it to quit.
- A user can change his own password using Users & Groups. If a user forgets a password, an administrator can reset the password, but the user will have a new, empty keychain associated with the new password. An administrator should configure her account so that she can reset her password using an Apple account.
- Use the Finder preferences pane to make folders display in the Finder sidebar.
- Erase and partition volumes and repair a damaged disk with Disk First Aid in the Disk Utility.
- The macOS CLI is the Terminal window where you can run macOS UNIX commands at the $ prompt.
- Open a Terminal window from the Utilities directory.
- You can open multiple Terminal windows, and each window can have multiple tabs open.
- The default Terminal $ prompt begins with the computer name followed by a colon and a tilde (~) to represent the home directory. These are followed by the user name of the currently logged-on user and the $ sign.
- The Terminal window has a menu at the top of the macOS screen. Use the Shell menu to open new windows and/or new tabs within an open Terminal window.
- At the $ prompt press the Tab key twice and respond to the resulting message with a **y** to see a list of all command names (without descriptions).
- macOS Terminal is case-sensitive. Commands are usually in lower case, but options can vary.

Key Terms List

$ prompt *(284)*

address space layout randomization (ASLR) *(275)*

AirPlay *(273)*

Apple menu *(254)*

Automatic login *(278)*

Darwin *(250)*

Dock *(255)*

Finder *(260)*

Gatekeeper *(274)*

Guest User *(278)*

Home folder *(260)*

iCloud Keychain *(276)*

keychain *(276)*

Keychain Access *(276)*

Launchpad *(268)*

macOS *(250)*

macOS Setup Assistant *(253)*

Mac OS X Server *(250)*

Manpage *(285)*

Menu Extras *(272)*

Mission Control *(270)*

Notification Center *(271)*

recovery key *(275)*

sandboxed *(275)*

Secure Virtual Memory *(276)*

Shared folder *(277)*

Sharing Only account *(278)*

shell *(284)*

shell command *(284)*

Spaces *(269)*

Split View *(271)*

Spotlight *(259)*

Standard account *(277)*

System Preferences *(266)*

Terminal *(284)*

Time Machine *(254)*

Key Terms Quiz

Use the Key Terms List to complete the sentences that follow:

1. In a safe environment, such as your home, you can avoid entering your password at login by enabling _____.

2. To search for files, use _____, a feature found in the desktop menu bar and at the top of every Finder window.

3. A user's passwords for logging on to various servers and websites from a single computer are saved in a secure database called a/an _____.

4. At the core of macOS is a powerful UNIX system called _____.

5. The _____ screen displays icons for all installed apps.

6. The _____ account does not require a password, and any file or folder it creates is deleted when this user logs out.

7. _____, allows two full-screen apps to share the desktop.

8. The _____ is a GUI object on the macOS desktop that holds program icons for fast launching, as well as icons for open applications you can use for task switching.

9. The _____ limits the online sources from which you can download programs.

10. The _____, accessed through a small icon at the extreme top left of the macOS screen, sounds like something the hostess hands you in a vegetarian restaurant.

Multiple-Choice Quiz

1. When did the first Apple Mac OS appear?
   a. 1976
   b. 1983
   c. 1999
   d. 1984
   e. 2000

2. What voice-activated iPhone feature was added to recent versions of macOS?
   a. Cortana
   b. Gatekeeper
   c. Notification Center
   d. Siri
   e. Mission Control

3. When you first power up a new Mac, what program starts automatically and prompts you for information?
   a. Dock
   b. Safari
   c. macOS Setup Assistant
   d. iChat
   e. System Preferences

4. Complete this sentence: In macOS forced quits of applications . . .
   a. often cause other applications to fail.
   b. always require a restart of the OS.
   c. is not an option.
   d. usually cause system crashes.
   e. rarely affect the performance of the rest of the computer's functions.

5. Where will you quickly find version information about your macOS installation?
   a. Recent items
   b. Window menu
   c. Help menu
   d. Apple menu
   e. Finder

6. Which of the following is one of the four views available in Finder windows?
   a. Date
   b. Columns
   c. Reverse
   d. Finder
   e. Jukebox

7. The Applications folder has disappeared from the Finder Sidebar. Where in the GUI can you go to put the Applications folder back into the Sidebar?
   a. System Preferences | General
   b. Utilities
   c. Sidebar | Preferences
   d. Finder | Preferences
   e. Window | Restore

8. In addition to having an upgradable version of macOS running on one of the compatible models of Apple computer, you should also check to see if this (another system requirement) is up-to-date before upgrading to a new version of macOS.
   a. Apple ID
   b. Video drivers
   c. Firmware
   d. FileVault
   e. Gatekeeper

9. Which all-powerful account is used by the operating system, but is disabled for interactive users?
   a. Standard
   b. Group
   c. Administrator
   d. Root
   e. Global

10. You have an external hard drive from another Mac, and you would like to remove all the data on it and use it as backup for your new Mac. What will you use to prepare this disk for use?
   a. Finder
   b. Boot Camp Assistant
   c. System Preferences
   d. Tools
   e. Disk Utility

11. What type of service should you disable as a precaution before beginning an upgrade macOS?
   a. Networking
   b. Launchpad
   c. Mission Control
   d. Sharing
   e. Disk encryption

12. What keyboard shortcut can you use to force an application to quit?
   a. COMMAND+POWER key
   b. SHIFT-ESC
   c. SHIFT-RETURN
   d. COMMAND-OPTION-ESC
   e. Press C during startup

13. A Sharing Only type of account is not allowed to do which of the following?
   a. Connect over a network.
   b. Access shared folders.
   c. Log in locally.
   d. Enter a password.
   e. Enter a user name.

14. This account is automatically created by macOS it does not require a password associated with it, has limited local access, and when this user logs out, the contents of its Home folder are deleted.
   a. Sharing Only
   b. Administrator
   c. Root
   d. Guest User
   e. Standard Account

15. Which of the following preference panes allows you to configure settings for Spaces, Dashboard, and shortcuts?
   a. Finder
   b. Mission Control
   c. Desktop & Screen Saver
   d. Dock
   e. Notifications

Essay Quiz

1. Research the significance of the UNIX core of macOS and write a few sentences describing your findings.

2. Your Mac laptop has both personal financial information and files for all your in-process school projects, including data from research for a major project in one of your classes. This laptop has two equal-sized partitions on the hard drive, and is always with you at home, at school, and at work. Describe how you will ensure the security of your valuable data.

3. Your copy of Microsoft Word suddenly freezes in midsentence. Describe the best way to regain control of your Mac.

4. When you brought your new iMac home and completed the information in the Setup Assistant, you did not have Internet access. You have signed up for Internet access and the setup instructions from your ISP request the hardware address (MAC address) of your Wireless network card. First research and then explain where you will find this information within the macOS GUI and describe how it represents this value.

5. Describe the purpose of the Dock.

Lab Projects

LAB PROJECT 7.1

One of the users on your network, Helen Bandora, married Jon Moz, and changed her name to Helen Moz.

While it is simple enough to log into macOS as an administrator and alter her long user name to reflect her name change, changing her short name is not possible in macOS because it was used to create the Home directory *hbandora*. Her Home directory is not particularly full, with some Microsoft Word files in the Documents folder and some MP3s in her Music folder.

You decide that it would be polite to change both login names. What do you do to give her a correctly named account?

You will need a computer with macOS installed on which you have administrator rights.

You will need to do the following:

1. Research the solution for setting up Mrs. Moz with a correctly named account.
2. Find Helen's Home directory on the hard drive.
3. Implement your solution on the lab computer.

LAB PROJECT 7.2

macOS has a feature called Smart Folders that was not described in the chapter. Research Smart Folders and create at least one Smart Folder for yourself. Then, in your own words, write a short definition of Smart Folders, and describe a practical application of Smart Folders giving specifics.

LAB PROJECT 7.3

If you ever find yourself the administrator of a large network, you would want to minimize your network's electricity consumption by instituting good energy practices.

You will need a computer with macOS installed to do the following:

1. Go into the Energy Saver preferences pane and assess the various options you have for controlling the display and hard disk sleep features. Your goal is to reduce the display and hard disk sleep times to the minimum possible without causing the display to dim or the hard disk to spin down intrusively for users.

2. This is a chance to be creative and aware of the types of users of your network, and how they interact with the lab environment. Are computers used constantly, requiring a generous display or hard disk sleep time? Is the amount of RAM sufficient for working with files in memory or does the hard disk need to be accessed constantly? What kinds of software do your users use: processor and hard drive-intensive programs such as image manipulation and multimedia programs, or email and word processing software?

chapter

8 Linux on the Desktop

©Image Source/Getty Images

Learning Outcomes

In this chapter, you will learn how to:

LO **8.1** Describe Linux and its origins, and list benefits and drawbacks.

LO **8.2** Select, acquire, and install a distribution of Linux for the desktop.

LO **8.3** Identify certain features and utilities in a Linux GUI for customizing it and performing common tasks.

LO **8.4** Demonstrate the use of shell commands to accomplish common tasks.

LO **8.5** Secure a Linux desktop by creating user accounts, assigning passwords, and applying file and folder permissions.

Linux, a free operating system with many of the same qualities as UNIX, has the potential to save corporations millions of dollars. To grasp how important a free operating system is, think of an operating system as the software engine of your computer. Then consider the engine in your car. An engine costs thousands of dollars, but if a company started making and distributing free engines, the cost of your new car would drop dramatically, requiring just the cost of the body and chassis, electrical system, radiator, passenger heater and air conditioner, radio, and many other components. Of course, the Linux community offers many of the additional software components for the OS free.

In this chapter, learn the basics of Linux on the desktop with one of the many GUIs available. Linux is far too broad a topic to give a detailed exploration here, but you will learn why Linux is growing in popularity. You will learn where to obtain Linux to test on your computer and basic configuration and navigation tasks in a Linux environment. If you have never worked with Linux before, this chapter will serve as an introduction to this OS and perhaps inspire you to study it further. ✸

LO 8.1 | Linux Overview

Linux is an open-source operating system based on UNIX. In this section, discover why you should learn Linux, the features and benefits of Linux, and how and why Linux is used today.

Why Learn Linux?

Learning Linux can be very beneficial to your future career because of its growing importance on all types of computers. Like Windows and macOS you will find Linux on both desktops and servers.

Qualifying for a Job

If you are interested in a job in Information Technology (IT) or a related field, you should familiarize yourself with Linux. Because it is similar to UNIX, learning Linux prepares you for working with UNIX. Both Linux and UNIX are recognized as stable and used on servers worldwide. By learning Linux you are advertising your intelligence, initiative, and computer ability. A potential employer reviewing your résumé would see Linux knowledge as a big plus for an employee in many technology-related areas. Their reasoning is simple—if you can learn Linux, then you should quickly learn the idiosyncrasies of an organization's internal computer systems.

Improving Your Skills

Another reason to learn Linux is to improve your computer skills for working in a non-GUI environment, thus forcing you to be precise. Any OS is unforgiving when given the wrong instructions, but it doesn't take precision to browse a GUI and select the correct graphical object, which is how a GUI buffers users from the precision the operating system requires. The command-line interface (CLI) does not offer that buffer. In the IT networking environment, the typical router or switch is managed using shell commands in a CLI.

The Evolution of Linux

In the early 1970s, Ken Thompson, a developer working at Bell Labs, was criticized for playing a computer game on company equipment. He then found an unused computer and wrote an operating system that would run his game. This operating system became the foundation of UNIX, which has gone on to power the computers of many universities, corporations, and governments of the world. It is a powerful, stable, and fast system. While UNIX is not Linux, the latter does owe its existence to individuals who looked at what Thompson had done with UNIX and decided to create something similar. Below are just some of the important milestones in the evolution of Linux.

1984

In 1984, interested persons created the **GNU** organization to develop a free version of a UNIX-like operating system (GNU is a recursive acronym for GNU's Not Unix). Since its founding, GNU members have developed versions of Linux, as well as thousands of applications that run on UNIX and Linux platforms. Some of these apps are bundled with distributions of Linux.

Note: Learn more about GNU at www.gnu.org.

1988

In 1988, a group of UNIX licensees formed the Open Systems Foundation (OSF) to lobby for an "open" UNIX after AT&T formed a partnership with Sun Microsystems to develop a single proprietary UNIX. In response, AT&T and other licensees formed UNIX International to oppose the OSF. The trade press called the maneuverings of these two groups the "UNIX wars."

1991

In 1991, Linus Torvalds wanted to write a better, open-source version of MINIX, a UNIX-like operating system. Open-source software is distributed with all of its source code, which is the uncompiled program statements that can be viewed and edited with a text editor or special programming software. Linux is written in the C language as one or more text files, and then compiled, using a program called a C compiler, into binary object code. Object code is, essentially, an executable program in yet another language (machine language) that can be interpreted by a computer's CPU and loaded into memory as a running program. Object code cannot be edited.

Torvalds and a team of programmers succeeded in his original goal, but he receives no direct financial gain because he does not own Linux—just the name—and the open-source community could easily decide to rename it. But we don't believe that will happen because of Torvalds' fame and the very nature of the Linux community.

1994

Because the software was open source, many individuals and several companies modified the kernel. Two of the versions available in 1994 were the Slackware and Red Hat kernels, both written in the C++ language; both with TCP/IP functionality for communicating on the Internet as well as primitive Web servers. To obtain a copy, one simply went to an Internet site and selected the distribution to download. This is true today, with many more sources for the code.

> *Note:* The **World Wide Web (WWW)** (also called the **Web**) is the graphical Internet consisting of a vast array of documents located on millions of specialized servers worldwide. **Hypertext Transfer Protocol (HTTP)** is the protocol for transferring the files that make up the rich graphical Web pages we view on the Web.

Linux Today

The open-source movement has gained credibility in part because vendors such as Novell and IBM integrated open-source software into their product mix. The notion of free and open software, with no one entity owning the source code, thrives today and has the support of many organizations that previously opposed it. Several vendors offer inexpensive Linux servers running the open-source Apache HTTP Server, often simply called "Apache." This Web server software was originally written for UNIX but also runs on Linux. Separate versions have been available for other operating systems, including Windows. Apache is one of the most widely used Web servers due to its stability, security, and cost (free).

try this!

Learn from the Linux Foundation

Explore what is happening in the world of Linux. Try this:

1. Point your browser to www.linux.com, a website sponsored by the Linux Foundation.
2. Click on the Learn link, and select "What is Linux?"
3. Read the tutorial on Linux, and then scroll to the bottom for links to other helpful resources.

Linux Distributions

As mentioned in Chapter 1, when you buy or download a version of Linux you get a distribution, sometimes called a "distro," that includes the Linux kernel and a whole set of programs that work together to make a functional version of Linux. Most distributions include a number of applications. A distribution targeting desktop users will include an office suite and other productivity apps, while a server distribution will include server-related tools. A good source of the latest information about Linux distributions

try this!

Research Linux Distributions

You can learn a lot about the various Linux distributions at the DistroWatch website. Try this:

1. Point your web browser to **distrowatch.com**.
2. Notice the organization of this site. The large center column of the Home page contains announcements of new releases, with the latest first.
3. The middle column also contains a brief description with links to the *DistroWatch Weekly,* an online newsletter containing reviews, news, tips, and other articles of interest to the Linux community. Click on links to read the articles. Read a few articles that interest you.
4. Return to the DistroWatch Home page at any time; clicking the Home page link at the top of each page will return you to the DistroWatch Home page.
5. On the Home page, look for the list of distributions ranked by page hits.
6. Close your browser when you have finished.

Note: Terminology for Linux is a little different from other OSs. When you buy or download a version of Linux you get a distribution, sometimes called a "distro," that includes the Linux kernel and a whole set of programs that work together to make a functioning version of Linux. Most distributions include a number of Linux applications. There are many distributions of Linux!

is DistroWatch. First published in May 2001, this website has grown from a simple comparison of a handful of distributions to the go-to source for the latest information on Linux distributions. Learn more about Linux distributions in the Try This!

Benefits of Linux

There are several benefits to using Linux on your desktop computer.

Linux Is Free

The first benefit of Linux is cost. You may freely download many versions of Linux from the Web. Many sites offer Linux distributions in convenient ISO images. If you don't want to download these distributions, you may purchase prepackaged versions of Linux online or in computer stores for modest cost.

Canonical is the company behind the open-source Ubuntu Linux distributions, updating the OS frequently. In addition, they are involved in other open-source projects and offer consulting services, which is how they pay their employees and keep the lights on and the servers running.

The Fedora Project is the organization founded in 2003 by Red Hat and other contributors. The resulting Fedora Linux distributions are open source, and also the basis for Red Hat's commercially available Red Hat Enterprise Linux (RHEL).

Linux Can Run on Old Equipment

In addition to being free or inexpensive, Linux can run on old equipment. A nonprofit organization can provide computers for its employees with donated or very inexpensive equipment. There are countless situations in which computers too underpowered to run even an outdated version of Windows continue to run reliably for years—as Web servers! The requirements for the latest version of the Ubuntu Linux Desktop Edition are:

- 2 GHz dual-core processor or better.
- 2 GB system RAM.
- 25 GB of free space on a hard drive, USB thumb drive, or external hard drive.
- A DVD drive or a USB port if using USB-attached installation media.

Linux Is Fast

While Linux runs respectably well on old computers, it is even faster on newer computers. This is because Linux programs are very lean and efficient. They use as few resources as possible, graphics use in Linux is optional, and many Linux applications use few, if any, graphics. Graphics can slow a system's response time, making it seem slower than it truly is.

Linux Can Have a GUI

Unlike Windows, Linux was not intended to have a GUI, but rather just a text-only shell. A shell is the user interface to an OS; it accepts commands and displays error messages and other screen output. The traditional Linux shell is a command-line interface (CLI), such as the BASH shell. The term "shell command" is most often applied to text commands entered through a CLI shell.

Note: BASH is an acronym for Bourne-Again SHell. The BASH shell in use today (the default in most Linux systems) is an enhanced version of the original shell program written by Steve Bourne.

Many distributions of Linux, especially those for desktop computers, come with a GUI shell created to a standard for Linux, X Window System. This standard was developed in 1984 at MIT for use with UNIX. The X Consortium then continued development of the X Window System (commonly called X Window or simply "X"). Today the Open Group continues the work.

Many Linux GUIs are available today, including but not limited to GNOME (usually pronounced "nome") and KDE. These competing Linux GUIs have improved over the years and various groups have developed their own GUIs, targeting different types of users. We find them as easy to work with as the Microsoft Windows or macOS GUIs, after some practice. Figure 8-1 shows the KDE GUI bundled with a Fedora distribution. It has a bar across the bottom, much like the Windows taskbar, as well as a Fedora button (with a script "f" on it) on the far left of the bar. This button opens Kickoff Application Launcher. Figure 8-1 shows the result of clicking this button.

Linux Is Stable

Linux code is well written, which increases the speed at which Linux runs and improves the stability of the operating system. Linux is next to impossible to crash. If an application crashes, you can simply remove the program from memory and restart it (the program). This is why people use Linux on Web servers where stability is crucial.

Linux Is Secure

Linux is a secure operating system with all the appropriate security options, as well as the benefit of not being as much of a hacker target as Windows operating systems are. As open-source software, Linux has the advantage of having legions of programmers working to make it a better and more secure OS.

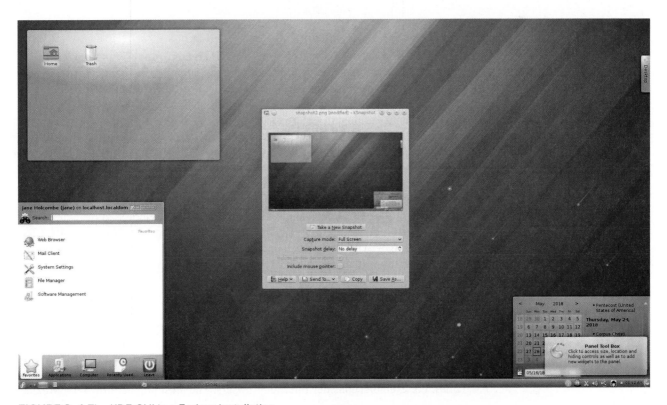

FIGURE 8–1 The KDE GUI in a Fedora installation.
Source: Fedora Project by Red Hat

Note: If you have a recent distribution of Linux with the Linux GNOME desktop, look for accessibility options listed under Universal Access in the System category of System Settings.

Linux Is Open Source

Finally, Linux is open-source software; users can read the source code and modify it as needed. This probably means little to the average user of the final version of a Linux kernel. However, during development, "beta" releases of the kernel are available to developers who download the code and test it thoroughly, searching for problems and correcting the code. This process helps to ensure an as-well-written-as-possible final release of the kernel.

Once they release a final version, developers can adjust the kernel as needed. We know a developer who modified his kernel to be more usable for vision-impaired users. He added better support for large-print output and a command-line narrator that reads the information on the command line out loud. Being Open source lets the developer modify his code to suit his needs.

Drawbacks of Linux

Even though Linux is widely used on corporate servers, websites, and large-scale networking environments, you still won't find many people using it on their home desktop computers. There are several reasons for this.

Lack of Centralized Support

No system is 100 percent secure; however, both Apple and Microsoft products have extensive documentation and support. Both release service packs and frequent updates to fix discovered vulnerabilities. Because Linux does not have this centralized support, the support and documentation for free Linux can be spotty. A user who downloads Linux from the Internet may receive only a downloadable manual and access to online help pages. It is true that the Linux community is growing, and there are many active user groups, but one must search them out and expend considerable time and effort to get questions answered.

Choice of GUIs Is Confusing

The fact that you can choose from various GUIs is confusing. Users want what they know, and the Linux GUIs, while responding to some of the same mouse and keyboard shortcuts as Windows and macOS, are still different from both. Working in Linux requires some exploration and self-training. For instance, the desktop shown in the Ubuntu example in Figure 8-2 shows the GNOME desktop with a menu bar across the top, similar to macOS and a Launcher/Dock bar along the side, unlike the GUIs for either macOS or Windows. However, the GUI shown in a Fedora distribution with a KDE GUI in Figure 8-1 has an entirely different look that is closer to the Windows Desktop with a bar across the bottom and a menu that opens from a button on the far left similar to the Windows Start Menu. Need we say more?

To add to the GUI confusion, several years ago Ubuntu moved to the Unity GUI, a departure from the previous GNOME GUI. Beginning with Ubuntu 16.04 LTS, Ubuntu has moved back to a much-updated GNOME GUI. Most of the screenshots in this chapter are with an Ubuntu LTS distro and the improved GNOME GUI.

Limited Software Selection

People purchase computers to run applications—whether for business or for pleasure. There are important titles for Windows that are not available for Linux, so you need to check the software selection before moving to Linux on the desktop. But more titles are becoming available for Linux every year—even some very well-known titles. For example, consider Internet browsers. The most popular browsers, Mozilla

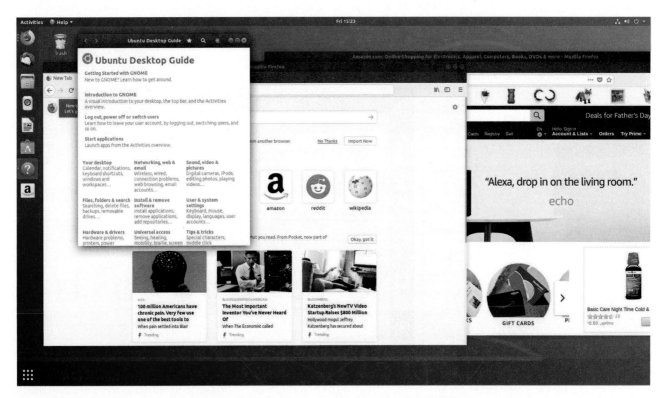

FIGURE 8–2 The GNOME GUI desktop in an Ubuntu installation.
Source: Ubuntu by Canonical

Firefox, Google Chrome, and Microsoft Internet Explorer, are available for Linux, as are other browsers.

You are also limited in your choice of word processors. The most popular word processor is Microsoft Word. Chances are good that every desktop computer in your school uses Word. But Word is not available for Linux, although there are open-source programs that allow Word to work under Linux in certain circumstances. Various distributions of Linux have bundled excellent substitutions, including LibreOffice and Apache OpenOffice. Each of these is an applications suite that contains a word processor and other office productivity tools. However, although both are very nice products, a proficient Microsoft Office user would have to learn how to use one with the same level of proficiency.

Figure 8-3 shows the Ubuntu Software Center, where you can search for software for an Ubuntu installation. Three tabs labeled All, Installed, and Updates give quick access to the three general modes for working in the Software Center. You can browse for new apps (All), view a list of previously installed apps (Installed), and update your apps (Updates). This is similar to what Apple and Microsoft offer for their OS platforms.

> *Note:* Versions of both LibreOffice and Apache OpenOffice are available for macOS and Windows as well as Linux.

Limited Hardware Support

Not all hardware products work with Linux, but we see this situation improving. Linux vendors work very hard to support the more common devices by providing drivers for them. Having the correct driver is crucial. If you have a new or unusual device, you may need to search the Internet for a driver. Maybe the vendor has not created a Linux driver for your new device, but there is great support among Linux users who create drivers and make them available on the Internet.

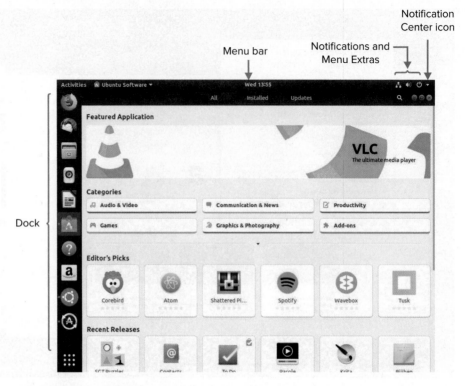

FIGURE 8–3 The Ubuntu Software Center.
Source: Ubuntu by Canonical

Complexity

The last block in the wall between Linux and greater success as a desktop OS is Linux's difficulty of use at the command shell, which continues to be where advanced tasks must be done. Only a limited subset of users will invest the time and effort to learn its intricacies. Linux, like UNIX, assumes that you know what you are doing, and it assumes that you know the consequences of every command you type.

Even with the new, improved GUI shells for Linux, it is not as easy to use as the more common operating systems. So if you implement Linux as a desktop OS, be prepared to spend time configuring Linux and providing training for other users who might need to use your computer.

Don't let this discourage you, however. By now, you have spent sufficient time working with operating systems so that you know the basic theory. You'll do fine in Linux. In this chapter, we will explore how to work in Linux in a GUI as well as the basics of working in the Linux terminal window.

LO 8.2 | Linux on Your Desktop

So now that you know some of the history of Linux and its benefits and drawbacks, how will you experience it? Do you have a computer to dedicate to Linux so that you can install it? Do you plan to install it in a dual-boot configuration and continue to boot into another OS? Do you have a computer with a hypervisor in which you can create a virtual machine for testing Linux? In this section, we will describe the sources of Linux distributions for desktop computers and test an option you may not have considered for experiencing Linux: a live image.

Acquiring Linux for the Desktop

There are many distributions of Linux, and many sources for them. The most important criterion to keep in mind before selecting one is the role you wish the Linux computer to play—will it be a server or a desktop? When selecting a source, select one that meets your support needs. Are you a developer who wants to participate in the further development of Linux and Linux apps? If so, you can join a community of like-minded people at one of many websites where they gather. Since this is a survey class, we will assume that most students reading this are only interested in getting acquainted with Linux to understand its place in the world.

Our criteria for a distribution to feature in this chapter was for a desktop version of Linux that we can download and use quickly and easily. We selected two: Ubuntu and Fedora. Learn more about each of these distributions at the following websites:

- Ubuntu (**www.ubuntu.com**)
- Fedora (**getfedora.org**)

While we have downloaded and installed Linux from both sources, we chose Ubuntu Desktop Edition for the examples in this chapter mainly because we have worked with it with some success in the past. Both sources provide an ISO file that allows you to create a bootable flash drive or DVD disc. When you boot from either type of media, you choose to install Linux onto the local computer or to boot into a live image of Linux. A *live image* is a bootable image of the operating system that will run from bootable media without requiring the OS be installed on the local computer. Many system administrators create custom live images that include both an OS and handy utilities. When an OS fails, an administrator can boot up with the live image and use the utilities for diagnostics, troubleshooting, and data recovery.

The Ubuntu distribution we selected includes a complete software bundle: the GNOME GUI desktop and a number of GUI applications including LibreOffice, Firefox, and software selections for many other functions, such as email, chat, social networking, music streaming, photo management and editing, and more. The download for this edition is under 2 GB.

The various versions of Linux have many things in common, so what you learn about one version will carry over to another version.

Please read all the information on the download page of the distribution you plan to install, paying attention to the system requirements for the installation. Usually, you have a choice of the very solid version that may be labeled LTS which stands for long-term support. In the case of Ubuntu Desktop, this support lasts up to five years and includes free security and maintenance updates. If you prefer to live on the bleeding edge, consider a newer version that has a shorter support window.

Note: The term **burn** traditionally refers to the writing of digital data to a disc (CD-R, DVD-R, or DB-R).

Note: In discussions of Linux distributions, people often mention FreeBSD, but it is not a version of Linux. FreeBSD is an operating system based on the Berkeley UNIX distribution and is primarily used on servers, whereas Linux was designed for and focused on desktop architectures.

Step-by-Step 8.01

Downloading Linux and Creating Bootable Media

This step-by-step exercise takes you through downloading a distribution of Linux and burning the image to a disc, which you can then use in the remainder of the class. The instructions and illustrations are for using a Windows computer to download an Ubuntu Linux ISO file and to create a bootable DVD. You can complete this exercise using a different distribution of Linux, and the steps will be similar. To complete this exercise you will need:

- A Windows computer (if using another OS, the steps and screens will differ from those shown here).
- An optical drive capable of burning a disc.
- A blank DVD disc.
- Broadband Internet access.

Step 1

Use your browser to connect to **www.ubuntu.com**. Open the downloads menu and click Desktop.

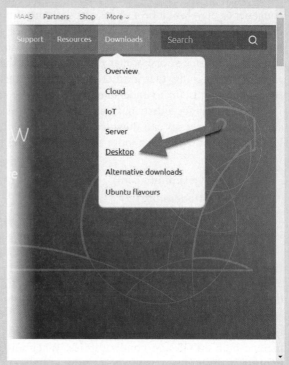

Source: Ubuntu by Canonical

Step 2

On the Download Ubuntu Desktop page, the latest LTS distribution of Ubuntu is at the top. View the system requirements information on this page and scroll down for links to instructions on various options for downloading Linux and creating bootable media. Then click the *Download* button.

Source: Ubuntu by Canonical

Step 3

Your browser will now open a dialog box asking you to open or save the file. Select Save to have it saved in the Downloads folder on your computer. Then click OK.

Step 4

The Ubuntu *Thank you* page will display, and you can check on the progress which will display on the menu bar in some browsers or at the bottom of the windows in others, such as the Chrome browser, shown here.

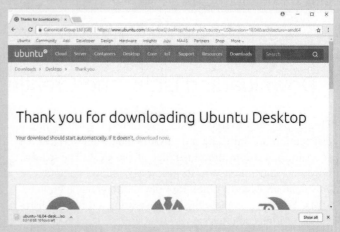

Source: Ubuntu by Canonical

Create the bootable disc by using the ISO image you downloaded. To do that in Windows, browse to the Downloads folder, right-click on the Ubuntu file, and select *Burn disc image*.

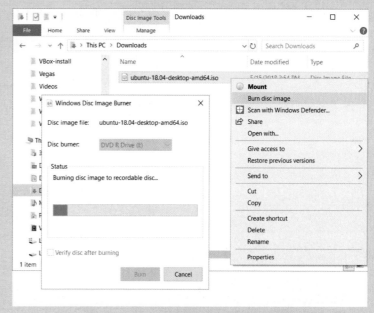

Source: Ubuntu by Canonical

Now test the disc by rebooting the computer with the disc inserted. After a brief delay during which you will see text on a black background, the Ubuntu Welcome screen displays. You have successfully downloaded Ubuntu Linux, created a bootable DVD, and are ready either to boot into Linux and explore it as a Guest or to proceed with an installation. Stay at this screen as you continue.

Source: Ubuntu by Canonical

Installing Linux or Using a Live Image

If you completed Step-by-Step 8.01, you should be at the Welcome screen. If so, select a language, and then click *Try Ubuntu* if you just want to try out Ubuntu without installing it, using the live image. If you run the live image, you will not need to log in, as you will be automatically logged in with the Guest account.

Only select the second option, *Install Ubuntu,* if you are ready to install it on the same computer. If you plan to install it to another location, click the System (gear) icon on the title bar in the upper right (see the illustration in Step 6), select *Shut Down* from the System menu and remove the disc before selecting *Shut Down* again in the confirmation box.

There are several possible scenarios for installing Linux. Just a few include a clean installation on a spare computer, a clean installation onto a second drive on a computer running another OS to create a dual-boot configuration, or an installation into a virtual machine. We installed both distributions of Linux into virtual machines on Windows 10 and iMac computers. We used VirtualBox as our hypervisor on both systems and found Ubuntu worked well without tweaking it in the virtual machine. Your experience may be different, as may the distribution you select.

FIGURE 8-4 The Software Updater message displayed in Ubuntu soon after installing the OS.
Source: Ubuntu by Canonical

Note: We recommend that you create a virtual machine for Linux, even if you plan only to boot into the live image because when you use a live image in a virtual machine you will still have access to your computer and can take notes, browse the Web, or take screen shots of the contents of the virtual machine.

If you did the exercises in Chapter 3 and installed a hypervisor, you only need to create a virtual machine for Linux, insert the disc you created, and start the virtual machine. If the virtual machine does not see the disc, you may need to modify the settings for the virtual machine to include the disc. If it recognizes the disc, the VM should start up and boot into the Ubuntu Welcome screen.

For the remainder of this chapter, leave Linux open—using the live image or an installation of Linux. If you choose to install it, you will find the installation is very similar to a clean installation of macOS or Windows, and shortly after you install Linux, you will see a notice (Figure 8-4) that updates are ready to install. If you are installing Linux in a school lab and have limited time, do not install the updates at this point; select *Remind Me Later* and wait until you have the time for them to install. Plan on restarting after installing updates.

LO 8.3 | Exploring a Linux GUI

In this section, you will practice certain tasks in Linux using a GUI, beginning with logging in, exploring the GUI Desktop, locating tools for changing settings, modifying the desktop, and ending a Linux session.

Deciding How to Log In to Ubuntu Linux

Note: The Ubuntu user manual is available at **Ubuntu.com** for those who want to peruse it ahead of time. However, once Linux is installed, the manual is available through the Help utility. In the latest GNOME GUI used in this chapter, open Help from the question mark icon on the Launcher/Dock.

In Linux, as in most modern operating systems, you are always logged in as a user—even when you do not see a login page and do not enter a username and credentials. When you run a live image of Linux, you are automatically logged in as the Guest, with limited privileges. However, if you opt to install Linux, the installation prompts you to create a username and password. You must do this, even if you plan to enable Automatic Login option. If you choose that option, you will not need to enter a password to log in and will go directly to the desktop. However, if you make a significant settings change or install software, you will be prompted for the password for the currently logged in user.

Figure 8-5 shows the log in prompt. The user JH is the only user (other than Guest) on this installation, but if other accounts exist, they will also display here. Notice that you can also select *Guest Session* and log in as a Guest with no password. In that case, as in a live image, you will have limited access compared to other users, but you will still be able to experience Linux.

FIGURE 8-5 Log in to the Linux GUI.
Source: Ubuntu by Canonical

The Ubuntu GNOME Desktop

The first time you log in to Ubuntu a *Welcome to Ubuntu* tutorial displays. Take time to go through this tutorial. Figure 8-6 shows one page from this tutorial, identifying the new features of the desktop. Notice the bar across the top, like the bar in macOS. The Window switcher is on the left, then the Application menu for the current app on the desktop, followed by the Clock and calendar. On the far right is the System menu. The Launcher bar is along the left side of the desktop, with the Apps button at the bottom.

The Ubuntu GNOME desktop includes the Launcher, a bar on the left side of the screen that serves the same purpose as the macOS Dock or the pinned items feature on the taskbar on the Windows Desktop. Simply pause the mouse cursor over one of the icons on the Launcher and a title will pop out. Figure 8-7 is a screenshot we modified with a photo editor to show all the titles for the standard set of Launcher icons.

Note: The latest Ubuntu documentation uses the terms "Launcher" and "Dock" interchangeably for the bar that, by default is located along the left edge of the screen. In Figure 8–6, it is labeled "Launcher" while in the manual/Help the term "Dock" is more often used. In the Settings window, the term "Dock" is used.

Searching in the Ubuntu GNOME Desktop

Use the search tool for finding apps and all types of files. To open it, click the Activities button at the top of the Launcher or simply press the WINDOWS key (located next to the Ctrl key on many keyboards). A Search box opens at the top of the desktop, as shown in Figure 8-8. To search for a file or app, enter a search string into the Search box.

Search results will find matches in both files and apps, as shown in Figure 8-9. The Try This! exercise will walk you through a search.

Use a Linux GUI Search Tool

Whether you are using the Ubuntu GNOME desktop or another GUI, it will have a search utility. If it is not apparent to you how to open the Search utility, use the Help utility for your distribution of Linux, which should be readily available from a menu. Try this:

1. Locate and open the Search utility.
2. In the Search box, enter a search string and press the ENTER key.
3. What were the results? Did it find both apps and files that matched the search string?
4. Compare your results to others in your class.

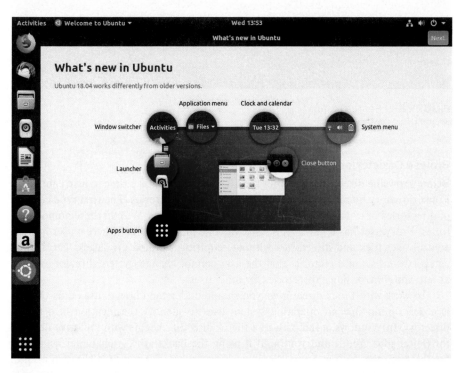

FIGURE 8–6 This page of the *Welcome to Ubuntu* tutorial identifies Desktop objects.
Source: Ubuntu by Canonical

FIGURE 8–7 The Launcher with icons labeled.
Source: Ubuntu by Canonical

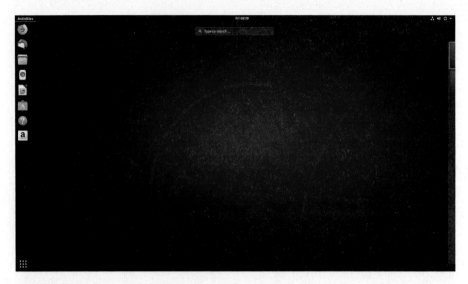

FIGURE 8–8 The search utility opens a Search box at the top of the desktop.
Source: Ubuntu by Canonical

FIGURE 8–9 Search results.
Source: Ubuntu by Canonical

Note: Every user on a Linux computer has a home directory with the exception of Guest.

Note: While working in a GUI, you will not normally need to type in a path, nor will you often even see this notation in the GUI, but you should understand Linux paths as you navigate. You will need to understand paths if you decide to work in Linux at the CLI.

Browse Directories in the GUI

Before browsing directories in either the GUI or the CLI, take time to learn about the Linux directory hierarchy. It contains two types of directories. The first type consists of directories in which an ordinary user can make changes. We call these home directories. Every user has a **home directory**, the one place in Linux where a user has full control over files and directories without requiring elevated privileges. The second category consists of directories that the user cannot change: system directories, such as /etc and /bin, or home directories for other users.

To work with Linux directories, you should understand how to use paths. A **path** is a description that an operating system uses to identify the location of a file or directory. In Windows, a full path to a file or directory begins with the drive designator (letter plus colon) and you build it using the backslash (\) character as separators between the drive and root directory (first back-slash) and then between each of the subsequent directories in the path. Thus, one example of a Windows path is C:\ Winnt\System32. In Linux, you do not use a drive letter in a path, you use a forward

TABLE 8–1 Linux Default Directories

Directory	Purpose or Contents
/	The top, or root directory of a storage volume
/bin	Linux commands
/boot	Files to be loaded during Linux boot up
/dev	Files that represent physical devices
/etc	Linux system configuration files
/home	Home directories for each user
/lib	Shared libraries for programs and commands to use
/mnt	Mount points for removable devices
/opt	Optional (add-on) software packages
/proc	Current status of OS processes
/root	Root account home directory
/sbin	System commands and binary files
/tmp	Temporary files
/usr	Secondary hierarchy
/var	Several directories containing variable data

slash (/) at the beginning of a path to represent the root and a forward slash (/) to separate directories in a path. A valid path is **/etc/gtk.** In Linux, everything is a file identified within the file system. Files represent drives and other devices, as well as directories and files.

When you log in to Linux, your home directory becomes your current (working) directory. If you installed Linux with the defaults, your home directory path is **/home/***username,* where *username* is the user name for the account you used to log in. The default installation includes several other directories. The **/bin** directory within your home directory contains many of the Linux commands. The **/usr/bin** directory is an example of a symbolic link that points to another directory, in this case, **/bin.** Table 8–1 shows some of the default directories with brief descriptions.

Now that you know something about the directory structure on your Linux computer, find a tool in the Linux GUI for browsing the Linux directories and explore the directories on your computer. A big advantage of working in a GUI is that you do not need to carefully type the names of files and directories—a fact made more important, since Linux is case-sensitive, meaning that it preserves the case used in the characters of a file name when created, and requires that you enter the correct case to open or manage the file. Step-by-Step 8.02 will guide you through the process of browsing the Linux directory structure. Notice that some directories have upper and lower case. You will want to remember that later when you explore Linux directories from the CLI.

Note: While Linux is case-sensitive, Windows is case-aware, meaning that it will preserve the case used for the characters in a file name when you create it, but it does not require the correct case when retrieving or managing the file.

Step-by-Step 8.02

Browsing the Linux File System in a GUI

In this exercise, use a GUI to browse the Linux directory structure. You will need the following:

- A computer running Linux with a GUI.
- The username and password for a user account.

Step 1

Log in to a Linux installation with a GUI. In our case, we logged in to Ubuntu Linux with the GNOME GUI.

Step 2

Click on the Files icon in the Launcher and a window opens focused on the currently logged-on user's home directory. This home directory contains directories created during the installation of this distribution of Linux, as well as directories created by the user.

Source: Ubuntu by Canonical

Step 3

Browse through the directories in the home directory, then return to the home directory, and click the item on the left labeled Other Locations. Then select the drive containing the Linux OS. This opens focused on the root (the top level of the file system).

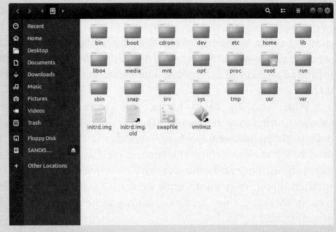

Source: Ubuntu by Canonical

Step 4

Double-click the *home* folder to open the top-level home directory. A home directory should display for each user. In our example, the only user is Jane. Notice that the Guest user does not have a home folder. When a Guest user logs in, they are given a Home folder, but it is deleted when they exit. Therefore, you will not see a Guest Home folder when you are logged in as another user.

Source: Ubuntu by Canonical

Step 5

When you are finished browsing the directories, close the window.

Updating Ubuntu from the GNOME Desktop

When updates to Ubuntu are available, the Software Updater message box opens on the desktop. From here, you can click to *Settings* button to open the Software & Updates settings dialog (Figure 8-10), the *Remind Me Later* button to postpone the update, or the *Install Now* button.

System Settings

Click the small down arrow on the far right of the top bar to open the small drop-down System menu, shown in Figure 8-11. Locate the icon that resembles a pair of hand tools positioned in an "x." Tap this button to open Settings, shown in the middle of Figure 8-11. In Settings, work your way through the categories in the left column to configure your system settings.

Modify the Desktop

Modify the desktop to suit your personal tastes. The Settings windows (Figure 8-11) is the place to modify the Desktop using various categories in the left column, such as Background, Dock, Notifications, Search, Region & Language, and Universal Access (accessibility). Step-by-Step 8.03 describes how to make changes to your Desktop.

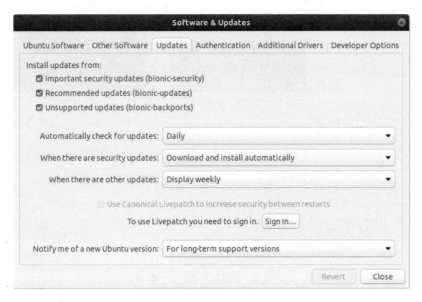

FIGURE 8-10 Software and Updates settings.
Source: Ubuntu by Canonical

FIGURE 8-11 The Settings window contains system settings.
Source: Ubuntu by Canonical

Step-by-Step **8.03**

Modifying the Desktop

You will need the following:

- A computer with Ubuntu installed. The steps are written for Ubuntu with the GNOME GUI.

- The username and password of an administrator account for this computer.

Step 1

Click the small down arrow on the far right of the top bar to open the drop-down System menu. Locate the icon that resembles a pair of hand tools positioned in an "x." Tap this button to open Settings. In the left column select Background.

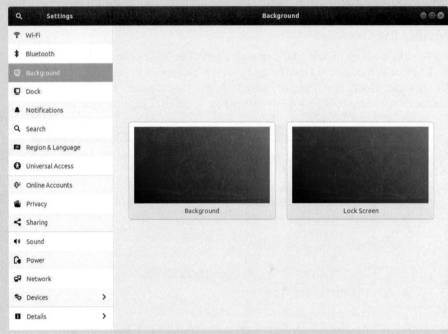

Source: Ubuntu by Canonical

Step 2

The Background control panel lets you select to make changes on the background for the Desktop as well as the Lock screen. Click the Background screen to open a window with three tabs: Wallpapers, Pictures, and Colors. Click Wallpapers, then as you click on a wallpaper selection, it appears on the desktop behind the control panel window.

Source: Ubuntu by Canonical

Step 3

Click on *Dock* in the left column of Settings. This is where you can choose to auto-hide the Dock, change the icon size on the Dock, and select the position of the Dock: left, bottom, or right.

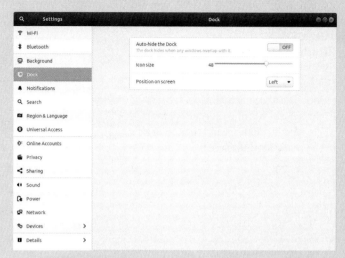

Source: Ubuntu by Canonical

Step 4

No need to click an OK button; changes are made as soon as you select them. In our case, we selected a new wallpaper but did not change the behavior of the Dock.

Source: Ubuntu by Canonical

Step 5

Return to Settings and open Devices (near bottom or list) and Display. Here you can select settings for Orientation, Resolution, Scale, and Night Light (uses warmer screen color). Make desired changes and then return to the main Settings screen.

Source: Ubuntu by Canonical

Step 6

Return to the main Settings windows and select *Universal Access*. This is where you can customize this installation of Linux to make it more accessible to someone who needs adjustments made for viewing the screen, listening, typing, or using a pointing device. When you are finished close the window.

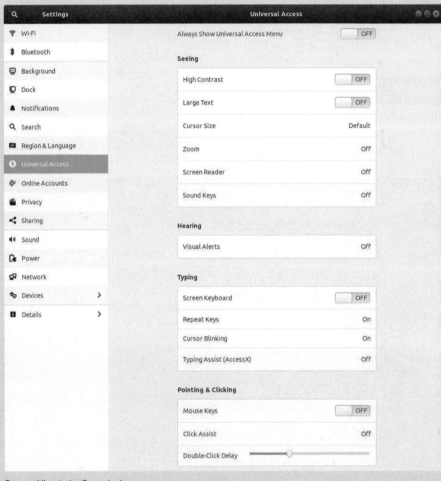

Source: Ubuntu by Canonical

Ending a Linux Session from the GUI

As with Windows and macOS, you have choices for ending your session in Windows. You can simply log out, which is a reasonable choice if you are sharing a computer with someone else. You can shut down, which will both log you out and shut down your computer. You can restart Linux.

Logging Out of a Linux GUI Session

When you log out of Linux it ends your session, giving you an opportunity to save files before closing down all apps (and your desktop if in a GUI), but does not turn off the computer. After logging out, another user can log in, as Guest or using another account on that computer. How you log on or off a Linux GUI session depends on which GUI you are using.

If you are using the Ubuntu GNOME desktop, click on the System menu in the upper-right corner to open the drop-down menu shown in Figure 8-12. Then select your user name to open the User options menu in Figure 8-13. Finally, select *Log Out*. You will need to respond to the "Are you sure" to continue with Log Out. Then the session will end and after a delay a login page similar to the one shown back in Figure 8-5 will display.

Switching Users

If you have multiple accounts on a Linux computer you can take advantage of switch users, a feature that allows the currently logged-on user to leave their apps and data open in memory, switching away so that another user can log in to a separate session. Each user's session is protected, requiring a password to access again.

To switch users in GNOME GUI in Ubuntu, open the Switch User Accounts menu by clicking the user icon on the right of the Desktop bar. Then either select another user to log on or click on **Switch User** from the items below the current user's name. This opens a login screen where you can select a local account and enter a password to switch to another account.

Shutting Down, Restarting, or Suspending a Linux GUI

When you shut down a Linux computer, you are logged out and the operating system closes all files and powers off the computer. When you select restart on a Linux computer, you are logged out and the operating system closes all files and then issues a restart command to the computer, without turning the power off. The operating system is then restarted and the login screen displays.

To shut down a computer from the Linux GNOME GUI, first select the Power button from the System menu, shown in Figure 8-15. Then the screen will dim and display the message shown in Figure 8-16. Here you have the choices *Cancel, Restart,* and *Power Off.* In spite of the different term used here, you know what to do.

Note: The switch users feature is also available in Windows and macOS.

FIGURE 8–12 The Ubuntu GNOME System menu.
Source: Ubuntu by Canonical

FIGURE 8–13 From the System menu open the options for a single user.
Source: Ubuntu by Canonical

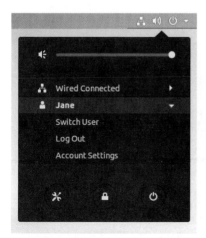

FIGURE 8–14 Select Switch User.
Source: Ubuntu by Canonical

FIGURE 8–15 Select the Power button.
Source: Ubuntu by Canonical

FIGURE 8–16 Select *Power Off.*
Source: Ubuntu by Canonical

LO 8.4 | Linux Command-Line Interface

The native Linux user interface is the command-line interface (CLI). Many installations of Linux, especially on servers, have only a CLI. Although there are great GUI options for working in Linux, system administrators still do much of the real work of supporting and managing Linux from the CLI, which forces you to be precise when entering commands. Any OS is unforgiving when given the wrong instructions, but it doesn't take precision to browse a GUI and select the correct graphical object, which is how a GUI buffers users from the precision required from a command prompt. Acquiring the habit of being precise now will help you succeed in future computer work.

To learn the commands, you must enter them at a Linux prompt. Sit at a Linux computer while reading the following sections because, as we examine various commands, you will have frequent opportunities to try them. Feel free also to experiment on your own. Note that your screen may not look exactly like the examples shown.

The Terminal Window in Linux

If you installed Linux with a GUI or are running it from a live image booted into a GUI, you can open a terminal window, equivalent to a Windows Command Prompt window, where you can experience the Linux CLI. How you do this depends on the GUI. For instance, in the Ubuntu GNOME GUI, click on Activities and type "terminal" in the Activities Search box (Figure 8-17). Then select the *Terminal* icon from the results list. That will open a terminal window, similar to the one shown in Figure 8-18.

When you open a terminal window you will see the $ prompt, which consists of the name of the currently logged-on user and the computer name. These are separated by the @ sign, which in turn is followed by a tilde (~) representing the path to your home directory. When you start a session at the $ prompt, the current directory is your logged-on user's Home directory. The prompt ends with the dollar sign ($).

Later in this chapter you will learn how to use the **cd** command to change the current directory. If you make another directory current, the name of that directory will be included in the $ prompt. The appearance of the $ prompt may vary somewhat among Linux versions. The blinking cursor that follows the $ prompt, seen in Figure 8-18 as a white rectangle, indicates that it is awaiting your command.

Using Linux Shell Commands

The most important thing to learn and remember about working in the Linux shell (in a terminal window or in Linux without a GUI) is that it is case-sensitive. Commands are entered in lowercase, and so are most options.

FIGURE 8–17 Type "terminal" in the Activities Search box.
Source: Ubuntu by Canonical

FIGURE 8–18 A terminal window in the Ubuntu GNOME GUI.
Source: Ubuntu by Canonical

Linux Shell Command Syntax

When working at the CLI, the Linux shell command syntax follows these rules:

- All lines start with a Linux command (the first string of characters).
- A space must follow the command.
- Next come options, specific to the command, that modify its behavior. Most options are short options using a single character, while more recent options may be long (more than one character).
- Order of options is usually of little importance.
- Use a space between each option.
- Short options are preceded by a hyphen (-d); long options are preceded by two hyphens (--help).
- If you want to use multiple short options for a command, you can combine them into one long option with a single hyphen at the beginning.
- Some commands are followed by a parameter, which is a file name, directory, or device name. A parameter is the object that the command action targets.

In general, the command syntax in Linux follows this format:

    command option parameter

Combining Options

Now let's practice combining options. Consider the **ls** command, which lists contents of a directory, as shown in Figure 8-19, in which the command is run without any options or parameters.

try this!

Test Case Sensitivity in Linux

Test Linux case sensitivity while using the **man** command that, when entered correctly, opens the user manual page for the command you provide, such as the **list directory contents** command, **ls.** Try this:

1. At the Linux $ prompt enter the following command in all caps: MAN LS
2. Notice the resulting error message.
3. Now reenter the command in all lower case. The result is that the Linux user manual will open to the page on the command **ls.**
4. Use the SPACEBAR and UP and DOWN arrow keys to move through the manual page.
5. To quit a manual page, press **q.**

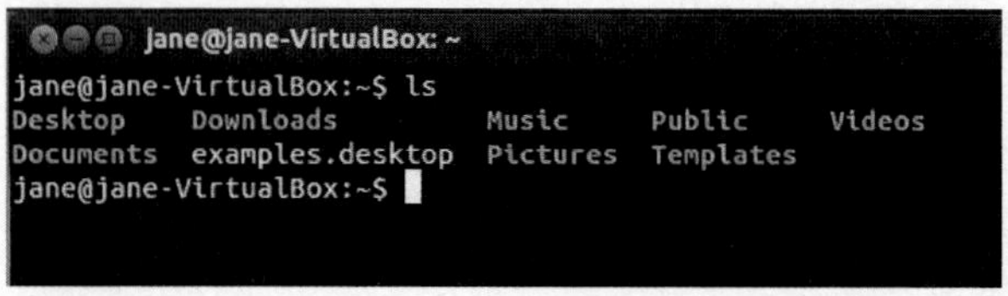

FIGURE 8–19 The **ls** command showing a simple listing of the current directory.
Source: Ubuntu by Canonical

FIGURE 8–20 The **ls -a** command showing a listing of all items in the current directory.
Source: Ubuntu by Canonical

FIGURE 8–21 The **ls** command using two options (-a and -l) showing a listing of all items in the current directory and the "long" information on each item.
Source: Ubuntu by Canonical

try this!

Using Multiple Options

Practice using **ls.** Run the command with a single option and then with multiple options. Try this:

1. Enter the command **ls.**
2. Notice that **ls** defaults to a column output (four across).
3. To get a long listing of this directory, enter **ls -l.** This runs the -l option on the current directory.
4. Now use multiple options. Enter **ls -la.** This provides a long listing for all files, including hidden files, in the current directory.

It has several options, two of which are **a** (all files including hidden files) and **l** (lowercase "L") for long format listing that will include permissions, owner, size, modification time, and more. Figures 8-20 and 8-21 show the use of each of these commands alone. To use **ls** with the **a** option enter **ls -a,** which will simply list the files, as shown in Figure 8-20, but give no information about them, other than the color coding for the type of file, explained later. To use both options at once, enter **ls -al** or **ls -la,** as shown in Figure 8-21. Either will work. When too much text displays for the size of the terminal window, a scroll bar appears on the side, and you can use it to scroll through the results.

The Help Manual

Help is always at hand in the form of the online user manual, accessed with the **man** command. Type **man** *command,* where *command* is the shell command you wish to learn more about. Figure 8-22 shows the result of entering **man ls.** This is the first page of the explanation for the **ls** command. Notice the instructions in white at the bottom of the screen. Press *h* to see an explanation of how to move through the manual. Press *q* to quit the **man** command. You can even see the documentation for the **man** command itself by entering **man man** at the $ prompt.

Command-Line History

Linux saves the shell commands you enter for the duration of the session (called command-line history), and you can scroll through these commands while at the $ prompt. Simply use the up and down arrow keys to move through the history. When you find the command you would like to reuse, you can edit the command by moving back and forth through it with the left and right arrow keys. When you are ready

Note: The screen (or terminal window) gets pretty cluttered. To clear the screen and return the $ prompt to the top of an empty screen, enter the **clear** command. If the screen has unusual characters on it that do not disappear with the **clear** command, use the **reset** command for a more thorough reset of the terminal window.

to use the command, simply press ENTER. Linux saves these commands in a file called .bash_history, but you do not need to know anything about this file to take advantage of this feature.

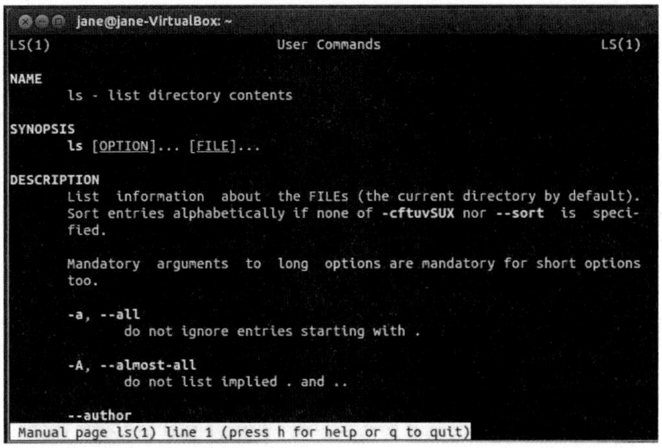

Command Completion

As you enter a command at the $ prompt, experiment with the command completion feature. Enter the command name and a few more characters of the options, then press the TAB key. Linux tries to automatically fill in partially typed commands, and is especially clever at doing this when it looks like you are entering a directory name, indicated by the forward slash (/), but you need to give it more information than just the forward slash. For instance, when using the **cd** (change directory) command, if you enter **cd /e** and then press the TAB key, it will guess that you intended to type "etc/" and will complete it that way so that it reads **cd /etc/**. A more general term for this feature, when used in applications and search engines, is *autocompletion*.

Linux Feedback

When it comes to feedback, Linux commands are actually similar to Windows Command Prompt commands, in that they all provide cryptic feedback, communicating with you only if there is a problem. A Linux BASH command does not report when it is successful, though you'll get an error message if the command is incorrect. In this example, we first tried to change to the documents directory using the command **cd documents.** The second line shows an error. We then ran the **ls** command (third line) to see the contents (fourth and fifth lines) that showed the directory was actually named "Documents." We entered it again (sixth line), using the correct case: **cd Documents.** No message resulted from this command, although it is clear that we changed directories because the dollar prompt on the seventh line now shows Documents as the current location.

Like Windows, Linux relies heavily on a directory structure that has several predefined directories created by default during installation. Some hold important system files, and others hold user data. Linux is very similar. It has several directories for system files and a home directory for each user. You have already been introduced to a few of the file and directory management tools: **ls** and **cd** while learning the basics of working with shell commands. In this section, you will use these and other commands to explore the default directories and learn more about working with Linux at the CLI.

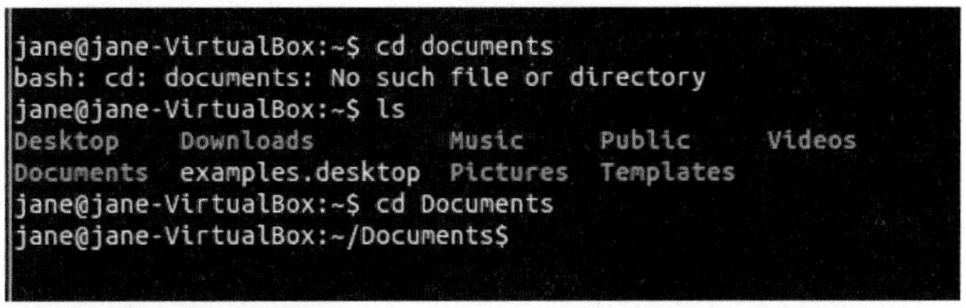

Using Shell Commands for the Linux File System

A shorthand for the path, or location, of the Home directory both at the $ prompt and in a shell command is the tilde (~). Use the **ls** command to see other directories. Some have rather strange names.

In Linux everything is a file, even physical objects like a hard drive or other storage devices. Therefore, Linux shows each drive and other device simply as a part of the file system and gives it a path that begins at the root of the file system (/). Drives and other devices have assigned names, such as **/dev/sda0,** the first hard drive on a SCSI interface (indicated by **sda**); or **/dev/hda1,** the first hard drive on an IDE interface (**hda**).

FIGURE 8-22 Enter the **man ls** command to see the manual page for the **ls** command.
Source: Ubuntu by Canonical

try this!

What Time Is It?

Practice entering the date and calendar commands. Try this:

1. Type the command **date** and press ENTER. This will display the current date, along with the day of the week and time.
2. Now type the command **cal** and press ENTER. This will display the calendar for the current month with the day highlighted.

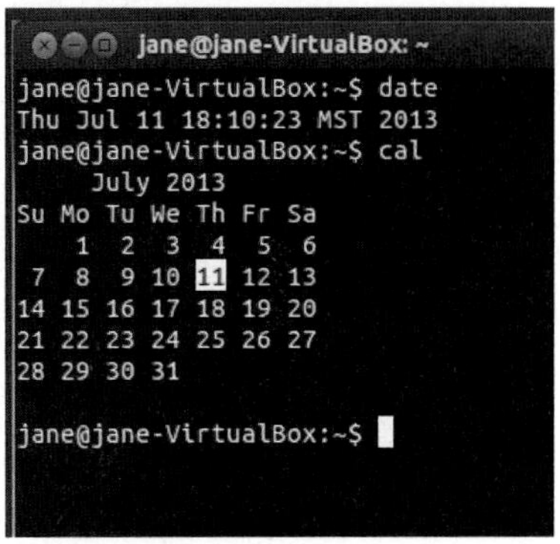

The date and cal commands.
Source: Ubuntu by Canonical

A message appears only if a command causes an error.
Source: Ubuntu by Canonical

Note: The terms folder and directory are synonymous in Linux, as they are in Windows. However, it is customary to use the term folder in a GUI and directory in a command-line interface. Suit yourself!

Practice using shell commands to work with files and directories on your computer. Table 8-2 provides a list of basic file management commands for your reference.

You were introduced to the **ls** command earlier in this chapter, and Figure 8-12 showed the use of the **man ls** command to display the manual page for this command. Table 8-3 lists and explains the commonly used options for **ls**. Recall that Linux is case-sensitive, so pay attention to the case of each option. By itself, **ls** provides only the names of visible files in the current directory, and the **–a** option that you learned about earlier lists all files and directories, even hidden files. Hidden files have names that begin with a period (.).

Listing the Contents of a Specified Directory. If you do not specify the directory you want **ls** to work on, it uses the current directory. To point ls to another directory, use the directory name and the appropriate path as a parameter in the command. Figure 8-23 shows the result of typing **ls /etc.** The colors of the names tell you more about that file or directory.

- Blue = directory
- Green = program or binary data file such as jpeg
- Light blue or aqua = link to files in a different directory
- Pink = image file
- Red = compressed archive file
- White = text file
- Yellow = device

To view more details of the files in the **/etc** directory enter the command **ls -l /etc;** the output will be similar to that shown in Figure 8-24. This listing does not include hidden files because we did not use the **-a** option to see hidden files, as we did back in Figure 8-12.

In the results from using the **-l** option, the first column is 10 characters wide and lists the attributes on the file or folder, which you will examine a little later in this chapter. The next column indicates the number of links to a file. The next two columns list the owner (normally the user who created the file) and last modifier of the file,

TABLE 8–2 Basic Shell Commands for File Management

Command	Description
cd	Changes to another directory
chmod	Changes the mode or file permissions
cp	Copies a file
ls	Lists contents of a directory
mkdir	Makes a directory
more	Displays a text file, one screenful at a time
pwd	Prints the working directory
rm	Deletes a file

TABLE 8–3 Commonly Used Options for the ls Command

ls Option	Description
-a	Lists all files in the directory, including the hidden files. Files are hidden in Linux by making the first character a period, like this: **.bash_profile**
-l	Displays a long listing of the directory contents with all file attributes and permissions listed
-F	Classifies the listed objects. In particular, directory names have a / character after the name
-S	Sorts the output by size
-t	Sorts the output by time

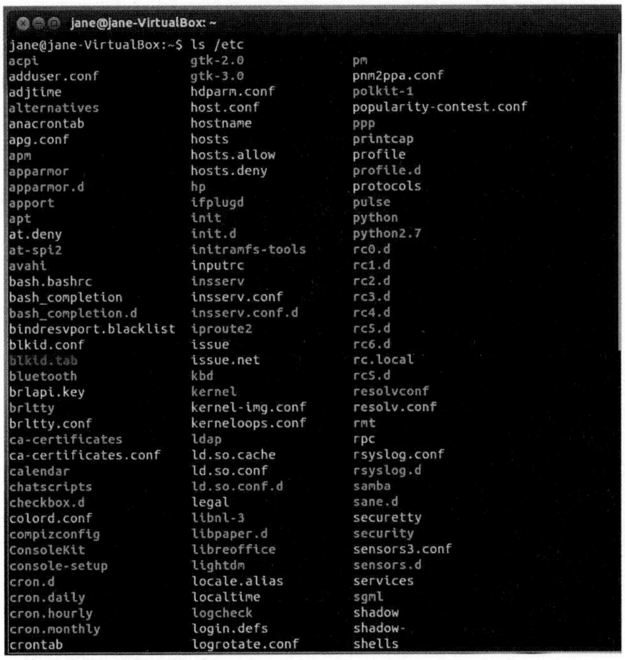

FIGURE 8-23 A listing of the /**etc** directory.
Source: Ubuntu by Canonical

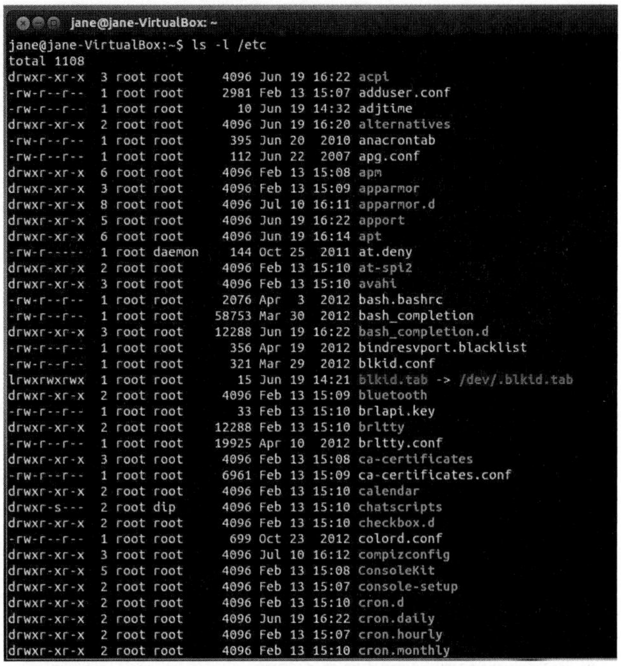

FIGURE 8-24 A listing of the /**etc** directory with more details.
Source: Ubuntu by Canonical

respectively. The next number indicates the size of the file. The next columns indicate the file creation date and time. Lastly, it shows the name of the file. If a file is a link, it next lists the link location; the file after the arrow is the original file.

Changing the Current Directory. The command to change the current directory in Linux is **cd.** The **cd** command was used in previous examples in this chapter to illustrate the command completion feature and the need to pay attention to letter case. Let's focus on this command for itself now.

The **cd** command requires one parameter: the directory to change to. If the directory is a child of the current directory, then you only need the name to change to this directory. For example, suppose that in your home directory you have a child directory called private. To change to this directory, you enter **cd private.** If the directory is not a child of the current directory, you will need to enter the path to the directory. An absolute path will start with **/** (the root directory). Each directory in the path is listed after the **/** and separated from the next by another **/.** For example, to change to the **sbin** directory under the **/ usr** directory, you would enter **cd /usr/sbin.** It is called an absolute path because you clearly provide its location beginning with the top level, which in Linux is the root directory.

When you correctly use **cd** to change to a different directory, it rewards you with a change in your prompt. In Figure 8-25, the user started in the Home directory of the user jane, as indicated by the tilde (~) in the $ prompt, and changed to the /usr/ sbin directory. The prompt changed to reflect the new directory. You can quickly change back to your personal home directory from any directory by entering **cd ~ .** Figure 8-26 shows the result of entering this command.

WARNING!

To avoid seeing error messages in place of results, whenever you need to use a shell command to perform an operation on a hidden file or directory, be sure to include the (.) at the beginning of the name.

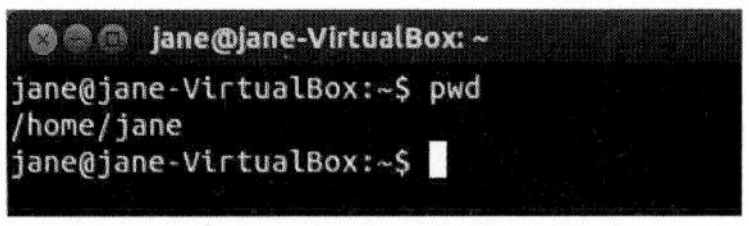

Use the **pwd** command to display the path to the current directory.
Source: Ubuntu by Canonical

FIGURE 8-25 Changing to the /**usr/ sbin** directory.
Source: Ubuntu by Canonical

FIGURE 8-26 Changing to the Home directory using the tilde (~).
Source: Ubuntu by Canonical

Where Am I? Unfortunately, the Linux prompt does not (by default) show the entire path to the current directory. If you are unsure of where you are, use the command **pwd,** which stands for print working directory. It does not send anything to your printer; rather it displays (prints) the path to the working (current) directory on your screen, as shown here where the **pwd** command shows the path to the current directory (/home/jane) on the second line and then returns to the $ prompt on the third line.

try this!

Display the Contents of a File

Use the **more** command to display the contents of a file on the screen. Try this:

1. If a terminal window is not open, open it now.
2. If the prompt does not include a tilde (~), enter **cd ~** to ensure that you are in the Home directory.
3. Enter the command: **more .bash_history.** This will display the contents of the hidden file .bash_history, pausing after the screen is full.
4. Press the ENTER key (repeatedly) to scroll one line at a time or press the SPACEBAR to scroll one screenful at a time. Continue to the end of the output.

```
jane@jane-VirtualBox: /home
jane@jane-VirtualBox:~$ pwd
/home/jane
jane@jane-VirtualBox:~$ cd ..
jane@jane-VirtualBox:/home$
```

FIGURE 8–27 Use the command **cd** .. to move to the parent directory of the current directory.
Source: Ubuntu by Canonical

Relative Path. Linux allows you to use commands to navigate directories, using special symbols as shorthand for moving to directories that are relative to your current directory. For instance, the command **cd ..** will change the current directory to the next directory up in the hierarchy. If you are in your personal home directory, this command will move you to the home directory, one level up. In Figure 8-27, the first two lines show the **pwd** command and its result, showing that the /home/jane directory is current. The third line shows the command **cd ..** followed by the resulting $ prompt on the fourth line in which the /home directory is current. The /home directory is the parent directory of all the home directories on a Linux computer.

Place the **..** characters between forward slashes (/) to move up additional levels. In addition, throw in a specific directory that exists at that level. For example, the command **cd ../../etc** moves up two levels and then to the etc directory. Be sure you know where you want to go, and remember, using one of these characters is supposed to save you typing. Rather than use the command string **cd ../../etc,** it is shorter to type **cd /etc.** Another special symbol is the single dot (.), which refers to the current directory.

try this!

Using Relative Path Statements

A little practice with relative paths is helpful. Try this:

1. Type the command: **cd ..**
2. Return to your home directory by typing: **cd ~**
3. Now move to the /etc directory using a relative path: **cd ../../etc**
4. Return to your home directory by typing: **cd ~**

Wildcards. Linux supports the use of wildcards. A wildcard is a symbol that replaces any character or string of characters in a command parameter. It is also supported in other CLIs for other OSs. The use of the asterisk (*) as a wildcard in a file name or directory name replaces all the characters from the point at which you place the asterisk to the end of the name. For instance, **ls bi*** would list all files or directories that begin with "bi."

Linux wildcard support is flexible. You can enter a range of characters as a wildcard. For instance, if you enter **ls [c-d]*** the **ls** command will display all files in the current directory that begin with the letters *c* through *d*. The bracket symbols ([]) are part of a Linux feature called regular expressions. Linux also allows you to use the dollar sign ($) to represent a single character within a file name, a feature also supported by DOS and the Windows Command Prompt. We considered ourselves very experienced DOS users (back in its heyday), and we found that using the dollar sign was rarely worth the bother.

When a parameter for the **ls** command is the name of a directory, the result will include the contents of that directory. Therefore, if you try the command in the example given in the previous paragraph from within the **/etc** directory, the **ls [c-d]*** command will result in a long listing because each of the items that begins with either a "c" or "d" that is also a directory will cause **ls** to list the contents of that directory. Figure 8-28 shows just a portion of the output from running this command with the /etc directory current. Each line that ends with a colon is for a directory and the following line or lines display the contents of that directory.

Creating Directories

Create a directory in Linux with the **mkdir** command, which requires at least one parameter: the name of the directory to create. For example, to create a directory called junk within the current directory, enter the command **mkdir junk.** Because Linux gives you no feedback after you create a directory, use **ls** to verify that it built the directory.

If you list more than one parameter, then it will create a directory for each. Therefore, to create two directories named "sales" and "marketing" with one command, enter the command **mkdir sales marketing** (see Figure 8-29).

Copying Files in Linux

The command to copy files is **cp.** We recommend you make a copy of a file before you change it. This allows you to recover from any changes you make.

The **cp** command requires two parameters. The first is the source file, which can be a file in the current directory or a file in another directory, as long as you provide the correct path. The second parameter is the target, which can be a target location to copy to and/or a name for the file. This makes more sense after you practice using the command.

As you can see in Figure 8-30, the file named hosts was copied from the /etc directory to the current directory. (The period at the end of the command represents the current directory.) This is just a copy, leaving the original hosts file in the /etc directory. Notice that Linux does not report that it copied a file. The figure also shows that we used the **ls** command to verify a successful copy of the file.

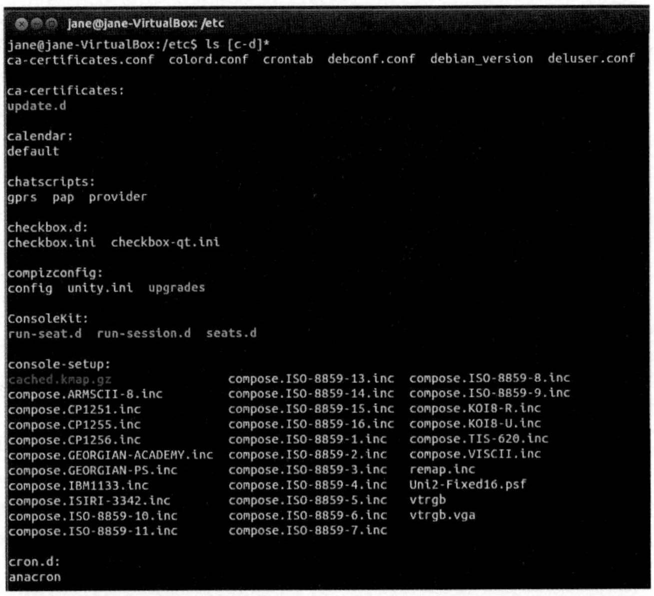

FIGURE 8–28 A portion of the results of the command **ls [c-d]***
when run from the /**etc** directory.
Source: Ubuntu by Canonical

try this!

Using Wildcards

1. Change to the /etc directory (enter **cd /etc**).
2. Enter the command **ls e*.** You'll see all files that begin with the letter *e.*
3. Now enter the command **ls [c-d]* /etc.**

try this!

Create Directories

Create directories in your home folder. Try this:

1. Enter the command **mkdir data.**
2. Use the **ls** command to confirm that it created the data directory.
3. Make several directories by entering the **mkdir** command followed by two or more names for new directories.
4. Use the **ls** command to confirm that it created the new directories.

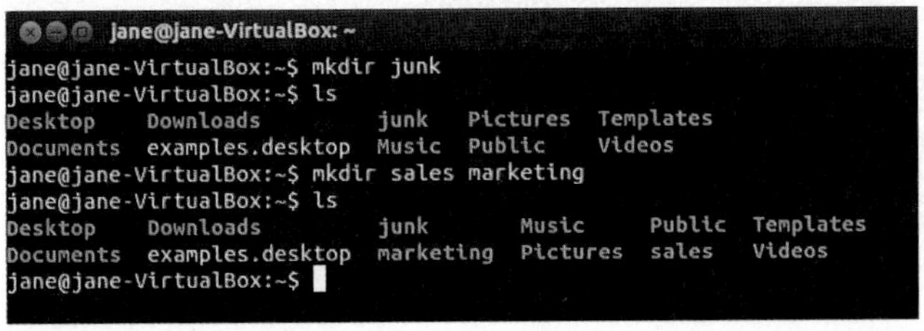

FIGURE 8–29 Use **mkdir** to create directories and **ls** to confirm that they were created.
Source: Ubuntu by Canonical

FIGURE 8–30 Copying the hosts file from the /**etc** directory to the user's home directory.
Source: Ubuntu by Canonical

LO 8.5 | Securing a Linux Desktop

Linux is a very secure OS—whether you are using a GUI or a CLI. It is important to know how to configure a computer for the needs of its users. This includes managing user accounts and applying security to directories.

Keeping Linux Up-to-Date

Since security updates are an important part of updates to any software, ensure that your installation of Linux continues to get updates. The Software Updater app in the Ubuntu GNOME GUI will by default download and install updates; it requires interaction from the user to restart. This can cause delays in keeping your installation of Ubuntu up-to-date.

Ubuntu now includes Livepatch, an optional service that applies updates that would normally require restarting. In other words, it patches (another term for updating) the operating system without restarting it. We encountered this in Ubuntu 18.04 during the personalization stage. It has two requirements:

1. You must enter your user password for that installation of Linux (Figure 8–31). You will need to use your local password, even if you do not require a password to login.

2. You must sign in with an Ubuntu Single Sign-On Account, an online service requiring an email address and password (Figure 8–32). These credentials are usable and reusable across multiple instances.

Managing Users

Linux allows several users to use one computer, but each user should have a unique account. When you create a user account, Linux also creates a home directory within the **/home** directory, using the user's name for the directory name. This is the place in the Linux file system where an ordinary user account has full control over directories and files. The user can both save files and create new subdirectories. Users can further protect files from other users by changing the permissions on files and folders in their home directories.

FIGURE 8–31 Enter your local password.
Source: Ubuntu by Canonical

Livepatch

Canonical Livepatch helps keep your computer secure, by applying some updates that would normally require restarting.

Would you like to set up Livepatch now?

| Cancel | Ubuntu Single Sign-On Account |

Email address: [   ]

⊙ I have an Ubuntu Single Sign-On account

Password: [   ]

○ I want to register for an account now

○ I've forgotten my password

FIGURE 8–32 Enter credentials for a Single Sign-On Account.
Source: Ubuntu by Canonical

The Linux Root Account

Each installation of Linux has a root account, an all-powerful account that is only used when absolutely necessary to do advanced tasks. Ubuntu Linux comes with this account disabled in such a way that no one can log in directly with the account, but there is a way to temporarily use it whenever you need it for tasks, such as creating or deleting users. However, you must be logged on with an administrator-type account to do this. You can do this from within a GUI or at a CLI in Linux. You will practice this when you create a user account in the next section.

Creating a User Account in a GUI

Step-by-Step 8.04 describes how to temporarily take on the power of the root account and add a new user in the Ubuntu GNOME GUI. If you are using a different GUI, you will need to locate the GUI tool for administering user accounts. In GNOME for Ubuntu, this is User Accounts.

Step-by-Step 8.04

Add a New User Account in GNOME for Ubuntu

If you are adding no more than a few users to a desktop installation of Ubuntu, a GUI tool is the easiest to use. In this example, we use the User Accounts tool in GNOME for Ubuntu.

To complete this exercise you will need:

- A computer running Ubuntu with the GNOME GUI.
- The username and password of an administrator-type account for this computer.

Open *Settings* in the Ubuntu GNOME GUI and select *Details* (bottom left), then select *Users* to open the Users pane in the Settings Window. Select *Unlock* in the top right.

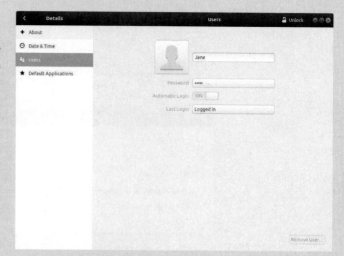

Source: Ubuntu by Canonical

When prompted enter your password. The Users window now has a green button labeled *Add User* in place of the *Unlock* button.

Source: Ubuntu by Canonical

Click *Add User.* This opens the Add User dialog box. Notice that you can choose to make this user a Standard user or an Administrator. If you wish to remain the sole administrator on the computer, be sure that Standard is selected, as shown.

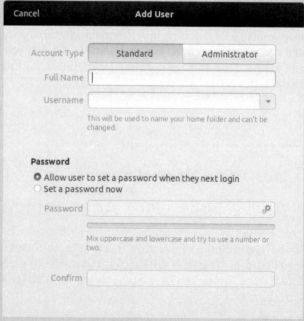

Source: Ubuntu by Canonical

Step 4

Enter a full name for the new user. The system will generate a username from this full name. You may change it at this point, as we did, shortening the username. Leave the Password setting as is, so that the first time the user logs in they will need to create their own password. Then click *Add*.

Source: Ubuntu by Canonical

Step 5

The new user is added to the *Users* window. Notice that you can continue to create users one-by-one by click *Add User*. Once you close out of this window, when you return, it will be locked again, as it was before you unlocked it and created the user.

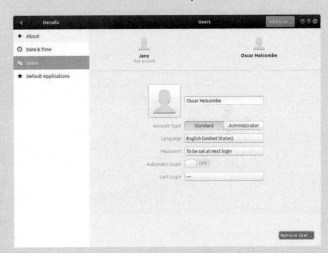

Source: Ubuntu by Canonical

Step 6

The next time you log out of restart the computer, the sign-in screen will include the new user. When that user signs in the dialog box will require that they create and confirm a password.

Managing User Accounts with Shell Commands

When adding many users to either a Linux desktop or server, an advanced Linux administrator will add users by creating a special script that will create a list of users much faster than using a GUI. We believe that if you need to create only a few users on a few computers, it is easier to work through the GUI. However, if you need to manage users on a Linux computer without a GUI, you will need to know how to work with shell commands. Table 8–4 lists useful commands for managing users with shell commands.

Note: When you enter a password in a Linux CLI, the characters you enter do not show on the line as you enter them. In fact nothing shows. The cursor does not move. Don't forget to press ENTER at the end of the password.

TABLE 8–4	Shell Commands for User Management
Command	**Description**
useradd	Adds a user to the system
userdel	Removes a user from the system
passwd	Changes a user's password
finger	Finds a username

When working from a Linux CLI, temporarily assign root account (also called Superuser) privileges to the currently logged-on user (who must be an administrator-type account) by preceding the command you wish to run with the **sudo** (Superuser Do) command. When you use **sudo** it will prompt you to enter your password (not the root password). Then, for the next five minutes (by default) you will be able to run **sudo** without requiring a password. After this time has passed, if you run **sudo** again, you will need to enter your password. The following includes examples of using the **sudo** command to run administrative commands, beginning with the installation of software to add a command to Linux.

The **finger** command allows you to look up user information, but some installations of Linux (including Ubuntu) do not automatically install it. Therefore, if you want to experiment with the **finger** command, you must install the finger daemon. A daemon is a program that runs in background until it is activated by a command. Once installed, the **finger** daemon is activated by running the **finger** command. Install the **finger** daemon with this command: **sudo apt-get install finger.** This should result in the output shown here.

```
jane@jane-VirtualBox: ~
jane@jane-VirtualBox:~$ sudo apt-get install finger
[sudo] password for jane:
Reading package lists... Done
Building dependency tree
Reading state information... Done
The following packages were automatically installed and are no longer required:
  linux-headers-3.5.0-23-generic linux-headers-3.5.0-23
Use 'apt-get autoremove' to remove then.
The following NEW packages will be installed:
  finger
0 upgraded, 1 newly installed, 0 to remove and 0 not upgraded.
Need to get 19.6 kB of archives.
After this operation, 81.9 kB of additional disk space will be used.
Get:1 http://us.archive.ubuntu.com/ubuntu/ precise/main finger amd64 0.17-14 [19
.6 kB]
Fetched 19.6 kB in 0s (33.6 kB/s)
Selecting previously unselected package finger.
(Reading database ... 195632 files and directories currently installed.)
Unpacking finger (from .../finger_0.17-14_amd64.deb) ...
Processing triggers for man-db ...
Setting up finger (0.17-14) ...
jane@jane-VirtualBox:~$
```

Installing the **finger** daemon.
Source: Ubuntu by Canonical

```
jane@jane-VirtualBox: ~
jane@jane-VirtualBox:~$ sudo useradd -p pa22w0rD aphoenix
[sudo] password for jane:
jane@jane-VirtualBox:~$ sudo finger aphoenix
Login: aphoenix                    Name:
Directory: /home/aphoenix          Shell: /bin/sh
Never logged in.
No mail.
No Plan.
jane@jane-VirtualBox:~$
```

FIGURE 8–33 Create a user with the **useradd** command. Confirm its creation with the **finger** command.
Source: Ubuntu by Canonical

From the command shell, use the **useradd** command preceded by **sudo** to create a user. This command requires at least one parameter, the username you want to add. If you want to create a password for this user in the same operation, use the **useradd** option **-p** followed by the password. For instance, to create an account for Ashley Phoenix using the username of aphoenix with the password pa22w0rD, enter the command **sudo useradd -p pa22w0rD aphoenix.** To verify that it created the user account, use **finger aphoenix** (see Figure 8–33).

Changing User Passwords

Changing a user's password involves the command **passwd.** Entering **passwd** without any additional parameters will let you change your own password. Any user can change his or her own password, but only a user with root privileges can change the password on other user accounts. For example, enter **sudo passwd aphoenix** to change the password for the aphoenix account. The administrator doing this does not need to know the current password for the account before changing it to the new one, but can simply enter the new password twice. Note that, as always, Linux doesn't display passwords, but it does provide the useful feedback that the password was updated successfully.

Deleting Users

In any organization, employees leave. For security reasons, you should remove these accounts from the system shortly after the employee leaves. The command **userdel** allows you to remove a user from a Linux account, but you must run this command using **sudo.**

The syntax for userdel is similar to that for **passwd** and **useradd.** For example, you can remove the aphoenix account with the command **sudo userdel aphoenix.**

Recall that every user has a home directory in which to store his or her files. When you delete a user you do not remove this directory—you must remove these files manually. The long explanation for doing this is to delete the files contained in the user's home directory first; then delete the user's home directory itself. It will have the user's name. However, if a directory has subdirectories, you first need to switch into each subdirectory and delete all files in those as well. Once you have deleted the files, you change the directory to one level above and use the **rmdir** command. The syntax for **rmdir** is as follows: **rmdir *directoryname.***

Now, for the quicker method for deleting a directory and its contents. The **rmdir** command can only remove empty directories, but the **rm** command removes a file or a directory and its contents. Use the **rm** command with the -r (remove) and -f (force) type **rm -rf** *directory-or-file-name* to remove a directory and everything below it.

WARNING!

The **rm** command is very dangerous. Be very careful, and check your spelling before hitting the ENTER key.

File and Folder Permissions

To implement security for a file or folder, you must first understand Linux file and folder attributes. When you use the **-l** option with the **ls** command, you will see the attributes listed in a column of 10 characters on the far left. Each character is significant in both its placement (first, second, etc.) and in what each single character represents. The first character at the far left indicates whether the entry is a file (-), directory (**d**), or link (**l**). The next nine characters show the permissions on the file or folder for three different entities. Figure 8-34 shows a listing of a directory using the -l option to show all the attributes of nonhidden entries. To decode the permissions, use the following list:

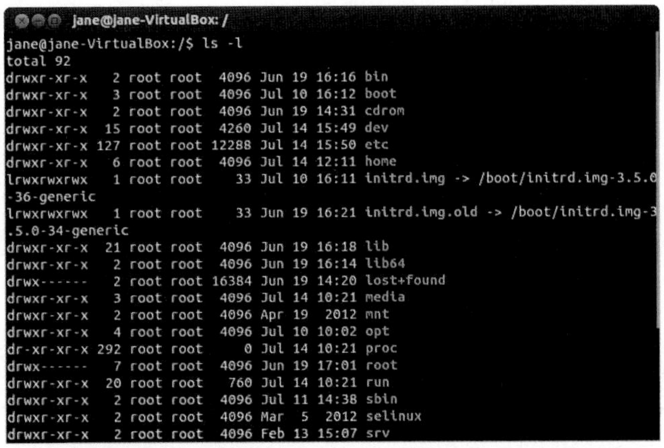

FIGURE 8–34 A sample listing showing attributes.
Source: Ubuntu by Canonical

r = read
w = write
x = execute
- = disabled

Notice the set of permissions for the link named **initrd.img.** The attributes r (read), w (write), and x (execute) repeat three times. Linux is not repeating itself; it is listing permissions for three different individuals or groups. The first set of three permissions applies to the user who owns the files. Normally, if you create a file, then you are the owner.

The second set of three permissions applies to the group the user belongs to. We use groups to organize users, joining those with similar needs and access privileges. For example, a school may group all faculty members into a single group. This will allow instructors to create files that other instructors can read, but that students cannot read.

The third set of three permissions applies to all others. So the read, write, and execute permissions on initrd.img apply to the owner (root, in this case), the owner's group, and all others. Look at the permissions for the first entry, **bin.** The permissions on this directory are set so that the owner has read, write, and execute permissions, but the owner's group and all others have only read and execute permissions, meaning only the owner can change or delete the file.

Note: To remember the order of the groups, think of the name UGO. UGO stands for User, Group, Other.

The command to change a file's or a directory's permissions is **chmod** (called change mode). The **chmod** command requires two options. The first option is the access mode number. The second option is the file to change.

There is a small calculation to perform to determine the access mode number. In Figure 8-34, the link named **initrd.img** has access mode number 777, and the directory **bin** has access mode number 755. You can calculate this number by using the values in Table 8-5. Determine the permission for each user or group by adding the values together. Therefore, if the owner needs to read, write, and execute a file, the first number is 4 + 2 + 1 + 7. If the group is also to read, write, and execute the file, the second number is also 7. If a user has permission only to read and execute a file, the value is 4 + 1 + 5.

WARNING!

Always be sure the file owner has at least an access mode number of 6 for a file, which allows for read and write permissions. If the mode for the owner drops below 6, on some Linux installations any future access to this file is blocked. You should rarely have a file with permissions of 777 because it means that anyone can change the file.

TABLE 8–5 Access Mode Numbers

Permission	Value
Read	4
Write	2
Execute	1

Step-by-Step 8.05

Working with Directories

Imagine that a marketing firm that uses Linux as its primary OS hired you. You will work with a group of users. You need to create a series of directories that the group can see as well as a private directory that no one else but you can see. The following steps will allow you to create directories and set permissions on the directories. You will create these directories in your own home directory.

You will need the following:

- An account on a Linux computer with or without a GUI. If you log in to a GUI, open the terminal.
- Read access to the /etc directory.

Step 1

First create the directories needed to work. Use **mkdir** to create two directories, called wineProject and private, entering this command: **mkdir wineProject private.**

Step 2

Use the command **ls -l** to verify that Linux created the directories and to view the permissions assigned to the directories by default.

Source: Ubuntu by Canonical

Step 3

You are now the owner of these directories. Set the permissions on the private directory so that only you can access it, and on the wineProject directory give yourself read, write, and execute permissions, only read and write permissions to users in your group, and no permissions for others. To set the permissions appropriately enter these two commands: **chmod 700 private** and **chmod 760 wineProject.**

Confirm the new permissions using **ls -l.**

```
[jh@classlab01 jh]$ chmod 700 private
[jh@classlab01 jh]$ chmod 760 wineProject
[jh@classlab01 jh]$ ls -l
total 216
-rw-rw-r--   1 jh      jh          70 Dec  3 08:14 busplan2006
-rw-rw-r--   1 jh      jh         178 Dec  2 19:51 instructor_letter
-rw-r--r--   1 jh      jh        9283 Dec  2 22:03 mailcap
-rw-r--r--   1 jh      jh         112 Dec  2 22:03 mail.rc
-rw-r--r--   1 jh      jh        4426 Dec  2 22:03 man.config
-rw-r--r--   1 jh      jh       36823 Dec  3 06:49 mime-magic
-rw-r--r--   1 jh      jh       99960 Dec  2 22:03 mime-magic.dat
-rw-r--r--   1 jh      jh       12786 Dec  2 22:03 mime.types
-rw-r--r--   1 jh      jh        1110 Dec  2 22:03 minicom.users
-rw-r--r--   1 jh      jh         311 Dec  2 22:03 modules.conf
-rw-r--r--   1 jh      jh         281 Dec  2 22:03 modules.conf~
-rw-r--r--   1 jh      jh           0 Dec  2 22:03 motd
-rw-r--r--   1 jh      jh         242 Dec  2 22:03 mtab
-rw-r--r--   1 jh      jh        1913 Dec  2 22:04 mtools.conf
drwx------   2 jh      jh        4096 Dec  3 10:10 private
drwxrw----   2 jh      jh        4096 Dec  3 10:11 wineProject
[jh@classlab01 jh]$ _
```

Source: Ubuntu by Canonical

Populate the wineProject directory by copying two files into it from your home directory, using the **cp** command. For instance, to copy the file named "letter" type **cp letter wineProject.**

Change to the wineProject directory by entering the command **cd wineProject.** Confirm that the files are there and view the permissions on the files. They do not inherit the permissions of the directory. You will need to modify the permissions on the files if you wish permissions more restrictive than those assigned to the directory. However, any restrictive directory permissions will keep users from accessing the contents of the directory.

```
[jh@classlab01 jh]$ cp instructor_letter wineProject
[jh@classlab01 jh]$ cp busplan2006 wineProject
[jh@classlab01 jh]$ cd wineProject
[jh@classlab01 wineProject]$ ls
busplan2006  instructor_letter
[jh@classlab01 wineProject]$ ls -l
total 8
-rw-rw-r--   1 jh      jh          70 Dec  3 10:11 busplan2006
-rw-rw-r--   1 jh      jh         178 Dec  3 10:10 instructor_letter
[jh@classlab01 wineProject]$ _
```

Source: Ubuntu by Canonical

Chapter 8 REVIEW

Chapter Summary

After reading this chapter and completing the Step-by-Step tutorials and Try This! exercises, you should understand the following facts about Linux:

Linux Overview

- Linux, originally created by Linus Torvalds, is free, open-source software that is like UNIX in stability and function.
- Many versions of Linux exist for all types of computers, and it is used on many Web servers.
- Linux benefits include cost (it is free or inexpensively bundled), the ability to run on old hardware, speed, and stability.
- Drawbacks of Linux include lack of centralized support, choice of GUIs is confusing, limited software selection, limited hardware support, and complexity.

Linux on Your Desktop

- There are many sources of Linux distributions: just two are Ubuntu (www.ubuntu.com) and Fedora (getfedora.org).

- Software distributions are available with GUIs and a complete software bundle of apps.
- Download a distribution as an ISO file and create a bootable DVD or USB flash drive for installing. Popular distributions include a live image from which you can boot and run Linux without having to install it.
- Install Linux as a clean installation on a spare computer, in a dual boot configuration, or into a virtual machine.
- After installing Linux, initiate updates, as you would with Windows.

Exploring a Linux GUI

- If you boot into a live image of Ubuntu Linux, you are logged in as a Guest, but if you install Ubuntu Linux, you will log in with the username and password you provided during the installation.
- In a GUI, or at the CLI, Linux is case-sensitive.

- A Linux distribution with a GUI will have graphical objects similar, but not identical, to those in Windows and macOS.
- The Ubuntu Desktop bar displays at the top of the screen in the GNOME GUI.
- The Ubuntu GNOME desktop includes the Launcher, a bar on the left side of the screen.
- The Ubuntu GNOME desktop has a search tool for locating files and applications.
- Every user on a Linux computer has a home directory, the one place in Linux where a user has full control over files and directories without requiring elevated privileges. Users cannot normally change system directories, such as /etc and /bin or the directories of other users.
- A path is a description that an operating system uses to identify the location of a file or directory. In Linux, you do not use a drive letter; you use a forward slash (/) character at the beginning of a path to represent the top level (root) of the file system.
- The path to a user's home directory is/home/username.
- The **bin** directory within each user's home directory contains many of the Linux commands.
- The **/etc** directory resides in the root of the file system and contains settings and configuration data for a Linux installation.
- It is far easier to browse the Linux directory structure in a GUI than in a Linux CLI.
- The GNOME GUI on Ubuntu includes an Update Manager utility for downloading and installing updates.
- Unity's System Settings window serves the same purpose as Windows' Control Panel and macOS System Preferences.
- Modify the GNOME Desktop using GUI tools similar to those in Windows and macOS.
- End a GNOME Ubuntu Linux session with the Shutdown command, which will log out the currently logged-on user and turn off the computer. You can also choose to restart or suspend.

Linux Command-Line Interface

- The Linux native user interface is the CLI, and many installations, especially on servers, only have a CLI.
- If you installed Linux with a GUI or are running it from a live image booted into a GUI, you can open a terminal window, where you can try the Linux CLI.
- You can combine short options and precede them with a single hyphen (-).

- Some options are followed by a parameter, such as a file name, directory, or device name that the command action targets.
- The command syntax in Linux follows this format: command -option parameter
- The **reset** command clears the screen and returns the $ prompt to the top:
- The **man** command gives you access to the Linux manual.
- Linux saves the shell commands you enter for the duration of the session, and you can scroll through these commands while at the $ prompt.
- Linux has a command completion feature in which it tries to guess what you want to type next.
- The **date** command displays the day, date, and time. The **cal** command displays the calendar for the month with the current day highlighted.
- Linux gives very little feedback at the CLI, but it does issue error messages when you enter something wrong.
- Certain shell commands are useful when managing the file system. They are **cd, chmod, cp, ls, mkdir, more, pwd,** and **rm.**
- When you list the contents of a directory, the items are color coded to identify different types of entries.
- Linux allows you to use commands to navigate directories, using special symbols as shorthand for moving to directories that are relative to your current directory.
- The wildcard asterisk (*) is a symbol that replaces any character or string of characters, in a command parameter.
- Create a directory in Linux with the **mkdir** command, which requires at least one parameter: the name of the directory to create. Use multiple parameters to create multiple directories with one command.
- Use the **cp** command to copy files. It requires a parameter for the source file, and one for the target location and/or name of a file.

Securing a Linux Desktop

- If multiple people need to use one computer, each should have a unique account.
- When you create a Linux account, it also creates a home directory for the account using the user's name for the directory name.
- The **root account** is an all-powerful account that is only used when absolutely necessary to do advanced tasks. Ubuntu Linux comes with this account disabled in such a way that no one can log in directly with the account, but there is a way to temporarily use it.

- Create an account using a GUI tool or by using the **useradd** command at the CLI. The **userdel** command will delete specified users, **passwd** is used to change a user's password, and the **finger** daemon will confirm that a user has been created.

- Temporarily assign root account privileges to the currently logged-on user by preceding the command you intend to run with the **sudo** command. **Sudo** will prompt you to enter your password (not the root password). Then, for the next five minutes (by default), you will be able to run **sudo** without requiring a password.

- The **rmdir** command can only delete empty directories, while the **rm** command will delete a directory and its contents. This is a very dangerous command.

- When you use the **ls** command with the **-l** option it lists files and directory details. The first 10 characters are attributes. The first character is the type of entry: file (**-**), directory (**d**), or link (**l**). The next nine characters show the permission on the file or folder for three different entities (owner, group, and others).

- The characters that represent permissions are **r** for read, **w** for write, **x** for execute, and **-** for disabled.

- The command to change a file's or a directory's permissions is **chmod.**

- Access mode values are 4 for read, 2 for write, and 1 for execute. These are added together to create the access mode number. If the owner, group, or other has read (4), write (2), and execute (1) permission to a file, the access mode number for that entity on that file is 7.

Key Terms List

absolute path *(319)*	**GNU** *(294)*	**Red Hat Enterprise Linux (RHEL)** *(296)*
access mode number *(327)*	**home directory** *(306)*	**root account** *(323)*
Apache HTTP Server *(295)*	**Hypertext Transfer Protocol (HTTP)** *(295)*	**source code** *(295)*
BASH *(296)*	**Kickoff Application Launcher** *(297)*	**switch users** *(313)*
burn *(301)*	**Launcher** *(305)*	**symbolic link** *(307)*
case-aware *(307)*	**Linux** *(294)*	**terminal window** *(314)*
case-sensitive *(307)*	**live image** *(301)*	**Ubuntu** *(296)*
command completion *(317)*	**object code** *(295)*	**Web** *(295)*
command-line history *(316)*	**open-source software** *(295)*	**wildcard** *(320)*
daemon *(326)*	**owner** *(327)*	**World Wide Web (WWW)** *(295)*
GNOME *(297)*	**path** *(306)*	**X Window System** *(297)*

Key Terms Quiz

Use the Key Terms List to complete the sentences that follow. Not all terms will be used.

1. To access the CLI in the GNOME GUI, you open a _____.

2. GNOME is an example of a/an _____ GUI.

3. A/an _____ is a bootable image of the operating system that will run from bootable media without requiring that the OS be installed on the local computer.

4. When you create a user in Linux, the OS creates a _____ on disk for that user.

5. When you write digital data to an optical disc, you are said to _____ the disc.

6. A/an _____ is a program that runs in background until it is activated by a command.

7. The _____ organization was created in 1984 to develop a free UNIX-like operating system.

8. A/an _____ is a special symbol, such as an asterisk (*), that replaces a character or string of characters in a command parameter.

9. _____ is the uncompiled program statements that can be viewed and edited.

10. The most powerful account in Linux is the _____.

Multiple-Choice Quiz

1. Linux is modeled on which operating system?
   a. Windows
   b. UNIX
   c. Chrome OS
   d. VMS
   e. CP/M

2. If the access mode number for the owner of a file or directory drops below this on some Linux installations, any future access to this file is blocked.
   a. 5
   b. 8
   c. 1
   d. 7
   e. 6

3. Who was the initial developer responsible for Linux?
   a. Ken Thompson
   b. Linus Torvalds
   c. Steve Jobs
   d. Dennis Ritchie
   e. Fred Linux

4. Which user has the most power and privileges in Linux?
   a. Administrator
   b. Admin
   c. Absolute
   d. Root
   e. Linus

5. What is the command a user invokes to log off when working at the Linux shell?
   a. **exit**
   b. **shutdown**
   c. **bye**
   d. **log off**
   e. **quit**

6. What is the Linux shell command to copy a file?
   a. **cpy**
   b. **rm**
   c. **mv**
   d. **copy**
   e. **cp**

7. What option for the **ls** command lists all files in a directory, including the hidden files?
   a. **-S**
   b. **-F**
   c. **-l**
   d. **-a**
   e. **-t**

8. What is the shell command (and option) to turn off a Linux computer immediately?
   a. **sudo down**
   b. **sudo shutdown now**
   c. **exit stat**
   d. **off now**
   e. **power off**

9. What feature preserves your open apps and data, but allows another user to log in to his or her own session on the same computer?
   a. Daemon
   b. Lock screen
   c. Live image
   d. Switch users
   e. Guest

10. What organization formed in 1988 to lobby for an "open" UNIX after AT&T formed a partnership with Sun Microsystems to develop a single proprietary UNIX?
    a. GNU
    b. Apache
    c. Ubuntu
    d. BASH
    e. OSF

11. Which command displays a text file one page (screenful) at a time?
    a. **mkdir**
    b. **more**
    c. **pwd**
    d. **cd**
    e. **rm**

12. What command can you use at the CLI to temporarily borrow the privileges of the most powerful account in a Linux system?
    a. **sudo**
    b. **root**
    c. **rm**
    d. **switch users**
    e. **chmod**

13. Which Linux command can you use to change file permissions?
    a. **cd**
    b. **ls**
    c. **more**
    d. **chmod**
    e. **rm**

14. Why would a Linux administrator use shell commands rather than a Linux GUI when creating many users at once?
    a. The shell commands are more intuitive.
    b. Linux GUIs are too cryptic.

c. Shell commands are faster.

d. The Linux CLI is more secure.

e. You cannot create users from a Linux GUI.

15. When in the terminal window, which command would return you to your Home directory, no matter what directory is current?

a. **cd ..**

b. **cd ~**

c. **cd /**

d. **chmod ~**

e. **cd.**

Essay Quiz

1. List and explain the reasons that Linux has not yet taken over the desktop OS market.

2. Discuss how your school or work could use Linux.

3. Discuss how open-source software can benefit an organization.

4. The Helping Hand, a charitable organization, has asked you to set up its computer systems. The organization has a very limited budget. Describe how Linux can allow users to be productive while costing very little.

5. Explain the merits of **sudo,** as implemented in Ubuntu Linux.

Lab Projects

LAB PROJECT 8.1

The GNOME GUI includes workspaces, a feature not described in this chapter. Research the workspaces and write a few sentences describing the notion of workspaces in Linux.

LAB PROJECT 8.2

Research the open-source debate.

Search on-line for recent articles on the open-source debate.

Look at the arguments in favor of open source versus those in favor of proprietary operating systems.

Determine which side of this debate you support and give your reasons.

LAB PROJECT 8.3

Research and describe the Suspend and Hibernate options sometimes available from the GNOME Shutdown menu (accessed from the icon on the far right of the menu bar).

chapter

9 Chromebooks and Chrome OS

Source: Google LLC

Learning Outcomes

In this chapter, you will learn how to:

LO **9.1** Personalize Chrome OS on a Chromebook.

LO **9.2** Use the features of Chrome OS and Google.

LO **9.3** Install apps into Chrome OS.

LO **9.4** Manage files in Chrome OS.

LO **9.5** Configure security in Chrome OS.

Chrome OS, the desktop operating system by Google, is based on their popular Chrome browser. Both the Chrome browser and Chrome OS have their roots in Linux. Earlier browsers were written in the 1990s to support how we experienced the Internet then, and they were added to as new uses and services evolved on the web. The Chrome browser, introduced in 2008, was created to support how we work on the web in the new millennium.

Similarly, the existing desktop operating systems have decades of added features and often contain code to support obsolete hardware and software. When Google announced their Google Chrome Operating System project in July of 2009, they described their vision: the new OS would be open source and "lightweight," meaning the software would be small and fast. They also promised "speed, simplicity, and security."

Competitors dismissed the idea of an operating system based on a browser. Google, perhaps more than other tech giants, appreciated that millions of people, especially millennials, spent most of their time on the Internet using a browser. So, they went ahead despite the naysayers. Now, the most popular vehicle for the Chrome OS, Chromebooks, have taken the education market by storm, squeezing out the more expensive Apple iPads, the longtime leader in the classroom. ❋

LO 9.1 | Getting Started with Chrome OS

What became known as the Chromium OS project moved quickly. Google released the Chrome OS source code, based on the Linux kernel, to developers late in 2009. By 2011, you could buy a Chromebook, a laptop with the Chrome OS preinstalled. Chromebooks have also come a long way since their introduction. Several manufacturers produce them, and most of them come with a modified keyboard to support Chrome OS features. There are other types of computers that manufacturers sell with Chrome OS preinstalled, such as the Chromebox, a desktop computer, and the tiny Chromebit dongle that plugs into a TV or computer display's HDMI port. Add a wireless mouse and/or keyboard, and you have a Chrome OS computer. However, to keep things simple, and to focus primarily on the operating system, we will use the term Chromebook when discussing a computer manufactured to support Chrome OS. In this section, we begin with the out-of-box setup of a Chromebook. Your experience may be different, as both the Chrome OS and the hardware products that support it are quickly changing and often improving.

First Power Up and Sign In

As you prepare to unpack a new Chromebook, let's set expectations about what you will eventually see on the screen. If you are familiar with the publicity around the introduction of the Chromebook, you may expect what they promised at that time: "you can do everything on the web," "no programs," and "no desktop background (no rolling hills of green)." Chrome OS on Chromebooks has all those features that they promised would not be there. In addition to a full-screen mode, the Chrome browser can be resized, revealing a customizable desktop background. Oh, and you can choose to have that background be rolling hills of green or anything else you want. Chrome OS, while still a platform for working and storing your data completely in the cloud (if you wish), now allows you to access local files and devices. Many of us still have ties to the apps running on our desktops or mobile devices, as well as those devices sitting on our desks or local networks, and Chrome OS now supports apps created for the mobile Android OS. You might call this being "downward compatible."

Before unpacking and powering up a new Chromebook, ensure that you have Internet connectivity via a Wi-Fi network (unless your Chromebook can directly connect to a cellular network). You will need to know the network name and password. Then follow the manufacturer's instructions for unpacking, connecting to a power source, and turning on. After that, the steps are nearly identical across Chromebooks.

Initial Setup and Sign in with an existing Google account

When you power up a new Chromebook, the first screen contains a Welcome window on a colorful background. Select your language, keyboard, and your Wi-Fi network and click the Continue button. Next review and accept the Terms of Use. After this, the Chrome OS updates, then it connects to Google, and the Google Sign-in prompt appears. If you already have a Google user account, a Google Account, sign in now by entering your username, selecting Next, and entering your password. If you do not have a Google account, you can create one at this point by selecting Create account at the bottom of the sign-in box as shown in Figure 9-1. The account you use for this initial sign in will be the owner of the Chromebook—the only account that can make significant changes to Chromebook settings.

Creating a Google Account

Google accounts are based on the Google Mail service with an email address ending in *@gmail.com*. A Google account gives you access to all the Google apps. Create a

Google account from any device with a browser and Internet connection. You will be required to enter your first and last names. These do not have to be unique because you will be giving Google other identifying information. What must be unique is your username, a name of at least 6 characters, but less than 30, that may include letters, numbers, and periods. When you enter your first and last names, Google will generate a possible username—one that is unique to Gmail. If you do not accept that username, you must create one that is unique.

Before you create a Google account be prepared with several options for your username. Google mail is so popular, the username you want to use may well be rejected because it belongs to someone else. The authors have both had Google accounts for several years. A lot of things have changed since then, so we both decided we needed to experience creating a new Google account. It took Chuck five attempts to create a unique username that Google would accept as his new Gmail address. He entered that name in frustration, not really expecting it to be accepted. Step-by-Step 9.01 will walk you through creating a Google Account and performing some simple tasks in Google to get you started with the Google Account features.

FIGURE 9–1 The Google sign-in box.
Source: Google LLC

Step-by-Step 9.01

Creating a New Google Account

In this hands-on exercise, create a Google account. To complete this exercise, you will need:

- Any computing device with a browser and Internet connection.

- One or more possible usernames and a complex password of eight or more characters with a mix of letters, numbers, and symbols.

Step 1

Point your browser to **https://accounts.google.com/signup**. The *Create your Google Account* page opens. Enter your first and last names. Then either accept the username generated by Google or create a new one that passes their uniqueness test. Then enter a password, twice, and select *Next*.

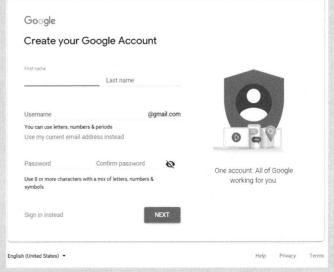

Source: Google LLC

Step 2

On the next page, there are two optional fields (phone number and recovery email address) and two mandatory fields (birthday and gender). Complete this page and select *Next*.

Source: Google LLC

Step 3

On the Privacy and Terms page, read the Terms of Service, scrolling down to the bottom as you read. Before you accept these terms, select *More Options*.

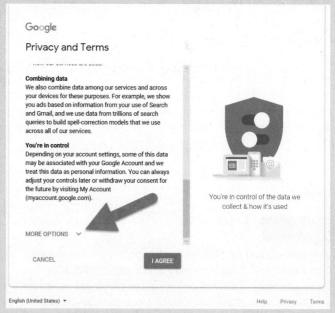

Source: Google LLC

Review the additional options and make any necessary changes. Then, if you accept the terms, select *I Agree*.

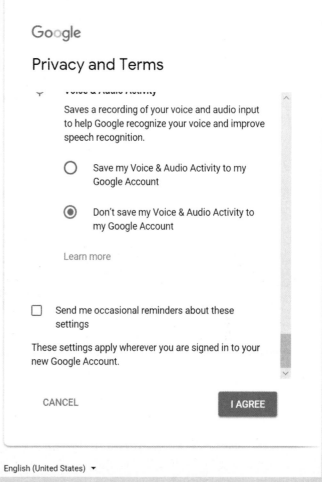

Source: Google LLC

Next Google opens your *My Account* page where you can make a variety of changes to security and privacy settings. You may take time to make changes here or wait until later in this chapter when we look more closely at some of these options.

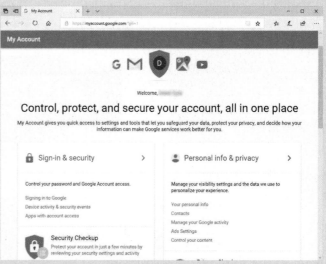

Source: Google LLC

First Look at the Chrome OS Desktop

After signing in to a new Chromebook, your first look at the desktop includes an invitation to take a tour (Figure 9–2). If you are new to the Chrome OS, take the time to do this. In this chapter, we will give a brief tour of some of the highlights to get you started in the Chrome OS, but there is much more to know about Chrome OS, and how to navigate all the services available to you. Google's tutorials are a great beginning.

The area along the bottom of the screen is the shelf. Shortcuts to features and apps reside here. It acts much like the Windows taskbar. The shelf starts out with a few shortcuts, but as you use Chrome OS, you can choose to pin apps to the shelf to launch them directly from there. However, there are other ways to launch apps.

The shortcut on the far left of the shelf, a white circle on a black background, opens the Launcher, which scrolls up from the bottom of the screen like a vertical drawer behind the shelf. Click the Launcher shortcut to see shortcuts for recent apps, shown in Figure 9-3. The Launcher is more than an app launcher; it shows you all the apps installed into your Chrome OS. It has multiple pages, depending on how many apps are installed. A small button sits on the Launcher, just above the shelf, as shown in Figure 9-3. Click this to see more apps (Figure 9-4). Look carefully on the right side of this page of the Launcher to see two small buttons. The white one represents the current page of apps. Click on the second button to open another page. When you find an app you wish to launch, click on its shortcut in the launcher or on the shelf.

Any time you wish to learn more about your Chromebook and the Chrome OS, simply open the Get Help app, a green square with a white question mark (Figure 9-5). On a new Chromebook, the *Get Help* shortcut is visible on the shelf, but if you pin many apps to the shelf, the Get Help shortcut will not be visible until you open the Launcher. It may depend on the screen size and resolution, but we found that once fourteen apps are pinned to the shelf, Chrome OS creates an additional row of

> *Note:* The shelf in Figures 9–3 and 9–4 has many more shortcuts than shown in Figure 9–2. These last two screenshots were taken after several days of working with a new Chromebook. As experienced Windows users, we decided to pin our favorite apps to the shelf. Learn how to pin apps to the shelf later in this chapter.

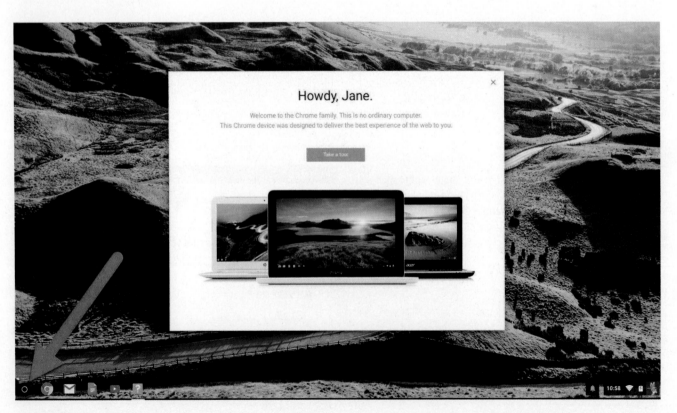

FIGURE 9–2 The Chrome OS desktop. Take a tour or open the Launcher from the button on the far left of the shelf.
Source: Google LLC

FIGURE 9–3 The Launcher showing recent apps. Click the button on the bottom to access more apps.
Source: Google LLC

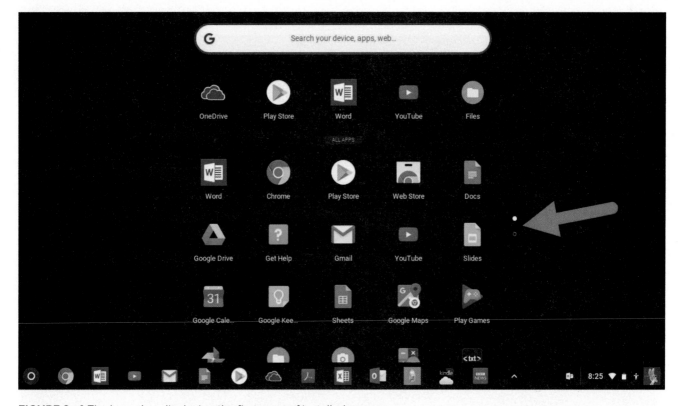

FIGURE 9–4 The Launcher displaying the first page of installed apps.
Source: Google LLC

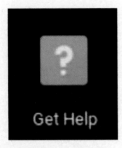

FIGURE 9–5 Click or tap to open the Get Help app.
Source: Google LLC

shortcuts that only displays when you click an up arrow added to the shelf between app shortcuts and the notification area, a shortcut with a bell icon that expands to a bar to hold the shortcuts of apps and services with notices for you. Next to that is the status tray. The status tray resides on the far right of the shelf. Click anywhere on the status tray and a pop-up message box gives the current status of network connections, battery life, who is signed in, and more.

The Chrome OS *Get Help* app is easy to use; the *Take a Tour* option on the *Get started* page takes you directly to the desktop where pop-up windows identify objects and their use, as shown in Figure 9–6. *Get Help* offers tutorials in very small doses so that you can stop at any time or continue. For instance, the image in Figure 9–6 is the beginning of Take a Tour. Clicking next moves the focus to the status tray, explaining its purpose.

Options for Ending Your Chrome OS Session

OK, imagine you have been researching a paper or entertaining yourself with videos on your Chromebook. Now you need to go to lunch, exit from a commuter train, go out for the evening, or simply stop what you are doing for now. You can sign out, put Chrome OS (and your Chromebook) to sleep, lock the screen, switch users, or power off.

Sign Out from Chrome OS

To sign out of Chrome OS, click or tap the Status bar and then in the pop-up (Figure 9–7) select *Sign out*. The Chrome OS ends your session and returns to the

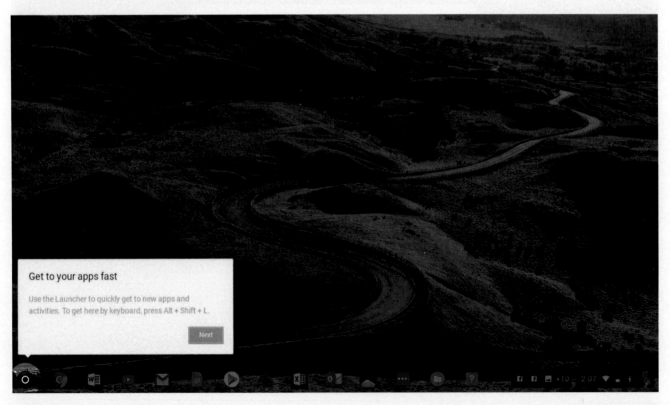

Get to your apps fast

Use the Launcher to quickly get to new apps and activities. To get here by keyboard, press Alt + Shift + L.

Next

FIGURE 9–6 Take a tour with Get Help.
Source: Google LLC

sign-in screen with the sign-in box in the center of the screen and a few other options along the bottom. From the sign-in screen, you can choose to browse as a Guest, add a user, shut down, or sign in with another Google account. You can also sign out of Chrome OS quickly using the Ctrl+Search+Q keyboard shortcut twice.

Put a Chromebook to Sleep

Put your Chromebook to sleep by simply closing the lid. That's it. At present, we are not aware of shortcut keys for this action. Sleep keeps your open apps and windows intact, keeps you signed in, and simply puts the computer into low power mode. If you are on battery power, do not leave it in sleep for a long time (overnight, days) or you could draw down the battery. Then you will not be able to bring it back up until you plug it in to power. To resume, simply open the lid and Chrome resumes with all your open apps and windows.

Lock the Screen

To lock the screen, click or tap the Status bar. Then, in the pop-up, select the Lock, as shown in Figure 9-8. The keyboard shortcut for locking the screen is Search+L. Locking the screen does not sign you out and leaves everything open, behind the sign-in screen. You are locked out until you sign in.

Switch Users

If you have added another Google Account to your device, you may choose to switch users to give the other user time on the Chromebook. To do this, sign out and click *Sign in another user.* Later we will look at how to add a user to your Chromebook.

Power off Your Device

To power off your Chromebook, click or tap the Status bar. Then, in the pop-up, select the Power button, as shown in Figure 9-9. You can also do this by holding the physical power button on the device until it completely powers down to a black screen.

LO 9.2 | Getting Acquainted with Chrome OS and Google Features

In this section, learn how to find the Chrome OS version number, personalize the Chrome OS desktop, and prepare to print from Chrome OS.

Finding the Chrome OS Version Number

An important feature of Chrome OS is its automatic update. You might be thinking that we claimed this was true of all the other operating systems discussed so far, and you would be correct. Maybe the difference is that, for the most part, you don't know that Chrome OS is updating and, more importantly, you don't need to care what version is installed, but sometimes you want to know the version number of Chrome OS installed on your device. Perhaps someone on your favorite social media site boasted of doing things in the Chrome OS, but you can't seem to do those things.

What comes to mind is printing to the printer sitting on your desk. It was more challenging in earlier versions of the OS but has greatly improved. Some users experienced it ahead of others because they participated in a preview program, but others may not have had that ability simply because their Chrome OS was a few days late in updating, compared to the computers of your social media friends.

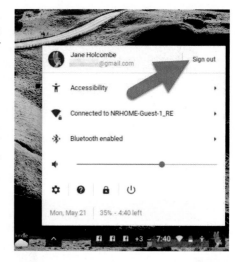

FIGURE 9–7 Sign Out.
Source: Google LLC

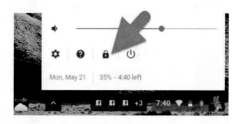

FIGURE 9–8 Lock the screen.
Source: Google LLC

FIGURE 9–9 Power off the computer.
Source: Google LLC

try this!

Practice leaving your Chromebook session.

Experiment with different ways to leave and return to your Chrome OS desktop. Try this:

1. Sign out and sign in again. First sign out from the Status menu, sign back in and then sign out using the keyboard shortcut Search+Q (twice).
2. Put the Chromebook to sleep by closing the lid. Wait a few minutes, and then open the lid again and resume working.
3. Lock the screen by selecting the Lock from the Status menu. Sign back in.
4. Turn off your Chromebook.

FIGURE 9–10 The Main menu button for Settings.
Source: Google LLC

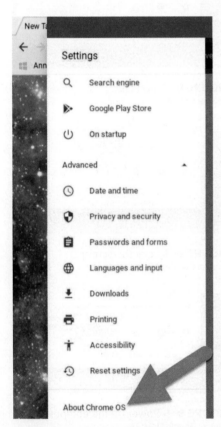

FIGURE 9–11 *About Chrome OS* is at the very bottom of the Settings Main menu.
Source: Google LLC

To see the version of Chrome OS on your Chromebook, click or tap the Status bar and then in the pop-up open Settings. In Settings, click on the Main menu button at the top left of the window, as shown in Figure 9-10. When the Settings menu opens scroll down and click or tap About Chrome OS (Figure 9-11). This opens the About Chrome OS settings, shown in Figure 9-12.

Personalizing the Desktop

Personalize Chrome OS by changing Shelf settings, selecting wallpaper or a solid background.

Shelf Settings

Personalize the background of your Chrome OS desktop. The quickest way to access these settings is to right-click on an empty area of the desktop. This opens the context menu, shown in Figure 9-13. In this example, moving the pointer to Shelf position opened choices for that option. As with the Windows task bar, you can move the shelf to either side or back to the default position on the bottom of the screen. The top choice allows you to autohide the shelf so that it is hidden until you move your cursor to its position, then it opens.

Wallpaper

The desktop setting with the most impact is *Set wallpaper.* As you can see in Figure 9-14, set wallpaper offers a variety of background wallpaper pictures in categories: Landscape, Urban, and Nature. You can also select a solid for the background or you can create a custom wallpaper from a file of your choice by selecting the Custom choice.

Appearance Settings

Beyond the Wallpaper settings, personalize Chrome OS with the Appearance settings. To do that, select the Settings button from the Status pop-up box (Figure 9-15). This opens the Settings window, containing many of the same settings you would see from the Chrome browser running in other operating systems. There are a few additional settings in Chrome OS to take care of some necessary system-wide settings, such as Wi-Fi and Bluetooth. Currently, the Chrome OS browser settings begin with the

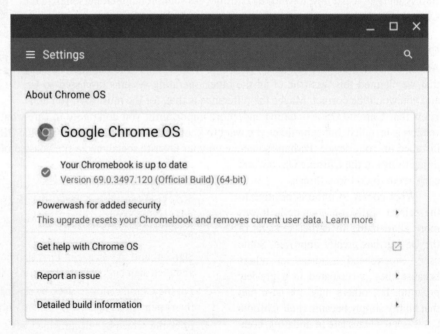

FIGURE 9–12 The Chrome OS version information.
Source: Google LLC

People category, but within some of the categories, there are settings that are found in the Chrome OS, but not in the browser on other OSs.

To see the Appearance settings, scroll down to *Appearance,* as shown in Figure 9-16. This group of settings includes Wallpaper—just another way to access those settings. While Wallpaper lets you modify the desktop background, these other settings are mainly for within the Chrome browser window. Figure 9-17 shows the browser window with a theme selected from the Chrome Web Store.

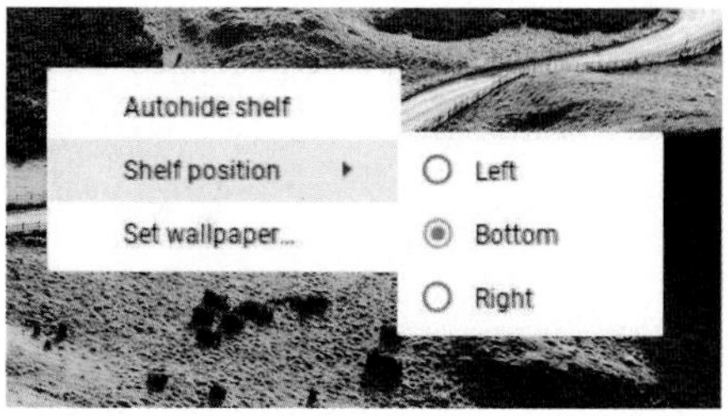

Printing in Chrome OS

Many tasks are easy to do in Chrome OS, thanks to our familiarity with working in the cloud. Printing is not one of those easy tasks, at least not at first. Let's take the example of our new Chromebook; before we could print, we first connected our printer to Google Cloud Print, and then we could print from our Chromebook or any device on which we signed in with the same Google account. We expect this to become easier as time goes on.

Connect Your Printer to Google Cloud Print

Before you can print in Chrome OS you must associate your printer with your Google Account and connect it to Google Cloud Print. First, sign in to a Windows or Apple computer, con-

nect your printer to that computer, ensure that the printer is connected to power, and then power-on the printer. Follow the instructions in Step-by-Step 9.02 to associate printers with your Google Account and Google Cloud Print.

FIGURE 9–13 The *Shelf position* settings.
Source: Google LLC

try this!

Use Appearance Setting in Chrome OS

Do you want to change the looks of the windows in Chrome? Try this:

1. In Settings, Appearance, select *Browser themes.* In the Google Web Store, select a free theme for the Chrome browser. Try out the theme. If you do not want it, simply return to the *Browser themes* and select *Reset to Default.*

2. In Settings, Appearance, use the Show home button to display (or not) the home button displays in the bar at the top of the Chrome browser window. Leave it at the setting you prefer.

3. In Settings, Appearance, experiment with turning the bookmarks bar on and off and select the setting you prefer.

4. Experiment with the two font settings and the page zoom, going back and forth between the Settings window and the Chrome browser to view your changes. When you are finished, close the Settings window.

FIGURE 9–14 The *Set Wallpaper* options.
Source: Google LLC

FIGURE 9–15 The Settings button.
Source: Google LLC

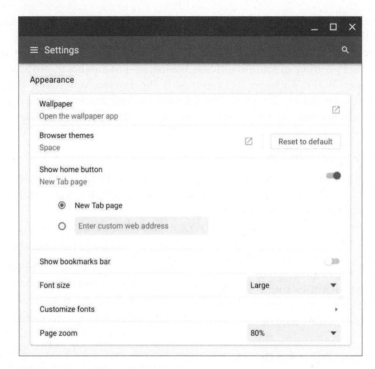

FIGURE 9–16 The Appearance category in Settings.
Source: Google LLC

FIGURE 9–17 The Chrome browser with a theme selected from the Google Web Store.
Source: Google LLC

Step-by-Step 9.02

Preparing to Print in Chrome OS

In this hands-on exercise, you will associate printers to your account in Google Cloud Print. To complete this exercise, you will need:

- A Windows PC or Apple running the macOS.
- A printer connected to the Windows or macOS computer.
- The Chrome browser installed and running in Windows or macOS.

- To be signed in to the Chrome browser with a Google account.
- A Chromebook or other device with the Chrome OS installed.
- To be logged on to the Chromebook with the same Google account.

Step 1

With the printer powered on and connected to the computer, open the Chrome browser on the computer and click the menu button in the upper corner of the Chrome browser.

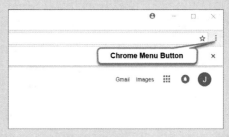

Source: Google LLC

Step 2

In the Chrome browser menu, select Settings.

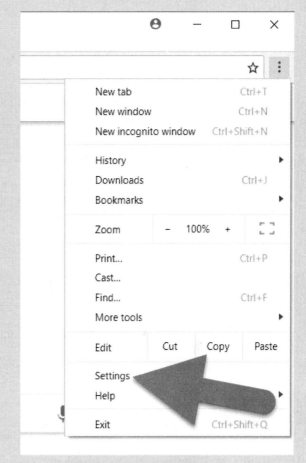

Source: Google LLC

Step 3

The Chrome browser's settings open in a new tab. Scroll down to the bottom until Advanced is available. Click *Advanced.* Advanced settings will display in the same window.

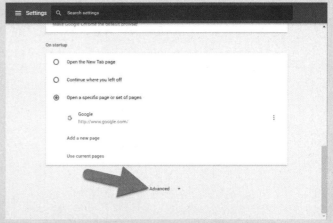

Source: Google LLC

Step 4

Scroll down through the Advanced settings to the Printing category. Select Google Cloud Print.

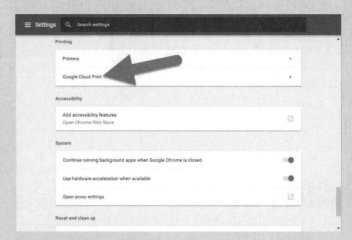

Source: Google LLC

Step 5

Click *Manage Cloud Print devices.* If prompted, sign in with your Google Account.

Source: Google LLC

Step 6

Select the printers you want to connect, and then click *Add printer(s).*

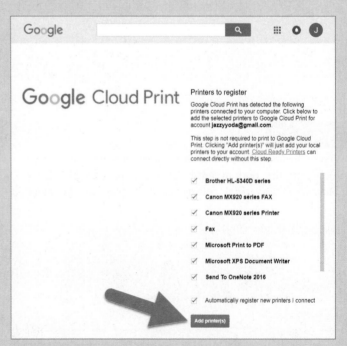

Source: Google LLC

Now you are ready to print from any app installed on your Chromebook if you are signed in with the same Google account.

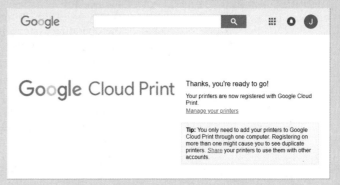

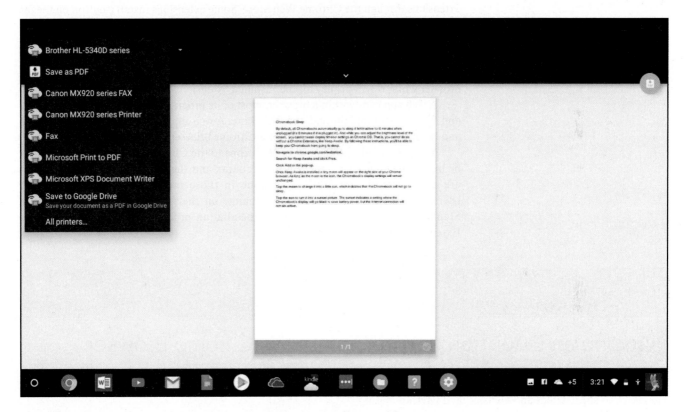

FIGURE 9–18 Selecting a printer using Microsoft Word in the Chrome OS.

Printing from Apps in the Chrome OS

Once a printer is associated with your Google account and connected to Google Cloud Print, you can print to that printer from your Chromebook using just about any app, including the Chrome browser, Microsoft Office apps, and Google's Web apps, such as Docs, Gmail, and more. Figure 9–18 shows the Microsoft Word print page and the list of printers available.

LO 9.3 | Installing Extensions and Apps into Chrome OS

While all operating systems evolve and gain new features over time, Chrome OS seems to have evolved in leaps and bounds in its short lifetime, especially regarding the apps it supports. At first both the apps (web apps) and data resided in the Google cloud.

A web app runs from a website within the Chrome browser and is not installed into the operating system. In contrast, a browser extension adds features to the Chrome browser. Shop for Web apps and browser extensions at the Google Web Store. This tethering to Google continues, but the OS has been beefed up to support more and more types of apps, including Linux apps.

In this section, we first look at adding browser extensions and web apps. Then we will look at installing such standard productivity tools as Microsoft Office. Finally, check out how Android apps are installed and run in Chrome OS.

Chrome Browser Extensions and Web Apps

Strictly speaking, a browser extension is not an app, but an add-on that adds features to the Chrome browser. Examples of extensions are password managers for storing your passwords and many aids to better and more secure browsing. Acquire Chrome extensions through the Chrome Web Store. Some extensions install a button on the far right of the Chrome browser toolbar.

To see what extensions are installed into your Chrome browser (in Chrome OS or in other operating systems), open the Chrome menu button on the far right of the tools bar, point to *More Tools,* in the pop-up menu select *Extensions.* The Chrome browser window will display all the installed extensions and web apps.

A web app runs within a browser, most of its program code is run from a website, and it is also acquired through the Web Store. A web app will be listed in the Launcher and launched as an app, albeit within a Chrome browser window.

You cannot add extensions or Web apps to the Chrome browser using a school or business Google account. Those accounts and the systems on which they run are administered centrally by someone in those organizations, and individual users are limited in what they can change on their school or work computers. Step-by-Step 9.03 walks through the installation procedure for Chrome Browser Extensions and Chrome Web apps.

Step-by-Step 9.03

Adding an Extension or Web App to the Chrome Browser

In this hands-on exercise, you will browse through the Google Web store, select an extension and later an app for installation into your Chrome browser. To complete this exercise, you will need the following:

- A Chromebook or other device with the Chrome OS installed.
- You must be logged on to the Chromebook with your personal Google account.

Step 1

Locate the Web Store app on the Chrome OS shelf and click or tap it.

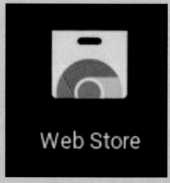

Source: Google LLC

Step 2

In the Web Store window, select Extensions in the left column, the right pane displays extension choices. From here, you can search or scroll down to browse for extensions.

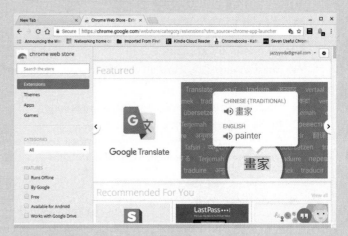

Source: Google LLC

Step 3

Select an extension and check it out. Here we are looking at LastPass, a Password Manager. Notice the tabs labeled Overview, Reviews, Support, and Related. We find the reviews very helpful—the more numerous the reviews the more we trust them.

Source: Google LLC

Step 4

When you find an extension you want, simply click the blue *Add to Chrome* button in the upper right of the window. Before Chrome installs the extension, it asks you to confirm that you want it and may give you a warning about the extension. For instance, the warning for LastPass looked like this:

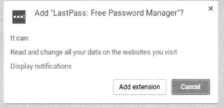

Source: Google LLC

Step 5

After you install an extension, it will appear on the far right on the Chrome browser toolbar. Here we have three extension buttons on the toolbar. They are, from left to right: Wayback Machine, Ghostery, and LastPass.

Source: Google LLC

try this!

Sync Apps and Extensions

You can sync your data across all your devices, selecting what type of data you want to sync. Try this:

1. Open the Status bar and select the Settings button.
2. In the People category, click or tap Sync.
3. Continue to browse through categories, then, to exit *Get Help,* use the close button (an "x") on the upper right of the window.

Select and install Chrome Web apps from the Web Store. Browse for them in the Apps category, as shown in Figure 9-19. Installed Web apps are listed in the Launcher, and you can pin a Web app's shortcut to the Shelf.

You can synchronize your apps and extensions across your devices, if you are signed into your Chrome account. Chrome allows you to select just which type of data you want to sync, or you can choose to sync all data. Figures 9-20 and 9-21 show the complete list of data types.

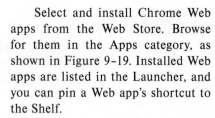

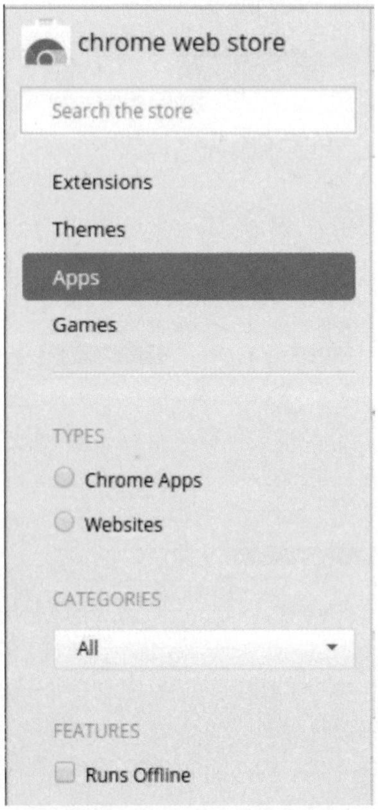

FIGURE 9–19 Select Web Apps from the Web Store.
Source: Google LLC

Android Apps on Chrome OS

The type of app that runs on an Android phone is an **Android app**. There are thousands of Android apps available, and if you have both an Android phone and a device running Chrome OS (a close relative of Android), you want the same apps on both devices.

Installing Android Apps into Chrome OS

Android operating system and the apps that run on it use a small native screen size, so the transition from mobile devices to a different (but related) OS on a much larger screen was a challenge to Chrome OS developers, and perhaps to the Android app developers, but they succeeded. Beginning with Chrome OS version 53, you can install and run your favorite Android apps on your Chromebook. Let's say you use what your learned earlier about finding the version number of your Chrome OS, and you confirm that you have a Chrome OS version 53 or newer. So, you're all set and ready to install Android apps. Well, not quite.

Android apps are installed from the Google Play store. Look for the Play Store shortcut (Figure 9-22) on the Launcher. If the Google Play Store app is not already available in the Launcher, you need to enable it in Chrome OS Settings. Then open the Play Store app (Figure 9-23) from the Launcher and browse for the apps you want and need for your Chromebook.

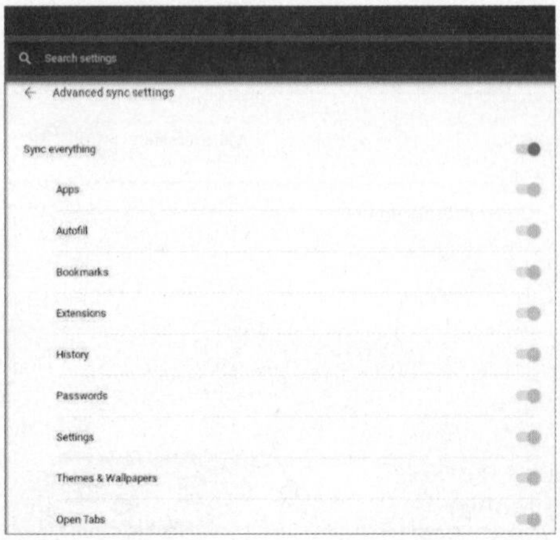

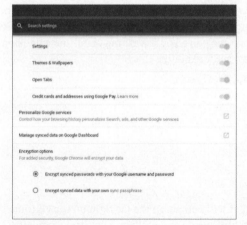

FIGURE 9–20 The top portion of the list of data types for syncing.
Source: Google LLC

FIGURE 9–21 The remaining data types for syncing.
Source: Google LLC

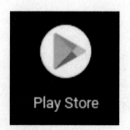

FIGURE 9–22 Launch Play Store.
Source: Google LLC

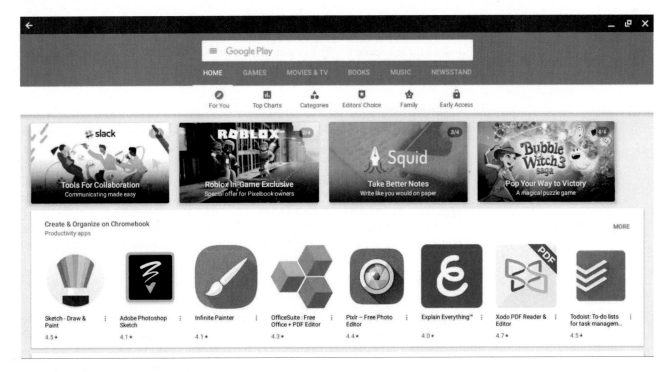

FIGURE 9–23 The Google Play Store app.
Source: Google LLC

As you install and experiment with Android apps on your Chromebook, keep in mind that Android apps were designed to work on smartphone screens, which are a lot smaller than even the smallest Chromebook screens. And when you work in an Android app on a Chromebook, you can use the window maximize, minimize, and restore buttons that switch your window from full screen to minimized to a shortcut on the shelf, to a return to smartphone screen. There are presently some apps that only work in smartphone size. Sure, you can click the maxi button and the window will expand, but the app stays in smart screen mode.

As long-time users of Microsoft Office, we are pleased that the app we need the most, Word, works in both full screen and smartphone screen sizes. And full screen is resizable. Although it does have not all the advanced editing features that we like to use, it is certainly handy. Things are improving rapidly for many Android apps on Chromebooks, but some are not yet available, and some only let you view files, not edit them.

try this!

Enable the Google Play Store App

If your version of Chrome OS is 53 or newer, enable the Google Play Store App in Settings. Try this:

1. Open the Status bar and select the Settings button.
2. Scroll down to the Google Play Store category and click or tap inside that box.
3. Then select the checkbox labeled *Enable Google Play Store*.
4. Now you are ready to shop for Android apps for your Chromebook.

LO 9.4 | File Management in Chrome OS

In this section, we will explore file management in Chrome OS on the Chromebook. The Chrome OS Files app file management program is your main tool for working with files, whether they are local to your OS device or in the cloud. Look on the Launcher or the Shelf for the round shortcut with white folder against a blue background.

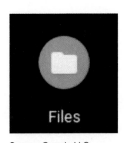

Source: Google LLC

We first look at working with Google Drive, beginning with some basic cloud concepts and then explore Google Drive features, such as their rather complicated calculations for the space devoted to your files. Then we will examine the use of the Files app to access several file types in various locations.

Using Google Drive in Chrome OS

Google Drive is an online storage service for keeping your files, photos, videos, or anything you need to store in a location you can access from your computer, smartphone, or tablet. As you would expect, you can give others access to just what you want them to be able to see or use. Google Drive, like other cloud storage services, is available as a consumer service as well as a business product. Google Drive includes the Google apps that you can use to create and edit many types of documents.

Before we take a closer look at the Chrome OS, let's explore the phenomenon that has made the Chrome OS and the hardware that supports it so timely: cloud computing.

Cloud Basics

The Internet is a worldwide network of networks, an internetwork. For decades, the Internet has been represented in diagrams by a cloud, an image that evolved to hide the complexity of any internetwork. The Internet is the most famous and largest internetwork, but there are also millions of internetworks privately owned by organizations of all types and sizes worldwide, secured behind firewalls, and accessed by authorized users. Such a private internetwork is an intranet.

From the use of an image of a cloud to hide the physical complexity of an internetwork, the term cloud now encompasses all the services offered over the Internet and on intranets, such as storage and apps that run from remote servers. Cloud computing is the use of those services, regardless of their actual location. The simplest and most common cloud-based service is data storage, called cloud storage. Cloud storage services are provided by many sources for all sizes and types of data storage needs. Google offers cloud storage and much more in the way of cloud computing. Their basic services are offered for free. To see a list of Google services, open your Chrome browser. Click on the Google Apps button in the upper right (Figure 9–24) and scroll through the list of apps, as shown in Figure 9–25. In addition to those listed, Google offers a personal assistant (Google Assistant), "smart" messaging through Google Allo and Google Duo, and much more. They also offer hardware products. To learn more about Google services and hardware products, open your browser and do a search on "Google products."

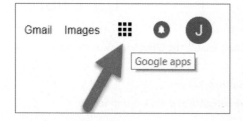

FIGURE 9–24 The Google Apps button opens the apps menu.
Source: Google LLC

Private Cloud

A private cloud is an intranet that is owned or managed for the benefit of a single organization and offers a variety of cloud services to members or employees. A private cloud may physically reside on the organization's servers and networks, or it may be hosted by a service provider who charges by the number of users and the services used. These services are not available to the general public, nor are the services visible to outsiders. Google offers private cloud services to organizations. Your school or employer may use Google or one of several other providers for their private cloud services. In which case, you may have a user account for one of these services at school or work.

Public Cloud

The term public cloud describes the hosting of a variety of free and/or fee-based services over the Internet available to anyone who enrolls in the service. Google offers

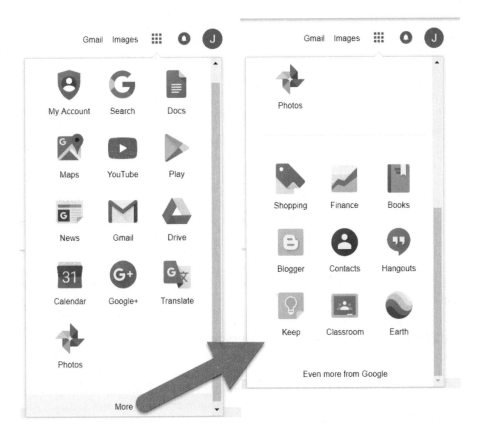

FIGURE 9–25 The Apps menu lists Google apps and services.
Source: Google LLC

public cloud services to individuals. If you have a personal Google account, it is part of their public cloud service.

Why Use Cloud Storage

Everyone has their own reason for moving to cloud storage. As the millennium neared, the authors did not expect to ever need cloud storage because we maintained a file server in our office, saved all our work in one place, and shared our data as we worked together on projects. In that same home office, Jane maintained an Internet-connected email server. The email server was the first to go when we made a major lifestyle change that made moving our email service to the cloud necessary. In 2003, we decided to sell our home in the upper Midwest and live and work full time in a recreational vehicle (RV). We became RVers! We outfitted our motorhome as a home and modified it to give both of us office space. Our dream was to travel the open roads, picking a warm and sunny place with a great view, where we could park for a spell while working to meet our deadlines. This was made possible by cell phones and a mobile satellite dish. Jane even did some remote server management from national parks and roadside rests. To make this change in lifestyle, we found the courage to trust a hosting service with our email needs, but we continued to maintain a local file server—both on the road and eventually in the home base we settled in after three years. The move to replace a private file server with cloud services happened gradually over several years.

For Jane, the move to the cloud happened as she found herself needing to access her personal and work data from multiple computers and devices in her home office as well as from two other locations. Chuck moved to the cloud when his most important client required that he work in the cloud with collaboration services that allow two or more people to work together on documents and entire projects.

The Operating System Connection

You may have heard that all you need to connect to cloud services is a browser, but that is only part of the story. To have data from your local computer synchronize with the cloud storage, you must install client software (an app) that is compatible with the operating system on that computer. The app interacts with the local file system and in most cases appears as a folder in your file management utility. We have found this very true when accessing Google Drive from Windows. When accessing Microsoft's OneDrive cloud storage from Chrome OS, we do indeed need a special app. While the Chrome OS Files app does not give OneDrive a folder, it does allow you to upload to OneDrive.

Getting Started with Google Drive Storage

Your Google account gives you 15 GB of free online storage shared by Google Drive, Gmail, and Google Photos. In addition to Gmail and Google Photos, you have the use of free online Google apps. Google Drive can store individual files up to 5 TB in size if they do not exceed the total storage available for your account. Any files you create with the Google productivity apps (Docs, Sheets, or Slides) won't count against your Google Drive limit. However, it's important to understand the very complex rules about how the type of data you store impacts your Google Drive storage limit:

- Your Gmail messages and attachments (both sent and received) count against your storage limit.
- If you use the Original format option for files saved in Google Photos, they count against your limit and are saved without compression in their original format. You may quickly run out of space using this option, especially if your camera is set to save in the RAW format preferred by professional photographers and many hobbyists. RAW format saves all the unprocessed data for an image and creates very large files.
- You have free unlimited storage for photos and videos saved using Google Photos' High Quality option. The photos must be 16 megapixels or less and videos must have a resolution of 1080p or lower. The High Quality option will compress photos and videos that exceed these limits, and they will also be compressed when synced to the original device that uploaded them.

Upgrading Your Google Drive Plan

If you need more than 15 GB of Google Drive Storage, you can upgrade to one of Google's fee-based plans. If you bought a Chromebook, you may have had the opportunity for a free upgrade for a limited time. In our case, we received 100 GB of Google Drive storage for two years, a plan that would otherwise cost $19.99 a year. This is in addition to the 15 GB of free storage. There are offers of various Google apps and services, depending on the manufacturer of the Chromebook. Google also has various incentives for which they reward account holders with storage upgrades. To see how much space you have available, open the Files app. With My Drive selected, click on the More menu button (three dots) on the right side of the Files window and the menu in Figure 9–26 displays. At the bottom of the menu, it displays the amount of Google Drive space you have available. If you want to buy more

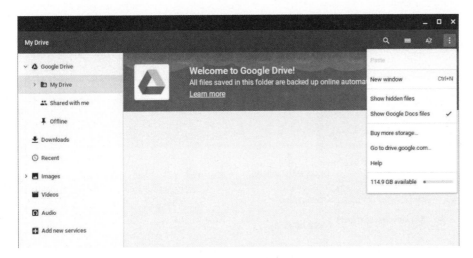

FIGURE 9-26 The menu on the right shows space available and includes the option to buy more storage on Google Drive.
Source: Google LLC

space, then, from this menu, select Buy more storage and you will be connected to Google's Drive Storage page where you can select a plan.

Sharing Files and Folders in Google Drive

Share files and folders by inviting others to view or download files or to collaborate with you. You can store files, save email attachments, and back up photos directly to Drive. Of course, those with whom you share files do not need to have Chrome OS because Google Drive works with Microsoft Windows and with macOS operating systems. It also has apps for Apple iOS and Android. It currently isn't available for Linux operating systems, although there are Linux apps for that. Google Drive also works with the Android and iOS mobile operating systems.

To share files and folders with other Google subscribers, open the Files app, select one or more files or folders in the My Drive to share and right click your selection. When the menu in Figure 9-27 opens select Share with Others. In the *Share with Others* box (see Figure 9-28), enter the email address of one or more people then select the permission and then click Send. You can give people three levels of permission to files and folders, as shown on the right. The permissions are:

- **Can View** allows a person the right to only view a file
- **Can Comment** allows a person to add comments, but not to change a file with edits.
- **Can Edit** grants the permission to edit a file.

On the receiving end of sharing, each person receives an email message like the one shown in Figure 9-29. The recipient simply clicks the *Open button.* This will open the document in the appropriate Google app for the document format (Docs, Sheets, or Slides). To open the document using other software, such as a Microsoft Office app, download the file. Then locate the file in your local Downloads folder and open it with another program. For instance, if we download the asdf.docx file we would then open it using Microsoft Word.

Another way to share is with a Link share. Link sharing is a way to share files and folders with someone who is not a Google subscriber. If you share a link using the *Public on the web* option, or enable the option *Anyone with the link,* then the link is all that is required to access the file or folder and the recipient does not need to sign in to Google to access it. However, if you choose the option *Specific people,* you are back in the Google-verse because you must specify the name or email of the recipients, and they are required to sign in to Google.

Note: While you may share a link with another Google subscriber, sharing via email is more appropriate between Google subscribers, because you may assign permissions.

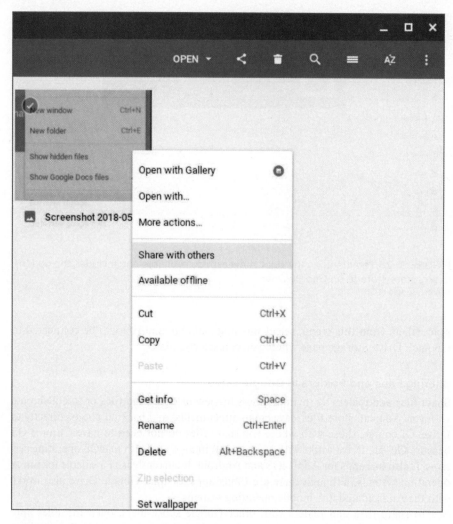

FIGURE 9–27 Select *Share with Others.*
Source: Google LLC

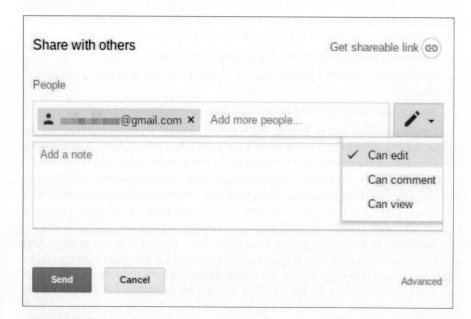

FIGURE 9–28 Enter an email address, select a permission, and send.
Source: Google LLC

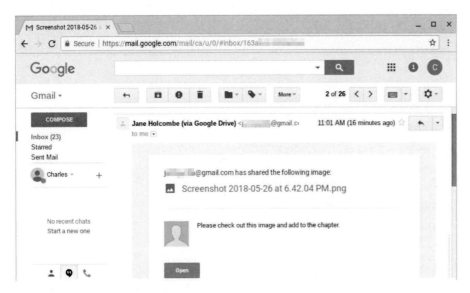

FIGURE 9–29 The email received by the sharing recipient.
Source: Google LLC

Using Local Storage in Chrome OS

The Chrome OS Files app file management program supports several locations for files including:

- Local files on a Chrome OS device,
- Files on directly connected storage devices,
  - USB-connected hard drives and flash drives
  - USB-connected CD and DVD drives (read-only).
- Files in your Google Drive,
- Files stored in another cloud storage service, such as Microsoft OneDrive, Box, and Dropbox.

Location is just one of your concerns about your data files. The file format is very important, and Chrome OS supports many files formats including:

- Microsoft Office Files with these filename extensions: doc, docx, xls, xlsx, ppt (read-only), and pptx (read-only).
- Popular Media Files with these filename extensions: 3gp, avi, mov, mp4, m4a, mp3, mkv, ogv, ogg, oga, webm, and wav.
- Photos and other image files with these filename extensions: bmp, gif, jpg, jpeg, png, and webp
- Compressed files with zip or rar filename extensions.
- Plain text files with the txt extension can be viewed but not edited.
- Portable document files with the pdf extension can be viewed, but not edited.

The Files app is your Chrome OS tool for accessing, moving, copying, deleting, and otherwise managing files. Figure 9–30 shows the Files app opened and focused on the My Drive folder in List view, which shows thumbnail icons.

The Files app also previews files, as shown in Figure 9–31 in Thumbnail view in which the files appear as recognizable images. Other apps are required for opening a file for better viewing or for editing. By default, when you double-click (or double-tap) one of these files, Google will open the appropriate Google app for that file format. Some file types can only be viewed, not edited. This is also referred to as read-only. Many formats, such as most Microsoft Office file types, can be edited with Google

FIGURE 9-30 The Files app in List view showing the My Drive folder.
Source: Google LLC

FIGURE 9-31 The Files app showing previews of the files in the My Drive folder.
Sources: Google LLC; photos ©Jane Holcombe

apps or with other apps, including Microsoft apps, if installed. Yet, others can be launched (run), as in the case of media (video and sound) files. Again, these actions are done with the appropriate Google app for the file format.

Working Offline in Chrome OS

What happens when you do not have an Internet connection, but have a deadline and need to work offline on data normally stored in the cloud? Major Cloud providers saw this problem years ago, and each has a solution (usually an app) for that. In Google's case, they have several offline file viewers so that you can view PDFs and play video or MP3 files offline, but the data must be downloaded beforehand. So, don't wait until you are confronted with that deadline-without-connectivity problem. Prepare.

Add an Extension for Google Drive

Google Docs Offline is the extension you need to work offline with your Google apps. You may already have this extension. To see if it is already installed, open the Chrome menu button on the far right of the tools bar, point to *More Tools,* in the pop-up menu select *Extensions.* The Chrome browser window will display all the installed extensions and web apps. If it is not installed, open the Web store and search on *google docs offline extension.* Then install the extension.

Working on Files Offline

With the Google Docs Offline extension installed, you are ready to turn on syncing between your Google Drive data and your local computer. To do that open My Drive, which opens your Google Drive folders in a Chrome window. Within the window, look for the Settings button (a gear icon) located on the right of the Google Drive (not Chrome browser) button bar near the Help button (a question mark). Select the Settings button, and select Settings (again) from the pop-up menu. In the Offline category, click or tap the check box (if empty) to add a check mark and turn on Syncing of your Google Drive data to the local device. Now Google will automatically save your most recent files to your device for offline. Now you are ready to work with your data offline, as if you were still connected. When your device reconnects to the Internet, your offline data will be synced with Google Drive.

LO 9.5 | Google and Chrome OS Security

To keep your data safe when working in Chrome OS, secure your Google Account and make modifications to the Privacy and Security settings on your Chrome OS computer.

Securing Your Google Account

The Google My Account home page is where you will find settings to make your Google account more secure, change your privacy settings, and manage your account preference.

Step-by-Step 9-4 explores security and privacy settings for your Google account. Among the tasks we will explore is Security Checkup, which enumerates devices from which you have logged in and used Google services, recent security activity, and whether or not you have Two-step Verification turned on. Then check your settings for *Find Your Phone,* which can be enabled on any mobile device running Android or Apple iOS. Google already knows any device on which you have used your Google account. However, Google does not turn on the Find Your Phone service for each device; you get to decide if you want to do that.

The last task in Step-by-Step 9.04 is turning on 2-Step Verification. Google is just one of many online services offering two-step verification to add an additional step to signing in beyond entering the correct password. We highly recommend it. After all, your password could be stolen or guessed. When you enable 2-Step Verification, you give the online service a method of sending a one-time verification code back to you via a predefined method. Originally, the choices were e-mail, voice message, or text message. The voice and text message options are also referred to as Over the Phone (OTP). All of these require that you have a way of retrieving the code at the time you are attempting to sign in. Many services, including Google now offer enhancements to 2-Step Verification that makes it possible to verify your sign in when it is inconvenient or impossible to retrieve the code. You can have Google generate a list of Backup codes that you save to a file and/or print out and keep handy for those when you cannot be directly verified, such as when you are traveling and need to sign in but do not have cellular service. Another option, once you have 2-step verification enabled in your account, is the *Google Prompt* app. Add this to your phone so that when you are asked for the 2-step verification code on another device, you will see the Google Prompt on your phone with *Yes* and *No* options. Then you only need to tap *Yes.* Add this app to your phone through your Google Account 2-Step Verification settings page. There are even more options that you can explore in your Google Account's security settings.

Note: Google requires JavaScript for the Security Checkup, Privacy Checkup, and other wizard-type features that guide you through steps for configuring settings. If you have disabled JavaScript, you will see a message, and you can enable your browser's JavaScript or choose to run an "alternate version" of the Account Settings. This means that you will not be helped through the steps, but will have a simpler interface to the settings.

Step-by-Step 9.04

Exploring Google Account Security and Privacy Settings

In this hands-on exercise, browse through your Google Account settings and determine the settings that will keep you more secure while allowing you to work within the Google environment. The exercise is written for any device that allows you to connect to Google and manage your Account settings. We used the Chrome browser on a Chromebook for the screenshots.

- An Internet-connected device with a browser.
- Your personal Google account.

Step 1

From your browser (any browser), sign in to Google unless you are already signed in. In the upper right corner of the page, click on the button representing your user account. Then click on the *My Account* button.

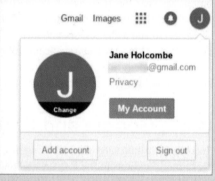

Source: Google LLC

Step 2

This page will display. Under *Sign-in & security,* locate *Security Checkup* and select *Get Started.*

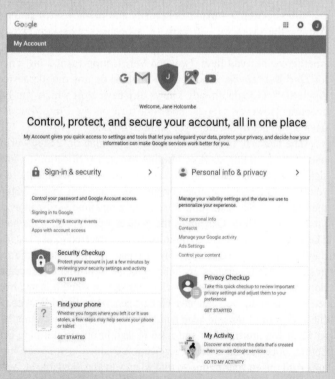

Source: Google LLC

On the Sign-in and Security page, select *Security Checkup*. Note the results and select *Continue to Your Google Account* to return to the main My Account page.

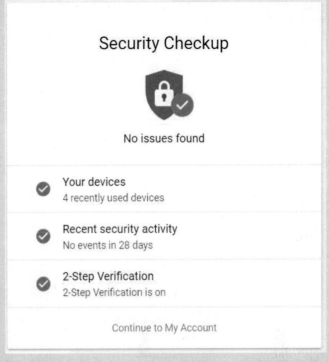

Source: Google LLC

Under *Find your phone*, select *Get Started*. Even if you have never configured this service, it will be aware of any Android or Apple iOS device if you used your Google account in any way on that device. This shows that Google is aware of Jane's iPhone and her old iPad but is not aware of her new iPad. If you wish to turn on the Find Your Phone service for a device, select that device. You will be prompted to provide your Google password to enable it.

Source: Google LLC

Select the back arrow on the top left of *Find your phone* and return to the main *My Account page.* Under *Sign-in & Security,* select *Signing in to Google.* Then select *2-Step* Verification. When requested, provide your password and click *Next.* If you are setting this up for the first time, you will need to provide a mobile phone number. Now, whenever you sign in to a new device, or make an Account change, a code will be sent to your mobile phone, and you must enter it into the box, shown here.

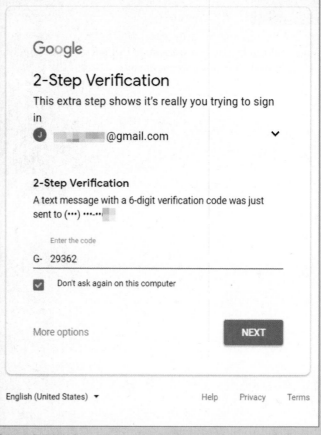

Source: Google LLC

Securing Chrome OS

In addition to securing your Google account, Secure Chrome OS through the *Privacy and Security* settings and the *Passwords and Forms* settings. Both are located in the Advanced Settings.

Privacy and Security

Some settings ask you to allow or disallow Google to gather your data and other information about your activities in Chrome OS. Other settings help to protect you from outside threats. The *Privacy and Security* page has an exhaustive list of possible settings, as you can see in Figure 9-32. Most of these are simply turned on and off like a light switch, but the three at the bottom require more work. We suggest you ignore Manage certificates unless you know how to manage them. Some of these settings are about data gathered by Google to provide their services, such as Manage Certificates, carefully review Content settings, which impact your privacy because this is where you control what data is collected (Cookies), whether apps can access your location or control your camera or microphone. Explore these settings and decide how to configure these options.

Finally, Chrome OS has both an autofill service and a password manager. These settings are lumped together under *Passwords and Forms,* located just below the *Privacy and Security* settings, as shown in Figure 9-33. Autofill settings lets you enable or disable Chrome's autofill service, that saves your personal information and provides it when

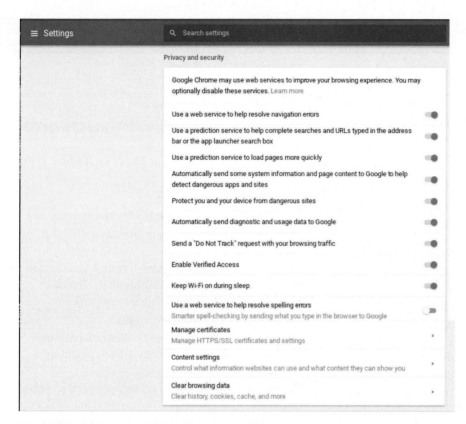

FIGURE 9–32 *Privacy and Security* settings.
Source: Google LLC

Passwords and forms

Autofill settings
Enable Autofill to fill out forms in a single click

Manage passwords
Offer to save your web passwords

FIGURE 9–33 *Passwords and Forms* settings.
Source: Google LLC

you are completing forms online. Control what information is saved and used by Autofill through settings for saved addresses and saved credit cards.

Select *manage passwords* to open a page where you can control this service (off or on), allow or disallow auto sign-in, centrally manage your passwords, and configure passwords for each website.

try this!

Explore Chrome OS Security Settings

There are dozens of security settings for Chrome OS. Have you explored these settings and thought about how they impact you? Try this:

1. Open Chrome OS Settings, scroll to the bottom of the list, and click or tap Advanced.
2. Scroll down to *Privacy and Security* and consider each setting. Chrome OS comes with most of these turned on. Experiment with turning them off and see how it affects how you work in Chrome OS.
3. Move on to *Passwords and Forms*. Check out the Forms settings. Have you added saved addresses or credit cards?
4. Check out *Manage Passwords*. If you have been using Chrome OS for a while, you may have allowed it to automatically sign you in to websites. Is there a list of websites and passwords saved? Decide if you want to remove any.
5. When finished, close the Settings window.

Chapter Summary

After reading this chapter and completing the exercises, you should understand the following facts about the Chrome OS.

Getting Started with Chrome OS

- The Chrome OS operating system is based on the Chrome web browser.
- Chrome OS comes preinstalled on computers, such as the Chromebook, Chromebox, and Chrome promises that you can do everything on the web, with web apps and browser extensions.
- Chrome OS supports Android mobile apps.
- Be ready to use or create a Google Account during the first power-on of a Chromebook. This first account is the owner of that device and the only person who can make significant changes to the Chromebook settings.
- The Get Help app and Google's tutorials and are worth taking the time to browse through. They present steps and concepts in a few minutes, and you pick the time to learn.
- Desktop objects include the Launcher, shelf, notification area, status tray, and more.
- To end a Chrome OS session sign out, put the device to sleep, lock the screen, switch user, or power off the device.

Getting Acquainted with Chrome OS and Google Features

- Find the Chrome OS version number in the About Chrome OS option on the main Settings menu of the devices Settings.
- Personalize the Chrome OS desktop by changing the wallpaper or background settings.
- The Appearance category in Chrome OS Settings gives more options, including browser themes and other settings that affect the browser.
- Associate printers with your account through Google Cloud Print.
- Print to both network and directly connected printers.

Installing Apps into Chrome OS

- A Google Account gives you access to several free Google Apps.
- The Chrome Web Store is your source for Chrome browser extensions and web apps.
- Chrome browser extensions add features to the Chrome browser.
- A web app is not installed into the operating system and runs from a website within the Chrome browser.
- Android mobile apps can be installed into Chrome OS version 53 or newer.
- The Google Play Store is your source for Android apps.

File Management in Chrome OS

- The Files app is the Chrome OS file management tool.
- Manage data stored in Google Drive as well as that stored locally.
- Google Drive is an online (cloud) storage service, one of many types of services available on the Internet, which itself is an example of an internetwork.
- An intranet is a private internetwork.
- The term cloud was first used on illustrations of internetworks to hide the complexity. Cloud computing is the use of cloud services.
- A private cloud is an owned or managed for the benefit of a single organization and to provide cloud services.
- The public cloud is the hosting of a variety of free and/or fee-based services over the Internet. They are available to anyone who enrolls in the services. Google offers both public cloud and private cloud services.
- Cloud storage can be accessed from nearly any device from anywhere you can connect to the Internet.
- To synchronize locally stored data with the cloud, you need an app that is compatible with the local operating system.
- Google offers up to 15 GB of free online storage to account holders, but there are complex rules for how this storage is used and what Google services and file formats do or do not count against storage limits. Upgrade to one of Google's paid plans if you exceed the storage limits.
- When you share files and folders in Google drive with other Google users you can assign three levels of permissions: Can View, Can Comment, and Can Edit. For this type of sharing you need the other person's Gmail address.
- You can also share with anyone (Google account or not) by using a link share that you send to someone. You can send to non-Google accounts using the *Public on the web* or *Anyone with a link* options. If you share a link using the *Specific people* option, you must specify the name or email address for a Gmail account.
- Google apps can view and/or open many file types. Some file types can only be viewed by Google apps, and require other apps to open them.

Securing Chrome OS

- Secure your Google Account by connecting to the Google My Account home page.
- The Security Checkup option will give you a quick snapshot of your Account security settings.
- Google is aware of any device from which you sign in to Google.
- If you sign in to your Google account from an iPhone, iPad, Android tablet, or Android phone, Google will save that information with your account and you can enable the *Find your phone service* for that phone or tablet.

- Google's 2-Step Verification makes your account more secure.
- Secure Chrome OS through Settings accessed via the Status bar of the computer. Then open the *Privacy and Security* settings for a long list of options that help to protect you from outside threats.
- Under *Passwords and forms,* select *Autofill settings* to have Chrome save personal information and automate entering that information into online forms.
- Also under *Passwords and forms* select *Manage passwords* to centrally manage your web passwords.

Key Terms List

Android apps *(352)*	cloud storage *(354)*	notification area *(342)*
browser extension *(350)*	collaboration services *(355)*	Original format *(356)*
Can Comment *(357)*	Files app *(353)*	Over the Phone (OTP) *(361)*
Can Edit *(357)*	Google Account *(336)*	private cloud *(354)*
Can View *(357)*	Google Drive *(354)*	public cloud *(354)*
Chromebit *(336)*	Google Mail *(337)*	RAW format *(356)*
Chromebook *(336)*	High Quality option *(356)*	shelf *(340)*
Chromebox *(336)*	internetwork *(354)*	status tray *(342)*
cloud *(354)*	intranet *(354)*	web app *(350)*
cloud computing *(354)*	Launcher *(340)*	

Key Terms Quiz

Use the Key Terms List to complete the sentences that follow. Not all terms will be used.

1. The _____, popular with professional photographers, creates large files and will count against your available storage in Google Drive

2. _____ is the practice of using Internet- or intranet-based services, such as apps and data storage.

3. Free or fee-based services available over the Internet to anyone who signs up are said to be in the _____.

4. _____, created to run on smartphones, are available for the Chrome OS through the Google Play Store.

5. Google Drive is an example of a _____ service.

6. A/an _____ is a laptop that comes with the Chrome OS preinstalled.

7. A/an _____ is not an app, but an add-on that adds features to a browser.

8. A group of people can work together on documents and projects through _____.

9. The _____ on Google Chrome OS desktop functions much like the taskbar in Windows.

10. If you want to give someone read-only rights to a shared document, the Google Drive share permission you will use is _____.

Multiple-Choice Quiz

1. Which of the following is a privately owned network of networks, secured behind a firewall, and accessible only by authorized users?
   a. Intranet
   b. Internet
   c. Internetwork
   d. Cloud
   e. Private cloud

2. With this feature, you don't need to worry if your Chrome OS is running the latest version.
   a. Accessibility
   b. Wi-Fi

c. Cloud storage

d. Automatic update

e. Launcher

3. This optional Google account security feature sends you a message with a code that you must enter, in addition to your correct password, when you attempt to sign in from a new device?

   a. Do Not Track

   b. Autofill

   c. 2-Step verification

   d. Private cloud

   e. Password manager

4. If you save photos and videos using this option in Google Photos, the files are counted against your Google Drive storage limit.

   a. Cloud storage

   b. Original format

   c. Enhanced uploader

   d. Basic uploader

   e. High Quality

5. The kernel of the Chrome OS operating system is based on which of the following?

   a. Linux

   b. Microsoft Windows

   c. macOS

   d. iOS

   e. Android

6. Which of the following is a Google Drive share permission? Select all correct answers.

   a. Simple file sharing

   b. RAW

   c. Can Comment

   d. Can Edit

   e. Original format

7. Which of the following is the official source for Android apps?

   a. App Store

   b. Web Store

   c. Play Store

   d. Amazon

   e. Google Drive

8. Which of the following is not found on the status pop-up?

   a. Accessibility

   b. Network connection

   c. Shelf

   d. Settings button

   e. Lock button

9. Which of these Google apps negatively impact an individual's Google Drive storage capacity? Select all that apply.

   a. Gmail

   b. Docs

c. Photos

d. Sheets

e. Slides

10. Which file format, used by digital cameras, saves all the unprocessed data for an image, creating large files?

   a. Original

   b. RAW

   c. High Quality

   d. Enhanced

   e. Extended

11. To synchronize files between a cloud service and your computer, you must install an app for that service that interacts with this OS function.

   a. User Interface

   b. Memory

   c. Task management

   d. Security

   e. File system

12. Of the following choices, which are reasons for using cloud storage? Select all that apply.

   a. Collaboration

   b. Access from many locations

   c. Security

   d. Unlimited free storage

   e. Access from many devices

13. Which of the following will enable you to work with your Google Drive data when your computer does not have a network connect?

   a. Android app

   b. Collaboration services

   c. Over the Phone (OTP)

   d. Web app

   e. Google Docs Offline

14. If you have two-step verification enabled to send a text message, have Google create this handy list for those times when cannot pick up a text message and you need to sign in on another device.

   a. Chromebit

   b. Backup codes

   c. Google Prompt

   d. Calculator

   e. Google +

15. If your account is configured for 2-step verification, add this app to your phone to greatly simplify the verification process when you sign in to your account from another device.

   a. Chromebit

   b. Backup codes

   c. Google Prompt

   d. Calculator

   e. Google +

Essay Quiz

1. Explain a significant difference between Google's 2009 vision of the user interface of the Chrome operating system and the Chrome OS GUI we see today.

2. Describe how to prepare to use Google Cloud Print.

3. Compare and contrast browser extensions and web apps in Chrome OS and how you add them to your Chromebook.

4. Explain what an Android app is, why you would want one (or more) installed on your Chrome OS device, and the official source of Android apps.

5. Compare and contrast the three levels of permissions available for shared files and folders on Google Drive.

Lab Projects

LAB PROJECT 9.1

Research significant changes in Chrome OS in the year immediately before you read this chapter. Are there more types of apps, or do web apps and Android apps have more abilities? Have there been more changes in security? Describe your findings.

LAB PROJECT 9.2

Research the term *Shadow IT* and how it relates to cloud computing. Something similar occurred in the 1980s after the IBM PC was available. See if you can find parallels to the Shadow IT caused by cloud computing to what happened in the first years after the IBM PC was introduced.

LAB PROJECT 9.3

There is a small "gotcha" to Google's support for working offline. By default, it syncs the files you have worked on recently to the local computer. What happens when you are offline and need to open a file from Google Drive that you have not worked on in months? Research how to prepare for this scenario, describe what you will do, and then test it on your Chromebook or in the Chrome browser in another operating system.

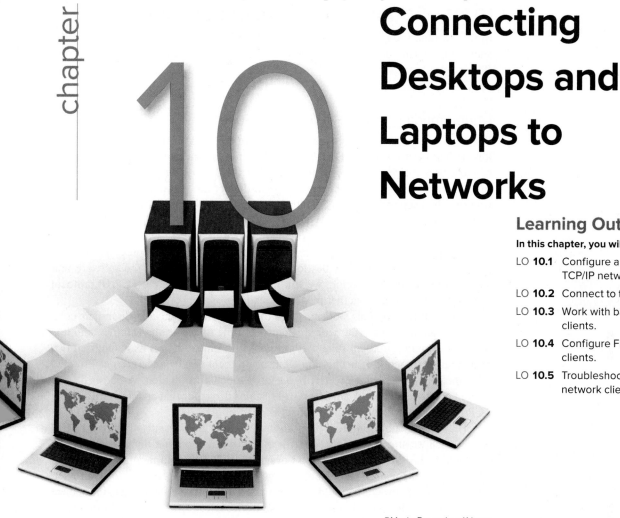

chapter

10

Connecting Desktops and Laptops to Networks

Learning Outcomes

In this chapter, you will learn how to:

LO **10.1** Configure a computer for a TCP/IP network.

LO **10.2** Connect to the Internet.

LO **10.3** Work with basic Internet clients.

LO **10.4** Configure File and Printer clients.

LO **10.5** Troubleshoot common network client problems.

©Yuriy Panyukov/Alamy

A stand-alone PC—one with no connection whatsoever to a network—is a rare thing today. Most of us can find some reason or need to connect to a network, whether it is a small home network, a corporate intranet, or the Internet. Without a network connection, a PC is like a remote island where the inhabitants have resolved to be isolated from civilization. And it does take resolve today to be so isolated because there are means by which a computer in the most remote location can connect to the Internet or another network. The heart and soul of all networks are the servers that provide the services we, as clients, seek on a network. These services are as simple as those that give us access to files and printers, Web pages, applications, and much more. Each of these services provides an important role on a network.

At work, at school, and at home, computer users depend on client software components that connect to services—whether for online research, playing games, engaging in a community through social media, using email, or downloading and uploading files.

In this chapter, you will study the client side of networking. Because a client computer cannot interact with network servers unless you properly configure it to communicate on a network, we begin with how to configure network connection settings on a client computer. Then move on to the Internet, first examine methods for connecting to the Internet, and then look at the most common Internet clients for browsing and email. Finally, practice methods for troubleshooting common connection problems. 🌐

LO 10.1 | Configuring a Network Connection

In this section, we will briefly describe the TCP/IP protocol suite, the basics of the addressing scheme of the IP protocol, and how to view and configure the important IP settings on your devices.

Understanding the TCP/IP Protocol Suite

TCP/IP is a group of protocols that evolved from the work of the Defense Advanced Research Projects Agency (DARPA); the Internet Engineering Task Force (IETF) now oversees TCP/IP development. TCP/IP is the underlying protocol suite of the Internet and nearly all private networks, regardless of the network medium (wired or wireless). It is supported by all operating systems on desktops, servers, and common mobile devices.

Each software implementation of a component of TCP/IP is a protocol, regardless of whether it is a driver, a service, or an application. So, in computer networking, a **protocol** is both the set of rules for doing some task as well as the software that accomplishes it. In this section, we will work at understanding the TCP/IP protocol suite, software bundled together in what we call a **protocol stack**.

The TCP/IP protocols work together to allow both similar and dissimilar computers to communicate. You need this protocol suite to access the Internet, and it is the most common protocol suite used on private intranets. It gets its name from two of its many protocols: Transmission Control Protocol (TCP) and Internet Protocol (IP)—the core protocols of TCP/IP. If, during Windows installation, Windows detects a wired or wireless network adapter it will install a driver for that adapter card and the TCP/IP protocol will automatically install.

TCP/IP is a subject of epic proportions! We offer only an introduction to TCP/IP, in which we attempt to arm you with useful information, but not overwhelm you with detail. Our goal is to give you an overview of TCP/IP and familiarize you with the settings that you may need to enter or modify for your desktop or laptop computer. Of course, this knowledge should also help you with your mobile devices, the subject of Chapter 11. Most computers and mobile devices need little or no help in acquiring the address they need to connect to a network, but knowing more about how this works is very helpful when things don't work as they should.

Note: TCP/IP was developed for connecting networks to networks. For this reason it is routable, meaning that messages can be sent from one TCP/IP network to another through routers, the devices that connect networks. The Internet consists of millions of such connected networks.

Note: For an entertaining overview of TCP/IP and the workings of network devices (routers, switches, and firewalls), check out YouTube video *TCP/IP the Movie* (Parts 1 and 2).

Transmission Control Protocol

Transmission Control Protocol (TCP) is the protocol responsible for the accurate delivery of messages, verifying and resending any pieces that fail to make the trip from source to destination. Several other protocols act as subprotocols, helping TCP accomplish this.

Internet Protocol

Internet Protocol (IP) is the protocol that delivers each IP **packet** (a small "package" containing chunks of data) from a source to a destination over a network on an Internetwork (a network of networks connected through routers). Special routing protocols use a destination IP address to choose the best route for a packet to take through a very complex internetwork. IP has subprotocols that help it accomplish its work, but we will not discuss the subprotocols.

Presently, there are two versions of Internet Protocol: IPv4 and IPv6, each with its own addressing scheme. Both protocols are present on the Internet, as it slowly transitions away from the older **IPv4** (the standard since 1983) to IPv6. A lot of attention is focused on the differences in addresses used by these two protocols, but there are many reasons for the Internet's move to **IPv6**.

Note: What progress has the Internet community made in moving toward an IPv4-free world? Check out the website **www.world ipv6launch.org** to see where things stand in the IP protocol world.

The short list of reasons IPv6 is better than IPv4 includes:

- IPv4 has run out of addresses.
- IPv6 has many more addresses: 340 trillion trillion trillion unique identifiers.
- IPv6 works better with mobile devices using a subprotocol, Mobile IP.
- IPv6 automatically assigns addresses to devices in a very reliable and no-fuss way.
- IPv6 manages addresses better.
- IPv6 has subprotocols that support better security.

It is important for you to learn about IP addresses because you cannot participate on a TCP/IP network without a valid IP address.

IP Addressing Basics

Let's explore the basics of IP addressing. First, an IP address is not assigned to a computer but to a network interface card (NIC) on a TCP/IP network, whether wired (Ethernet) or wireless (Wi-Fi). A modem (whether it is a cable modem, DSL modem, or an old analog "dial-up" modem) also has an address when you use it to connect to the Internet. If your computer or mobile device has multiple network connection devices connected to different networks, such as an Ethernet network adapter connected to a LAN and a Wi-Fi or cellular connection, each must have an address when it connects to a network.

That is why you see the Internet Protocol as a component of a connection in Windows (see Figure 10-1). The Connect Using box near the top of the Ethernet Properties dialog box identifies the connecting device to which these settings apply. Figure 10-1 shows that Windows supports both IPv4 and IPv6.

An IP address, along with a subnet mask (explained later) identifies your network card (a "host" in Internet terms), and the network on which it resides. An IP address, when added to a message packet as the destination address, allows the message to move from one network to another until it reaches its destination. At the connecting point between networks, a special network device called a router uses its routing protocols to determine the route to the destination IP address, before sending each packet along to the next router closer to the destination network. Each computer that directly attaches to the Internet must have a globally unique IP address. Both versions of IP have this much, and more, in common. Following are short explanations of IPv4 and IPv6 addresses.

IPv4 Addresses. IPv4 has been used on the Internet and other internetworks for over three decades. With 32-bit addressing, calculated by raising 2 to the 32nd power (2^{32}), IPv4 offers almost 4.3 billion possible IP addresses, but the way in which they were initially allocated to organizations greatly reduced the number of usable addresses, and we have now run out of IPv4 addresses.

An IPv4 address is 32 bits long in binary notation, but it usually appears as four decimal numbers, each in the range of 0–255, separated by a period. See examples of IPv4 addresses in Figures 10-2, 10-3, and 10-4. Figure 10-2 shows the Windows 10 Network Connection Details with the address of the local connection set as 192.168.1.10. The other IP addresses shown are to other network devices. If you have a Windows computer you can open the Details dialog box by following the instructions in the Try This!

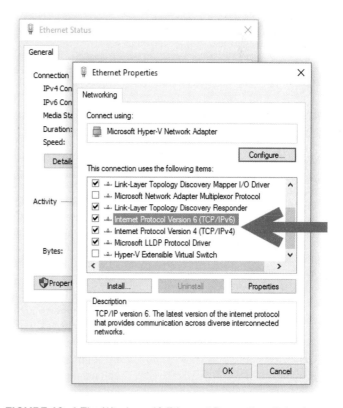

FIGURE 10-1 The Windows 10 Ethernet Properties dialog box.
Source: Microsoft Corporation

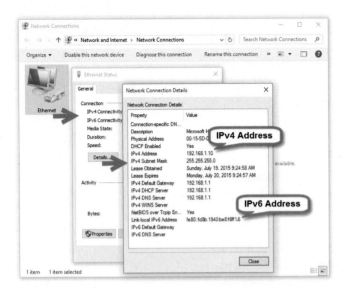

FIGURE 10–2 The Windows 10 Network Connection
Details box.
Source: Microsoft Corporation

FIGURE 10–3 The macOS Network preferences pane.
Source: Apple Inc.

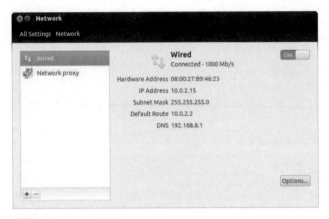

FIGURE 10–4 The Network dialog box in the Ubuntu Linux GUI.
Source: Ubuntu by Canonical

Note: What happened to IPv5? An
IPv5 standard was developed in
the 1980s in an effort to better support nontext traffic, such as audio,
video, and simulations.
However, it did not replace
IPv4, which was then still a
recent standard.

In the macOS Network preferences pane, shown
in Figure 10-3, the Wi-Fi device has an IPv4 address
of 192.168.1.16. Figure 10-4 shows the Network dialog
box from Ubuntu's Unity GUI with an IPv4 address of
10.0.2.15. Because this is a very simplified explanation, we
will not go into the exact rules for these addresses, just an
overview. And, as you can see, there is more to an IP configuration than the address of the device itself, but we will
tell you more about IP addresses before we discuss these
other settings.

IPv6 Addresses. The Internet is currently transitioning to
Internet Protocol version 6 (IPv6) with a new addressing
scheme that provides astronomically more addresses. For
many years, manufacturers and standards organizations
worked toward the day when they could fully support IPv6 on the Internet. In fact, the
World IPv6 Launch Day was June 6, 2012. On that day, however, the Internet world
did not become an IPv6-only world. What did happen was that many important Internet service providers and websites became available to computers using either IPv4 or
IPv6. They included Bing, Facebook, Google, and Yahoo!, and many more continue
to join them. For the near future (perhaps decades), IPv4 and IPv6 will coexist on the
Internet and on private and governmental internetworks of the world. Recent versions
of operating systems and all new networking equipment come with support for IPv6
built in.

IPv6 has 128-bit addressing, calculated by raising 2 to the 128th power (2^{128}),
which supports a huge number of unique addresses—340,282,366,920,938,463,463,
374,607,431,768,211,456 to be exact. An IPv6 address appears as eight groups of four
hexadecimal digits separated by colons. You will often see an IPv6 address shortened
by eliminating leading zeros in a group, and if there are all zeros between a set of
colons, the zeros won't show, and you will see just two colons together. If two or more
groups of all zeros are adjacent, there will still only be two colons. In Figure 10-5,
an IPv6 address is first shown in full hexadecimal notation, then with leading zeros
removed, and finally as eight groups of binary numbers.

An IPv6 Address in hexadecimal notation:

2002:0470:b8f9:0000:020c:29ff:fe53:45ca

The same address in hexadecimal notation with leading zeros removed:

2002:470:b8f9::20c:29ff:fe53:45ca

The same address in binary notation:

```
0010000000000010 0000010001110000 1011100011111001 0000000000000000
0000001000001100 0010100111111111 1111111001010011 0100010111001010
```

FIGURE 10–5 An IPv6 address expressed in both hexadecimal and binary notation.

Which Addresses Can You Use?

While we described both IPv4 and IPv6 addresses above, our discussion here centers around IPv4 because it will be around for a while, and you are more likely to need help resolving a problem with an IPv4 address than with an IPv6 address. We doubt anyone other than a network administrator will be concerned about IPv6 addresses.

There are billions of addresses, so how do you pick an address to use? Of course, the answer is—it all depends. Will you be using the address on a public network (the Internet) or on a private network? A central organization decides how to allocate all these addresses for use on the public Internet. They also understand that organizations need to use IP addresses within their private networks, and schemes were developed to slow down the depletion of addresses. One of those schemes involved dividing the possible IP addresses into two broad categories: public addresses and private addresses.

Public Addresses. Public IP addresses are designated for hosts on the Internet. In IP terminology, a host is any computer or device that has an IP address. To communicate over the Internet, you must send your message from an IP address that is unique on the entire Internet, and your message must go to a unique IP address. The centrally responsible organization for allocation of public IP addresses is the Internet Assigned Numbers Authority (IANA). This organization allocates numbers to various Regional Internet Registries (RIRs), which have the task of allocating IP addresses to Internet service providers. The largest ISPs, in turn, allocate addresses to other ISPs. You or your school or employer receive addresses for each Internet connection from your ISP. The addresses provided are from selected portions of those many billions of possible addresses specifically used on the Internet.

Private Addresses. A private IP address is an address from one of three ranges of IPv4 addresses designated for use only on private networks, so they are unusable on the Internet. All the IPv4 addresses in Figures 10-2, 10-3, and 10-4 are private addresses. In fact, many organizations use these addresses on their private IP networks, and you do not need to get permission to do so.

If a computer with a private address connects to the Internet, it will not be able to communicate because Internet routers will not forward packets with private addresses. Therefore, the same private address can be in use on millions of private networks, thus relieving some of the pressure on the limited supply of IPv4 addresses. Table 10-1 shows the three ranges used as private IPv4 addresses. All other IPv4 addresses either have specialized uses or are public addresses valid for computers and devices that are on the Internet.

TABLE 10–1 IPv4 Private IP Address Ranges		
Private IPv4 Address Ranges		
10.0.0.0 through 10.255.255.255		
172.16.0.0 through 172.31.255.255		
192.168.0.0 through 192.168.255.255		

If a user on a private network using private IP addresses wishes to connect to the Internet, a device between the local network and the Internet must intercept, repackage, and give a public IP address as its source address to each data packet before it goes onto the Internet. Then, if there is a response, each returning packet will go through the same process in reverse before returning to the private address.

If you connect to the Internet from home, school, or work, there is a device between your computer and the ISP that substitutes (or translates) your actual IP address to a unique Internet IP address. There are a couple of methods for doing this. One involves a special network service called a proxy server, and another involves a special service called network address translation (NAT). These are services that your ISP or network administrator manages for your school or organization. Such services also exist in the devices called Internet routers, which allow home or small-office computers to connect to the Internet, usually through a cable or DSL connection. A cable provider or telephone company will normally supply this equipment along with the Internet service.

How Does a NIC Get an IP Address?

Recall from the earlier discussion under IP Addressing Basics that an address is assigned to a network interface card (NIC). A NIC gets an IP address in one of two ways: static address assignment or automatic address assignment. Automatic address assignment is the most common method used today and there are two methods.

Static Address Assignment. A static IP address is manually configured by an administrator and can, therefore, be considered semipermanent—that is, it stays with the NIC until someone changes it. Manually configuring an IP address involves entering the IP address and other necessary IP settings. Most organizations only use static IP addressing on servers, network printers, and network devices such as routers that are required to have static addresses.

Where will you find this information on your desktop or laptop computer? Actually, unless you are setting up your own TCP/IP network (a very advanced task!), you will be given the IP addressing information by a network administrator, if you are connecting to a LAN at school or work, or by your Internet service provider. But most ISPs automate all the configuration of home Internet connections.

If you need to manually configure an address, be sure to carefully enter the numbers given to you, and double-check them! In Windows, you will enter these in the TCP/IP properties found in the properties dialog box for the network connection (see Figure 10-6).

Automatic Address Assignment. One nearly universal method is used for assigning IP addresses to computers: automatic IP addressing. Another method is used as a sort of fail-safe: Automatic Private IP Addressing (APIPA).

- Most organizations use automatic IP addressing for their desktop computers. It requires a special server or service on the network, called a Dynamic Host Configuration Protocol (DHCP) server, which issues IP addresses and settings to computers configured to obtain an IP address automatically, thus making them DHCP clients. The news gets even better since the default configuration of TCP/IP in Windows, macOS, Linux, and Chrome OS is to obtain an IP address automatically. Look for the line in Figure 10-2 that shows that DHCP is enabled for Windows 10, and Figure 10-3 shows that it is using DHCP to configure IPv4. However, in the Ubuntu Linux Network dialog box in Figure 10-4, you would need to click the Options button and bring up the Editing Wired connection 1 dialog box (not shown) to learn how the network card receives an IP address.

- Do not confuse *automatic* with *automatic private*. Most operating systems will enable a feature of DHCP—**Automatic Private IP Addressing (APIPA)**, whereby a DHCP client computer that fails to receive an address from a DHCP server will automatically give itself an address from a special range that has 169.254 in the first two octets of the IPv4 address. This is also called a link-local address, and IPv6 uses link-local addresses that begin with fe80. If a computer uses a link-local address, it will only be able to communicate on the local network segment, and then only with other devices and computers that use the same network ID. *When a computer is using an APIPA address, it continues to look for a DHCP server. Windows will check every 5 minutes.*

APIPA allows a novice to set up a small TCP/IP network without needing to learn about IP addressing. Each computer would use APIPA to assign itself an address, first testing that no other computer on the LAN is also using that same host ID.

Note: Flip back to Figure 10–2 showing the Network Connection Details. The third line from the bottom contains the link-local IPv6 address fe80:fd8b:1940:be8:f6ff%6. In this case, the NIC assigned this address to itself because it did not receive an IPv6 address. This NIC communicates on the network using the IPv4 address.

WARNING!

An APIPA address can indicate that a router is turned off or faulty.

IP Configuration Settings

If you must manually configure IPv4, you will need to understand the other settings to enter in addition to the IP address. Refer to the Windows 10 Internet Protocol Version 4 Properties dialog box in Figure 10-6 while reading the following descriptions of the various IP settings.

Subnet Mask. When a network device gets an IP address, it must also get a subnet mask. The subnet mask for an IPv4 address is as critical as the address itself because it takes what looks like a single address and divides it into two addresses by masking off part of the address. It is a little like your house address. The house number gives the address on the street, but you also need the street name. If you look at the Properties dialog box in Figure 10-6, the IPv4 address 192.168.1.132 has a mask of 255.255.255.0. The IP protocol now knows that this network device has the host address of 132 (its

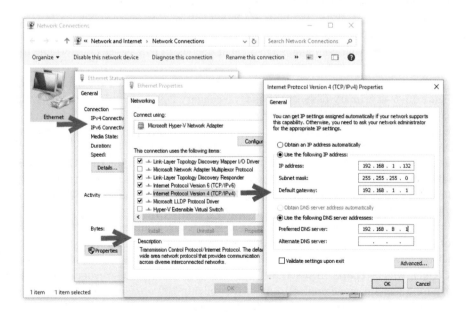

FIGURE 10–6 Manually configure TCP/IP in Windows 10 using the Internet Protocol Version 4 (TCP/IPv4) Properties dialog box.
Source: Microsoft Corporation

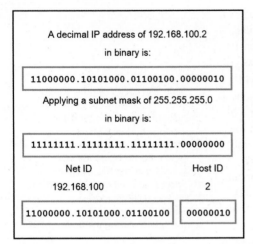

A decimal IP address of 192.168.100.2

in binary is:

11000000 . 10101000 . 01100100 . 00000010

Applying a subnet mask of 255.255.255.0

in binary is:

11111111 . 11111111 . 11111111 . 00000000

Net ID	Host ID
192.168.100	2

11000000 . 10101000 . 01100100	00000010

FIGURE 10–7 A subnet mask covers a portion of an IP address.

house number) on network 192.168.1 (its street name). The host address is the host ID, and the network address is the net ID.

Let's take a brief look at how masking works. Technically, it is done using binary math (base-2 math that uses only 0s and 1s), but you do not have to be a binary math whiz to understand the concept of masking; just look at the IP address and the mask in its binary form. You can use the scientific setting of the Calculator program that comes with Windows to convert each octet (a group of eight binary digits) of an IP address from binary to decimal or vice versa. As an example, if you convert an address of 192.168.100.2 to binary it looks like this:

11000000.10101000.01100100.00000010

If you convert the mask of 255.255.255.0 to binary, it looks like this:

11111111.11111111.11111111.00000000

If you lay the mask on top of the IP address, the ones cover (mask) the first 24 bits (short for binary digits). What falls under the ones of the mask is the network address, and what falls under the zeros of the mask is the host address. Figure 10-7 should make this concept clearer.

Default Gateway. The next entry shown back in Figure 10-6 is the default gateway. This is the IP address of the router connected to your network. The router is the network device that directs traffic to destinations beyond the local network. The net ID of the gateway address should be identical to the net ID of your NIC. Without a properly configured router, as well as the correct address (Default Gateway) for reaching this router, you cannot communicate with computers beyond your network. In our example in Figure 10-6, the router connects network 192.168.1 to other networks. Anytime your computer has a packet destined for a network with a network address other than 192.168.1, IP will send the packet to the gateway address to be forwarded to a host on another network.

DNS Servers. The last two settings are addresses of Domain Name System (DNS) servers. DNS is a distributed hierarchical online database containing registered domain names mapped to IP addresses. Thousands of name servers on the Internet maintain this distributed database. When you attempt to connect to a website, such as www.mhhe.com, your computer's DNS client queries a DNS server to determine the IP address for that website.

You may enter two addresses in the Microsoft Properties dialog shown in Figure 10-6—a primary DNS server and a secondary DNS server. The primary DNS server is the server the DNS client on your computer contacts any time you make a request to connect to a server using a domain name rather than an IP address. The DNS server will attempt to resolve the name to an IP address. The DNS client contacts the second DNS server only if there is no response from the first DNS server, but it does not use the second DNS server when the first DNS server responds that it cannot resolve the name. This is when you see an error similar to: "DNS query for www.somedomainname.com failed: host not found."

The Internet Corporation for Assigned Names and Numbers (ICANN), a California nonprofit corporation, currently oversees the Domain Name System, after having replaced an organization called InterNIC. The U.S. government sanctions ICANN, which reports to the U.S. Department of Commerce. Anyone wishing to acquire a domain name contacts one of the roughly 200 domain name registrars of top-level domains (.com, .org, .pro, .info, .biz, and so on) accredited by ICANN. Once registered with ICANN, each domain name and its IP address go on the Internet Domain Name Servers so that users can access Internet services offered under those domain names.

Step-by-Step 10.01

Examine a Connection's IP Configuration in a GUI

In this step-by-step exercise, you will examine a connection's IP configuration in the Windows GUI. The illustrations are from Windows 7, but this also works in Windows 10. You will need:

- A computer running Windows 7 or Windows 10.
- An administrator account and password for the computer.

Step 1

In Control Panel open the Network and Sharing Center. In the task list on the left side of the Network and Sharing Center, select **Change adapter settings** to open the Network Connections window.

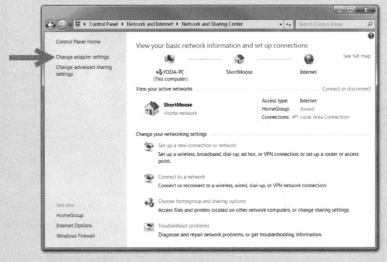

Source: Microsoft Corporation

Step 2

The Network Connections window will show all network connections. Our example shows only one network connection, but you may have several listed.

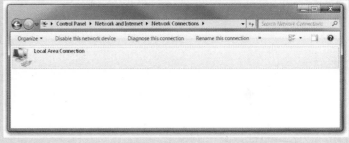

Source: Microsoft Corporation

Step 3

Double-click on the network connection you wish to examine. This opens the Status dialog box for the connection. Click the **Details** button to learn more about this connection.

Source: Microsoft Corporation

Step 4

The Network Connection Details box shows information about your NIC, including both IPv4 and IPv6 addresses. The Windows 10 version of this dialog box is shown back in Figure 10-2. If you wish to make changes to the configuration, click the Close button to return to the Status dialog box.

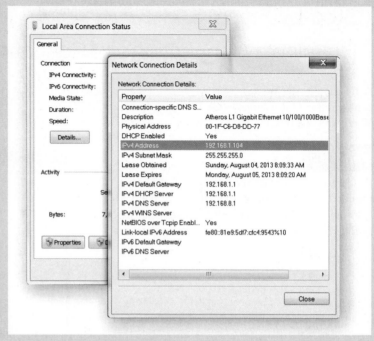

Source: Microsoft Corporation

Step 5

In the Status dialog box, click the Properties button to open the properties for this connection.

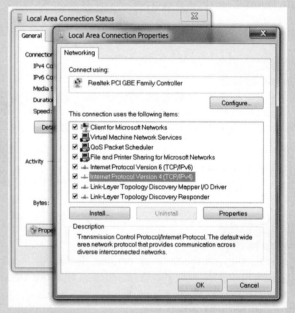

Source: Microsoft Corporation

Step 6

Keep in mind that only an advanced user should make changes to the network configuration. To look at the Properties dialog box for IPv4 for this connection, double-click Internet Protocol Version 4 (TCP/IPv4).

Step 7

When you have examined the configuration, click Cancel to close each open box without making changes. Then click Close to close the connection you examined, and then close the Network Connections window.

```
D:\Windows\system32\cmd.exe                                            _ □ X

D:\Users\Yoda>ipconfig /all

Windows IP Configuration

    Host Name . . . . . . . . . . . . : Yoda-PC
    Primary Dns Suffix  . . . . . . . :
    Node Type . . . . . . . . . . . . : Hybrid
    IP Routing Enabled. . . . . . . . : No
    WINS Proxy Enabled. . . . . . . . : No

Ethernet adapter Local Area Connection:

    Connection-specific DNS Suffix  . :
    Description . . . . . . . . . . . : Realtek PCI GBE Family Controller
    Physical Address. . . . . . . . . : 00-27-19-CD-2F-C2
    DHCP Enabled. . . . . . . . . . . : Yes
    Autoconfiguration Enabled . . . . : Yes
    Link-local IPv6 Address . . . . . : fe80::607f:c2b:3650:edcb%11(Preferred)
    IPv4 Address. . . . . . . . . . . : 192.168.1.134(Preferred)
    Subnet Mask . . . . . . . . . . . : 255.255.255.0
    Lease Obtained. . . . . . . . . . : Sunday, November 21, 2010 7:05:43 AM
    Lease Expires . . . . . . . . . . : Monday, November 22, 2010 7:05:51 AM
    Default Gateway . . . . . . . . . : 192.168.1.1
    DHCP Server . . . . . . . . . . . : 192.168.1.1
    DHCPv6 IAID . . . . . . . . . . . : 234891033
    DHCPv6 Client DUID. . . . . . . . : 00-01-00-01-14-2D-C9-A0-00-27-19-CD-2F-C2

    DNS Servers . . . . . . . . . . . : 192.168.8.1
    NetBIOS over Tcpip. . . . . . . . : Enabled
```

FIGURE 10–8 The output from running the command ipconfig /all.
Source: Microsoft Corporation

Viewing an IP Configuration from a Command-Line Interface

View the IP configuration of a computer from the command-line interface (CLI) in all of the desktop operating systems included in this text. In Windows you have two options for a CLI. They are the Command Prompt and the PowerShell. Both were described in Chapter 6, and the commands we describe in this chapter for the Windows CLI work in both Windows CLIs. If you have a Linux or macOS computer, open a terminal window and run similar commands.

In either Windows CLI use the **ipconfig** command without any command-line switches to have it display only the IP address (both IPv4 and IPv6, when present), subnet mask, and default gateway for each NIC that is connected to a network. Using the command with the **/all** switch will display much more information for each NIC. For instance, without this switch no detail is listed under Windows IP Configuration, but with the **/all** switch, as shown in Figure 10–8, several lines display, beginning with the Host Name. Then, for each adapter, in addition to the basic IP address, subnet mask, and default gateway, all the IP configuration information for each NIC displays. This includes the physical address, several lines of information pertaining to DHCP, and one or more DNS server addresses, if available, as well as the status of NetBIOS over TCP/IP, a protocol used for downward compatibility in networks with older Windows versions.

The equivalent of the Windows **ipconfig** command in the macOS Terminal window or at a $ prompt in Linux is the **ifconfig** command. Open a Terminal window in macOS or access the $ prompt in Linux and enter the **ifconfig** command with the **-a** switch to see all information about all network interfaces in that computer. The results for a macOS Terminal window are shown in

try this!

View Your IP Configuration from a Windows Command Prompt

Check out your current IP configuration using the **ipconfig** command. Try this:

1. Open a Command Prompt.
2. At the prompt type **ipconfig**.
3. After viewing the results of the command, type the command again with the **/all** switch: **ipconfig /all**.
4. Notice the additional information the **/all** switch provides.
5. Learn about other options for **ipconfig** using the **/?** switch.

Figure 10-9 and from the $ prompt in Linux in Figure 10-10. Notice that the information in macOS and in Linux is more difficult to decipher than it is in Windows. For instance, in both Figures 10-9 and 10-10 the lines labeled "inet6" refer to IPv6, while those beginning with "inet" refer to IPv4. You'll find the physical addresses of installed NICs in Figure 10-9 on lines beginning with "ether." In Figure 10-10, the line containing the physical address of the Ethernet NIC is in the first line of the section labeled eth0.

```
                        Terminal — bash — 79×35
Last login: Sun Nov 21 15:46:24 on ttys000
Janes-iMac:~ janeholcombe$ ifconfig -a
lo0: flags=8049<UP,LOOPBACK,RUNNING,MULTICAST> mtu 16384
        inet6 ::1 prefixlen 128
        inet6 fe80::1%lo0 prefixlen 64 scopeid 0x1
        inet 127.0.0.1 netmask 0xff000000
gif0: flags=8010<POINTOPOINT,MULTICAST> mtu 1280
stf0: flags=0<> mtu 1280
en0: flags=8863<UP,BROADCAST,SMART,RUNNING,SIMPLEX,MULTICAST> mtu 1500
        ether c4:2c:03:11:f5:1b
        media: autoselect
        status: inactive
fw0: flags=8863<UP,BROADCAST,SMART,RUNNING,SIMPLEX,MULTICAST> mtu 4078
        lladdr e8:06:88:ff:fe:fb:26:62
        media: autoselect <full-duplex>
        status: inactive
en1: flags=8863<UP,BROADCAST,SMART,RUNNING,SIMPLEX,MULTICAST> mtu 1500
        ether d8:30:62:57:17:fc
        inet6 fe80::da30:62ff:fe57:17fc%en1 prefixlen 64 scopeid 0x6
        inet 192.168.1.135 netmask 0xffffff00 broadcast 192.168.1.255
        media: autoselect
        status: active
vboxnet0: flags=8842<BROADCAST,RUNNING,SIMPLEX,MULTICAST> mtu 1500
        ether 0a:00:27:00:00:00
vnic0: flags=8843<UP,BROADCAST,RUNNING,SIMPLEX,MULTICAST> mtu 1500
        ether 00:1c:42:00:00:08
        inet 10.211.55.2 netmask 0xffffff00 broadcast 10.211.55.255
        media: autoselect
        status: active
vnic1: flags=8843<UP,BROADCAST,RUNNING,SIMPLEX,MULTICAST> mtu 1500
        ether 00:1c:42:00:00:09
        inet 10.37.129.2 netmask 0xffffff00 broadcast 10.37.129.255
        media: autoselect
        status: active
Janes-iMac:~ janeholcombe$
```

FIGURE 10–9 The result of running the **ifconfig -a** command in a Terminal window in macOS.
Source: Apple Inc.

```
chuck@chuck-linux:~$ ifconfig -a
eth0      Link encap:Ethernet  HWaddr 08:00:27:17:fe:b0
          inet addr:10.0.2.15  Bcast:10.0.2.255  Mask:255.255.255.0
          inet6 addr: fe80::a00:27ff:fe17:feb0/64 Scope:Link
          UP BROADCAST RUNNING MULTICAST  MTU:1500  Metric:1
          RX packets:2286 errors:0 dropped:0 overruns:0 frame:0
          TX packets:1853 errors:0 dropped:0 overruns:0 carrier:0
          collisions:0 txqueuelen:1000
          RX bytes:1718199 (1.7 MB)  TX bytes:247442 (247.4 KB)

lo        Link encap:Local Loopback
          inet addr:127.0.0.1  Mask:255.0.0.0
          inet6 addr: ::1/128 Scope:Host
          UP LOOPBACK RUNNING  MTU:16436  Metric:1
          RX packets:9 errors:0 dropped:0 overruns:0 frame:0
          TX packets:9 errors:0 dropped:0 overruns:0 carrier:0
          collisions:0 txqueuelen:0
          RX bytes:1056 (1.0 KB)  TX bytes:1056 (1.0 KB)

chuck@chuck-linux:~$
```

FIGURE 10–10 The result of running the **ifconfig -a** command at the $ prompt in Linux.
Source: Ubuntu by Canonical

LO 10.2 | Connecting to the Internet

A connection to the Internet is a wide area network (WAN) connection. A wide area network (WAN) is a network that covers a very large geographic area (miles). There are several WAN technologies to choose from. Some of these are wired technologies, and some are wireless. Most connection methods described here remain available 24/7, in which case, Internet access is as simple as opening your browser or sending an email. The connections include a wide range of speeds. In this section, we will compare the various means of connecting a network or computer to the Internet and discuss the most common methods for doing so from home or a small business so that you can decide for yourself. This will also help you to understand something about how you are connecting to the Internet from school or work, although we will not discuss the very expensive high-speed WAN services for connecting a large enterprise (commercial, government, or educational) to the Internet.

The choice of physical means of connecting to the Internet closely relates to your choice of an organization that will give you access to the Internet. This section includes an overview of these organizations first. Then you will learn about the technologies used at the connection point to the Internet, regardless of whether it is a single computer or a LAN connection.

Internet Service Providers

An **Internet service provider (ISP)** is an organization that provides access to the Internet for individuals and organizations. For a fee, an ISP provides you with this connection service and may offer other Internet-related services, such as Web-server hosting and email. Some ISPs specialize in certain connection types. For instance, HughesNet and Dish are both ISPs that specialize in satellite Internet services. T-Mobile (**www.tmobile.com**), Verizon, and AT&T all provide ISP services for their cellular customers; and your local telephone company may provide ISP services for dial-up, DSL, and cable customers. Virtually, all cable TV providers also provide Internet service.

> ## try this!
>
> ### Find Internet Service Providers
>
> You can use the Internet to find ISPs you might want to use. Try this:
>
> 1. Use your Web browser to connect to your favorite search engine, search on "Internet Service Provider," and brace yourself for a *long* list of ISPs and sites related to ISPs.
> 2. To find ISPs that specialize in satellite connections, for example, search on "Internet Satellite Data Service Provider."
> 3. Then, further refine your search to just one country by entering a country name in the search by results box.

Computer-to-Internet versus LAN-to-Internet

A **local area network (LAN)** is a network that covers a building, home, office, or campus. It can be wired or wireless. The traditional wired network uses Ethernet connectors and cables; Ethernet connectors are still standard on many desktops and some laptops. A **Wi-Fi network** is a **wireless LAN (WLAN)** that complies with IEEE 802.11 standards. The maximum distance covered by WLAN signals or LAN cabling is measured in hundreds of feet. Almost any computer will first connect to a LAN or WLAN, which in turn connects to a router connected (directly or indirectly) to the Internet. There is usually at least one router between your computing device and the Internet. More likely, there are many routers.

At the point of connection at home, you will have some sort of modem (cable, DSL, or analog). One port of the modem connects to a WAN connection and through that to an ISP. The other port may connect directly to a computer or, most often, to a router that in many cases is also a wireless access point (WAP) and an Ethernet switch. Therefore, you are connecting via a WLAN (Wi-Fi) or LAN (Ethernet) to the Internet. This is also the case at school or work, only on a larger scale, because the LAN or WLAN ultimately connects through a router to a high-speed Internet connection. Figure 10–11 shows these two scenarios.

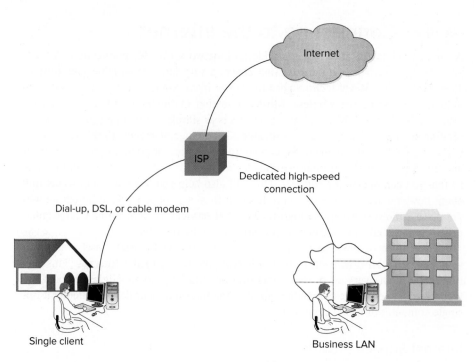

FIGURE 10–11 Connecting to the Internet from a single computer or from a LAN.

Wired Connectivity Technologies

Many wired WAN technologies for connecting to the Internet utilize the telecommunications infrastructure of the telephone system—either in its traditional state or with upgrades and equipment added to that infrastructure. Another private network often used for wired Internet connections belongs to the cable TV companies, which provide Internet access for their customers.

Dial-Up Connections Using Analog Modems

A technology that clearly takes advantage of the traditional phone system is dial-up, an inexpensive choice available to anyone with a standard phone line and an analog modem. At one time every laptop came with an internal analog modem.

Analog modems as standard equipment in laptops have gone the way of the buggy whip. Never heard of buggy whips? That's our point. However, dial-up is the only low-cost means of connecting to the Internet in remote areas of the world, including some within the United States, and millions still use dial-up, so we will devote some space to this topic.

The longtime speed standard for dial-up is 56 kilobits per second (Kbps). The dial-up connection at 56 Kbps is very slow compared to a LAN running at 100 megabits per second (Mbps) or 1 gigabit per second (Gbps). In addition to a standard phone line (what we often call a "land line"), you also need to subscribe to an Internet connection service from an ISP. The cost of the ISP subscription should be your only cost in addition to your phone service. When using an analog modem, you may not use the phone line simultaneously for voice or fax.

In a dial-up connection to the Internet, your computer uses its modem to dial a telephone number provided by the ISP (hence the term *dial-up connection*). One of many modems maintained by the ISP at its facility answers your computer's call; a server maintained by the ISP for authenticating customers authenticates you, and then the ISP routes traffic between your computer and the Internet for that session. Like a voice phone conversation, the connection is only temporary and ends when either your PC or the ISP's server ends the call. Most ISP servers disconnect a dial-up connection automatically after a certain period of inactivity.

Note: Several ISPs advertise dial-up service, including (but not limited to) NetZero and EarthLink.

High-Speed Wired Access

If multiple users need to share an Internet connection, the connection between the network and the ISP must be adequate to simultaneously carry the traffic created by all the users at peak usage times. The authors presently have a Wi-Fi router connected to a DSL modem. Through that wireless router we connect five desktop computers (three Windows PCs, one Linux computer, one iMac), two Windows laptops, two Kindles, two smartphones, an iPad, an Android tablet, an ASUS 2-in-1, a TiVO DVR, and a ROKU device. That's 15 devices for just two people. Many families exceed that number. For this you need high-speed WAN connections, such as the three wired options we describe here, or one of the wireless options detailed later.

Integrated Services Digital Network. Integrated services digital network (ISDN) is a digital telephone service that simultaneously transmits voice, data, and control signaling over a single telephone line. ISDN service operates on standard telephone lines but requires a special modem and phone service, which adds to the cost. An ISDN data connection can transfer data at up to 128,000 bits per second (128 Kbps). This seems extremely slow to most of us with faster options. While rarely used in homes in the United States, ISDN may be all that is available for a wired WAN connection in some areas, especially outside of the United States.

The benefits of ISDN (beyond the faster speed compared to a dial-up connection) include being able to connect a PC, telephone, and fax machine to a single ISDN line and use them simultaneously.

ISDN has fallen out of favor in many areas where there are higher performance options, such as cable and DSL. In remote parts of the world, another optional broadband service, satellite communications, may be a more viable option than ISDN because it does not require the wired infrastructure needed by ISDN.

Digital Subscriber Line. Digital subscriber line (DSL) service is similar to ISDN in its use of the telephone network, but it uses more advanced digital signal processing to compress more signals through the telephone lines. DSL requires component changes in the telephone network before they can offer it. DSL service can provide simultaneous data, voice, and fax transmissions on the same line. It gives you a dedicated circuit from your home or office to the central office and the service can usually guarantee consistent upload and download speeds.

Several versions of DSL services are available for home and business use. Each version provides a different level of service, speed, and distance, and each normally provides full-time connections. The two most common are asynchronous DSL (ADSL) and synchronous DSL (SDSL). ADSL is the type of service normally available to home users. Other versions include high-data-rate DSL (HDSL) and very high-data-rate DSL (VDSL). The abbreviation often used to refer to DSL service in general begins with an x (xDSL), reflecting the varied first character in the DSL implementations.

Across the DSL services offered by various ISPs, data transmission speeds range from 128 Kbps for basic DSL service through 24 Mbps for high-end service. When describing DSL speeds, they usually refer to the speed of traffic flowing "downstream"—that is, from the ISP to your computer. For instance, the authors subscribe to a rural phone company's ADSL service, which provides a downstream speed of 15 Mbps, but an upstream speed of 1 Mbps. While SDSL provides the same speed in each direction, it is much more expensive and not widely available. Most home users only require the higher speeds for downloads (browsing the Internet, downloading streaming video, and so on), so SDSL service is only practical for customers who must upload a great deal of data.

Because servers must upload a great deal of data in response to user requests, commercial Internet servers are normally hosted on much faster links than those discussed here.

Cable. Many cable television companies now use a portion of their network's bandwidth to offer Internet access through existing cable television connections. They call this Internet connection option cable modem service because of the need to use a special cable modem to connect.

Cable networks use coaxial cable, which can transmit data as much as 100 times faster than common telephone lines. Coaxial cable allows transmission over several channels simultaneously. Internet data can be on one channel while transmitting audio, video, and control signals separately. A user can access the Internet from his or her computer and watch cable television at the same time, over the same cable connection, without the two data streams interfering with one another.

The biggest drawback to cable modem service is the fact that the subscribers in a defined area share the signal. As the number of users in an area increases, less bandwidth is available to each user. Therefore, while cable providers advertise higher speeds than DSL, they cannot guarantee consistent speeds.

Wireless Connectivity Technologies

Like wired communications, wireless has moved from analog to digital over the years. Today, you can connect to the Internet through cellular networks, wireless wide area networks (WWANs), wireless LAN (WLAN) connections (if the WLAN ultimately connects to the Internet), and by satellite.

Smartphones support both voice and high-speed cellular data service, allowing users to surf the Internet from any location offering the required signal. Cellular Internet companies usually meter their connections, meaning that your plan allows only a predetermined amount of downstream data per month. Extra charges apply if you exceed the permitted amount.

In addition, modern smartphones also come with Wi-Fi. This allows users to configure their phones to use a Wi-Fi connection, when available, for connecting to a router that, in turn, is connected to the Internet, thus saving on connection and data charges from their cellular provider.

Tablets optionally have cellular communications features as well as Wi-Fi, allowing Web browsing and communicating by email and other features.

Wireless WAN Connections

A wireless wide area network (WWAN) is a digital network that extends over a large geographical area. A WWAN receives and transmits data using radio signals over cellular sites and satellites, which makes the network accessible to mobile computer systems. At the switching center, the WWAN splits off into segments and then connects to a public or private network via telephone or other high-speed communication links. The data then links to an organization's existing LAN/WAN infrastructure (see Figure 10–12). The coverage area for a WWAN, normally measured in miles or kilometers, makes it therefore more susceptible than wired networks to environmental factors such as weather and terrain.

A WWAN is a fully bidirectional wireless network capable of data transfer at speeds in excess of 100 Mbps. Usually, basic WWAN services offer connection speeds between 1 and 10 Mbps. With dedicated equipment, the downlink speeds can reach 100 Mbps. The uplink speeds are less. A WWAN system requires an antenna tuned to receive the proper radio frequency (RF).

A cellular Internet connection is an example of a WWAN. Many cellular services offer Internet data service. In addition to using your smartphone or tablet on a cellular network, providers offer cellular hotspot plans, in which your smartphone or a separate hotspot device acts as a Wi-Fi router for your other computers and devices to access the Internet.

Satellite

Satellite connections are as suitable for large businesses as for small offices, cybercafés, individuals, homes, and the armed forces. Satellite is the WAN of choice when it is

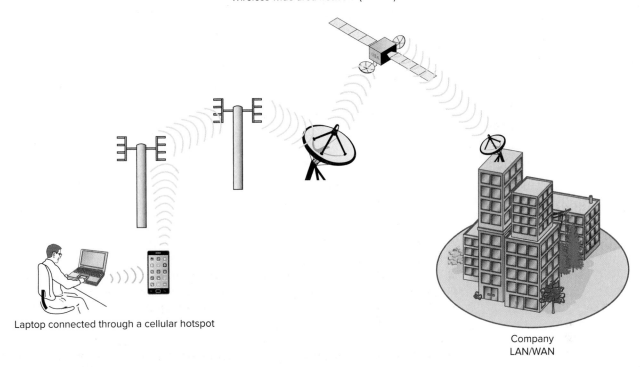

Wireless wide area network (WWAN) structure

Laptop connected through a cellular hotspot

Company
LAN/WAN

FIGURE 10-12 A WWAN includes devices that retransmit the wireless signal.

not possible or practical to use a wired connection and when cellular WAN services are not available or are too slow or costly. Satellite Internet providers offer several levels of service based on speed and they offer either stationary installations or mobile installations. The hardware cost for a mobile satellite installation is considerably higher than that for a stationary installation, and the ongoing service fees are higher, too.

Satellite Internet Connection Speeds. Like ADSL, satellite data communication is usually faster downstream than upstream. The discrepancy can be huge, as we found when we had our own mobile satellite system installed on our motor home in 2003. During our three years of living and working on the road, we often achieved download speeds of 400 to 800 Kbps (and occasionally more), but upload speeds were only in the range of 25 to 45 Kbps. While these speeds seem minimal compared to the mobile satellite options available today, the system worked well for us because, like most Internet users, our greatest need was for fast downloads as we browsed the Internet or downloaded files. At the time, cellular service was slow or simply did not exist in most locations, and so we found a mobile satellite connection was the best solution as long as we were careful not to park under trees or other obstacles to the satellite signal.

Satellite Internet Connection Costs. Today, the price of consumer-grade mobile satellite equipment and the basic monthly service fees are generally more expensive than they were in 2003. But the base plan speeds are much faster, at 3 or more Mbps down. If you are willing to spend the money on the appropriate equipment and service, you can have mobile satellite speeds of up to 5 Mbps down and 2 Mbps up.

Satellite Internet Connection Latency. Satellite communications tend to have a higher latency, or lag. Think of watching a news broadcast that includes a foreign correspondent reporting over a satellite link. The news anchor in the studio asks a question, and you see the correspondent on the screen with a frozen smile while he or she waits to hear the question in its entirety. While it is barely noticeable when someone is reporting the news, such latency is very undesirable for real-time Internet applications, such

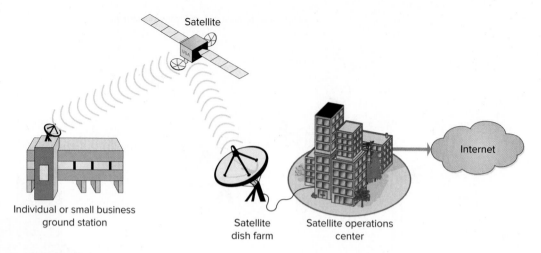

Satellite

Internet

Individual or small business
ground station

Satellite
dish farm

Satellite operations
center

FIGURE 10–13 Accessing the Internet through a satellite WAN connection.

as online games. Many IT professionals consider satellite connections unreliable, but it can be the best solution for Internet communications in remote areas.

When individuals or organizations contract with an ISP for stationary satellite service, they install an Earth-based communications station. It usually includes three parts: a transceiver (a combined transmitter and receiver), a device that for simplicity we call a modem, and the satellite dish on its mount. You place the satellite dish outdoors in direct line-of-sight of one of several data satellites in geostationary orbit around the Earth. The modem connects the other components to the computer or LAN. A mobile installation (on a land- or water-based vehicle) is generally much more expensive than a stationary installation because the mount must allow for moving the dish to align on the satellite, and therefore requires controlling circuitry and a costly motor-driven mount to achieve this with precision. The monthly service plans for mobile satellite communications are also more expensive than those for stationary installations.

Because a satellite traveling in a geostationary orbit moves at the same speed as the Earth's rotation, it hovers over the same location on the Earth—therefore, you can align a satellite dish antenna precisely on the satellite. The satellite links the user's satellite dish to a land-based satellite operations center, through which the signal goes to the Internet (see Figure 10–13).

WLAN Connections

A is a local area network, usually using one of the standards referred to as Wi-Fi (for wireless fidelity). The Wi-Fi standards of the Institute of Electrical and Electronics Engineers include 802.11a, 802.11b, 802.11g, 802.11n, and 802.11ac listed from oldest to newest. The maximum distance covered by a WLAN is a few hundred feet rather than miles. Therefore, this is not a technology that connects directly to an ISP (as a WWAN or satellite connection will) but can be used to connect to another LAN or device with a WAN connection. This is the technology of Internet cafés, wireless laptops, tablets, and smartphones. With enough wireless hubs, called wireless access points (WAPs), an entire community can offer wireless access to a shared Internet connection.

Many of us have one of the high-speed WAN technologies described above and connect multiple devices to them through a device that is both a wireless access point (WAP) and an Internet router. The authors presently have a Wi-Fi router connected to an ADSL connection. Through that wireless router, we connect all our computing devices to the Internet.

The latest IEEE 802.11 standards are both faster and more secure owing to encryption technology. Therefore, we regularly replace our Wi-Fi devices with newer ones that are up to the new standards.

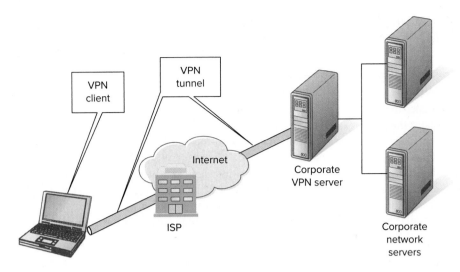

FIGURE 10-14 A remote access VPN.

Using a Virtual Private Network

Mobile users and remote offices often need to connect to a corporate intranet through the Internet using any of the connection technologies discussed earlier. You can make such a connection more secure by connecting through a virtual private network (VPN), over an existing WAN connection. Think of a VPN as a simulated private network that runs inside a "tunnel" from end point to end point. When an individual connects from a computer or mobile device, we call this connection a remote access VPN (see Figure 10-14). One end is a computer connected to the Internet, while the other end is a VPN server in the private network. When two networks connect by VPN, we call it a site-to-site VPN.

The tunnel effect is the result of encapsulating each data packet sent at one end of the tunnel and removing it from the encapsulation at the receiving end. Because the encapsulation itself provides only a very small amount of protection, VPN providers apply other measures to protect the data, such as encrypting the data, and requiring authentication at both ends of the tunnel.

Anyone who connects to the Internet while away from home, school, or work should consider using a VPN for secure access. Organizations often provide this service to their employees. Individuals can subscribe to VPN services targeted to consumers, such as Private Internet Access (PIA) or TunnelBear. This is not an endorsement of either of these services. If you are interested in protecting yourself while connected to public hotspots, research VPN services to find one that meets your needs and budget.

LO 10.3 | Using Internet Clients

The growth in the number and type of Internet services has increased the number of client types required to access those services. We will limit our discussion of Internet clients to Web browsers and email clients. Many services are accessible through Web browsers. Email may be the most important service on the Internet—many people, who have no other use for the Internet, use email.

Web Browsers

While the World Wide Web (the Web) is just one of many services that exist on the Internet, it alone is responsible for most of the huge growth in Internet use that began after the Web's introduction in the early 1990s. Web technologies changed the look of Internet content from all text to rich and colorful graphics, and made it simple to navigate the Web by using a special type of client called a Web browser. In this section, learn about common browser features and the most common browsers used on desktop and laptop computers.

Common Browser Features

The Web browser's ease of use hides the complexity of the Internet, as protocols help to transfer the content of a Web page to the user's computer. There the Web browser translates the plain-text language into a rich, colorful document that may contain links to other pages—often at disparate locations on the Internet. Today, the popular free Web browsers come in versions for macOS, Microsoft Windows, and Linux. Beyond the desktop, you'll find versions of these and other Web browsers with scaled-down screens for smartphones and tablets. In short, just about any electronic device that can connect to the Internet and has a display includes a Web browser.

Popular browsers share many of the same features for both general browsing and security. General browser features found in most browsers include:

- Active search
- Add-ons
- Autofill
- Automatic updates
- Bookmarks
- Integrated search engine
- Password manager

- Reading mode
- Personalization
- RSS feeds
- Search within page
- Synchronization
- Tabbed browsing
- Zoom

Google Chrome

Google Chrome is software from the Chromium open-source project and other sources. It is in its 44th major version at this writing and has a clean look with no menu bar, but a small button on the right called the Chrome button that opens the Customize and Control menu (shown in Figure 10–15). From this menu, you can

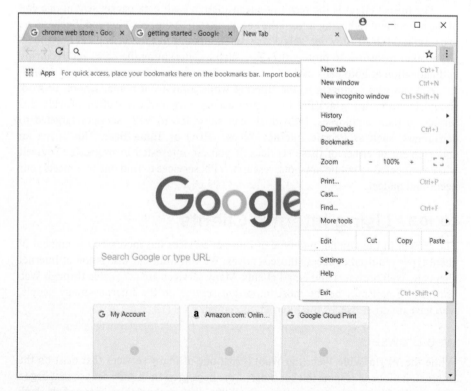

FIGURE 10–15 Google Chrome with three tabs open across the top and the Chrome menu open on the right.
Source: Google LLC

access any feature you would find in a menu bar. The Settings option opens your personal settings page (saved with your Google account). The Help option connects to Chrome's online help.

Mozilla Firefox

Mozilla Firefox is a product of the Mozilla Foundation. In the latest versions of Firefox, a menu button has been added to the right side of the button bar containing the most-used functions. If you don't find what you need there, check out the menu bar. If it is not visible, press the ALT key to open it whenever you need it. If you wish to keep the menu bar visible, press ALT, select the View menu and select Toolbars. Then click to place a check by Menu Bar and any other toolbar you want to stay visible. We believe that Firefox will eventually do away with the menu bar, but until they do, it is there for those who expect it to be. Figure 10–16 shows Firefox with the menu open on the right.

Internet Explorer

Microsoft introduced the Internet Explorer (IE) Web browser with the Windows 95 operating system, and IE is still bundled with Windows and available for free for Windows and macOS at the Microsoft website. Figure 10–17 shows the open Tools menu for IE version 11 running in Windows 10. As with Firefox, the IE menu bar is hidden until you press the ALT key. And, like Firefox, you can use the View options to select what toolbars you want to stay visible in IE. Microsoft's replacement for IE, Microsoft Edge, comes with Windows 10. Internet Explorer is also included with Windows 10, for use with websites that require features of IE.

Microsoft Edge

Microsoft Edge was introduced with Windows 10 as a replacement for IE. It is a Universal app, capable of adapting itself to all devices and screen sizes supported by

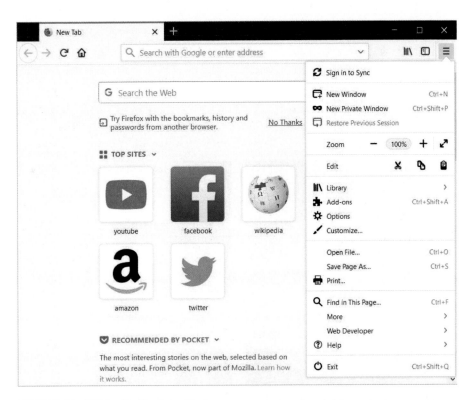

FIGURE 10–16 Mozilla Firefox with the menu open on the right.
Source: Mozilla Corporation

Windows 10. Like Chrome, Edge has a very clean look. It will be kept up-to-date with Windows Update. Figure 10–18 shows Microsoft Edge with the menu open on the right.

Other Browsers

Other browsers include Opera (**www.opera.com**) and Apple Safari (**www.apple.com/safari**) for macOS and Windows PCs.

FIGURE 10–17 Microsoft Internet Explorer 11 with the Tools menu open on the right.
Source: Microsoft Corporation

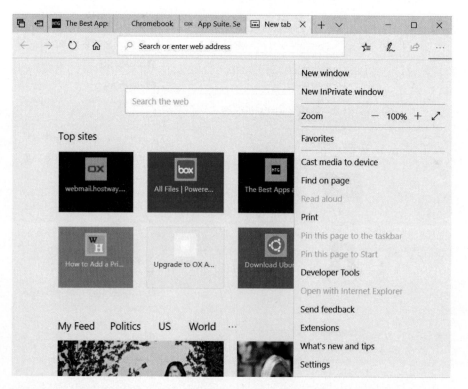

FIGURE 10–18 Microsoft Edge with its menu open.
Source: Microsoft Corporation

Security and Web Browsers

Rather than dive into the details of every security setting in your Web browser, we'll define certain security threats and describe how to manage them through modern Web browsers.

Cookies. As you learned in Chapter 2, cookies are good—mostly. Under some circumstances people can use them for the wrong purposes, but for the most part, their benefits outweigh the negatives. Normally, only the website that creates the cookies can access them. However, some advertisers on websites have the browser create so-called third-party cookies, which other sites that include this advertiser can use. Look for options to manage cookies when configuring a Web browser. Figure 10-19 shows the Content settings where you can change how Chrome handles cookies.

To check out the cookies settings for Firefox click the menu button, select Options, and click the Privacy button from the sidebar (a mask). Figure 10-20 shows the Firefox Privacy page with the settings for History. When you click on the down arrow in the box labeled *Firefox will,* and select *Use custom settings for history,* Firefox displays the options for controlling how it treats history. Notice that under *Cookies and Site Data* we configured it to never accept third-party cookies.

In IE, you need to dig a little deeper to find the settings for cookies. Open the Privacy page in Internet Options and click the Advanced button. On the Advanced Privacy Settings dialog box, you can manage first-party and second-party cookies,

Disable Third-Party Cookies in Chrome

Locate the settings for Cookies in the Chrome browser. Try this:

1. In the Chrome browser click the Chrome button on the far right of the menu bar to open the Chrome menu and select Settings.
2. On the Settings page scroll down to the bottom. If the last item is Hide Advanced Settings, skip to Step 3. If the last item on the Settings page is *Advanced,* click it.
3. Locate the *Privacy and security* category and click Content Settings.
4. The Cookies category shows your current settings for cookies. If it is not enabled, turn on **Block third-party cookies.**
5. When you are done click the back arrow at the top of the page until you return to your home settings page.

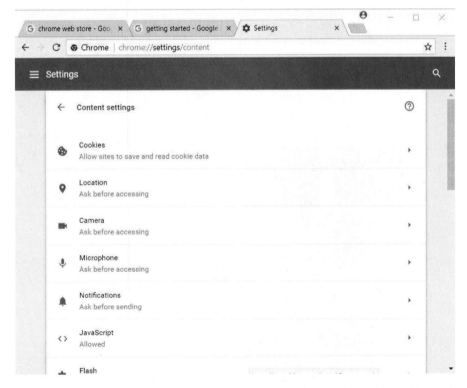

FIGURE 10–19 The Chrome Content Settings page includes settings for cookies.
Source: Google LLC

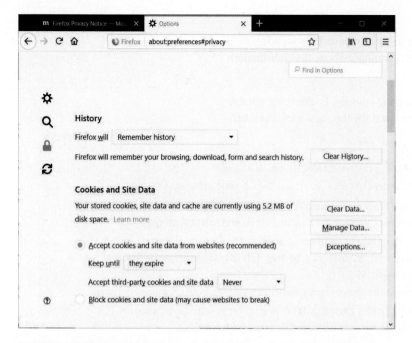

FIGURE 10–20 The Firefox privacy page with settings to protect you while browsing.
Source: Mozilla Corporation

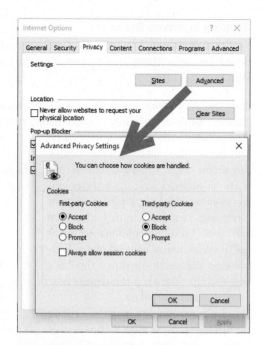

FIGURE 10–21 The Internet Explorer privacy page with settings to protect you while browsing.
Source: Microsoft Corporation

with options to accept, block, or prompt you for first-party and third-party cookies, as shown in Figure 10–21.

To change the Cookies settings in Microsoft Edge, click or tap the menu button on the far right of the button bar, select *Settings, Advanced Settings.* Scroll down to Cookies and select a setting. Figure 10–22 shows the advanced settings.

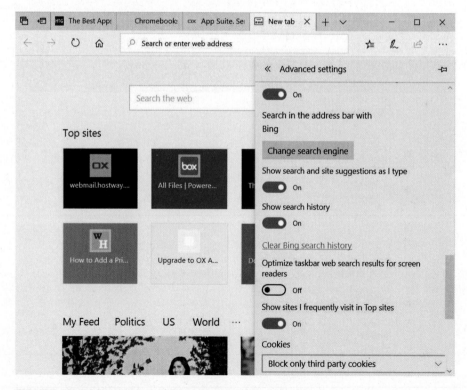

FIGURE 10–22 The Microsoft Edge Advanced Settings box.
Source: Microsoft Corporation

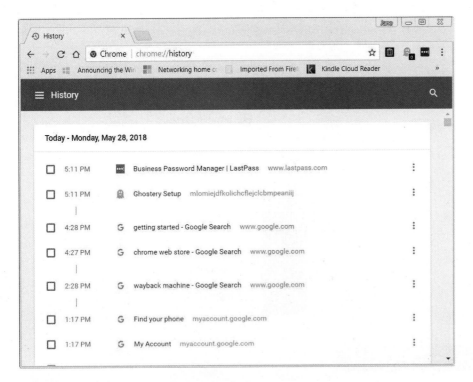

FIGURE 10-23 The Chrome History page.
Source: Google LLC

Browsing History. Your browsing history is useful information to marketers and others who want to learn more about you. At the same time, this information also makes life a bit easier for you when you return to favorite sites. While your browser does not divulge this information, a system compromised by spyware or malware could reveal this information to the wrong persons. Additionally, if you leave your computer unattended but logged on with your account, anyone with access to your computer could look at your browsing history; system administrators or others who have administrative access to your computer can do the same. Once again, your security needs may be at odds with your need for convenience on the Web. Therefore, Web browsers allow you to manage your browsing history.

Access the Chrome browser History page by selecting History from the Chrome menu. Figure 10-23 shows the History page. From this page, you can search through the history (see button at top), clear all browsing history, and select items using the check boxes to the left of each one. Or you can click the Actions button to the right of each item, which allows you to see more items from that site (searching) or remove the item from history.

In Firefox, manage browsing history settings on the Privacy page in the Options dialog box, shown previously.

In IE, if you want to quickly delete all browsing history, press CTRL-SHIFT-DELETE. When the Delete Browsing History box opens (Figure 10-24), select or deselect items and then click the Delete button.

In Microsoft Edge, the CTRL-SHIFT-DELETE shortcut works as it does in Internet Explorer, opening the browser settings to the *Clear browsing data* page, shown in Figure 10-25.

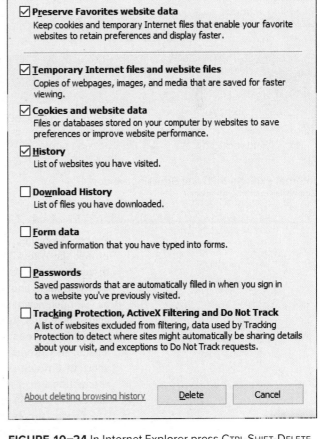

FIGURE 10-24 In Internet Explorer press CTRL-SHIFT-DELETE to open the Delete Browsing History page.
Source: Microsoft Corporation

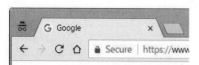

While a Chrome incognito window is open, this character at the upper left watches over the window.
Source: Google LLC

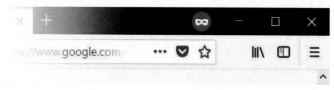

A purple mask appears at the top of a Firefox Private Browsing window.
Source: Mozilla Corporation

Internet Explorer InPrivate Browsing window.
Source: Microsoft Corporation

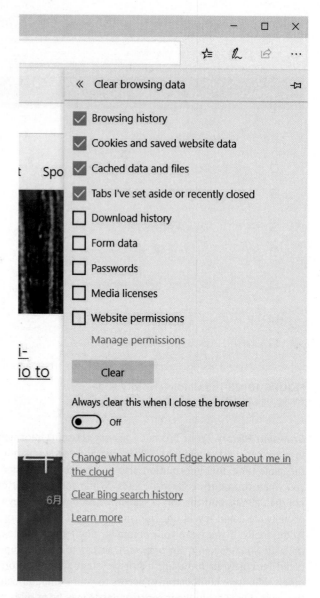

FIGURE 10–25 In Microsoft Edge press CTRL-SHIFT-DELETE to open the Clear browsing data page.
Source: Microsoft Corporation

Private Browsing. Private browsing is a browser security feature that allows you to browse the Web without saving any history on the local computer. All of the browsers discussed here offer private browsing. When you turn on private browsing you open a new window, and your protection exists as long as you remain in that window, even as you open new tabs within the window. Always use private browsing when you use a shared computer, as in a library or school lab.

Chrome's name for private browsing is incognito. To start a private browsing session in Chrome, select **new incognito window** from the Chrome menu or use the shortcut CTRL-SHIFT-N. Then notice the icon in the upper-left corner, shown here, resembling a man with dark glasses and hat peering down on your folders. As long as this is present, you are browsing incognito in Chrome.

Firefox simply calls the feature Private Browsing, and to use it click on the menu button on the right side of the button bar and select **New Private Window** or use the shortcut CTRL-SHIFT-P. The Firefox Private Browsing window is clearly marked, with a purple mask on the top of the window, as shown here.

Both Microsoft Edge and Internet Explorer call private browsing InPrivate Browsing. In Internet Explorer, open the Tools menu and select InPrivate Browsing. In Microsoft Edge, click the menu button on the far right of the button bar and select *New InPrivate window*. When you open an InPrivate window in either browser, the address box is clearly labeled, as shown here. It opens a page that alerts you that InPrivate is turned on and provides a link to online information about this feature, which opens in a new InPrivate browsing window. When you are ready to continue browsing, simply enter a universal resource locator (URL) or a search string in the address box.

Passwords. Do you like to have your browser remember your password to websites, or would you rather enter your user name and password every time you access a site? While it is convenient to have the browser remember passwords, this practice is a security risk if your computer is not protected with a strong password, or if you leave your computer unattended while you are logged in. Configure the browser password settings that work best for you.

In Chrome, open the Chrome menu and select Settings. In Settings, enter **password** in the search box. The search results will resemble Figure 10-26, showing all the settings having to do with passwords in Chrome. The first one is for synchronizing your settings across your devices, a handy feature if you sign in to Chrome with a Google account and want all your Google preferences synchronized across your devices. The last section in the Search results for password is the section Passwords and forms. The first setting allows you to enable Autofill with information such as your mailing address, so if you start typing this into a form in the Chrome browser, it will complete it. Finally, the last item includes the link **Manage passwords.** Click on this to see what passwords are saved and to delete those you no longer want to save.

Manage passwords in Firefox on the Options Privacy and Security page (Figure 10-27) where you can add a master password to your password list by clicking to place a "√" by **Use a master password.** If you decide to set a password, it will prompt you to enter it once per Firefox session in which Firefox retrieves a password for a

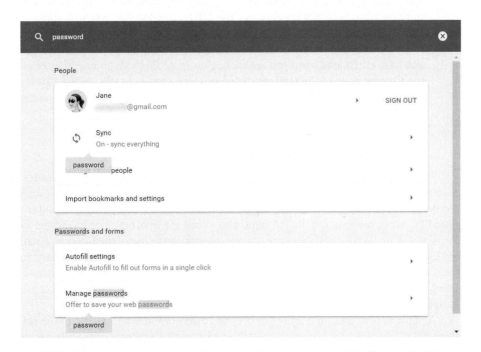

FIGURE 10–26 The Search results from searching on **password** in Chrome Settings.
Source: Google LLC

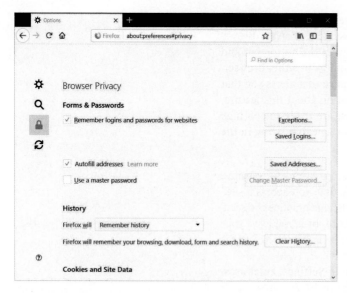

FIGURE 10–27 The Firefox Security Options with the Change Master Password dialog box open.
Source: Mozilla Corporation

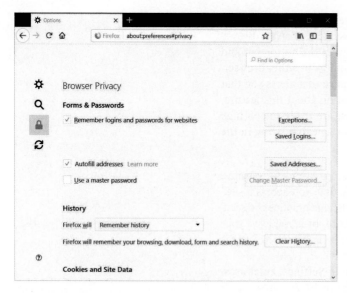

FIGURE 10–28 The Internet Explorer AutoComplete Settings dialog box.
Source: Microsoft Corporation

website. Back in the Security dialog box click on the Saved Logins button to see and manage the saved passwords.

Internet Explorer also saves passwords and other information you enter at websites. To turn this on, select Internet Options from the tools menu. In Internet Options, open the **Content** tab and then select **Settings** under AutoComplete. Figure 10–28 shows the AutoComplete Settings dialog box in Windows 10. Select the types of entries you want AutoComplete to save.

In Microsoft Edge, open Advanced settings and select **Manage my saved passwords** (Figure 10–29). This will open a list of websites with your user name for each site. Click on a website to make changes to your username or password.

Pop-Ups. We've all seen them. Those windows that pop up on top of your browser from a website advertising products, wanting to show you videos, or any number of excuses to get your attention and interrupt your stream of thought. We call them pop-ups, and not all pop-ups are bad. Some of our favorite websites use pop-up windows to open something we requested, such as a downloaded page or a login page, but the latest standard for creating Web pages discourages pop-ups because they do not work on all platforms and they interfere with assistive browsing technologies. Therefore, the use of pop-ups should wane in coming years. For the foreseeable future software that blocks pop-ups is necessary, but it also needs to be configurable so you can block pop-ups from all but the sites you trust.

To access the Pop-up settings for Chrome click on the menu button on the far right of the button bar, then click **Settings.** In the Settings page, scroll down to the bottom and click **Show advanced settings.** This expands the settings. Under **Privacy,** click the **Content settings** button and then scroll down through the Content settings list to **Pop-ups.** Here you can either allow all sites to show pop-ups or select **Do not allow any site to show pop-ups.** If you select the second option, you can click the Manage exceptions button to open a box where you can enter the URLs of sites that you will allow to show pop-ups.

Firefox and Internet Explorer also allow you to enable/disable pop-ups and have exceptions when you enable it. Configure Firefox's pop-up blocker on the **Content** page of the **Options** dialog box and configure IE's on the **Privacy** page of Internet Options. Turn on the pop-up blocker in Microsoft Edge on the Advanced Settings page.

Email Clients

The scope of Internet email has made several major jumps in the past decades.

It evolved from a service used by academics and government workers, through the period when early PC users accessed services such as CompuServ, to today's casual PC users, numbered in the billions, who joined the Internet since the advent of the World Wide Web in 1991. Because of the explosion in the use of the Internet, email has long been the most compelling reason to own a PC—but today you do not need to use a PC to send and receive email. Many people access their personal and business email from their mobile devices. Further, you do not need to own the device you use for Internet access.

An email client used in a school or corporate network may be specific to the private mail servers the user connects to, such as Microsoft Exchange, or the client may be one that you can use for different types of mail servers. Many users have access to email client software such as Microsoft Outlook, Apple Mail, or Mozilla Thunderbird. Users who subscribe to Web mail or free email services such as Gmail, MSN, or Yahoo! can use a Web browser rather than special email client software. Regardless of the type of client software, they all accomplish the task of sending and receiving in the same way.

The client software will show a list of all the messages in the mailbox by displaying information it reads from the message headers. The message header is information added to the beginning of the message that contains details such as who sent it and the subject, and also may show the time and date of the message along with the message's size. Then the user may click on a message to open it and read the body of the email. Users can then respond to the message, save the message, create a new message, add attachments, and/or send it to the intended recipient.

Email clients have become much easier to use, even to the point of automatically detecting and configuring the underlying settings for connecting to an email server, given your personal account information. They also will import your email and contact information from other accounts.

Email Protocols

There are three types of email accounts: POP, IMAP, and Web mail. The first two are protocols, while the third describes email that you access via the Web, and therefore, the protocol is some form of HTTP. When you configure an email client, you need to know the address and type of server, defined by the account type.

POP. Post Office Protocol (POP) is a protocol that enables email client computers to pick up email from mail servers, so that you can open it and read it in your email client. When it picks up a message, it deletes it from the POP server. The current version is POP3. This has been very popular with ISPs because it minimizes the amount of disk space required on the email server for each account. The user is responsible for maintaining and backing up messages. When the client computer does not connect to the email server, the user can still access all the locally stored messages.

IMAP. Internet Message Access Protocol (IMAP) is a protocol that will allow users to maintain the messages stored on an email server (usually on the Internet) without removing them from the server. This type of account allows you to log in and access your message store from any computer. Of course, the message store is not available to you when you are offline, and you may run out of allotted disk space on the mail server, at which point it rejects new messages.

Web Mail. Web mail is a generic term for using a Web browser (and therefore, either HTTPS or HTTP) to retrieve email, often replacing the traditional email client, such as Microsoft Outlook. In fact, this may be the method the tech support at school or work instructs you to use, allowing you to access your email from any browser on any device. With the increase in Internet hosting services offering a wide range of services, many individuals as well as both small and large organizations have their own Internet domains. The hosting services typically include hosting and management of both websites and email accounts for each domain. To do that, consult the Help utility at the provider.

Configuring and Using an Email Client

Whether you use Outlook, Apple Mail, or one of many third-party email clients, you should be prepared with the information to configure your email client. This includes:

- The protocol used by the mail server you are accessing (POP3, IMAP, HTTPS, or HTTP).

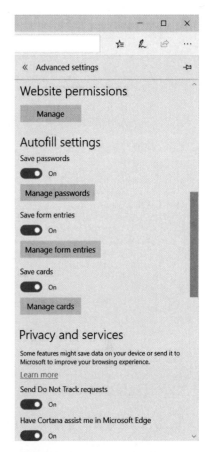

FIGURE 10–29 Select **Manage passwords** in Edge's Advanced settings.
Source: Microsoft Corporation

Note: A variation on a pop-up is a pop-under, a window that opens behind your browser window. Anytime you close a browser window and are puzzled to see a browser window (usually with an advertisement) lurking behind it, you have encountered a pop-under. These are also controlled through the pop-up settings for each browser.

Note: Don't confuse Microsoft Outlook, the email client, with Microsoft **Outlook.com**, the Web mail service.

- Your account name and password.
- The DNS name of the incoming mail server.
- If you are preparing to connect to a POP3 or IMAP server, you will also need to know the name of an outgoing mail server.

If you do not have this information, ask your ISP, in the case of a private account, or ask a network administrator if your mail server is a school or corporate mail server. ISPs often provide email configuration information on their websites. Check this out before configuring your email client because it will help you avoid certain pitfalls. For instance, when configuring a client using a cell data connection, you may have to configure it to authenticate to a certain mail server in the home service area.

In Step-by-Step 10.02, we use Microsoft Outlook 2016 to demonstrate how to configure an email account. Although we stated that you need the information listed above, you might be lucky because email clients, such as Apple Mail and Outlook, can automatically configure some types of email accounts given just the user name and password. This is where you should start. Then, if that doesn't work, use the other information you gathered.

Step-by-Step 10.02

Connecting a Client to an Email Account

To complete this step-by-step exercise, you will need a PC with an Internet connection and an email client. In this exercise, we use Microsoft Outlook 2016 running on a Mac. The basic steps are similar in other email clients. We assume you are adding an account and that the email client already has one account configured. If this is the first account for this email client, you may have introductory screens that will walk you through the process. To complete the exercise, you will need the first two items listed here for all accounts, and the last four only if the client fails to automatically connect to your account with the basic login information.

- The type of account.
- Your password, account name, and email address. The last two are often just the email address.
- The DNS names of the outgoing and incoming mail server.
- The DNS name or IP address of an incoming mail server for POP3, IMAP, or HTTP.
- The DNS name or IP address of an outgoing mail server (SMTP).
- If using a provider, such as Gmail, you may need to change the settings for your Gmail account to allow IMAP access.

Step 1

Locate the option for adding an account. In Outlook first select the Tools ribbon, and then select Accounts on the far left of the ribbon.

Source: Microsoft Corporation

In the Accounts dialog box, locate the list of accounts and click the plus (+) button at the bottom to open the **Add New Account** page.

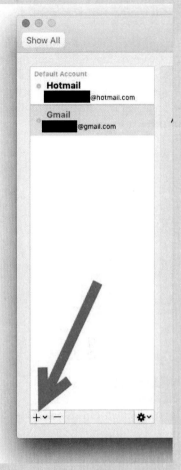

Source: Microsoft Corporation

Select the account type.

Source: Microsoft Corporation

If you select Exchange or Office 365, enter the account information on the following page. Click the scroll button on the right of the **Method** box to select an authentication method.

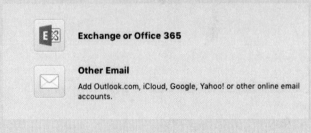

Source: Microsoft Corporation

Step 5

If you select **Other Email,** try using just your email address and password. If that fails, enter the information you obtained from your provider. For instance, we have an account with our hosted domain, so we had to enter the names of the incoming and outgoing mail servers. *Note:* Identifying information is obscured in this image.

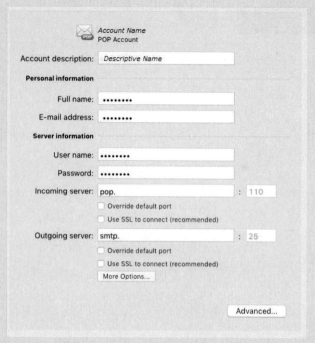

Source: Microsoft Corporation

Step 6

If you connect to this email account from multiple devices, you should configure the email clients on each device to leave messages on the server. To do that in Outlook, select the Advanced button in the Account page, shown in Step 5, and choose if and when you want messages deleted on the server. Outlook also allows you to delete messages individually from Inbox.

Source: Microsoft Corporation

Step 7

Select **Security** to enable digital signing and encryption, if supported by your email provider.

Source: Microsoft Corporation

LO 10.4 | Sharing Files and Printers

The file and printer sharing service allows users to share and access files and printers over a network. All the OSs discussed in this book have methods for allowing file and printer sharing. There are two sides to file and printer sharing: the server side and the client side, and before you implement either side of this equation, take a few minutes to understand how they interact. Both sides must use complementary file and printer services that can talk to each other. Then you can implement sharing on the server side (even on a desktop computer) and users can access it from the client side. For our examples, we'll use Microsoft Windows 7.

The Server Side of File and Printer Sharing

A **file and printer server** (often simply called a file server), is a computer that gives client computers access to files and printers over a network. The actual folder or printer being shared acts as a connecting point on the server and is called a **share**. A share is visible as a folder over the network, but it is a separate entity from the disk folder or printer to which it points. Like other file-sharing services, the one installed with Windows allows you to share both files and printers. This service is installed and enabled by default, although it is up to you to decide how to use it. On a Windows desktop computer, look for File and Printer Sharing for Microsoft Networks in the Properties dialog box for a network connection, as shown in Figure 10–30.

try this!

Find Microsoft File and Printer Servers

You can use Windows Explorer in Windows 7 or open File Explorer on newer versions of Windows to look for the file and printer servers on your network. Try this:

1. Open Windows Explorer/File Explorer.
2. Browse to the Network folder in the left pane.
3. View the icons in the contents pane. The icons resembling a computer with a blue screen are file and printer servers.
4. If any file and printer servers are visible, double-click one to access it and browse. If you do not have permissions, you will see a Network Error message. If you have permissions to a server, you will be able to browse the folders to which you have permissions.

The Client Side of File and Printer Sharing

A file and printer client includes both the user interface and the underlying file-sharing protocols to access its matching file-sharing server service on a network server. The client for Microsoft file and printer sharing is installed and enabled by default. With the client installed, you can use the Windows GUI to see those Microsoft computers on the network that have file and printer sharing turned on. You can see both dedicated Windows network servers and Windows desktops that have this service turned on. Your ability to connect to any shares on those computers depends on the permissions applied to each share. Figure 10–31 shows four computers and a printer (EPSON0E0C4E) that are visible because they have the file and printer service turned on.

With appropriate permissions, you will be able to browse to the shared folders on a server and perform file operations, such as copying, moving, deleting, and opening files in your locally installed applications.

Note: As a rule, a desktop computer should not have File and Printer Sharing turned on, especially if the computer is a member of a domain and connects to dedicated servers for file and printer services. The exception to this is when a desktop computer is participating in a HomeGroup or work group and must share local files and printers with other computers. This is common in the small office/home office (SOHO) situation.

LO 10.5 | Troubleshooting Common Network Client Problems

If you are unable to access another computer on the network, several command-line utilities will help in pinpointing the source of a problem and arriving at a solution. In this section, you will learn to troubleshoot common client connection problems using each of these utilities, as indicated by the symptoms. Each utility provides different information and is most valuable when used appropriately. For instance, you should

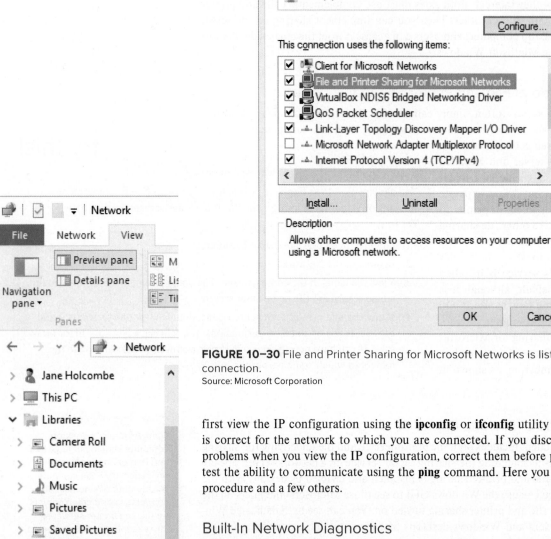

FIGURE 10–30 File and Printer Sharing for Microsoft Networks is listed for a network connection.
Source: Microsoft Corporation

FIGURE 10–31 The computers and printer listed at the bottom under Network have File and Printer Sharing turned on.
Source: Microsoft Corporation

first view the IP configuration using the **ipconfig** or **ifconfig** utility and verify that it is correct for the network to which you are connected. If you discover any obvious problems when you view the IP configuration, correct them before proceeding. Then test the ability to communicate using the **ping** command. Here you will practice this procedure and a few others.

Built-In Network Diagnostics

Each of the operating systems surveyed in this book has a variety of utilities for diagnosing network problems. From the command-line utilities discussed later in this section to GUI tools that combine the functions of several tools into one broad-stroke diagnostics tool, each generation of OS brings improvements in these tools. In Windows 7 and Windows 8, the Windows Network Diagnostics, the Windows 7 version of which is shown in Figure 10–32, will diagnose the problem area (the broadband modem in this example) and instruct you on how to solve the problem. Similarly, if your Internet connection fails, the Network Diagnostics window will display and attempt to diagnose the problem.

The Network Utility in macOS, shown in Figure 10–33, requires more knowledge of the individual tools, but it does spare you from entering the commands from the macOS Terminal window.

Testing IP Configurations and Connectivity

When the TCP/IP suite is installed on a computer, it includes many protocols and many handy little programs that network professionals quickly learn to use. You should learn two right away, for those times when you find yourself sitting at your computer and talking to a network professional while trying to resolve a network problem. These are commands you enter at a command line. In Windows these commands are **ipconfig** and **ping**. In macOS and Linux they are **ifconfig** and **ping**. Learn about these commands below, and then do Step-by-Step 10.03, in which you will use both of these commands to test a network connection.

Verifying IP Configuration with ipconfig

The **ipconfig** command will display the IP configuration of all network interface cards, including those that receive their addresses and configuration through DHCP. Using this command shows whether the IP settings have been successfully bound to your network adapter. *Bound* means that there is a linking relationship, called a binding, between network components—in this case, between the network protocol and the adapter. A binding establishes the order in which each network component handles network communications. When troubleshooting network connectivity problems on an IP network, always use the **ipconfig** command to verify the IP configuration.

If the **ipconfig** command reveals an address beginning with 169.254, it is an APIPA address and a symptom of a failure of a Windows DHCP client to receive an IP address from a DHCP server (for whatever reason). Troubleshoot the DHCP server on your network (such as the DHCP service in a broadband router).

Troubleshooting Connection Errors with the ping Command

The **ping** command is useful for testing the communications between two computers. The name of this command is actually an acronym for packet Internet groper, but we prefer to think (as many do) that it was named after the sound of underwater sonar. Instead of bouncing sound waves off surfaces, the **ping** command uses data packets, and it sends them to specific IP addresses, requesting a response (hence the idea of pinging). This is a great test to see if you can access a certain computer.

To use the **ping** command, give it an address and it sends packets to the specified address, "listens" for a reply, and then displays the results.

1. Pinging the IP address of the computer's own NIC and receiving a successful response indicates that the IP protocol and the local address is working. Using the example in Figure 10–34, from Host_1-1 you would type: **ping 192.168.1.101** to ping the local NIC.

FIGURE 10–32 The Windows 7 Network Diagnostics tool.
Source: Microsoft Corporation

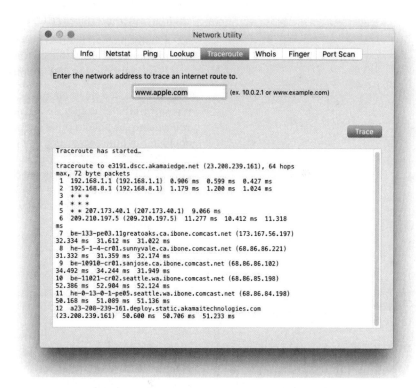

FIGURE 10–33 The macOS Network Utility at work (notice the various network diagnostic tools listed across the top).
Source: Apple Inc.

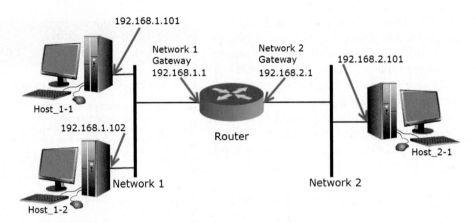

FIGURE 10–34 Two networks connected by a router.

2. Then ping another computer on the same network to test the ability to communicate between the two computers. Again, from Host_1-1 you would type **ping 192.168.1.102** to ping Host_1-2, a computer on the same network.

3. Next, ping the gateway address to ensure that your computer can communicate with the router. Again, working from Host_1-1 in Figure 10–34, type **ping 192.168.1.1** to ping the gateway address for Network 1, which is the address of the router interface (NIC) connected to Network 1.

4. Finally, ping an address beyond your network, to test the router and the ability to communicate with a computer via the router. Using Figure 10–34, from Host_1-1 type **ping 192.168.2.101** to ping the address of Host_2-1 on Network 2.

Now the bad news about the **ping** command. First, a firewall can block specific types of traffic or configure an individual computer not to respond to a ping. Hence, you may not be able to ping a computer, even if you can communicate with that same computer in other ways such as by Web browsing or downloading email.

The reason firewalls or individual computers block or ignore the requests from a **ping** command is because people can use this command in malicious ways—most notoriously in a denial of service (DoS) attack, in which someone sends a large number of ping requests to an address, overwhelming the server so that it is unavailable to accept other traffic.

Step-by-Step 10.03

Testing an IP Configuration

In this step-by-step exercise, you will first open a command-line interface (CLI) in Windows—either Command Prompt or Windows PowerShell. Then, you will run a CLI command to determine if the IP settings are automatic or static. Next, you will verify that you can communicate with a computer on your network and then test your connection to a router on your network. Finally, test to confirm that you can communicate with a computer beyond your network. To complete this exercise, you will need the following:

- A computer with Windows 7 or later.

- A working connection to the Internet.
- The IP address of another computer on your local network (use this when a step asks for *NearbyIPaddress*). Enter this in the appropriate line in Step 3.
- The IP address of a computer beyond your local network (use this when a step asks for *RemoteIPaddress*). Enter this in the appropriate line in Step 3.
- The user name and password of an account that is a member of your computer's Administrators group.

Step 1

Begin by opening a CLI where you will run commands to view settings and test connectivity. In Windows 8, 8.1, or 10, open the Command Prompt or PowerShell per the instructions in Step 6 of Step-by-Step 6.02 in Chapter 6. In Windows 7, open a Command Prompt by selecting Start | Run. In the Open dialog box, type "cmd" and press Enter. At the prompt in the CLI type **ipconfig/all**.

```
C:\Documents and Settings\Jane>ipconfig /all

Windows IP Configuration

        Host Name . . . . . . . . . . . . : Wickenburg
        Primary Dns Suffix  . . . . . . . :
        Node Type . . . . . . . . . . . . : Hybrid
        IP Routing Enabled. . . . . . . . : No
        WINS Proxy Enabled. . . . . . . . : No

Ethernet adapter Local Area Connection:

        Connection-specific DNS Suffix  . :
        Description . . . . . . . . . . . : Realtek RTL8139/810x Family Fast Eth
ernet NIC
        Physical Address. . . . . . . . . : 08-00-46-A7-29-3B
        Dhcp Enabled. . . . . . . . . . . : No
        IP Address. . . . . . . . . . . . : 192.168.100.48
        Subnet Mask . . . . . . . . . . . : 255.255.255.0
        Default Gateway . . . . . . . . . : 192.168.100.1
        DNS Servers . . . . . . . . . . . : 192.168.100.1

C:\Documents and Settings\Jane>
```

Source: Microsoft Corporation

Step 2

If the current settings show an IP address other than 0.0.0.0, IP has successfully bound an IP address to the network adapter. If the current settings include DHCP enabled = **Yes,** and shows an IP address for a DHCP server, then your network adapter is configured to receive an address automatically and has received its address from the DHCP server whose address is listed. If your DHCP Enabled setting = **No** and your computer has a set of values for the IP address and subnet mask, then it has a static IP configuration that is successfully bound to the network adapter.

Step 3

Gather the information from the **ipconfig /all** command and fill in the first three lines provided below. Your instructor will give you the last two items, *NearbyIPaddress* and *RemoteIPaddress.* You will need these addresses in the following steps.

IPaddress: _____

Default GatewayIPaddress: _____

DNSServerIPaddress: _____

NearbyIPaddress: _____

RemoteIPaddress: _____

Step 4

At the Command Prompt, enter **ping** *IPaddress,* where "*IPaddress*" is the address of your computer from Step 3. You should receive four replies if your computer is properly configured. If you receive an error message or fewer than four replies, report this to your instructor.

Step 5

At the Command Prompt, enter **ping** *NearbyIPaddress,* where "*NearbyIPaddress*" is the address of another computer on your same network. You should receive four replies if your computer is properly configured and if the other computer is also powered up and properly configured. If you receive an error message or fewer than four replies, report this to your instructor.

```
C:\Documents and Settings\Jane>ping 192.168.100.48

Pinging 192.168.100.48 with 32 bytes of data:

Reply from 192.168.100.48: bytes=32 time<1ms TTL=128
Reply from 192.168.100.48: bytes=32 time<1ms TTL=128
Reply from 192.168.100.48: bytes=32 time<1ms TTL=128
Reply from 192.168.100.48: bytes=32 time<1ms TTL=128

Ping statistics for 192.168.100.48:
    Packets: Sent = 4, Received = 4, Lost = 0 (0% loss),
Approximate round trip times in milli-seconds:
    Minimum = 0ms, Maximum = 0ms, Average = 0ms

C:\Documents and Settings\Jane>_
```

Source: Microsoft Corporation

If the last test was successful, and if your computer has a gateway address, test this address now. Return to the Command Prompt and enter **ping** *Default gatewayIPaddress,* where "*Default gatewayIPaddress*" equals the Default Gateway address recorded in Step 3. You should receive four replies if your computer is properly configured and if the default gateway is active on your network.

```
C:\Documents and Settings\Jane>ping 192.168.100.1

Pinging 192.168.100.1 with 32 bytes of data:

Reply from 192.168.100.1: bytes=32 time<1ms TTL=128
Reply from 192.168.100.1: bytes=32 time=1ms TTL=128
Reply from 192.168.100.1: bytes=32 time<1ms TTL=128
Reply from 192.168.100.1: bytes=32 time<1ms TTL=128

Ping statistics for 192.168.100.1:
    Packets: Sent = 4, Received = 4, Lost = 0 (0% loss),
Approximate round trip times in milli-seconds:
    Minimum = 0ms, Maximum = 1ms, Average = 0ms

C:\Documents and Settings\Jane>
```

Source: Microsoft Corporation

If your IP configuration includes the address of a DNS server, you should test connectivity to the DNS server now. Return to the Command Prompt and enter **ping** *DNSServerIPaddress,* where "*DNSServerIPaddress*" equals the DNSServer address recorded in Step 3. You should receive four replies if your computer is properly configured and if the default gateway is active on your network.

If you were given the address of a computer beyond your local network, test this address now by returning to the Command Prompt and entering **ping** *RemoteIPaddress,* where "*RemoteIPaddress*" is the address of the remote computer.

Note: The equivalent command in Linux or macOS Terminal is **traceroute.**

Troubleshooting Connection Problems with tracert

You may have situations in which you can connect to a website or other remote resource, but the connection is very slow. If this connection is critical to business, you will want to gather information so that a network administrator or ISP can troubleshoot the source of the bottleneck. You can use the **tracert** command to gather this information. **tracert** is a command-line utility that traces the route taken by packets to a destination. When you use this command with the name or IP address of the target host, it will **ping** each of the intervening routers, from the nearest to the farthest, as shown in Figure 10–35. You see the length of the delay at each router, and you will be able to determine the location of the bottleneck. You can then provide this information to the people who will troubleshoot it for you. Consider a scenario in which your connection to the Google search engine (www.google.com) is extremely slow. You can use this command to run **tracert** and save the results to a file: **tracert www.google.com tracegoogle.txt.**

try this!

Use tracert

You can use **tracert** to determine where a problem is occurring. Try this:

1. Open a Command Prompt.
2. Type **tracert www.google.com**.
3. If the command runs successfully, you will see output similar to Figure 10–35, but with different intervening routers.

```
C:\>tracert www.google.com

Tracing route to www.google.akadns.net [216.239.41.99]
over a maximum of 30 hops:

  1    <1 ms    <1 ms    <1 ms   192.168.100.1
  2   858 ms   810 ms   812 ms   hh1095067.direcpc.com [205.177.62.67]
  3   875 ms   819 ms   807 ms   dpc6682016181.direcpc.com [66.82.16.181]
  4   803 ms   746 ms   872 ms   dpc6682016073.direcpc.com [66.82.16.73]
  5   749 ms   820 ms   747 ms   so-5-1.hsa1.Washington1.Level3.net [63.215.128.129]
  6   806 ms   867 ms   879 ms   ge-9-2.ipcolo2.Washington1.Level3.net [4.68.121.172]

  7   815 ms   806 ms   760 ms   unknown.Level3.net [166.90.148.174]
  8   749 ms   812 ms   811 ms   216.239.47.69
  9   821 ms   805 ms   812 ms   216.239.47.154
 10   871 ms   747 ms   811 ms   216.239.48.77
 11   755 ms   867 ms   880 ms   216.239.41.99

Trace complete.

C:\>_
```

FIGURE 10–35 The tracert results.
Source: Microsoft Corporation

Troubleshooting DNS Errors Using ping, netstat, and nslookup

Have you ever attempted to browse to a Web page, only to have your browser display an error message such as "Cannot find server or DNS Error"? This may be a name resolution problem because the fully qualified domain name (FQDN) portion of a URL, such as www.google.com, must be resolved to an IP address before a single packet goes to the website.

Using the ping Command to Troubleshoot DNS

One way to test if the problem is a connectivity problem or a DNS error is to first test for connectivity by either pinging the IP address of the website or using the IP address in place of the FQDN in the URL. If you cannot reach the website by using its IP address, then it is a connectivity problem and you should resolve it by contacting your network administrator or ISP and telling them the symptoms and the results of the **ping** test.

If you can reach the website by pinging the IP address but cannot access it through your browser, then it is a name resolution problem. A simple test to see if DNS name resolution is working is to ping the FQDN. Figure 10–36 shows the result of pinging the FQDN www.google.com. Notice that this displays the IP address of the website, confirming the DNS name-to-IP address resolution is working.

Troubleshooting with the netstat Command

When you are troubleshooting networking problems, it is very helpful to have a second computer that does not display the same problems. Then you can use the second computer to discover the IP address of a website by using your browser to connect. Once connected, you can use the **netstat** command to discover the IP address of the website. **netstat** displays network statistics, protocol statistics, and information about current

> *Note:* If you want to save a copy of the information displayed by a command-line command (such as **tracert**), you can send the screen output of this command to a text file, using the command-line redirection symbol (>). You can use any file name and any path to which you have write access. For instance, type **tracert www.google.com >tracegoogle.txt**. No output will appear on the screen.

```
C:\>ping www.google.com

Pinging www.google.akadns.net [216.239.41.104] with 32 bytes of data:

Reply from 216.239.41.104: bytes=32 time=923ms TTL=245
Reply from 216.239.41.104: bytes=32 time=856ms TTL=245
Reply from 216.239.41.104: bytes=32 time=855ms TTL=245
Reply from 216.239.41.104: bytes=32 time=858ms TTL=245

Ping statistics for 216.239.41.104:
    Packets: Sent = 4, Received = 4, Lost = 0 (0% loss),
Approximate round trip times in milli-seconds:
    Minimum = 855ms, Maximum = 923ms, Average = 873ms

C:\>
```

FIGURE 10–36 Pinging the FQDN www.google.com reveals the IP address.
Source: Microsoft Corporation

```
C:\>netstat

Active Connections

  Proto  Local Address          Foreign Address         State
  TCP    Wickenburg:1175        216.239.41.104:http     ESTABLISHED

C:\>
```

FIGURE 10–37 The **netstat** command displays the IP address and protocol information of current connections.
Source: Microsoft Corporation

```
C:\>nslookup
*** Can't find server name for address 192.168.100.1: Non-existent domain
*** Default servers are not available
Default Server:  UnKnown
Address:  192.168.100.1

>
```

FIGURE 10–38 The **nslookup** command reveals a DNS problem.
Source: Microsoft Corporation

TCP/IP connections. Figure 10-37 shows the result of running the **netstat** command after connecting to a website with a browser. The IP address for this website, **www.google.com**, is shown under Foreign Address, and the protocol used to connect to the website, http, is shown after the colon.

Using the nslookup Command to Troubleshoot DNS

Finally, the classic command for troubleshooting DNS, used for many years on the Internet and other TCP/IP networks, is **nslookup.** The NS in this command name stands for "name server." This command allows you to send queries to a DNS name server directly and see the results. It is a very powerful command, but you can use it to test your DNS setting without learning all of its subcommands. Running **nslookup** in a Command Prompt without any additional command-line parameters will cause it to attempt to connect to the name server address in your IP configuration. Then it displays the **nslookup** prompt, a greater-than sign (>). You may enter subcommands at this prompt. If it cannot connect to the DNS server, it will display an error, as shown in Figure 10–38. If you see this error, contact your network administrator or ISP. Type **exit** at the **nslookup** prompt to exit from the command. Then type **exit** again to exit from the Command Prompt.

Note: To learn more about the **nslookup** command, search on **nslookup** in the Windows Help program.

Chapter 10 REVIEW

Chapter Summary

After reading this chapter and completing the Step-by-Step tutorials and Try This! exercises, you should understand the following facts about networking:

Configuring a Network Connection
- A protocol is a set of rules, usually formalized in a standard published by one of many standards organizations. A software implementation of a protocol is also called a protocol.

- TCP/IP is the protocol suite needed to access the Internet.

- Transmission Control Protocol (TCP) and Internet Protocol (IP) are the core protocols of TCP/IP.

- An IP address assigned to a network adapter or modem connects it to a network.
- IPv4, an old version of the protocol, is slowly being replaced by IPv6.
- Public IP addresses are for hosts on the Internet, and each address must be unique on the entire Internet.
- A private IP address is one of three ranges of IP addresses designated for use only on private networks. They are not for use on the Internet, and you do not need to obtain permission to use these addresses on a private network.
- Computers on a private network using private IP addresses get access to the Internet through a specialized device, usually a router.
- Each host on a TCP/IP network must have an IP address. A host receives an address by two general methods: automatically as a DHCP client via a network DHCP server (or a self-assigned APIPA address), or as a static address.
- In addition to the IP address there are several IP configuration settings including subnet mask, default gateway, DNS server, advanced DNS settings, and WINS settings.

Connecting to the Internet

- A connection to the Internet is a wide area network (WAN) connection.
- An Internet service provider (ISP) is an organization that provides individuals or entire companies access to the Internet.
- Common wired WAN technologies include dial-up, ISDN, DSL, and cable.
- ISDN is a digital telephone service that simultaneously transmits voice, data, and control signaling over a single telephone line and can transfer data at up to 128,000 bits per second (128 Kbps).
- Digital subscriber line (DSL) service is similar to ISDN in its use of the telephone network, but it uses more advanced digital signal processing to compress more signals through the telephone lines and so is much faster than ISDN.
- Many cable television companies now offer Internet access through existing cable television connections using special cable modems.
- Wireless options for connecting to the Internet include cellular networks, wireless wide area networks (WWANs), wireless LAN (WLAN) connections (if the WLAN ultimately connects to the Internet), and satellite.
- Mobile users and remote offices often need to connect to the corporate intranet through the Internet using any of the connection technologies discussed

previously, with the addition of a virtual private network (VPN) for security.

Using Internet Clients

- Web technologies changed the look of Internet content from all text to rich and colorful graphics and made it simple to navigate the Web by using a special type of client called a Web browser.
- The top Web browsers are Google Chrome, Mozilla Firefox, and Internet Explorer.
- Both Firefox and IE have many configuration settings that range from GUI preferences to settings critical to protecting your privacy and maintaining security for your computer and personal data.
- An email service and client are defined by the protocols they use, which are POP3, IMAP, and Web mail (HTML protocol).
- While some email services require dedicated clients, some email clients can interact with a variety of email server types.
- To configure any email client you need a specific set of information. This includes:
  - The type of mail server you are accessing (POP3, IMAP, or HTTP).
  - Your account name and password.
  - The DNS name of the incoming mail server.
  - If you are preparing to connect to a POP3 or IMAP server, you will also need to know the name of an outgoing mail server.

Sharing Files and Printers

- A file and printer sharing protocol allows a computer to share files and printers with compatible clients.
- A file and printer client includes both the user interface and the underlying file-sharing protocols to access a file-sharing system on a network file and printer server.
- Windows installs with both the server and client components for file and printer sharing.

Troubleshooting Common Network Client Connection Problems

- All the OSs surveyed in this book have GUI-based Network Diagnostics that combine many functions.
- Several command-line commands help in diagnosing and solving network client connection problems. These utilities include:
  - **ipconfig**
  - **ifconfig**
  - **ping**
  - **tracert**
  - **netstat**
  - **nslookup**

Key Terms List

Key Terms Quiz

Use the Key Terms List to complete the sentences that follow:

1. The IP addresses designated for hosts connected directly to the Internet are _____.

2. _____ is the version of the Internet Protocol that is slowly replacing the version that has been in use since 1983.

3. A/an _____ uses encapsulation to protect data sent over a public network. Encryption makes the data more secure.

4. An IPv4 address beginning with 169.254 is a/an _____ address.

5. A/an _____ is not used for hosts on the Internet.

6. A/an _____ is an organization that provides individuals or entire companies with access to the Internet.

7. In an IPv4 address, each grouping of decimal numbers is called a/an _____ because it represent eight bits.

8. Among IP configuration settings, the _____ is the IP address of the router used to send packets beyond the local network.

9. _____ is a term for a group of wired high-speed technologies offered through the phone company, and capable of much greater speeds than ISDN.

10. Most organizations use a _____ to assign IP addresses to desktop computers.

Multiple-Choice Quiz

1. The IPv4 address 192.168.30.24 is an example of one of these.
   a. DNS server address
   b. Public IP address
   c. Private IP address
   d. Automatic private IP address
   e. WINS server address

2. This protocol has 340 trillion, trillion, trillion unique identifiers.
   a. DNS
   b. IPv6

   c. DSL
   d. DHCP
   e. IMAP

3. In the chapter, which form of DSL is described as having the same speed upstream as downstream?
   a. ADSL
   b. *x*DSL
   c. VDSL
   d. HDSL
   e. SDSL

4. Your neighbor tells you that his Internet connection at home is much slower than the connection he enjoys at work—and he is disconnected if there is a period of inactivity. From his description, which type of connection would you assume he has?
   a. ISDN
   b. Dial-up
   c. ADSL
   d. SDSL
   e. Cable

5. What appears in the Windows Connect Using box in the connection properties dialog box?
   a. A connection device
   b. An ISP name
   c. A user name
   d. A password
   e. A phone number

6. Which of the following is obviously *not* a valid IPv4 address?
   a. 192.168.100.48
   b. 10.0.33.50
   c. 172.300.256.100
   d. 30.88.29.1
   e. 200.100.99.99

7. You connect to Wi-Fi from your smartphone or laptop in public places, such as airports and coffee shops. What type of service should you use to protect your communications?
   a. VPN
   b. Firewall
   c. Private browsing
   d. IPv6
   e. Private IP address

8. What command can you use to view the status of current connections, including the IP address and protocol used for each connection?
   a. **ipconfig**
   b. **cmd**
   c. **ping**
   d. **netstat**
   e. **tracert**

9. Which of the following is an example of an IPv6 address with the leading zeros removed?
   a. 2002:0470:b8f9:0000:020c:29ff:fe53:45ca
   b. 192.168.1.1
   c. 10.0.0.1
   d. 2002:470:b8f9::20c:29ff:fe53:45ca
   e. 0.0.0.0

10. Which command would you use as a test to see if a DNS server will respond to a request to resolve a name?
    a. **ping**
    b. **nslookup**
    c. **ipconfig**
    d. **netstat**
    e. **tracert**

11. This IPv4 configuration setting defines the two parts of an IP address: the Host ID and the Net ID.
    a. Gateway
    b. Subnet mask
    c. DNS
    d. DHCP
    e. Host name

12. Where in Internet Options can you configure how IE manages cookies?
    a. General page
    b. Security page
    c. Tabs page
    d. Advanced Privacy Settings dialog box
    e. Exceptions button

13. Your neighbor, a retiree on a modest fixed income, has asked your help in acquiring an Internet connection for his computer, a desktop computer running Windows 7. His only interest in Internet access is to use email to keep in touch with his children, who live in other states. He has a reliable phone connection. Based on this information, which service will you recommend?
    a. Cable
    b. ISDN
    c. Dial-up
    d. DSL
    e. Satellite

14. If you wanted to see the IP configuration from the $ prompt on a MAC, Linux, or UNIX system, which command would you use?
    a. **ipconfig**
    b. **netstat**
    c. **nslookup**
    d. **ping**
    e. **ifconfig**

15. What protocol is responsible for the accurate delivery of messages, verifying and resending pieces that fail to make the trip from source to destination?
    a. Internet Protocol
    b. Transmit Control Protocol (TCP)
    c. Secure Sockets Layer (SSL)
    d. File Transfer Protocol (FTP)
    e. Transmission Control Protocol (TCP)

Essay Quiz

1. Your computer was recently connected via a network adapter to a LAN that includes a router through which traffic passes to the Internet. You know the adapter was configured to use TCP/IP, and you need to test its ability to communicate with computers on the LAN and on the Internet. In your own words describe the steps you will take.

2. After reviewing Web browsers in this chapter, do you see a commonality in the user interface and in the less obvious features of these different apps? Describe your observations.

3. In a large western state an agency that dispatches mobile units to disaster areas to monitor the disaster sites for hazardous chemical and biological contamination requires reliable Internet access for these units from any location in the state. They need to keep up-to-date with technical information via postings on federal websites and to upload their data to state and federal sites. Which Internet connection option is the best fit for their needs? Explain your answer.

4. In Step-by-Step 10.02, Step 6, you are instructed to configure when messages should be deleted from a mail server. This is a setting in most email clients. Consider how you would configure your email clients on several devices connecting to the same email service, including an explanation of why you would (or would not) configure all your clients to delete messages as soon as they are picked up.

5. Explain subnet masking in simple terms, including why a subnet mask is required when an adapter is configured with an IP address.

Lab Projects

LAB PROJECT 10.1

Research VPN services for individuals and answer these questions.

1. How do the various VPN services differ?

2. What is the advantage of the feature called geo-shifting?

3. What does it mean when a provider says that they do not keep logs?

4. Why is it important to know where the VPN servers are located when selecting a VPN service?

5. Why would someone want the feature that makes it appear that they are connected from a different country?

6. What are the advantages to hiding the type of content you are downloading?

LAB PROJECT 10.2

This project requires the use of a Windows, Linux, or Mac computer that has Internet access. Using methods you learned in this chapter, find the answers to the following questions:

1. How is an IP address assigned to the lab computer?

2. Record the IP configuration settings for the lab computer below:
   a. IP address
   b. Subnet mask
   c. Default gateway
   d. DNS server

LAB PROJECT 10.3

Interview the IT staff at your school, place of work, or another organization and determine what Internet services they offer to students (Web pages, email, etc.). The list will usually go beyond the basic services studied in this chapter. Create a list of these services and the clients they require.

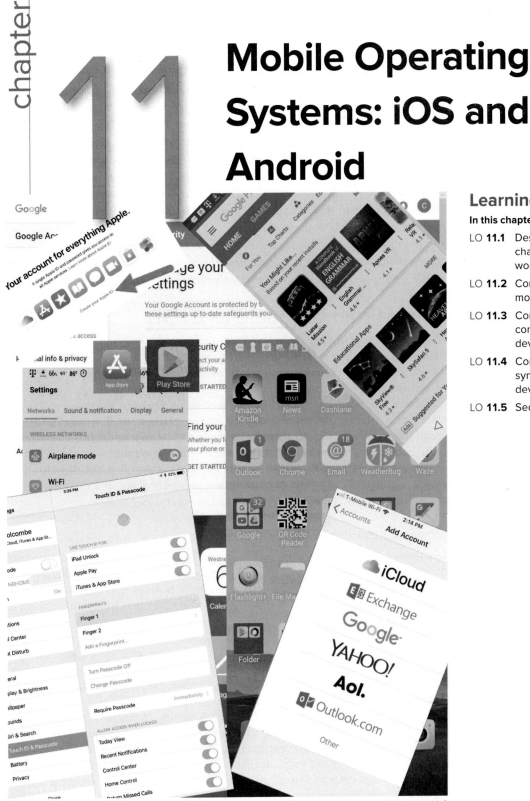

chapter

11

Mobile Operating Systems: iOS and Android

Learning Outcomes

In this chapter, you will learn how to:

LO **11.1** Describe the benefits and challenges of BYOD in the workplace.

LO **11.2** Configure accounts for mobile devices.

LO **11.3** Configure wireless connections on mobile devices.

LO **11.4** Configure email, apps, and synchronization on mobile devices.

LO **11.5** Secure mobile devices.

Source: Apple Inc. and Google LLC

Mobile computing in the 21st century has evolved from two branches of the technology tree: the telephony branch and the personal computing branch. Today's mobile devices only remotely resemble their awkward ancestors because today's devices are remarkably tiny and powerful, more like fictional *Star Trek* communicators than any 20th-century phones or computers. The versatility and widespread consumer appeal of today's mobile devices exceeds the extraordinary imagination and vision of *Star Trek* creator Gene Roddenberry, at least in their use by consumers. Perhaps no one could have predicted five decades ago how tiny and powerful computing and communicating devices would become, and that they would be so common that individuals would insist on using them at work.

Chapter 1 introduced mobile devices and mobile operating systems. Before reading this chapter, we urge you to review the Chapter 1 section titled "Today's Mobile Operating Systems." The coverage includes a description of the hardware features of popular smartphones and tablets. They include cameras, speakers, speaker jacks, adapters for a growing number of wireless technologies, and several types of sensors. Sensors include the accelerometer (described in the overview of mobile devices in Chapter 1), GPS, magnetometer, proximity sensor, compass, and ambient light sensors. We will also look at a few mobile accessories.

In this chapter, we first explore the issues surrounding employees using their personal mobile devices at work, then we describe common configuration tasks for your mobile device, and finally we look at security for mobile devices. 🌐

LO 11.1 | From Luggable to BYOD

Mobile computing was once something only certain business travelers did using computers that were just luggable versions of the PCs they left at the office. Mobile computing has evolved, and in just the last few years the mobile computing market has been flooded with tiny and powerful mobile devices. Now consumers in every walk of life practice mobile computing, children carry smartphones to preschool, and teachers uncrate boxes of iPads preloaded with student coursework. The "mobile" aspect seems to mean that we are not tethered to power and data lines, even as we practice mobile computing at home and everyplace else we go day or night.

In this section, you'll peek at the past of mobile computing, which wasn't very mobile, rarely connected, and involved little computing power. Then you'll examine the issue of using personal mobile devices in the workplace.

Mobile Computing Then and Now

In a span of 30 years, mobile computing devices went from a few heavy underpowered devices to today's large number of mobile devices that fit nicely in the hand and whose weight is measured in ounces rather than in tens of pounds. Hence, personal mobile devices are rarely out of reach of their owners, who have come to depend on them at home, school, work, and play. Some of us have lived through this history.

Sometime in the mid-1980s, our friend Amber was waiting in the baggage area of an airport as a gray plastic bin rose into view at the center of the baggage carousel and made a precarious slide down to the moving stainless-steel track. She recognized its clattering contents as the components of a Compaq portable computer, its cracked case the size of a 21st-century gaming tower.

Obviously, some road warrior had wearied of lugging 28 pounds of technology and checked it as baggage. Amber smugly snatched up her own suitcase and placed it on top of her luggage cart that already contained her carry-on: a 16-pound Zenith Data Systems Z-180 Portable PC. She had spent the flight with her feet resting uneasily on the portion of the laptop that did not fit under the passenger seat in front of her, while the luggage cart rode in the overhead compartment. There was no way she could actually put the laptop on her lap and get real work done. Computer professionals like Amber, rather than the typical consumer of the time, were the target market for portable computers. To quote the Welcome page of the Zenith Data Systems Z-180 Owner's Manual:

This Owner's Manual is for you, the new computer user. In the first part of this manual, you will learn how to set up and operate your new computer for the first time. In

The Home screen on an iPhone.
Source: Apple Inc.

the second part, you will learn about the firmware of the computer and how to program it. In the third part, you will learn about the hardware and how to use the programmable registers in the computer.

Programmable registers? Times have changed. Three decades later we no longer expect or need a manual for a new tablet or smartphone. Another big change is that modern mobile devices are almost always connected to one or more networks, whereas the old devices did not connect to any network while in transit. Amber had to wait until she arrived in a classroom with a connection to a local area network (LAN) or hotel room that included a "modem line" for a slow dial-up connection. The more expensive the hotel, the more they charged for this service. Today's travelers demand that hotels provide free high-speed Internet access, and many people have cellular data plans so that their mobile devices can wirelessly connect to the Internet 24/7.

And consider what they do with those connections! Mobile device users collectively upload and share hundreds of millions of photos every day. They upload an estimated 300 hours of video to YouTube per minute. And this type of traffic is increasing as more and more mobile users stay in touch, sharing their thoughts and opinions via social media, and keeping up with work and personal email. This pervasiveness of mobile devices has led to a phenomenon in the workplace that we explore next.

Mobile Devices and BYOD

Smartphones and tablets present a challenge for schools and employers because most people come to school or work armed with a pocket or a backpack full of technology. And they don't care to spend any time separated from these devices. Many demand to be able to use these devices for accessing work email, text messages, and data. This practice is called bring your own device (BYOD), and it occurs in many organizations, whether or not they officially condone it.

The Home screen on an Android smartphone.
Source: Google LLC

There are variations of policies (or lack of them) governing BYOD in the workplace. Here are just a few examples:

- Companies may reimburse an employee who uses their own device for cellular voice and data usage. This is important, because cellular voice charges are usually by the minute, and cellular data services are metered, with the cost going up with the amount of data downloaded. Charges can quickly mount up for someone using their personal device for work.
- In a form of shared ownership, an employer subsidizes the purchase of an employee's personal mobile device, giving the employee the option of buying a more expensive device than budgeted.
- An employer may allow or require use of personal mobile devices but not compensate the employee or have any clear policies regarding how to protect work data.

Advantages of BYOD to Employers

BYOD has certain advantages for employers:

- Quicker response by the employee using email and text messaging.
- It saves the employer the cost of the device.
- Some jobs require, or at least benefit from, the use of mobile devices.
- Acceptance of employees' use of mobile devices attracts tech-savvy people.
- Employees are inclined to work outside of normal work hours.
- You can deliver important job training to mobile devices that employees can use when needed.

The Home screen on an iPad.
Source: Apple Inc.

Disadvantages of BYOD to Employers

There are risks to allowing employees access email and corporate data using their personal mobile devices. A few of the issues include:

- Personal mobile devices can significantly increase the load on the employer's network infrastructure.
- It may conflict with corporate security policy.
- It may violate government regulations for employees to have certain data on their mobile devices.
- If a device is lost or stolen, it puts the employer at risk.
- Employees may leave a job and still have sensitive work-related data on their personal devices.
- Normally, intellectual property created as part of a job belongs to the employer. It is unclear who owns the intellectual property if it is created on the employee's device.

Risks of BYOD to Employees

There are risks and concerns for the employee. Consider these issues:

- Who will pay for the cost of the device?
- Who will pay for added voice and data usage due to business use?
- What protects the employees if the employer's policy mandates monitoring BYOD devices?
- Can an employer or law enforcement agency confiscate an employee's device for any work-related reason?

Basic BYOD Policies

Basic BYOD policies should address these areas:

- Who owns intellectual property created on an employee's device—the employee or the employer?
- What security requirements should there be and how should they be enforced, including but not limited to passwords, encryption, and remote wipe (remotely deleting data from a lost or stolen device)?
- How and when does the employee back up the employer's data?
- Will video- and audio-recording features in BYOD devices be allowed in the workplace?
- Will the employer take advantage of location services on devices to monitor an employee's location during working hours? A location service is one that allows an app to track your location, using one or more methods, often with the help of the Internet.

Managing BYOD

Managing BYOD begins with company policies covering work behavior, security, and employee reimbursement. Existing policies may cover the use of personal devices in very broad terms and need updating. Employers have many options for managing BYOD to protect themselves and their employees. They also want to make the mobile devices more useful to the employees.

Employers' awareness of BYOD and the need to manage it varies. Therefore, some experts on security and BYOD promote a bottom-up approach, seeking to educate the employees so that they will be aware of the risks to themselves and request more

Note: In an interesting twist on BYOD, some cellular providers now advertise "Bring your own Device" or "Bring your own Phone." What they are offering is switching your existing mobile device from another provider to their service, with incentives.

clarity in BYOD policies from their employers.

In addition to modifying policies for BYOD, employers can enforce those policies and manage mobile devices using a category of software called **mobile device management (MDM)**. Companies such as Citrix, VMware, Sophos, MobileIron, Acronis, and Microsoft offer such products—sometimes integrated into existing suites of products. Mobile device management is a broad term for the variety of features offered and the different approaches by the vendors of this type of software.

To isolate work apps and data from personal, some employers use products that include some form of virtualization. That may be in the form of a virtual machine running on the remote device or some variation of application virtualization—with processing occurring either on the mobile device or on the remote servers.

Others prefer to create a Web-based portal to work apps and data, making this available to a wider range of devices, since the only required client software is a browser.

LO 11.2 | Configure Accounts for Mobile Devices

There are two or more accounts associated with a mobile device. First, there is the credit account with the cellular provider. It is the account we set up and forget until we see our monthly statement. Then there is the account associated with the operating system on the device. Beyond that, many of us have one or more other accounts for additional cloud services we use on that device. Of course, we also need wireless connections for these mobile devices. That's what makes them mobile. The accounts and the connections are equally important, so the question is, which to address first? Other than the credit account with the cellular provider, the other accounts can be created and configured before you purchase your mobile device. After all, you are probably already using cloud services through your employer or school and/or have a personal account with Google, Microsoft, DropBox, or other cloud services. Of course, then there are the social media accounts (Facebook, Twitter, and many more). For that reason, we will consider the accounts first, using the account associated with your mobile OS as an example. The security settings you create on this account affect your privacy and safety on your device. Later, in this chapter, we will return to the topic of security and the settings you can configure on the device itself to further secure your data privacy.

Mobile Provider Accounts

When you purchase a smartphone or cellular-enabled tablet (one with an internal cellular modem) at one of Verizon's, AT&T's, T-Mobile's, or any cellular provider's brick-and-mortar store, they check your credit and you provide a payment method for the monthly charges, all associated with your account with them. They then program the device for their cellular network. This activation process often includes inserting a card called a Subscriber Identity Module (SIM). If you purchase the device over the Internet, the SIM card may come with the device, with instructions for installing it and activating the phone yourself. Beyond the personal billing and contract information tied to this account, configure settings that affect your usage of that service on each mobile device included in your plan to keep from incurring more costs. To see how an iPhone is using cellular data, open *Settings* and select *Cellular,* as shown in Figure 11-1. On an Android device, open

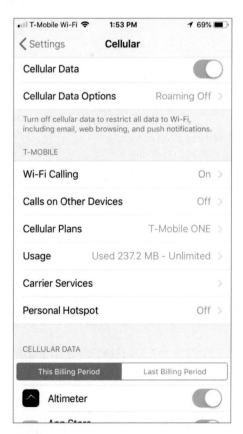

FIGURE 11–1 Cellular settings on an iPhone.
Source: Apple Inc.

FIGURE 11–2 Cellular settings on an Android phone.
Source: Google LLC

Note: Your Apple ID credentials include an email address (any working email address) and a password you create just for the Apple ID—*not* the password for using the email account.

Settings and scroll down to the *Connectivity* category and tap *More. More* includes settings for Wi-Fi Calling, VPN, and Mobile networks. Select *Mobile networks* to open the page shown in Figure 11–2.

Accounts Tied to Mobile Operating Systems

You also have an account tied to the operating system on each mobile device. The most common are Google accounts for the Android devices and Apple IDs for the Apple iOS mobile devices. An Android tablet may or may not include a cellular modem, in which case it still has Wi-Fi. And yes, you may have a cellular-enabled tablet running Microsoft Windows, or a Wi-Fi-only Windows tablet. In that case, the account associated with the operating system is a Microsoft Account (MSA), which you will want to use on a Windows 10 device if you use Microsoft services. You can configure the account associated with the operating system before purchasing a mobile device and we recommend that you do so. If you already have the account for the operating system, this is an opportunity to examine the security settings for those accounts. See Chapter 5 for information on creating and configuring a Microsoft Account.

On your device with Apple iOS, Google Android, or Windows, you can also subscribe to any of the other cloud services available: Apple services on Windows or Google devices, Google services on Apple or Windows devices, and Windows services on Apple or Google devices. There are many more cloud services that we have not mentioned here, and you can have multiple cloud providers on each device. What you learn here configuring an Account for Apple or Google services generally applies to other cloud services.

Sign in with a Google account

When you power up a new Android smartphone or tablet, you must sign in with a Google account. The account you use for this initial sign in will be the owner of the device—the only account that can make significant changes to device settings. A Google account is free, including the use of many Google apps, but some of the services, such as Google Drive space over the 4GB free service limit, are fee-based. If you are unfamiliar with Google accounts, please review the information on this topic in Chapter 9.

Sign in with an Apple ID.

When you power up a new iPhone or iPad, you must sign in with an **Apple ID**, your customer account for all Apple services and products. The Apple ID includes an email address you provide when you create the account. The basic account is free, and you can opt for additional, fee-based services. Your payment information for those services is saved with your account. Your Apple ID you use for the initial sign in to an Apple device will be the owner of the device—the only account that can make significant changes to device settings.

Step-by-Step 11.01 will walk you through the process of logging in with an existing or new Apple ID. It includes instructions on creating a new Apple ID and retrieving an Apple ID after you have forgotten the Apple ID or password.

Step-by-Step **11.01**

Sign in with Your Apple ID or Create a New One

In this hands-on exercise, you will use a browser to sign in with your existing Apple ID or create a new one.

- A computer or mobile device with an Internet connection.
- The username (email address) and password for your existing Apple ID or,

- One or more possible usernames and a complex password of eight or more characters with a mix of letters, numbers, and symbols.

Point your browser to **appleid.apple.com**.

> **If you do not have an Apple ID,** and wish to create one, scroll down to the bottom of the Apple ID page and proceed to Step 2.
>
> **If you do have an Apple ID,** sign in now. Your Apple Account page will open. Skip the remaining steps of this exercise and move on to the section titled *Exploring your Apple ID Account Settings*.
>
> **If you do have an Apple ID,** but have forgotten either the Apple ID or the password, click or tap *Forgot Apple ID or password?* Then skip to Step 4.

Source: Apple Inc.

Step 2

Click or tap *Create your Apple ID*.

Source: Apple Inc.

Step 3

On the *Create Your Apple ID* page fill in all the information, scrolling down to complete the form. Tap *Next* as you complete each page. In addition to a password, you will also need to choose three security questions. At this point Apple sends a single-use verification email to you. You need to pick up this email and enter the code on the website. Apple creates your Apple ID. Once you successfully create your Apple ID, you have completed this exercise. Stay signed in to your account, which we will explore in the section titled *Exploring your Apple ID Account Settings*.

Source: Apple Inc.

If you have an existing Apple ID, but cannot sign in, look for this link on the bottom of the Apple ID page: *Forgot Apple ID or password.* Click or tap it to open this page and enter your email address or look it up and then tap Continue.

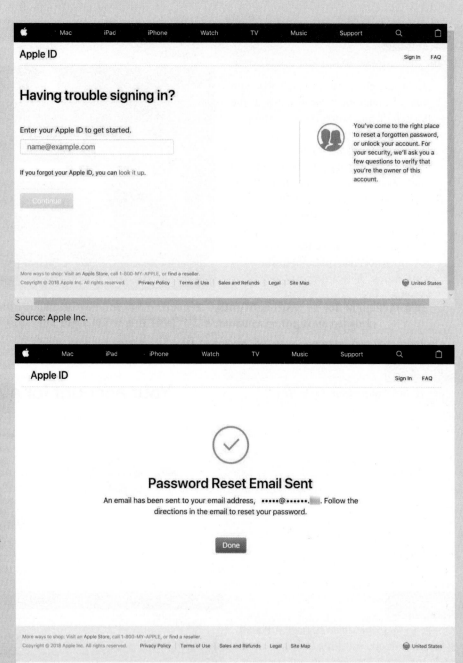

Source: Apple Inc.

Once you provide an email address, and it is confirmed to be a valid Apple ID email, Apple will send a password reset email. When you receive that email, follow the instructions which take you to a web page where you can provide confirming information and create a new password. Once you are signed in, keep the Apple Account page open and move on to the section titled *Exploring your Apple ID Account Settings.*

Source: Apple Inc.

Exploring Your Apple ID Account Settings

After signing in to your Apple ID, check out the account settings and make a few decisions about securing your account and Apple devices. On your Apple ID settings page (Figure 11-3), verify that the information in the Account section is correct. If you find an error, or wish to change something in any section, click or tap the Edit button at the top right of the section and make the changes.

Now explore the Security section. This is where you can change your password, add a rescue email, change the security questions, and additional security for your Apple ID. We will leave the password and security questions for now, assuming they are recent, and look at the other options for securing your account.

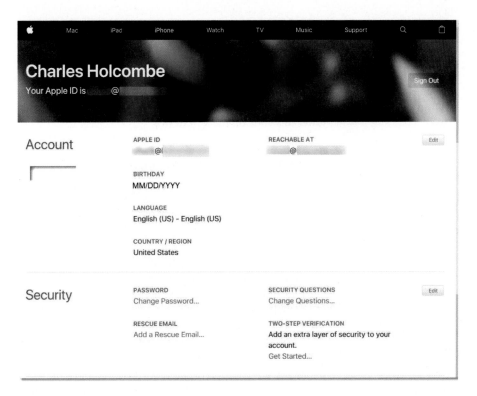

FIGURE 11-3 Manage your Apple ID settings.
Source: Apple Inc.

If you have a second email that you frequently check, use it as your rescue email and to reset your password and security questions. To add a rescue email, simply select *Add a Rescue Email* and provide the email address.

Apple has two extra security options with similar names: Two-Step Verification, shown as an option in Figure 11-3 and Two-Factor Authentication, a newer more secure option.

Two-Step Verification. Apple added the Two-Step Verification to Apple accounts several years ago and it is still available in the Apple ID Security settings. When you enable this feature, you must register at least one device that can receive a verification code via an Apple push notification or text message (SMS). In addition to that device, you can provide a phone number for a voice message. Apple can also contact you through Find My iPhone. When you turn this on, Apple provides a Recovery Key for use in the event you forget your Apple ID password or lose the device associated with your Apple ID. Save this Recovery Key in a file and/or print it out. In both cases, be sure you have quick access to the Recovery Key. Once Two-Step Verification is enabled, whenever you sign in to your Apple account using a device that is not trusted by your account, you will need to enter your account password after which a dialog box will open into which you must enter a single-use code sent by Apple to the registered device. Therefore, you need access to both devices. If you do not have access to the trusted device, you will need your Recovery Key.

Note: Other online services, such as Microsoft and Google, offer two-step verification, or multifactor authentication. The name may be the same (or it may just be similar), but the implementation varies, and most of these services now have enhancements to two-step verification.

Two-Factor Authentication. Apple has a newer implementation of multifactor authentication they call Two-Factor Authentication. This feature is not available in your Apple ID settings until you register at least one device running iOS 9 or greater or OS X 10.11 (El Capitan) or greater. Once you have a qualifying device registered with your account, Two-Factor Authentication is available in your Security settings. With this enabled, when someone attempts to sign in with your account from an unknown

FIGURE 11-4 Select *Don't Allow* or *Allow*.
Source: Apple Inc.

FIGURE 11-5 Enter this single-use code on the new device.
Source: Apple Inc.

(to your Apple account) device, you will receive two dialog boxes on the trusted device. The first, shown in Figure 11-4, informs you that your Apple ID is being used to sign in to a new device, giving a location and a map, and you can allow or disallow this attempt. If you allow it, a second dialog box provides the single-use verification code, shown in Figure 11-5. Enter this code on the new device.

LO 11.3 | Configure Wireless Connections on Mobile Devices

When preparing to buy a smartphone, first shop for the cellular provider, such as Verizon, AT&T, T-Mobile, or others, and look for the best service and options in your area. If you live in an area with multiple providers visit several stores or websites to compare plans and costs before making your final choice. There are many plans and a great deal of competition among providers, especially in metro areas. These include plans with a flat rate for a certain amount of cellular data usage or even unlimited data. The data portion of the plan is important if you are using your smartphone for services other than just voice, and most of us use our smartphones all day long for various types of data—email, text messaging, browsing the Internet, and using a variety of apps.

After selecting the carrier and the plan you would like, select the device. Once you have selected the device that fits your needs and budget, you normally sign a contract for a certain level of service and for a credit account with the provider. Before you receive the phone, the cellular service provider will program it for your cellular account. This process often includes inserting a card called a **Subscriber Identity Module (SIM)** into the device. If you purchase the device over the Internet, the SIM card may come with the device, with instructions for installing it and activating the phone. If you purchase a smartphone in a brick-and-mortar store, you will usually configure the cellular connection while still in the store, or the salesperson may do it for you.

Connecting to Cellular Networks

The first time you power up a new smartphone that has not been prepared or one that has the basic configuration but still needs your personal settings, a setup screen will display and lead you through the process. This will include accepting a language and terms of use. You will also have an opportunity to read a privacy statement and then go through steps for setting up your phone.

Cellular data communications is optional in a tablet, adding a premium to the cost of the device because of the required internal cellular modem as well as the ongoing cost for the cellular data plan. As with a smartphone, the cellular provider will either configure the device or give you special instructions. The device may come preconfigured for connecting to the cellular network, and the first time you start it up, you personalize it by moving through screens where you answer questions.

Cellular Data Settings

An important money-saving feature is enabled by default in most mobile devices with both cellular and Wi-Fi connections. When the device is connected to a Wi-Fi network with a good signal, it will use that rather than the cellular network for data.

Look back at Figure 11-1, which shows the cellular settings on an iPhone with Cellular Data turned on. If you have a limited data plan and are often connected to a trusted Wi-Fi network, turn cellular data off, or turn it on and scroll down to the list of apps using cellular data and turn off the use of cellular data in those apps that are not critical.

Sharing Your Cellular Connection

A mobile hotspot is a generic term for sharing a cellular connection with nearby devices connected by Wi-Fi, Bluetooth, or USB. The device at the core of the mobile hotspot is a cellular wireless router within the device. This may be a smartphone or tablet with cellular access or a dedicated mobile hotspot device. Novatel has a trademarked name for the hotspot device they manufacture, MiFi Figure 11-6 shows the mobile hotspot setting on an iPhone, where it is referred to as *Personal Hotspot*. Once you have arranged for this service with your provider, you would turn on Personal Hotspot. This device allows for three methods of sharing this connection with local computers: Wi-Fi (for which they provide a password), Bluetooth, and USB.

Similarly, Android has settings for sharing a cellular connection, which is called Tethering, as shown in Figure 11-7. To enable this, first turn on Mobile data, then, under Tethering, configure the connection between the device and other local devices. The two options are via USB or Wi-Fi. For USB, you need to directly connect a device via USB cable, which is a one-to-one sharing of the cellular connection. Wi-Fi on this Android tablet allows for up to eight connections. To connect via Wi-Fi, you need to turn on the Mobile HotSpot and configure the settings for the Wi-Fi connection, shown in Figure 11-8.

FIGURE 11-6 Personal Hotspot settings on an iPhone.
Source: Apple Inc.

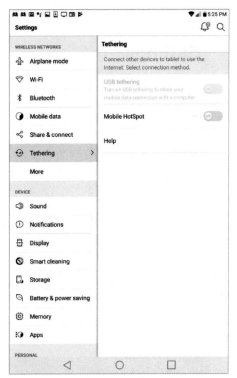

FIGURE 11-7 Tethering settings on an Android tablet.
Source: Google LLC

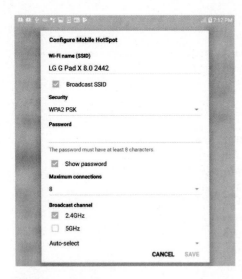

FIGURE 11–8 Mobile Hotspot settings on an Android tablet.
Source: Google LLC

Note: Tethering is also used to describe a connection between your mobile device and another mobile device or computer for the sake of synchronizing or backing up data.

Connecting to Wi-Fi Networks

To connect to a Wi-Fi network for the first time, open the Settings app on your device. Then select the option for Wireless (or Wi-Fi) and turn on Wi-Fi, if necessary. It will then scan for Wi-Fi networks and list detected Wi-Fi networks, using the SSID of each network. A Service Set ID (SSID) is a network name used to identify a wireless network. Consisting of up to 32 characters, the SSID travels with the messages on a Wi-Fi network, and all wireless devices on a WLAN must use the same SSID to communicate.

In the list of available Wi-Fi networks, select one and enter the required password. The device will remember this network and the password, maintain a list of Wi-Fi networks it has successfully connected to, and automatically provide the password you entered when you first connect to that network. Figure 11–9 shows an iPad Wi-Fi Settings page with a successful connection to a Wi-Fi network named NRHOME. The Android Wi-Fi settings page is nearly identical to this.

For additional security, the network administrator may turn off broadcasting of the SSID, so the network name will not show in the list of networks displayed when your device attempts to connect. In that case, the administrator gives authorized users the name of the network and the password to enter. On an iOS device, select *Other* (shown in the list of networks in Figure 11–9) to open the dialog box and manually enter the network name and password.

Connecting to Bluetooth Devices

Bluetooth is a wireless standard used for communicating over very short distances. You can connect a Bluetooth headset or keyboard to your mobile device, connect your smartphone to your car stereo, or connect your phone or tablet to a PC or Mac to synchronize data. Bluetooth consumes battery power, so it is disabled by default. To connect

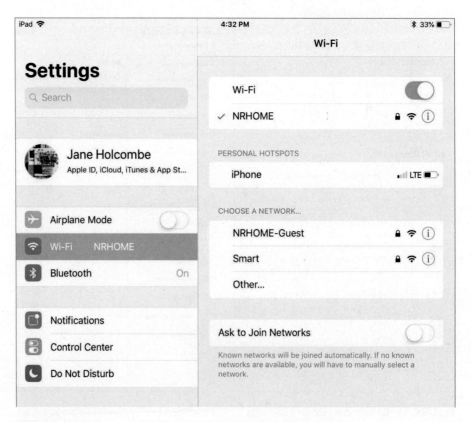

FIGURE 11–9 Choose a Wi-Fi network and provide a password.
Source: Google LLC

devices via Bluetooth, first open the Settings app on your mobile device and enable Bluetooth. When connecting to a device without a user interface, such as a headset or keyboard, Bluetooth is enabled on that device every time you turn it on, so you simply use the Bluetooth settings on your mobile device to detect the device and select it. The connection between two Bluetooth devices is a pairing.

When connecting two computing devices, such as an iMac and an iPhone or iPad, go to the Settings screen on each one and select the other device for pairing. After a short pause a message will display with a pairing code (also called a passkey or PIN code), as shown in Figure 11–10, an Android tablet pairing with an iPhone. Simply confirm that the same code shows on the screen for both devices and tap the *Pair* button. In cases like this, you do not need to type in the pairing code.

Enable or Disable Wi-Fi

If you have a mobile device, it will have a setting for enabling or disabling Wi-Fi networking. Try this:

1. Open the Settings utility on your mobile device.
2. Search for the Wi-Fi settings.
3. Enable or disable Wi-Fi.
4. Test the setting by opening an app that requires Wi-Fi access.
5. Return the Wi-Fi setting to its previous configuration.

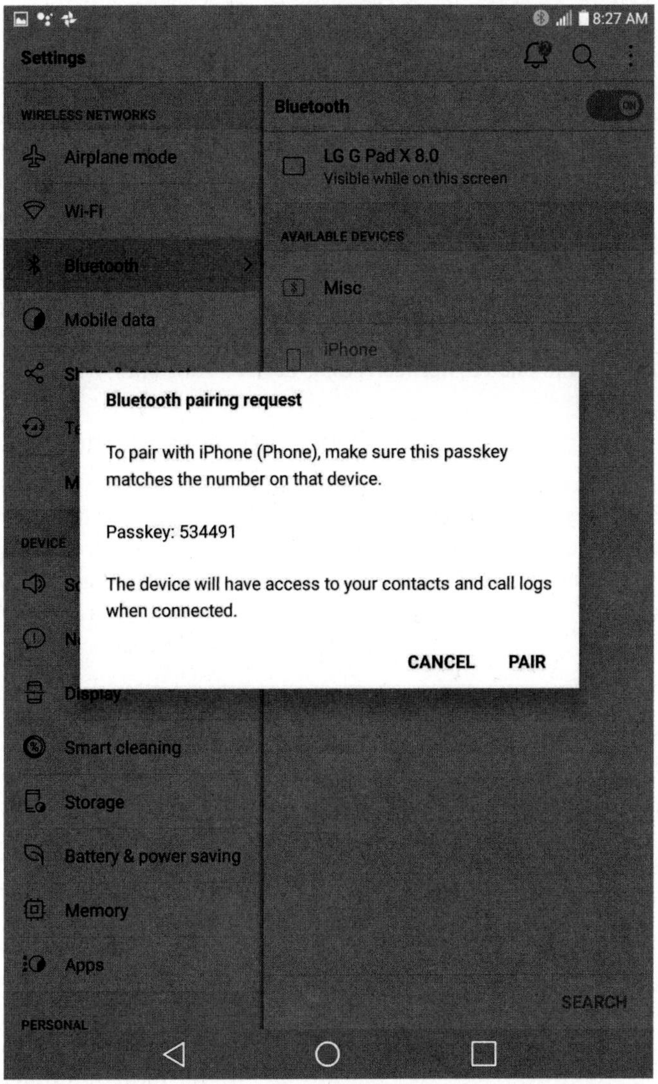

FIGURE 11–10 Tap *Pair* to confirm the pairing.
Source: Google LLC

Always test connectivity between devices. We have found that just entering the pairing code on a Bluetooth keyboard is not enough confirmation that the connection is working, so we open an app that accepts keyboard input and start typing on the keyboard. If it does not work, you may not have confirmed the pairing on both sides (not usually necessary). A failure to connect may simply be a case of impatience, so a short wait is in order. If the pairing problem persists, disable Bluetooth on both devices and start over again.

Making Bluetooth Easier

While pairing Bluetooth devices is not difficult, it usually requires opening the Settings app on your mobile device. In the future, that may not be necessary. For instance, Google's **Fast Pair** feature scans for nearby Bluetooth signals and displays a prompt identifying the device. Tap the box, and your phone connects to the device. Following that first connection the user is prompted to download an app, providing one is available for the device. Fast Pair is relatively new, and it will take time for manufacturers to provide a Fast Pair companion app for their devices. When this or other solutions become common, we will avoid having to go into the Settings app to connect to Bluetooth devices.

Combining Bluetooth and Wi-Fi

Apple, Google, Microsoft, and other tech companies offer enhanced Bluetooth capabilities or combine Bluetooth with other technologies. Apple requires that Bluetooth be enabled on their devices for AirDrop, AirPlay, and location services, even when the service uses other wireless types of signals. In addition, their **AirDrop** service uses Bluetooth or Wi-Fi to transfer files between Apple devices (Mac, iPad, iPhone, iPod Touch). Apple AirPlay, originally designed for audio data, is Apple's technology for streaming several types of data (audio, video, and photos) between Apple devices using both Wi-Fi and Bluetooth.

Connecting with Other Short-Range Wireless Methods

Some mobile devices include the ability to use **Near Field Communication (NFC)**. With this enabled, you can position your phone very close to another device that also has NFC enabled and share data and even pay for purchases at location using this type of device. Apple uses NFC technology for their Apple Pay, Wallet, Touch ID, and Face ID services.

Airplane Mode

When traveling by commercial airliner you may be required to turn off all wireless signals (Wi-Fi, cellular, Bluetooth, NFC) on mobile devices. This may be only during takeoff and landing or during the entire trip. Some airlines allow Wi-Fi use via their provided in-flight Wi-Fi service, and some offer cellular service. The policy concerning wireless devices on airliners varies by airline company and by country. Complying is much easier than it was with early mobile devices that had to be powered down to turn off those transmissions. Modern devices have **airplane mode** to turn off the wireless features without the need

try this!

Pair Two Devices with Bluetooth

Connect your mobile device to a computer or peripheral using Bluetooth. Try this:

1. Open the Settings utility on your mobile device.
2. Locate the Bluetooth setting and turn it on.
3. Turn on your Bluetooth device.
4. The mobile device should show that it is searching, connecting, and pairing.
5. If it is a keyboard, enter the code that appears on the mobile device.
6. Test the connection: for instance, play music to test a Bluetooth headset.
7. Disable Bluetooth when you are finished.

try this!

Enable or Disable Airplane Mode

If you have a mobile device, experiment with enabling or disabling Airplane Mode. Try this:

1. Open the Settings utility on your mobile device.
2. Locate the *Airplane Mode* settings.
3. Turn Airplane mode on.
4. Test Airplane mode by opening a browser and attempting to connect to a website.
5. When you have tested it, turn Airplane mode off.

to power off the device, so you can continue to do other tasks that do not require wireless connections.

Airplane mode is useful beyond its use on airlines because it prevents your device from repeatedly attempting to connect to Wi-Fi while you are out of range. Similarly, when you are traveling (especially by air), it may deplete your battery as it repeatedly attempts to detect cell towers as you fly over the landscape. Look for *Airplane Mode* in Settings, as shown in Figure 11-11, the *Settings* screen on an Android smartphone containing the switch for enabling or disabling airplane mode. When enabled, an airplane icon will display in the notification bar at the top of your device—on the left side on Apple devices, and on the right on Android devices.

LO 11.4 | Email, Apps, Wallets, and Synchronization

Once you know how to work with your mobile device's connection settings, you will want to configure email, acquire new apps, and enable synchronization.

Configuring Email

In order to use your mobile device to access your email, begin by adding the email account. Mobile devices support several types of accounts for email, social networking, data backup, and more. And you can configure a single device to use several accounts. Mobile operating systems know the basic connection information for many types of accounts. Therefore, for many accounts, you only need to provide your personal login information to the account, which is usually an email address and password. Figure 11-12 shows a list of account types supported on an iPhone or iPad. Chapter 10 described email account types as well as the settings required to connect to an email account.

Web Mail Accounts

For Web mail accounts, such as Hotmail or Gmail, you do not have to specify a sending and receiving server. All you need to enter is your user name and password. All the mobile OSs described here work with Web mail accounts.

Accounts Requiring IMAP, POP, or SMTP Settings

If you want to use an account type other than a Web mail service, you will need server names for the incoming and outgoing mail servers. Obtain these from your mail server administrator. To receive mail you will need a name for a Post Office Protocol 3 (POP3) or an Internet Message Access Protocol 4 (IMAP4) server that receives your incoming mail and forwards it to you. An email client uses one or the other of these. To send email you usually need the name of your Simple Mail Transfer Protocol (SMTP) server that accepts your outgoing email and forwards it to the recipient's mail server.

A POP3 name will simply be the name of a mail server in an Internet domain and may resemble this: **pop.domainname.com**; while the name for an IMAP4 server might look something like this: **imap.domainname.com**. Then, we probably don't need to say this, but the SMTP name might look like this: **smtp.domainname.com**. These are just examples, and you need to get the names for these servers from your email administrator.

Armed with the needed information, locate the email settings on your mobile device and carefully enter the information. On an iPhone or iPad, open the Settings app and tap *Accounts & Passwords.* Then, in *Accounts & Passwords* tap **Add Account.** Does the list include the type of email account you need to use? If it does, tap it and continue. If not, tap **Other** at the bottom of the list and then

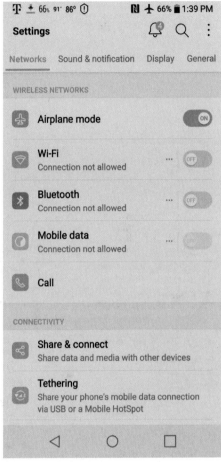

FIGURE 11–11 The *Airplane Mode* setting on an Android phone.
Source: Google LLC

FIGURE 11–12 Mobile OSs offer many types of accounts for email and social networking.
Source: Apple Inc.

FIGURE 11–13 The settings for a POP email account.
Source: Apple Inc.

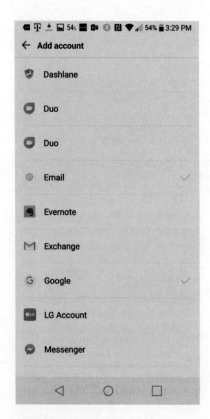

FIGURE 11–14 Select the account type from the list in the Android **Add account** page.
Source: Google LLC

tap **Add Mail Account.** The **New Account** dialog box will display, along with the virtual keyboard (unless you have an external keyboard connected). Enter your name (not a user account name), email address, password for that email account, and a description for the email account that will identify it for you in the list of accounts. Tap **Next,** and follow the instructions, using the addresses you obtained from your mail server administrator. Figure 11-13 shows the settings for a POP account named "Holcombe" by the user. The green button to the right shows that this account is enabled. If you slide that button left, you will disable the account without deleting it. To delete an account, scroll down in this list of settings to the Delete Account option.

On an Android device, you will have a Google account for accessing Google services and Gmail. To add another type of account in Android, open **Settings.** Then under the **General** tab select **Accounts & sync,** and tap **Add Account** (located at the bottom). This opens the **Add Account** screen (Figure 11-14) listing a variety of account types, not just email accounts but social networking sites, photo sharing sites, data backup sites, and other accounts added as you install certain apps.

From the **Add Account** screen, scroll through the list of account types and select the type of account you wish to add. Then enter the appropriate information for that account type.

Configuring an Exchange Client

Many organizations use internally maintained Microsoft Exchange mail servers for employee email accounts and for email within the organization as well as over the Internet. Also, many hosting services for Internet domain names offer Exchange email hosting services to their clients. Exchange gives the organization full administrative control, while providing users with a central location for their email history, contacts, tasks, and many collaborative tools.

If you need to connect your device to an Exchange server, first open Accounts from Settings. All the mobile OSs described in this chapter list Microsoft Exchange as an account type. Select it and enter the email address, user name, password, and a description for the list of accounts.

The organization owning the Exchange server and domain, such as a company or university, centrally manages and owns all Exchange accounts stored in one Exchange accounts database. Due to the complexity and cost of managing large numbers of email accounts, organizations are increasingly outsourcing email services to companies like Google and Microsoft.

Source: Google LLC

Mobile Apps

Apps are what make your mobile device the high-tech version of a Swiss Army knife. All mobile devices come with some built-in apps, but everyone installs more apps. Whatever mobile OS you select, you can choose from among hundreds of thousands of mobile apps. Apps are OS specific, so you must find apps that work with your OS and device. The Home screen on a mobile device will normally have an icon for connecting to an online retail site for buying apps for that mobile OS and (sometimes) device type.

When you find an app that sounds like what you need, read through the description, paying close attention to the requirements. An app may require certain services in order to work as advertised. For instance, you may need to give the app full control of your device or turn on the location service and/or global positioning system (GPS) service.

Source: Apple Inc.

Apps for Android

Play Store is an Android app that connects you to the Google Play online app store, the official source for Android apps, but since this is an open OS, there are other sources in the open-source market. Pay very close attention to the specs for an app, as there are many versions of Android, with features that are only supported on some devices. Figure 11–15 shows a small sampling of the Android apps at the Google Play store.

Apps for Apple iOS

Apple's online App Store or the brick-and-mortar Apple stores are the only app sources for Apple devices of any type. They sell only Apple-sanctioned software from many publishers. Because of the screen size differences some apps display best on the device for which they were written. Tap the App Store on the home page of your iOS device to connect to the App Store; the first time you connect from a device you will need to provide your Apple ID and password. Figure 11–16 shows the App Store. Update apps through the App Store, and when one or more updates are ready, the number of updates will appear on the App Store icon. When you open the App Store, the updates will display, and if you decide to update or download an app, you will need to enter your Apple ID and password (or use *Touch ID* or *Face ID*) before continuing.

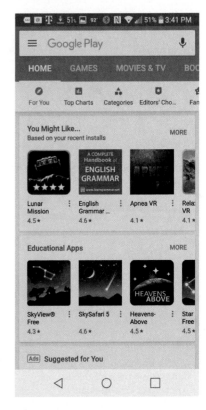

FIGURE 11–15 A small sampling of apps in the Google Play online app store.
Source: Google LLC

Replacing Your Wallet with a Mobile Device

If you still carry a stack of plastic to pay for purchases, consider checking out one of the virtual wallets available to you for your mobile device. Both Apple and Google offer payment services that are accepted at a growing number of brick and mortar locations, as well as online.

FIGURE 11–16 The Apple online App Store.
Source: Apple Inc.

Google Pay

Google Pay, the combined and renamed Android Pay and Google Wallet services. It uses payment methods saved in your Google Account. Use this service to pay anyone via their email address or phone number. Store loyalty membership cards and movie tickets in Google Pay. Do you commute to work in London, Chicago, Las Vegas, or Portland? Store your transit tickets in Google Pay and then use your phone as a ticket before you board. This service is available in other cities, too.

Apple Pay and Wallet

Wallet is an Apple iOS app for storing (in digital form) those plastic cards overflowing your physical wallet. Wallet does more than store those cards—it lets you use them for making payments and even for other purposes. For example, you can store and use coupons, boarding passes, tickets, credit cards, student IDs, and much more, using them just like the physical cards with other services that accept them. This data is stored online with your Apple ID and can be used from any of your iOS devices with Wallet enabled.

Apple Pay does not store coupons, boarding passes, tickets, and other types of plastic cards, but does store payment information that you can use to digitally pay for services and products at NFC point-of-sale-terminals. To blur the lines a bit more, you can use credit and debit cards stored in Wallet to make purchases with Apple Pay. Turn on Apple Pay and configure it with payment sources by opening *Wallet & Apple Pay* in iOS Settings.

Synchronization

Some of us have multiple computing devices. The authors each have a desktop PC, a laptop, and a smartphone. In addition, Jane has an iMac and iPad and Chuck has an Android tablet. With so many devices (and we know people with more), it is a challenge to keep track of our data. Therefore, we synchronize certain data

Note: Depending on the device and the options available to you, you can synchronize data using four connection types: USB cable, Wi-Fi, Bluetooth, or cellular data network.

between devices. When data is synchronized between two locations, the files are examined and newer files replace the older files—sometimes, but not always, in both directions so that the contents match. Synchronizing can be to another computer or mobile device or to a cloud-based service to ensure against data loss if the device is lost or stolen.

We don't do this between the two users, but each of us synchronizes our own data on all of our devices with a cloud service.

Connecting Mobile Devices for Syncing

You can synchronize your smartphone or tablet with your computer, using a USB cable, Wi-Fi, Bluetooth, or over the Internet using a cloud-based service. If you choose a cable, use the USB cable that came with the smartphone; it is usually attached to an alternating current (AC) adapter for charging. Disconnect it from the AC adapter and connect the end previously connected to the power supply (usually a standard USB connector) to the computer and connect the other end to the device. On smartphones, this will usually be a micro-USB connector; on older iPads and some other tablets, it was a proprietary 30-pin connector. Apple introduced their much smaller Lightening connector on the iPhone 5 in 2011, and later on the iPad 4. On some devices, this connection will cause two programs to run on the PC—one from your cellular provider (if the device has cellular service) for configuring your online account (if you already have one, you simply log in). The second program will be device-specific to aid in transferring files.

Syncing Android Devices

When you connect an Android device to your computer it is treated like an external drive, and you can copy files back and forth once you figure out the directory structure and locate the files you want to copy or back up. Strictly speaking, this isn't syncing. There are individual solutions for various types of data. For instance, when you create a contact in Android it asks you to pick an account to store (or back up) the contact information. The choices are Google or one provided by your cellular carrier. Select Google and they will be automatically backed up and synced to Google over the Internet, either through a cellular connection or via Wi-Fi. Who do you expect to have the longest relationship with, Google or your cellular provider? We use Google to back up our contacts on Android devices because it will be available to use if we cancel the contract with the cellular provider.

Syncing an iOS Device with a Mac or PC

Use Apple iTunes for syncing an iOS device with a Mac or PC. It comes with all Apple computers and is a free download for Windows PCs from the Microsoft Store. You can synchronize apps, several types of audio content, books, contacts, calendars, movies, TV shows, photos, notes, documents, and ringtones.

If you have a Mac, you may still need to update to the latest version of iTunes.

There are other requirements for playing music and video through iTunes on a PC, but we are only concerned with the requirements to synchronize your contacts, email, pictures, music, and videos from the device to the Mac or PC. You cannot copy files from the Mac or PC to the mobile device, but you can back up (not sync) your apps using iTunes.

Another option that is more of a backup than a synchronizing option is iCloud, an Apple Internet-based service for backing up your data from any Apple device to the iCloud service. This data is available to all devices from any location with Internet access.

Step-by-Step 11.02

Configuring Synchronization in iOS Using iTunes

This step-by-step exercise goes through the steps for synchronizing your iPad or iPhone data using iTunes. The steps are written for using a direct connection via a USB cable, but you can also synchronize using Wi-Fi. To complete this exercise, you will need the following:

- The latest version of iTunes on your Mac or Windows PC.
- An iPhone or iPad as well as the USB cable that came with the device.

Step 1

Open iTunes on your Mac or Windows PC and sign in, if prompted. Connect the USB cable between the iPad or iPhone and the computer. The first time you do this on a Windows PC, there will be a slight delay while it installs the driver. When the iPad is recognized, the iPad button will appear in the button bar of the iTunes app. Tap the iPad button.

Source: Apple Inc.

Step 2

In the iTunes app locate Backups and select *This computer.* If you want to encrypt your account passwords and data, select that box, and then select *Backup now.*

Source: Apple Inc.

Step 3

During the backup a progress bar displays at the top of the iTunes app.

Source: Apple Inc.

Step 4

When the backup is complete, the date and time shown under Latest Backup will change.

Step 5

When you disconnect the iPhone or iPad iTunes will return to its Home page, shown in Step 1. Exit iTunes.

LO 11.5 | Securing Mobile Devices

How do you protect a mobile device from malware? How do you keep the wrong people from logging on to a device they stole or found? How do you keep mobile operating systems up to date? How can you find lost devices? Mobile operating systems have many built-in security features. In this section, we describe the steps you can take to make your mobile device more secure using those built-in features, as well as features tied to your Google or Apple ID accounts for protecting your devices.

Patching and OS Updates

As with any computer, you need to keep your device updated with operating system patches and security updates to protect it from malware and other threats. The mobile OSs described here update automatically. You can check on the status for each OS.

Android has updates turned on by default, but the cellular carriers control what updates download and install on specific phone models. Check out the status of updates on your Android device by opening **Settings.** Then select the General tab and tap **About tablet** or **About phone** (Figure 11-17). This opens a list of information about your device, as shown in Figure 11-18. Locate and tap **Software info** (or System updates), shown in Figure 11-18 to see the status of updates. On some devices, you can disable or enable updates. We recommend that you leave it turned on.

On an Apple iOS device, open *Settings,* tap *General,* and then tap *About.* This opens a page of information about your device, such as the cellular network it uses, what types of data and apps are using local storage, and how much available space is left. In this list, *Version* shows the version number of iOS installed on that device. To check the status of updates, open Settings, tap General, and on that page locate Software Update, which will show the numeral 1 inside a red circle if an update is available.

Securing Lock Screens on Mobile Devices

A mobile device has a lock screen that keeps you from accidental touch actions, such as inadvertently "pocket dialing" your boss when you are at lunch. By default, the lock screen displays when you first start up your device or after a period of inactivity

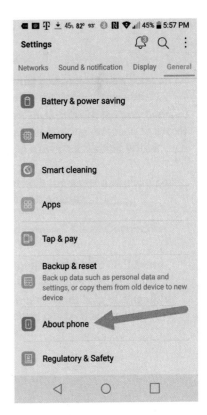

FIGURE 11–17 Select *About phone.*
Source: Google LLC

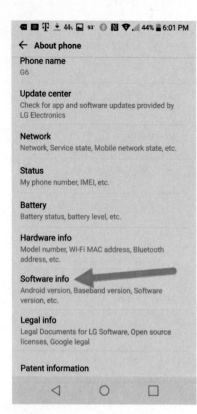

FIGURE 11–18 Select *Software info.*
Source: Google LLC

on the device. Mobile devices usually have an optional setting for a passcode lock that keeps the lock screen in place until you perform some action, such as entering a code or password or using a biometric sign-in, such as Apple's Touch ID or Face ID. Without a passcode lock a simple swipe closes the lock screen and gives anyone access to the device. Android, iOS, and Windows include this feature, although they use different terms to describe it as well as different options.

Android Screen Lock

Android has several settings for Screen lock. Open the Android Settings app and tap *Display,* then *Lock screen* and tap *Select screen lock.* Figure 11-19 shows the list of options for screen lock. The top six are on most recent Android devices. These settings go from least secure (*None* or *Swipe*) to a variety of security settings: *Knock Code, Pattern, PIN,* and *Password.* The settings at the bottom under *Biometrics* (*Fingerprints and Face recognition*) are only available on devices that have hardware support for biometrics. Before selecting a biometric option, you must have another way to unlock your phone, selected from *Knock Code, pattern, PIN,* or *password.*

iOS Passcode, Face ID, and Touch ID

Apple offers several options for securing the lock screen, depending on the vintage of the iPad or iPhone. Of course, on all iOS devices, you can still opt to have no security on the lock screen, "unlocking" it with a simple swipe, or you can use a passcode. On certain devices you can use one of Apple's biometric methods—either Touch ID or Face ID. As for which devices have these features, Apple introduced Touch ID on the iPhone 5S, and it is on newer iPads and iPhones that have the Home button with its special sensors. Face ID was introduced with the iPhone X, which does not have a Home button. As with Android devices, you must have a passcode in place and enter it before you can enable one of the biometric authentication methods or make any changes to these settings.

Touch ID When you first enable Touch ID (using *Touch ID and Passcode* settings), you go through the process of having a finger scanned several times, moving it slightly before each scan. You can add multiple fingers, which is a very good idea. Figure 11-20 shows the *Touch ID & Passcode* Settings page on an iPad with iOS 11. Touch ID is great when you are in a low-light environment or want to authenticate quickly with just one hand.

Face ID The iPhone X uses infrared facial recognition for its Face ID feature, but it does not support Touch ID because Apple removed the physical Home button on the iPhone X. In Settings on an iPhone X look for *Face ID & Passcode.* When you first enable Face ID, follow the instructions for moving your head while the device uses infrared light and an infrared scanner to scan your face creating a mathematical model that is stored in the device. Then, when someone attempts to unlock your phone with Face ID, it scans the face and compares it to the stored mathematical model, unlocking the phone if there is a match.

With either Touch ID or Face ID, you still need to remember your passcode because there are situations when you are required to use it rather than Touch ID. According to Apple's Security Guide for iOS 11, these scenarios include:

- After turning off and restarting the device.
- After the device has been locked for over 48 hours.
- If the passcode has not been used to unlock the device in the last 6.5 days, and Face ID has not unlocked the device in the last 4 hours.
- If the device received a remote lock command.
- After five unsuccessful attempts to unlock with Touch ID or Face ID.
- After a power off/Emergency SOS.

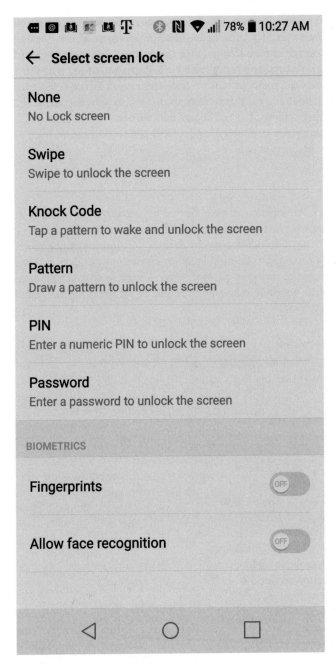

FIGURE 11–19 Android screen lock settings.
Source: Google LLC

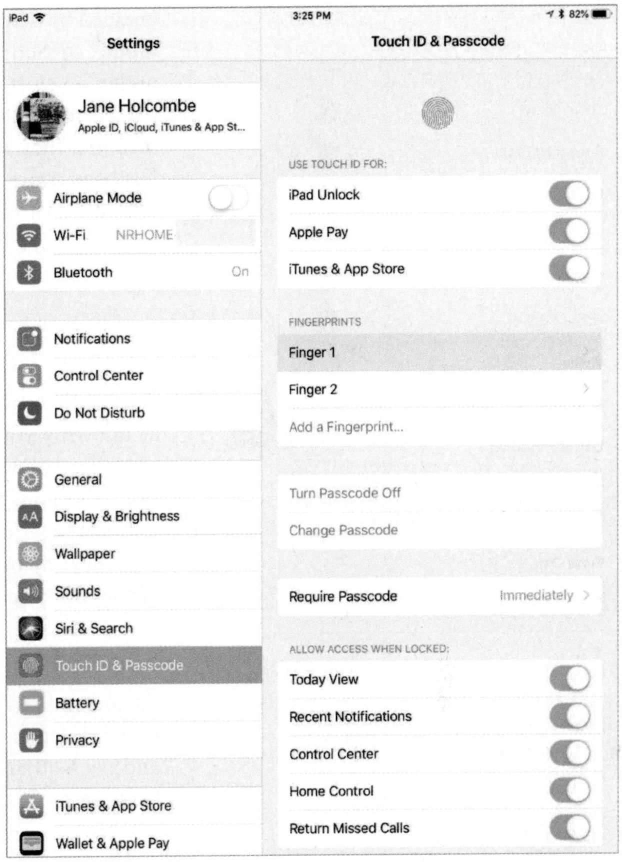

FIGURE 11–20 *Touch ID & Passcode* settings on an iPad.
Source: Apple Inc.

Use any of the three methods—Passcode, Touch ID, or Face ID—to authenticate yourself for purchases made in iTunes or the App Store or through many other sources using Wallet or Apple Pay. Enable the use of Touch ID and Passcode for Apple Pay and for Wallet by locating each of these under *Touch ID & Passcode* in iOS Settings. Until you do this, you will need to authenticate with your Apple ID.

USB Restricted Mode A serious security vulnerability in iOS devices has been exploited by unauthorized persons to bypass Apple's security using a special USB accessory plugged into the iOS device's USB port, the Lightning port. Beginning with iOS version 11.4.1, Apple added a new security feature, USB Restricted Mode, that is

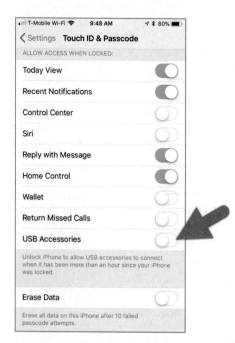

enabled by default. But presently, you won't find it by searching on "USB restricted mode" in Settings. The setting for this mode, titled *USB Accessories,* is located under *Touch ID and Passcode* or *Face ID and Passcode,* as shown in Figure 11-21. In reverse logic, when USB Accessories is disabled, USB Restricted Mode is enabled meaning that a USB accessory cannot make a data connection to the device if it has been more than an hour since it was locked. In this mode, you can charge the phone via the Lightening connect, but not access data. When USB Accessories is enabled, USB Restricted Mode is disabled, and a USB connection can be used to both charge the phone and access data.

Location Settings

Applications that track the location of your device have a variety of uses, such as allowing you to find your lost or stolen mobile device from another device or computer, plotting driving directions from your current location, and much more. For these apps to work you need to enable a location service on your device. Apps that use location services are expected to inform you, and once you turn on location services for a device, you should be able to enable or disable it for individual apps in all operating systems.

Android Location Services

FIGURE 11–21 *When USB Accessories is disabled, USB Restricted Mode is* enabled.
Source: Google LLC

On an Android device, Locations settings, shown in Figure 11-22, shows the Location Service enabled and using the High accuracy mode that detects GPS signals and uses other wireless technologies to detect the location of the device. Other location modes include a battery saving mode that does not use GPS, but does use other networks that only uses device sensors (GPS). To enable it, set the slider switch to *On.* Google will then prompt for your consent to allow your phone to share its approximate location with apps and services. Both the High accuracy and Battery saving modes use the cellular network, in which case data usage charges will apply. The Emergency 911 (E911) location service is enabled by default and cannot be disabled on a mobile cellular phone.

try this!

Enable or Disable Location Services

If you have a mobile device, it should have a setting for enabling or disabling location services. Try this:

1. Open the Settings utility in your mobile device.
2. Look for a setting for location and tap it.
3. If you do not see a setting for location, look for "privacy."
4. Once you find it, disable it and test it by opening a mapping program and trying to find your location. It will fail if you turned the location service off, and it will succeed if you turned it on.

iOS Location Services

In iOS, open **Settings,** select **Privacy,** and then tap **Location Services** to open the list of settings shown in Figure 11-23. Notice that you can enable or disable location services for various components and apps on this device.

Lost or Stolen Devices

Mobile devices are easily stolen or lost. Therefore, take steps ahead of time to protect your data and to help you locate the lost or stolen device. This will usually involve enabling a locator service on the device that tracks its location. Those services for Apple Devices are associated with your Apple ID, and similar services for an Android device are included with your Google Account.

Google Find My Device

When you sign in to Google from any mobile device (regardless of the OS), Google adds it to your list of devices in your Google Account. However, when it comes to Google's Find My Device service, it is designed for your Android devices, not for Apple devices. If an Android device is lost or stolen, sign in to your Google

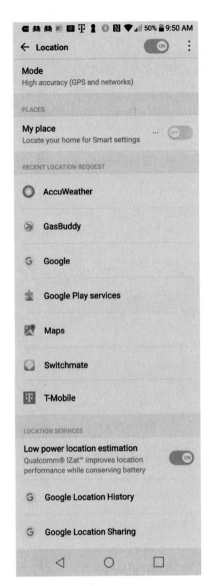

FIGURE 11–22 Android location
settings.
Source: Google LLC

FIGURE 11–23 Apple iOS location
settings.
Source: Apple Inc.

Account in the browser of any device. On the Google Account page, locate *Find your phone* under *Sign-in & security* (Figure 11-24). Select *Get Started.* On the next page, select your phone or tablet from the list of detected devices. You will need to sign in again and tap *Next.*

Figure 11-25 shows the Google page with *Ring or locate your phone* options in the *Find your phone* option. Select Ring to make it ring, which is useful when it is "lost" nearby. If you do not hear it ring, then tap *Locate,* and a map will display showing its approximate location.

Apple iCloud Find My iPhone

On an Apple macOS or iOS device you can enable a free feature that uses iCloud to locate a lost or stolen iMac, iPad, iPhone, or iPod and then select from several actions, including a remote wipe if your device is lost or stolen. Find my iPhone is a service associated with your Apple ID. On the iOS device, open Settings, tap your Apple ID, and select iCloud to open the page shown in Figure 11-26. Scroll down on the iCloud page and select Find My iPhone to open the Find My iPhone page. Then enable **Find My iPhone** (or iPad or iPod) and enable **Send Last Location,** as shown in Figure 11-27. Tap **Allow** in the confirmation message that displays.

Once enabled, you can connect to **www.icloud.com** from another computer and log in with your Apple ID. On the iCloud home screen (Figure 11-28), select **Find iPhone** (i.e., the name of this service, whether you have an iPhone or not). You may be

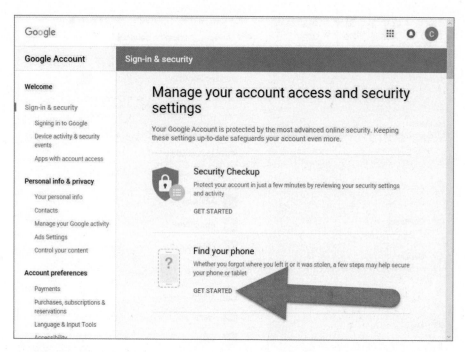

FIGURE 11–24 Get started with Google *Find your phone*.
Source: Google LLC

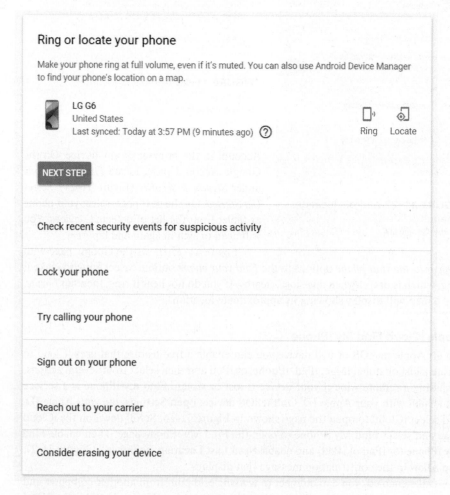

FIGURE 11–25 Ring or locate your Android phone or tablet.
Source: Google LLC

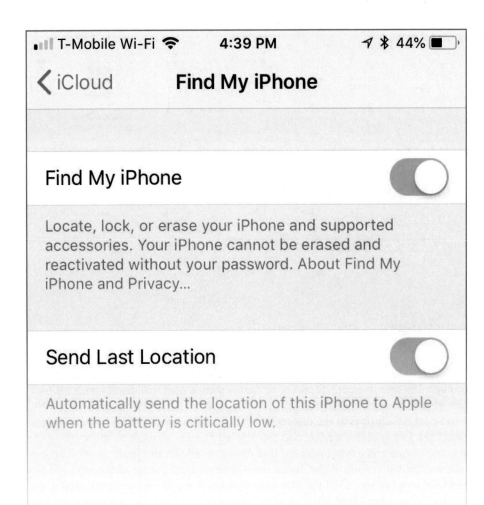

FIGURE 11–26 On the iCloud page select *Find My iPhone*.
Source: Google LLC

FIGURE 11–27 On the *Find My iPhone* page enable **Find My iPhone** and **Send Last Location.**
Source: Apple Inc.

FIGURE 11–28 After signing in to the iCloud Home page select Find iPhone.
Source: Apple Inc.

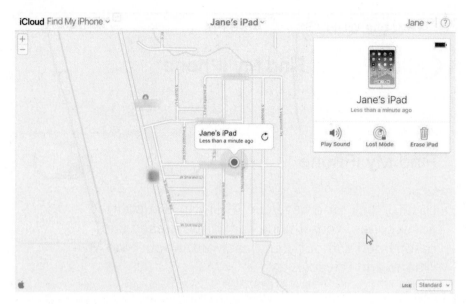

FIGURE 11–29 Select the actions for a lost device.
Source: Apple Inc.

prompted to sign in again. Then on the next screen, a map will display with the location of your devices.

Select All Devices at the top center of this page to open a menu of your devices. Select the lost or stolen device, and the title **All Devices** changes to the name of the selected device and a box opens for that device, as shown in Figure 11–29. This box tells you the battery life of the device (see the upper-right corner of the box) and lets you take some action. Clicking **Play Sound** causes a sound on the device, and it will display the message "Find My iPad Alert" on the device. This is very handy when your device is hiding under a pile of papers in your office. Select **Lost Mode** and enter a passcode to lock the device (this appears if the device does not already have a passcode). Once someone enters the passcode on the device itself, it is no longer in Lost Mode and can be used. The last option is **Erase iPad.** Select this if you are convinced it is stolen.

Chapter 11 REVIEW

Chapter Summary

After reading this chapter and completing the step-by-step tutorial and Try This! exercises, you should understand the following facts about mobile operating systems.

From Luggable to BYOD

- Just 30 years ago, mobile computing involved lugging heavy computers that could not connect to a network when in transit.
- Today's mobile devices are popular consumer devices that are tiny, powerful, and connected 24/7.

- People bring their personal mobile devices to school and work, a practice called bring your own device (BYOD).
- Most employers do not have an adequate policy for BYOD to address the many issues of security, ownership, and cost.
- Mobile device management (MDM) is a category of software for managing mobile devices.

Configure Accounts for Mobile Devices

- A cellular mobile device needs a credit account with the provider that you use for paying the monthly fees.
- All popular smartphones and tablets require a user account associated with the operating system.
- An Android device has a Google account associated with it for accessing Google services.
- An Apple ID is a customer account for accessing Apple services and products.
- Configure accounts for additional cloud services you use on the device.
- The security settings on the account associated with the device OS affect your privacy and safety on all your devices.

Configure Wireless Connections on Mobile Devices

- A smartphone requires a cellular connection from a cellular provider.
- A cellular data connection is an extra option for a tablet, adding a premium to the cost of the device, plus requiring a cellular data plan.
- All popular mobile devices offer Wi-Fi connections, which you can enable and connect to hotspots using appropriate credentials.
- A mobile device with a cellular connection may be able to share that connection, turning the device into a mobile hotspot. Cellular providers charge a service fee for allowing you to do this.
- You can purchase a separate device to use as a dedicated mobile hotspot. Novatel calls their mobile hotspot device MiFi.
- Tethering is a feature that allows you to share your smartphone's cellular data connection.
- Near Field Communication (NFC) is a special chipset in some mobile devices that allows you to position your device close to another that also has NFC enabled and share data, pair with a Bluetooth device, or pay for purchases.

- Airplane mode is a feature of mobile devices that, when enabled, turns off all radio frequency (RF) signals. It complies with commercial airline requirements.

Email, Apps, Wallets, and Synchronization

- Any popular mobile device can support multiple accounts of different types at once.
- Mobile operating systems understand the basic connection information required for many types of accounts, so you may only need to enter the personal login information for the account and it will attempt to connect.
- Sometimes when configuring an email account you may have to provide more information, such as the name of POP, IMAP, or SMTP servers.
- Replace your physical wallet with Google Pay or Apple's Wallet and Apple Pay.
- Each mobile OS has some service for synchronizing data between the mobile device and other devices or to the cloud.

Securing Mobile Devices

- Mobile OSs have many security features built in.
- By default, mobile operating systems have updates enabled, so that security patches and updates of the OS are downloaded and installed automatically.
- A mobile device has a lock screen to prevent accidental touch actions. You can protect a lock screen with various security measures so that a simple swiping gesture does not give the wrong person access to the device.
- Enable the location on your mobile device then use settings to control which apps can use it.
- Google *Find your phone* is a free service from Google that will help you locate and manage a lost or stolen device, remotely wipe the device, and cause it to ring. Locate a lost or stolen device using *Find your phone* on your Google Account page.
- Apple iCloud has the free Find My iPhone service. Enable it through iCloud settings on your device.

Key Terms List

AirDrop *(428)*

airplane mode *(428)*

Apple ID *(420)*

Apple Pay *(432)*

Bluetooth *(426)*

bring your own device (BYOD) *(417)*

Face ID *(436)*

Fast Pair *(428)*

Google Pay *(432)*

Lightning port *(437)*

location service *(418)*

MiFi *(425)*

mobile device management (MDM) *(419)*

mobile hotspot *(425)*

Near Field Communication (NFC) *(428)*

pairing *(427)*

passcode lock *(436)*

Service Set ID (SSID) *(426)*

Subscriber Identity Module (SIM) *(424)*

synchronize *(432)*

tethering *(425)*

Touch ID *(436)*

Two-Factor Authentication *(423)*

USB Restricted Mode *(437)*

Wallet *(432)*

Key Terms Quiz

Use the Key Terms List to complete the sentences that follow:

1. If you turn on the _____ feature of a cell-enabled mobile device the device serves as a cellular modem for an attached computer.

2. Turn on _____ to turn off all radios in your mobile device.

3. The list of available Wi-Fi networks that display on your device or computer are each identified by a/an _____.

4. The practice of people using their own mobile devices at work is called _____.

5. One company uses the trademarked name of _____ to identify their line of small devices that act as dedicated mobile hotspots.

6. A connection between two Bluetooth devices is called a _____.

7. Some organizations use a type of software called _____ to manage mobile devices used by their employees.

8. Transfer files via Bluetooth or Wi-Fi between two Apple devices using the _____ feature.

9. A/an _____ secures the lock screen on a mobile device.

10. _____ is a service offered by Apple on their newer devices that have both Touch ID and NFC, allowing the user to pay for purchases wirelessly.

Multiple-Choice Quiz

1. Which of the following is *not* true concerning BYOD?
   a. Employees may personally incur higher voice and data costs when they bring their own devices to work.
   b. A lost or stolen device can put the employer at risk.
   c. It is unclear who owns intellectual property created.
   d. An employee's private data on their personally owned device may be at risk.
   e. Most organizations have adequate policies in place for BYOD.

2. Which of the following is not a type of wireless communications?
   a. NFC
   b. USB
   c. Wi-Fi
   d. Cellular
   e. Bluetooth

3. Which of the following is an account required for using an Android smartphone?
   a. Apple ID
   b. Microsoft account
   c. Yahoo!
   d. Google account
   e. Hotmail

4. Which type of connection is the primary connection type for a smartphone?
   a. NFC
   b. USB
   c. Wi-Fi
   d. Cellular
   e. Bluetooth

5. Which type of connection is an option for a tablet that adds cost to the hardware as well as a fee for data usage?
   a. NFC
   b. USB
   c. Wi-Fi
   d. Cellular
   e. Bluetooth

6. Which feature, if available, allows you to share your smartphone's cellular data connection with another device over a USB cable?
   a. Mobile hotspot
   b. Tethering
   c. MiFi
   d. SSID
   e. BYOD

7. Which mode turns off all radio frequency (RF) signals on a device?
   a. Tethering
   b. Mobile hotspot
   c. Airplane mode
   d. Synchronization
   e. Data protection

8. What wireless connection feature, if available in your phone, would allow you to pay for purchases by simply positioning the device very close to another device with this feature?
   a. NFC
   b. USB
   c. Wi-Fi
   d. Cellular
   e. Bluetooth

9. Without this type of feature on a mobile device, a simple swipe gives anyone access to the device. What is the term for this feature?

   a. Location service

   b. Passcode lock

   c. Updates

   d. Screen saver

   e. Device manager

10. This very short-range wireless connection option is often used to connect keyboard and headsets to mobile devices.

    a. NFC

    b. USB

    c. Wi-Fi

    d. Cellular

    e. Bluetooth

11. What free Google service is available to all Google accounts, allowing them to locate their lost or stolen Android mobile devices?

    a. iCloud

    b. Find Your Phone

    c. Web apps

    d. Find My iPhone

    e. Google Play

12. Use this Apple service to synchronize your iOS device with a Mac or PC.

    a. iCloud

    b. Apple ID

    c. Find My iPhone

    d. iTunes

    e. iMac

13. What Apple service allows you to back up your data from any Apple device so that it is available to all your devices?

    a. iCloud

    b. Apple ID

    c. Find My iPhone

    d. iTunes

    e. iMac

14. What type of card inserted into a mobile device programs it for a user's cellular account information?

    a. NFC

    b. SSID

    c. MDM

    d. SIM

    e. MiFi

15. This name identifies a Wi-Fi network.

    a. NFC

    b. SSID

    c. MDM

    d. SIM

    e. MiFi

Essay Quiz

1. Describe your ideal mobile device, whether it exists or not.

2. What options do you have for cellular service in your area? Write a paragraph listing the cellular providers who service your area and which one you would choose if you were shopping for a mobile device today. Explain your choice.

3. Take a poll of your fellow students or coworkers. What mobile operating systems are on their mobile devices? Record the results of your poll and compute the percentage between Android and iOS devices.

4. What is the U.S. Federal Aviation Administration policy for the use of electronic devices on an airliner? If you live or travel outside the United States, research the policy of the equivalent agency in another country. Does this policy allow for Airplane mode?

5. Research how mobile devices are being used in both virtual reality (VR) and augmented reality (AR) scenarios for education and on-the-job training. Find some free VR or AR apps and experiment with them on a mobile device.

Lab Projects

LAB PROJECT 11.1

Research mobile device management (MDM) software products by searching for recent product reviews and answer the following questions.

① What mobile operating systems did the majority of the MDM products you found support?

② How many of the reviewed products included support for desktop OSs in addition to mobile OSs? List the OSs and the number of MDM products you found that supported them.

③ How many of the MDM products reviewed included a feature that would block devices from accessing email if MDM policies were violated?

LAB PROJECT 11.2

An organization that hosts email services for clients does not need to view the content of the messages in order to provide this service. They can deliver messages by simply examining the header information of the packets that comprise each message. Storing email messages on servers also does not require scanning the content.

Two popular email service providers, Microsoft (**hotmail .com** and **outlook.com**) and Google (Gmail), both include advertising next to your messages in their Web-based email GUIs. Research this practice by these two providers and see if you discern any difference in their use of advertising. Write up your findings and share them with your instructor or class.

LAB PROJECT 11.3

What do you see as the most significant change in mobile devices over the last five years? Is it a new type of mobile device or a revolutionary new app? Is this change a law concerning mobile devices? Discuss this change with your classmates, and tell why you believe it is the most significant change.

Appendix A

Windows Mouse and Keyboard Shortcuts

Mouse Action or Mouse + Key Combination	Result in Windows 7 and Earlier	Result in Windows 8 and Newer
ALT + PRTSCR	Captures the current window and saves it in the Clipboard.	
CTRL + −	Zoom out (where supported in the GUI).	
CTRL + +	Zoom in (after a zoom out and where supported in the GUI).	
CTRL + A	Select all.	
CTRL + F1	Expand or minimize the ribbon in an app with the ribbon includes File Explorer in Windows 8 and newer versions.	
CTRL + Roll middle scroll wheel	Semantic zoom (in and out).	
CTRL + SHIFT + ESC	Opens Task Manager.	
CTRL + ALT + DELETE	Opens the CTRL + ALT + DELETE menu.	
Double left-click	Selects or activates the object, performing the default command. If the pointer is in a document, this action selects the word at the insertion point, and a third click selects the sentence or paragraph (depending on the application and the version of the application). The third click for selecting an entire paragraph disappeared from Microsoft Word several versions ago.	
Drag and drop	After pointing at a graphic object, hold the primary pointing device button down while moving the pointing device to visually drag the object. At the destination, release the button to drop the object.	
F1	Opens context-sensitive Help where supported.	Opens context-sensitive Help where supported on the Desktop. It does not work in Modern apps or the Start screen.
Hover	The object the mouse pointer hovers over will display a tooltip, infotip, or similar information, if enabled for the object.	
PGDN	Depending on context, moves cursor/current screen to next screen.	
PGUP	Depending on context, moves cursor/current screen to previous screen.	
PRTSCR	Captures the screen and saves it in the Clipboard.	
SHIFT + single left-click	For selectable objects, this action contiguously extends the selection.	
Single left-click	Selects or activates an object, depending on the current context and location of the pointer. For instance, if the pointer is in a document, this action sets the insertion point.	
Single right-click	Selects the object and displays its context menu.	
WINDOWS KEY + F1	Opens Windows Help and Support window.	Opens Windows Help and Support window on the Desktop.
WINDOWS KEY ALONE	Opens the Start menu.	Returns to Start screen or returns to previous app from Start screen.

Mouse Action or Mouse + Key Combination	Result in Windows 7 and Earlier	Result in Windows 8 and Newer
WINDOWS KEY + PRTSCR	Captures the screen and saves it in the Clipboard.	Captures the screen and saves it in a folder named *Screenshots* in the Pictures folder.
WINDOWS KEY + TAB KEY (repeat)	N/A	Cycles through Modern app history in the task switcher bar on the left of the screen. Desktop apps appear as one app (Windows 8.*x*).
WINDOWS KEY + TAB KEY (release)	N/A	Opens Task view for current virtual desktop (Windows 10).
WINDOWS KEY + SHIFT + LEFT ARROW KEY	On dual display system, switches contents of windows.	On dual display system moves desktop window to left display.
WINDOWS KEY + SHIFT + RIGHT ARROW KEY	On dual display system, switches contents of windows.	On dual display system moves desktop window to right display.
WINDOWS KEY + +	Opens Magnifier to magnify all or part of the screen.	
WINDOWS KEY + ESC	Closes Magnifier.	
WINDOWS KEY + , (COMMA)	N/A	Peek at the Desktop. Release to return to previous screen or Desktop window.
WINDOWS KEY + HOME	Minimize nonactive desktop windows.	
WINDOWS KEY + LEFT ARROW KEY	Snaps current desktop window to left.	
WINDOWS KEY + RIGHT ARROW KEY	Snaps current desktop window to right.	
WINDOWS KEY + UP ARROW KEY	Maximizes current desktop window.	
WINDOWS KEY + DOWN ARROW KEY	Restores/minimizes current desktop window.	
WINDOWS KEY + PGUP KEY	Same as PGUP KEY alone.	Moves Start screen to left monitor.
WINDOWS KEY + PGDN KEY	Same as PGDN KEY alone.	Moves Start screen to right monitor.
WINDOWS KEY + 1–9	Opens desktop app at the given position on the task bar.	
WINDOWS KEY + C	N/A	Opens Charms bar (Windows 8.*x*). Opens Cortana (Windows 10).
WINDOWS KEY + D	Minimizes all open windows and displays the desktop.	Same as Windows 7 (Windows 8.*x*). From Start screen or Modern app, opens the Desktop or returns to Desktop (Windows 8.*x*).
WINDOWS KEY + E	Opens a Windows Explorer window.	Opens a File Explorer window on the Desktop.
WINDOWS KEY + F	Opens a Search window.	Opens Search focused on files (Windows 8.*x*).
WINDOWS KEY + H	N/A	Opens the Share bar.
WINDOWS KEY + I	N/A	Opens the Settings bar (Windows 8.*x*). Opens Settings (Windows 10).
WINDOWS KEY + J	N/A	When using Snap, switches focus between apps (Windows 8.*x*).

Mouse Action or Mouse + Key Combination	Result in Windows 7 and Earlier	Result in Windows 8 and Newer
WINDOWS KEY + K	N/A	Opens the Devices bar (Windows 8.*x*). Opens Connect bar (Windows 10).
WINDOWS KEY + L	Locks the PC displaying the Sign-In screen.	Locks the PC displaying either the Lock screen (if enabled) or the Sign-In screen.
WINDOWS KEY + M	Minimizes all windows.	Minimizes all Desktop windows.
WINDOWS KEY + O	N/A	Toggles the device orientation of mobile devices on and off in portrait or landscape.
WINDOWS KEY + P	Opens projection/second monitor options.	
WINDOWS KEY + Q	N/A	Opens the Apps Search bar (Windows 8.*x*). Opens Cortana Home (Windows 10).
WINDOWS KEY + R	Opens the Desktop Run box.	
WINDOWS KEY + T	Cycles through open Desktop apps.	
WINDOWS KEY + U	Opens Ease of Access Center.	
WINDOWS KEY + W	N/A	Opens Settings Search (Windows 8.*x*).
WINDOWS KEY + X	N/A	Opens Power User menu.
WINDOWS KEY + Z	N/A	When in Start screen or a Modern app, opens Apps bar on bottom of screen (Windows 8.*x*).
WINDOWS KEY + CTRL + D	N/A	Opens New virtual desktop (Windows 10).
WINDOWS KEY + CTRL + F4	N/A	Closes current virtual desktop (Windows 10).
WINDOWS KEY + CTRL + RIGHT ARROW KEY	N/A	Switches to next virtual desktop (Windows 10).
WINDOWS KEY + CTRL + LEFT ARROW KEY	N/A	Switches to previous virtual desktop (Windows 10).
WIN + CTRL + SHIFT + B	N/A	Restarts graphics drivers.

Chromebook & Chrome Browser Keyboard Shortcuts

Chromebook System-Wide Keyboard Shortcuts

Key Combination	Action	Notes
CTRL + ALT + ?	Display a list of keyboard shortcuts	
SEARCH + L	Lock the Chromebook screen	
CTRL + SEARCH + Q (twice)	Log out	
ALT + 1	Opens the first app on the Chrome shelf	
ALT + (Number from 2 to 8)	Opens app in the indicated numeric position on the Chrome shelf	
ALT + [	Docks current window to left side of screen	Does not work in all apps
ALT +]	Docks current window to right side of screen	Does not work in all apps
ALT + TAB	Switches between open programs.	
CTRL + SWITCHER (*aka F5)	Takes a screenshot and saves to the Downloads folder	
CTRL + SHIFT + SWITCHER (*aka F5)	Takes a screenshot of a selection from screen and saves to the Downloads folder	
SEARCH	Opens shelf to display Search box.	
ALT + SEARCH	Toggles Caps Lock on and off	
SEARCH + ESC	Launches Task Manager	
CTRL + SEARCH + +	Increases size of items on screen	Does not work in all apps
CTRL + SEARCH + −	Decrease size of items on screen	Does not work in all apps
CTRL + SEARCH +)	Reset screen scale to default	Does not work in all apps
CTRL + SEARCH + REFRESH** (aka F3)	Rotate screen 90 degrees	
CTRL + IMMERSIVE*** (aka F4)	Configure display settings when an external display is connected.	

*Switcher key is in the position occupied by the F5 key on a PC keyboard.
**Refresh key is in the position of the F3 key on a PC keyboard.
***Immersive key is in the position of the F4 key on a PC keyboard.

Chrome Browser Shortcuts

Key Combination	Action
ALT + E	Open Chrome Browser menu
CTRL + 1	Switches to first tab in current window
CTRL + 2	Switches to second tab in current window
CTRL + T	Opens a new tab in current windows
CTRL + W	Closes current tab
CTRL + L	Makes location bar current

Chrome Editing Shortcuts

Key Combination	Action
CTRL + BACKSPACE	Delete previous word
CTRL + Z	Undo
CTRL + X	Cut
CTRL + C	Copy
CTRL + V	Paste

Glossary

The number at the end of the entry refers to the chapter where the term is introduced.

$ prompt (Pronounced "dollar prompt.") The command prompt displayed in a Terminal window in macOS. The $ prompt is also used in the Linux CLI. (7)

absolute path A directory path that begins with the top level. In Linux, an absolute path begins with a forward slash (/) to indicate the root directory. (8)

accelerometer A component of a mobile device that detects the physical tilt and acceleration of the device, allowing the device to change the screen orientation for readability. (1)

Access Control Entry (ACE) An entry in an Access Control List, containing just one user or group account name and the permissions assigned to this account for that file or folder. (4)

Access Control List (ACL) A table of users and/or groups and their permissions to access the file or folder associated with the ACL. (4)

access mode number A value assigned to a file permission in Linux. The user (owner), group, and others each have a different access mode number calculated using the following values: read = 4, write = 2, and execute = 1. (8)

Action Center A Windows feature, represented by the small flag icon on the right of the toolbar; it will briefly display a message balloon when there is a problem with security programs or backup. (4)

activation A method of combating software piracy, intended to ensure that each software license is used solely on a single computer. (4)

Add Printer wizard A series of onscreen instructions that guide you through the installation of a printer's driver and utilities. (4)

address space layout randomization (ASLR) A security feature of macOS that loads the kernel, into random locations in memory, rather than loading into the same memory addresses every time. (7)

administrator account type An account type in an OS that can perform system-wide tasks such as changing computer settings and installing or removing software and hardware. (2)

adware A form of spyware downloaded to a computer without permission. It collects information about the user. (2)

Aero Peek A Windows 7 feature that allows the user to peek at the underlying desktop by hovering the mouse over the Show Desktop button on the far right of the taskbar. (4)

Aero Shake A Windows Aero feature that lets you quickly minimize all but one window by giving that window a quick shake. (4)

Aero Snap A Windows Aero feature that lets you manipulate windows quickly. To maximize a window, drag it until its title bar touches the top edge of your display. Restore a maximized window by dragging it away from the top of the display. (4)

AirDrop An Apple service that uses Bluetooth or Wi-Fi to transfer files between Apple devices. (11)

airplane mode A feature of mobile devices that turns off all wireless communications (cellular, Wi-Fi, Bluetooth, and NFC) without powering off the device. (11)

AirPlay A feature for connecting an iOS or macOS device to an Apple TV, which acts as an intermediary device for sending iTunes songs, video, pictures, and other data from the computer to a high definition (HD) TV via Wi-Fi. (7)

Android apps Apps created for the Google Android operating system and available at the Play Store. (9)

Apache HTTP Server Open source Web server software, originally written for UNIX, runs on Linux. (8)

Apple ID A free account that identifies the holder as a customer of Apple for all Apple services and products. (11)

Apple menu A pop-up menu opened by clicking on the Apple icon in the upper left of the macOS desktop. (7)

Apple Pay An automatic payment system for Apple Watch and iPhones that uses NFC wireless technology. It can also be used from a Mac computer. (11)

application Software that allows a user to perform useful functions such as writing a report or calculating a budget. (1)

application virtualization Virtualization of an application whereby a user connects to a server and accesses only the application rather than an entire desktop environment. (3)

AppLocker A feature introduced in Windows 7 for controlling which applications each user can run, reducing the chance of malware running on the user's computer. (4)

augmented reality (AR) Viewing something in real time through a smartphone or special eyeglasses while the image (or other input) is digitally modified. (3)

authentication Validation of a user account and password that occurs before the security components of an OS give a user access to the computer or network. (2)

authorization The process of both authenticating a user and determining the permissions that the user has for a resource. (2)

automatic IP addressing A method by which a host can be automatically assigned an IP address and all the additional configuration settings. (10)

Automatic login In macOS (and other operating systems), a setting that bypasses the login when the computer powers on, page and logs into the selected user account without requiring a user to enter a password or passcode. (7)

Automatic Private IP Addressing (APIPA) A method by which a DHCP client computer that fails to receive an address from a DHCP server will automatically give itself an address from a special range that has the value 169 (base-10) in the first octet (eight binary digits) of the IP address. (10)

avatar An animated computer-generated being used in a virtual world to represent an individual. (3)

back door A way to use software to bypass security and gain access to a computer. (2)

BASH An acronym for Bourne Again Shell; the Linux component (shell) that provides the character-mode user interface for entering and processing commands, issuing error messages, and other feedback. (8)

binary file A file that contains program code, as opposed to a file containing data. (6)

bitcoin An online payment system. (2)

BitLocker A feature introduced in the Enterprise and Ultimate editions of Windows Vista and Windows 7 for encrypting the drive on which the Windows OS resides and other drives beyond the system drive. (4)

BitLocker To Go An enhanced feature of BitLocker that includes encryption of removable devices. (4)

black hat hacker Someone who breaks into computers (hacks) to do harm. (2)

bloatware Slang for the software added to a computer when it is purchased with Windows preinstalled. Some of these programs are useful, but most are annoying or may be free trial software that you can try, but must purchase to use after the trial period (often 30 days) expires. (5)

bluesnarfing The act of covertly collecting information broadcast from wireless Bluetooth devices. (2)

Bluetooth A wireless standard for using radio waves to communicate over very short distances between devices. (11)

bootloader OS startup code that must be loaded into early in the startup process. The Windows bootloader is a file named BOOTMGR. (6)

bootstrap loader A firmware program that uses hardware configuration settings stored in nonvolatile memory, to determine what devices can start an OS and the order in which the system will search these devices while attempting to begin the OS startup process. It then loads the bootloader program. (6)

botherder Someone who initiates and controls a botnet. (2)

botnet A group of networked computers that, usually unbeknown to their owners, have been infected with programs that forward information to other computers over the network (usually the Internet). (2)

bring your own device (BYOD) The practice of using personal mobile devices at work. (11)

browser extension An add-on to a browser that adds features. (9)

browser hijacking Malware installed on a computer that causes the Internet Explorer home page to always point to a specific site, often advertising something. (2)

burn To write digital data just once to a CD or DVD disc. (8)

Can Comment A Google Drive file permission that allows a person to add comments to a shared file. (9)

Can Edit A Google Drive file permission that allows a person to edit a shared file. (9)

Can View A Google Drive file permission that allows a person to only view a shared file. (9)

case-aware In an operating system, a feature that allows the OS to preserve the case used for the characters in a file name when creating it, but does not require the correct case when opening or managing the file. (8)

case-sensitive In an operating system, a feature that allows the OS to preserve the case used for the characters in a file name when creating it, and requires the correct case to open or manage the file. (8)

cellular hotspot A service offered by cell providers in which a customer's smartphone or a separate device acts as a Wi-Fi router to allow other computers and devices to access the Internet. (10)

central processing unit (CPU) An integrated circuit (chip) that performs the calculations, or processing, for a computer. See also *microprocessor.* (1)

Chromebit A dongle containing the Chrome OS that plugs into a TV or computer display's HDMI port. (9)

Chromebook A laptop with the Chrome OS preinstalled. (9)

Chromebox A desktop computer with the Chrome OS preinstalled. (9)

Chrome OS Google's OS based on their Chrome browser. (1)

clean installation An installation of an OS onto a completely empty hard disk or one from which all data is removed during the installation. (4)

Click bait Content in an email, web page, social networking page, or any online app, designed to lure the user to click on it and its associated link. (2)

client A software component on a computer that accesses services from a network server. (1)

cloud All services offered over the Internet and on intranets. (9)

cloud computing The use of services offered in the cloud. (9)

cloud storage Services offering data storage in the cloud. (9)

code signing A Windows feature in which all of the operating system code is digitally signed to show that it has not been tampered with. See also *driver signing.* (6)

cold boot A method of starting up a computer and operating system by turning on the power switch. (6)

collaboration services Cloud-based services that allow two or more people to work together on documents and projects. (9)

command completion A feature of Linux and UNIX (and macOS Terminal) that completes what is entered at the command line with a command name or file or directory name. (8)

Command Prompt In Windows, the command-line interface that is launched from within Windows or in Safe Mode or as a Recovery option. (6)

command-line history The Linux and UNIX (and macOS Terminal) feature that saves command-line history in a file named bash_history. (8)

command-line interface (CLI) A user interface that includes a character-based command line that requires text input. (1)

computer. A device that calculates. (1)

Consent Prompt Part of the Windows User Account Control security feature, this prompt appears when a user is logged on as an administrator and a program attempts to perform a task requiring administrative permissions. (6)

content filter Software that blocks Web content based on predetermined rules. (2)

Continuum A feature of Windows 10 that senses when a keyboard is attached versus when a keyboard is removed and presents the appropriate desktop for each configuration. (5)

cookies Very small text files an Internet browser saves on the local hard drive at the request of a website. (2)

Cortana An intelligent search system introduced in Windows Phone 8.1, and improved on as a personal assistant in Windows 10. (5)

Credentials Prompt Part of the Windows User Account Control security feature, this prompt appears when a user is logged on as a standard user and a program attempts to perform a task requiring administrative permission. The user must provide an administrator password to continue. (6)

cursor In a command-line interface (CLI), a marker for where the next character you type on the keyboard will appear on the screen. In a GUI the cursor is replaced by both an insertion point as well as by a graphical pointer that can have a variety of shapes you can move around on the screen by manipulating a pointing device. (1)

cybercrime Illegal activity performed using computer technology. (2)

cybercriminal A person who breaks laws using computer technology. (2)

cyberterrorism A computer-based attack that wreaks havoc on victims. (2)

cyberterrorist A person who commits a computer-based attack that wreaks havoc on victims. (2)

daemon In Linux, software that runs in background until it is activated. (8)

Darwin The name of the core operating system on which macOS is based. A product of the open-source community. (7)

data type In the Windows registry, a special data format. There are several registry data types, such as REG_BINARY, REG_DWORD, and so forth. (6)

data wiping The permanent removal of data from a storage device. (2)

default gateway The IP address of the router connected to your network. (10)

Desktop mode A feature of Windows 10 that displays the desktop and apps appropriately for a computer with a keyboard attached. (5)

desktop virtualization The virtualization of a desktop computer into which you can install an operating system, its unique configuration, applications, and user data. (3)

device driver Software that is added to an OS to control a physical component (device). (1)

device management An OS function that controls hardware devices through the use of device drivers. (1)

Device Manager A Windows recovery tool that aids in troubleshooting device problems. (5)

Device Stage A feature introduced in Windows 7 that, if the device supports it, will bring up a page from which you can make many choices for managing the device; it often includes an accurate image of the device. (6)

dial-up An inexpensive WAN option available to anyone with a phone line and a standard analog modem (the longtime standard runs at 56 Kbps). (10)

digital certificate A special file stored on a computer that may hold a secret key for decrypting data. (2)

digital signature In Windows, encrypted data that can be unencrypted by Windows in a process called file signature verification. (6)

digital subscriber line (DSL) A WAN service similar to ISDN in its use of the telephone network, but using more advanced digital signal processing to compress signals through the telephone lines. (10)

directory A special file on a storage device that can contain files as well as other directories. This term is often used with non-GUI operating systems, while *folder* is often used when describing a directory in a GUI. (1)

distribution A bundling of the Linux kernel and software—both enhancements to the OS and applications—such as word processors, spreadsheets, media players, and more. (1)

DMZ A network between a private network and the Internet with a firewall on both sides. (2)

Dock A floating bar on the macOS desktop that holds icons for commonly used programs, as well as icons for open applications. A single click on an icon launches the program. (7)

Domain Joined A feature that allows a Windows computer to join a Microsoft Active Directory Domain. (5)

Domain Name System (DNS) A distributed online database containing registered domain names mapped to IP addresses. (10)

drive-by download A program downloaded to a user's computer without consent. (2)

driver signing Code signing of device drivers that indicates two things: the integrity of the file or files, and that the device driver has passed Microsoft's tests for compatibility. (6)

dual-boot A multiboot configuration with just two choices of operating systems. (4)

dumb terminal A device consisting of little more than a keyboard and display with a connection to a host computer and having no native processing power of its own. (3)

Dynamic Host Configuration Protocol (DHCP) server A server that issues IP addresses and settings to computers that are configured to obtain an IP address automatically, thus making them DHCP clients. (10)

Early Launch Anti-Malware (ELAM) A security feature, introduced in Windows 8, that examines all device drivers before they are loaded into memory, preventing suspicious drivers from loading. (6)

Ease of Access A group of Windows settings for audio and visual aids. (5)

email spoofing Forging of a sender's address in the email message's header so that an incorrect address appears in the "from" field of an email message. (2)

embedded OS An operating system stored in firmware, as in a mobile device (1)

Encrypting File System (EFS) An NTFS file encryption feature for encrypting selected files and folders (not entire drives). (2)

encryption The transformation of data into a code that can be decrypted only through the use of a secret key or password. (2)

exploit A malware attack. (2)

Face ID Apple's infrared facial recognition technology introduced on the iPhone X. (11)

Fast Boot A feature of Windows 8 and newer in which startup takes advantage of the hibernated kernel (if the last shutdown was a Hybrid Shutdown), bringing the hibernated system session out of hibernation, saving all the work of the Kernel Loading phase. (6)

Fast Pair A Google Android feature that scans for nearby Bluetooth signals, displaying a prompt identifying the device. Tap the box, and the phone connects to the device. (11)

FAT file systems Several related file systems based on the original FAT file system. They include FAT12, FAT16, FAT32, and exFAT. Each has a logical structure that includes a file allocation table (FAT) and a directory structure. (4)

FIDO Alliance An industry consortium that works together on solutions that will allow users to securely access online services and conduct financial transactions without using password authentication and reduce the risk of fraud. (5)

file and printer server A network server that gives client computers access to files and printers. Also simply called a file server. (10)

File Explorer Previously named Windows Explorer, the name of the Windows file management tool. (5)

file management An operating system function that allows the operating system to read, write, and modify data and programs organized into files and directories. (1)

file signature verification The process by which Windows unencrypts a digital signature and verifies that the file has not been tampered with. (6)

file system The logical structure used on a storage device for the purpose of storing files, as well as the code within an operating system that allows the OS to store and manage files on a storage device. (1)

Files app The Chrome OS file management app. (9)

FileVault A feature in macOs that, in earlier versions, encrypted the Home folder. In recent versions, it encrypts the entire startup disk. (2)

Finder The foundation of the macOS GUI and the equivalent to Windows Explorer, the Windows file management tool. (7)

firewall A firewall is software or a physical device that examines network traffic. Based on predefined rules, a firewall rejects certain traffic coming into a computer or network. The two general types of firewalls are network-based firewalls and personal firewalls on individual computers. (2)

firmware Software resident in integrated circuits. (1)

first-party cookie A cookie that originates with the domain name of the URL to which you directly connect. (2)

Flip 3D A Windows Aero feature that lets you switch through your open windows as if they were in a stack of cards or photos. (4)

folder A special file that can contain files as well as other directories. This term is often used with GUI operating systems, while *directory* is often used when describing a directory in a non-GUI. (1)

forged email address An address that appears in the "from" field of an email address because the sender address was modified in the email message's header. This type of forgery is also called *email spoofing.* (2)

formatting The action of an operating system when it maps the logical organization of a file system to physical locations on the storage device so that it can store and retrieve the data. (1)

fraud The use of deceit and trickery to persuade someone to hand over money or other valuables. (2)

fully qualified domain name (FQDN) The human-readable name corresponding to the TCP/IP address of a host, as found on a computer, router, or other networked device. It includes both its host name and its domain name. (10)

gadget In Windows 7 a small program represented by an icon on the desktop. Gadgets are no longer recommended because they are potential security holes. (4)

Gatekeeper A security feature of macOS that limits sources from which you can download apps. (7)

GNOME An acronym for GNU network object model environment, a Linux GUI that uses the Linux X Windows system. (8)

GNU An organization created in 1984 to develop a free version of a UNIX-like operating system. GNU develops applications that run on UNIX and Linux platforms. Many are distributed with versions of Linux. (8)

Google Account A free account that gives the account holder access to basic Google services. (9)

Google Drive Google's online file storage service. (9)

Google Mail Google's electronic mail service. (9)

Google Pay Google's virtual wallet that stores a variety of membership cards, movie tickets, transit tickets, and other card information. It uses payment methods stored with a Google Account. (11)

graphical user interface (GUI) A user interface that takes advantage of a computer's graphics capabilities to make it easier to use with graphical elements that a user can manipulate to perform tasks. (1)

group account A security account that may contain one or more individual or group accounts. (2)

guest account A special account used when someone connects to a computer but is not a member of a security account recognized on that computer. That person connects as a guest (if the guest account is enabled) and will have the limited permissions assigned to the guest account. (2)

guest OS An operating system running within a virtual machine. (3)

Guest User An account created by macOS (and other operating systems) that does not require a password, has access only to the Guest Home folder, and when this account logs out, all files and folders created during that session are deleted. (7)

hacker Someone with a great deal of computing expertise. One who does no harm is a white hat hacker. One who does harm is a black hat hacker. (2)

header The information that accompanies a message but does not appear in the message. (2)

Hey Cortana The voice activation options for the Cortana feature of Windows 10. (5)

hibernate A Windows power or shutdown option that, if enabled, saves both the system state and the user session in a file named hiberfil.sys. (6)

High Quality option A photo file storage option that does not count against your Google Drive unless the file is larger than 16 MB. (9)

hive The portion of the Windows registry represented in one registry file. (6)

home directory In Linux, a directory created for a user, using the user's login name, and located under the /home directory. This is the one place in Linux where an ordinary user account has full control over files without logging in as the root account. (8)

Home folder A folder created by macOS for a user that displays in the Finder when that user is logged on, identified in the sidebar by a house icon and the user's name. (7)

honey pot A server created as a decoy to draw malware attacks and gather information about attackers. (2)

host ID The portion of an IP address that identifies the host on a network, as determined using the subnet mask. (10)

host key A key or key combination that releases the mouse and keyboard from a virtual machine to the host OS. (3)

host OS The operating system installed directly on a computer. (3)

hotspot A Wi-Fi network that connects to the Internet through a router. (2)

Hybrid Shutdown The default when you select Shutdown from the Windows 8 (or newer version) Power menu: Windows closes the session for each logged-on user, and hibernates the Windows session, saving it in a file. (6)

Hypertext Transfer Protocol (HTTP) The protocol for transferring the files that make up the rich graphical Web pages we view on the World Wide Web (WWW). (8)

hypervisor The software layer that emulates the necessary hardware for an operating system to run in, creating a virtual machine within which a guest OS can run. (3)

iCloud keychain A database of user names passwords to various locations stored in a user's iCloud and accessible to all devices that support it and that have been enabled by the user. (7)

identity theft The collection of personal information belonging to another person and the use of that information to fraudulently make purchases, open new credit accounts, or even obtain new driver's licenses and other forms of identification in the victim's name. (2)

image An exact duplicate of the entire hard drive contents, including the OS and all installed software, that is used to install copies of an OS and associated applications on multiple computers. (4)

input/output (I/O) Anything sent into a computer (input); anything coming out of a computer (output). (1)

integrated circuit (IC) A small electronic component made up of transistors (tiny switches) and other miniaturized parts. (1)

integrated services digital network (ISDN) A digital telephone service that simultaneously transmits voice, data, and control signaling over a single telephone line. An ISDN data connection can transfer data at up to 128,000 bits per second (128 Kbps). (10)

Internet of Things (IoT) Not really a separate Internet, but a term that describes the trend to have devices such as appliances connected to networks—even to the Internet. (1)

Internet Protocol (IP) The core TCP/IP protocol that delivers communications in chunks, called packets. It uses a logical address called an IP address. (10)

Internet service provider (ISP) An organization that provides individuals or entire organizations access to the Internet. (10)

internetwork A network of interconnected networks. (9)

intranet A privately owned network of networks. (9)

IP address The logical address used on a TCP/IP network to identify a network interface card (NIC). (10)

IPv4 The version of the Internet Protocol in use since 1983 (with updates). (10)

IPv6 The latest version of the Internet Protocol that is gradually replacing IPv4. (10)

ISO file A copy of the entire contents of a CD or DVD that can be easily transferred to a writable CD or DVD with ISO image copy software. (3)

job management An operating system function that controls the order and time in which programs are run. (1)

Jump List In Windows, a list of recently opened items such as files, folders, and websites that appear when you right-click on a program on the Start menu or taskbar. (4)

kernel The main component of an operating system that always remains in memory while a computer is running. (1)

key In the Windows registry, a folder object that may contain one or more sets of settings as well as other keys. (6)

keyboard shortcut A key combination that performs an assigned action, saving you several mouse or keyboard actions. (5)

keychain A database in which macOS saves encrypted passwords for a single computer. The first keychain, login, is created for each user and associated with the user's login password. (7)

Keychain Access The macOS utility for managing the keychain. (7)

keylogger See *keystroke logger.* (2)

keystroke logger A hardware device or a program that monitors and records a user's every keystroke, usually without the user's knowledge. Also called a keylogger. (2)

Kickoff Application Launcher A GUI object on the KDE GUI bundled with Fedora that, when clicked, opens a menu (similar to the Windows Start menu) for launching programs. (8)

killer app An application that is so useful or otherwise desirable that customers buy a device in order to use that app. (1)

Last Known Good (LKG) Configuration A Windows start-up option for start-up failures due to a configuration change. It lets you restore the system to a single restore point (not called that). You must use LKG on the first reboot after making a configuration change, and *before* logging on. (6)

Launcher A GUI object (a bar) on the left side of the Ubuntu Unity desktop that serves the same purpose as the macOS Dock and the pinned items feature on the taskbar on the Windows Desktop. This same term is used in Chrome OS. (8)

Launchpad A feature in macOS that resembles the home screen on Apple iOS devices. It consists of one or more screens holding icons for all installed apps. Apps can be grouped together and/or launched from the Launchpad. (7)

library A feature introduced in Windows 7, in which a library is a special folder with pointers to disk folders that can be in many locations, but will all appear to be in the same library. (4)

Lightning port The USB port on an iOS device used for charging the device, as well as for file transfer. (11)

Linux An open source operating system based on UNIX that was developed by Linus Torvalds and others beginning in 1991. (8)

Live File System A file format used by Windows to burn discs that will only be used on newer Apple Macs and newer PCs. Using Live File System you can directly copy items to a CD or DVD without requiring extra hard drive space. You can copy items individually, multiple times. (4)

live image A bootable image of the operating system that will run from disc or other bootable media without requiring that the OS be installed on the local compute. (8)

live tile A rectangle on the Windows 10 Start screen that when tapped with a finger or clicked with a mouse launches an app. The "live" part of the name is due to each tile's ability to display active content related to the app without requiring that you launch the app. (5)

local area network (LAN) A network that covers a building, home, office, or campus. It can be wireless or wired. (10)

local security The security options available and limited to a local computer. In Windows, this includes local security accounts and local security for files and folders, Windows BitLocker drive encryption, Windows Defender antispam protection, and Windows Firewall. (4)

location service A service on a computer or mobile device that allows an app to track your location, using one or more methods, often with the help of the Internet. (11)

Lock screen A screen that displays at startup of a Windows 8 or Windows 10 computer, when Windows is locked, or when a period of inactivity triggers the screen saver. You must use a swiping motion (with finger or mouse) to close the Lock screen and access either the Sign-in screen or the Start screen. (5)

logon phase A phase of Windows startup during which a user is authenticated, the service control manager starts, logon scripts run, startup programs run, and noncritical services start. Plug-and-play detection occurs during this startup phase. (6)

Mac The product name for Apple's desktop computers. (1)

macOS The Apple desktop operating system. (7)

macOS Setup Assistant In a new computer with macOS preinstalled, the OS is not configured, so the first time it is powered up, this program prompts you for the user preferences information. (7)

Mac OS X Server The first of the macOS line designed for Mac Server computers. It was introduced in 1999, shipping preinstalled on Mac Server. Today you can only buy it as an add-on to macOS. (7)

malware A shortened form of "malicious software" that covers a large and growing list of threats such as viruses, worms, Trojan horses, and spam. (2)

manpage In Linux, UNIX, and the macOS Terminal window, a manual page is the documentation for a command, accessed with the **man** command. (7)

Mastered When burning a disc in Windows this option allows you to use the burned CD or DVD in a conventional CD or DVD player or in any computer. (4)

master file table (MFT) The main logical structure of the NTFS file system that is expandable and uses transaction processing to track changes to files. (4)

Measured Boot A UEFI firmware feature that logs the startup process. Antimalware software can analyze this log to determine if malware is on the computer or if the boot components were tampered with. (6)

memory The physical chips that store programs and data. There are two basic types: random-access memory (RAM) and read-only memory (ROM). (1)

memory management An operating system function that manages and tracks the placement of programs and data in memory. (1)

Menu Extras Icons on the right side of the macOS menu bar that give quick access to some System Preferences settings. (7)

microcomputer A computer built around a microprocessor. (1)

microprocessor An integrated circuit (chip) that performs the calculations, or processing, for a computer. Also called a processor or central processing unit (CPU). (1)

Microsoft account (MSA) A free account with Microsoft that gives the subscriber access to Microsoft services, such as Hotmail, Messenger, SkyDrive, Windows Phone, Xbox LIVE, and Outlook.com. (5)

Microsoft Edge The Internet browser introduced with Windows 10. (5)

Microsoft family A free service that allows an administrator to create new accounts for family members or invite someone with a Microsoft account to join the family. It includes tools for protecting children. (2)

Microsoft Passport A feature that securely signs in to network resources without sending a password or PIN over the network. (5)

Microsoft Product Activation (MPA) Microsoft's method of combating software piracy, intended to ensure that each software license is used solely on a single computer. Many other software vendors require activation. See *activation*. (4)

MiFi Novatel's trademarked name for the hotspot device they manufactured. It stands for "my Wi-Fi." (11)

Mission Control A screen in macOS where you can create and organize Spaces. (7)

mobile device A device that uses wireless technologies and offers a variety of functions to the user. (1)

mobile device management (MDM) A category of software for enforcing policies and managing mobile devices. (11)

mobile hotspot A mobile device that shares its data cellular connection with nearby devices connected via Wi-Fi. (11)

motherboard The central circuit board of a computer to which all other devices connect. (1)

MSCONFIG The System Configuration Utility, a Windows tool for modifying system startup, allows you to modify and test start-up configuration settings without having to alter the settings directly. (6)

multiboot An installation that leaves an old OS in place, installing a new OS in a separate location. This allows you to select the OS you want to boot into every time you start the computer. (4)

multitasking Two or more programs (tasks) running simultaneously on a computer. (1)

multitouch The ability to interpret multiple simultaneous touch gestures, such as the pinching gesture in which fingers first touch the device (screen, touch mouse, or touch pad) at separate locations and then pinch them together. (5)

Near Field Communication (NFC) A technology that supports a short-distance wireless standard that requires two devices to touch before communicating. (11)

net ID The network portion of an IP address, as determined through the subnet mask. (10)

network virtualization A network addressing space that exists within one or more physical networks, but which is logically independent of the physical network structure. (3)

New Technology File System (NTFS) The Windows file system that is expandable and uses a transaction processing system to track changes to files, so that it can roll back incomplete transactions. It also includes several other features: file compression, file encryption, file and folder security, and indexing. (1)

Notification area In Chrome OS, an area on the shelf located to the right of app shortcuts and to the left of the status bar. (9)

Notification Center A macOS feature that displays important status messages, notifying the user of important events, such as a new email or text message or that an update is available. Windows, Linux, and Chrome OS also have this feature. (7)

object code An executable program, the result of compiling programming statements, that can be interpreted by a computer's CPU or operating system and loaded into memory as a running program. (8)

octet A group of eight binary digits. (10)

on-screen keyboard A virtual keyboard that is available as an accessibility option. It also displays in Windows 8 and Windows 10 devices without a keyboard when you need to enter alphanumeric characters. (5)

open source software Software distributed with all its source code, allowing developers to customize it as necessary. (8)

operating system (OS) A collection of programs that provides a computer with critical functionality, such as a user interface, management of hardware and software, and ways of creating, managing, and using files. (1)

Original format An option for files saved in Google Photos that counts against your Google storage limit. (9)

Out of Box Experience (OOBE) A feature on a new computer with Windows 8 or Windows 10 preinstalled. When you take it out of the box and turn it on, you will be greeted with this last phase of Windows installation where you personalize the GUI and configure how you will sign in. (5)

over the phone (OTP) The use of voice or text for sending a verification code for sign in. (9)

owner In Linux, the user account that creates a file or directory. This term is also used in Windows. (8)

packet A piece of a message packaged by the Internet Protocol. Each packet includes a header that contains information including the source address (local host address) and the destination address. (10)

pairing A connection between two devices using the Bluetooth wireless standard. (11)

Parental Controls A feature in macOS that allows parents to protect their children from harm by setting specific Parental Controls for a child's user account. (2)

partition An area of a physical hard disk that defines space used for a logical drive. (1)

passcode lock A string of characters (or gestures) that a user enters to close the lock screen and access a device. (11)

password A string of characters that a user enters (along with a user name) in order to be authenticated. (2)

password cracker A program used to discover a password. (2)

password manager Software that creates and remembers passwords, and can manage your use of passwords across all your devices. (2)

path A description that an operating system uses to identify the location of a file or directory. (8)

permission A level of access to an object, such as a file or folder, that is granted to a user account or group account. (2)

personal computer (PC) A microcomputer that complies with the Microsoft/Intel standards. (1)

personal folders A set of folders created by Windows for each user account to hold user data files. (4)

phishing A fraudulent method of obtaining personal financial information through Web page pop-ups, email, and even paper letters mailed via the postal service. Phishing is a form of social engineering. (2)

picture-in-picture (PIP) A TV display feature supported by the Xbox app in which one show displays on the screen while another displays in a small box. (5)

pinning A feature introduced in Windows 7 that allows you to place icons for applications and destinations on the taskbar and Start menu. Once pinned, an item's icon remains on the toolbar regardless of whether the program is open or closed. Click it to open the application or destination. (4)

plug-and-play (PnP) The ability of a computer to detect and configure a hardware device automatically. To work, the computer, the device, and the OS must all comply with the same plug-and-play standard. (1)

pop-up An ad that runs in a separate browser window you must close before continuing with the present task. (2)

pop-up blocker A program that works against pop-ups. (2)

pop-up download A program that is downloaded to a user's computer through the use of a pop-up page that appears while surfing the Web. (2)

portable operating system An operating system that you can use on a variety of computer system platforms, with only minor alterations required. (1)

power-on self-test (POST) Tests of system hardware that runs from firmware when a computer starts up. (6)

Power User menu A Windows 8 and Windows 10 menu that opens when you use the WINDOWS KEY+X shortcut. This menu contains many handy utilities. (6)

predictive notification A feature of Cortana by which it provides a notice or other information in anticipation of a need. (5)

private browsing A security feature available in browsers that allows you to browse the Web without saving any history on the local computer of the sites visited. (10)

private cloud An intranet that is owned and manage for one organization, offering a variety of cloud services. (9)

private IP address An address from one of three ranges designated for use only on private networks. The private IP address ranges are 10.0.0.0 through 10.255.255.255, 172.16.0.0 through 172.31.255.255, and 192.168.0.0 through 192.168.255.255. (10)

processes Components of a program active in memory. (1)

Program Compatibility Troubleshooter A wizard that you run from Help and Support to set compatibility options for an older application that will "trick" the older program into thinking that the OS is actually the earlier version of Windows required by the application (such as Windows XP). (4)

protocol In computer technology and networking a set of rules, usually formalized in a standard published by one of many standards organizations. This is also the term for the software that implements a certain set of rules. (10)

protocol stack A group of bundled programs based on networking protocols and designed to work together. (10)

public cloud The hosting of a variety of free and/or fee-based services over the Internet available to anyone who enrolls in the service. (9)

public IP addresses IP addresses assigned to hosts on the Internet. (10)

Quick link The name for a shortcut on the Windows 10 Start menu. (5)

random-access memory (RAM) Memory in a computer that acts as the main memory for holding active programs. (1)

ransomware Malware that threatens to do damage or lock a user out of a computer unless the user pays a "ransom." (2)

RAW format A photo file format, generated within a camera, that saves all unprocessed data for an image, creating a very large file. (9)

recovery key A code generated by macOS when it encrypts the start disk with FileVault. (7)

Red Hat Enterprise Linux (RHEL) Red Hat's commercially available version of Linux. (8)

registry A database of all configuration settings in Windows. (6)

remote access VPN A connection between an individual computer or mobile device using a VPN over a WAN connection. (10)

restore point A snapshot of Windows, its configuration, and all installed programs. If your computer has problems after you have made a change, you can use System Restore to roll it back to a restore point. (4)

root account In Linux, an all-powerful account that is used only when absolutely necessary to do advanced tasks. (8)

root key In the Windows registry, each of the top five folders is a root key, sometimes called a subtree in Microsoft documentation. Each of these root keys is the top of a hierarchical structure containing folders called keys. (6)

rootkit Malware that hides within the OS code or another program running on the computer. (2)

router A network device that sits between networks and directs (routes) traffic to destinations beyond the local network. (10)

Safe Mode A start-up mode in which Windows starts without using all of the drivers and components that would normally be loaded. Use Safe Mode when your Windows computer will not start normally. (6)

Safe Mode with Command Prompt A start-up mode in which Windows starts without using all of the drivers and components that would normally be loaded and opens an Administrator Command Prompt window against a black background with the words "Safe Mode" in the four corners of the screen. Use Safe Mode when your Windows computer will not start normally. (6)

sandboxed A feature in macOS that isolates an app so that it cannot access any code or device it is not authorized to access. (7)

scareware A vector technique that uses threatening messages. (2)

screen rotation A feature of mobile operating systems that takes advantage of the built-in hardware accelerometer by rotating the image on the screen to accommodate the position and allow you to read the screen. (1)

secret key A special code that can be used to decrypt encrypted data. (2)

Second-Level Address Translation (SLAT) A feature of many newer Intel and AMD CPUs, required by some hypervisors. (3)

Secure Boot A UEFI firmware feature that loads only trusted operating system bootloaders. This is one of the UEFI security features required on computers that come with Windows 8 pre-installed. (6)

Secure HTTP (HTTPS) A form of the HTTP protocol that supports encryption of the communications. HTTPS uses the Secure Sockets Layer (SSL) security protocol. (2)

Secure Sockets Layer (SSL) A security protocol for encrypting network data. (2)

Secure Virtual Memory A macOS feature that encrypts the swap file (virtual memory). (7)

security An operating system function that provides password-protected authentication of the user before allowing access to the local computer. (1)

security account In a security accounts database, a listing of information about a user, group, or computer. A security account is used for authentication. (2)

security ID (SID) A unique string of numbers preceded by *S-1-5* that identifies a security principal in a Windows security accounts database. (6)

server A computer that plays one or more of several roles on a network, providing services to other computers (clients). (1)

server virtualization The hosting of multiple virtual servers on a single computer. (3)

Service Set ID (SSID) A network name that identifies a Wi-Fi network. (11)

share A connecting point to which network clients may connect. Visible as a folder over the network, it is a separate entity from the disk folder to which it points. (10)

Shared folder A folder created by macOS in each user's Home folder. It is accessible to other users without restriction. (7)

Sharing Only account In macOS, an account that allows a user to log in remotely and access shared folders, but that does not have a Home folder and cannot be used to log in locally on that computer. (7)

shelf In the Chrome OS desktop, a bar on the edge of the screen containing shortcuts to features and apps. (9)

shell The operating system component that provides the character-mode user interface—processing commands and issuing error messages and other limited feedback. (7)

shell command A command entered through a CLI shell. (7)

shortcut An icon that represents a link to an object, such as a file or program. Activating a shortcut (by clicking on it) is a quick way to access an object or to start a program from any location. (4)

shoulder surfing The gathering of information by reading information on a screen as a user works on the device. (2)

site-to-site VPN A VPN connection between two networks. (10)

Sleep A Windows power down option that leaves the computer in a very-low-power mode in which the system state and user session (applications and data) are saved in RAM, but the screen turns off. (6)

smartphone A cell phone that connects to the Internet and runs a variety of apps for entertainment, education, and work. (1)

social engineering The use of persuasion techniques to gain the confidence of individuals—for both good and bad purposes. (2)

social media A service (Internet-based or other) that provides a place where people can interact in online communities, sharing information in various forms. (2)

social networking The use of social media. (2)

solid-state drive (SSD) A storage device that uses integrated circuits, which are faster than conventional hard disk drives and optical drives. (1)

source code The uncompiled text program statements that can be viewed and edited with a text editor or special software. (8)

Spaces A macOS feature in which a space is a virtual screen; macOS supports up to 16 Spaces. Use Spaces for separating categories of files, such as those for work, play, and school projects. (7)

spam Unsolicited email. This includes email from a legitimate source selling a real service or product, but if you did not give permission to send such information to you, it is spam. (2)

spam filter Software designed to combat spam by examining incoming messages and filtering out those that have characteristics of spam. (2)

spear phishing Targeted phishing attacks that often target high-value individuals. (2)

spim An acronym for Spam over Instant Messaging; the perpetrators are called spimmers. (2)

Split View A feature introduced in macOS 10.11 El Capitan that allows two full-screen apps to share the screen. (7)

Spotlight A Mac macOS search utility that, much like Search in Windows, is a live search, so it starts presenting results as soon as you start typing. (7)

spyware A category of software that runs surreptitiously on a user's computer, gathers information without permission from the user, and then sends that information to the people who requested the information. (2)

Standard account In macOS an account type that can only access files in that user's Home folder and the Shared folder and is denied access to higher-level system settings. (7)

standard user account An account for an "ordinary" user without administrator status. (2)

Start button A button on the Windows 7 and Windows 10 taskbar that opens the Start menu. In Windows 8.1 the Start button returns you to the Start screen. (5)

Startup Repair A Windows recovery tool that will scan for problems with missing or damaged system files and attempt to replace the problem files. (4)

static IP address An IP address that is manually configured for a host and can, therefore, be considered semipermanent in that, it stays with the device until someone changes it. (10)

status tray A bar on the far right of the Chrome OS shelf that opens a pop-up with the current status of network connections, battery life, who is signed in, and more. (9)

storage virtualization Multiple networked hard drives functioning as a single logical drive. (3)

subkey In the Windows registry, a key that exists within another key. (6)

subnet mask An important IP configuration parameter as critical as the address itself, because it divides what looks like a single address into two addresses by masking off part of the address. (10)

Subscriber Identity Module (SIM) An integrated circuit card that, when inserted into a mobile device, programs it for a customer's use on a cellular network. (11)

switch users A feature of most operating systems that allows the currently logged-on users to leave their apps and data open in memory, switching away so that another user can log in to a separate session. (8)

symbolic link In Linux, a string of characters, such as **/usr/bin**, that points to another directory. (8)

synchronize To match the contents of two locations, sometimes in both directions, so that the contents match. (11)

system firmware Software resident in integrated circuits that contains program code for interacting with the hardware. (1)

System Image Recovery A Windows recovery tool that will let you restore a complete PC Image backup, provided you created one. (4)

system-on-a-chip (SoC) A term used to describe a microchip containing all or most of the electronic circuitry for a small computing device, such as a smartphone. (1)

System Preferences The macOS equivalent of the Windows Control Panel. (7)

System Recovery Command Prompt A command prompt accessed by starting a computer from the Windows 7 disc and navigating through the menus to the Recovery Options screen and select Command Prompt. (6)

System Restore A recovery tool that creates restore points, which are snapshots of Windows, its configuration, and all installed programs. Use System Restore to roll a Windows installation back to a restore point. (4)

tablet A mobile computing device with a touch screen, usually no integrated keyboard, and it is larger than a smartphone but more portable than a laptop. (1)

Tablet mode Beginning in Windows 10, the mode for displaying the desktop and applications when no keyboard is attached to a device. (5)

task management An operating system function in multitasking OSs that controls the focus. (1)

Task Manager A Windows utility that allows you to see the state of the individual processes and programs running on the computer and to stop one, if necessary. (4)

Task view A feature of Windows 10 that lets the user quickly view all open apps. (5)

TCP/IP A suite of protocols that work together to allow both similar and dissimilar computers to communicate. It is needed to access the Internet and is the most common protocol suite used on private intranets. (10)

Terminal A window in the macOS GUI that provides a command-line interface (CLI) for entering UNIX shell commands. The default Terminal shell is BASH. (7)

terminal client Software that establishes a connection to a terminal server. (3)

terminal services Software running on servers to which users connect from their desktop PCs using terminal client software. (3)

terminal window A window in a Linux GUI that provides a command-line interface (CLI) for entering Linux shell commands. (8)

tethering A feature that allows you to share your smartphone's cellular data connection with another device. The connection between the smartphone and the computer, laptop, or tablet can be via USB cable, Wi-Fi, or Bluetooth. (11)

thin client A minimally configured network computer. (3)

third-party cookie A cookie that originates with a domain name beyond the one shown in the URL for the current Web page. (2)

Time Machine An macOS backup utility that automatically backs up files to a dedicated drive that is always available when the computer is turned on. (7)

token A physical device that can be used in authentication, either alone or together with a user name and password. (2)

Touch ID A feature in iPhone 5s and newer incorporating a fingerprint scanner into the Home button for authentication. (11)

Transmission Control Protocol (TCP) The protocol responsible for the accurate delivery of messages, verifying and resending pieces that fail to make the trip from source to destination. (10)

Trojan horse A program that is installed and activated on a computer by appearing to be something harmless. This is a common vector. (2)

Trusted Boot A feature of Windows 8 and newer that examines each of the system files loaded during the boot process before it is loaded into memory. (6)

Two-Factor Authentication In an Apple ID account, a security service that adds an extra layer of protection to an account. It differs from Two-Step Verification in that it first sends a message stating that someone is attempting to access a device. (11)

two-step verification A security measure used by Microsoft and others (sometimes with different names) that requires, in addition to your credentials, a numeric code sent to your smartphone or other device, identified in your account information. (5)

Type I hypervisor A hypervisor that can run directly on a computer without an underlying host operating system—sometimes called a bare-metal hypervisor. (3)

Type II hypervisor A hypervisor that requires a host operating system. (3)

Ubuntu A group of Linux distributions supported by a company named Canonical. (8)

Unified Extensible Firmware Interface (UEFI) The specification for system firmware that replaced ROM-BIOS. (6)

Universal app A type of app, introduced in Windows 10, that adapts to the screen size and type so that it displays in a usable fashion on all Windows 10 devices. (5)

Upgrade An installation of an OS installed directly into the folders in which a previous version was installed, preserving preferences and data. (4)

USB Restricted Mode An Apple security feature that prevents a USB accessory from making a data connection to a device if it has been more than an hour since it was locked. (11)

user account A record in an accounts database that represents a single person and that is used for authentication. (2)

User Account Control (UAC) A security feature that prevents unauthorized changes to Windows. A user logged on with an administrator type account only has the privileges of a standard account until the user (or a malicious program) attempts to do something that requires higher privileges. (2)

user interface (UI) The software layer, or shell, through which the user communicates with the OS. (1)

user right The privilege to perform a systemwide function, such as access the computer from the network, log on locally, log on from the network, back up files, change the system time, or load and unload device drivers. (2)

User tile A small image representing the user. A user tile appears in various places in Windows: in the Start menu in Windows 7 and Windows 10 and on the top right of the Start screen in Windows 8.x. Beginning in Windows 8, click or tap the User tile to open User settings. (5)

value entry A setting within a Windows registry key. (6)

vector A mode of malware infection, such as email, code on websites, Trojan horse, searching out unprotected computers, sneakernet, back doors, rootkits, pop-up downloads, drive-by downloads, war driving, and bluesnarfing. (2)

Virtual Desktop A feature introduced in Windows 10 that supports multiple unique instances of the desktop. (5)

virtual desktop infrastructure (VDI) Hosting and managing multiple virtual desktops on network servers. (3)

virtual keyboard An onscreen image of a keyboard with labeled keys that you can tap. (1)

virtual machine (VM) A software simulation of a computer. (3)

virtual machine monitor (VMM) Another name for a hypervisor. A software layer that emulates the necessary hardware for an operating system to run in. (3)

virtual private network (VPN) A virtual tunnel created between two end points over a real network or internetwork. (10)

virtual reality (VR) A virtual environment that includes three-dimensional images and involves other senses, giving the participant a feeling of actually being present in that time and space. (3)

virtual world An online simulated communal environment within which users, often using an animated computer-generated human (avatar), can interact with one another and create and use various objects. (3)

virtualization The creation of an environment that seems real, but isn't. (3)

virus In the broadest sense, malware, a program that is installed and activated on a computer without the knowledge or permission of the user. (2)

Wallet The Apple app that holds credit and debit card data for use with Apple Pay. It also digitally stores other data normally carried in a physical wallet, such as tickets, boarding passes, and students IDs. (11)

war driving The act of moving through a neighborhood in a vehicle or on foot, using a Wi-Fi sensor to exploit unsecured Wi-Fi networks. (2)

warm boot Restarting a computer without a power-down and power-up cycle. (6)

Web A shortened version of the term World Wide Web (WWW). (8)

Web app An app that runs entirely within a browser and resides on a website. (9)

Web-based setup An online installer, available through the Microsoft website for installing Windows 10. (5)

Web browser A special type of client software used to navigate the Web. (10)

Web mail A generic term for Web-based email services such as Hotmail, Gmail, and Yahoo! that keep your messages stored on the Internet, allowing you to access them from any computer via a Web browser. (10)

Web Note A feature of Microsoft Edge that allows the user to draw and make notes on a Web page and save a copy of the notated page. (5)

white hat hacker A hacker who is not a cybercriminal. (2)

wide area network (WAN) A network that covers a very large geographic area (miles). (10)

Wi-Fi network A wireless LAN (WLAN) that complies with IEEE 802.11 standards. (10)

wildcard A symbol that replaces a character or string of characters as a parameter in a CLI command. (8)

Windows 10 Home The basic consumer edition of Windows 10. (5)

Windows 10 Pro The Windows 10 edition for professional users. (5)

Windows Aero Microsoft's name for a group of GUI desktop features and visual themes introduced in Windows Vista. (4)

Windows Defender A free built-in antispyware product in Windows 7. Beginning in Windows 8, this is an improved product with added capabilities that make it a multifunction security program. (4)

Windows Easy Transfer (WET) A utility that will transfer your data, and settings for the Windows desktop and your applications from an old installation of Windows to Windows 7. (4)

Windows Explorer The name of the primary tool for copying, moving, renaming, and deleting files in Windows. Beginning in Windows 8, it was renamed File Explorer. (4)

Windows Hello A Windows 10 biometric sign-in feature that uses fingerprint scanning, facial recognition, or iris scanning. It requires special hardware. (5)

Windows key (⊡) A key located near the bottom left of most keyboards that displays a Windows logo and is used in combination with other keys to create keyboard shortcuts. (5)

Windows Memory Diagnostic Tool A Windows recovery tool that tests the system's RAM because RAM problems can prevent Windows from starting. (4)

Windows PowerShell A Windows CLI scripting environment for advanced users and administrators. (6)

Windows Preinstallation Environment (Windows PE) A scaled-down Windows operating system. Windows PE supports the Windows Setup GUI, collecting configuration information. (4)

Windows Recovery Environment (Windows RE) A powerful group of Windows diagnostics and repair tools that runs in the Windows Preinstallation Environment (Windows PE). (6)

Windows setup The traditional program for installing and upgrading Windows. (5)

Windows Update A Windows program that can automatically connect to the Microsoft site and download and install updates. (4)

Windows XP Mode Introduced in Windows 7; Windows Virtual PC with a free and legal Windows XP VM preinstalled. (3)

wireless LAN (WLAN) A local area network using one of the standards referred to as Wi-Fi (for wireless fidelity). The distance covered by a WLAN is measured in a hundreds of feet rather than miles. (10)

wireless wide area network (WWAN) A digital wireless network that extends over a large geographical area. (10)

World Wide Web (WWW) The graphical Internet consisting of a vast array of documents located on millions of specialized servers worldwide. (8)

worm A self-replicating computer virus. (2)

X Window System The program code used as the basis for many GUIs for Linux or UNIX. (8)

Xbox Game bar A bar that displays as part of the Xbox app. It contains buttons for working with Xbox. (5)

zero-day exploit A software vulnerability in an operating system or application that is unknown to the publisher of the software. (2)

zombie An individual computer in a botnet. (2)

Index

Note: Page numbers followed by *f* or *t* represent figures or tables, respectively.